T0374942

THE

PUBLICATIONS

OF THE

Lincoln Record Society

FOUNDED IN THE YEAR

1910

VOLUME 79

ISSN 0267–2634

FOR THE YEAR ENDING 31 AUGUST 1988

A
BIBLIOGRAPHY
OF PRINTED ITEMS RELATING TO
THE CITY OF LINCOLN

compiled by
D. Mary Short, M.A.

The Lincoln Record Society

The Boydell Press

The Francis Hill Commemoration Trust
Andrew & Co., Solicitors, St Swithin's Square, Lincoln

A Lincoln Record Society publication
First published 1990 by The Boydell Press
an imprint of Boydell & Brewer Ltd
PO Box 9, Woodbridge, Suffolk IP12 3DF
and of Boydell & Brewer Inc.
Wolfeboro, New Hampshire 03894–2069, USA

ISBN 0 901503 52 5

British Library Cataloguing in Publication Data
Short, D. Mary
  A bibliography of printed items relating to the city
  of Lincoln. – (The publications of the Lincoln Record
  Society ISSN: 0267–2634; 79).
  1. Lincolnshire. Lincoln, history – Bibliographies
  I. Title   II. Lincoln Record Society   III. Series
  016.9425'34
  ISBN 0–901503–52–5

Library of Congress Cataloging-in-Publication Data
Short, D. Mary.
    A bibliography of printed items relating to the city of Lincoln /
  compiled by D. Mary Short.
      p.   cm. – (The Publications of the Lincoln Record Society,
  ISSN 0267–2634 ; v. 79)
    ISBN 0–901503–52–5 (alk. paper)
    1. Lincoln (England) – Bibliography.   I. Title.   II. Series
  DA670.L69R5   vol. 79
  [Z2024.L6]
  [DA690.L67]
  942.5'31   s –dc20
  [016.9425'31]   89–13040
                                                                         CIP

This publication is printed on acid-free paper

Printed in Great Britain by St Edmundsbury Press, Bury St Edmunds, Suffolk

Contents

THE BIBLIOGRAPHY

Numbers here and in the index refer to records rather than pages.

Sir Francis Hill
Reproduced by permission of the Municipal Mutual Insurance Society

Sir Francis Hill, Kt., C.B.E., M.A., LL.D., Litt.D., F.S.A.

James William Francis Hill was born at 38 Tentercroft Street in downhill Lincoln on 15 September 1899, the son of a Scottish draper. His father's family lived around Dornoch; his mother's were Lincoln people, his ancestors on that side including a great-grandmother Steeper who kept a girls' school at Atton Place and also a former teacher at the Lincoln Bluecoat School. He was baptized into the Newland Congregational Church of which he was a lifelong member. He attended the Municipal Technical Day School, later the City School, where his abilities were recognised and from where he made his way to Trinity College, Cambridge. He was commissioned and served briefly in the King's Royal Rifle Corps. After leaving Cambridge he returned to Lincoln, his base for the rest of his life. He joined a partnership of solicitors, eventually becoming the senior partner of Andrew and Co., and remaining so until his death. He quickly became involved in local affairs and societies from which he entered a wider world.

While at Cambridge, as he wrote in the preface to his *Mediaeval Lincoln*, he was inspired by those teaching in the school of Maitland to do some work of his own, and had already become a member of local learned societies in Lincoln. He found much encouragement through these and in the friendship of Canon C.W. Foster, of the Stentons and later of Miss Kathleen Major. His papers in local Proceedings led eventually to his four volumes, *Mediaeval Lincoln* (1948), *Tudor and Stuart Lincoln* (1959), *Georgian Lincoln* (1966), and *Victorian Lincoln* (1974), published by the Cambridge University Press, which gave a new dimension to the history of cities. His *Short History of Lincoln*, published by the Lincoln Civic Trust (his brainchild), appeared just before his death. He contributed *The Letters and Papers of the Banks Family of Revesby Abbey, 1704–1760* to the Lincoln Record Society in 1952.

It was, however, his legal knowledge and grasp of affairs, coupled with his scholarship, that enabled him to play a variety of parts. His involvement in the affairs of the Lincoln city council, from 1932, led to his membership, and later presidency of the council of the University of Nottingham, and eventually to his becoming its Chancellor from 1972 to 1978. He was chairman of the Association of Municipal Corporations from 1957 to 1966 and representative of that association on the British Records Association Council from 1947 to 1973. Similarly he was honorary solicitor of the Royal Historical Society from 1961 to 1975, and honorary vice-president from 1977 until his death. Again arising from his local government service was his appointment to the Royal Commission on Local Government in England (1966–69), and his service as president of the European Conference of Local Authorities at Strasbourg (1966–68) and as president of the International Union of Local Authorities (1967–71). In his semi-retirement local and national service went together in his trusteeship of the Lincolnshire Old Churches Trust, his chairmanship of the Lincoln Cathedral Fabric Appeal and his membership of the Advisory Board for Redundant Churches (1969–75).

One of his great interests in local government service was the provision of an archive service in Lincolnshire. He had been treasurer of the Lincoln Diocesan Record Office from 1935, and while I was its archivist, from 1945 to 1948, combined in one person parts normally played by fellow officers and commmittee in local government. The consequent relationship continued while he was vice-chairman of the Lincolnshire Archives Committee and chairman of its Technical and Advisory Sub-committee. In spite of his many commitments he very rarely missed the committee's meetings. His recollections of the processes by which four independent authorities, the city and the three parts of the county, were persuaded to join together, and the bishop (and dean and chapter) to deposit their records with them, are given in ''From Canon Foster to Lincolnshire Archives Office'' in *Lincolnshire History and Archaeology*, vol.13 (1978). He was responsible for securing for the office many deposits and gifts, both from his own collections and those of others. His last gift, under his will, was of his personal papers and correspondence which are in process of being sorted and from which some information has been taken for this notice.

People often wonder how Sir Francis could do so much and in many varying fields. He had remarkable powers of concentration and in the organisation of his time, to a certain extent limiting time for social life and relaxation. His charm of manner and persuasiveness were helpful in attracting the interest and labour of others for his causes. He suceeded in much but had his disappointments, such as his failure to get into parliament and his feelings on the outcome of the Maude Report. His friends remember his generosity and interest in their affairs, and his sudden death on 6 January 1980 was a sad blow to them.

JOAN VARLEY
(Obituary reprinted from *Archives*,
vol.XV, no.65, April 1981)

Foreword

On the initiative of the Lincoln Civic Trust, a public appeal was issued with a view to the establishment of a fund to commemorate Sir Francis' life of scholarship and public service. There was an excellent response and as a result the Francis Hill Commemoration Trust was formed and registered as a charity, its principal object being to promote studies in history and local government. To this end the Trust has commissioned the research for and preparation of this bibliography. It was known that Sir Francis hoped such work would be done and the bibliography is seen as a complement to his own four volumes of Lincoln history.

Amongst the many contributions to the fund, mention should perhaps be made of those of the Lincoln City Council, Lincolnshire County Council, The Ferens Education Trust of the University of Hull, under the aegis of Professor B. Jennings and Dr. R.W. Ambler of the School of Adult and Continuing Education, and the partners of Andrew & Co., Sir Francis' former firm, for their generous allocation of office space.

The Trustees would like to express their warm thanks to our researcher, Miss Mary Short, M.A., who has been engaged full-time in this task for more than a year and a half. We are confident that we could not have made a better appointment and believe that all interested in the history of Lincoln for many years to come will benefit from her careful and scholarly work.

We would like to record our appreciation of the co-operation so readily afforded to her in her work by the Lincolnshire Library Service and many others.

We wish her well in her new appointment as Assistant Librarian at the Royal Botanic Gardens at Kew.

PHILIP RACE
Chairman

February 1989

Preface

A.R. Corns' *Bibliotheca Lincolniensis*, published in 1904 and based upon the holdings of the newly formed Lincoln City Library, is the only previous bibliography covering the city. The first section of the present work shows that since this time the main contributions to the bibliographic coverage of the city have been commercial auction and booksellers' lists. There are also two bibliographies in periodical format, which have contained relevant material: the Lincolnshire section of the regional lists formerly produced by the Library Association; and the ongoing *East Midlands bibliography*.

SUBJECT COVERAGE

While Corns included items relating to the county of Lincoln, the present bibliography is deliberately limited to the city itself. The Cathedral has also been largely excluded, apart from the substantial amount of material common to both the city and the Church; items concerning the Bishops of Lincoln, for example. More detailed coverage of the Cathedral will be found in a bibliography prepared by Dr D.M. Owen, which is to comprise part of a forthcoming volume on Lincoln Cathedral.

TYPES OF MATERIAL

The brief for the project was to compile a bibliography of printed items relating to the city of Lincoln. Most of the records describe monographs, journal articles, parts of books or pamphlets, but some typescript material and occasionally manuscript material has also been included where necessary. Unpublished dissertations have proved to be major sources of specialised information and have been included in many instances. The greater part of such unpublished material is to be found in the collection of the Lincoln Central Library.

Newspaper articles are only included on an ad hoc basis, though several obituaries are cited. Similarly, there is no systematic coverage of non-book material, such as photographs or maps.

A great deal of pamphlet and broadsheet material was included; the mass of primary material relating to nineteenth century elections is a notable example of this. There was no attempt to discard primary sources such as this ephemeral matter, though it undoubtedly lengthened the bibliography. To ignore this kind of information, which is not listed elsewhere, is to lose a rich and interesting resource relating to the life of the city. Also included are a number of incomplete records which, although they are not entirely satisfactory from a cataloguing point of view, may nonetheless prove helpful to users of the bibliography.

On the other hand, references to some classes of ephemera have had to be limited on the grounds of their sheer volume. For instance, catalogues and prospectuses concerned with industrial products have largely been excluded; material produced by Ruston's alone might well have doubled the number of entries. Another category of literature where sample items are noted is the in-house newsletter or journal.

DATES

No specific dates were set for inclusion or exclusion of material; new material was collected up to the end of 1988. Most of the earlier literature dates from the eighteenth century, though there are a few older items.

SOURCES

The bibliography is based as far as possible on the collections of Lincoln Central Library. Other sources visited during the project include the Lincolnshire Archives Office, Ruston Gas Turbines, the Bodleian Library, the British Library and the Library of the University of Nottingham. After much deliberation, I decided that the printed volume should not include a location code with each record, on the grounds that in most cases this would give a false impression of availability. It is, however, my intention to deposit in the Lincoln Central Library a printout of this work annotated with the locations current in January, 1989.

LINCOLN CENTRAL LIBRARY

The Local Studies Collection contains a mass of non-book material relating to the city, such as maps, illustrations, theatre bills, broadsheets, microfilm, newspapers and newspaper-cuttings, scrapbooks and manuscript items.

The illustrations collection comprises many postcards and portraits, amounting to more than 8,000 items featuring the city of Lincoln. An index provides access by subject, district or street name. The newspaper cuttings file dates back to the 1970s. For earlier coverage there are the 60 scrapbooks compiled by E.I. Abell, dating from the 1940s and each devoted to a different topic.

Lady Monson has deposited Ross' manuscript 'Civitas Lincolniae' at the Library and his 'Annales' are held on microfilm. Also available on microfilm is the whole of the E.J. Willson collection. The Library possesses the Banks collection, an illustrated survey of most of the important buildings of Lincolnshire. The manuscript of the Torrington diaries, dating from the 1790s, is also held at the Library. There are many manuscript letters relating to Christ's Hospital School to be found in the collections. Unique holdings relating to the more recent past include 30 volumes of photographs showing parts and machines from Robey Globe Works.

The period of work upon this bibliography coincided with the process of computerization of the catalogue of books in the Lincoln Central Library Local Studies Collection. This will give more flexible access to bibliographic records relating to the whole of Lincolnshire as well as to the city. As yet, only part of the large pamphlet collection has been entered into the database.

SECONDARY BIBLIOGRAPHIC SOURCES

In the later stages of this project a number of printed bibliographies were consulted. These were particularly helpful when locating references for the sections on archaeology and history. Wilfred Bonser's *A Prehistoric bibliography*, *An Anglo-Saxon and Celtic bibliography, (450–1087)* and *A Romano-British bibliography, (55 BC – AD 449)* have all been extremely useful, as were Charles Gross' *A Bibliography of English history to 1485* and *A Bibliography of British municipal history. The Annual bibliography of British and Irish history* produced by the Royal Historical Society and the *International medieval bibliography* provided further information. The notes on local books to be found in the *Bulletin of local history: East Midlands region* have been informative.

ARRANGEMENT

The arrangement of this bibliography is roughly that of the classified order developed by Cordeaux and Merry in their *Bibliography of printed works relating to the city of Oxford* and the other two volumes covering the county and the University of Oxford, with modifications reflecting the distinctive character of the city of Lincoln and the literature relating to it. Within each section, items have usually been ordered by date rather than by author or title. In sections such as biography or parts of topography, however, ordering by date was subordinated to arrangement by biographical subject or location respectively. Some of the sections relating to particular, named institutions have been similarly treated, with the organisation's name taking precedence over dates.

STRUCTURE OF RECORDS

The form of records describing items is based upon the recommendations in the *Anglo-American cataloguing rules*, second edition (1978, reprinted with corrections, 1984). There are three types of entry: monographs, journal articles and unpublished material. The arrangement for monographs follows the pattern outlined below.

AUTHOR/MAIN HEADING
Title: subtitle
Statement of responsibility if this differs from the main heading. Edition statement.
Place of publication: publisher, date of publication. Physical description.
(Series)
Bibliographic notes, about previous editions, etc.
ISBN
    Notes and annotations.

The other two categories follow this basic pattern too, except that the publication details are replaced by either a journal citation or a statement referring to the unpublished item's format. The titles of published works are printed in italics. Ordinary type-face is used to indicate the titles of journal articles and unpublished material.

ABBREVIATIONS

In order to produce records which are both clear and concise, a number of abbreviations have been used. When a main heading is repeated in successive records, this is denoted by a long unbroken line, thus —————. A similar device is occasionally employed in the notes field to avoid the repetition of identical titles.

Publication details have been simplified by citing the names of the publishing bodies in the briefest form necessary for identification. In the case of defective records, the absence of place, publisher and/or date is recorded by the use of s.l. (sine loco), s.n. (sine nomine) and ? respectively. Square brackets signify that the information given has been supplied by the compiler.

Lastly, two journal titles which occur frequently have been abbreviated throughout the text as follows:
Lincolnshire notes and queries becomes *LN&Q*;
Associated Architectural Societies reports and papers becomes *AAS reports and papers*.

ACKNOWLEDGEMENTS

I would like to thank in the first place the Trustees of the Francis Hill Commemoration Trust who gave me every encouragement and help. I am grateful to Miss F. A. R. Murray, Dr. D. M. Owen, Mr P. H. Race and Mr F. T. Baker for advice, hospitality and friendship. Dr. K. Major gave important guidance.

It is impossible sufficiently to express my gratitude to the people who have helped me in so many ways throughout this project. I am only sorry that I cannot mention everybody by name: the Lincolnshire County Library Service (with personal thanks to Mrs R. Boyce, Mr J. English, Miss S. Gates and Miss E. Nannestad); the Lincolnshire Archives Office (in particular Miss A. Goode and Miss J. Williams); the staff of Andrew & Co.; the Bodleian Library (especially Mr and Mrs A. J. Flavell); Mr M. Brook, former Local Studies Librarian at the University of Nottingham Arts Library; Mr R. Hooley of Ruston Gas Turbines; Spalding Gentlemen's Society; Professor C. Garton of the State University of New York, for his information on the Lincoln School.

Three people gave a great deal of their time, energy and patience to the preparation of the final text and index. Dr. A. H. Short advised on the computerization of the project. He and Mrs M. R. Short contributed substantially to the editing and prepared the index. I owe a special debt to Mr J. A. Dawson for his tireless assistance. The omissions and errors remain of course my own.

Mary Short
Bakewell, Derbyshire
8 April 1989.

BIBLIOGRAPHY

GENERAL

1.
The Bibliography of Lincolnshire and the great county history
pp.9–14 in *Old Lincolnshire*, vol.1, 1885.
> Contains list of books in the library of Thomas Phillipps, the Thirlestaine House collection.

2.
Materials for a complete list of Lincolnshire topographical books
[Lincoln]: [s.n.], [1888].   32p.
Bound with volume 1 of *LN&Q*, 1888–89.
> pp.22–26: Lincoln.

3.
*Topographical history of Leicestershire, Lincolnshire, Middlesex, Monmouthshire: a classified collection of the chief contents of **The Gentleman's magazine** from 1731–1868*
edited by George Laurence Gomme.
London: Elliot Stock, 1896.   xiii, 345p.
> pp.57–191: Lincolnshire; pp.138–145: Lincoln.

4.   **CORNS, A.R.**
Bibliotheca Lincolniensis: a catalogue of the books, pamphlets, etc., relating to the city and county of Lincoln, preserved in the Reference Department of the City of Lincoln Public Library
Lincoln: printed W.K. Morton, 1904.   274p.
> Part III, pp.59–94: city of Lincoln, general works; Part IV: city of Lincoln, works relating to particular subjects. Also available in 2 vols. with interleaved annotations.

5.
Local history: its interest and value
Lincoln: Lindsey Local History Society, [1930s].   31p.
> Includes list of books of local interest.

6.   **VARLEY, Joan**
Some books, articles and pamphlets bearing on the history of Lincolnshire towns
1955.   7 leaves.
Typescript.
> pp.3–4: Lincoln.   Prepared for students of weekend school at Stoke Rochford, January, 1955.

7.
[Calendar of documents deposited by Burton, Scorer & Co. at Lincolnshire Archives Office, 1957]
[1957].   [8] leaves.
Typescript.
> Much material relating to the city.

8.   **EXLEY, C.L.**
Papers of the late C.L. Exley, Esq. of Lincoln, deposited by Mrs. F. Exley, February, 1957:   [list]
45 leaves.
Typescript.
> Important collection of material concerning city of Lincoln deposited at the Lincolnshire Archives Office.

9.
[Calendar of documents deposited by J.W.F. Hill at the Lincolnshire Archives Office] [1957].   [10] leaves.
Typescript.
> Some items of Lincoln interest, e.g. many apprenticeship indentures and other legal documents.

10.   **MILLS, Dennis R.**
A Bibliography of post-war work relating to the geography of Lincolnshire
pp.175–183 in *AAS reports and papers*, vol.7, no.2, 1957–58.

11.
Bibliotheca Lincolnshire: [catalogue]
Lincoln: Harlequin Gallery, 1970.   [48]p.
Includes index.
> Local history and topography.

12.
A Catalogue of Lincolnshire books and pamphlets
Stamford: Staniland (Booksellers), 1988.   [28]p.
(Catalogue of old and second-hand books, no.38, winter, 1988)
> 'Most of the items in this catalogue formerly belonged to the late Sir Francis Hill...'

AUCTION CATALOGUES

Book Collections

13.
Auction sale of rare, antiquarian and out-of-print books principally of Lincolnshire...on Thursday, 26th September, 1974 at the Old Hall, Parnell Street, Gainsborough, Lincolnshire
Sleaford: William H. Brown, 1974.   34p.

14.
Auction sale: valuable and antiquarian printed books, mainly relating to the history & topography of Lincolnshire and Nottinghamshire, to be held on Thursday, November 20th, 1975 at the Guildhall, Grantham, Lincolnshire
Nottingham: Frank Innes, 1975.   18p.: ill.

15.
Auction sale: valuable, rare and antiquarian printed books, mainly relating to the history & topography of Nottinghamshire and Lincolnshire...on Thursday, December 2nd, 1976 at the Robin Hood Hotel, Lombard Street, Newark, Notts...
Newark: Earl & Lawrence, 1976.   19p.

16.
*By instructions from the estate of the late H. Hammerton of Lincoln: important sale of
antiquarian books of Lincolnshire, manuscripts, photographs, maps, postcards,
magazines, Lincolnshire guides, etc., dating from 1275 A.D. to the present*
Lincoln: Earl & Lawrence, 1977. 28p.

17.
*A Catalogue of the library of the late Rev. W. Gray, which will be sold by auction by Mr.
Harmston, at his late dwelling-house, in the Vicars' Court, Lincoln, on Wednesday and
Thursday, the 19th and 20th days of July, 1826*
Lincoln: printed W. Brooke, 1826. 19p.

18.
*A Catalogue of the valuable library of a clergyman of the Church of England, deceased,
comprising about twelve hundred volumes...sold by auction...at Mr Reynold's
show-rooms, Silver-Street, Lincoln on Tuesday, May 7th, 1833*
Lincoln: printed by W. Brooke, 1833. 12p.

19.
*A Catalogue of the valuable and extensive library, a great portion of which is
theological, choice prints and pictures, household furniture, china, glass, and other
effects, of the late George Moore... sold by auction...31st May, 1841...*
Lincoln: printed W. and B. Brooke, [1841]. 32p.

Catalogues of Personal Collections

20.
*Catalogue of the library of Ernest L. Grange, Esq...consisting of a large and important
collection of books, manuscripts, tracts, engravings, etc., relating to the county of
Lincoln...sold by auction...14th March, 1892...*
London: Sotheby, Wilkinson & Hodge, 1892. 49p.

21.
*Catalogue of books to be sold on the premises of the Rev. J. Penrose, Minster Yard,
Lincoln, on Monday, the 27th day of February, 1837*
Lincoln: printed by W. and B. Brooke, 1837. 1 sheet.

22.
*312, High-Street, Lincoln: condensed catalogue of the superior stock of stationery,
library of books...valuable collection of prints...to be sold by auction by Mr. T.J.N.
Brogden, on the premises in High Street, Lincoln, lately occupied by J.W. Drury,
deceased, on Monday 10th March & following days*
Lincoln: printed J.W. Drury, [1851]. 14p.

23.
*A Catalogue of the extensive and valuable collection of books, prints, paintings, ancient
and mediaeval remains, antique porcelain, household furniture and other effects of the
late Edward James Willson sold by auction...November, 1854*
Lincoln: printed W. and B. Brooke, [1854]. 32p.

24.

A Catalogue of tracts, pamphlets, prints, and drawings, illustrating Lincolnshire, on sale for ready money
London: Alfred Russell Smith, 1878.   pp.187–193, 1–13.
> Books from the collection of William Upcott who published a bibliography of Great Britain in 1818.

25.

Catalogue of the...books, manuscripts, original drawings, engravings, maps, coins, tokens, seals, &c., formed by the late E.J. Willson...illustrative of or relating to the city and county of Lincoln...sold by auction...on Wednesday, the 30th day of May, 1888, by Messrs. Sotheby, Wilkinson & Hodge
London: Dryden, [1888].   32p.

26.

A Catalogue of...books including the library of the late Rev. W.O. Massingberd removed from Ormsby Rectory...and other properties, comprising topographical, antiquarian and genealogical works relating to the county of Lincoln...sold by auction
London: Hodgson, 1911.   55p.

27.

A Catalogue of valuable miscellaneous books, including the library of the late Rev. W.O. Massingberd...comprising topographical, antiquarian, and genealogical works relating to the county of Lincoln, &c...sold by auction...January 18th, 1911
London: Hodgson, 1911.   pp.19–26.

28.   **JEFFERSON, J.K.**
Richard William Goulding collection: a handlist
[Lincoln]: [Lincolnshire Library Service], [197?].   150p.
> Contains subject and author listings. Collection based at Louth Library; particularly strong on history of Louth, but some city of Lincoln items listed.

MAPS

29.
Catalogue of the manuscript maps, charts, and plans, and of the topographical drawings in the British Museum.   Vol.1
London: Trustees of the British Museum, 1844.   481p.
> pp.462–481: Lincolnshire.   Includes many items relating to Lincoln.

SOCIETY PUBLICATIONS

30.   **SOCIETY FOR LINCOLNSHIRE HISTORY AND ARCHAEOLOGY**
Catalogue of publications
[Lincoln]: [The Society], [c.1974].   25p.

NATURAL HISTORY

GEOLOGY

31.   **BEDFORD, William**
The Geology of Lincoln
pp.15–28, [1] plan, [1]p. of plates in *A Selection of papers relative to the county of Lincoln*, 1843.
>   Paper read before the Lincolnshire Topographical Society, March 16th, 1841.

32.   **USSHER, W.A.E.**
Memoirs of the Geological Survey, England and Wales: the geology of the country around Lincoln (explanation of sheet 83)
by W.A.E. Ussher, A.J. Jukes-Browne and Aubrey Strahan.
London: HMSO, 1888.   x, 218p.: ill.
Includes index.

33.   **WALTON, F.F.**
The Lincoln lias and its fossils
pp.18–21 in *Transactions of the Hull Geological Society*, vol.V, pt.1, 1898–99.
>   Mainly list of fossils found.

34.   **TRUEMAN, A.E.**
The Lias of South Lincolnshire
pp.64–111: ill. in *The Geological magazine*, new series, decade VI, vol.V, 1918.
>   pp.103–107: the Lincoln district.

35.   **RICHARDSON, L.**
'Field meeting at Lincoln', Whitsun 1940: report
pp.246–256: ill. in *Proceedings of the Geologists' Association*, vol.LI, pt.3, 1940.

36.   **EVANS, W. David**
The Jurassic rocks of the Lincoln district
pp.316–335, [3] folded leaves of plates in *Proceedings of the Geological Association*, vol.LXIII, pt.4, 1952.

37.   **STRAW, Allan**
The Quaternary evolution of the lower and middle Trent
pp.171–189, maps in *The East Midland geographer*, vol.3, pt.4, no.20, 1963.
>   Much of paper concerned with glaciation and drainage around Lincoln.

38.   **KENT, P.E.**
A Review of the correlation of the Lincolnshire limestone (inferior oolite)
pp.57–69: ill. in *Transactions of the Leicester Literary and Philosophical Society*, vol.LX, 1966.
>   pp.61–62: the Lincoln district.

39.   **BATE, Raymond Holmes**
Stratigraphy and palaeogeography of the Yorkshire oolites and their relationships with the Lincolnshire limestone
pp.113–141: ill., [3] folded plates in *Bulletin of the British Museum (Natural History): geology*, vol.14, no.4, 1967.
  pp.121–123: refers to the Kirton cementstone series found at Greetwell Quarry.

40.   **KENT, Peter**
British regional geology: eastern England from the Tees to the Wash
2nd ed.
London: HMSO, 1980.
Originally published: 1948.   Includes index.
ISBN 0118841211
  Includes references to Lincoln area.

41.   **STRAW, Allan**
Pre-Devensian glaciation of Lincolnshire (eastern England) and adjacent areas
pp.239–260: ill. in *Quaternary science review*, vol.2, 1983.

WILD LIFE

42.   **ERNSTSONS, Emma L. Bundulis**
Summer of the swans
with photographs by Fricis Ernstsons.
Syracuse, N.Y.: Central New Yorker Printing Division, 1973. 127p.: ill.
  Photographs of swans near Lincoln in 1957.   There is very little on Lincoln: interest focussed on the birds rather than their environment.

43.   **EAST MIDLAND BIRD STUDY & CONSERVATION GROUP**
Management possibilities for Hartsholme Country Park
compiled by Trevor Kerry.
Lincoln: The Group, 1979.   17 leaves.

44.   ————————
Hartsholme park nature trail: annual report [nos.2–4]
[compiled by] Trevor Kerry.
[Lincoln]: The Group, 1977–79.

45.   **KERRY, Trevor**
Birds of a Lincoln garden
pp.46–48: ill. in *Lincolnshire life*, vol.19, no.7, October, 1979.

46.   **LINCOLN, Department of Planning and Architecture**
Hartsholme Country Park: development plan
Lincoln: The Department, 1985.   [15]p.: ill., maps.

HISTORY

GENERAL

47.   **ALLEN, Thomas**
The History of the county of Lincoln, from the earliest period to the present time
by the author of the histories of London, Yorkshire, Lambeth, Surrey, Essex, &c., &c.,
&c.
London; Lincoln: John Saunders, Jr., 1834.   2 vols.
Includes index.
> Vol.1, p.100–210: thorough survey of Lincoln, including its history, buildings, charities, etc.
> See also Allen's *Illustrations*, 1830.   Note in BM catalogue says 'The first portion of the work
> was published at Leeds in 1830, with a different title page, bearing Allen's name. The present
> copy contains additional illustrations.'

48.
*Remarkable occurrences that have happened in Lincoln, for upwards of a 1000 [years]
and the number of inhabitants, in each parish, as taken on March, 1801*
New ed. with additions.
Lincoln: printed and sold John Smith, 1805.   36p.

49.
Remarkable occurrences that have happened at Lincoln for upwards of a 1000 years
Lincoln: John Smith, [c.1809].   36p.

50.
A Condensed history of the county of Lincoln
[London]: [printed Stevens and Pardon], [1835].   207p.

51.
Remarkable occurrences that have happened in Lincoln
[Lincoln]: [s.n.], [1837?].   22p.

52.
*A Chronological history of Lincoln containing an account of every remarkable
occurrence that has happened therein, from the earliest period to the present time,
collected from authentic sources*
Lincoln: printed S. Thorpe, [c.1837].   1 sheet.

53.
*A Chronological history of Lincoln, containing an account of every remarkable
occurrence that has happened therein, from the earliest period to the present time, from
authentic source*
Lincoln: printed R.E. Leary, [1847].   1 sheet: ill.
> Includes executions at Lincoln since 1722.

54.
A Chronological history of Lincoln, containing an account of every remarkable occurrence that has happened therein, from the earliest period to the present time, from authentic sources
Lincoln: printed R.E. Leary, [1849].   1 sheet: ill.
   Members of Parliament, executions since 1769.

55.
Chronological history [of] Lincoln: containing an account of every remarkable occurrence that has happened therein, from the earliest period to the present, taken fron authentic sources
Lincoln: R.E. Leary, [1850s].   1 sheet.

56.   STARK, Adam
History of the bishopric of Lincoln from its commencement at Sidnacester or Lindisse: its connection with Lichfield and Leicester: its junction with Dorchester: until the seat of the see was fixed at Lincoln, immediately after the Conquest
London: Longman, Brown, Green, 1852.   xviii, 529p.
   No index but detailed 'contents'.

57.
The Lincoln date book, from the earliest time to the present, collected with care and from the most authentic sources
Lincoln: printed and published R.E. Leary, [1858].   126p., [c.60]p.
   Final section is list of medicines and applications for which Leary was agent.

58.
The Date book for Lincoln and neighbourhood, from the earliest time to the present
Lincoln: printed and published by R.E. Leary, [1866].   425p.

59.   BROCKLEHURST, J.W.
General index to Lincoln date book from earliest times to 1866
prepared by J.W. Brocklehurst.
1957.   33p.
Typescript.
   Date book produced by R.E. Leary, 1866.

60.
History of Lincoln, Big Tom, executions, etc.
Lincoln: Robert Leary, [c.1868].   1 sheet: ill.

61.
History of Lincoln
3rd ed.
Lincoln: Samuel Ward, [post 1872].   1 sheet: ill

62.   FREEMAN, Edward A.
English towns and districts: a series of addresses and sketches
London: Macmillan, 1883.   455p., [12] leaves of plates.
   pp.191–221: Lindum colonia, a paper read before Lincolnshire Architectural Society at Grantham, June 16, 1875, with some material from article in *Saturday review*, October 1st, 1870.

63.
Bygone Lincolnshire
edited by William Andrews.
Hull: A. Brown, 1891.   2 vols.
> Vol.1, pp.79–80: Roman arch; pp.131–142: the Pilgrimage of Grace; vol.2, pp.25–42: Lincoln
> Castle; pp.151–60: the Battle of Lincoln; pp.161–169: Lincoln Fair.

64.
The Victoria history of the county of Lincoln.   Vol.2
edited by William Page.
London: James Street, 1906.   xv, 528p., [5] leaves of plates.
Only vol.2 published.
> Covers ecclesiastical history and religious houses, political history, social and economic
> history, industries, agriculture, forestry, schools and sport.

65.   **BREARS, Charles**
A Short history of Lincolnshire
London: A. Brown, 1927.   216p.: ill.
Includes index.

66.   **HILL, J.W.F.**
The Beginnings of Lincolnshire
pp.5–7 in *Lincolnshire magazine*, vol.1, 1932–34.

67.   **LAMBERT, M.R.**
Lincoln
by M.R. Lambert and M.S. Sprague with illustrations by R. Walker.
Oxford: Blackwell, 1933.   xv, 258p., [18]p. of plates, plans.
Includes index.

68.   **ABELL, E.I.**
The Story of Lincoln: an introduction to the history of the city
by E.I. Abell and J.D. Chambers.   2nd ed.
Lincoln: Lincoln, Education Committee, 1946.   239p., [12]p. of plates: ill.
Originally published: 1939.   Includes bibliography and index.
> Also available in reprint of revised 2nd ed., with introduction and additional title page: East
> Ardsley: S.R. Publishers, 1971.

69.   **KING, Stanley H.**
Contributions towards the study of the historical geography of Lincolnshire
Thesis [Ph.D.] – University of London, 1946.   2 vols.
> pp.256–311: development of the city from earliest time to 1485, development in modern times,
> medieval commerce of the city, economic geography of Lincoln since 1485.

70.   **BYGOTT, John**
Lincolnshire
London: Hale, 1952.   xii, 280p., [39]p. of plates.
Includes index.
> pp.201–219: Lincoln.

71.   **GREEN, Herbert**
Forgotten Lincoln: a history of the city from the earliest times
East Ardsley: EP Publishing, 1974.   163p.: ill.
Facsimile of 2nd ed. originally published: Lincoln, 1898.
ISBN 0854099662
> Wide-ranging, including: Roman city; St Benedict's; High Bridge; Black-, Grey- and White-Friars; Jews; Stonebow and Guildford; Mint; Royal visits; war; St Mary's Guild; mayors; sheriffs; Castle; Bishop's Palace; Bluecoat School.   Articles first appeared in the *Lincoln gazette & times*

72.   **HILL, J.W.F.**
A Short history of Lincoln
Lincoln: Lincoln Civic Trust, 1979.   113p., maps, [16]p. of plates.
Includes index.
> Based on Hill's 4 volume work but with additional information on this century.

73.   **GILBERT, Bernard S.**
Living Lincoln
Gainsborough: Thorndyke, [1983].   103p.: ill.
ISBN 0905840319

74.   **COUPAR, Richard**
Lincoln comes of age
pp.28–31: ill. in *Lincolnshire life*, vol.24, no.1, April, 1984.
> Article about the archaeology and history of the city and in particular the contribution of the Lincoln Archaeological Trust as reflected by the exhibition 'Lincoln comes of age'.

75.
Lincoln: 21 centuries of living history
Lincoln: Lincoln Archaeological Trust, 1984.   60p.: ill.
ISBN 0905086058
> Booklet sponsored by Yorkshire Television to accompany the exhibition 'Lincoln comes of age'.

76.
Lincoln, 1984: coming of age
pp.7–8: ill. in *Popular archaeology*, vol.5, pt.10, April, 1984.
About exhibition 'Lincoln comes of age'.

77.
A Prospect of Lincolnshire: being collected articles in the history & traditions of Lincolnshire in honour of Ethel H. Rudkin
edited by Naomi Field & Andrew White.
Lincoln: F.N. Field and A.J. White, 1984.   145p.: ill., maps.
Includes index.
ISBN 0950982105

GENERAL ARCHAEOLOGY

78.   **NICHOLSON, W.A.**
Advantage of recording the discovery of local antiquities
pp.87–90 in *A Selection of papers relative to the county of Lincoln*, 1843.
> Illustrative examples from his 15 years of residence in Lincoln.

79.
[Proceedings of the committee: Mr. Smith read extracts from private correspondents at Lincoln respecting the antiquities of that city]
pp.258–259 in *The Journal of the British Archaeological Association*, vol.1, 1846.

80.   **ROYAL ARCHAEOLOGICAL INSTITUTE**
Catalogue of antiquities exhibited in the museum formed during the annual meeting of the Archaeological Institute, held at Lincoln, in July, 1848
36p., [13] leaves of plates.
> From the volume of *Proceedings of the Archaeological Institute, at the annual meeting at Lincoln*, 1848.

81.
Meeting of the Archaeological Institute at Lincoln
pp.72–76: ill. in *The Illustrated London news*, no.329, vol.XIII, Saturday, August 5th, 1848.

82.
Memoirs illustrative of the history and antiquities of the county and city of Lincoln, communicated to...the Archaeological Institute of Great Britain and Ireland, held at Lincoln, July, 1848...
London: The Institute, 1850.   lx, 327p., 4 plans, [60] leaves of plates.

83.   **WORDSWORTH, Christopher**
Inaugural address of the Right Rev. the Bishop of Lincoln to the annual meeting of the Institute held at Lincoln
pp.345–350 in *The Archaeological journal*, vol.XXXVII, 1880.

84.   **BRITISH ARCHAEOLOGICAL ASSOCIATION**
[Proceedings of the congress at Lincoln]
pp.60–69, 62–169 in *The Journal of the British Archaeological Association*, vol.XLVI, 1890.

85.   **VENABLES, Edmund**
Some recent archaeological discoveries in Lincoln
by the Rev. Precentor Venables.
pp.186–189 in *The Archaeological journal*, vol.XLVIII, 1891.
> Covers Roman city walls and villa in Greetwell fields.   Also St Catherine's Priory.

86.   **ROYAL ARCHAEOLOGICAL INSTITUTE**
Lincoln meeting, 1909: [programme of proceedings]
[London]: [The Institute], [1909].   28p: ill., [4] folded plates.

87.   _____
Lincoln meeting, 1909: [proceedings at meetings]
pp.343–399: ill., [3] plates in *The Archaeological journal*, vol.LXVI, 1909.
> pp.352–353: St Peter-at-Gowts and St Mary-le-Wigford; pp.353–354: Roman remains; pp.354–357: the Close, Castle and Bishop's Palace.

88.   **BRITISH ARCHAEOLOGICAL ASSOCIATION**
Report of the seventy-eighth congress, 1921, June 27 to July 2, at Lincoln: [programme and proceedings]
pp.3–60 in *The Journal of the British Archaeological Association*, new series, vol.XVVII, 1921.

89.   **PHILLIPS, Charles W.**
The Present state of archaeology in Lincolnshire
pp.106–149, 15p. of plates in *The Archaeological journal*, vol.XC, 1934.
Continued: pp.97–187: ill., maps, [12]p. of plates in vol.XCI, 1935.
    Includes: Witham shield; anthropoid hilted dagger; Roman Lincoln; list of finds in Lincoln.

90.
Archaeology: an exhibition held in the Usher Art Gallery, Lincoln, 8–28 July, 1946:
[arranged in connection with the meeting of the Royal Archaeological Institute in
Lincoln, 1946]
Lincoln: Lincoln, Libraries, Museum and Art Gallery Committee, 1946. [18]p.: ill.

91.   **ROYAL ARCHAEOLOGICAL INSTITUTE**
The Archaeological journal
London: The Institute, 1947. vi, 219p., 30p. of plates.
    Special volume, CIII for the year 1946, of *The Archaeological journal*, 1947. Individual papers
    relating to Lincoln specifically are catalogued under individual author.

92.   **BAKER, F.T.**
Ten seasons' digging, 1945–1954
Lincoln: Lincoln Archaeological Research Committee, 1955. 32p.: ill., maps.

93.   _____
Historic cities and boroughs. XXV: majestic Lincoln
pp.383–386: ill. in *The Municipal review*, vol.34, no.402, June, 1963.
    Discusses evidence of occupation since the Bronze Age.

94.
Archaeological notes
in *Lincolnshire history and archaeology*, no.1, 1966– .
    Annual round-up of archaeological news, including that of Lincoln.

95.
Report on ancient monuments and listed buildings in the ~ity of Lincoln
Lincoln Industrial Archaeology Group.
1972. 35 leaves.
Typescript.

96.   **LINCOLN ARCHAEOLOGICAL TRUST**
First annual report, 1972–1973
    First seven of this series of reports were issued in typescript. Excavations on Roman and
    medieval defences at: the Park; Lucy Tower St. Early Roman occupation: the Park and
    Holmes Grainwarehouses. Also reports on work at Flaxengate, Westgate, the Brayford and
    Dickinson's Mill.

97.   _____
Second annual report, 1973–1974
    Excavations at: East Bight; St Paul-in-the-Bail; Castle; Flaxengate; Silver St.; Broadgate East;
    Saltergate; Chaplin St.

98.   _____
Third annual report, 1974–1975
    Excavations at: Danes Terrace; Flaxengate; Grantham St.; Steep Hill; and St Paul-in-the-Bail.

99.   _____
Fourth annual report, 1975–1976
    Excavations at: Flaxengate; St Mark's; Washingborough tile kiln; Brayford Wharf North.

100. ——————
Fifth annual report, 1976–1977
> Excavations at: Flaxengate; St Mark's; St Paul-in-the-Bail; Westgate/West Bight.

101. ——————
Sixth annual report, 1977–1978
> Excavations at: St Paul-in-the-Bail; St Mark-in-Wigford; Danes Terrace.

102. ——————
Seventh annual report, 1978–1979

103. ——————
Eighth annual report, 1979–1980
> Excavations at: St Paul-in-the-Bail; West Bight; Orchard St.   Site research at Roman traders' houses in St Mark's.   Conservation of iron padlock discovered in Flaxengate. Finds of Roman jewellery, Roman coins and pottery; animal bones from Flaxengate.

104. ——————
Ninth annual report, 1980–1981
> Excavations at: East Bight; St Mary's Guildhall. Site research at Flaxengate. Conservation of hanging basket from St Paul-in-the-Bail.

105. ——————
Archaeology in Lincoln, 1981–1982: [tenth annual report of Lincoln Archaeological Trust]
> Excavations at: Grantham Place; St Mary's Guildhall; Monson St.; Brayford Wharf East; Lincoln Castle west gate; Grantham St.; Laboratory work on Flaxengate glass-working.

106. ——————
Archaeology in Lincoln, 1982–1983: [eleventh annual report of the Lincoln Archaeological Trust]
> Archaeology and tourism in Lincoln.   Excavations at: Grantham St.; Lincoln Castle. Laboratory work on non-ferrous metal from Flaxengate.

107. ——————
Archaeology in Lincoln, 1983–1984: [twelfth and final report of the Lincoln Archaeological Trust]
> Excavations at: Hungate; Spring Hill; Roman well at St Paul-in-the-Bail; Mint wall stables.

108
Lincoln Archaeological Trust appeal
[Lincoln]: [The Trust], [1973].   [4]p.: ill., plan.

109
City of Lincoln: past, present, future
Lincoln: LSG, 1976.   16p.: ill.
> pp.8–9, 12: 'A future for Lincoln's past: delving into the city's history', by Christina Colyer.

110. **LINCOLNSHIRE COUNTY MUSEUMS**
Scheduled sites in Lincolnshire and South Humberside
1974.   [26]p.
Typescript.
> [2]p.: Lincoln.

111. **COLYER, Christina**
Lincoln: the archaeology of an historic city
Lincoln: Lincoln Archaeological Trust, 1975.   48p.: ill., maps.

112.   **MOORE, C.N.**
Archaeology in Lincolnshire, 1974
p.57–65: ill. in *Lincolnshire history and archaeology*, vol.10, 1975.
> pp.57–58: Greetwell Villa; Lincoln Archaeological Trust excavations; Roman aqueduct; East Bight.

113.   **WHITE, A.J.**
Archaeology in Lincolnshire and South Humberside, 1975
pp.55–64 in *Lincolnshire history and archaeology*, vol.11, 1976.

114.   ──────────
Archaeology in Lincolnshire and South Humberside, 1976
pp.71–79: ill. in *Lincolnshire history and archaeology*, vol.12, 1977.
> pp.75–76: Roman aqueduct; Bishop Grosseteste College; Flaxengate; St Mark's Church.

115.   **AMBROSE, Timothy**
A Guide to Roman Lincoln
by Timothy Ambrose and Andrew White.
Lincoln: Lincolnshire Museums, 1978.   11p.: ill., map.
Cover title: 'A Visitor's guide: Roman Lincoln'.

116.   **WHITE, A.J.**
Archaeology in Lincolnshire and South Humberside, 1977
pp.75–89: ill. in *Lincolnshire history and archaeology*, vol.13, 1978.
> p.79: aqueduct; Bishop Grosseteste College; Flaxengate; St Mark's; West Gate; West Bight; St Paul-in-the-Bail; Vicars' Court.

117.
Excavations at Lincoln: second interim report: excavations in the lower town, 1972–8
edited by Christina Colyer and M.J. Jones.
pp.50–91: ill., 11p. of plates in *The Antiquaries journal*, vol.LIX, pt.1, 1979.
> With contributions from R.H. Jones, D. Perring, N.M. Reynolds and J.S. Wacher.

118.   **WHITE, A.J.**
Archaeology in Lincolnshire and South Humberside, 1978
pp.65–85: ill. in *Lincolnshire history and archaeology*, vol.14, 1979.
> pp.70–73: aqueduct; St Paul-in-the-Bail; Danes Terrace; Vicars' Court.

119.   **WHITE, A.J.**
Archaeology in Lincolnshire and South Humberside, 1979
pp.67–91: ill. in *Lincolnshire history and archaeology*, vol.15, 1980.
> pp.73–78: Castle; Castle Square; St Paul-in-the-Bail, by G. Gilmour and M. J. Jones; North District School, by B. Gilmour and M.J. Jones; Nettleham Glebe.

120.
Excavations at Lincoln: third interim report: sites outside the walled city, 1972–1977
edited by M.J. Jones with contributions from Margaret J. Darling, Brian Gilmour, R.H. Jones and K.F. Wood.
pp.83–114: ill., [8]p. of plates in *The Antiquaries journal*, vol.LXI, pt.1, 1981.

121.   **JONES, Michael**
Lincoln: a city set on a hill
pp.36–40: ill. in *Popular archaeology*, January, 1981.
Also reprinted by F.L.A.R.E. as 8p. booklet.

122.   **WHITE, A.J.**
Archaeology in Lincolnshire and South Humberside, 1980
pp.63–84: ill. in *Lincolnshire history and archaeology*, vol.16, 1981.
   pp.72–75: West Bight; Orchard St.; East Bight; High St.; Hawhill; Swanpool.

123.   **JONES, Michael**
Lincoln latest
pp.14–18: ill. in *Popular archaeology*, October, 1982.

124   **WHITE, A.J.**
Archaeology in Lincolnshire and South Humberside, 1981
pp.71–83: ill. in *Lincolnshire history and archaeology*, vol.17, 1982.
   pp.72–74: Bishop's Palace; East Bight; Grantham Place.

125.   ───────────
Archaeology in Lincolnshire and South Humberside, 1982
compiled by A.J. White and M.C. Solly.
pp.91–112: ill. in *Lincolnshire history and archaeology*, vol.18, 1983.
   pp.98–100: Monson Street Roman cemetery; Roman houses in the southern suburbs, by J.R. Magilton.

126.   **JONES, Barri**
Past imperfect: the story of Rescue Archaeology
London: Heinemann, 1984.   xii, 164p.: ill., maps, plans.
Includes bibliography and index.
ISBN 043532974X
   pp.80–85: Lincoln.

127.   **BAKER, F.T.**
Archaeology in Lincolnshire: looking back over 60 years
pp.5–14: ill. in *Lincolnshire history and archaeology*, vol.20, 1985.
   Account of discoveries and of the personalities involved.   Much of the excavation discussed took place in Lincoln itself.

128.   **JONES, Michael J.**
Archaeology in Lincoln
pp.1–8, plans in *British Archaeological Association conference transactions for the year 1982*, vol.VIII, 1986.

129.   **PAGE, Tony**
Archaeology in Lincolnshire and South Humberside, 1985
compiled by Tony Page and Naomi Field.
pp.71–80: ill. in *Lincolnshire history and archaeology*, vol.21, 1986.
   pp.72–74: 'Archaeology in Lincoln', by M.J. Jones.

130.
[Lincoln: excavations by Trust for Lincolnshire Archaeology]
pp.157–158 in *Medieval archaeology*, vol.30, 1986.

131.
Report of Committee of Inquiry into Archaeology in Lincolnshire
Lincoln: Trust for Lincolnshire Archaeology, 1986.   65p.

132.   **TRUST FOR LINCOLNSHIRE ARCHAEOLOGY**
Archaeology in Lincolnshire, 1985–86: [second annual report]
Lincoln: The Trust, 1986.   32p.: ill.
   pp.18–30: St Mary's Guildhall; Monks Abbey; Lawn Hospital; Cathedral; St Benedict's Square; Chapel Lane; Hungate.

133.   **PHILLIPS, Charles W.**
My life in archaeology
Gloucester: Alan Sutton, 1987.   xiv, 175p., [24]p. of plates.
p.19: observations on Lincoln Museum, Arthur Smith and archaeology in the city.

134.   **TRUST FOR LINCOLNSHIRE ARCHAEOLOGY**
Archaeology in Lincolnshire, 1986–1987: third annual report of the Trust for Lincolnshire Archaeology, October 1987
Lincoln: The Trust, 1987.   40p.: ill.
ISBN 0948639024
pp.20–35: Castle West Gate; the Lawn; Cathedral; Greetwellgate; Swanpool; Waterside North.

ROMAN PERIOD

General

135.   **NICHOLSON, W.A.**
[Mr W.A. Nicholson, architect of Lincoln...communicated the following description of a Roman tessellated pavement discovered in that city]
p.186 in *The Journal of the British Archaeological Association*, vol.1, 1846.

136.   **DRURY, Michael**
Notes on the excavations for sewer works at Lincoln
[1878].   11p.: ill.
Typescript.
Author was architect and surveyor who practised between 1860–1890.   Recorded his observations of strata exposed by sewer trenches; of archaeological interest particularly for evidence of Roman occupation.

137.   **MAYHEW, S.M.**
Recent discoveries at Colonia Lindum
pp.308–316, [3] leaves of plates in *The Journal of the British Archaeological Association*, vol.35, 1879.
Paper read December 4, 1878 and June 18, 1879.

138.
Roman antiquities at Lincoln
pp.125–126 in *The Journal of the British Archaeological Association*, vol.40, 1884.

139.
[Proceedings of the association: Mr. E.P. Loftus Brock...laid on the table a drawing of a well-know mass of Roman masonry which formed part of the Roman north wall of Lincoln
p.188 in *The Journal of the British Archaeological Association*, vol.47, 1891.

140.   **TATHAM, Edward H.R.**
Lincolnshire in Roman times: a paper read before the Louth Antiquarian and Naturalists' Society
Louth: J.W. Goulding, 1902.   52p.
pp.16–21: concerned with Lincoln, especially the canal system.

141.   **McELDERRY, R. Knox**
Some notes on Roman Britain.   1: the date of the Roman colony at Lincoln
pp.398–399 in *The Classical review*, vol.XVIII, 1904.

142.   **WELBY, Alfred C.E.**
Legion IX at Lincoln
p.5–6 in *LN&Q*, vol.11, no.1, 1910.

143.
Stone cist found at Lincoln
pp.225–226, [1] leaf of plates in *LN&Q*, vol.11, no.8, 1911.

144.
Memorials of old Lincolnshire
edited by E. Mansel Sympson.
London: George Allen, 1911.   xv, 348p., [30] leaves of plates.

145.   **SMITH, Arthur**
Some notes on Roman Lincoln
pp.82–86 in *Birmingham Archaeological Society transactions and proceedings*, vol.36,
1911.

146.   **TATHAM, E.R.H.**
The Romans in Lincolnshire
pp.24–52 in *Memorials of old Lincolnshire*, 1911.
        pp.28–32: Lindum.

147.   **BEVAN, J.O.**
The towns of Roman Britain
London: Chapman & Hall, 1917.   viii, 66p., 2 leaves of maps.
        pp.41–42: Lindum Colonia.

148.   **SYMPSON, E. Mansel**
Roman Lincoln: lecture
pp.595–607 in *The Journal of the Institution of Mechanical Engineers*, October, 1920.

149.   **WEIGALL, Arthur**
Wanderings in Roman Britain
London: Thornton Butterworth, 1926.   341p.: ill., [2] leaves of maps, [11] leaves of
plates.
        pp.158–166: Lincoln.

150.   **OSWALD, Felix**
Un indice presumable de la presence de la huitieme legion en Angleterre
pp.269–271: ill. in *Homagem a Martins Sarmento*, 1933.

151.   **STANWELL, R.H.**
The Newport earthwork, Lincoln: excavations during July-August, 1937
by R.H. Stanwell and F.T. Baker.
pp.255–261: ill. in *Lincolnshire magazine*, vol.3, 1936–38.

152.   **COLLINGWOOD, R.G.**
Roman Britain and the English settlements
R.G. Collingwood and J.N.L. Myres.   2nd ed.
Oxford: Clarendon Press, 1937.   xxv, 515p., 10 maps.
Originally published: 1936.   Includes index.
        Lincoln mentioned passim.

153.   **BAKER, F.T.**
Roman Lincoln
Lincoln: Lincoln Branch of the Historical Association, 1938. 27p., [7]p. of plates, 1 leaf map.

154.   **RICHMOND, Ian A.**
A Project for the excavation of Roman Lincoln
p.1–4 in *AAS reports and papers*, vol.3, pt.1, 1941.

155.
Roman Lincoln, 1945–46: two years' excavation in Lincoln: report of the Lincoln Archaeological Research Committee
[Lincoln]: [The Committee], 1946. 27p.: ill.

156.   **RICHMOND, I.A.**
The Roman city of Lincoln
pp.26–56: ill., [6]p. of plates, map in *The Archaeological journal*, vol.CIII, 1946.

157.   ————————
The Four Coloniae of Roman Britain
pp.57–84: ill., plans in *The Archaeological journal*, vol.CIII, 1946.

158.   **NASH-WILLIAMS, E.V.**
Review: Roman Lincoln, 1945–46
p.84 in *The Archaeological journal*, vol.CIII, 1946.

159.   **BAKER, F.T.**
The Pre-historic settlement of Lincolnshire
299p.: ill., 8 maps, 26 plates.
Thesis [M.A.] - University of Nottingham, 1954.
   Contains gazeteer and location list of pre-historic discoveries in Lincolnshire, of which
   pp.278–279 concerns Lincoln.

160.
Lindum Colonia: a brief account of excavations on the northern defences and the east gate of the Roman legionary fortress and town at Lincoln
[Lincoln]: [Lincoln Archaeological Research Committee], [196?].   [6]p.: ill.

161.   **PETCH, Denis F.**
Excavations at Lincoln, 1955–58: the southern defences of the legionary fortress and the upper Colonia, at the Sub-deanery and the Old Bishop's Palace
pp.40–70: ill., [5]p. of plates in *The Archaeological journal*, vol. CXVII, 1962.

162.   **DUDLEY, Donald R.**
The Roman conquest of Britain, A.D.43–57
by Donald R. Dudley & Graham Webster.
London: Batsford, 1965.   216p.: ill., plans, [frontis].
(British battles series)
   Includes several references to Lincoln.

163.   **WHITWELL, J.B.**
Roman Lincoln
pp.351–353: ill. in *History today*, May, 1968.

164.   **COLLINGWOOD, R.G.**
The Archaeology of Roman Britain
R.G. Collingwood and Ian Richmond.   Revised ed.
London: Methuen, 1969.   xxiv, 349p.: ill., [24]p. of plates.
(Methuen handbooks of archaeology)
Originally published: 1930.   Includes index.
    pp.100–101: defences; pp.124–125: pipelines and sewers; pp.272–273: pottery.

165.   **WHITWELL, J.B.**
Roman Lincolnshire
Lincoln: History of Lincolnshire Committee, 1970.   xxv, 155p.: ill., [8]p. of plates.
(History of Lincolnshire, 2)
Includes index.
    pp.17–43: Roman Lincoln.

166.   **COLYER, Christina**
Dig this
pp.8–9: ill. in *ETC: the house magazine of the GEC Electronic Tube Co. Ltd.*, no.10,
August, 1971.
    Roman archæology.

167.   ─────────────
Lincoln
pp.67–71: ill. in *Current archaeology*, no.26, vol.3, no.3, May, 1971.
    Mainly Roman.

168.   **SALMON, M.**
From Roman fort to Cathedral City
pp.325–326: ill. in *The Townswoman*, vol.XXXVIII, no.9, Eastern counties issue,
October, 1971.
    Mainly Roman.

169.   **DAVEY, P.J.**
Bronze age metalwork from Lincolnshire
pp.51–127: ill., map, [1]p. of plates in *Archaeologia*, vol.CIV, 1973.
    Includes items found at Lincoln.

170.   **TODD, Malcolm**
The Coritani
London: Duckworth, 1973.   164p.: ill., maps.
(Peoples of Roman Britain)
Includes index.
ISBN 0715606492
    pp.28–29: fortress; pp.34–35: Lindum Colonia; pp.132–133: post Roman.

171.   **JONES, Michael J.**
Roman fort-defences to A.D.117, with special reference to Britain
Oxford: British Archaeological Reports, 1975.   192p.: ill., maps.
(BAR, 21)

172.   **WACHER, John**
The Towns of Roman Britain
London: Batsford, 1975.   460p.: ill., maps, plans.
Includes index.
ISBN 0713427949
    pp.120–137: discussion of relationship between sewerage system and aqueduct.

173.   **MAY, Jeffrey**
Prehistoric Lincolnshire
Lincoln: History of Lincolnshire Committee, 1976.   xix, 215p.: ill., 9p. of plates.
(History of Lincolnshire, 1)
Includes index.
> p.214: Lincoln City and County Museum; pp.130–133: dagger and shield found in the Witham.

174.   **SORRELL, Alan**
Roman towns in Britain
London: Batsford, 1976.   80p.: ill.
Includes index.
ISBN 017343237
> pp.51–53: Lincoln and references passim.

175.   **AMBROSE, Timothy**
Gaius Valerius: a Roman soldier in Lincoln
Lincoln: Lincolnshire Museums, 1978.   [4]p.: ill.
(Lincolnshire Museums information sheet.   Archaeology series, no.1)

176.
Lincoln in Roman times: the Roman army
[Lincoln]: F.L.A.R.E. Education Group, 1978.   57p.: ill.
> For children.

177.
Lincoln in Roman times: the city
[Lincoln]: F.L.A.R.E. Education Group, 1979.   48p.: ill.
Includes bibliography.
> For children.

178.   **JONES, Michael J.**
The Defences of the upper Roman enclosure
Michael J. Jones with Margaret J. Darling, Sarah Dobson et al.
London: Council for British Archaeology, 1980.   62p.: ill., plans.
(The Archaeology of Lincoln, vol.VII–1)
Includes bibliography. Text in English with summaries in French and German.
ISBN 0906780004

179.   ⸺⸺⸺⸺
Roman Britain
Oxford: Oxford University Press, 1981.   xx, 824p., [12]p. of maps.
ISBN 0192851438
> pp.152–153: Colonia.

180.
Lincoln in Roman times
Lincoln: F.L.A.R.E. Education Group, [1982?].   [6]p.

181.   **JONES, Michael**
Lincoln
by Michael Jones, Brian Gilmour and Kevin Camidge.
pp.366–369: ill. in *Current archaeology*, no.83, vol.VII, no.12, August, 1982.
> Mainly Roman.

182.
A Roman walk: an illustrated archaeological walk
Lincoln: F.L.A.R.E., 1983.   4p.: ill.
[2 unbound cards].
ISBN 0946853002

183.   **FRERE, Sheppard**
Britannia: a history of Roman Britain
3rd ed., revised.
London: Routledge & Kegan Paul, 1987.   423p., map, 32p. of plates.
Originally published: 1967; 2nd revised ed.: 1978.
    pp.55–57: Ninth Legion and various other references.

184.
Fortress into city: the consolidation of Roman Britain, first century A.D.
edited by Graham Webster
London: Batsford, 1988.   178p.: ill., maps.
Includes bibliography and index.
ISBN 0713455187
    pp.145–166: 'Lincoln', by Michael Jones.

Specific Finds

185.   **POWNALL, John**
Account of some sepulchral antiquities discovered at Lincoln: [read March 10, 1791]
pp.345–349, [1]p. of plates in *Archaeologia*, vol.X, 1792.
    Roman remains found half a mile east of East Gate.

186.   **CARTER, John**
Account of sepulchral monuments discovered at Lincoln...in a letter to John Pownall
pp.107–113, [3]p. of plates in *Archaeologia*, vol.XII, 1795.
    Concerns artefacts associated with Roman burials.

187.
 Discovery of a Roman tombstone at Lincoln
p.16 in *The Reliquary*, vol.VII, 1866–67.
    Situated at the corner of Salt House Lane.

188.   **WORDSWORTH, J.**
Roman milestone of the Emperor M. Piavonius Victorinus, 265–267 A.D., found in the
centre of ancient Roman Lincoln, April 2, 1879
p.13–16, [1] leaf of plates in *AAS reports and papers*, vol.15, 1879–80.

189.   **VENABLES, Edmund**
Roman altar to the Parcae discovered at Lincoln
by the Rev. Precentor Venables.
pp.32–39 in *AAS reports and papers*, vol.17, 1883–84.

190.   **O'NEILL, William**
Discovery of Roman remains at Lincoln
pp.182–184 in *Old Lincolnshire*, vol.1, 1885.
    Letter originally appeared in *The Lancet*, June 20, 1884.   Concerns remains found on the
    corner between Bailgate and Eastgate.

191. ―――――――
Discovery of Roman remains at Lincoln
pp.210–212 in *Old Lincolnshire*, vol.1, 1885.
    Supplements previous paper.

192. ―――――――
Discovery of Roman remains in Lincoln
pp.107–109 in *Chambers journal*, 5th series, pt.14, March 2, 1885.

193. ―――――――
Further notes on the Roman crematorium at Lincoln
pp.225–228: ill., [2]p. of plates in *Old Lincolnshire*, vol.1, 1885.

194. **FOWLER, J.**
Roman wall in Lincoln
p.144 in *LN&Q*, vol.1, no.5, 1889.

195. **G., E.L.**
Notes: [on Roman pavement found at Lincoln in 1846]
pp.161–163, [2] leaves of plates in *LN&Q*, vol.1, no.6, 1889.

196.
Roman pavements at Lincoln
p.207 in *LN&Q*, vol.1, no.7, 1889.

197. **DRURY, Michael**
On a concrete causeway, supposed to be Roman, at Lincoln
pp.221–226, [1] leaf plan in *The Journal of the British Archaeological Association*,
September 30, 1890.

198. **SMITH, C. Roach**
Notes on Roman antiquities at Lincoln during the Lincoln congress
pp.53–57 in *The Journal of the British Archaeological Association*,
vol.46, 1890.

199. **VENABLES, Edmund**
Some account of the discovery of a Roman villa in the Greetwell fields, near Lincoln
pp.48–52, [1] folded plate in *AAS reports and papers*, vol.21, 1891–92.

200. ―――――――
Some account of the Roman colonnade discovered in Bailgate, Lincoln
pp.3–6, [1] folded plate in *AAS reports and papers*, vol.21, 1891–92.

201. ―――――――
[Notes on the discovery of a beautiful pilaster of Roman work at Lincoln]
Rev. Precentor Venables.
p.260 in *The Archaeological journal*, vol.XLVIII, 1891.
    Discovered while digging foundations of new School of Art & Science.

202. **FOX, George E.**
Recent discoveries of Roman remains in Lincoln
pp.233–238, [1] leaf plan in *Archaeologia*, vol.LIII, 1892.

203. **VENABLES, Edmund**
Some account of the Roman colonnade discovered in Bailgate, Lincoln
by the Rev. Precentor Venables.
pp.131–135: ill. in *The Archaeological journal*, vol.XLIX, 1892.

204. ───────────
Some account of the discovery of a Roman villa in the Greetwell fields, near Lincoln
pp.258–262, 1 folded plan in *The Archaeological journal*, vol.XLIX, 1892.

205.　**O'NEILL, William**
An Account of Roman remains discovered in Lincoln
pp.56–69 in *AAS reports and papers*, vol.22, 1893–94.

206.
Roman pavement at Lincoln
pp.179–180 in *LN&Q*, vol.3, no.22, 1893.

207.　**SYMPSON, E. Mansel**
The First Roman south wall of Lindum Colonia
pp.129–130, [1] leaf of plates in *LN&Q*, vol.7, no.57, 1903.

208. ───────────
The Original west gate of the Roman city of Lindum Colonia
pp.225–226, [1] leaf of plates in *LN&Q*, vol.8, no.68, 1905.

209 ───────────
The Western half of the north wall of Lindum Colonia
pp.33–35, [1] leaf of plates in *LN&Q, vol.9, no.70, 1906.*

210.　**SMITH, Arthur**
Roman antiquities in the City & County Museum, Lincoln (part 1)
Lincoln: Lincoln City and County Museum, 1908.　12p.: ill.
(Lincoln City and County Museum publications, no.3)

211. ───────────
Roman antiquities in the City & County Museum, Lincoln (part 2)
Lincoln: Lincoln City and County Museum, 1908.　10p., [2] leaves of plates.
(Lincoln City and County Museum publications, no.5)

212. ───────────
Roman antiquities in the City & County Museum, Lincoln (part 3)
Lincoln: Lincoln City and County Museum, 1909.　10p., [2] leaves of plates.
(Lincoln City and County Museum publications, no.7)

213. ───────────
Roman antiquities in the City & County Museum, Lincoln (part 4)
Lincoln: Lincoln City and County Museum, 1912.　[7]p.: ill.
(Lincoln City and County Museum publications, no.14)

214. ───────────
Roman antiquities in the City & County Museum, Lincoln (part 5)
Lincoln: Lincoln City and County Museum, 1913.　22p.: ill., [1] leaf of plates.
(Lincoln City and County Museum publications, no.16)

215.　**HAVERFIELD, F.**
[Notes on discovery of tombstone of Gaius Valerius]
pp.193–196, [1] leaf of plates in *LN&Q*, vol.10, no.7, 1909.

216.
Roman antiquities: [catalogue of specimens of terra sigillata ware – ie. Samian – in the
Lincoln Museum]
Lincoln: Lincoln City and County Museum, [1910?].　22p.: ill., [frontis].

217.   **SMITH, Arthur**
Roman antiquities in Westgate, Lincoln
pp.129–132: ill., [1] leaf of plates in *LN&Q*, vol.11, no.5, 1911.

218.   ─────────────
A Catalogue of the Roman inscribed stones found in the city of Lincoln
Lincoln: Lincolnshire Publishing, [1929].   vii, 24p.: ill.

219.   **ABELL, E.I.**
The Cold bath: [notes]
[193?].   2 leaves.
Typescript.
    Refers to the Roman bath.

220.   **SMITH, Arthur**
Roman inscribed stones found in the city of Lincoln: [since the publication in 1929 of
A Catalogue of inscribed stones...]
pp.1–2, [1] leaf of plates in *LN&Q*, vol.23, 1934–35.

221.   **BAKER, F.T.**
Roman pottery kiln at Lincoln
pp.187–190: ill. in *Lincolnshire magazine*, vol.3, 1936–38.

222.   **FARADAY, Laurence**
Relics from Lincolnshire in the British Museum.   2: the Roman era
pp.9–13: ill. in *Lincolnshire magazine*, vol.4, 1938–40.
Includes items found in Lincoln.

223.   **RICHMOND, I.A.**
Three fragments of Roman official statues, from York, Lincoln, and Silchester
pp.1–9, [4]p. of plates in *The Antiquaries journal*, vol.XXIV, 1944.
    pp.5–7: bronze leg of a horse from an equestrian statue from Lincoln.

224.   **WEBSTER, Graham**
The Legionary fortress at Lincoln
pp.37–78: ill., [3] leaves of plates in *Journal of Roman studies*, vol.XXXIX, 1949.

225.
[Notes on excavations of the East Colonia, carried out by Lincoln Archaeological
Research Committee]
pp.91–92 in *Journal of Roman studies*, vol.XLIV, 1954.

226.   **THOMPSON, F. Hugh**
The Roman aqueduct at Lincoln
pp.106–128: ill., plans, [6]p. of plates in *The Archaeological journal*, vol.CXI, 1955.
    Author was curator of Lincoln Museum.

227.   ─────────────
Roman Lincoln, 1953: (i) defences of the legionary fortress and Colonia in East Bight;
(ii) a fountain basin at nos.191–2, High Street
pp.22–36: ill., plans, [3]p. of plates in *Journal of Roman studies*, vol.XLVI, 1956.

228.   **BAKER, F.T.**
Ancient monuments scheduled in Lincolnshire.   Part 3: IV Roman remains
pp.38–42 in *The Lincolnshire historian*, vol.II, no.5, 1958.
    pp.39–40: Lincoln.

229.   **PETCH, D.F.**
A Roman temple near Lincoln
p.27 in *Lincolnshire life*, vol.1, no.4, winter, 1962.
> Discovery of inscription describing dedication of an arch to Mars Rigonemetos.

230.   **COLLINGWOOD, R.G.**
The Roman inscriptions of Britain
by R.G. Collingwood and R.P.Wright.
Oxford: Clarendon Press, 1965.   xxxiii, 790p.: ill., xix plates.
Includes index.
> pp.80–91: Lincoln; pp.91–92: Fossdyke.

231.   **TODD, Malcolm**
Roman stamped tiles from Lincoln and their origin
pp.29–31 in *Lincolnshire history and archaeology*, no.1, 1966.

232.   **THOMPSON, F.H.**
Some lost Roman bronzes from Lincoln
pp.100–103, [4] plates in *The Antiquaries journal*, vol.51, 1971.
> Drawings and notes by E.J. Willson of finds which are no longer extant.

233.
A New office block for Lincoln CBC: and the Roman wall and gateway on the site at 'The Park', Lincoln
[Sheffield]: [F.P.A. Finnegan], [1972?].   1 folded sheet: ill.
> Archaeology of the site by Christina Colyer.

234.   **THOMPSON, F. H.**
The Gates of Roman Lincoln
by F.H. Thompson and J.B. Whitwell.
pp.129–207: ill., plans, [26]p. of plates in *Archaeologia*, vol.CIV, 1973.

235.   **BOGAERS, J.E.**
Roman tile stamps from Lincoln (Lindum) and the Legio V Alaudae
pp.275–278 in *Britannia*, vol.8, 1977.

236.   **DARLING, Margaret J.**
A Group of late Roman pottery from Lincoln
London: Council for British Archaeology for the Lincoln Archaeological Trust, 1977.
42p.: ill.
(Lincoln Archaeological Trust monograph series, vol.XVI–I)
Includes bibliography.
> Group found in 1970 outside the west gate of lower Colonia at the Park.

237.   **WHITE, Andrew**
Antiquities from the River Witham.   Part 1: Prehistoric and Roman
Lincoln: Lincolnshire Museums, 1979.   6p.: ill.
(Lincolnshire Museums information sheet.   Archaeology series, no.12)

238.   _____
Parisian ware: a study of stamped wares of the Roman period in Lincolnshire, Humberside and South Yorkshire
Highworth: VORDA Archaeological and Historical Publications, 1982.   56p.: ill.
(VORDA research series, 4)
ISBN 0907246036
> Some references to material found at Lincoln.

ROMANO-BRITISH PERIOD

General

239.   **MYERS, J.N.L.**
Lincoln in the fifth century A.D.
pp.85–88: ill. in *The Archaeological journal*, vol.CIII, 1946.

240.   **WHITWELL, J.B.**
The Coritani: some aspects of the Iron Age tribe and the Roman civitas
Oxford: British Archaeological Reports, 1982.   406p., maps.
ISBN 0860541622
(BAR British series, 99)

241.   **CRICKMORE, Julie**
Romano-British defences
Oxford: British Archaeological Reports, 1984.   205p., maps.
(BAR British series, 126)
ISBN 0860542645
    Includes references to Lincoln as one of the Coloniae.

242.   **MYERS, J.N.L.**
The English settlements
Oxford: Clarendon Press, 1986.   xxviii, 248p.: ill., 4p. of maps.
(Oxford history of England, 1B)
ISBN 0198217196
    Covers period between collapse of Roman government and arrival of St Augustine in A.D.597.
    Lincoln pp.177–179 and 181–182 and other references.

Specific Finds

243.   **WEBSTER, Graham**
A Romano-British pottery kiln at Swanpool, near Lincoln
by Graham Webster and Norman Booth.
pp.61–79: ill., [1] leaf of plates in *The Antiquaries journal*,
vol.XXVII, 1947.

244.   **CORDER, Philip**
A Romano-British pottery kiln on the Lincoln racecourse
Nottingham: Department of Adult Education, University of Nottingham, 1950.   18p.:
ill., [2]p. of plates.
    Based on the work of the members of the Summer School in Archaeology, Lincoln, 1949.

245.   ——————
The Structure of Romano-British pottery kilns
pp.10–27: ill., [5]p. of plates in *The Archaeological journal*, 1957.
    Photograph and diagram of Lincoln Race Course kiln with references in text.

246   **THOMPSON, F.H.**
A Romano-British pottery kiln at North Hykeham, Lincolnshire:
with an appendix on the typology, dating and distribution of 'Rustic' ware in Great Britain
pp.15–51: ill., [4]p. of plates in *The Antiquaries journal*,
vol. 38, 1958.
    Information about kiln sites in Lincoln contained in appendix.

247.   **WEBSTER, Graham**
A Romano-British pottery kiln at Rookery Lane, Lincoln
pp.214–220: ill. in *The Antiquaries journal*, vol.40, 1960.

248.   **WHITWELL, J.B.**
Three pottery kiln sites in Lincolnshire, located by proton gradiometer (Maxbleep) survey
and confirmed by excavation
pp.125–129: ill. in *Estratto da prospezioni archeologiche*, 1969.
Text in English with Italian summary.
    pp.125–126: Swanpool, Romano-British remains.

ANGLO-SAXON PERIOD

General

249.   **TROLLOPE, Edward**
The Introduction of Christianity into Lincolnshire during the Saxon period: a paper read
at the Lincoln meeting, May 26, 1857
pp.1–8, [2] leaves of plates in *AAS reports and papers*, vol.4, 1857–58.
    Refers to Paulinus in Lincoln.

250.
*Documents illustrative of the social and economic history of the Danelaw from various
collections*
edited by F.M. Stenton.
London: published for the British Academy by Oxford University Press, 1920.   cxliv,
554p.
Includes index. Text in Latin.
    Many references to buildings and inhabitants within the city.

251.   **HILL, J.W.F.**
Danish and Norman Lincoln
pp.7–22, plans in *AAS reports and papers*, vol.41, 1932–33.

252.   **MARYON, Herbert**
A Sword of the Viking period from the River Witham
pp.175–179, [2]p. of plates in *The Antiquaries journal*, vol.XXX, 1950.

253.   **STENTON, F.M.**
The Free peasantry of the northern Danelaw
Oxford: Clarendon Press, 1969.   191p.
Includes index.
    Brief references to Lincoln.

254.   ——————
Anglo-Saxon England
3rd ed.
Oxford: Clarendon Press, 1971.   xli, 765p., folded map.
    References to Lincoln passim, especially to Paulinus and Blaecca.

255.
The Archaeology of Anglo-Saxon England
edited by David M. Wilson.
London: Methuen, 1976.   xvi, 532p.: ill., [21]p. of plates.
Includes index.
ISBN 041615090X
    Various references to Lincoln; p.328: Lincoln-type war.

256.   **ADAMS, Lauren**
Lincoln: a Viking town
Lauren Adams and others.
Lincoln: Lincolnshire Museums, 1980.   8p.: ill.
(Lincolnshire Museums information sheet.   Archaeology series, no.20)

Specific Finds

257.   **ALLEN, J. Romilly**
Anglo-Saxon pins found at Lincoln
pp.52–53 in *The Reliquary and illustrated archaeologist*, new series, vol.X, 1904.

258.   **FARADAY, Laurence**
Relics from Lincolnshire in the British Museum.   4: late Anglo-Saxon & Viking
pp.89–91: ill. in *Lincolnshire magazine*, vol.4, 1938–40.
    Includes number of items found in Lincoln.

259.   **KENDRICK, T.D.**
A Late Saxon hanging bowl
pp.161–162, [2]p. of plates in *The Antiquaries journal*, vol.XXI, 1941.
    Found in the River Witham near Lincoln.

260.   **WHITWELL, J.B.**
Archaeological notes for 1963
p.66: ill. in *AAS reports and papers*, new series, vol.10, 1963–64.
    Disc brooch and seal box found in Lincoln.

261.   **WILSON, David M.**
Anglo-Saxon ornamental metalwork, 700–1100, in the British Museum
London: Trustees of the British Museum, 1964.   xii, 248p.: ill., XLIV plates.
(Catalogue of antiquities of the later Saxon period, vol.1)
Includes bibliography and index.
    References to Lincoln mount and sword found in the Witham.

262.
Medieval Britain in [19__]
in *Medieval archaeology*, 1973– .
    A summary of excavation work in Britain, often including that at Lincoln.

263.   **WHITE, Andrew**
Antiquities from the River Witham, 1979.   6p.: ill.
(Lincolnshire Museums information sheet.   Archaeology series, no.13)

MIDDLE AGES

Specific Finds

264.   **HURST, J.G.**
Post mediaeval French imports and English copies at Lincoln
pp.54–56, [2]p. of plates in *Lincolnshire history and archaeology*, no.1, 1966.
　　　Chafing dishes and lobed cups found in Lincoln.

265.   **HEALEY, R. Hilary**
Medieval and sub-medieval pottery in Lincolnshire
viii, 179, [85] leaves, [27] leaves of maps.
Thesis [M. Phil.] – University of Nottingham, 1975.
　　　Includes reference to Lincoln and Lincoln types of pottery.

266.   **REYNOLDS, Nicholas**
Investigations in the Observatory Tower, Lincoln Castle
pp.201–205: ill. in *Medieval archaeology*, vol.XIX, 1975.

267.   **ADAMS, Lauren**
Medieval pottery from Broadgate East, Lincoln, 1973
London: Council for British Archaeology for the Lincoln Archaeological Trust, 1977.
54p.: ill.
(Lincoln Archaeological Trust monograph series, vol.XVII–I)
Includes bibliography.

268.   **MANN, J.E.**
Early medieval finds from Flaxengate. 1: Objects of antler, bone, stone, horn, amber and jet
London: Council for British Archaeology, 1982.   68p.: ill., plans.
(The Archaeology of Lincoln, vol.XIV–1)
Includes bibliography.
ISBN 0906780209

269.   **HURST, J.G.**
The Development of medieval pottery research in Lincolnshire
pp.64–68 in *A Prospect of Lincolnshire*, 1984.
　　　Describes work of the Lincoln Archaeological Research Committee.

Excavations at Particular Sites

270.   **TROLLOPE, Edward**
Notice of a sepulchral slab discovered on the site of the Hospital of the Holy Innocents, near Lincoln.
pp.212–217, 1 leaf of plates in *The Archaeological journal*, vol.XIII, 1856.
　　　Other names under which the hospital has been known include: Malandery; Maladeria; Maladrerie; Maladerie; Leprosery; Domus Leprosorum.

271.
Sepulchral slab found in the malandery field near Lincoln
p.xi, [1] leaf of plates in *AAS reports and papers*, vol.8, 1865–66.

272.
An Account of some ancient arms and utensils found in Lincolnshire, chiefly in the bed of the River Witham between Kirkstead and Lincoln, when it was scoured out in 1787 and 1788: from Sir Joseph Banks' Ms. at Revesby
pp.196–201 in *LN&Q*, vol.3, no.23, 1893.
  Continued: pp.232–236, vol.3, no.24, 1893.

273.   **PANTIN, W.A.**
Chantry priests' houses and other medieval lodgings
pp.216–258: ill. in *Medieval archaeology*, vol.3, 1959.
  pp.247–248: Vicars' Court, Lincoln.

274.
[Notes on excavations carried out at the Old Bishop's Palace by Lincoln Archaeological Research Committee]
pp.109–111: ill. in *Journal of Roman studies*, vol.XLIX, 1959.

275.   **HANKEY, T.**
A Short history of the Eastgate site
[Lincoln]: Trust House Hotels, [1964?].   13p.: ill., plan.

276.   **COPPACK, Glyn**
The Excavation of a Roman and medieval site at Flaxengate, Lincoln
pp.73–114: ill. in *Lincolnshire history and archaeology*, vol.8, 1973.

277.   **CHAPMAN, Hugh**
Excavations at the Bishop's Palace, 1968–72
by Hugh Chapman, Glyn Coppack, Peter Drewett.
Sleaford: Society for Lincolnshire History and Archaeology, 1975.   62p.: ill.
(Occasional papers in Lincolnshire history and archaeology)
ISBN 0904680010

278.   **COLYER, Christina**
Excavations at Lincoln, 1970–72: the western defences of the lower town: an interim report
pp.227–266: ill., [10]p. of plates in *The Antiquaries journal*, vol.LV, 1975.

279.   **LINCOLN ARCHAEOLOGICAL TRUST**
Excavations at St Paul-in-the-Bail, March, 1975
Lincoln: Lincoln Archaeological Trust and Lloyds Bank, 1975.   [3]p.

280.   **REYNOLDS, Nicholas**
Investigations in the Observatory Tower, Lincoln Castle
pp.201–205: ill. in *Medieval archaeology*, vol.19, 1975.

281.   **COLYER, Christina**
St Paul-in-the-Bail, Lincoln
by Christina Colyer and Brian Gilmour.
pp.102–105: ill. in *Current archaeology*, vol.6, 1978.

282.   **GILMOUR, Brian**
The Anglo-Saxon church at St Paul-in-the-Bail, Lincoln
pp.214–218: ill. in *Medieval archaeology*, vol.23, 1979.

283.   **ADAMS, Lauren**
Early Islamic pottery from Flaxengate, Lincoln
pp.218–219 in *Medieval archaeology*, vol.23, 1979.

284.   **JONES, Michael**
Excavations at East Bight
pp.370–371: ill. in *Current archaeology*, no.83, vol.VII, no.12, 1982.

285   **COULSON, Charles**
Hierarchism in conventual crenellation: an essay in the sociology and metaphysics of medieval fortification
pp.69–100 in *Medieval archaeology*, vol.26, 1982.
    pp.72, 75–77: the Close Wall, Lincoln.

286.   **WILFORD, John**
Beneath the Stonebow Centre: 2000 years of Lincoln's history
drawings by David Vale.
Lincoln: F.L.A.R.E., 1983.   24p.: ill., plans.

287.   **PAGE, A.B.**
Archaeology in Lincolnshire and South Humberside, 1983
pp.99–111: ill. in *Lincolnshire history and archaeology*, vol.19, 1984.
    pp.102–105: Monks Abbey.

288.   **STOCKER, D.A.**
The Remains of the Franciscan friary in Lincoln: a reassessment
pp.137–144: ill. in *Archaeological papers from York presented to M.W. Barley*, 1984.
ISBN 09050629723

289.   **PAGE, A.B.**
Archaeology in Lincolnshire and South Humberside, 1984
pp.69–72: ill. in *Lincolnshire history and archaeology*, vol.20, 1985.
    pp.70–72: Lincoln bypass.

290.   **STOCKER, D.A.**
Excavations to the south of Lincoln Minster, 1984 and 1985: an interim report
pp.15–19: ill. in *Lincolnshire history and archaeology*, vol.20, 1985.

291.   **TRUST FOR LINCOLNSHIRE ARCHAEOLOGY**
The Story of Hungate
Lincoln: The Trust, [1985?].   [4]p.: ill.

292.   **GILMOUR, B.J.J.**
St Mark's Church and cemetery
B.J.J. Gilmour and D.A. Stocker.
London: Council for British Archaeology, 1986.   97p.: ill., 1 folded map + 1 microfiche.
(The Archaeology of Lincoln, vol.XIII–1)
Includes bibliography
ISBN 0906780586
    Contributors: Jean Dawes; Sarah Jennings; David King;, Jenny Mann; and Jane Young.   Text in English with summaries in French and German.

293.
The West gate, Lincoln Castle: archaeological excavation, 1987
Lincoln: Lincoln County Council, Recreational Services, [1987].
[3] leaves.

294.   **WILSON, E.M.**
Bygones of Monks Road
[Lincoln]: [The Author], [1989].   18p.

Tobacco Pipes

295.   **MANN, Jenny E.**
Clay tobacco pipes from excavations in Lincoln, 1970–74
London: Council for British Archaeology for the Lincoln Archaeological Trust, 1977.
60p.: ill.
(Lincoln Archaeological Trust monograph series, vol.XV–1)
Includes bibliography.
> Includes: 'The pipe-making industry in Lincoln, 1600–1900', by M.J. Jones; 'The contexts of the finds', by Christina Colyer and M.J. Jones.

296.   **WELLS, Peter**
Lincolnshire clay pipe makers: [list]
[197?].   9p.
Typescript.
> Arranged by town.   pp.5–7: Lincoln.

297.
The Archaeology of the clay tobacco pipe.   1 : Britain: the Midlands and eastern England
edited by Peter Davey.
Oxford: British Archaeological Reports, 1979.
(BAR British series, 63)
ISBN 0860540510

298.   **WALKER, Iain C.**
Regional varieties of clay tobacco-pipe markings in eastern England
Iain C. Walker and Peter K. Wells.
pp.3–66 in *The Archaeology of the clay tobacco pipe.   1 : Britain: the Midlands and eastern England*, 1979.

299.   **WELLS, P.K.**
The Pipe-makers of Lincolnshire
pp.123–169 in *The Archaeology of the clay tobacco pipe.   1 : Britain: the Midlands and eastern England*, 1979.
> pp.123–169: Lincoln.

300.   **WHITE, A.J.**
Clay pipes from Vicars' Court, Lincoln
pp.171–178 in *The Archaeology of the clay tobacco pipe.   1 : Britain: the Midlands and eastern England*, 1979.

NUMISMATICS

Lincoln Mint

301.   **HAWKINS, Edward**
The Ancient Mint of Lincoln
pp.49–57 in *Memoirs illustrative of the history and antiquities of the county and city of Lincoln*, 1850.

302.   **SIMPSON, Justin**
The Lincoln Mint
p.79 in *LN&Q*, vol.1, no.3, 1888.

303.   **MOOR, C.T.J.**
The Lincoln Mint
pp.25–26 in *LN&Q*, vol.2, no.1, 1890.

304.   **DOLLEY, R.H.M.**
Three more late Saxon notes: a possible sixth Anglo-Saxon mint in Lincolnshire
pp.51–54: ill. in *British numismatic journal*, vol.XXIX, pt.1, 1959.
Mentions Lincoln Mint.

305.   **MOSSOP, H.R.**
The Lincoln Mint, c.890–1279
edited by Veronica Smart.
Newcastle-upon-Tyne: Corbitt & Hunter, 1970.   32, cip., [c.200]p. of plates.
Includes index.
Contains chart showing Lincoln moneyers.

306.   **BLUNT, C.E.**
The Lincoln and Stamford Mints in the tenth and eleventh centuries
Lincoln: Lincolnshire Museums, 1981.   7p.: ill.
(Lincolnshire Museums information sheet.   Numismatic series, no.5)

Finds from Particular Periods

307.   **COMBE, Taylor**
Description of a large collection of pennies of Henry II, discovered at Tealby, in
Lincolnshire
pp.1–8 in *Archaeologia*, vol.XVIII, 1817.
Lincoln mentioned as a mint and also lists inscriptions on Lincoln coins.

308.   **HAWKINS, Edward**
Description of a large collection of coins of William the Conqueror, discovered at
Beaworth, in Hampshire, with an attempt at a chronological arrangement of the coins of
William I and II
pp.1–25, [1] leaf of plates in *Archaeologia*, vol.XXVI, pt.1, 1835.

309.   **ANDREW, W.J.**
A Numismatic history of the reign of Henry I, 1100–1135
London: Quaritch, 1901.   35, 16, 515p., 8 leaves of plates.
(Numismatic chronicle and journal of the Numismatic Society, 4th series, vol.1)
Includes index.
Lincoln mentioned passim, but particularly pp.257–273.

310.   **SMITH, Arthur**
Coins of the Roman period found in Lincolnshire: [parts 1–4]
Lincoln: printed W.K. Morton, 1910.   32p.
(Lincoln City and County Museum publications, nos.10–13)

311.   _____
Roman coins made in Lincolnshire
pp.1–14, [2] leaves of plates in *AAS reports and papers*, vol.41, pt.1, 1932.

312.   **STEWART, Ian**
The St Martin coins of Lincoln
pp.46–54 in *British numismatic journal*, vol.XXXVII, 1968.
    Refers to Viking coinage of Lincoln in first half of tenth century.

313.   **WHITWELL, J.B.**
Archaeological notes, 1968
J.B. Whitwell and C.M. Wilson.
pp.99–119, [6]p. of plates in *Lincolnshire history and archaeology*, vol.1, no.4, 1969.
    Some references to artefacts from Lincoln, especially coins.

314.   **GUNSTONE, Anthony**
Lincoln: Ellis' Mill hoard, 1977
in *Spink's numismatic circular*, July/August, 1978.
    Twentieth century coins found hidden in the Mill.

315.   **MANN, J.E.**
Roman coins from Lincoln, 1970–1979
J.E. Mann and Richard Reece.
London: Council for British Archaeology for the Lincoln
Archaeological Trust, 1983.   pp.47–72, maps.
(The Archaeology of Lincoln, vol.VI–2)
Includes bibliography.

316.
*Catalogue of part 1 of the important collection of Plantagenet coins from the Conquest of
William I in 1066 to the Reform of Edward III in 1351 formed by the late Elmore
Jones...day of sale...Wednesday, 13th April, 1983*
catalogued by A.H. Baldwin & Sons Ltd. for the auctioneers Glendinning & Co.
London: Baldwin, 1983.   37p., 7p. of plates.
    Coins listed under reign and then alphabetically by place.   Largest number of Lincoln coins:
    'Tealby' coinage, 1158–80.

317.   **HEYWOOD, Nathan**
Some Roman brass coins found at Lincoln
pp.229–234 in *British numismatic journal*, vol.IV, 1908.

Coin Collections

318.
*The Ceremony of the presentation of the Sir Francis Hill collection of coins to the city of
Lincoln, the Usher Gallery...Saturday, the 23rd day of March, 1974*: [programme]
[Lincoln]: [Lincoln, Libraries, Museum and Art Gallery Committee], [1974].   5p.: ill.

319.   **ROBINSON, David N.**
Poachings: the Sir Francis Hill coin collection
pp.20–21 in *Lincolnshire life*, vol.14, no.2, April, 1974.

320.   **BLUNT, Christopher**
*Address on the occasion of the opening of the Usher Coin Gallery on Thursday, 12th
March, 1976*
Lincoln: Lincolnshire Museums, 1976.   5p.
    Hill collection and the Lincoln Mint.

321.   **GUNSTONE, Andrew**
Gold coins in the Lincolnshire museums: [catalogue]
Lincoln: Lincolnshire Museums, 1982.   8p., [2]p. of plates.
(Lincolnshire Museums information sheet.   Numismatic series, no.4)

Tradesmen's Tokens

322.   **SIMPSON, Justin**
A List of the Lincolnshire series of tradesmen's tokens and two pieces of the seventeenth century, with biographical and genealogical notes
London: Bemrose, [1872].   xvii, 136p., III plates.
> pp.31–36: Lincoln.

323.   **CASWELL, C.J.**
Notes: [on Lincolnshire town and traders' tokens]
C.J.C.
pp.225–232, [1] leaf of plates in *LN&Q*, vol.2, no.8, 1891.

324.   **SHEPPARD, Thomas**
A List of the seventeenth century tokens of Lincolnshire in the Hull Museum, with descriptions of hitherto unpublished tokens and varieties
pp.115–144: ill. in *Transactions of the Hull Scientific and Field Naturalists' Club*, vol.IV, pt.III, 1911.
> Reprinted as: Hull Museum publications, no.79.

325.   **SMITH, Arthur**
A Catalogue of the town and trade tokens of Lincolnshire issued in the seventeenth century
Horncastle: W.K. Morton, 1931.   51p., [15] leaves of plates.
Includes blank leaves for annotation.
> pp.25–34: Lincoln.

326.   **GUNSTONE, Anthony**
Nineteenth century Lincolnshire beer tickets
Lincoln: Lincolnshire Museums, 1979.   8p.: ill.
(Lincolnshire Museums information sheet.   Numismatic series, no.1)
> Includes Lincoln pubs.

327.   _____
Lincolnshire nineteenth century and later tickets, checks and passes
Lincoln: Lincolnshire Museums, 1980.   11p.: ill.
(Lincolnshire Museums information sheet.   Numismatic series, no.2)

328.   **WHITE, Andrew**
Seventeenth century Lincolnshire tradesmen and their tokens
Lincoln: Lincolnshire Museums, 1980.   6p.: ill.
(Lincolnshire Museums information sheet.   Numismatic series, no.3)
> Includes photograph of city of Lincoln's own halfpenny and drawing of that of Henry Wanless of the Two Dolphins.

329.   **TOWNSEND, T.W.**
Seventeenth century tradesmen's tokens of Lincolnshire: the issuers: [catalogue]
edited by Anthony Gunstone.
Lincoln: Lincolnshire Museums, 1983.   61p., 10p. of plates.
(Lincolnshire Museums occasional papers, 2)
ISBN 0861110056
    pp.38–43: Lincoln

RECORDS RELATING TO LINCOLN

Charters

330.
*A Copy of the charter of the city of Lincoln, granted by King Charles the First, in the
year of our Lord 1628*
Lincoln: printed and sold by J.W. Drury, 1793.   41p.

331.
*The Manuscripts of Lincoln, Bury St Edmund's; and of the Deans and Chapters of
Worcester and Lichfield, &c.*
edited by W.D. Macray
London: HMSO, 1895.   351p.
(Fourteenth report, appendix, pt.VIII)
    pp.1–121: Lincoln Corporation. I. Royal charters, 1154–1509; II. Miscellaneous records
    tempore Edward II, 1798; III. Chamberlains rolls, 1685–1747; IV. Registers, 1421–1800.
    Section on civic insignia. Provides continuous record from 1511 onwards with very full
    bibliographic descriptions.

332.
*Lincolnshire record: abstracts of final concords temp. Richard I,
John and Henry III.   Vol.1*
edited by W. Boyd and W.O. Massingberd.
London: Spottiswoode, 1896.   vii, 394p.
Includes index.

333.   **BIRCH, Walter de Gray**
*The Royal charters and grants to the city of Lincoln: a lecture delivered before the mayor
and Corporation of Lincoln*
London: Bedford, 1906.   42p.

334.   _____
*Catalogue of the royal charters and other documents and list of books belonging to the
Corporation of Lincoln, now preserved in the Muniment Room of the Corporation*
Lincoln: printed W.K. Morton, 1906.   68p.

335.   _____
The Royal charters of the city of Lincoln, Henry II to William III
transcribed and translated by Walter de Gray Birch.
Cambridge: Cambridge University Press, 1911.   xlix, 308p., 5 leaves of plates.
Includes glossary and index.   Parallel Latin and English text.

336.   **GALBRAITH, V.H.**
Seven charters of Henry II at Lincoln Cathedral
pp.269–278, [7]p. of plates in *The Antiquaries journal*, vol.XII,
pt.III, July, 1932.

337.   **TASKER, Lynn**
[Essay assessing the value of the charter for an understanding of the historical processes
at work in Lincoln, c.1500–1780]
[1981].   11 leaves.
Typescript.
>   Open University course work.

Domesday

338.   **SMITH, Charles Gowen**
*A Translation of the portion of Domesday book which relates to Lincolnshire and
Rutlandshire*
London: Simkin, Marshall, [1870].   xlviii, 276p., folded map.
>   pp.1–4: city of Lincoln.

339.
The Lincolnshire Domesday and the Lindsey survey
translated and edited by C.W. Foster and Thomas Longley.
Lincoln: Lincoln Record Society, 1924.   xc, 315p., [frontis].
(Lincoln Record Society, 19)
Includes index.
>   pp.3–9: city of Lincoln.

340.
*Domesday, 1086–1986: an exhibition to celebrate the 900th anniversary of
Domesday book mounted by the Public Record Office*
London: Millbank, 1986.   77p.: ill.
ISBN 0946171734
>   pp.66–70: 'Lincoln, a Domesday city through the ages'.

Exchequer

341.   **MADOX, Thomas**
The History and antiquities of the Exchequer of the Kings of England in two periods...
London: William Owen, 1769.   2 vols.
Includes index.
>   Many references to Lincoln.

342.   **TOUT, T.F.**
*Chapters in the administrative history of medieval England. 1: the Wardrobe, the
Chamber and the Small Seals*
Manchester: Manchester University Press, 1920–23.   6 vols.
(Publications of the University of Manchester.   Historical series, nos.34, 35, 48, 49, 57,
64)
Includes index in vol.6.
>   Successor to Madox's *The History and antiquities of the Exchequer...*, which includes many
>   references to Lincoln.

Inquisitions

343.
Inquisitions and assessments relating to feudal aids: with other analogous documents preserved in the Public Records Office, A.D. 1284–1431. Vol.3: Kent – Norfolk
London: HMSO, 1904. xii, 818p.
Includes index.
    pp.127–371: Lincoln.

Miscellaneous

344.
Bracton's note book: a collection of cases decided in the King's courts during the reign of Henry the Third, annotated by a lawyer of that time, seemingly by Henry of Bratton
edited by F.W. Maitland
London: C.J. Clay, 1887. 3 vols.
Includes index. Text in Latin.
    About a dozen cases in Lincoln.

345.
Lincoln marriage licences: an abstract of the allegation books preserved in the registry of the Bishop of Lincoln, 1598–1628
edited by A. Gibbons.
London: Mitchell and Hughes, 1888. 163p.
Includes index.

346.   **GIBBONS, Alfred**
Early Lincoln wills: an abstract of all the wills & administrations recorded in the episcopal registers of the old diocese of Lincoln...1228–1547
Lincoln: James Williamson, 1888. 244p.
Includes indexes of persons, places and subjects.

347.   **MADDISON, A.R.**
Lincolnshire wills. First series, A.D. 1500–1600, with notes and an introductory sketch
Lincoln: James Williamson, 1888. lx, 165p.
    Unfortunately no index to place.

348.
The Manuscripts of the Duke of Beaufort, KG., the Earl of Donoughmore, and others
London: HMSO, 1891. 640p.
(Twelfth report, appendix, pt.IX)
    pp.553–573: the Dean and Chapter of Lincoln; pp.573–580: the Lincoln District Registry.
    Lists classes of documents preserved in the registry of the Bishop of Lincoln, such as marriage bonds, court rolls, etc.

349.   **MADDISON, A.R.**
An Early Lincoln will
pp.99–100 in *LN&Q*, vol.4, no.28, 1894.
    Will of J.N. Thorold.

350.
Marriages, 1813–1837, from the transcripts, marriage bonds and original registers: [of St Peter-in-Eastgate]
[19??].   23 leaves.
Typescript.
Includes index.

351.   **SWAN, Robert**
A Practical treatise on the jurisdiction of the ecclesiastical courts, relating to probates and administrations...
London: S. Sweet, 1830.   112p.
> Includes an appendix containing an account of all the courts in the diocese of Lincoln, the extent of their jurisdiction and the places where the wills are proved and deposited. The author was registrar of the diocese of Lincoln.

352.
Calendars of Lincoln wills.   Vol.I: 1320–1600
edited by C.W. Foster.
London: British Record Society, 1902.   xii, 349p.
(The Index library, XXVIII)

353.
Calendars of Lincoln wills.   Vol.II: 1601–1652, Consistory Court wills
edited by C.W. Foster.
London: British Record Society, 1910.   234p.
(The Index library, XLI)

354.
Lincoln wills registered in the District Probate Registry at Lincoln. Vol.1: A.D. 1271 to A.D. 1526
edited by C.W. Foster.
Lincoln: Lincoln Record Society, 1914.   xi, 264p.
(Lincoln Record Society, no.5)
Includes index.

355.
Lincoln wills registered in the District Probate Registry at Lincoln. Vol.II: A.D. 1505 to May, 1530
edited by C.W. Foster.
Lincoln: Lincoln Record Society, 1918.   xxviii, 300p.
(Lincoln Record Society, no.10)
Includes index.

356.
Final concords of the county of Lincoln from the feet of fines preserved in the Public Record Office, A.D. 1244–1272, with additions from various sources. A.D. 1176–1250.   Vol.II
edited by C.W. Foster.
Lincoln: Lincoln Record Society, 1920.   lxxxi, 448p., [frontis].
(Lincoln Record Society, no.17)
Includes index.

357.
Calendars of wills and administrations at Lincoln. Vol.IV
edited by C.W. Foster.
London: British Record Society, 1930.   xii, 510p.
(The Index library, vol.LVII)
Includes index.

358.
*Lincoln wills registered in the District Probate Registry at Lincoln.
Vol.III. A.D. 1530–1532*
edited by C.W. Foster.
Lincoln: Lincoln Record Society, 1930.   301p.
(Lincoln Record Society, no.24)
Includes index.

359.   **REED, Vi**
Lincoln city marriage index, 1813–1837
compiled by Vi Reed, Anne Cole.
Lincoln: Society for Lincolnshire History and Archaeology, 1983.   68p.
ISBN 0904680223

360.   **JOHNSON, C.P.C.**
Lincoln city marriages, 1754–1812: surnames A–L
compiled by C.P.C. Johnson, Vera Miller, Vi Reed.
Lincoln: Society for Lincolnshire History and Archaeology, 1985.   71p.
(Lincolnshire marriage index series, vol.3A)
ISBN 0904680320

361.   ─────────────
Lincoln city marriages, 1754–1812: surnames M–Z
compiled by C.P.C. Johnson, Vera Miller, Vi Reed.
Lincoln: Society for Lincolnshire History and Archaeology, 1985.   129p.
(Lincolnshire marriage index series, vol.3B)

362.   **BOSLINGTON, Colen**
*Alphabetical index of surnames in the 1851 census of Lincolnshire.
Part 6: Lincoln registration district*
compiled by Colen and Gwen Boslington.
Lincoln: Society for Lincolnshire History and Archaeology,
Family History Subcommittee, 1985.   94, vip.
ISBN 0904680363

MEDIEVAL HISTORY

General

363.   **HUNTER, Joseph**
On the death of Eleanor of Castile, consort of King Edward the First, and the honours
paid to her memory.
pp.167–191 in *Archaeologia*, vol.XXIX, 1842.
   pp.171–172: the procession at Lincoln; p.182: account of the cross.

364. **HARTSHORNE, Charles Henry**
The Parliaments of Lincoln, the Castle of Lincoln, and the Palace and Parliament of
Clipstone
32p.: ill., [2] leaves of plates in *Proceedings of the Archaeological Institute at the annual
meeting at Lincoln*, 1848.

365. ──────────
The Parliaments of Lincoln
pp.19–38 in *Memoirs illustrative of the history and antiquities of the county and city of
Lincoln*, 1850.

366. **FOXE, John**
The Acts and monuments of John Foxe
Revised and corrected by Josiah Pratt. 4th ed.
London: Religious Tract Society, [1877]. 8 vols.
> Includes references to siege of Lincoln Castle by the Bishop of Ely in 1191, Battle of Lincoln
> in 1217 and many references to Bishops of Lincoln.

367.
*English gilds: the original ordinances of more than one hundred early
English gilds...and a preliminary essay in five parts on the history and development
of gilds by Lujo Brentano*
edited by Toulmin Smith.
London: published by N. Trubner for the Early English Text Society, 1870.
cxcix, 483p.
Includes index.
> pp.172–185: Lincoln.

368. **STUBBS, William**
The Constitutional history of England in its origin and development
Library ed.
Oxford: Clarendon Press, 1880. 3 vols.
Includes index.
> Lincoln Parliaments of 1301 and 1316.

369. **NORGATE, Kate**
England under the Angevin kings
London: Macmillan, 1887. 2 vols.
Includes index.
> Includes account of Battle of Lincoln.

370. **PERRY, George G.**
The Gilds of Lincolnshire
pp.69–71 in *LN&Q*, vol.1, no.3, 1888.
> Information about the guilds of St Benedict, St Michael-on-the-Hill, and the Fullers, extracted
> from returns in Toulmin Smith's *Early English gilds*.

371. **LAMPLOUGH, Edward**
The Battle of Lincoln
pp.151–160 in *Bygone Lincolnshire*, vol.2, 1891.

372. ──────────
Lincoln Fair
pp.161–169 in *Bygone Lincolnshire*, vol.2, 1891.

373.   **MORGAN, T.**
The Rose of Provence and lilies of France in a vision of Lincoln
pp.25–55 in *The Journal of the British Archaeological Association*, vol.XLVII, 1891.

374.   **GREEN, Mrs. J.R.**
Town life in the fifteenth century
London: Macmillan, 1894.   2 vols.
Includes index.
    Contains references to the Guild of St Benedict and bailiffs; especially in the second volume.

375.   **HUGHES, Arthur**
The Parliament of Lincoln, 1316
pp.41–58 in *Transactions of the Royal Historical Society*, new series, vol.X, 1896.

376.   **TOUT, Thomas Frederick**
The Fair of Lincoln and the 'Histoire de Guillaume le Marechal'
pp.240–265 in *English historical review*, XVIII, 1903.

377.   **RAMSEY, James H.**
The Dawn of the constitution, or The reigns of Henry III and Edward I, A.D. 1216–1307
London: Swan Sonnenschein, 1908.   xxxi, 591p., [2] leaves of plates, [3] folded maps.
    pp.8–11: the Fair of Lincoln.

378.   **ROUND, J.H.**
Feudal England: historical studies on the XIth and XIIth centuries
London: Swan Sonnenschein, 1909.   xvi, 587p.
Includes index.
    pp.328–329: Thorold the Sheriff (Turoldus); pp.528–535: Bishop Hugh of Lincoln's refusal to give money for Richard's war in France.

379.   **CUNNINGHAM, W.**
The Growth of English industry and commerce during the early and Middle Ages
5th ed.
Cambridge: Cambridge University Press, 1910.   xxvi, 724p., [2] leaves of plates.
Originally published: 1882.   Includes index.
    Lincoln mentioned briefly passim.

380.   **COLE, R.E.G.**
The Manor and rectory of Kettlethorpe, in the parts of Lindsey, in the county of Lincoln
pp.41–86, [2] leaves of plates in *AAS reports and papers*, vol.31, 1911–12.
    Of interest because of Lincoln connections of Katherine Swynford and John of Gaunt.

381.   **NORGATE, Kate**
The Minority of Henry the Third
London: Macmillan, 1912.   307p.
Includes index.
    Reference to the city, but mainly account of the Castle and the Battle of Lincoln and role of Hugh II, Bishop of Lincoln.

382.
Public works in mediaeval law.   Vol.1
edited by C.T. Flower.
London: Quaritch, 1915.   xxxviii, 343p.
(Selden Society, vol.XXXII)
Includes index.   Text in English and Latin.
    Legal cases about failure to maintain public roads, sewers, bridges, etc. taken from ancient indictments and Coram Rege rolls.

383.   **WESTLAKE, H.F.**
The Parish gilds of mediaeval England
London: SPCK, 1919.   242p., [6] leaves of plates.
Includes index.
     p.17: Gild of St Edmund of Pontigny.

384.   **BROOKS, F.W.**
The Campaign and Battle of Lincoln, 1217
by F.W. Brooks and F. Oakley.
pp.295–312 in *AAS reports and papers*, vol.36, 1921–22.

385.   **JOHNSTONE, Hilda**
The Parliament of Lincoln of 1316
pp.53–57 in *English historical review*, January, 1921.

386.   **EDGAR, J.G.**
Runnymede and Lincoln Fair: a story of the great charter
London: Dent, [1923].   xiv, 279p.
Originally published: by S.O. Beeton, 1866; this edition first issued, 1908.

387.   **DEPREZ, Eugene**
La Conference d'Avignon, 1344: l'arbitrage pontifical entre la France et l'Angleterre
pp.301–320 in *Essays in medieval history presented to Thomas Frederick Tout*, 1925.
     Refers to role of Jean d'Ufford, Dean of Lincoln.

388.   **JACOB, E.F.**
Studies in the period of baronial reform and rebellion, 1258–1267
Oxford: Clarendon Press, 1925.   xiv, 443p.
(Oxford studies in social and legal history, XIV)
     Includes brief references to Lincoln.

389.   **HILL, J.W.F.**
The Manor of Hungate, or Beaumont Fee, in the city of Lincoln
pp.175–208 in *AAS reports and papers*, vol.38, 1926–27.

390.   **MONMOUTH, Geoffrey of**
*The Historia regum Britanniae of Geoffrey of Monmouth with contributions to the study
of its place in early British history by Acton Griscom, together with a literal translation
of the Welsh manuscript no.LXI of Jesus College, Oxford by Robert Ellis Jones*
London: Longmans, Green, 1929.   xii, 627p., 16 leaves of plates.
Text in Latin and English.
     Introduction sums up what various sources say about the Battle of Lincoln, but actual
     references in Latin text sparse.

391.   **RICHARDSON, H.G.**
Select documents.   XXV: the Parliament of Lincoln, 1316
H.G. Richardson, G.O. Sayles.
pp.105–107 in *Bulletin of the Institute of Historical Research*,
vol.XII, 1934–35.

392.   **WILLARD, James Field**
*Parliamentary taxes on personal property, 1290 to 1334: a study in mediaeval English
financial administration*
Cambridge, Mass.: Mediaeval Academy of America, 1934.   xii, 357p.
(Mediaeval Academy of America publication, no.19.   Monograph, no.9)
Includes index.
     Brief references to Lincoln passim, especially to the Parliament of 1316.

393. RICHARDSON, H.G.
Select documents. XXV: the Parliament of Lincoln, 1316
H.G. Richardson, G.O. Sayles.
pp.105–107 in *Bulletin of the Institute of Historical Research,*
vol.XII, 1934–35.

394. MAJOR, Kathleen
Lincoln copy of the Magna Carta
pp.109–111: ill. in *Lincolnshire magazine,* vol.4, 1938–40.

395. MEARNS, David C.
Magna Carta: the Lincoln Cathedral copy exhibited in the Library of Congress
David C. Mearns and Verner W. Clapp.
Washington, D.C.: Government Printing Office, 1939.   10p., [1] leaf of facsims.
    Also published: 1941, without the facsimile.

396. HILL, J.W.F.
Medieval Lincoln
Cambridge: Cambridge University Press, 1948.   xvii, 487p., plans,
[22]p. of plates.
Includes index.

397. PELHAM, R.A.
The Provisioning of the Lincoln Parliament of 1301
pp.16–32, maps in *University of Birmingham historical journal,*
vol.III, no.1, 1951.

398. STENTON, Doris Mary
English society in the early Middle Ages: 1066–1307
Harmondsworth: Penguin, 1951.   287p.
Includes index.
    Lincoln mentioned passim.

399. POOLE, Austin Lane
From Domesday book to Magna Carta, 1087–1216
2nd ed.
Oxford: Clarendon Press, 1955.   xv, 541p.
(Oxford history of England, III)
Originally published: 1951.
    pp.85–86: cloth industry; pp.141–142: account of Battle of Lincoln.

400. McKISACK, May
The Fourteenth century, 1307–1399
Oxford: Clarendon Press, 1959.   xix, 598p., map, [frontis].
Includes index.
pp.47–48: Lincoln Parliament.

401. STENTON, Frank
*The First century of English feudalism, 1066–1166, being the Ford lectures,
delivered in the University of Oxford in Hilary term, 1929*
2nd ed.
Oxford: Clarendon Press, 1961.   ix, 312p.
Originally published: 1932.   Includes index.
    Various references to Lincoln, especially to Castle and Battle of Lincoln.

402.   **POWICKE, Maurice**
The Thirteenth century, 1216–1307
2nd ed.
Oxford: Clarendon Press, 1962.   xiv, 829p., [frontis].
Originally published: 1953.
>   pp.11–12: Battle of Lincoln; pp.701–705: Parliament of Lincoln.

403.   **COOK, A.M.**
The Lincolnshire background of Shakespeare's tragedy King Richard II
[Lincoln]: Lincoln Civic Trust and Friends of Lincoln Cathedral, 1964.
[12]p.: ill.

404.   **ORDERICUS, Vitalis**
The Ecclesiastical history of Orderic Vitalis
edited by Marjorie Chibnall.
Oxford: Clarendon Press, 1968–80.   6 vols.
(Oxford medieval texts)
Includes index in each volume.
>   References to Lincoln passim, especially in vol.6, pp.538–547: Battle of Lincoln.

405.   **ZIEGLER, Philip**
The Black Death
London: Collins, 1969.   319p.
ISBN 0002110857
>   pp.178–179: Lincoln outbreak in 1349.

406.   **OWEN, B.J.**
Mediaeval Lincoln: a history trail
by B.J. Owen and D.J. Longlands.
Lincoln: Lincoln Teachers' Centre, [1972].   52p.: ill., maps.

407.   **MacGREGOR, Patricia**
Monuments to a much-loved queen: the Eleanor crosses
by Patricia and Alasdair Alpin MacGregor.
pp.1651–1652: ill. in *Country life*, June 7, 1973.
>   Reference to cross at St Catherine's.

408.
Gesta Stephani
edited and translated by K.R. Potter.
Oxford: Clarendon Press, 1976.   xl, 249p., map.
Parallel Latin text and English translation.
>   pp.110–115: Battle of Lincoln.   Introductory note to the effect that 'his account of the Battle of
>   Lincoln suggests strongly that he had not seen the place'.

409.   **PLATT, Colin**
The English medieval town
London: Secker & Warburg, 1976.   219p.: ill.
Includes index.
ISBN 0436375524
>   Lincoln mentioned briefly.

410.   **REYNOLDS, Susan**
An Introduction to the history of English medieval towns
Oxford: Clarendon Press, 1977.   xiii, 234p.: ill., maps.
Includes bibliography, glossary and index.
>   Lincoln mentioned passim.

411.
Early trailbaston proceedings from the Lincoln roll of 1305
edited by Alan Harding.
pp.144–168 in *Medieval legal records edited in memory of C.A.F. Meekings*, 1978.

412.   **JONES, R.H.**
Medieval houses at Flaxengate, Lincoln
London: Council for British Archaeology for Lincoln
Archaeological Trust, 1980.   56p.: ill.
(The Archaeology of Lincoln, vol.XI–I)
Includes bibliography.   Text in English, French and German.
    Vol.XI concerns the lower city of medieval times.

413.
The English medieval landscapes
edited by Leonard Cantor.
London: Croom Helm, 1982.   225p.
Includes index.
ISBN 0709907079
    Various brief references to Lincoln.

414.   **OWEN, Dorothy**
The Norman Cathedral at Lincoln
pp.188–199 in *Anglo Norman studies*, vol.VI, 1984.
    Founding of Cathedral, but also strategic significance of the Castle.

415.   **PLATTS, Graham**
Land and people in medieval Lincolnshire
Lincoln: History of Lincolnshire Committee, 1985.   340p.: ill., [frontis].
(History of Lincolnshire, IV)
    Many references to Lincoln, covering the Jews, commerce, the ecclesiastical community and
    politics.

416.   **STAFFORD, Pauline**
The East Midlands in the early Middle Ages
Leicester: Leicester University Press, 1985.   230p.: ill., maps.
(Studies in the early history of Britain)
Includes index.
ISBN 071851257X
    Includes many references to Lincoln, particularly to trade and the Mint.

417.   **BRITISH ARCHAEOLOGICAL ASSOCIATION**
Conference transactions for the year 1982.   VIII: Medieval art and
architecture at Lincoln Cathedral
[London]: The Association, 1986.   157p.: ill., [32] leaves of plates.
Includes bibliographies.
ISBN 0907307159

418.   **DUKE, Dulcie**
The Growth of a medieval town: Lincoln from the Norman Conquest to the
Wars of the Roses
2nd ed.
Cambridge: Cambridge University Press, 1988.   47p.: ill., maps.
Originally published: as *Lincoln: the growth of the medieval town*, 1974.
For children.
ISBN 0521337259

The Jews of Lincoln

419.
*Calendar of the Plea Rolls of the Exchequer of the Jews preserved in the
Public Record Office*
London: Jewish Historical Society of England, 1905, 1910, 1929.   3 vols.
Includes indexes of persons and places.
> Many substantial references to Lincoln and to individual Jews, such as Benedict, Aaron and
> Hagan.

420.
English and Scotch historical ballads
edited, with introduction, notes and glossary by A. Milman.
London: Longmans, Green, 1871.
> pp.39–44: Hugh of Lincoln.

421.   **LETHIEULLIER, Smart**
A Letter from Mr. Smart Lethieullier to Mr. Gale, relating to the shrine of St Hugh, the
crucified child at Lincoln: [read at the Society of Antiquaries, Nov. 11, 1736]
pp.26–29 in *Archaeologia*, vol.I, 1770.

422.   **MICHEL, Francisque**
*Hughes de Lincoln: recueil de ballades anglo-normande et ecossoises relatives au
meurtre de cet enfant commis par les Juifs en MCCLV*: [verse]
Paris: Silvastre, 1834.   ix, 64p.

423.   **NOTTINGHAM, Edward, Bishop of**
Little St Hugh of Lincoln
by the Right Rev. Edward, Bishop Suffragen of Nottingham.
pp.126–131, [1] leaf of plates in *AAS reports and papers*, vol.15, 1879–80.

424.   **DAVIS, M.D.**
The Medieval Jews of Lincoln
pp.178–200 in *The Archaeological journal*, vol.XXXVIII, 1880.

425.   **YOUNG, Jessie**
St Hugh of Lincoln
pp.65–68, 81–86 in *Old Lincolnshire*, vol.1, 1885.

426.
*Simon de Montfort & his cause, 1251–1266: extracts from the writings of Robert of
Gloucester, Matthew Paris, William Rishanger, Thomas of Wykes, etc., etc.*
selected and arranged by W.H. Hutton.
London: David Nutt, 1888.   189p., [3] folded plates.
> Includes references to Grosseteste; pp.55–58: Paris' account of murder of St Hugh; p.60: trial
> of the Jews.

427.   **VENABLES, Emund**
Fines of Lincoln citizens for an assault on the Jews, A.D. 1190
pp.109–112 in *LN&Q*, vol.2, no.4, 1890.

428.   **ABRAHAMS, B. Lionel**
The Conditions of the Jews of England at the time of their expulsion in 1290
pp.76–105 in *The Jewish Historical Society of England transactions*, session 1894–95.
> All the information on Lincoln is contained in the appendix between pp.94–96 which consists
> of 2p. of tables listing names, bonds and other property owned.

429.   **JACOBS, Joseph**
Jewish ideals and other essays
London: David Nutt, 1896   xviii, 242p.
    pp.192–224: Little St Hugh of Lincoln.

430.   **HAES, Frank**
Lincoln, 1898: a report
pp.180–186: ill. in *Transcripts of the Jewish Historical Society of England*, 1896–98.
    Survey of Aaron of Lincoln's house and the Jews Court.

431.
*Select pleas, starrs, and other records from the Rolls of the
Exchequer of the Jews, A.D. 1220–1284*
edited by J.M. Rigg.
London: Quaritch, 1902.   lxi, 134, 134, [32]p.
(Publications of the Selden Society, vol.XV)
Includes index.   Parallel Latin text and English translation.
    pp.xxx–xxxii: Hugh myth; also mention of Lincoln Jews, including Benedict and Hagan.

432.   **HOWITT, Thos. R.**
Jews Court and the legend of Little St Hugh of Lincoln
Lincoln: [s.n.], [1911].   12p., [6]p. of plates.
    Author actually appears to give credence to the myth and revels in the bloodthirsty details.

433.   **ROTH, Cecil**
Essays and portraits in Anglo-Jewish history
Philadelphia: Jewish Publication Society of America, 1962.   xii, 318p.: ill., 10p. of
plates.
    Ch.6: medieval Lincoln Jewry and its synagogue; discusses Bellassez's house, the betrothal
    contract of 1271 and argues that the so-called Jews Court was in fact a synagogue.

434.
[Report of visit of the Jewish Historical Society to Lincoln, particularly concerning
attitudes to the ritual murder myth]
p.10 in *The Jewish chronicle*, no.3, 403, Friday, June 29th, 1934.

435.   **ROTH, Cecil**
Mediaeval Lincoln Jewry and its synagogue
London: Jewish Historical Society of England, 1934.   28p., 4p. of plates.
    pp.11–15: 'Lincoln and pre-expulsion Jewry'; the Jewish Historical Society's visit; pp.15–28:
    'Mediaeval Lincoln Jewry and its synagogue: retrospect and a reconstruction'.

436.   **WINDHAM, Joan**
Six o'clock saints
London: Sheed & Ward, 1942.   107p.: ill.
Originally published: 1934.
For children.
    pp.62–69: story of Little St Hugh, where the protagonists have become the 'Christians' and the
    'Unchristians'.

437.   **HUME, ABRAHAM**
*Sir Hugh of Lincoln, or An examination of a curious tradition respecting the Jews, with a
notice of the popular poetry connected with it*
London: John Rusell Smith, 1849.   54p.

438. **EKBERG, Charles**
The Murder of Little St Hugh
p.31 in *Lincolnshire life*, vol.2, no.1, spring, 1962.

439. **ROTH, Cecil**
A History of the Jews of England
3rd ed.
Oxford: Clarendon Press, 1964.   xiii, 311p.
  Originally published: 1941; 2nd ed.: 1949. Includes index.
  Lincoln mentioned passim. Especially Hugh, pp.56–57; also Aaron, Belaset, etc.

440. **DAWSON, Elizabeth**
A Shouting in the streets: [theatre programme]
[Lincoln]: [Lincoln Theatre Royal], [1967].   [12]p.: ill.
  Includes 1p. on the story of Little St Hugh.

441. **LANGMUIR, Gavin I.**
The Knight's tale of young Hugh of Lincoln
pp.459–482 in *Speculum*, vol.XLVII, no.4, 1972.

442. **ROBINSON, David N.**
Poachings: Jews Court, Lincoln
pp.16–18 in *Lincolnshire life*, vol.15, no.11, January, 1976.
  Short article pointing out that the story of Little St Hugh is unsupported legend
  and includes an account of the manufacturing of the 'well'.

443. **FISK, Roy**
Lincolnshire gleanings
[Lincoln]: [The Author], [198?].   110p.: ill.
  Includes story about Little St Hugh.

444. **STOCKER, David**
The Shrine of Little St Hugh
pp.109–117, plans in *British Archaeological Association conference transactions for the year 1982*, vol.VIII, 1986.

TUDOR AND EARLY STUART PERIOD

445. **MADDEN, Frederic**
Account of King Henry the Eighth's entry into Lincoln in 1541...[and transcription of]
Ms. Add. 6113.f.179b
p.334–338 in *Archaeologia*, vol.XXIII, 1831.

446. **TRIVET, F. Nicholas**
Annales sex regum angliae, qui a comitibus andegavensibus originem traxerunt, A.D. MCXXXVI–MCCCVII, ad fidem codicum manuscriptorum recensuit Thomas Hog
London: English Historical Society, 1845.   xii, 434p.
  Brief references to the Bishops;   pp.200–201: account of the Fair of Lincoln.

447. **ROSS, Frederick**
The Pilgrimage of Grace
pp.131–142 in *Bygone Lincolnshire*, vol.1, 1891.

448.　**GOFF, Cecilie**
A Woman of the Tudor age
London: John Murray, 1930.　326p., [7] leaves of plates.
Includes index.
> Concerns Katherine Willoughby, Duchess of Suffolk and refers to her husband's actions during
> the Lincolnshire Rebellion of 1536.　Includes account of the sacking of the Bishop's Palace.

449.　**MUIR, Dorothy**
Lincolnshire Rising, 1536
pp.3–8: ill. in *Lincolnshire magazine*, vol.3, 1936–38.

450.　**BATES, John G.**
A Forlorn hope: an account of the Lincolnshire Rebellion, 1536
pp.367–381 in *Durham University journal*, vol.XXX, no.5, March, 1938.

451.　**HILL, J.W.F.**
Tudor and Stuart Lincoln
Cambridge: Cambridge University Press, 1956.　xiv, 254p., 2 maps, [17] leaves of plates.
Includes index.

452.　**REEVES, Marjorie**
Elizabethan citizen
Marjorie Reeves and Paule Hodgson.　4th impression.
London: Longmans, 1967.　93p.: ill., map.
(Then and there series)
Originally published: 1961.
For children.
> pp.5–54: 'The citizen at home' features Simon Fulbeck, a cordwainer of Lincoln; account
> based upon household records.

453.　**JAMES, M.E.**
Obedience and dissent in Henrician England: the Lincolnshire Rebellion, 1536
pp.3–78 in *Past and present*, no.48, August, 1970.
> Lincoln mentioned passim, but particularly pp.48–51 in connection with the dissenting politics
> of the 'new' families.

454.　**DODDS, Madeleine Hope**
The Pilgrimage of Grace, 1536–1537, and the Exeter conspiracy, 1538
by Madeleine Hope Dodds and Ruth Dodds.
London: Frank Cass, 1971.　2 vols.
Includes index.
> Vol.1, pp.89–140: Lincolnshire Rising.

455.　**OAKESHOTT, R. Ewart**
A Knight in battle
London: Lutterworth, [1971].　116p.: ill., plans.
For children.
ISBN 0718816145
> pp.44–66: Battle of Lincoln, 1217.

456.　**WILSON, Derek**
A Tudor tapestry: men, women and society in Reformation England
London: Heinemann, 1972.　viii, 287p., map, [12]p. of plates.
ISBN 0434872253
> pp.60–84: Lincolnshire Rising.

457.   **HODGETT, Gerald A.J.**
Tudor Lincolnshire
Lincoln: History of Lincolnshire Committee, 1975.   xvii, 212p., [16]p. of plates.
(History of Lincolnshire, VI)
> Includes many references to the city.

458.
Visit of James I to Lincoln, 1617
[Lincoln]: [Lincoln Teachers' Centre], [c.1977].   4 leaves.
(Archives, 5)
> Based upon information from the *Register of municipal proceedings* produced by the Historical
> Manuscripts Commission.

459.
The Lincolnshire Rising, 1536: a brief history and programme of events in 1986 to mark
the 450th anniversary
Lincolnshire Rising 1536–1986 Coordinating Group.
[Lincoln]: [Lincoln County Council, Recreation Services], [1986]. 1 folded sheet: ill.

460.   **WARD, Anne**
The Lincolnshire Rising, 1536
Nottingham: WEA, 1986.   35p.: ill.
ISBN 0901977063
> pp.28–30: Lincoln.

461.   **MADDISON, A.R.**
Lincolnshire gentry during the sixteenth century
pp.174–222 in *AAS reports and papers*, vol.22, 1893.
> Part played by the Lincolnshire gentry in the Rising of 1536.

ENGLISH CIVIL WAR

General

462.   **HYDE, Edward**
The History of the rebellion and civil wars in England, together with an historical view of
the affairs of Ireland
by Edward, Earl of Clarendon.
Oxford: Oxford University Press, 1849.   7 vols.
> Vol.2, pp.268–269: account of King's visit to Lincoln, but little on Lincoln itself because of
> author's royalist standpoint.

463.
The Quarrel between the Earl of Manchester and Oliver Cromwell, an episode of the
English Civil War: unpublished documents relating thereto collected by the late John
Bruce, FSA
annotated and completed by David Masson.
London: Camden Society, 1875.   xcvii, 102p.
(New series, XII)
> More than half letters written when Manchester was at Lincoln.

464.   PEACOCK, Edward
Lincoln in 1644
pp.167–177, 1 folded map in *The Archaeological journal*, vol.XXXVIII, 1881.
    About the Civil War.

465.
The Monckton papers
edited by Edward Peacock.
London: Philobiblon Society, [1885].   viii, 204p.
    p.22 and pp.178–179: Lincoln during the Civil War.

466.   CAVENDISH, Margaret
*The Life of William Cavendish, Duke of Newcastle, to which is added the true relation of
my birth, breeding, and life by Margaret, Duchess of Newcastle*
edited by C.H. Firth.
London: John C. Nimmo, 1886.   lxviii, 388p., [4] leaves of plates.
Includes index.
    Covers period of Civil War.

467.   GRANGE, Ernest L.
A List of Civil War tracts and broadsides relating to the county of Lincoln
Horncastle: W.K. Morton, 1889.   24p.
Published in 75 copies, privately printed.

468.   HUTCHINSON, Lucy
Memoirs of the life of Colonel Hutchinson
by his widow, Lucy.   New ed.
London: George Routledge, 1906.   467p.
Originally published: 1806.
    Hutchinson played part in Civil War.   p.39: brief account of schooling at Lincoln under Mr.
    Clarke.

469.   TATHAM, Edward H.R.
Lincolnshire and the Great Civil War
pp.249–279 in *Memorials of old Lincolnshire*, 1911.

470.   HENSMAN, E.W.
The East Midlands and the second Civil War, May to July, 1648
pp.126–159 in *Transactions of the Royal Historical Society*, 4th series, vol.VI, 1923.

471.   WOOD, Alfred C.
Nottinghamshire in the Civil War
Oxford: Clarendon Press, 1937.   x, 240p.
Includes index.
    References to Lincoln passim.

472.   BISHOP, J.K.
The Civil War in Lincolnshire
30, xiii leaves.
Thesis [B.A.] – University of Manchester, 1962.

473.   ALLISON, Michael
Lincolnshire worthies.   No.3: Edward Rossiter, Lincolnshire's Civil War hero
pp.32–35: ill. in *Lincolnshire life*, vol.19, no.12, March, 1980.
    Rossiter was from Somerby but the article does describe events in Lincoln.

Civil War Tracts

474.
*Propositions for peace, propounded by the King's most excellent Majestie to the High
Court of Parliament...also the King's Majestie's letter to the Lord Willoughby at Lincoln,
concerning the militia, and mustering of the trained bands of that county*
London: printed for William Arding, 1642.   [8]p.

475.
*The Declaration and protestation of divers the knights, gentry, and freeholders, and
others of the foresaid country, whose names are subscribed to the Right Honorable
Francis, Lord Willoughby, lord lieutenant of the county of Lincolne, and of the city
of the county of Lincolne*
London: printed by A. Norton for Edward Husbands and John Frank, 1642.   1 sheet.

476.
*A True relation of His Majestie's reception and royall entertainment at Lincoln by the
knights, esquires, gentlemen, and freeholders of the said countie*
York; London: John Thomas, 1642.   [5]p.

477.
*The Lord Willoughby of Parham, his letter to an Honorable Member of the House of
Parliament...*
[London]: printed for Joseph Hunscott and John Wright, [1642].   4p.
    Written from Lincoln.

478.
*Instructions of the Lords and Commons assembled in Parliament for the Right
Honourable Francis, Lord Willoughby of Parham, lord lieutenant of the county of
Lincoln...for the setting & preserving the peace of that county and city, and the parts
adjoyning*
London: printed for W.B., 1642.   [8]p.

479.
*The Humble petition of divers baronets, knights, esquiers, gentlemen, clergy, and
freeholders of the county of Lincolne...with a letter sent to master speaker, from the
knights, esquiers, gentry, and freeholders of the same county...*
[London]: first printed at York and now reprinted for John Thomas, 1642.   8p.

480.
*A Declaration of the Lords and Commons assembled in Parliament, for the association of
all well-affected persons in Lincolnshire ..likewise an order of both Houses for removing
the prisoners out of Lincoln Castle, and for the speedy fortifying of the same*
London: printed for I. Wright, 1642.   [6]p.

481.
*His Majestie's two speeches: one to the knights, gentlemen, and freeholders of the county
of Nottingham at Newark: the other to the knights, gentlemen, and freeholders of the
county of Lincoln at Lincoln*
London: printed by Robert Baker...by the assignes of John Bill, 1642.   5p.

482.
*The King's Majestie's letter to the Lord Willoughby of Parham, June the fourth, with his
Lordship's answer thereunto, together with a letter sent by the Lord Willoughby to an
Honourable Member of the Parliament, read at a conference between both Houses
this eighth day of June, 1642*
London: printed for A.N., 1642. 6p.

483.
*Speech delivered to His Majesty, by the recorder of Lincoln: at his reception into the city,
July, 1642*
London: 'T.J.', 1642. [7]p.

484.
*A Particular relation of the several removes, services, and successes of the Right
Honorable, the Earle of Manchester's army...since he went from Bedford, April 20, to the
compleating of the great victory at Lincolne, May the 6th, 1644, sent by Mr. William
Goode from the Earle's quarters at Lincoln, to Mr. Simeon Ash...both chaplaines to the
said noble Earl*
London: printed for Thomas Underhill, 1644. 6, [2]p.

485.
*Mercurius aulicus, communicating the intelligence and affaires of the court to the rest of
the kingdome*: [the 38th week, ending September 21st, 1644]
p.1168.
    Entry for Monday, September 16th gives account of Cromwell ransacking Lincoln Cathedral.

486.
*An Ordinance of the Lords and Commons assembled in Parliament, for putting the
associated counties of Suffolk, Norfolk, Essex, Huntingdon, Hartford, Cambridge,
Lincoln, the Isles of Ely, and the cities of Lincoln and Norwich into a posture of defence...*
London: printed for Edward Husbands, 1644. 15p.

487.
*A True relation of the taking of the city, Minster and Castle of Lincolne, with all their
ordinance, ammunition and horse by the Right Honourable, the Earle of Manchester...*
London: printed by R. Cotes for Joh. Bellamy, 1644. 6p.

488.
*An Ordinance of the Lords and Commons assembled in Parliament, for a monethly
charge and tax of two thousand eight hundred pounds upon the county of Lincoln for the
defence and safety of the said county*
London: printed for Edward Husbands, 1645. 7p.
    The city of Lincoln is mentioned.

489.
*An Impartial and true relation of the great victory obtained through the blessing of God,
after a very sharpe dispute, by the conjoyned forces of Lincolne, Nottingham, Lecester,
Derby, and Rutland, under the command of Col. Edw. Rossiter, with a list of the names
and number of prisoners, colours, armes, and carriages taken on Tuesday, July 5, 1648*
London: printed Edw. Griffin, 1648. [6]p.

POST CIVIL WAR AND EIGHTEENTH CENTURY PERIOD

490.   MERES, Thomas
[Report of speech made on behalf of the city of Lincoln to the King by Sir Thomas Meres]
pp.446–448 in *The Parliamentary intelligencer*, no.28, Monday, July 2 to Monday,
July 9, 1660.

491.
[Notice of meeting to consider ways to 'check the spirit of the disaffected to the King',
11th December, 1792]
[Lincoln]: [s.n.], 1792.   1 sheet.

492.
*Lincoln: at a general meeting of the inhabitants of the town of Lincoln...held at the
Guildhall...on Wednesday, the 19th day of December, 1792...to consider of the most
effectual steps to be adopted to check the spirit of the disaffected to the King...*
[Lincoln]: [s.n.], 1792.   3p.

493.
[Resolutions of meeting of the inhabitants of the city of Lincoln on Wednesday, the 19th
day of December, 1792 to consider the most effectual steps to be adopted to check the
spirit of the disaffected to the King]
[Lincoln]: [s.n.], 1792.   1 sheet.

494.
[Notice of meeting to discuss paper about diminishing the consumption of wheat, July 16,
1795]
[Lincoln]: [s.n.], 1795.   1 sheet.

495.
[Copy of agreement for reducing the consumption of wheat: recommendation of this to
the citizens by the mayor, January 12, 1796]
[Lincoln]: [s.n.], 1796.   1 sheet.

496.
[Resolutions]: *at a meeting of the proprietors of estates..within the city of Lincoln...21st
September, 1799*
[Lincoln]: [s.n.], [1799].   1 sheet.

497.   PEACOCK, Edward
Lincoln and the revolution of 1688
pp.146–147 in *LN&Q*, vol.2, no.5, 1891.

498.   BINNALL, Peter B.G.
Lincolnshire echoes of the 'forty-five
pp.181–183 in *The Lincolnshire historian*, no.4, 1949.
> Lincolnshire and Lincoln involvement in the Jacobite rebellion.

499.   NAMIER, Lewis Bernstein
The Structure of politics at the accession of George III
2nd ed.
London: Macmillan, 1960.   vii, 514p.
Includes index.
> p.107: Monsons and Sibthorps' lengthy representation of the city.

500.   **HILL, J.W.F.**
Georgian Lincoln
Cambridge: Cambridge University Press, 1966.   xvi, 336p., [20]p. of plates.
Includes index.

501.   **COPPACK, Glyn**
Two eighteenth century pit groups from Lincoln
pp.115–125: ill. in *Lincolnshire history and archaeology*, vol.8, 1973.
    Groups at the Bishop's Palace and the Guildhall.

502.   **JAMES, Joy**
The Blacksmith's house
photographs by Chris Fairclough.
London: Black, 1979.   25p.: ill.
(Beans)
For children.
ISBN 0713619732
    Compares the lifestyles of John Hird, a 17th century blacksmith, who lived in parish of
    St Swithin's, and a modern family whose house is on the same spot. Based upon an inventory
    of the original house drawn up in 1643.

NINETEENTH CENTURY

503.
[Resolutions of a meeting for considering the best mode of testifying that joy which every
Briton must feel on the happy occasion of a general peace between this country and
France, 11th June, 1814]
[Lincoln]: [s.n.], 1814.   1 sheet.

504.
[Request for meeting to discuss presentation of congratulatory address to Her Majesty the
Queen, 'on her recent triumph over conspiracy and perjury', 27th November, 1820]
Lincoln: printed Drury, 1830.   1 sheet.

505.
 [Request for meeting of the freemen and inhabitants, 11th December, 1820]
Lincoln: printed Drury, 1820.   1 sheet.

506.
[Copy of anti-slavery petition to the Commons from the inhabitants of Lincoln and its
vicinity, February 13th, 1826]
Lincoln: printed W. Brooke, 1826.   1 sheet.

507.
[Letter to the mayor on the subject of the corn laws, 16th January, 1839]
Lincoln: printed James Drury, 1839.   1 sheet.

508.
[Letter to mayor requesting public meeting to consider petitioning Parliament for
alteration in the corn and provision laws, February 21st, 1842]
Lincoln: printed R.E. Leary, 1842.   1 sheet.

509.
Opinions of the metropolitan press on the protectionist meeting, held at Lincoln, on Monday last: [from *Times* daily news]
Lincoln: printed Lincolnshire Times, [1842?].   1 sheet.

510.
[Letter to the mayor requesting meeting to discuss suspension of duties on imported corn, December 29th, 1846]
Lincoln: printed James Drury, 1846.   1 sheet.

511.
[Letter to the mayor requesting meeting to prevent augmentation of 5d. in the pound income tax, February, 1848]
Lincoln: printed William Doncaster, 1848.   1 sheet.

512.
Funeral of the Duke of Wellington: [notice about closure of shop windows, 12th November, 1852]
Lincoln: printed W. and B. Brooke [for the Lincoln Corporation], 1852.   1 sheet.

513.
Peace rejoicings in Lincoln, Thursday, May the 29th, 1856: [programme]
Lincoln: printed R.E. Leary, 1856.   1 sheet.

514.
*The **Lincolnshire chronicle and leader** centenary supplement: bridging the century*: [1833–1933]
Lincoln: Lincolnshire Newspapers, 1933.   64p.: ill.
Includes index.
> Includes articles on: government of Lincoln, by J.W.F. Hill; transport; education, by C.W. Hooton; assizes; typhoid epidemic; religion; industry; 1832 election contest between Colonel Sibthorp, Mr. Heneage and Mr. Bulwer; Lincoln inns.

515.   **DAVIES, Susan**
Migration: the mobility of women in the mid-1800s: a survey of the migration paths taken, by women and girls, into the city of Lincoln in order to enter into domestic service
[197?].   4p.: ill.
Typescript.

516.   **MIDDLETON, Kathleen**
General living conditions in Lincoln during the latter part of the 19th century and the beginning of the 20th century
[197?].   6p.
Typescript.

517.   **HILL, J.W.F.**
Victorian Lincoln
Cambridge: Cambridge University Press, 1974.   ix, 341p., maps, [8]p. of plates.
Includes index.
ISBN 0521203341

518.   **EBERY, Mark**
Domestic service in late Victorian and Edwardian England, 1871–1914
Mark Ebery, Brian Preston.
Reading: University of Reading, Department of Geography, 1976. 117p.
(Geographical papers, 42)
> Lincoln is one of 17 urban centres which are examined more closely using census enumeration
> schedules.

519.   **PRESTON, Brian**
Occupations of father and son in mid-Victorian England
Reading: University of Reading, Department of Geography, 1977. ii, 40p.
(Geographical papers, 56)
ISBN 0704904667
> Lincoln is one of four sample areas.

520.   **WILSON, Catherine M.**
Industrial archaeology notes, 1976
pp.57–64: ill. in *Lincolnshire history and archaeology*, vol.12, 1977.
> p.63: Fisons Ltd., Carholme Rd.; Stamp End Lock footbridge.

521.   **ROBINSON, Michael James**
Two themes of life in Victorian Lincoln: drink and sewage
40p., plans.
Thesis [Certificate in local history] – University of Nottingham, 1978.
> Work done under auspices of the University of Nottingham in conjuction with Bishop
> Grosseteste College.

522.   **KNAPP, Malcolm G.**
Industrial archaeology notes, 1979
pp.55–63: ill. in *Lincolnshire history and archaeology*, vol.15, 1980.
> pp.57–60: street furniture of Motherby Hill, by Catherine M. Wilson.

523.   **TASKER, Lynn**
Lincolnshire in 1880
Lincoln: Lincolnshire Library Service, 1980.   38p., [12]p. of plates.
(Lincolnshire history series, 3)
> Extracts from Lincolnshire newspapers, including items about the city.

524.   **BOLLWORTHY, Claire J.**
Domestic service in Victorian England: recruitment, migration and work in Lincoln,
1851–1871
59p.: ill.
Thesis [B.A. Hons.] – University of Cambridge, 1981.
Includes bibliography.

525.   **BETTERIDGE, Stephen J.**
Industrial archaeology notes, 1983
pp.113–117: ill. in *Lincolnshire history and archaeology*, vol. 19, 1984.
> Stone railway sleepers at St.Mark's; p.114–117: maltings, Brayford Wharf North, Lincoln, by
> Tony Barlow.

526.   ―――――――――
Industrial archaeology notes, 1984
pp.65–67: ill. in *Lincolnshire history and archaeology*, vol.20, 1985.
> pp.65–66: Lincoln railways; Ruston Proctor boiler works.

527   **MILLS, Dennis R.**
A Lincolnshire guide to the nineteeth century censuses
pp.25–29 in *Lincolnshire history and archaeology*, vol.22, 1987.
     Mentions sources for city.

TWENTIETH CENTURY AND PAGEANTS

528.
*The Grand Empire Pageant organized and arranged by the members of and friends of
the 'Lindum', 'Central' and 'Nettleham' habitations of the Primrose League*
[Lincoln]: [The League], [1890s?].   [18]p.: ill.

529.
The City of Lincoln: temp. Edward VII
Brighton: W.T. Pike, [1909?].   1, 104p.: ill.
Cover title: Lincolnshire temp. Edward VII.

530.
[Lincoln strikes and riots, 1911: a folder containing photocopies of articles, letters,
telegrams and photographs relating to the strikes]
1 portfolio.
     Available at Lincoln Central Library.   Items have not been annotated consistently.

531.   **TOWNSEND, E.M.**
Scenes of pageantry connected with Lincoln Cathedral, 1186–1280 A.D.: [as produced
for the G.F.S. Festival, in the grounds of the Old Palace, May 13th, 1914]
Lincoln: W.K. Morton, [1914].   10p.

532.   **CRAIG, Hardin**
The Lincoln cordwainers' pageant
pp.605–615 in *Publications of the Modern Language Association of America*, new series,
vol.XXV, 1917.
     Includes transcriptions of portions of cordwainers' account book which refers to part played in
     the St Anne's day Sights Celebration.

533.   **NORTON, Harry**
The Food question
Lincoln: Lincolnshire Press, [1918].   14p.
     Reprint of series of articles which appeared in the *Lincoln leader*.   Mainly general but does
     refer to the situation in Lincolnshire and Col. Ruston's action on allotments.

534.   **TOWNSEND, E.M.**
Seven scenes of pageantry connected with Lincoln Cathedral, 648 to 1280 A.D.
Lincoln: Lincolnshire Publishing, [1920].   19p.
     Performed in Palace grounds, 1920.   Much intermingling of material from earlier production.

535.   _____
*Seven scenes of pageantry connected with Lincoln Cathedral, 628 to 1280 A.D., as
arranged to be held in the grounds of the Old Palace, 1926*
by Emily M. Townsend, aided by the Dean of Lincoln.
Lincoln: Lincolnshire Publishing, 1926.   23p.

536. ─────────────
Dramatic scenes from Lincolnshire history: [broadcast from Midland regional station of the BBC during the Lincolnshire Week, December, 1932]
Lincoln: J.W. Ruddock, 1932. 36p.

537.
Silver jubilee of His Majesty, King George the Fifth, 1910–1935: **Lincolnshire chronicle souvenir**
Lincoln: Lincolnshire Newspapers, 1935. 40p.: ill.
Includes index.
> Contains articles on: Lincoln 25 years ago; the royal visit; growth of the city; problems for trade caused by the Depression; the development of transport; educational changes; the Corporation gas and electricity undertakings.

538.
Air raids on Lincolnshire, 1940–1945
Lincoln: County Constabulary Headquarters, [1945]. 12p.
> Includes Lincoln.

539. **ELVIN, Laurence**
Looking back: Lincoln during 1917
pp.5–9: ill. in *The Fireside magazine*, vol.5, no.3, December, 1967.

540 ─────────────
Flashback: Christmas, 1903
pp.8–11: ill. in *The Fireside magazine*, vol.10, no.3, December, 1972.
> Information gleaned from the pages of the *Lincolnshire echo*.

541. **WINFIELD, Mame**
Lincoln in World War I
pp.28–29: ill. in *Lincolnshire life*, vol.25, no.8, November, 1985.
> Childhood reminiscence.

TOPOGRAPHY

LINCOLNSHIRE GENERAL GUIDES

542.   **COX, Thomas**
Magna Britannica et Hibernia, antiqua & nova, or A new survey of Great Britain
London: sold by M. Nutt, 1720.   6 vols.
> Vol.2 : *A Topographical, ecclesiastical and natural history of Lincolnshire*; pp.1436–1441:
> Lincoln.

543.
A New present state of England
London: printed for R. Baldwin, 1750.   2 vols.
Based on *The Present state of Great Britain*, by Guy Miege.
> Vol.1, pp.149–156: Lincolnshire; pp.150–151: Lincoln.

544.
*England described, or The traveller's companion, containing whatever is curious in the
several counties, cities, boroughs, market towns and villages of note in the kingdom...*
London: printed for R. Atkinson, 1788.   [16], 458p.
> pp.279–286: Lincoln.

545.
*England illustrated, or A compendium of the natural history, geography, topography and
antiquities ecclesiastical and civil, of England and Wales...*
London: R. & J. Dodsley, 1764.   2 vols.
> pp.403–404: Lincoln.

546.
*A Description of England and Wales containing a particular account of each county.
Vol.5*
London: printed for Newbery and Carnan, 1769.   288p., [4] leaves of maps, [16] leaves
of plates.
> pp.225–288: Lincolnshire; pp.279–286: Lincoln city.

547.
*A New display of the beauties of England, or A description of the most elegant or
magnificent public edifices, royal palaces, noblemen's and gentlemen's seats, and other
curiosities, natural or artificial, in different parts of the kingdom.   Vol.1*
3rd ed.
London: R. Goadby, 1777.
> pp.72–74: Lincoln.

548.
Britannica curiosa, or A description of the most remarkable curiosities, natural and artificial, of the island of Great Britain, in the several counties, cities, towns, villages, &c., the principal seats of the nobility and gentry
2nd ed.
London: Fielding and Walker, 1777. 6 vols.
Originally published: as *The Curiosities natural and artificial of Great Britain*, 1775.
 Vol.1, pp.306–312: Lincoln.

549. **LINCOLN LIBRARY**
Topographical catalogue
[18??]. 256p.
Ms.
Cover title.
 Lincolnshire rather than Lincoln in scope.

550. **DIBDIN, Charles**
Observations on a tour through almost the whole of England, and a considerable part of Scotland, in a series of letters, addressed to a large number of intelligent and respectable friends
by Mr. Dibdin.
London: G. Goulding, [1801]. 2 vols.
 Vol.1, p.377: Lincoln.

551. **BRITTON, John**
The Beauties of England and Wales. Vol.IX: A topographical and historical description of the county of Lincoln: containing an account of its towns, seats, antiquities, churches, public edifices, scenery, the residences of the gentry, etc.
London: Sherwood, Neely and Jones, 1807. 2 vols.
 Vol.1, pp.593–656: Lincoln.

552. **COOKE, G.A.**
Topographical and statistical description of the county of Lincoln...
London: Sherwood, Neely and Jones, [after 1811]. 144p.: ill., [3] leaves of plates.
Includes index.
 Forms part of the 47 volume work with the overall title *The Modern British traveller*, each part
 having a special title page beginning 'Topographical and statistical...'. pp.52–76: Lincoln.

553. **BREWER, James Norris**
The Picture of England, or Historical and descriptive delineations of the most curious works of nature and art in each county...
London: Harris, [1820]. 2 vols.
 Some five pages allotted to Lincoln.

554.
A Description of Lincoln, containing some account of its antiquities, public buildings, &c., particularly the Cathedral
Lincoln: printed Drury, [1820s?]. 52p.

555.
The History and topography of Lincolnshire, with biographical sketches, &c., &c., and a map of the county
London: printed for G. and W.B. Whittaker, 1824. 72p., map.
(Pinnock's county histories)
Originally published: 1823.
 Written in question and answer form. pp.20–27: Lincoln.

556.
An Historical and descriptive account of Lincolnshire, collected from the best authorities and illustrated by engravings
London: Sherwood, Jones, 1825.   48p., [frontis].
     pp.29–40: city of Lincoln; pp.40–48: Bishops.

557.
An Historical and descriptive account of Lincolnshire, collected fron the best authorities, and illustrated by numerous engravings. Vol.1 : Containing the city of Lincoln and division of Lindsey
London: Sherwood, Gilbert and Piper, 1828.   425p.: ill., [7] leaves of plates.
     pp.29–93: Lincoln.   Lincoln Central Library copy has interleaved Ms. notes.

558.   **MOULE, Thomas**
The English counties delineated, or A topographical description of England
London: George Virtue, 1837.   2 vols.
Cover title: The English counties in the nineteenth century.
Includes index.
     Vol. 2, pp.198–199: Lincoln.

559.   **LEWIS, Samuel**
A Topographical dictionary of England, comprising the several counties, cities, boroughs, corporated and market towns, parishes, chapelries, and townships...with historical and statistical descriptions...
5th ed.
London: S. Lewis, 1842.   4 vols.
Originally published: 1831; subsequent editions: 1833; 1835; 1840.
     Vol.III, pp.73–77: Lincoln.

560.
Slater's (late Pigot & Co.'s) pocket atlas, topography and gazetteer of England:
[Lincolnshire]

561.
A Selection of papers relative to the county of Lincoln, read before the Lincolnshire Topographical Society, 1841, 1842
Lincoln: printed W. and B. Brooke, 1843.   114p., 10 leaves of plates.

562   **WILLSON, E.J.**
Opening address: [to the Lincolnshire Topographical Society, February 23rd, 1841]
p.3–13 in *A Selection of papers relative to the county of Lincoln, read before the Lincolnshire Topographical Society*, 1843.
     Gives account of various major sources on Lincolnshire: Leland; Camden; Stukely; Howlett; *Beauties of England and Wales*; Marrat; Weir; Allen.

563.   **ANDERSON, Charles**
A Short guide to the county of Lincoln
Gainsborough: Alfred Smith, 1847.   v, 69, [12]p.
     pp.9–10: Lincoln.

564.   **WHITE, Walter**
Eastern England, from the Thames to the Humber
London: Chapman and Hall, 1865.   2 vols.
Includes index.
     Vol.2, pp.44–60: Lincoln.

565.
Chronicles of English counties: Lincolnshire. Part 1
pp.461–516 in *All the year round*, October 27, 1883.
> pp.461–465: Lincoln itself.

566. **WILKINSON, G.J.**
*Illustrated guide to Lincolnshire, what to see and how to see it: the tourists' handbook:
an illustrated, historic and descriptive guide to the beautiful and interesting district in
and around Lincolnshire*
Lincoln: The Author, 1900. 304p.: ill.
> pp.24–61: Lincoln.

567. **JEANS, G.E.**
Handbook for Lincolnshire
2nd ed.
London: Edward Stanford, 1903. vi, xl, 258p., map, plans.
Originally published: 1890. Includes index. Cover title: Murray's handbook
Lincolnshire.
> pp.27–66: Lincoln.

568.
*A Relation of a short survey of 26 counties observed in a seven weeks journey begun on
August 11, 1634 by a captain, a lieutenant, and an ancient, all three of the military
company in Norwich*
edited by L.G. Wickham Legg.
London: F.E. Robinson, 1904. xxvii, 200p., map, [frontis].
Includes index.
> pp.3–9 and notes pp.138–141: concerned with Lincoln. Mainly ecclesiastical and military
> interests. Taken from B.L. Lansdowne Ms. 213f.315.

569. **CORNS, A.R.**
The County of Lincoln
10p.: ill.
Supplements: *The Draper*, March 9, 1907.
> Includes informal history of the city.

570. **SYMPSON, E. Mansel**
Lincolnshire
Cambridge: Cambridge University Press, 1913. viii, 193p.: ill., maps.
(Cambridge county geographies)
> Thematic rather than geographical approach.

571 **RAWNSLEY, Willingham Franklin**
Highways and byways in Lincolnshire
London: Macmillan, 1914. xviii, 519p.
> pp.91–136: Lincoln.

572. **BARRAS DE ARAGON, Franciso de las**
Notas tomadas en Inglaterra, Escocia e Irlanda en 1909
Seville: Placentines, 1915. 111p.
Text in Spanish.
> pp.16–20: Lincoln.

573 **COX, J. Charles**
Lincolnshire
London: Methuen, 1916. xv, 363p., maps, [30] leaves of plates.
> pp.196–217: Lincoln.

574.
Holidays in England: by the cathedral cities, the Tennyson and Dickens' country, and the homes of the Pilgrim fathers
edited by Percy Lindley.
New York: H.J. Ketcham, [1930s?].   97p.: ill., [4] leaves of plates.

575.   **SHEARS, W.S.**
This England: a book of the shires and counties
3rd ed.
London: Hutchinson, 1939.   703p., [frontis].
Originally published: 1936.
   pp.557–562: Lincoln.

576.   **WYMER, Norman**
A Breath of England.   Book 2: Wheatsheaf and willow: the eastern shires
London: Lutterworth, 1949.   267p.: ill.

577.   **PEVSNER, Nikolaus**
Lincolnshire
by Nikolaus Pevsner and John Harris.
Harmondsworth: Penguin, 1964.   768p.: ill., map, 64p. of plates.
(The Buildings of England)
   pp.81–164: Lincoln.

578.
Lincolnshire buildings: a list of amendments and additions to Pevsner's *Lincolnshire*
compiled by members of the Society for Lincolnshire History and Archaeology.
[1964?].   34p.
Typescript.
   pp.1–5: Lincoln.

579.   **MEE, Arthur**
The King's England: Lincolnshire
fully revised and edited by F.T. Baker.   New ed.
London: Hodder and Stoughton, 1970.   440p., [16]p. of plates.
(The King's England)
Originally published: 1949; 2nd impression: 1952.
ISBN 0340127287
   pp.214–250: Lincoln.

580.   **ROGERS, A.**
A History of Lincolnshire with maps and pictures
Henley-on-Thames: Darwen Finlayson, 1970.   96p., maps, 12p. of plates.
Includes bibliography and index.
ISBN 0852080603
   Lincoln mentioned passim and in particular pp.45–51 and 83–85.

581.   **BARLEY, M.W.**
Lincolnshire and the Fens
2nd ed.
Wakefield: EP Publishing, 1972.   192p.: ill.
Originally published: 1952.   Includes index.
ISBN 0854097643
   Various references to Lincoln.

582.   **MARSDEN, Walter**
Lincolnshire
London: Batsford, 1977.   208p.: ill.
Includes index.
ISBN 0713406836
      pp.111–131: Lincoln.

583.   **FISK, Roy**
Reflecting Lincolnshire
[Lincoln]: [The Author], [1981].   109p.: ill.
ISBN 0950837903

584.   **LLOYD, Michael**
Portrait of Lincolnshire
London: Hale, 1983.   224p., [22]p. of plates.
ISBN 0709008465
      pp.200–209: Lincoln.

GEOGRAPHY

585.   **ARCHBOLD, Thomas**
Geography of Lincolnshire adapted to the new code
London: William Collins, [1872].   24p.:ill., [2] leaves of maps.
(Collins' county geographies)
      pp.13–15: Lincoln.

586.
An Historical geography of England before A.D. 1800: fourteen studies
edited by H.C. Darby.
Cambridge: Cambridge University Press, 1951.   xii, 566p., maps.
Originally published: 1936; reissued with corrections: 1948.   Includes index.
      Various references to Lincoln from Roman times onwards.

587.   **EDWARDS, K.C.**
Lincoln: a geographical excursion: maps and explanatory notes
Lincoln: Lincoln Training College, [1953].   11p., maps.
      Notes and maps for excursion arranged for members of Spring Conference of the Geographical
      Association held at Lincoln in April, 1953.

588.
Nottingham and its region
edited by K.C. Edwards.
Nottingham: British Association for the Advancement of Science, 1966.   538p.: ill.,
[15]p. of plates.
      pp.467–473: 'Lincoln', by E. Joan Garlick.

589.
*Outside the geography room: 15 geographical excursions in the East Midlands for
schools and colleges*
compiled by members of the Geography Advisory Committee of the Institute of
Education of the University of Nottingham.

Nottingham: University of Nottingham, Institute of Education, [1966].   56p., maps.
(University of Nottingham, Institute of Education occasional papers, 4)
For schools.
    pp.44–52: Lincoln.

590.   **DALTON, Roger**
Lincolnshire landscapes: an approach to geographical study
by Roger Dalton and Spencer Thomas.
Lincoln: Bishop Grosseteste College, [1968].   76p.: ill.
    pp.43–49: Lincoln.

591.   **THOMAS, Spencer**
A County and Cathedral city: Lincoln
London: Longmans, Green, 1968.   32p.: ill.
(On the spot geographies, 4)
    For children.

592.   **DARBY, H.C.**
The Domesday geography of eastern England
3rd ed.
Cambridge: Cambridge University Press, 1971.   xiv, 400p., maps.
Originally published: 1952.

CITY OF LINCOLN

General Books

593.
Abbeys and cathedrals of the world.   No.2
pp.274–288: ill., plan in *Architecture*, July, 1896.
    Also describes surroundings and more general history.

594.   **LONGLEY, F.E.**
*Our eastern cathedrals: a concise illustrated handbook to the cathedrals of Ely, Lincoln,
Norwich and Peterborough...a short description of the cities themselves: a panoramic
itinerary of the routes by which they are reached from the metropolis...*
London: F.E. Longley, [189?].   16p.: ill., map.
(Longley's holiday guides)

595.   **SYMPSON, E. Mansel**
Lincoln: a historical and topographical account of the city
illustrated by E.H. New.
London: Methuen, 1906.   147p.: ill.
(Ancient cities)

596.   **HAVERFIELD, F.**
Ancient town-planning
Oxford: Clarendon Press, 1913.   152p.: ill., maps, [7] leaves of plates.
    pp.117–118 and 143: Lincoln.

597.   ANDREWS, William
Old English towns
by William Andrews and Elsie M. Lang.
London: T. Werner Laurie, 1925.   438p., [33]p. of plates.
Includes index.
>pp.114–125: descriptive and historical account of Lincoln.

598.   STEPHENSON, Carl
Borough and town: a study of urban origins in England
Cambridge, Mass.: Mediaeval Academy of America, 1933.   xv, 236p.
(Mediaeval Academy of America publications, no.15.   Monograph, no.7)
>pp.192–194: topography of the city of Lincoln.   Numerous other references to Lincoln.

599.
The British Isles: Lincoln
London: British Travel Association, [1966].   1 folded sheet: ill., map.

600   WILSON, Roger J.A.
A Guide to the Roman remains in Britain
Lincoln: Constable, 1975.   xvi, 365p.: ill.
Includes index.
ISBN 094598703
>pp.150–160: Roman remains to be seen in Lincoln rather than archaeology.

601.
The Plans and topography of medieval towns in England and Wales
edited by M.W. Barley.
London: Council for British Archaeology, 1976.   vi, 92p.: ill., maps, plans.
(CBA research report, no.14)
Includes bibliography and index.
>References to Lincoln passim.   Includes a plan of Lincoln town defences after 1066 and a plan
>of the medieval built-up area.

602.   MAITLAND, Alan
Cathedral towns of England: Lincoln, an impish mixture of grandeur and grime
pp.48–52: ill. in *This England*, autumn, 1978.

Historical and Descriptive Guides Pre–1820

603.
An Historical account of the antiquities in the Cathedral Church of St.Mary, Lincoln...
Lincoln: printed and sold by W. Wood, [1771].   iv, 55p.

604.
Lincoln: a survey and descriptive account of the city and Cathedral
pp.407–411, 1 leaf of plates in *The New Christians magazine*, May, 1783.

605.
An Historical account of Lincoln and the Cathedral
Lincoln: printed and sold by J.W. Drury, 1793.   58p.
Accompanied by: charter of the city, 41p.; mayors and bailiffs: [list], xxvip.;
memorandums 1794, [10]p.
>Lincoln Central Library includes [36]p. of Ms. notes.

606.
*An Historical account of Lincoln and the Cathedral, with a list of remarkable occurences
that have happened in Lincoln for upwards of 700 years, and the number of inhabitants
in each parish, &c.*
New ed.
Lincoln: printed and sold by John Smith, [1801?]. 48p.: ill.

607.
An Historical account of Lincoln and the Cathedral
Lincoln: printed and sold by J.W. Drury, 1802. 54p.

608.
*An Historical account of Lincoln and the Cathedral, with a list of remarkable occurences
that have happened in Lincoln for upwards of 1000 years, and the number of inhabitants
in each parish, as taken in March, 1802*
New ed. with additions.
Lincoln: John Smith, 1804. 48p.

609.
An Historical account of Lincoln and the Cathedral...
New ed. with additions.
Lincoln: John Smith, 1805. 36p.

610.
*An Historical account of the Cathedral Church of Lincoln and the city, Bail and Close of
Lincoln*
Lincoln: J.W. Drury, 1808. 58p.

611.
*A Description of Lincoln, containing some account of its antiquities, public buildings,
&c., particularly the Cathedral*
Lincoln: printed Drury, [1808]. 48p.

612.
*The History of Lincoln: with an appendix, containing a list of the Members returned to
serve in Parliament, as also of the mayors and sheriffs of the city*
Lincoln: A. Stark, 1810. 312, 27, viip.: ill.

613.
*An Historical account and description of the Cathedral Church of St.Mary, Lincoln, with
a short sketch of the Bishops who have presided over this Church*
Lincoln: printed and sold John Smith, 1810. 32p.

614.
*The History of Lincoln: containing an account of the antiquities, edifices, trade and
customs...to which is added an appendix, comprising the charter and a list of mayors and
sheriffs*
Lincoln: Drury, 1816. 223p., 3 leaves of plates.
    The British Library possess E.J. Willson's annotated copy. One copy at the Lincolnshire
    Archives Office also has copious Ms. notes constituting some 180 pages.

615.
The History of Lincoln: and guide to its curiosities and antiquities
Lincoln: printed for J. Cole by A. Stark, 1818. 160p.
    Lincoln Central Library own copy interleaved with annotations by E.J. Willson.

616.

An Abridged history of Lincoln and its Cathedral Church, with an engraved south-east view of that edifice
Lincoln: printed W. Brooke, [1820s?]. 12p.
> History 'given...to purchasers of books almanacks'.

617.

A Description of the antiquities, public objects, &c., in Lincoln
Lincoln: printed W. and B. Brooke, [1820s?]. 68p., [1] leaf of plates.

618.

Ward's historical guide to Lincoln
Lincoln: printed Samuel Ward, [1875?]. 1 sheet: ill.

Historical and Descriptive Guides Post–1820

619.

The Hand book guide to Lincoln, and business intelligencer
Lincoln: printed and published by R.E. Leary, [1841]. 68, [41]p.

620.

A Sketch, historical and descriptive, of the Minster and antiquities of the city of Lincoln
Lincoln: E.B. Drury, 1831. 88p.: ill., [2] leaves of plates.
> 'Along the water, beautiful views of the town, Castle, lunatic asylum and Cathedral, present themselves.'

621.

The History of Lincoln: containing an account of its antiquities, edifices, trade and customs and a description of the Cathedral
Lincoln: Drury, 1825. 153p.
Originally published: 1823.

622

The History of Lincoln: containing an account of the Minster and antiquities of the city of Lincoln
Lincoln: Drury, 1826. 54, [38]p.: ill.

623.

A Sketch, illustrative of the Minster and antiquities of the city of Lincoln
Lincoln: E.B. Drury, 1835. 108p.: ill., [2] leaves of plates.

624.

The Stranger's guide through Lincoln Cathedral, also the Castle, Bishop's Palace, Newport Gate, Roman Walls, and a general survey of the various antiquities, public objects...completed to the present time
Lincoln: printed and sold by W. and B. Brooke, [1836?]. 30p., plan, 1 leaf of plates.
Includes: 'A new guide to the antiquities, &c., of Lincoln', 60p., [4] leaves of plates.

625.

A Survey of the antiquities of the city of Lincoln, with illustrations
Lincoln: W. and B. Brooke, [1840?]. 32, xvip., [3] leaves of plates.

626.
A Topographical and historical description of the city of Lincoln and its immediate vicinity...together with a chronological register of every remarkable and extraordinary event
Lincoln: R.E. Leary, 1843.   28p., 1 leaf of maps, [frontis].

627.
The Strangers' guide to Lincoln: historical sketch, Castle and Cathedral, antiquities, public buildings, charities, geology, botany, etc.
Lincoln: James Drury, 1846.   138p.: ill., [11] leaves of plates.

628.
The Handbook guide to Lincoln, and business intelligencer
2nd ed.
Lincoln: printed for R. Bulman [by] R.E. Leary, [1848].   72p.: ill., maps.

629.
The Handbook guide to Lincoln, and business intelligencer
2nd ed.
Lincoln: R.E. Leary, [1848].   72p.: ill., maps.
    Same as edition produced for Bulman but with green frontispiece.

630
The Handbook guide to Lincoln, and business intelligencer
2nd ed.
Lincoln: printed & published for W. Doncaster, [1848?].   72p.: ill., [5] leaves of plates.

631.
The Handbook guide to Lincoln, and business intelligencer
Lincoln: R.E. Leary, [1848?].   68, [41], 15p.: ill., map.

632.
The Handbook guide to Lincoln, and business intelligencer
Lincoln: R.E. Leary, [c.1849–52].   68p., map, [4] leaves of plates.

633.
The Illustrated hand book guide to Lincoln
Lincoln: R.E. Leary, [c.1850].   49p.: ill., map.

634.
The Illustrated strangers' guide to Lincoln: historical sketch, Castle, Cathedral and antiquities, public buildings, charities, etc.
6th ed.
Lincoln: printed and sold by James Drury, 1850.   60p.: ill., 8 leaves of plates.

635.
A Survey of the antiquities of the city of Lincoln with illustrations
Lincoln: W. and B. Brooke, 1840–48.   Various pagings.

636.
The Strangers' illustrated guide through Lincoln: giving a descriptive account of the Castle, Cathedral and its antiquities, public buildings, charities etc., and an historical sketch of the city
9th ed.
Lincoln: George J. Lockyer, 1856.   110p.: ill., 7 leaves of plates.

637.
The Strangers' guide to Lincoln, the Castle, Cathedral and antiquities: with an historical sketch of the city
Lincoln: printed Edward R. Cousans, 1858. 110p., [5] leaves of plates.

638.
The Illustrated hand book guide to Lincoln
Lincoln: R.E. Leary, [1859?]. 52p.: ill., 6p. of plates.

639.
The Handbook guide to Lincoln, and business intelligencer
3rd ed.
Lincoln: R.E. Leary, [1860?]. 72p.: ill., 1 leaf of plans.

640.
Leary's annual advertiser for 1860, attached to the Lincoln guide and trade register
Lincoln: R.E. Leary, 1860. 55p.: ill., 2 leaves of plates.

641.
Lincoln illustrated guide and general annual advertiser: directory for visitors & travellers
New ed.
Lincoln: F.H. Tomlinson, [after 1861]. 26, [10]p., [4] leaves of plates.

642.
The Strangers' illustrated guide through Lincoln: containing a graphic descriptive account of the Castle, Cathedral and antiquities, public buildings, charities, etc., and an historical sketch of the city
10th ed.
Lincoln: Richard Loder, 1861. 112p.: ill.

643.
Lincoln as it is! what there is to see! and where to see it!, or The illustrated hand book guide
Lincoln: R.E. Leary, 1862. 45, [37]p.: ill.
Accompanies: Leary's *Annual advertiser*.

644.
Tracts and miscellanies relating to Lincoln Cathedral, the city, Castle, Palace ruins, etc., with some original letters and curious documents hitherto unpublished
Lincoln: Brookes & Vibert, 1863. Various pagings: ill.
> Apart from subjects mentioned in title, also: brief annals from the Norman Conquest; letters from Mr. Sympson of Lincoln with Browne Willis; extracts from municipal records; Anne Askew; notes on Lincolnshire words.

645.
Williamson's guide through Lincoln
Lincoln: James Williamson, [187?]. 99p.: ill., [frontis].

646.
History of Lincoln and Big Tom
Lincoln: printed and published for H. Brummitt, [c.1870]. 1 sheet: ill.

647.
Brummitt's illustrated guide through Lincoln with an account of the Cathedral, Castle and antiquities
Lincoln: Henry H. Brummitt, [after 1873]. 34p.

648.
The City of Lincoln described, its Cathedral, Castle, Palace ruins, parish churches,
religious houses, gateways, Roman remains, &c., with numerous plans and cuts: Speed's
curious plan in 1610, &c. and a copious narrative of historical events
Lincoln: Brookes & Vibert, [1873].   34p.: ill., [8]p. of plates.

649.   **ANDERSON, C.H.J.**
The Lincoln pocket guide: being a short account of the churches and antiquities of the
county, and of the Cathedral of the Blessed Virgin Mary of Lincoln, commonly called the
Minster
Lincoln: printed Edward Ralph Cousans, 1874.   196p.

650.   —————————
The Lincoln pocket guide
[Enlarged ed.]
London: Edward Stanford, 1880.   192p., maps, [5]p. of plates.

651.   —————————
The Lincoln pocket guide
2nd ed.
London: Edward Stanford, 1881.   192p.: ill., [5]p. of plates.

652.   —————————
The Lincoln pocket guide
edited and revised by A.R. Maddison.   3rd ed.
London: Edward Stanford, 1892.   192p., maps, [5]p. of plates.

653.
Ward's historical guide to Lincoln
Lincoln: printed Samuel Ward, [c.1877].   1 sheet: ill.

654.
The City of Lincoln described: its Cathedral, Castle, Palace-ruins, parish churches,
religious houses, gateways, Roman remains, &c.
Lincoln: James Williamson, [188?].   Various pagings.

655.   **PERKYNS, J.H.H.**
Akrill's visitors' guide to Lincoln and its Cathedral Church, with a brief sketch of the
neighbourhood
Lincoln: Charles Akrill, [1881].   96p., [10] leaves of plates.

656.
Williamson's guide through Lincoln
2nd and revised ed.
Lincoln: James Williamson, 1881.   128p.: ill., [9]p. of plates.

657.   **VENABLES, Edmund**
A Walk through the streets of Lincoln: a lecture delivered...to the YMCA...11th
December, 1883
Lincoln: printed Chas. Akrill, [1884].   32p.

658.
Williamson's illustrated guide through Lincoln with map of city and plan of Cathedral: a
complete and authentic description of the many places of historical interest in and
around Lincoln
Lincoln: James Williamson, [c.1885].   142p.: ill.

659.
Williamson's illustrated guide through Lincoln
3rd revised ed.
Lincoln: James Williamson, 1887.   viii, 160p.

660.   **VENABLES, Edmund**
Walks through the streets of Lincoln: two lectures
5th ed.
Lincoln: J.W. Ruddock, [1888].   84p.

661.
Ward and Lock's illustrated handbook to Lincoln Cathedral, with a topographical account of the city
London: Ward, Lock, 1889.   220p.: ill., 10 leaves of plates.
> Coloured engravings by Winkles of the Cathedral as used in *Cathedral churches of England and Wales*, with line drawings of other landmarks complementing the text.

662.   **PERKYNS, J.H.H.**
Akrill's visitor's guide to Lincoln and its Cathedral Church, with a brief sketch of the neighbourhood
Lincoln: Akrill, Ruddock & Keyworth, [1890?].   96p.: ill., 10 leaves of plates.
Includes index.

663.
Williamson's handbook to Lincoln city and Cathedral
Lincoln: James Williamson, [1890s?].   31p.

664.
Lincoln and Lincoln Cathedral: a descriptive guide to the city and Cathedral
Lincoln: Boots, [1899].   84p.: ill.
(Boots series of view books and guides)

665.   **F., A.**
Lincoln and Lincoln Cathedral: a descriptive guide to the city and Cathedral
New and revised ed.
Lincoln: Boots, 1899.   143p.: ill., [1] folded plan.
Includes index.

666
Lincoln and its Cathedral
2nd ed.
Lincoln: Keyworth, [18??].   66p.: ill.

667.
Lincoln city & Cathedral: a description for visitors and citizens
Lincoln: J.W. Ruddock, 1901.   185p.: ill.

668.
Melton's guide to Lincoln
Lincoln: Melton, [1913?].   24p.: ill., 1 map.

669.
Lincoln and its Minster
Lincoln: Melton, [1919?].   [16] leaves of plates.

670.
Lincoln and its Cathedral
Lincoln: Keyworth, [1920s?].   [58]p.

671.
Meltons' guide to Lincoln
Lincoln: Melton, [1920s?].   24p.: ill., 1 map.

672.
Lincoln
London: SPCK, [1940/50s?].   [15]p.: ill.
    Mainly photographs.

673.   **MEE, Arthur**
Lincoln
London: St.Hugh's, [1950s?].   52p.: ill., maps.
Maps on inside covers.

674.   **MARTINEAU, Hugh**
A Cameo of Lincoln.   Part one
pp.28–37: ill. in *Lincolnshire life*, vol.8, no.10, December, 1968.
    Brief history accompanied by photographs.

675.   ——————
A Cameo of Lincoln.   Part two
pp.18–25: ill. in *Lincolnshire life*, vol.8, no.11, January, 1969.
    Gives some coverage to 'below-hill' Lincoln.

676.
The Pocket guide to Lincoln and Lincoln Cathedral
Lincoln: Old Cathedral Store, [1969].   24p.: ill.

677.   **FISK, Roy**
About historic Lincoln: an illustrated talk-about walk-about
Lincoln: [The Author], [1986].   38p.: ill., map.

Official Guides

678.   **PAGE, C.F.**
The Official guide to Lincoln city and Cathedral
Lincoln: Lincoln Corporation, [1910?].   164p.: ill., [5] leaves of plates.

679.
The Official guide of the Lincoln Corporation: Lincoln city and Cathedral, with plans and illustrations: a handbook for visitors and residents
Lincoln: J.W. Ruddock; London: Homeland Association, [1921].   lxvii, 152p.: ill.
(Homeland handbooks, vol.90)
Includes indexes to subjects and advertisers.

680.
A Descriptive guide to the ancient city Lincoln and its Cathedral Church of St Mary
Lincoln: J.W. Ruddock, 1929.   xvi, 112p.: ill.
Includes index.
    'Being the official guide of the Corporation of Lincoln and of the Lincoln Chamber of
    Commerce'.

681.   **PAGE, C.F.**
*A Descriptive guide to the ancient city Lincoln and its Cathedral Church of
St Mary...being the official guide of the Corporation of Lincoln and of the Lincoln
Chamber of Commerce*
Lincoln: J.W. Ruddock, 1929.   112p.: ill., maps, plans.
Includes index.

682.
Lincoln: [guide book]
Cheltenham: Ed. J. Burrow, [193?].   16p.: ill., map.

683.
Lincoln
[Lincoln]: Lincoln Corporation, [1934].   10p.: ill.

684.
*The City of Lincoln: its history, the story of its Castle and Cathedral with notes on the
modern city: the official guide*
Cheltenham: E.J. Burrow for the Corporation, [1934?].   60p.: ill., maps, [13]p. of plates.

685.   **PAGE, C.F.**
Lincoln: a descriptive guide to the ancient city and its Cathedral Church of St Mary
2nd ed.
Lincoln: J.W. Ruddock, 1934.   96p.: ill.

686.
*The City of Lincoln: its history, the story of its Castle and Cathedral with notes on the
modern city: the official guide*
Cheltenham: Ed. J. Burrow, [1940?].   60p.: ill., maps, 3p. of plates.
    Paragraphs relating to: the Cathedral, by Canon J.H. Srawley; the architectural, archaeological
    and historical features of the city, by J.W.F. Hill.

687.
The City of Lincoln: the official guide
2nd ed.
Cheltenham: Ed. J. Burrow, [1942?].   60p.: ill., maps, 4p. of plates.

688.
The City of Lincoln: the official guide
3rd ed.
Cheltenham: Ed. J. Burrow, [1944?].   56p.: ill., maps, 6p. of plates.

689.
The City of Lincoln: the official guide
4th ed.
Cheltenham: Ed. J. Burrow, [1945?].   56p.: ill., map, 6p. of plates.

690.
City and county of the city of Lincoln
Lincoln: J.W. Ruddock, 1947.   56p.: ill., maps.
    Contains much of the same information as Burrow edition, updated and with different
    illustrations.

691
Lincoln official guide
Lincoln: J.W. Ruddock, [1948].   85p.: ill., maps.
    Includes section on industry in Lincoln: Ruston & Hornsby; Ruston Bucyrus; Robey & Co.

692.
Lincoln official guide
Lincoln: J.W. Ruddock, [1949].   94p.: ill., maps.

693.
Lincoln official guide
Lincoln: printed J.W. Ruddock, [1960?].   85p.: ill., maps, plans.

694.
Lincoln: [official guide]
Lincoln: Lincoln Corporation, [1967].   72p.: ill., map.

695
City of Lincoln official guide
Carshalton: Home Publishing, Northern, [1970?].   106p.: ill., maps.

696.
City of Lincoln official guide
Lincoln: Lincoln Corporation, 1972.   108p.: ill., maps.
    Includes series of local maps and a street index.

697.
City of Lincoln official guide
Carshalton: Home Publishing, Northern, [1973?].   108p.: ill., maps.

698.
City of Lincoln official guide
Carshalton: Home Publishing, Northern, [1976].   148p.: ill., maps.

699.
City of Lincoln official guide
Lincoln: Lincoln City Council, 1977.   148p.: ill., maps.

700.
Official street plan
Wallington: Forward Publicity, [1980?].   56p., maps.

701.
City of Lincoln official guide
Wallington: Home Publishing, [1982?].   120p.: ill., maps.

Other Brief Guides

702.
Guide through city of Lincoln
3rd ed.
Lincoln: J.B. Smith, [after 1877].   1 sheet: ill.

703.
Guide through the city of Lincoln
4th ed.
Lincoln: printed Charles Keyworth, [1881?].   1 sheet: ill.

704.   **HUNT, Alfred**
Objects of interest in Lincoln
Lincoln: Alfred Shuttleworth, 1917.   [4]p.
    In memory of Colonel S. Mason.

705. —————————
Objects of interest in Lincoln
2nd ed.
Lincoln: Echo and Gazette, 1918. [4]p.

706.
A Brief guide to Lincoln with view and a plan
Lincoln: J.W. Ruddock, [c.1918]. 40p.: ill.

707.
Some places of interest
Lincoln: City Information Office, [197?]. [3]p.

708.
Lincoln: a history-book city looks to the future: a special report to mark the 900th anniversary of the Cathedral's foundation
pp.I-IV: ill. in *The Times*, Friday, May 26, 1972.

709.
City of Lincoln: miniguide to the city
Lincoln: City Information Office, [1972?]. 12p.: ill., map.

710.
White Hart Hotel: [menu]
[Lincoln]: [The Hotel], [c.1972]. [4]p.: ill.
    With annotated plan of Lincoln giving details of historical events.

711.   **HILL, J.W.F.**
The City of Lincoln
by Sir Francis Hill for the Lincoln Civic Trust.
London: Pitkin Pictorials, [1975]. 24p.: ill., map.
(Pitkin pride of Britain books)

712.
Some places of interest
Lincoln: City Information Centre, [1976]. 1 folded sheet: ill., plan.

713.   **WILSON, C.M.**
History trail: Lincoln Castle to the Museum of Lincolnshire Life
Lincoln: Lincolnshire Museums, 1979. 1 folded sheet: ill.

714.
Lincoln
Huntingdon: Colourmaster, [1980]. 32p.: ill., map, plan.
(Colour master publication)
ISBN 0859331873

715.   **BAKER, F.T.**
Historic Lincoln
Norwich: Jarrold Colour Publications, 1983. [32]p.: ill., map.
Parallel English, French and German text.
ISBN 0711700966

716.
Lincoln's heritage: a pictorial guide
Lincoln: City Information Office, [1983]. 1 folded sheet: ill., map.

717.
Lincoln: [cassette]
Plymouth: Cassette Town Trails, 1986.
Cassette accompanied by 1p. of instructions and sketch map of Lincoln.

Guides for Special Occasions

718.
Archaeological Institute of Great Britain and Ireland: meeting at Lincoln, July, 1848: architectural notes of the churches and other ancient buildings of the city and neighbourhood of Lincoln
by a member of the Architectural Section.
[London]: [The Institute], [1848].   20p.
     pp.1–10: city of Lincoln.

719.   **TROLLOPE, Edward**
Handbook of the excursions proposed to be made by the Lincoln Diocesan Architectural Society, on the 27th & 28th of May, 1857
Sleaford: printed W. Fawcett, 1857.   72, [9]p.: ill., [1] leaf of maps.
     pp.1–13 and 40–51: Lincoln.

720.
Annual meeting at Lincoln...July 27 to August 2, 1880: general notes upon the places visited during the meeting
London: W.S. Johnson, 1880.   50p., map, [11] leaves of plates.
     pp.3–20: history of Lincoln.

721.   **SYMPSON, E. Mansel**
Handbook to Lincoln: city and Cathedral
Lincoln: printed James Williamson, 1892.   20p., [1] folded map.
     Prepared for the visit of the British Medical Association, July, 1892.

722.   **VICKERS, B.**
City of Lincoln and Stow Church: itinerary: [Quatuor Coronati Lodge, no.2076, London, 1903 summer outing, 25th to 28th June]
compiled by B. Vickers and H.H. Dunn.
[London]: [The Lodge], 1903.   16p.: ill., plans.

723.   **SYMPSON, Edward Mansel**
Lincoln: a guide for the excursion on Saturday, 20th August
Cambridge: British Association, Cambridge, 1904.   22p.

724.   **GREEN, H.**
Lincoln Royal Show, 1907: a history of the city and an interesting souvenir of the visit of the Royal Agricultural Society of England to Lincoln, June 25th-29th, 1907
Lincoln: Gazette and Echo, 1907.   [94]p.: ill., folded plan.
     Includes: 'Lincoln: a tour through the city'.

725.
A Souvenir of the Royal Show, Lincoln, June 25th-29th, 1907
Lincoln: Harrison and J.W. Ruddock, 1907.   120p.: ill., map.
     Includes brief history of Lincoln by E. Mansel Sympson as well as articles on agricultural
     matters.

726.
The Royal Show, Lincoln, June...1907: an attractive guide to the show and an interesting souvenir of the event, together with a profusely illustrated guide to the city and places of interest in the county
Lincoln: W.K. Morton, 1907.   [27], 92, [58]p.: ill.

727.   **BRITISH ARCHAEOLOGICAL ASSOCIATION**
Report of the seventy-eighth congress, 1921, June 27 to July 2, at Lincoln
pp.9–18 in *The Journal of the British Archaeological Association*, new series, vol.XXVII, 1921.
pp.9–11: St Peter-at-Gowts; pp.11–12: St Mary's Guild; p.12: St Mark's; pp.12–13: St Mary-le-Wigford; p.13: High Bridge; pp.13–14: Grey Friars; p.14: St Swithin's; pp.14–16: Jews House; pp.16–18: Aaron's House.

728.
Lincoln: [National Association of Head Teachers 1936 conference souvenir]
London: Gregg, [1936].   126, xiip., [31] leaves of plates.
pp.5–16: 'The story of Lincoln', by J.W.F. Hill; pp.67–78: 'Antiquities of Lincoln', by E.I. Abell; pp.79–85: 'Industry in Lincoln', by Wm. Tritton; pp.86–96: 'Education in Lincoln', by C.W. Hooton; pp.110–119: 'Art and the drama', by Austin Garland.

729.
City and county of the city of Lincoln...on the occasion of the Royal Agricultural Show, 1947
Lincoln: Lincoln Corporation, 1947.   56p.: ill., maps.

730.   **ROYAL ARCHAEOLOGICAL INSTITUTE**
Programme of the summer meeting at Lincoln, Monday, 22 July to Saturday, 27 July, 1974
London: The Institute, 1974.   122p.: ill., 62p. of plates.
Includes: the Chancery; the Priory; the Old Bishop's Palace; the Cardinal's Hat; St Mary-le-Wigford; St Peter-at-Gowts; Newport Arch; Eastgate; Lincoln Castle; the Park; Lincoln gateway and defences; Stonebow.

LINCOLN, HISTORIC AND INDUSTRIAL CITY

731.
Lincoln as an ancient Cathedral city and as a modern commercial centre: official handbook of the Lincoln Incorporated Chamber of Commerce
Cheltenham: Ed. J. Burrow, [1924].   62p.: ill., maps.

732.
Lincoln, England: city of history and industry: [*Lincolnshire chronicle & leader* special supplement, August, 1930]
Lincoln: Lincolnshire Newspapers, 1930.   48p.: ill.
Includes index.
Includes: 'The Story of Lincoln', by J.W.F. Hill; 'The Castle of the Conqueror: its stirring story through the centuries', by J.W.F. Hill; 'The Usher Art Gallery'; 'Lincoln worthies', by John Shallaker; articles on main firms of the city.

733.   **BROME, James**
Travels over England: giving a true and exact description of the chiefest cities, towns and corporations with the antiquities of other places
2nd ed. with large additions.
London: R. Gosling, 1707.   315p.
Originally published: 1700.
    Some 4 pages devoted to Lincoln.

734.   **LELAND, John**
Johannis Lelandi antiquarii de rebus Britannicis collectanea cum Thomae Hearnii praefatione notis et indice ad editionem primam
Editio altera.
London: Benjamin White, 1774.   6 vols.
Includes index.   Text in Latin with some English.
    Many brief references.

735.   ——————————
The Itinerary of John Leland in or about the years 1535–1543.   Parts I to III
edited by Lucy Toulmin Smith.
London: George Bell, 1907.   xliii, 352p., folded map.
Includes index.
    pp.28–31: Lincoln.

736.   **WALPOOLE, G.A.**
The New and complete British traveller, or A complete display of Great Britain and Ireland, being a new tour through England, Wales and Scotland, Ireland...
London: printed for A. Hogg, [1784].   520p.
    Chapter 2: Lincolnshire.

737.
Account of the city of Lincoln: [letter to 'Mr. Urban']
pp.209–211, [1] leaf of plates in *The Gentleman's magazine*, March, 1822.

738.   **HATFIELD, Miss**
The Terra incognita of Lincolnshire, with observations moral, descriptive, and historical, in original letters, written, purposely for the improvement of youth, during the months of May and October, 1815
3rd ed.
London: F. and H. Laking, 1832.   vi, 144p.
Originally published: 1816.
    pp.6–7: Lincoln.

739.
Cobbett's lecture speeches: [poster]
Lincoln: printed E.B. Drury, [1830].   1 sheet.

740.   **DIBDIN, Thomas Frognall**
A Bibliographical, antiquarian and picturesque tour in the northern counties of England and in Scotland
London: The Author, 1838.   3 vols.
    Vol.1, pp.84–119: details of contents of Honywood's library with asides on Lincoln.

741.   **GARDINER, William**
Music and friends, or Pleasant recollections of a dilettante
London: Longman, Orme, Brown and Longman, 1838.   3 vols.
> Vol.1, pp.293–296: music of Lincoln Cathedral; pp.406–407: hanging of Jane Flower and her daughter at Lincoln.   Vol.2, p.714: discovery of remains of shop at Dancing Lock (Dantzic Lock).

742.
Visit to Lincoln
pp.153–154 in *Chambers' Edinburgh journal*, no.488, Saturday, June 5, 1841.

743.   **COBBETT, William**
Rural rides in the counties of Surrey...Lincoln...and Northumberland, in the years 1821, 1822, 1823, 1825, 1826, 1829, 1830 and 1832, with economical and political observations...
New ed.
London: A. Cobbett, 1853.   679p., [frontis].
Originally published: 1830.
> pp.602–606: account of the meeting held in Lincoln with some reference to Cathedral and city.

744.   **WALCOTT, MacKenzie E.C.**
Memorials of Lincoln & the Cathedral
Lincoln: Chas. Akrill, 1866.   73p., [5] leaves of plates.

745.
As the crow flies: due north: Lincoln to Somersby
pp.536–540 in *All the year round: a weekly journal conducted by Charles Dickens with which is incorporated Household words*, no.49, new series, Saturday, November 6, 1869.
> Mainly Cathedral and Bishops of Lincoln.

746.   **THORNBURY, Walter**
A Tour round England
London: Hurst and Blackett, 1870.
> pp.164–181: Peterborough to Lincoln; pp.182–204: Lincoln.
> Papers originally published: in *All the year round*.

747.   **HAWTHORNE, Nathaniel**
Our old home
London: Chatto and Windus, 1890.   2 vols.
> pp.236–245: Lincoln.

748.   **LOVEDAY, John**
Diary of a tour in 1732 through parts of England, Wales, Ireland and Scotland made by John Loveday of Caversham
Edinburgh: Roxburghe Club, 1890.   xiv, 227, ixp.
> pp.204–210: Lincoln.

749.
The Book of the pilgrimage: a record of **The Congregationalist'**s *pilgrimage to England and Holland*
Boston, Mass.: Office of the Congregationalist, 1896.   156p.: ill.
> pp.98–101: Lincoln.

750.   **GILBERT, Bernard**
Living Lincoln
Lincoln: Lincolnshire Publishing, 1914.   81p.: ill.
> Includes articles about: Cathedral; public library; water tower; football; and general observations on life in the city.   Articles originally published: in *Lincolnshire echo*.

751.   **CANTON, William**
The Appeal of Lincoln Cathedral
pp.637–645: ill. in *The Review of reviews*, June 15th, 1922.
     Mostly Cathedral and appeal initiated by Dean Fry, but first writes of impresssions of city.

752.
Educational tours in eastern Britain
[York]: [London & North Eastern Railway], 1935.   39p.: ill.
     pp.23–26: 'Lincoln', by A.R. Corns.

753.   **SOUTHEY, Robert**
Letters from England
edited with an introduction by Jack Simmons.
London: Cresset, 1951.   xxvi, 494p.
Originally published: 1807.   Includes index.
     p.266: Lincoln.

754.   **COTTRELL, Leonard**
Seeing Roman Britain
London: Evans, 1956.   295p., [32]p. of plates.
Includes index.
     pp.179–187: Lincoln, in this 'personal account of travels in search of Roman Britain'.

755.   **MORLEY, Frank**
The Great North Road
London: Hutchinson, 1961.   327p.
     pp.97–100: mainly discussion of cloth industry and the colour of Lincoln 'green'.

756.   **EKBERG, Charles**
Lincoln
pp.21–26 in *Lincolnshire life*, vol.1, no.4, winter, 1962.
     Historical and contemporary view.

757.
Britain in miniature...statistically typical of the country as a whole: we explore Lincoln
pp.2–3, 5: ill. in *The Sunday times* colour section, 4th February, 1962.

758.   **BINNS, Kathleen**
City set on a hill
pp.8–10: ill. in *The Home owner*, no.110, May, 1963.

759.
On Lincoln: its people, its policies, its country: a selection of leaders published in the
Lincolnshire chronicle *since November, 1963.*
[Lincoln]: [The Chronicle], 1965.   16p.

760.   **HAWTHORNE, Nathaniel**
Hawthorne in England: selections from **Our old home** *and the* **English note-books**
edited by Cushing Strout.
Ithaca, N.Y.: Cornell University Press, 1965.   274p.
(Cornell paperbacks)
     pp.117–121: visit to Lincoln mentioned in 'Pilgrimage to Old Boston'.

761.   **JONES, H. Dennis**
Lincoln
pp.740–741: ill. in *The Lady*, 17th November, 1966.

762.
City of Lincoln: past, present, future: [*Lincolnshire chronicle* supplement, April, 1976]
Lincoln: The Chronicle, 1976.   16p.: ill.
Articles on: Cathedral; tourism; planning; archaeology; cinema.

763.   SEELY, Frank
Recollections of Bailgate, Lincoln, 1900–1914
as remembered by Frank Seely.
[1978].   3 leaves.
Typescript.

764.
Lincoln
[6]p. in *The Observer* colour supplement, 19th August, 1979.

765.   WHITE, A.J.
The Revd. John Skinner's tour to Lincolnshire, 1825
pp.93–98 in *Lincolnshire history and archaeology*, vol.19, 1984.
Visit to Lincolnshire recorded in *Journal of a northern tour*, vol.1 (B.M. Add. Ms. 33683) is
particulary valuable for its drawings of the collections of antiquities in the possession of J.
Fardell, E.J. Willson and the Dean and Chapter.   Article gives transcription of Lincolnshire
section; pp.94–96: Lincoln.

766.   DAVIES, Anita
A *Lincolnshire life* special feature: Lincoln today
pp.30–33: ill. in *Lincolnshire life*, vol.26, no.3, June, 1986.

767.   BOWDEN, Ken
Henry Stephenson's journey to Lincolnshire, July, 1877
pp.32–34: ill. in *Lincolnshire life*, vol.26, no.3, August, 1986.
Article is a condensed version of Stephenson's manuscript diary.

768.   SITWELL, Sacheverell
Sacheverell Sitwell's England
[S.l.]: Orbis, 1986.
pp.55–66: Lincolnshire; includes Lincoln, mainly the Cathedral.

INDIVIDUAL LOCATIONS

769.
Antiquarian and topographical cabinet
London: published for the proprietors by Murray, Nornaville and Fell, 1817–19.   6 vols.
Vol.II: [3] leaves on the Episcopal Palace; vol.III: [1] leaf on Jews House, Lincoln.

770.   PARKER, John Henry
A Glossary of terms used in Grecian, Roman, Italian and Gothic architecture
5th ed., enlarged.
Oxford: John Henry Parker, 1850.   2 vols. in 3 pts.
Originally published: 1836; subsequent eds.: 1838; 1840; 1845.   Includes index.
Includes: Cathedral; St Mary-le-Wigford; St Benedict's; St Peter-at-Gowts; Jews House;
St Mary's Guild; John of Gaunt's Palace; Newport Arch.

771.
Lincoln and its neighbourhood
pp.918–919 in *The Builder*, November 20, 1869.
> Concentrates upon history of the buildings.

772.   **MADDISON, A.R.**
A Ramble through the parish of St Mary Magdalene, Lincoln
[Lincoln]: James Williamson, 1892.   34p.
> Much information culled from the Chapter leases.

773.   ─────────────
A Ramble through the parish of St Margaret-within-the-Close
pp.1–31 in *AAS reports and papers*, vol.22, 1893–94.

774.   **WATKINS, W., & SON**
*Report on the proposed conversion of the building known as 'The Grey Friars' to the
purposes of a museum, with a brief archaeological history of the structure*
Lincoln: printed M.A. Doncaster, 1903.   7p.

775.   **COLVIN, H.M.**
A Biographical dictionary of English architects, 1660–1840
London: John Murray, 1954.   821p.
Includes index of places.
> Many references to Lincoln, though often very brief.

776.
Lincoln past, present & future
Lincoln: Allinson & Emerson, 1969.   20p.: ill.
> Articles by Laurence Elvin originally published in *The Fireside magazine*, about: Hartsholme
> Hall; Lincoln pleasure fair; Monks Rd.; Lincoln horse fair; the Palace Theatre; Lincoln races;
> and the Saracen's Head.

777   **JONES, Stanley R.**
Four Minster houses
Lincoln: Friends of Lincoln Cathedral, 1974.   56p.: ill.
Includes glossary.
ISBN 0903420066
> Covers: the Priory; the Chancery; the Subdeanery; nos.28–30, Steep Hill. Described as first
> fruit of a survey of medieval houses in Lincoln begun in 1969.

778.
*Looking at historic buildings in Lincoln: teachers' course at the Urban Studies Centre,
Bishop Grosseteste College, Lincoln, 1st Nov., 1979*
Lincoln: The College, 1979.   32 leaves: ill.
Cover title.
> Product of workshop activities; suggestions for study schemes with questionnaires for various
> age groups, etc.

779.   **FISK, Roy**
Lincolnshire gleanings
Lincoln: The Author, [1982].   110p.: ill.
ISBN 0950837911
> '...being a miscellany of drawings, stories, etc.: a companion book to *Reflecting Lincolnshire*'.

780.
Norman buildings in Lincoln
Lincoln: Lincoln City and County Museum, 1983.   12p.: ill., map.

781.   **JONES, Stanley**
The Survey of ancient houses in Lincoln.   I: Priorygate to Pottergate
by Stanley Jones, Kathleen Major and Joan Varley, with a contribution by Christopher
Johnson.
Lincoln: Lincoln Civic Trust, 1984.   106p.: ill. + 3 microfiches.
Includes glossary.
ISBN 0860760278

782.   _____
The Survey of ancient houses in Lincoln.   II: houses to the south and west of the Minster
by Stanley Jones, Kathleen Major and Joan Varley.
Lincoln: Lincoln Civic Trust, 1987.   109p.: ill., plans + 4 microfiches.
ISBN 0947693017
    Microfiches contain abstracts and excerpts from sources.

783.   **JOHNSON, C.P.C.**
The Arboretum
in *The Lincolnshire echo*, Thursday, July 21, 1977.
Continued: Wednesday, July 27th, 1977 and Thursday, August 4th, 1977.

784.   **ROUSE, E. Clive**
Wall paintings at Atherstone Place, the Close, Lincoln
[1984?].   [4] leaves.
Typescript.
    Includes 2 leaves of plans dating from 1984.

785.
The Newport Arch at Lincoln
[3]p.: ill. in *Discovery*, February, 1938.

786.
*Some account of domestic architecture in England, from Edward I to Richard II, with
notices of foreign examples and numerous illustrations of existing remains from original
drawings*
by the editor of *The Glossary of architecture*.
Oxford: John Henry Parker, 1853.   v, 352p.: ill., [96] leaves of plates.
    p.238: Cantilupe Chantry and the Priory.

787.
[Article on restoration of Cardinal's Hat]
p.5, [1]p. of plates in *Lincolnshire poacher*, vol.1, no.3, summer, 1953.

788.
*The Story of the Cardinal's Hat...restored 1952–53 by St.John Ambulance Brigade and
opened as county and corps headquarters on 30th April, 1953...*
Lincoln: printed Keyworth, [1953].   23p.: ill.
    pp.8–10: 'Documentary history', by J.W.F. Hill; p.11–19: 'Structural history', by W.A.
    Pantin.   Appendix is a probate inventory of 1616.

789.
The Struggle to restore the 'hidden place' of old Lincoln
pp.46, 69: ill. in *Lincolnshire life*, vol.6, no.7, September, 1966.
    About the Cardinal's Hat.

790.   **ROBERTS, David L.**
The Cardinal's Hat
pp.84–86 in *Royal Archaeological Institute: programme of the summer meeting at Lincoln*, 1974.

791.   **ENGLEFIELD, Henry Charles**
Additions to Mr. King's account of Lincoln Castle...read May 16, 1782
pp.376–380, [2] leaves of plates in *Archaeologia*, vol.VI, 1782.

792.   **KING, Edward**
Sequel to the observations on ancient castles, read Jan. 17, 1782 to the Rev. Doctor Milles, Dean of Exeter, president of the Society of Antiquaries
pp.231–392, [33]p. of plates in *Archaeologia*, vol.VI, 1782.
     pp.261–266: Lincoln Castle, including a plan.

793.
[Plans and drawings of Lincoln Castle from the E.J. Willson collection]
[183?].   1 portfolio.
Ms.

794.   **SMIRKE, Robert**
Reports of Sir Robert Smirke and Mr. Edward James Willson on the state of Lincoln Castle
Lincoln: printed T.J.N. Brogden, 1835.   13p., [1] folded plan.

795.   **HARTSHORNE, C.H.**
The Castle of Lincoln
pp.19–38 in *Memoirs illustrative of the history and antiquities of the county and city of Lincoln*, 1850.

796.   **WILLSON, Edward James**
Lincoln Castle, notices of its history and the existing remains: illustrated by a plan, from actual survey
pp.280–292 in *Memoirs illustrative of the history and antiquities of the county and city of Lincoln*, 1850.

797.
Some account of domestic architecture in England, from Richard II to Henry VIII, with numerous illustrations of existing remains from original drawings.   Part II
by the editor of *The Glossary of architecture.*
Oxford: John Henry Parker, 1859.   pp.201–491: ill., [60] leaves of plates.
Includes index.
     pp.227–229, [1] plate: Lincoln Castle.

798.   **TROLLOPE, Edward**
On the historic incidents connected with Lincoln Heath: [paper read before the Geological and Polytechnic Society of the West Riding of Yorkshire, held at Bradford, Feb. 10th, 1863]
pp.218–226: ill. in *The Reliquary*, vol.3, 1863.
Continued: pp.3–9, vol.4, 1864.

799.   **CLARK, G.T.**
Lincoln Castle: [paper] addressed to the Lincoln Diocesan Architectural Society at their meeting in June, 1875
pp.176–191, [1] leaf of plates in *AAS reports and papers*, vol.13, 1875–76.
     pp.189–190: 'Addenda', by Edmund Venables.

800.
Guide to Lincoln Castle and grounds
Lincoln: printed W.H. Leary, [189?].   [3]p.: ill.

801.   **SYMPSON, E. Mansel**
Lincoln Castle
pp.25–42 in *Bygone Lincolnshire*, vol.2, 1891.

802.
Guide to Lincoln Castle
Lincoln: printed W.K. Morton, 1906.   25p.: ill.

803.
The Guide to Lincoln Castle
Lincoln: printed W.K. Morton, 1906.   25p., 4p. of plates.

804.
The Development of the castle in England and Wales
London: Historical Association, 1910.   32p., [4]p. of plates.
(Leaflet, 22)

805.
Guide to Lincoln Castle
2nd ed.
Lincoln: printed W.K. Morton, 1912.   25p.: ill.

806.   **TIMBS, John**
Abbeys, castles and ancient halls of England & Wales: their legendary lore & popular history
by John Timbs and Alexander Gunn.   2nd ed.
London: Frederick Warne, [1925].   573p., [10] leaves of plates.
Originally published: 1870.   Includes index.
    pp.14–16: Lincoln Castle.

807.
Guide to Lincoln Castle
Lincoln: printed Lincolnshire Chronicle, 1927.   6p.: ill., plan.

808.   **WEIGALL, Arthur**
The Grand tour of Norman England
London: Hodder and Stoughton, [1927].   352p., 59p. of plates.
    pp.272–274: Castle and Jews House.

809.   **HILL, J.W.F.**
Lincoln Castle: official guide
Lincoln: Lincoln Corporation, [193?].   12p.: ill.
    Two issues printed by W.K. Morton and LSG, differing only in photograph on p.11.

810   ——————————
Lincoln Castle: official guide
Lincoln: Lincoln Corporation, [193?].   12p.: ill.
    Another issue printed by LSG but reverting to original picture.   Price 6 pence.

811.   ——————————
Lincoln Castle: the constables and the guard
pp.1–14: ill. in *AAS reports and papers*, vol.40, 1930–31.

812. ─────────────
Lincoln Castle
pp.157–159, plan in *The Archaeological journal*, vol.CIII, 1946.

813.
History of the king's works. II
edited by Brown, Colvin & Taylor.
London: HMSO, 1963.
> pp.704–705: Lincoln Castle.

814.　　**CLARK, A.R.**
The Western gate of Lincoln Castle
p.52 in *Lincolnshire life*, vol.8, no.3, May, 1968.

815.　　**HILL, J.W.F.**
Lincoln Castle: official guide
Lincoln: Lincoln Corporation, [1969].　12p.: ill.

816.　　**HOGG, Garry**
Castles of England
Newton Abbot: David & Charles, 1970.　112p.: ill.
ISBN 071534773X
> pp.50–51: brief account of Lincoln Castle.

817.　　**FOSTER, Glyn**
The History of the Castle of Lincoln
[1973].　60 leaves.
Typescript.

818.　　**HESSELL, Graham S.**
Lincoln Castle
pp.20–25: ill. in *Lincolnshire life*, vol.18, no.3, June, 1978.

819.　　**ELLIOTT, Helen**
Lincoln Castle in the Middle Ages: a guide for children
Lincoln: F.L.A.R.E. Education Group, 1980.　[8]p.: ill.

820 ─────────────
Lincoln Castle: [guide]
[by Helen Elliott and others].
Lincoln: Lincoln, Recreational Services, 1984.　34p.: ill.
ISBN 0861111095

821.　　**SANCHA, Sheila**
Lincoln Castle: the medieval story
Lincoln: Lincoln, Recreational Services, 1985.　48p.: ill.
For children.
ISBN 0861111214

822.　　**DAVIES, Anita**
Lincoln Castle
pp.32–33: ill. in *Lincolnshire life*, vol.26, no.6, September, 1986.

823.　　**JONES, Stanley R.**
The Chancery
pp.62–63 in *Royal Archaeological Institute: programme of the summer meeting at Lincoln*, 1974.

824.   **VENABLES, Edmund**
A Survey of the houses in the Minster Close of Lincoln, taken by order of Parliament in
1649 and 1641, with explanatory notes and additions
pp.43–75, [2] folded plans in *AAS reports and papers*, vol.19, 1887–88.

825.   ─────────────
Some account of the old houses in Lincoln Close pulled down in March, 1892
pp.44–48, [1] leaf of plates in *AAS reports and papers*, vol.21, 1891–92.

826.   **SYMPSON, E. Mansel**
The North gate of the Close of Lincoln
pp.161–162, [1] leaf of plates in *LN&Q*, vol.9, no.74, 1907.

827.   ─────────────
Old house in Corporation Street
pp.65–66, [1] leaf of plates in *LN&Q*, vol.5, no.37, 1897.
      Demolished during alterations for traffic.

828.   **ELVIN, Laurence**
Bygone Lincoln: the Cornhill
pp.4–8: ill. in *The Fireside magazine*, vol.4, no.6, March, 1967.

829.   **CROOK, J. Mordaunt**
The Building of Lincoln County Hall
pp.151–157 in *AAS reports and papers*, new series, vol.9, 1961–62.
      Designs of Sir Robert Smirke.

830.   **WILLSON, Edward James**
Notice of the ancient Deanery, Lincoln
pp.292–294 in *Memoirs illustrative of the history and antiquities of the county
and city of Lincoln*, 1850.

831.   **SYMPSON, E. Mansel**
Deloraine Court, Lincoln
pp.161–163, [2] leaves of plates in *LN&Q*, vol.6, no.50, 1901.

832.   **WOOD, M.E.**
Deloraine Court, Lincoln
pp.356–358, [1] folded leaf of plates in *The Lincolnshire historian*, no.10, 1952.

833.
Deloraine Court, James Street, Lincoln: [notes]
[1969].
Typescript.
      Includes plan dated 1959.

834.   **PANTIN, W.A.**
33–34, The Strait, Lincoln: report by W.A. Pantin
1963.   [5] leaves, [1] leaf of plans.
Typescript.
      Known as Dernstall House.

835.   **VARLEY, Joan**
Documents deposited temporarily for listing by Mr. L. Elvin on behalf of Mr. W.F.
Gadsby, May, 1963: [list]
1963.   [5] leaves.
Typescript.
      Concerning 33–34, The Strait.

836.
Dernstall House, 33 & 34, The Strait, Lincoln: restoration apppeal
Lincoln: Lincoln Civic Trust, [1965].   1 folded sheet: ill.

837.
Dernstall House, 33/34, The Strait, Lincoln: 15th century, restored 1969–70
[Lincoln]: [Lincoln Civic Trust], [1971].   [5]p.: ill.
    Includes structural notes by W.A. Pantin and historical note by J.W.F. Hill.

838.
Eastgate Hotel, Lincoln: historical notes
[1964?].   5 leaves.
Typescript.

839.
[Plan of the Eastgate Hotel]
[1965].   [4] leaves.

840.   **VARLEY, Joan**
The Exchequergate Arch
[196?].   9 leaves.
Typescript.

841.
Multi-storey car-park, Flaxengate, Lincoln
[Lincoln]: [Simons], [1970].   1 folded sheet: ill.

842.   **DRURY, Ray**
Frome Cottage, Lincoln
p.51: ill. in *Lincolnshire life*, vol.20, no.9, December, 1980.
    Renovation of 'Birdcage Cottages' off Michaelgate.

843.   **SYMPSON, E. Mansel**
The South wall of the city of Lincoln
pp.33–34, [1] leaf of plates in *LN&Q*, vol.13, no.2, 1914.

844.   —————————
The Palace of John of Gaunt, Lincoln
pp.1–3, [1] leaf of plates in *LN&Q*, vol.8, no.61, 1904.

845.   **ELVIN, Laurence**
Bygone Lincoln: the Great Northern Hotel
pp.11–15: ill. in *The Fireside magazine*, vol.3, no.1, October, 1965.

846.   **MASSINGBERD, Francis C.**
The Grecian Stairs, Lincoln
pp.58–64 in *Memoirs illustrative of the history and antiquities of the county and city of Lincoln*, 1850.

847.   **SYMPSON, E. Mansel**
The Grey Friary, Lincoln
pp.194–202, [2] leaves of plates in *LN&Q*, vol.7, no.59, 1903.
    History of the building until its use as a school.

848.   **BAKER, F.T.**
The Lincoln Greyfriars
p.166 in *The Archaeological journal*, vol.CIII, 1946.

849.   **TURNER, T. Hudson**
Some account of domestic architecture in England, from the Conquest to the end of the thirteenth century, with numerous illustrations of existing remains from original drawings
Oxford: John Henry Parker, 1851.   xxxii, 287p., [102] leaves of plates.
     pp.40–42: Lincoln; [2] plates showing St Mary's Guild and the Jews House.

850.   **WATKINS, W.**
The Buildings of St Mary's Guild, Lincoln, locally known as John o'Gaunt's stables
pp.157–164: ill. in *Journal of the Royal Institute of British Architects*, 3rd series, vol.XX, no.5, 11 January, 1913.

851.   ——————
St Mary's Guild, Lincoln and mediaeval builders
pp.282–288 in *Journal of the Royal Institute of British Architects*, 3rd series, vol.XXI, no.9, 14 March, 1914.

852.   **THOMPSON, A. Hamilton**
St Mary's Guildhall, Lincoln, popularly known as John of Gaunt's stables
Lincoln: printed J.W. Ruddock, 1935.   5p.: ill.

853.   **WOOD, Margaret**
St Mary's Guildhall and the Lincoln Jews Houses
by Margaret Wood and J.W.F. Hill.
pp.159–162, plan in *The Archaeological journal*, vol.CIII, 1946.

854.   **JOHNSON, C.P.C.**
St Mary's Guildhall: a brief historical and archaeological description
compiled by C.P.C. Johnson and D.A. Stocker.
Lincoln: Lincoln Civic Trust, 1986.   7p.: ill.

855.   **LINCOLN CIVIC TRUST**
St Mary's Guildhall, Lincoln
[196?].   5p.
Typescript.
     Notes outlining restoration work done and giving architectural details.

856.   **DAWKINS, A.T.**
Homes and gardens: Tanfield, Canwick, Lincoln
pp.22–24 in *Lincolnshire life*, vol.6, no.3, May, 1966.

857.   ——————
Homes and gardens: Manor Close, Lincoln
pp.20–23: ill. in *Lincolnshire life*, vol.7, no.4, June, 1967.

858   **STEPHENSON, Amanda**
Homes and gardens: St Clements, Lincoln
pp.20–23: ill. in *Lincolnshire life*, vol.6, no.12, February, 1967.

859.   **MARFLEET, Maple**
Homes and gardens: Atherstone Place, Eastgate, Lincoln
pp.16–17: ill. in *Lincolnshire life*, vol.8, no.11, January, 1969.

860.
*Report as to the structural condition of the bridge which spans the River Witham
beneath the High Street, Lincoln, and known as the 'High Bridge'*
W. Watkins & Son.
Lincoln: Lincoln Corporation, 1902.   9p., 4 plans.
> Analyses origin of different parts of the bridge as shown on the plans.   Mentions the sketch which is said to be in the Bodleian of the Wayside Chapel of St Thomas of Canterbury which formerly stood over the arch.

861.   **ELVIN, Laurence**
High Bridge Cafe
pp.9–12: ill. in *The Fireside magazine*, vol.13, no.5, March, 1976.

862.   **SYMPSON, E. Mansel**
Reredos, Lincoln
pp.97–98, [1] leaf of plates in *LN&Q*, vol.4, no.28, 1894.
> Stone reredos in no.4, James Street.

863.   **SMITH, W.H.**
Reredos at Lincoln
p.160 in *LN&Q*, vol.4, no.29, 1895.
> No.4, St James Street.

864.   **GIBSON, J.H.**
The Jews House at Lincoln
pp.179–180 in *LN&Q*, vol.16, no.6, 1920.

865.
Jews House and Jews Court, Steep Hill, Lincoln
Lincolnshire Archives Office.
1964.   [2] leaves.
Typescript.

866.   **WOOD, Margaret**
The English mediaeval house
London: Phoenix House, 1965.   xxx, 448p., LX plates.
Includes index.
> Many references to Lincoln buildings, especially Jews Houses, St Mary's Guild, Bishop's Palace and Vicars' Court.

867.   **BAKER, F.T.**
Jews Court, Lincoln: a brief history of the building
[Lincoln]: [Jews Court Trust], [c.1975].   [4]p.: ill.

868.
[Appeal for funds for Bardney Abbey and the Jews Court]
[Lincoln]: Lincolnshire Architectural and Archaeological Society, [196?].   [2]p.: ill.

869.   **ROBERTS, Rose**
Memories of life at Jews Court, Lincoln, 1905–1928
[transcribed by F.T. Baker].
[196?].   [2] leaves.
Typescript.

870.
The Judges Lodgings, Lincoln
[1975].   1 folded sheet: ill.
Typescript.
     Brief history.

871.   MARFLEET, Maple
Homes and gardens: 2/14, Minster Yard, Lincoln
pp.20–22: ill. in *Lincolnshire life*, vol.12, no.9, November, 1972.

872.
Minster Yard
Lincoln: Friends of Lincoln Cathedral, 1974.   31p.: ill.
ISBN 0903420058

873.   DUNN, David
Homes and gardens: 13, Minster Yard, Lincoln
pp.24–27: ill. in *Lincolnshire life*, vol.16, no.1, March, 1976.

874.   MAJOR, Kathleen
Houses in Minster Yard, Lincoln: documentary sources
pp.146–147 in *British Archaeological Association conference transactions
for the year 1982*, vol.VIII, 1986.

875.   SYMPSON, E. Mansel
Monk's Abbey, Lincoln
pp.225–227, [1] leaf of plates in *LN&Q*, vol.7, no.60, 1903.

876.
Roman arch, at Lincoln: [letter requesting presence at meeting on Wednesday, 26th
October]
[Lincoln]: [s.n.], [1825?].   1 sheet.

877.
[Resolutions of meeting about preservation of Newport Gate, 2nd December, 1825]
[1825].   1 sheet.

878.
Newport Gate, Lincoln
[Lincoln]: [s.n.], [1825?].   1 sheet.
     Resolutions passed at a meeting about preservation of the arch.

879.
To the lovers of antiquity and the public, Newport Arch, Lincoln
[Lincoln]: [s.n.], [1825?].   1 sheet.
Accompanied by: *Present list of subscribers*, 1 sheet.

880.   SYMPSON, E. Mansel
Newport Arch, Lincoln
pp.129–131, [1] leaf of plates in *LN&Q*, vol.10, no.5, 1909.

881.   WRIGLEY, H. Andrew
City walls and gates
pp.26–27: ill. in *The Queen's highway*, vol.XIX, no.2, July, 1952.
     Brief reference to Newport Arch and Stonebow.

882.   **BAKER, F.T.**
Newport Arch, Eastgate, Lincoln Castle
pp.117–120 in *Royal Archaeological Institute: programme of the summer meeting at Lincoln*, 1974.

883.   **AMBROSE, Timothy**
Newport Arch, Lincoln
Lincoln: Lincolnshire Museums, 1978.   6p.: ill., map.
(Lincolnshire Museums information sheet.   Archaeology series, no.4)

884.   **GROSE, Francis**
The Antiquities of England and Wales
London: printed for S. Hooper, 1773–76.   4 vols.
    One page of text on Lincoln, with plates of Newport Arch and Bishop's Palace.

885.   **WILLSON, Edward James**
The Ancient Episcopal Palace, Lincoln
pp.1–18 in *Memoirs illustrative of the history and antiquities of the county and city of Lincoln*, 1850.

886.   **VENABLES, Edmund**
Notes: [on the Old Episcopal Palace, Lincoln]
pp.33–36, [1] leaf of plates in *LN&Q*, vol.1, no.2, 1888–89.

887.   ————————
The Episcopal residence in Lincoln
pp.134–136 in *LN&Q*, vol.1, no.4, 1888–89.

888.   ————————
Subterranean chamber at the Old Palace, Lincoln
pp.31–32 in *LN&Q*, vol.1, no.2, 1888–89.

889.   ————————
Episcopal Palaces of England
by Edmund Venables and others.
London: Ibister, 1895.   253p.: ill., [frontis].
    pp.191–208: Lincoln Palace.

890.
English Episcopal Palaces, province of Canterbury
edited by R.S. Rait.
London: Constable, 1910.   344p., 15 leaves of plates.
    pp.155–209: the Old Palace at Lincoln set in the wider context of the history of Lincoln itself.
    By-product of the *Victoria history of the counties of England* which in the editor's note is
    described as being 'an investigation into the lighter side of history'.

891.   **WOOD, Margaret E.**
The Bishop's Palace, Lincoln
pp.278–280 in *The Lincolnshire historian*, vol.1, no.7, 1951.

892.   **FAULKNER, Patrick A.**
The Old Bishop's Palace
pp.80–84 in *Royal Archaeological Institute: programme of the summer meeting at Lincoln*, 1974.

893.   **AMBROSE, Timothy**
The Bishop's Palace, Lincoln
Lincoln: Lincolnshire Museums, 1980.   16p.: ill., map.
(Lincolnshire Museums information sheet.   Archaeology series, no.18)

894.   **COLYER, Christina**
The Park, Lincoln gateway and defences
pp.120–122 in *Royal Archaeological Institute: programme of the summer meeting at Lincoln*, 1974.

895.   **HEWLINGS, Richard**
A Palmyra ceiling in Lincoln
[1987].   [5] leaves.
Typescript.
> Surveyed on behalf of the Historic Buildings and Monuments Commission for England.
> Refers to no.5, Pottergate.

896.   **HILL, J.W.F.**
The Priory
pp.63–64 in *Royal Archaeological Institute: programme of the summer meeting at Lincoln*, 1974.

897.   **EXLEY, C.L.**
Some notes on St Andrew's Hall, Wigford
by C.L. Exley and D.M. Williamson.
pp.118–120, [2] leaves of plates in *AAS reports and papers*, new series, vol.6, 1955–56.

898.   **ELVIN, Laurence**
Bygone Lincoln: the Saracen's Head Hotel
pp.4–8: ill. in *The Fireside magazine*, November, 1965.

899.   **WILLSON, Edward James**
Notice of St Mary's Conduit, Lincoln
p.295 in *Memoirs illustrative of the history and antiquities of the county and city of Lincoln*, 1850.

900.   **WELBY, Alfred**
St Mary's Conduit, Lincoln
pp.65–66, [1] leaf of plates in *LN&Q*, vol.20, no.5, 1929.

901.   **WHITE, Andrew**
St Mary's Conduit, Lincoln
Lincoln: Lincolnshire Museums, 1980.   9p.: ill., map.
(Lincolnshire Museums information sheet.   Archaeology series, no.19)

902.   **MADDISON, A.R.**
Southam Place, Lincoln
p.23 in *LN&Q*, vol.5, no.34, 1896.
> Ancient canonical residence in the Close.

903.   **HILL, J.W.F.**
The Lincoln Stonebow, Guildhall, city charters and insignia
p.159 in *The Archaeological journal*, vol.CIII, 1946.

904.   ―――――――
Stonebow
p.122 in *Royal Archaeological Institute: programme of the summer meeting at Lincoln*, 1974.

905. AMBROSE, Timothy
The Stonebow and the Guildhall
Lincoln: Lincolnshire Museums, 1978. 6p.: ill., map.
(Lincolnshire Museums information sheet. Archaeology series, no.2)

906.
Swanpool Garden Suburb, Lincoln
pp.88, 90–91, 93 in *Architects journal*, 16 July, 1919.
Account of objectives of the scheme soon after its inception, under the auspices of Colonel Ruston. Also gives layout.

907. SWANPOOL COOPERATIVE HOUSING SOCIETY
Swanpool Cooperative Housing Society Limited...first annual balance sheet and report, 1920
[Lincoln]: [The Society], [1920]. 4p.

908.
Swanpool Garden Suburb, Lincoln
pp.749–758 in *Architects journal*, May 24th, 1922.
Tells how building began 1919 and continued until the next year when money problems halted work. Includes photographs of the houses that were finished.

909. JAMES, C.H.
Small houses for the community
by C.H. James and F.R. Yerbury.
London: Crosby, Lockwood, 1924. xi, 32, [121]p., 6 plans, 140 leaves of plates.
Plates XC-CII: Swanpool.

910. VENABLES, Edmund
The Vicars' Court, Lincoln, with the architectural history of the college and an account of the existing buildings
by the Rev. Precentor of Lincoln.
pp.235–250, [1] leaf of plans in *AAS reports and papers*, vol.17, 1883–84.

911. CLARK, Colin
Homes and gardens: Number Two, Vicars' Court, Lincoln
pp.20–21: ill. in *Lincolnshire life*, vol.7, no.11, January, 1968.

912.
The Wig & Mitre
pp.26–27: ill. in *Lincolnshire life*, vol.19, no.4, July, 1979.
About restoration of the building.

VIEWS

913.
Lincolnshire in 1835: with the rivers Humber, Trent & Witham, displayed in a series of views, each view accompanied by an explanatory and illustrative description
Lincoln: John Saunders, Jnr., 1835. 100p.: ill., [37] leaves of plates.

914.   **HOWLETT, Bartholomew**
A Selection of views in the county of Lincoln: comprising the principal towns and churches, the remains of castles and religious houses and seats of the nobility and gentry: with topographical and historical accounts of each view
London: William Miller, 1805.   [c.120p.], 1 map, [54] leaves of plates.
    1 engraving and 2p. of text: Lincoln; the same for the Cathedral.

915.
Remnants of feudal splendour and monastic times, comprising the beauties of antiquity, in a series of one hundred highly finished engraved cabinet views of the most interesting antiquarian and topographical subjects, accompanied with letter-press descriptions in two vols.
London: printed W. Smith for the proprietors, 1817.   2 vols.
    Includes: Episcopal Palace, Lincoln; Jews House; Monk's House.

916.   **ALLEN, T.**
Illustrations to the history of Lincolnshire
London: John Saunders, 1830.   26 plates.

917.
Lincolnshire in 1836: displayed in a series of nearly one hundred engravings on steel and wood: with accompanying descriptions, statistical and other important information, maps, &c.
Lincoln: John Saunders, Jnr., 1836.   179p.: ill., [50] leaves of plates.
    pp.55–81: Lincoln.

918.   **NOBLE, T.**
The Counties of Chester, Derby, Leicester, Lincoln and Rutland, illustrated from original drawings by Thomas Allom, with historical and topographic descriptions
by T. Noble and T. Rose.
London: Fisher, [1837].   76p., [35] leaves of plates.
    Includes: the Stonebow; view from the Castle; High Bridge; view from the Witham.

919.
Twelve views of Lincoln
London: Rock, Brothers & Payne, [1853?].   12 leaves of plates.

920.
Rock & Co's. views of Lincoln
London: Rock, [1853?].   [8] leaves of plates.
    Contains 18 engravings.

921.
[Views of Lincoln]
Lincoln: C. Akrill, [189?].   [12] plates.
    Engraved by Newman & Co.

922.
The Album of Lincoln views
[Lincoln?]: [Akrill, Ruddock & Keyworth], [189?].   14 leaves of plates.

923.
Album of Lincoln views
Lincoln: H.H. Brummitt, [1895?].   16p. of plates.

924.
*Beecham's photofolio: 24 choice photographic views: Lincoln, Peterborough &
Grantham*
St Helens: Thomas Beecham, [1897?].   [24] plates.
    Presented by Boots Ltd., the cash chemists.

925.
An Album of Lincoln views
London: Charles Reynolds, [19??].   [9]p. of plates.

926.
Six views of Lincoln Cathedral
Lincoln: C. Akrill, [19??].   [6] leaves.

927.
Snap-shots of Lincoln
Lincoln: W.K. Morton, [19??].   8p. of plates.

928.
Thirty-three views and pictures of Lincoln with Somersby, Tennyson's birthplace
Lincoln: J.W. Ruddock, [19??].   20p. of plates.

929.
Lincoln: [photographic reproductions]
[Lincoln?]: [s.n.], [19??].   17p. of plates.

930.
Lincoln: [album]
Lincoln: Boots, [1900?].   [16] leaves of plates.
Cover title.

931.
Photographic album of the city of Lincoln
3rd ed.
Lincoln: Boots, [1902–10?].   [20] leaves of plates.

932.   **LINCOLN CORPORATION**
[Reproduction of the address presented to King Edward VII on 26th June, 1907, on the
occasion of the Royal Show: illuminated address by A. MacKinder and six watercolours
of Lincoln by A.G. Webster]
Lincoln: J.W. Ruddock, 1907.   7 leaves: ill.

933.   **ROBINSON, Will B.**
Old Lincoln
from pen drawings by Will B. Robinson.
Lincoln: J.W. Ruddock, [1910?].   7 leaves of plates, [frontis].

934.
12 beautiful photographic reproductions of Lincoln
London: W.H. Smith, [1910?].   12 leaves of plates.

935.
Photographic views of Lincoln
[Lincoln?]: [s.n.], [192?].   6 leaves of plates.

936.   **SALWEY, Jasper**
Lincoln: a sketch-book
London: A. & C. Black, 1928.   24p.

937.
The Album of Lincoln views
[Lincoln?]: [s.n.], [1930?].   7p. of plates.
Plates with captions: general views; Cathedral; Newport Arch; Jews House; Arboretum; Stonebow; Bishop's Palace; John o'Gaunt's House.

938.   **SALWEY, Jasper**
Lincoln: a sketch-book
London: A. & C. Black, 1934.   [28]p.: ill.
(New artists' sketch books)
Originally published: 1928, as volume of sketches only.
Descriptive and historical notes by J.W.F. Hill.   Sketches include: Cathedral; Castle gate; Newport Arch; Potter Gate; house of Aaron the Jew; Stonebow; Glory Hole; St Benedict's; Whitefriars; John o'Gaunt's stables.

939.   **WOOD, Richard H.**
The Cathedral in art: an exhibition of significant paintings depicting Lincoln Cathedral, arranged in connection with the Cathedral's 900th anniversary celebrations
Lincoln: Usher Gallery, [1972].   [14]p.
Many of the pictures listed are general views of the city.

940.   **ELVIN, Laurence**
Lincoln as it was
Nelson: Hendon, 1974.   [43]p.: ill.
Photographs from local studies collection of Lincoln City Library.

941.   **FISK, Roy**
With Lincoln in view: 200 years in sketch & story
Lincoln: The Author, [1975].   35p.: ill.

942.   **ELVIN, Laurence**
Lincoln as it was.   Vol.II
Nelson: Hendon, 1976.   [43]p.: ill.

943.   _____
Lincoln as it was.   Vol.III
compiled on behalf of Lincolnshire Library Service by Laurence Elvin.
Nelson: Hendon, 1979.   [44]p.: ill.

944.   _____
Lincoln as it was.   Vol.IV
compiled on behalf of Lincolnshire Library Service by Laurence Elvin.
Nelson: Hendon, 1981.   [44]p.: ill.

945.   _____
Lincoln in the 1930s & 40s
compiled on behalf of Lincolnshire Library Service by Laurence Elvin.
Nelson: Hendon, 1982.   [43]p.: ill.

946.   **FISK, Roy**
Lincolnshire medley: being a miscellany of drawings, stories, etc.
Lincoln: The Author, [198?].   112p.: ill.
ISBN 095083792X
pp.44–45: conjectural nature of pre-Roman Lincoln; pp.46–47: fountain in the Arboretum; pp.46–47: urn to Simon, horse and friend; pp.50–51: view from Pottergate; pp.62–63: St Mary's Guild; pp.64–65: St Benedict; pp.66–67: postern gate under Stonebow Centre, conjectural Roman hypocaust; pp.82–85: story about Lincoln typhoid epidemic.

947.   **AMBROSE, Timothy**
Samuel Buck and eighteenth-century Lincolnshire
Lincoln: Lincolnshire Museums, 1981.   15p.: ill.
(Lincolnshire Museums information sheet.   Archaeology series, no.24)
    Includes engravings of Lincoln Castle and Bishop's Palace.

948.   **BANGAY, John**
Lincolnshire sketchbook: the Harlequin, Lincoln
pp.40–41: ill. in *Lincolnshire life*, vol.21, no.7, October, 1981.

949.   **HODSON, Maurice B.**
Lincoln then and now.   Vol.1
Lincoln: The Author, [1982].   84p.: ill., map.
Map on inside cover.
    Juxtaposition of contemporary photographs with those taken at beginning of century.

950.   **BANGAY, John**
Lincolnshire sketchbook: Ellis's Mill, Lincoln
pp.28–29: ill. in *Lincolnshire life*, vol.23, no.4, July, 1983.
    Sketch and brief history.

951.   **CUPPLEDITCH, David**
Lincoln in old picture postcards
Zaltbommel, Netherlands: European Library, 1984.   [126]p. of plates.
(In old picture postcards)

952.   **HODSON, Maurice B.**
Lincoln then and now.   Vol.2
Lincoln: The Author, 1984.   68p.: ill., map.
Map on inside cover.

953.   **BECKLEY, Mary**
Two views of Lincoln
illustrated by Colin Carr.
pp.42–43 in *Lincolnshire life*, vol.6, no.2, April, 1966.

954.   **HODSON, Maurice B.**
Lincoln then and now.   Vol.3
Lincoln: The Author, 1987.   70p.: ill.

955.
Reflections of a bygone age in Lincoln: 1982 calendar
[S.l.]: [s.n.], [1982].   [12] sheets.
    Photographs from postcard collection of Maurice Hodson.

SCRAPBOOKS

956.   **BAKER, W.**
[Scrapbook of early aviation in Lincoln]
[197?].   49 leaves.
    Includes dated newspaper articles, postcards and excerpts from books covering the period
    1912–18.   Particular interest in the career of pilot B.C. Hucks.

957.
[Scrapbook]
[given by E.H. Rudkin].
2 vols.
Many loose items.
> Mainly items printed in Lincoln between 1836–39 by T.O. Brumby, S. Thorpe, Keyworth.
> Subject matter: religious, carols, etc.; accounts of murders and hangings; 2nd vol.: coats of
> arms and printers' ornaments.

958.   WALLIS, Carrie A.
[Scrapbook of newspaper cuttings]
2 vols.
> Subject matter: mainly ceremonies and events taking place in the city but unfortunately not
> annotated.   'From the library of Sir Francis Hill'.

959.   PATE, Mary Howitt
[Scrapbook of newspaper cuttings, 1915–23]
[c.80]p.
> Lincoln during war, especially births, marriages and deaths.

960.   ─────────
[Scrapbook of newspaper cuttings, 1923–54]
[c.100]p.

961.   BRUNNER, Miss
[Cuttings]
collected by Miss Brunner.
[1925].   44 leaves.
> Subjects covered: Oxford House School; St.Martin's Church; R.A. Macbrair; Canon
> Akenhead; Carholme Golf Club; Lincoln links with Jewry.   Miss Brunner was headmistress of
> Oxford House School.

962.
[Photograph albums]
2 vols.
> Particular interest in building work on the Cathedral and ceremonies taking place there.

963.
[Photograph album showing demolition and building work on site of new NAAFI club,
Park St.]
[1950].   [19] leaves.

964.   PUGH, J.L.
A Photographic survey of Bailgate, Feb. 1967: [album]
[1967].   26 leaves.
> Small colour contact prints with detailed black and white prints.

965.   BAKER, W.
Scrapbook of old Lincoln
[197?].   [c.85] leaves.
> Photographs and postcards; typhoid epidemic and transport in particular.

PLACE NAMES

966. DRURY, Michael
The River Witham
pp.93–94 in *LN&Q*, vol.1, no.3, 1888.
> Concerning derivation of the name of the river.

967. WHEELER, W.H.
The River Witham
pp.53–54 in *LN&Q*, vol.1, no.2, 1888.
> Concerns the name of the river, Lindis from Lindum and Witham.

968.
The River Witham
pp.51–53 in *LN&Q*, vol.3, no.2, 1892.
> Derivation of the name.

969. BROWN, Robert
The Name Lincoln
pp.50–52 in *LN&Q*, vol.9, no.70, 1906.

970. EMINSON, T.B.F.
The River name Lindis
pp.241–250 in *LN&Q*, vol.14, no.8, 1917.

971. WELBY, Alfred C.E.
River name Lindis
pp.26–27 in *LN&Q*, vol.15, no.1, 1918.

972. ABBOTT, N.C.
Lincoln: name and place
pp.3–133 in *Publications of the Nebraska State Historical Society*, vol XXI, 1930.
> Paper deals with the derivation of the name with some reference to Lincoln, England, but most interest centred on American people and places which inherited the name.

973. ABELL, E.I.
City of Lincoln place names
p.268 in *Lincolnshire magazine*, vol.1, 1932–34.
Continued: pp.288, 298, 322, 331, 347, 355, 360, 367, 391.

MAPS

974. MARRAT, Wm.
Map of Lincoln dedicated by permission to Coningsby Waldo Sibthorpe, Esq., one of the representatives in Parliament for the city of Lincoln...
Lincoln: Wm. Marrat, 1848.
> Bound in Brookes & Vibert's *Tracts and miscellanies*.   Scale 3 chains to 1 inch.

COMMUNICATIONS

RIVERS AND CANALS

975.
[32 Geo.III, 1792]: *An Act for enlarging and improving the canal called Tattershall Canal...and rendering complete the navigable communication between the said River Witham and the Fosdike Canal through the High Bridge, in the city of Lincoln*
[London]: [s.n.], [1792]. 56p.

976.   DUGDALE, William
The History of imbanking and drayning of divers fenns and marshes, both in foreign parts and in this kingdom, and of the improvements thereby, extracted from records, manuscripts and other authentick testimonies
London: Alice Warren, 1662. 424p., [3] folded maps.
     pp.167–168: Fossdyke; pp.168–170: the Witham.

977.   GRUNDY, John
A Scheme for the restoring and making perfect the navigations of the River Witham from Boston to Lincoln, and also for draining the low-lands and fenns contiguous thereto
[Spalding?]: [s.n.], 1744. 48p.

978.
[Discussion of three proposals for a general drainage of the waters between Lincoln and Boston at a meeting held at Boston...October 19th, 1753]
[Boston]: [s.n.], [1753]. 23p.

979.   GRUNDY, John
Mr. Grundy's plan
Lincoln: printed W. Wood, [1753]. 15p., [1] map.

980.   ⸺⸺⸺⸺⸺⸺
The Report of Messr. John Grundy, Langley Edwards and John Smeaton, engineers, concerning the present ruinous state and condition of the River Witham, and the navigation thereof, from the city of Lincoln
Lincoln: printed W. Wood, [1761]. 26p., folded map.

981.
Observations on the bill now depending in Parliament for draining certain low lands in the county of Lincoln, and for preserving and restoring the navigation on the River Witham
[Lincoln]: [s.n.], [1761]. 9p.

982.
*Proposals or heads of a bill for restoring and preserving the outfall of the River Witham,
in the county of Lincoln: and of the drainage of the fens on both sides thereof: and also of
the navigation thereon from Brayeford, or Braydon Meer, on the west side of the city of
Lincoln, through the borough of Boston to the sea*
Lincoln: printed John Rose, [1761]. 48p.

983.
*The Case of...the city of Lincoln...against the bill for draining and preserving certain low
lands called the Fens...and for restoring and maintaining the navigation of the said river
from Brayford Meer, in the city of Lincoln...*
[Lincoln]: [s.n.], [1762?]. 3p.

984.
*An Act for draining and preserving certain low lands, called the Fens, lying on both sides
of the River Witham, in the county of Lincoln: and for restoring and maintaining the
navigation of the said river from the High Bridge in the city of Lincoln through the
borough of Boston, to the sea.*
London: printed R. Wilkes, 1762. 44p.

985.
*Some strictures on the Ancholme drainage, address'd to the smaller non-commission'd
freeholders and occupiers of land in that level*
Lincoln: printed W. Wood, 1773. 62p.

986.
[Notice of meeting of inhabitants of Lincoln to discuss navigations from Horncastle to
River Witham, November 7, 1791]
[Lincoln]: [s.n.], [1791]. 1 sheet.

987. **JESSOP, W.**
*The Report of William Jessop, engineer, on the practicability of widening and deepening
the communication between the River Witham and the Fossdike Canal, without injury to
the lowlands east of Lincoln*
[London]: [s.n.], 1792. 3p.
　　　Concerns High Bridge and Stamp End Lock.

988. **MORRIS, Jos.**
To all persons navigating on the River Witham, or the cut and trenches thereof
Jos. Morris [and] Mich. Pilley.
[Lincoln?]: [s.n.], 1794. 1 sheet.

989.
[Estimates for work]
Lincoln: [s.n.], 1794. 4p., [3] folded plans.
　　　Includes: Sincil Dyke; High Bridge; Stamp End Lock.

990.
Appeal to the owners and occupiers of land, respecting the Fossdyke Navigation
Lincoln: printed E.B. Drury, [18??]. 1 sheet.

991.
The Lincoln bridges: [letter signed 'Civis']
Lincoln: printed T.J.N. Brogden, [18??]. 1 sheet.
Extract from: *Lincolnshire chronicle.*

992.   CHAPMAN, William
*Facts and remarks relative to the Witham and the Welland, or A series of observations on
their past and present state: on the means of improving the channel of the Witham and
the port of Boston...*
Boston: printed J. Hellaby, 1800.   vii, 75p.
   pp.17–63: Witham.

993.   RENNIE, John
*To the commissioners for navigation on the River Witham: and to the proprietors of the
Foss Navigation, and the land-owners draining through the same:* [report, 26th October,
1803]
Boston: printed Kelsey, [1803].   7p.

994.   ─────────────
To the proprietors of land draining through the River Foss
Hull: printed J. Ferraby, 1804.   5p.

995.
[Notice that temporary dam to be built, July 22, 1805]
Lincoln: printed J.W. Drury, 1805.   1 sheet.

996.
[Notice that those washing sheep in Foss will be prosecuted, April 8, 1805]
Lincoln: printed J.W. Drury, 1805.   1 sheet.

997.   BOWER, Anthony
*To the general commission for drainage and navigation, by the River Witham, in the
county of Lincoln, and the land owners...:* [report respecting the improvement of the
River Witham from the Grand Sluice at Boston to Stamp End Lock at Lincoln]
Sleaford: printed Thornill, 1806.   [2]p.

998.
*A Letter to the editor of the **Stamford mercury** on the subject of a speech said to have
been delivered by Col. Ellison, at Lincoln, on Tuesday, May 5th, 1807:* [signed 'Verax']
Stamford: printed and sold by J. Drakard, [1807].   19p.

999.   RENNIE, John
*To the Earl of Buckinghamshire, chairman and the general commissioners of the River
Witham drainage and navigation:* [letter]
Sleaford: printed Thornill, 1807.   2p.
   Mentions effect upon trade.

1000.
*Resolutions of the general commissioners for drainage, and the commissioners for
navigation, by the River Witham, in the county of Lincoln, respecting the more effectual
drainage of the lands, and improvement of the navigation: with Mr Rennie's plan and
estimate relative thereto:* [April, 1807]
Sleaford: printed Thornill, 1807.   [2]p.

1001.
*Certain resolutions of the general commissioners for drainage, and the commissioners
for navigation, by the River Witham, in the county of Lincoln with Mr Rennie's report, in
consequence thereof:* [at meeting held in Boston, 19th September]
Sleaford: printed Thornill, [1807].   5p.

1002.
[48 Geo.III, Sess.1808]: *A Bill for rendering more effectual an Act of His Present Majesty, for draining certain low lands lying on both sides the River Witham, in the county of Lincoln, and for restoring the navigation of the said river from the High Bridge in the city of Lincoln to the sea*
[London]: [s.n.], 1808.   16p.

1003.   **JESSOP, W.**
To the worshipful the mayor and Corporation of the city of Lincoln: [report on scheme for improving drainage and navigation of the Witham]
Lincoln: printed J.W. Drury, 1808.   1 sheet.

1004.   **RENNIE, John**
To the Earl of Buckinghamshire and the other commissioners of the River Witham navigation and drainage: [letter, with Mr. Rennie's report and estimate for the improving of the drainage and navigation by the River Witham]
[London]: [s.n.], [1811].   [3]p.

1005.
Report of the committee appointed by the Witham commissioners to prepare the heads of a bill for improving the drainage and navigation by the River Witham: [with Mr Rennie's report of August 9th, 1811]
Boston: printed Hellaby, 1811.   3, [3]p.

1006.
[52 Geo.III, 1812]: *An Act for rendering more effectual an Act of His Present Majesty, for draining lands lying on both sides the River Witham, in the county of Lincoln, and restoring the navigation of the said river*
London: printed Luke Hansard, 1812.   86p.

1007.
[52 Geo.III, 1812]: *Observations on the execution of an Act of Parliament, for improving the drainage and navigation by the River Witham, from the city of Lincoln to the borough of Boston*
London: printed for R. Hunter, 1817.   28p.

1008.   **HANDLEY, B.**
Answer to a recent publication entitled 'Facts respecting the Witham Navigation'
London: printed for R. Hunter, 1817.   43p.

1009.   **SWAN, R.**
Facts respecting the Witham Navigation: respectfully addressed to the proprietors
London: printed Luke Hansard, 1817.   23p.

1010.
The Witham schism
by a byestander.
Lincoln: printed by W. Brooke, 1817.   19p.

1011.
Lease of the Fossdike Navigation, for nine hundred and ninety-nine years, from 1741: between the mayor, sheriffs, citizens and commonalty of the city of Lincoln and Richard Ellison...
Lincoln: printed J.W. Drury, 1826.   42p.

1012.
The Mayor, sheriffes, citizens and commonalty of the city of Lincoln, to Mr Richd.
Ellison: counterpart of a lease of the River Fossedike, for 999 years, from Michaelmas,
1741
Lincoln: printed R.E. Leary, [1826].   18p.

1013.
An Act of Parliament, passed in the reign of King Charles the Second, for restoring and
improving the navigation of the Fossdyke & Witham: to which is added a short historical
sketch with plans
Lincoln: printed J.W. Drury, 1826.   iv, 43p., [2] leaves of plans.

1014.
[Meeting about navigation of Fossdyke between Torksey and High Bridge, 19th August,
1826]
Lincoln: printed W. Brooke, 1826.   1 sheet.

1015.
[Resolutions of meeting about state of navigation between Torksey and High Bridge,
19th August, 1826]
Lincoln: printed W. Brooke, 1826.   1 sheet.

1016.
[Resolutions of meeting to discuss state of navigation between Torksey and the
High-Bridge in Lincoln, August 29th, 1826]
Lincoln: printed Drury, 1826.   1 sheet.

1017.
At a meeting of commissioners acting under and by virtue of an Act of the 22nd and 23rd
of King Charles the Second 'for improving the navigation between the town of Boston
and the River Trent', so far as relates to the River Fossdyke...: [held in the Guildhall,
15th November, 1826]
Lincoln: Lincoln Corporation, 1826.   3p.

1018.
[Letter to the mayor requesting meeting, 18th December, 1826]
Lincoln: printed W. Brooke, 1826.   1 sheet.

1019.
A Report of a public meeting, holden at the Guildhall in Lincoln, on Tuesday, Dec. 26,
1826, to consider the propriety of applying for a new Act of Parliament relative to the
Fossdyke Navigation
Boston: printed by H. Brooke, 1827.   32p.
    Extract from: *Boston gazette*, January 2, 1827.

1020.
The Petition and respectful requisition of a general meeting of merchants,
traders...affected by the present state of the Fossdyke Navigation...15th January, 1827
Lincoln: printed E.B. Drury, 1827.   1 sheet.

1021.
Some facts respecting the public river Fossdyke, February 10, 1827
Lincoln: printed W. Brooke, 1827.   1 sheet.

1022.
[Statement about tolls reprinted from *Boston gazette*, June 5th, 1827]
Lincoln: printed J.W. Drury, 1827.   1 sheet.

1023.
*Proceedings of the committee appointed to confer with the lessees of the Fossdyke
Navigation: with the communications received, the opinion of the counsel, and the
resolutions of the general meetings*
2nd ed.
Lincoln: printed E.B. Drury, 1827.   46p.

1024.
[Resolutions of meeting of owners and occupiers of land on the Lower Witham and
Fossdyke, 15th June, 1827]
Lincoln: printed E.B. Drury, 1827.   1 sheet.

1025.
[10 Geo. IV, 1829]: *A Bill to authorize the raising of a further sum of money for
completing the drainage and navigation by the River Witham and for amending the Acts
relating thereto*
[London]: [s.n.], 1829.   10p.

1026.
*An Abstract of the clauses of the Act, 52nd George III, cap.108: and the bye-laws,
regulating the trade upon the Witham Navigation*
Lincoln: printed M. Keyworth, 1829.   24p.

1027.
*Copy of the indenture between the commissioners for improving the navigation upon the
Fossdike and the mayor, &c., of Lincoln: ascertaining the tolls to be taken for vessels
navigating the said river, dated 10th of October, 23rd Charles 2nd*
Lincoln: printed E.B. Drury, [183?].   8p.

1028.   **PRIESTLY, Joseph**
Historical account of navigable canals & railways throughout Great Britain
London: Longman, 1831.   xii, 776, xp., chart, map.
Published as reference to Nichols, Priestley and Walker's *Map of the inland navigation,
canals and rail roads throughout Great Britain.*
     pp.684–690: River Witham.   Includes list of Acts relating to the river.   pp.276–278: Fossdyke.

1029.   **BEAUMONT, George**
[Letter respecting River Witham navigation, July 4, 1834]
[Lincoln], [s.n.], [1834].   1 sheet.

1030.
Launch of the London: dreadful accident
Lincoln: printed S. Thorpe, [1835].   1 sheet.
     Schooner built for Lincoln and London direct trade which sank at launch.

1031.
[Letter to the mayor of Lincoln, September 16th, 1839 about the Fossdyke Navigation]
Lincoln: printed James Drury, 1839.   1 sheet.

1032.
*Fossdyke suit: the decisive judgment of the vice-chancellor of England, Sir Lancelot
Shadwell, in favour of Mr. Ellison, delivered in Westminster-Hall, on Monday, January
21st, 1839*
Lincoln: printed by T.J.N. Brogden, 1839.   15p.

1033. **ELLISON, Richard**
To the owners, masters of vessels, and boatmen navigating the Fossdyke: [letter]
Lincoln: printed J.W. Drury, 1844. [2]p.
    Justifying his position on the troubled relationship between rail and water.

1034.
[8 Vict., 1845]: *An Act for enabling Richard Ellison, Esquire, and his trustees to grant leases of the Fossdyke Navigation, in the county of Lincoln, and for other purposes*
[London]: [s.n.], 1845. 32p.

1035.
[Post advertising sale of Witham Navigation shares, 21st September, 1847]
Lincoln: printed J. Stainton, 1847. 1 sheet.

1036.
Wharves and landing places: bye-laws
[Lincoln]: [Lincoln Corporation], [1854]. 4p.

1037.
The Public wharfs' question: Rudgard versus the city of Lincoln: an address from a committee of merchants and tradesmen of Lincoln to the citizens thereof, June 12th, 1855
Lincoln: printed W. Bellatti, 1855. 1 sheet.

1038. **HAWKSHAW, John**
Witham drainage: report of John Hawkshaw: also resolutions of the general commissioners for drainage by the River Witham: and of the landowners within the first, third and fifth districts draining by the Grand Sluice, passed...27th September, 1862
[London]: [Commissioners for Drainage], [1862]. 11p.
    Concerns Sincil Dyke and Bargate Sluice.

1039. —————
Witham drainage: report of John Hawkshaw
London: printed by G. MacLaran, 1877. 23p., [1] folded map.
    Includes discussion of drainage problems within the city.

1040.
Witham drainage reports, printed by the direction of the general commissioners for drainage by the River Witham, 5th May, 1877
London: printed by G. MacLaran, 1877. 136p., [1] folded map.
    Includes: Na. Kinderley's observations, 1736; Daniel Coppin's report, 1745; John Grundy's plan, 1753; Grundy, Langley Edwards and J. Smeaton's joint report, 1761; Smeaton and Grundy's report, 1762; John Smith and James Creassy's report, 1776; John Smeaton's report, 1782; Antony Bower's report, 1806; John Rennie's reports, 1807, 1811, 1813, 1816, 1818, 1830; Wm. Cubitt's report, 1850; Mr Lewin's report, 1860; Mr Hawkshaw's reports, 1861, 1862; statement of clerk, 1864; Edward Welsh's report, 1876.

1041.
Witham drainage reports, for the use of the general commissioners, 10th February, 1877
Boston: printed John G. Buck, 1877. 59p.
    Includes: Mr Rennie's reports of 1807, 1811, 1830; Mr Lewin's report, 1860; Mr Hawkshaw's reports of 1861, 1862; statement of clerk to the general commissioners, 1864; Mr Welsh's report, 1876.

1042.
Instructions for Sir John Hawkshaw, as settled at a meeting of the committee held at the residence of the Marquis of Ripon, in London, on Thursday, the 15th day of February, 1877
[London]: [s.n.], 1877. 1 sheet.

1043.   **PADLEY, J.S.**
The History of the floods of mid-Lincolnshire
[1882?].
Ms.

1044.   **SMILES, Samuel**
Lives of the engineers, with an account of their principal works comprising also a history of inland communication in Britain
New revised ed.
London: John Murray, 1874.   5 vols.
Originally published: 1861–62.   Includes index.
> Covers Smeaton and Rennie and their involvement in fen drainage, including its effect on the city.

1045.   **SMITH, Arthur**
An Old poster and what it records
pp.60–62: ill. in *Lincolnshire magazine*, vol.2, 1934–36.
> About steam packet trade, especially between Lincoln and Boston.

1046.   **WILLAN, T.S.**
River navigation in England, 1600–1750
Oxford: Oxford University Press, 1936.   163p.
(Oxford historical series)
Includes index.
> Includes references to Lincoln and Fossdyke Navigation.

1047.   **BARLEY, M.W.**
Lincolnshire rivers in the Middle Ages
pp.1–22, map in *AAS reports and papers*, new series, vol.1, 1936-37.
> References to Witham at Lincoln.

1048.   **AICKMAN, Robert**
Know your waterways
London: Coram, [1955].   119p.: ill.
> p.90: Fossdyke canal; p.92: River Witham.

1049.   **ROLT, L.T.C.**
The Inland waterways of England
London: Allen and Unwin, 1950.   221p., folded map, XLVIII plates.
> pp.20–22: Lincoln.

1050.   **SEYMOUR, John**
Sailing through England
London: Eyre & Spottiswoode, 1956.   256p.: ill.
> pp.105–109: Lincoln and the Fossdyke.

1051.   **GOODACRE, Don**
Brayford Pool, Lincoln
p.13: ill. in *Waterways*, vol.6, no.53, April, 1961.

1052.
Cruising on the Fossdyke and Witham Navigations: Torksey Lock to Boston
New ed.
London: British Waterways Board, 1965.   20p.: ill., [1] folded map.
Cover title.

1053.
Brayford Pool, Lincoln, 1966: a report on the rehabilitation of Brayford
by Bartlett and Gray
Lincoln: Lincoln Civic Trust, 1966.   [31] leaves: ill.

1054.   **CREASEY, John S.**
[Brayford-Pool, Lincoln, design project]
[c.70]p.: ill., 1 map, [6] leaves of plates.
Thesis [Diploma] – Leicester College of Art and Design, 1969.
Includes items of correspondence relating to the project, newspaper cuttings + 1
microfiche.
> Design for new premises for Lincoln Canoe Club, cafe, shop and WCs, with a sketch scheme
> for the area around Brayford.   Includes items of correspondence and newspaper cuttings
> relating to the project.

1055.   **ACTON, R.**
The Financing and operation of mid-Lincolnshire navigations, 1740–1830
112 leaves, [29] leaves of maps.
Thesis [M.A.] – University of Sheffield, 1971.
> Fossdyke and Witham are given coverage.

1056.   **GAGG, John**
Canals in camera.   2
London: Ian Allen, 1971.   112p.: ill.
ISBN 0711002193
> pp.92–103: Fossdyke and Witham.

1057.   **EDWARDS, L.A.**
Inland waterways of Great Britain: England, Wales and Scotland
5th revised and reset ed.
St Ives: Imray, Laurie, Norie and Wilson, 1972.   xii, 447p.: ill., [10]p. of plates.
Originally published: 1950.   Includes index.
ISBN 185288012X
> pp.87–88: Fossdyke; pp.336–339: Witham.   Gives specifications.

1058.
Witham Navigation improvement: extracts from Mr. Jessop's report: [*Lincoln &
Stamford mercury*, 6 May, 1808]
p.25 in *Journal of the Railway and Canal Historical Society*, vol.XXV, no.1, March,
1972.

1059.
*Lincoln water festival and rally of boats, Brayford Pool, 16–17 June, 1973: information
booklet*
[Lincoln]: [Lincoln Water Festival Committee], [1973].   30p.: ill.
> p.10: history of Brayford, by J.W.F. Hill; pp.12–13: Brayford Trust aims; pp.22–23: the
> waterways of Lincolnshire, by Ted Banks.

1060.
Lincoln water festival, 1974: souvenir brochure
[Lincoln]: [Lincoln Water Festival Committee], [1974].   28p.: ill.
> pp.5–11: 'Where do we go from here?', by Frederic Doerflinger about Fossdyke & Witham
> Navigation; pp.22–23: Brayford Trust.

1061.
Lincoln: the Brayford study: report to the Corporation of the city of Lincoln
by William Holford & Associates.
Edinburgh: William Holford, [1974?].   128p.: ill., maps, plans.

1062.   **BOYES, John**
The Canals of eastern England
by John Boyes and Ronald Russell.
Newton Abbot: David & Charles, 1977.   368p.: ill., [16]p. of plates.
(The Canals of the British Isles)
Includes index.
ISBN 071537415X
    pp.254–268: historical treatment of Fossdyke and Witham with references to city.

1063.   **CLARKE, Margaret**
A Description of the emergence of the steam-packet boat as a means of passenger
transport in the early 19th century and its subsequent decline
1977.   [13] leaves.
Typescript.
Submitted as part of year's work for B.A.
    Ch.2: development of the steam packet boat on the Witham and the activities of Charles West
    and Nathaniel Clayton.

1064.   **BLAKE, Amanda**
A Study of Brayford Pool: the rise and fall of an inland port
55p.: ill.
Thesis [B.Ed.] – Bishop Grosseteste College, 1979.

1065.   **HADFIELD, Charles**
William Jessop, engineer
Charles Hadfield and A.W. Skempton.
Newton Abbot: David & Charles, 1979.   315p.: ill.
Includes index.
ISBN 0715376039
    pp.56–58: Witham Navigation.

1066.   **SIMMONS, B.B.**
The Lincolnshire Car Dyke: navigation or drainage?
pp.183–196: ill. in *Britannia*, vol.10, 1979.
    Argues against assumption that there was a navigable channel connecting Cambridge and
    Lincolnshire with the Roman markets of Lincoln and York.

1067.   **ACTON, R.**
Navigations and the mid-Lincolnshire economy, 1790–1830
pp.47–54: ill. in *Lincolnshire history and archaeology*, vol.15, 1980.

1068.   **TAYLOR, Mike**
The Fossdyke Navigation
pp.22–25: ill. in *Lincolnshire life*, vol.26, no.7, October, 1986.
    Account of the 11 mile canal from Torksey to Lincoln.

1069.
At a public meeting held at the Guildhall in the city of Lincoln, on Tuesday, the 21st of October, 1834, for the purpose of considering the expediency of forming a railway, from London by Bishops-Stortford to Cambridge and from thence to Lincoln and York...
Lincoln: printed J.W. Drury, 1834. [2] leaves.

1070.   **CUNDY, N.W.**
Observations on the Midland counties' railroad: [letter to the committee of the Grand Northern Railway, 5th May, 1835]
Lincoln: printed E.B. Drury, 1835.   1 sheet.

1071.
Report of the committee appointed at Lincoln to examine the proposals for a northern railway: [March, 1835]
Lincoln: printed E.B. Drury, [1835].   16p.

1072.   **HULL, LINCOLN & NOTTINGHAM RAILWAY**
Hull, Lincoln & Nottingham Railway via Newark: [prospectus]
[London]: [The Railway], [1837/38?].   2p.

1073.
To the honourable the Commons of the United Kingdom of Great Britain and Ireland, in Parliament assembled: the humble petition of the undersigned noblemen, gentlemen, farmers, merchants and other inhabitants of the city of Lincoln: [letter about Great Grimsby & Sheffield Junction Railway]
[Lincoln]: [s.n.], [184?].   1 sheet.

1074.
To the farmers of Lincolnshire: [letter signed 'Humphrey Home-Thrust']
Lincoln: printed W. and B. Brooke, [1844].   1 sheet.

1075.   **DIRECT NORTHERN RAILWAY**
Statement of the case and merits of the Direct Northern Railway from London to York, by Lincoln
London: The Railway, 1844.   3p.

1076.   **DIRECT LINCOLN, EAST RETFORD AND SHEFFIELD JUNCTION RAILWAY**
[Prospectus for Direct Lincoln, East Retford and Sheffield Junction Railway]
[London?]: The Railway, [1844].   [3]p.

1077.
To the tradesmen and inhabitants of Lincoln: [letter signed 'A Lincoln tradesman']
[Lincoln]: [s.n.], [1844].   2p.
    Argument in favour of the Lincolnshire Junction.

1078.
To the inhabitants of Lincolnshire, and those of the city of Lincoln and town of Boston in particular
[Lincoln]: [s.n.], [1844].   [2]p.
    Against letter by 'A Lincoln tradesman'.

1079.
The Railway fight: [letter to the people of Lincoln, signed 'A tradesman of the city']
Lincoln: printed T.J.N. Brogden, [1844?].   1 sheet.

1080.   **SEELY, Charles**
Facts and figures.   No.2: Mr. Seely's speech at the Scarborough Arms, on Friday night last
Lincoln: printed T.J.N. Brogden, [1844].   1 sheet.

1081.   **LINCOLNSHIRE JUNCTION RAILWAY**
Proposed branch railway from the North Midland at Swinton, to Doncaster, Gainsburgh, and Lincoln...: [prospectus for Lincolnshire Junction Railway, February 20, 1844]
[Gainsborough]: The Railway, 1844.   1 sheet.

1082.   **CAMBRIDGE & YORK RAILWAY**
Prospectus: Cambridge & York Railway via Lincoln: [22nd February, 1844]
London: The Railway, 1844.   [2]p.

1083.
A Lincoln tradesman's second address on railways: [signed 'Alpha, the Lincoln tradesman', April 9th, 1844]
Lincoln: printed James Drury, 1844.   1 sheet.

1084.
Railways: [letter signed 'One of the interested']
Lincoln: printed James Drury, [1844?].   1 sheet.
Extract from: *Lincoln advertiser*, April 30.

1085.
Railways: [letter to the inhabitants of Lincoln, May 1st, 1844]
Lincoln: printed James Drury, 1844.   1 sheet.

1086.
[Letter to the inhabitants about railways, signed 'Alpha', May 1st, 1844]
Lincoln: printed James Drury, 1844.   1 sheet.

1087.
Railways: [letter signed 'Omega', May 4th, 1844]
Lincoln: printed James Drury, 1844.   1 sheet.

1088.
No.2 railways: [letter to the public, signed 'One of the interested']
Lincoln: printed J. Stainton, [1844].   1 sheet.

1089.
The Locomotive, vol.1, no.1, Monday, May 6th, 1844
Lincoln: printed T.J.N. Brogden, 1844.   8p.
    Discussion of benefits of Lincoln Junction Railway and of Wakefield and Lincoln Line.

1090.
Railways no.3: [letter to the public, May 10th, 1844]
Lincoln: printed James Drury, 1844.   1 sheet.

1091.
Alpha to the inhabitants of Lincoln: [letter, May 10, 1844]
Lincoln: printed James Drury, 1844.   1 sheet.

1092.
'Quid pro quo, or The day of dupes': [letter signed 'Another of the interested', 22nd May, 1844]
Lincoln: printed W. and B. Brooke, 1844.   1 sheet.

1093.
Railways: correspondence between Mr Thomas Wetherell and Mr. Seely: [June, 1844]
Lincoln: printed T.J.N. Brogden, 1844.   1 sheet.

1094.
Sheffield and Lincolnshire Railway
Lincoln: printed Leader, 1844.   1 sheet.
Extract from: *Sheffield and Rotherham independent*, June 1, 1844.

1095.
Railway meetings: [letter to the public, no.4, signed 'One of the interested', June 3, 1844]
Lincoln: printed James Drury, 1844.   1 sheet.

1096.
Most important news!!: quarrel between the Autocrat of all the Russias and the Prince of the Railroads: [squib, 7th June, 1844]
Lincoln: printed James Drury, 1844.   1 sheet.
    Refers to Thomas Wetherell and Charles Seely.

1097.
The Pig and Whistle papers, number 12: [spoof letter about railways]
Lincoln: printed T.J.N. Brogden, 1844.   1 sheet.
Extract from: *Lincolnshire herald*, Tuesday, June 11, 1844.

1098.
Railways: [letter to the farmers & others interested in agriculture, signed 'Investigator', July 5, 1844]
Lincoln: printed T.J.N. Brogden, 1844.   1 sheet.

1099.
Railway meeting: [notice, July 6th, 1844]
Lincoln: printed J. Hall, 1844.   1 sheet.

1100.
The London & York Line: [letter extracted from the *Lincolnshire herald* of Tuesday last, August 26th, 1844]
Lincoln: printed T.J.N. Brogden, 1844.   1 sheet.

1101.
Report of the Railway Department of the Board of Trade, on the schemes for extending railway communication between London and York, &c.
London: The Board, [1845].   61p.

1102.
Eastern Counties Railway, March and Lincoln extension: [notice for *Gazette*, 1845]
London: Roy, Blunt, 1845.   2p.
    Line to terminate in parish of St.Mark's.

1103.   **LINCOLN, HORNCASTLE, SPILSBY AND WAINFLEET HAVEN RAILWAY**
Preliminary prospectus: [Lincoln, Horncastle, Spilsby and Wainfleet Haven Railway]
Alford: Bourne, 1845.   [2] leaves.

1104.
[Letter to the mayor requesting meeting to consider the railways affecting Lincoln, March 20th, 1845]
Lincoln: printed T.O. Brumby, 1845. 1 sheet.

1105.
To the inhabitants of Lincoln: railway: [letter signed 'A tradesman of Lincoln', March 24th, 1845]
Lincoln: printed W. and B. Brooke, 1845. 1 sheet.

1106.
[Resolutions of meeting convened for the purpose of considering the decision of the Board of Trade as it regards the railways affecting Lincoln, 26th March, 1845]
Lincoln: printed Charles Brogden, 1845. 1 sheet.

1107.   **LINCOLN CORPORATION**
Council meeting, 13th March, 1846: [Mr Cubitt's report to the committee of directors of the London and York Railway Company]
Lincoln: printed for W. Peck, [1846]. 3p.

1108.
Extensions of the Nottingham and Lincoln Branch Railway at Lincoln, with connecting branch to the Lincoln Station, Birmingham
[S.l.]: Samuel Carter, 1846. [3]p.

1109.   **LINCOLN CORPORATION**
City of Lincoln: report of the Corporation committee on railways immediately affecting the interests of the city: and especially with reference to the proposed two crossings of the High Street
Lincoln: printed for W. Peck, 1847. 12p.

1110.
Great Northern Railway improvements: [poster about sale of building materials and elm trees, October 18th, 1847]
Lincoln: printed J. Stainton, 1847. 1 sheet.

1111.
Lincoln and Wakefield Railway: to the inhabitants of Lincolnshire and those of the city of Lincoln and town of Boston in particular
Lincoln: printed W. and B. Brooke, [1847]. 1 sheet.

1112.
Midland Railway Nottingham & Lincoln line: [notice of postponement of meeting, 18th February, 1847]
Lincoln: printed James Drury, 1847. 1 sheet.

1113.
[Typed transcript of extracts about railways from *The Lincolnshire chronicle* 1848–1862]
24, 7 leaves.
Typescript.

1114.
The Traveller's hand-book for the Lincoln and Nottingham Railway, describing in an attractive and pleasing form the towns, villages, scenery, &c., during the rapid ride
Lincoln: printed and sold by James Drury, [185?]. 48p.: ill.
    pp.4–11: sketch of Lincoln; pp.11–16: Lincoln Station to Doddington.

1115.　**MEASOM, George**
The Official illustrated guide to the Great Northern Railway, including all the branch lines and continuations
London: W.H. Smith, [1857].　200p.: ill., folded map.
    pp.76–93: Lincoln.

1116.　————————
Official illustrated guide to the Great Northern, Manchester, Sheffield and Lincolnshire, and Midland railways
[London]: Griffin, Bohn, 1861.　xii, 524p.: ill.
Originally published: 1857.
    pp.273–297: Lincoln.

1117.
[Light Railways Act, 1896]: *North Lincolnshire Light Railway: order authorising the construction of a light railway in the county of Lincoln from Lincoln to Scawby*
[London]: [Light Railway Commissioners], 1898.　33 leaves.

1118.
Estimate of cost: proposed North Lincolnshire Light Railway
Hull: Rollit, [1898].　[4] leaves.

1119.
[Light Railways Act, 1896]: *North Lincolnshire Light Railway: draft order authorising the construction of a light railway between Lincoln and Barton-on-Humber in the county of Lincoln*
Hull: Rollit, 1898.　28 leaves.

1120.
Railway operating maps and diagrams, Lincoln district
[Lincoln]: [Lincoln District Railways], [19??].　[11] leaves of plans.

1121.　**GRINLING, Charles H.**
The History of the Great Northern Railway, 1845–1902
London: Methuen, 1903.　xviii, 463p.: ill., [frontis].
Originally published: 1898.　Includes index.
    Substantial references passim.

1122.　**AHRONS, E.L.**
Locomotive and train working in the latter part of the nineteenth century
edited by L.L. Asher.
Cambridge: W. Heffer, 1953.　xii, 152p., [24]p. of plates.
Originally published: in *The Railway magazine*.
    pp.28–29: in favour of the two level crossings of Lincoln.

1123.　**PERREN, B.**
Resorts for railfans.　19: Lincoln
pp.432–439: ill. in *Trains illustrated*, vol.LX, no.9, September, 1956.
    State of railways and stations in Lincoln.

1124.　**DOW, George**
Great Central
London: Locomotive Publishing, 1959–65.　3 vols.
Vol.3 published by Ian Allen.
    Vol. 1: the progenitors, 1813–63; Vol. 2: dominion of Watkin, 1864–1899; these vols. contain references to Lincoln.

1125.
Railway accident: report on the derailment that occurred on 3rd June, 1962 at Lincoln in the Eastern Region, British Railways
London: Ministry of Transport, 1962.   7p., [2] folded plans.

1126.   **SMITH, J.N.**
E.R. rationalisation in Lincolnshire
pp.27–28: ill. in *Modern railways*, July, 1964.
    Discusses problem of two level crossings in Lincoln.

1127.   **CUPIT, J.**
The Lancashire, Derbyshire & East Coast Railway
by J. Cupit & W. Taylor.
Lingfield: Oakwood, 1966.   42p., map, [8]p. of plates.
(Oakwood library of railway history, 31)
    Various references to Lincoln and Pyewipe Junction.

1128.
[Train register: Bracebridge Gas Sidings from 17th Dec. 1968 to 20th April, 1970]
[1968].   [c.190]p.
Printed tables with Ms. entries.

1129.   **NICHOLSON, Pete**
British narrow gauge locomotive register.   Part 6: Ruston & Hornsby Ltd., Lincoln
pp.8–12: ill. in *Narrow gauge illustrated*, no.64, spring, 1973.

1130.   **RUDDOCK, J.G.**
The Railway history of Lincoln
J.G. Ruddock, R.E. Pearson.
Lincoln: J.G. Ruddock, 1974.   272p.: ill., maps.
Includes indexes.
ISBN 0904327000

1131.   **HEMINGWAY, G.Y.**
The Great Northern & Great Eastern Joint Railway
[1977].   144 leaves: ill.
Typescript.
    Various references to Lincoln.

1132.   ―――――――
The Louth & Lincoln Railway
pp.94–101 in *The Journal of the Railway and Canal Historical Society*, November, 1977.

1133.   ―――――――
The Louth and Lincoln Railway
[1977].   62 leaves.
Typescript.
    Excerpts from number of sources including: Bradshaw's *Railway manual*; White's directory; company minutes; G.N. records; and *Railway times*.

1134.   **BAYES, C.S.**
Lincoln, 1937
pp.16–17 in *Great Eastern journal*, no.13, January, 1978.

1135.   **BOREHAM, Andrew**
An Introduction to the G.N. & G.E. Joint
pp.4, 12 in *Great Eastern journal*, no.13, January, 1978.

1136. LAKE, R.
The Lancashire, Derbyshire and East Coast Railway
pp.10–12 in *Great Eastern journal*, no.13, January, 1978.

1137. RUSH, A.D.N.
Train working on the G.N.& G.E. Joint Line before 1914
pp.5–9 in *Great Eastern journal*, no.13, January, 1978.

1138. HEMINGWAY, G.Y.
Source material, Nottingham & Lincoln
[1979]. 226 leaves.
Typescript.

1139. WROTTESLEY, John
The Great Northern Railway
London: Batsford, 1979–81. 3 vols.
Includes index.
ISBN 0713415908
> Vol.1: origins & development; vol.2: expansion & competition; vol.3: twentieth century grouping. Much about Lincoln in each volume.

1140.
Called-in application for listed building consent to demolish St Mark's Station, Lincoln
p.852 in *Estates gazette*, May 30, 1981.
> Paragraph giving reasons for refusal of listed building consent for demolition.

1141. GREENING, David
Steam in the East Midlands
Norwich: Becknell, 1982. 96p.: ill.
ISBN 0907087094
> pp.69–74: pictures of Lincoln stations.

1142. DENMAN, Mr
Working lives recalled: Mr Denman and Mr Meanwell: [transcript of taped interview]
Lincoln: Lincolnshire Educational Aids Project, 1984. 16p.
(Railways, 1)
> Both men were railway workers in Lincoln.

1143. GOODE, C.T.
Midland Railway Derby-Lincoln
Hull: [The Author], 1984. 72p.: ill.
ISBN 0950823945
> Ch.4: out to Lincoln; ch.7: trains to Lincoln.

1144. LELEUX, Robin
A regional history of the railways of Great Britain.   Vol.IX: the East Midlands
2nd revised ed.
[S.l.]: David St John Thomas, 1984. 268p.: ill., 1 map, [31]p. of plates.
Originally published: 1976. Includes index.
> Includes references to Lincoln.

1145. REDFORD, Mr
Working lives recalled: Mr Redford
Lincoln: Lincolnshire Educational Aids Project, 1984. 12p.
(Railways, 5)
> Railway worker in Lincoln area.

1146.   **GOODE, C.T.**
The Railways of North Lincolnshire
Hull: [The Author], 1985.   96p.: ill.
ISBN 095082397X
> pp.17–19: Lincoln.

1147.   **LINCOLN RAILWAY SOCIETY**
Farewell, St Mark's!
The L.R.S. journal, May 11th, 1985.

1148.   **M., P.**
The Spiritual railway: [words and music]
[1985].   9p.
Ms.
> Most of words taken from tombstone in Ely Cathedral but with topical references to St Mark's and Central Stations.

1149.   **WELLS, P.H.**
Steam in the East Midlands
London: Ian Allen, 1985.   112p.: ill.
ISBN 0711014795
> Pictorial survey; pp.102–105: Lincoln.

1150.   **ANDERSON, P. Howard**
Regional railways handbooks.   No.1: The East Midlands
[S.l.]: David St John Thomas, 1986.   208p.: ill.
Includes index.
ISBN 0946537356

1151.   **VESSEY, Steve**
The Other side of the track: a traveller's guide to the journey from Lincoln to London by rail
Lincoln: Seas End Enterprise, 1986.   [72]p.: ill., maps.
ISBN 1870283015

1152.   ————————
The Other side of the track: a traveller's guide to the journey from Grimsby to London by rail
Lincoln : Seas End Enterprise, 1986.   [92]p.: ill., maps.
ISBN 1870283007
> Several pages on Lincoln but mainly illustration.

1153
Tomorrow's Lincoln needs tomorrow's railways
[Scunthorpe]: [Railway Development Society, Lincolnshire Branch], [1987].   [4]p.: ill.

ROADS

1154.   **OGILBY, John**
Britannia.   Volume the first, or An illustration of the kingdom of England and dominion of Wales, by a geographical and historical description of the principal roads thereof...
London: The Author, 1675.   200, [40]p., maps.
> p.81: Lincoln.

1155.
City of Lincoln tolls: [notice of re-imposition, April, 1797]
[Lincoln]: [Lincoln Corporation], [1797].   1 sheet.

1156.   **BOUMPHREY, G.M.**
Along the Roman roads
2nd ed.
London: George Allen & Unwin, 1964.   149p., [8] leaves of plates.
Originally published: 1935.
      pp.68–75: Fosseway and Ermine Street at Lincoln.

1157.   **CARRINGTON, C.E.**
Ermine Street: from London to York, under a succession of Roman governors, the great
road to the north was built during the first century A.D.
pp.321–328: ill. in *History today*, vol.XVIII, no.5, May, 1968.
      Includes references to the 9th Legion at Lincoln.

1158.
The Fosse Way in Nottinghamshire & Lincolnshire
compiled and edited by Trevor Dann.
Nottingham: BBC Radio Nottingham, 1976.   73p.: ill.
Includes index.
      To accompany a series of programmes broadcast by BBC Radio Nottingham.

1159.   **BARHAM, Jeffrey**
The Fosse Way
pp.32–35: ill. in *Popular archaeology*, August, 1980.

1160.
[Letter about new roads into Lincoln and alteration of Cross-o-cliff Hill, August 9, 1842]
Lincoln: [Lincoln Turnpike Road Trust], 1842.   1 sheet.
Accompanied by: [Notice raising subscriptions for the work], 1 sheet.

1161.
*City of Lincoln: Thorn Bridge, completed May, 1940: memorial tablet unveiled 23rd
October, 1940 by the Right Worshipful, the mayor of Lincoln*
[Lincoln]: [Lincoln Corporation], [1940].   [7]p.: ill.

1162.   **LINCOLN CORPORATION**
*Visit of Her Majesty, Queen Elizabeth and His Royal Highness, the Prince Philip, Duke
of Edinburgh: programme of events*: [27th June, 1958]
Lincoln: The Corporation, 1958.   24p.: ill.
      Includes 6p. on Pelham Bridge and its effect on traffic control in the city.

1163.
Pelham Bridge: history of a great project: [*Lincolnshire echo* supplement, June 27, 1958]
Lincoln: Lincolnshire Echo, 1958.   xiip.: ill.

1164.   **LINCOLN CORPORATION**
City of Lincoln traffic regulation: Bailgate area order, 1967
[1967].   [3] leaves.
Typescript.

1165.   **LINCOLN, Department of Planning & Architecture**
Cathedral relief road
[1967].   9 leaves, map.
Typescript.
Map on inside cover.

1166.   **SCORER, Sam**
Traffic in Lincoln: homes and work
p.6: ill. in *Lincolnshire echo*, Wednesday, March 29, 1967.

1167.   ——————
Traffic in Lincoln: the primary roads
p.12: ill. in *Lincolnshire echo*, Friday, March 31, 1967.

1168.
[Statutory instruments, 1969, no.455]: *Highways, England and Wales: the city of Lincoln (Brayford Head new bridge) scheme, 1965: confirmation instrument, 1969*
London: HMSO, 1969.   [2]p.

1169.   **LINCOLN CITY COUNCIL**
Traffic regulation in the Bailgate area: a summary of the proposals of the Lincoln City Council
Lincoln: The Council, 1970.   4 leaves, 4 leaves of plans.

1170.   ——————
Traffic regulation in the city: a summary of the proposals of the Lincoln City Council
Lincoln: The Council, 1970.   [12] leaves, [6] leaves of plans.

1171.   ——————
Traffic regulation in the city: a summary of the proposals of the Lincoln City Council
Lincoln: The Council, 1971.   15p., [7] leaves of plans.

1172.
Presidential visit to the city of Lincoln, 25th June, 1971 to inspect inner ring road: stage 1 and archaeological excavations
[1971].   7 leaves, [1] folded plan.
Typescript.
    Produced by the East Midlands District Branch of the Institute of Municipal Engineers.

1173.
[Statutory instruments, 1973, no.1511]: *Highways, England and Wales: the city of Lincoln (Fossdyke Bridge) scheme, 1972: confirmation instrument, 1973*
London: HMSO, 1973.   4p.: ill.

1174.
[Town and Country Planning Act, 1971]: Application for planning permission by Lincoln County Borough Council referred under section 35: western relief road, Lincoln
[1973].   [32] leaves.
Typescript.

1175.   **LINCOLN CITY COUNCIL**
Traffic regulations in the city: a summary of the proposed amendments and additions of the Lincoln City Council
Lincoln: The Council, 1975.   16 leaves, [2] leaves of maps.

1176.   **LINCOLNSHIRE COUNTY COUNCIL**
Lincoln area transportation strategy: report to Transportation Committee
Lincoln: The Council, 1975.   50, [7]p., [13]p. of maps.
Discusses various options aimed at reducing traffic congestion in the centre of Lincoln.

1177.   **LINCOLN, Department of Planning & Architecture**
Lincoln's approach roads: roads from the north
Lincoln: The Department, 1977.   28p.: ill., maps.

1178.   **DEPARTMENT OF TRANSPORT**
A Relief road for Lincoln: please give us your views
Harrogate: The Department [North Eastern Road Construction Unit], 1978.   1 folded
sheet: ill., maps.

1179.   ——————
Statement by the Department of Transport: preferred route for the Lincoln relief road
[1979].   [6] leaves, [1] leaf of maps.
Typescript.
Includes list of representative bodies who reported.

1180.   ——————
Lincoln relief road: statement on noise aspects
Acoustical Investigation Research Organisation Ltd.
[1981].   [13] leaves.
Typescript.

1181.   ——————
The Bath-Coventry-Lincoln trunk road: Lincoln relief road: traffic and economic
statement
[1981].   5 leaves, [3] folded maps.
Typescript.

1182.   ——————
Bath-Coventry-Lincoln trunk road: Lincoln relief road: statement of case
[1981].   38 leaves, maps.
Typescript.

1183.   ——————
[Statutory instruments, 1982, no.1749]: *Highways, England and Wales: the A46*
Bath-Coventry-Lincoln trunk road (Lincoln relief road) line order, 1982
London: HMSO, 1982.   3p., [2]p. of folded maps.

1184.   **LINCOLN, City Engineer**
Canwick Road tidal flow scheme
Lincoln: The Engineer, [c.1986].   1 folded sheet: ill.

1185.
Lincoln relief road opens ahead of schedule
pp.14–15: ill. in *Highway*, vol.54, pt.1909, January, 1986.

1186.   **RIDOUT, Graham**
Lincoln green: tidal flow keeps traffic on the move
pp.14–16: ill. in *Public works weekly surveyor*, 15 May, 1986.
Refers to Canwick Road system.

1187.   **LINCOLN, Planning & Property Department**
Cathedral relief road: development brief, June, 1987
[1987].   8p., [1] leaf of plans.
Typescript.

Road Repair

1188.
[Anno vicesimo nono Georgii II Regis]: *An Act for repairing and widening the roads
from the north end of Dunsby Lane...and the bridge over the River Witham, at
Bracebridge, to the city of Lincoln...and for enforcing the performance of statute...*
London: printed Thomas Baskett, 1756.   pp.1051–1087.

1189.
*An Act for repairing and widening the roads from the north end of Dunsby Lane to the
south-west corner of Riseholm Hedge...and the bridge over the River Witham, at
Bracebridge, to the city of Lincoln and from the foot of Canwicke Hill, to the great
Bar-Gates..*
[London]: [s.n.], 1756.   68p.

1190.
*An Act for enlarging the term amd powers of an Act made in the twenty-ninth year of the
reign of King George the Second, for repairing and widening certain roads leading to
and from the city of Lincoln...*
[London]: [s.n.], [1756].   18p.

1191.   **LINCOLN CORPORATION**
Turnpike tolls to be let: [notice, April 5, 1805]
Lincoln: printed J.W. Drury, 1805.   1 sheet.

1192.   **PADLEY, J.S.**
*To the committee of the Lincoln Turnpike Trust appointed to procure information and to
ascertain the best practical method for lowering Cross-o-cliff Hill, in the parish of
Bracebridge, near Lincoln*
Lincoln: printed J.W. Drury, 1831.   4p., [1] folded plan.

1193.   **LINCOLN TURNPIKE TRUST**
*General statement of the income and expenditure of the south-east and south-west district
of the Lincoln turnpike roads, between the sixth day of April, 1832 and the sixth day of
April, 1833*
Lincoln: printed J.W. Drury, 1832.   1 sheet.

1194.   ───────────
*General statement of the income and expenditure of the north-west district of the Lincoln
Turnpike Trust, in the city and the county of Lincoln and the county of Nottingham,
between the 1st day of January and the 31st day of December, 1835*
Lincoln: printed J.W. Drury, 1835.   1 sheet.

1195.   ───────────
General statement of the income and expenditure of the north-west district...1836
Lincoln: printed J.W. Drury, 1836.   1 sheet.

1196. ――――――
General statement of the income and expenditure of the south-east and south-west districts of the Lincoln Turnpike Trust, in the city and the county of Lincoln...1836
Lincoln: printed J.W. Drury, 1836.   1 sheet.

1197. ――――――
General statement of the income and expenditure of the south-east and south-west districts...1837
Lincoln: printed J.W. Drury, 1837.   1 sheet.

1198. ――――――
General statement of the income and expenditure of the north-west district...1837
Lincoln: printed J.W. Drury, 1837.   1 sheet.

1199. ――――――
General statement of the income and expenditure of the south-east and south-west districts...1838
Lincoln: printed J.W. Drury, 1838.   1 sheet.

1200. ――――――
General statement of the income and expediture of the north-west district...1838
Lincoln: printed J.W. Drury, 1838.   1 sheet.

1201.
[4 & 5 Vict., 1841]: *An Act...for repairing and widening certain roads leading to and from the city of Lincoln...*
[London]: [s.n.], [1841].   23p.

1202.   **LINCOLN TURNPIKE TRUST**
General statement of income and expenditure of the north-west district...1842
Lincoln: printed J.W. Drury, 1842.   1 sheet.

1203. ――――――
[Notice of annual general meeting, February 10th, 1849]
[Lincoln]: [s.n.], [1849].   1 sheet.

Road Transport

1204.
From horses to horsepower: long trail of Lincoln transport
in *Lincolnshire echo*, October 10, 1969.

1205.   **WHITE, Peter R.**
Passenger transport in Lincoln: Lincoln Corporation Transport and the Lincolnshire Road Car Company
London: Omnibus Society, [1974].   31p.: ill.
    History of trams and buses from late 19th century to 1973.

1206.   **HEMINGWAY, G.Y.**
Some Lincolnshire road services, 1815–1816
[1978].   25 leaves.
Typescript.
    Services between various Lincolnshire towns including Lincoln.

Stage Coaches

1207.
The Age coach from Lincoln to London in one day: [schedule, fares, etc.]
Lincoln: printed W. and B. Brooke, [18??].   1 sheet.

1208.   **HEMINGWAY, G.Y.**
The Great North Road and its early traffic
[1977].   154 leaves.
Typescript.
      pp.101–105: stage coaches from London to Lincoln & Barton, 1786.

1209.   ——————
Stage coaches to York and beyond
[1977].   pp.155–231.
Typescript.
      p.183: stage coaches from London to Lincoln & Barton, 1786–1815; pp.200–204: cross county
      services, Nottingham, Newark, Lincoln.

1210.   ——————
Coaches and waggons in the Lincoln area in the 18th century
[1977].   19p.
Typescript.

Tramways

1211.
The Electric tramway scheme for Lincoln
pp.127–128 in *Lincolnshire poacher*, vol.1, no.6, November, 1900.

1212.   **LINCOLN CORPORATION**
Byelaws
[Lincoln]: [The Corporation], [1906].   18p.
      pp.15–18: Tramways Act, 1870: 'The following provisions of the Tramways Act, 1870, are
      applicable to the Lincoln Tramways system'.   Includes the injunction that 'no person...shall
      eat anything which has an objectionable smell...'.

1213.   **BRADBURY, C.H.**
The Tramway in Lincoln
pp.20–22: ill. in *Lincolnshire life*, vol.10, no.8, October, 1970.

1214.   **YARNELL, D.H.**
The Tramways of the city of Lincoln
pp.163–172: ill., map in *Tramway review*, vol.8, no.63, autumn, 1970.

1215.   ——————
The Tramways of the city of Lincoln: [continued]
pp.195–205: ill., map in *Tramway review*, vol.8, no.64, winter, 1970.

1216.   ——————
The Tramways of the city of Lincoln: [continued]
pp.19–26: ill. in *Tramway review*, vol.9, no.65, spring, 1971.

1217.   **JOHNSON, C.P.C.**
The Tramways of old Lincoln
in *Lincolnshire echo*, 25th August, 1977.
Continued: 1st September, 1977.

The Motor Car

1218.   **NEWSUM, R.A.**
Lincolnshire's highway pioneers
pp.60–63 in *Lincolnshire life*, vol.8, no.3, May, 1968.
>   History of the Lincolnshire Automobile Club based in Lincoln.

TRADE, COMMERCE AND INDUSTRY

GENERAL SURVEYS

1219.   **LINCOLN CHAMBER OF COMMERCE**
Panoramic Lincoln
Gloucester: Panoramic, [1930s/40s].   16p.: ill.
   Aimed at attracting industry.

1220.
A Factual survey of Lincoln, Sleaford, Boston, Newark, Horncastle, Market Rasen,
Skegness and districts: [marketing information]
Lincoln: Lincolnshire Publishing, [1950].   15p.: ill., maps.

1221.
Marketing information for Lincoln and district, including Boston, Horncastle, Market
Rasen, Newark, Skegness, Sleaford
[Lincoln]: [Lincolnshire Publishing], [1954].   20p.: ill., maps.
   One of 10 sections of *Scanning the provinces*, 1954.

1222.   **LINCOLN JUNIOR CHAMBER OF COMMERCE**
Lincoln today & tomorrow: a report by the Commercial and Industrial Affairs Committee
[1966].   [20] leaves.
Typescript.
   Covers: education; industrial expansion; communications; city centre amenities and
   recreational facilities.

1223.
Scanning the provinces
6th ed.
Lincoln: Lincolnshire Echo, 1967.   30p., map.
Map on inside cover.

1224.   **LINCOLN, Town Planning Department**
Industry and employment
Lincoln: The Department, 1969.   26 leaves, [9] leaves of tables.
(Development plan studies, 4)
   Fourth in series of research studies undertaken by the city's Planning Department to investigate
   the economic and social factors which affect the development of Lincoln.   Includes survey of
   period 1951–66 of economic activity in town and district.

1225.
Scanning the provinces
7th ed.
Lincoln: Lincolnshire Echo, 1970.   24p.: ill.
   A survey concentrating upon the industrial side of Lincoln but also giving information on
   services and a demographic breakdown of the population.

1226.   **LINCOLN, Chief Executive's Department**
Lincoln: city for enterprise
Lincoln: The Department, [1972–   ].
  Twice yearly report giving plans and proposals of Lincoln City Council.

1227.
Industry: [Lincolnshire Standard/Chronicle Group supplement, Friday, January 28th, 1972]
Lincoln: Lincolnshire Standard/Chronicle, 1972.   24p.: ill.

1228.
Industry special supplement: [February, 1976]
Lincoln: Lincolnshire Standard/Chronicle, 1976.   28p.: ill.

1229.
Industry special supplement: [February, 1977]
Lincoln: Lincolnshire Standard, 1977.

1230.
Industry in Lincolnshire review
Lincoln: Lincolnshire Echo, 1982.   xp.: ill.
Supplement to: *Lincolnshire echo*, Monday, March 29, 1982.
  Adverts and articles on firms, including: Simons; Rilmac and Clarke's Crank and Forge.

1231.   **MARKS, Laurence**
Divided Lincoln: the city where former Labour M.P. Dick Taverne fell out with his local party
pp.37, 39, 41: ill. in *The Observer magazine*, 11 February, 1973.
  Mainly about Lincoln itself: engineering, unemployment, etc.

1232.   **LINCOLN CITY COUNCIL**
City of Lincoln industrial development handbook
Wallington: Home, [1979].   64p.: ill.

1233.   **LINCOLN, Housing & Estates Department**
Lincoln: a city for your industry
Lincoln: printed by J.W. Ruddock, [1980].   [12]p.: ill.

1234.
Work in Lincoln
edited by Roger Minshull.
Lincoln: Bishop Grosseteste College, Urban Study Group, 1982.   90p.: ill.
Includes bibliography.
  Material on manufacturing, wholesaling and similar services in Lincoln, collected by a group
  of teachers who met regularly at the College, 1980–81.   Intended to be of use in teaching
  urban geography.   See also *Shopping in Lincoln* below.

1235.   **COUSINS, P.R.**
Lincolnshire at work
compiled by P.R. Cousins and C.M. Wilson.
Lincoln: Lincolnshire Museums, 1982.   16p.: ill.
(Lincolnshire Museums information sheet.   Local history series, no.3)

1236.   **LINCOLN CITY COUNCIL**
Lincoln: [information pack]
Lincoln: The Council, [1984].   1 portfolio.
> Contains a variety of leaflets and booklets.   The pack is designed to attract businessmen to the
> area; not only includes information about industrial activities, but also history, tourism,
> property and schools.

TRADE ASSOCIATIONS

1237.   **LINCOLN GUARDIAN SOCIETY**
The Lincoln Guardian Society, for the protection of trade: [rules]
Lincoln: printed E.B. Drury, 1827.   16p.

1238.   **TRADESMAN'S UNION SOCIETY**
*The Seventeenth anniversary of the Tradesman's Union Society, held at the King's Arms
Inn, in the city of Lincoln, July 13th, 1840: statement of accounts, list of officers and
members*
Lincoln: printed W. and B. Brooke, 1840.   1 sheet.

1239.   ——————
The Eighteenth anniversary of the Tradesman's Union Society, July 12th, 1841:
[statement of accounts and list of members]
Lincoln: printed W. and B. Brooke, 1841.   1 sheet.

1240.   **LINCOLN INCORPORATED CHAMBER OF COMMERCE**
*Twentieth annual report and balance sheet of the council, for the year ending 31st
March, 1909*
Lincoln: M.A. Doncaster, 1909.   24p.

1241.   **LINCOLN TRADES COUNCIL**
Year book, 1944
Lincoln: The Council, 1944.   [18]p.

1242.   **LINCOLN CHAMBER OF COMMERCE**
*Sixty-eighth annual report, 1956–1957: also a list of the members with their business
classifications*
[Lincoln]: [The Chamber], [1956].   42p.: ill.

1243.   **LINCOLN PRODUCTIVITY ASSOCIATION**
Handbook: [1967/68–1970/71]
Lincoln: The Association, 1967–70.

1244.   **LINCOLN JUNIOR CHAMBER OF COMMERCE**
Lincolnshire expo '69: trade fair and exhibition, 22–24 May, 1969: [prospectus for
participants]
[Lincoln]: [The Chamber], 1969.   23p.: ill.

1245.   ——————
Expo '69: programme of events [and] catalogue of exhibitors, May 17 to May 26, 1969
Lincoln: The Chamber, 1969.   128p.
> Includes details of Lincoln industry.

1246.   **LINCOLN, Housing & Estates Department**
Lincoln Enterprise Agency: [promotional leaflet]
Lincoln: The Department, [1983?].   1 folded sheet: ill.

1247.   **LINCOLN ENTERPRISE AGENCY**
Lincoln Enterprise Agency: annual report, year ended 31st March, 1985
Lincoln: The Agency, 1985.   5p.
> Initiative to combat unemployment.   The Agency merged with the Lincoln Employers Forum, 1983–85.

1248.   **LINCOLN INCORPORATED CHAMBER OF COMMERCE**
The Voice of commerce
Lincoln: The Chamber, 1986.   1 folded sheet: ill.

AGRICULTURE

1249.   **LINCOLNSHIRE AGRICULTURAL SOCIETY**
The Rules of the Lincolnshire Agricultural Society, established 1819
Lincoln: printed by Drury, 1820.   22p.

1250.   **MAYDWELL, Isaac**
Copy of a speech, delivered in the Castle Yard at Lincoln, on Friday, March 29th, 1822, at a meeting...for considering the propriety of presenting petitions for Parliament, on the present alarming state of agricultural distress
Louth: printed H. Hurton, [1822].   8p.

1251.   **LINCOLNSHIRE AGRICULTURAL SOCIETY**
The Rules of the Lincolnshire Agricultural Society, established 1819
Lincoln: printed by Bradbury and Dent, 1823.   16p.

1252.
Important agricultural meeting at Lincoln
Lincoln: printed T.J.N. Brogden, [1836].   18p.
> Public meeting of the agriculturalists of Lincolnshire at the City Arms Hotel to discuss means of relieving agricultural distress.

1253.   **LINCOLN LONGWOOL SHEEP BREEDERS' ASSOCIATION**
Brief history of the Lincoln longwool sheep, from the year 1750
Lincoln: The Association, 1950.   18, 10p.: ill.

1254.   **THIRSK, Joan**
English peasant farming: the agrarian history of Lincolnshire from Tudor to recent times
London: Routledge & Kegan Paul, 1957.   xv, 350p.: ill, folded map, [4] leaves of plates.
Includes index.
> Lincoln as a market and especially in connection with Fen drainage and navigation.

1255.   **LINCOLN LONGWOOL SHEEP BREEDERS' ASSOCIATION**
Lincoln longwool sheep
Lincoln: The Association, [c.1964].   [11]p.: ill.

1256.   **UPRICHARD, R.J.H.**
The Lincoln Red Cattle Society
pp.43–45: ill. in *Lincolnshire life*, vol.16, no.2, April, 1976.

1257. **BEASTALL, Tom William**
The Agricultural revolution in Lincolnshire
Lincoln: History of Lincolnshire Committee, 1978. xii, 256p.: ill., [17]p. of plates.
(History of Lincolnshire, VIII)
Includes index.
ISBN 0902668072
> References to Lincoln, including pp.99–102: communications.

1258. **MARSHALL, J.R.**
The Lincoln longwool
pp.30–32: ill. in *Lincolnshire life*, vol.21, no.7, October, 1981.

CRAFTS

General

1259. **LINCOLNSHIRE GUILD OF MASTER CRAFTSMEN**
Rules of the Lincolnshire Guild of Master Craftsmen, Limited
Lincoln: The Guild, [1938]. 16p.
> Offices were at 86, Newland.

1260. **BARLEY, L.B.**
Lincolnshire craftsmen in the sixteenth and seventeenth centuries
by L.B. and M.W. Barley.
pp.7–22 in *The Lincolnshire historian*, vol.II, no.6, 1959.
> Includes: Lincoln leather workers, wood workers, etc.

Textiles

1261.
New woollen factory, Lincoln: [notice]
[Lincoln]: [s.n.], [178?].   1 sheet.

1262.
Proposals for establishing the manufacture of camblets and shalloons in the city of Lincoln
[Lincoln]: [s.n.], [1784?].   3p.

1263. **HEATON, Herbert**
The Yorkshire woollen and worsted industries
Oxford: Clarendon Press, 1920.   xii, 459p.
Includes index.
> Brief references to Lincoln.

1264. **ALEXANDRE, John P.**
The Jersey School at Lincoln, 1591–1830 circa: an old-time scheme for relieving unemployment
pp.289–291 in *The Lincolnshire magazine*, vol.1, 1932–34.

1265.   **HILL, J.W.F.**
Lincoln Jersey School
by J.W.F.H.
p.301 in *The Lincolnshire magazine*, vol.2, 1934–36.
>Note about mistake in fourteenth report of the Historical Commission, where 8 leaves of orders
>made in 1591 and 1592 in fact refer to York and not Lincoln, which lead to inaccuracies in
>Alexandre's article.

1266.   **BOLTON, Clement**
Contributions to the history of dyeing: Lincoln green: a professor's theory that it was
scarlet!: the legend that Flemings founded English textile industry: why Kendal and
Lincoln for greens
pp.667–668 in *The Dyer & textile printer*, December 31, 1937.

1267.   ─────────────
Contributions to the history of dyeing: yellow which might have been used to produce
Lincoln green: saw wort and buckthorn berries, quercitron bark and its sponsor, Edward
Bancroft, spy, physician, merchant and technologist
pp.19–20 in *The Dyer & textile printer*, January 14, 1938.

1268.
The Ordinance book of the merchants of the staple
with an introduction by E.E. Rich.
Cambridge: Cambridge University Press, 1937.   viii, 210p.
Includes index.
>Only four references to Lincoln, but of some interest.

1269.   **BISCHOFF, John Paul**
Economic change in thirteenth-century Lincoln: decline of an urban cloth industry
335p.
Thesis [Ph.D.] – Yale University, 1975.

Other Crafts

1270.   **CORDWAINERS' COMPANY**
[Cordwainers' Company account book, 1524–1785]
c.400 leaves.
Ms.
>To be found in Lincoln Central Library.

1271.   **BARRETT, Thomas**
*Thomas Barrett, wire-worker and machine maker, St Mary's Church-Lane, opposite the
Crown and Woolpack Inn, High-Street, Lincoln*: [prospectus for improved machines,
May 11, 1805]
Lincoln: printed J.W. Drury, 1805.   1 sheet.
>Another issue: dated July 4, 1805.

1272.   **BROMLEY AND CO.**
Manufacturers of earthen-ware: [announcement of intention to keep warehouse on
Waterside, Lincoln, June 21, 1805]
Lincoln: printed J.W. Drury, 1805.   1 sheet.
>Another issue: dated November 14, 1805.

1273.   **WRIGHT, Neil R.**
Tobacco manufacturing in Lincolnshire
pp.1–33: ill. in *Industrial archaeology*, vol.7, no.1, [19??].
    pp.7, 9: Lincoln.

1274.   **SYMPSON, E. Mansel**
The Church plates of the diocese of Lincoln
pp.213–222: ill., X plates in *The Archaeological journal*, 2nd series, vol.XVII, no.3, 1910.
    References to silversmith working in Lincoln.

1275.   **HOLLAND, Margaret**
Did Lincoln make silver?
pp.84–86: ill. in *The Antique dealer and collectors guide*, vol.23, no.11, June, 1969.

1276.   ─────────
A Lincoln jigsaw
pp.32–33: ill. in *Lincolnshire life*, vol.10, no.5, July, 1970.
    Discusses the possibility that silver was made at Lincoln.

1277.
Handmade: an exhibition of Lincolnshire crafts including work by the Guild of Lincolnshire Craftsmen
[Lincoln]: Lincolnshire Association for the Arts, [c.1974].   1 portfolio.
    Many of craftsmen working in Lincoln.

1278.   **DEPARTMENT OF EDUCATION AND SCIENCE**
Arts with the people
[London]: [HMSO], [1975].   [38]p.: ill.
    2p. on Lincolnshire and Humberside Arts and the Usher Art Gallery.

1279.
Regional Craft Centre, Lincoln
Lincoln: Lincolnshire and Humberside Arts, [c.1975].   [3]p., map.
    Set up in Jews Court.

1280.
Lincoln's first painter in residence: Timothy Hyman
Lincolnshire and Humberside Arts.
[1983].   3p.
Typescript.

SERVICES

Banking

1281.   **RHODES, Walter E.**
The Italian bankers in England and their loans to Edward I and Edward II
pp.137–168 in *Historical essays by members of the Owens College, Manchester, published in commemoration of its jubilee, 1851–1901*, 1902.
    pp.145–152: Frescobaldi family, including connections with Lincoln.

Lincoln Savings Bank

1282.   LINCOLN SAVINGS BANK
[Rules]
Lincoln: printed W. Brooke, [18??].   1 sheet.

1283.   ——————
Rules of the Lincoln Saving Bank
Lincoln: printed Drury, [1817?].   3p.

1284.   ——————
Rules of the Lincoln Savings Bank, conformable to the several Acts of Parliament passed for the regulation of such institutions
Lincoln: printed W. Brooke, 1825.   31, [12]p.

1285.   ——————
[Accounts, 1829, 1830, 1831, 1833, 1835]
Lincoln: The Bank, 1829–35.

1286.   ——————
Depositor's book
Lincoln: printed W. Bradbury, [after 1829].   31p.
   Includes rules.

1287.   ——————
Rules of the Lincoln Savings Bank, conformable to the several Acts of Parliament passed for the regulation of such institutions
Lincoln: printed E.B. Drury, 1829.   34p.

1288.   ——————
Rules of the Lincoln Savings Bank, conformable to the several Acts of Parliament passed for the regulation of such institutions
Lincoln: printed W. and B. Brooke, 1838.   30p.
Includes index.

1289.   ——————
[Notice of meeting, 24th November, 1849]
[Lincoln]: [The Bank].   1 sheet.

1290.   ——————
[Notice of meeting, 6th March, 1849]
[Lincoln]: [The Bank], 1849.   1 sheet.

1291.   PORTER, J.T.B.
[Applications for post of auditor at the Lincoln Savings Bank, 22nd November, 1849]
[Lincoln]: [The Author], 1849.   1 sheet.

1292.   ROBINSON, Henry Thomas
[Applications for post of auditor, 21st November, 1849]
[Lincoln]: [The Author], 1849.   1 sheet.

1293.   LINCOLN SAVINGS BANK
The Lincoln Savings Bank: [short history]
Derby: New Centurion Publishing and Publicity, [1957].   32p.: ill.

1294. HESSELL, Graham S.
Lincoln's new T.S.B. headquarters
pp.44–45: ill. in *Lincolnshire life*, vol.18, no.12, March, 1979.
> History of the Lincoln Savings Bank.

1295. HEBDEN, C. Donald
The Trustee Savings Bank of Yorkshire and Lincoln: the story of its formation and of the six savings banks from which it was constituted
Hull: The Bank, [1981]. 382p.
ISBN 0950791407
> pp.209–252: Lincoln Savings Bank.

Lincoln and Lindsey Bank

1296. LINCOLN AND LINDSEY BANK
Deed of settlement of the Lincoln and Lindsey Bank, established 12th August, 1833, under the authority of an Act of Parliament passed in the seventh year of the reign of George the Fourth: to which is appended an abstract of the Act
Lincoln: printed by E.B. Drury, 1833. xiii, 63p.

1297. —————
Lincoln & Lindsey Bank shares to be sold by auction...Friday, October 29th, 1847
Lincoln: printed W. and B. Brooke, 1847. 1 sheet.

1298. HOWARD, S.W.
Another historic site: the Lindsay [sic] Bank, Lincoln
pp.236–239: ill. in *The Midland venture: the magazine of the Midland Bank Staff Association*, July, 1926.

1299. KENDALL, G.H.
Centenary of the Lincoln and Lindsey Banking Company
pp.546–547 in *The Midland venture: the magazine of the Midland Bank Staff Association*, December, 1933.

1300. CRICK, W.F.
A Hundred years of joint stock banking
by W.F. Crick and J.E. Wadsworth.
London: Hodder & Stoughton, 1936. 464p., chart, 5p. of plates.
> Includes references to the Lincoln and Lindsey Bank.

1301. HOWARD, S.W.
Lincoln and Lindsey Banking Company, Ltd.: an account of the premises occupied by the Bank at Lincoln as its head office
[1980]. 6 leaves, [2] leaves of plates.
Typescript.

Smiths/National Westminster Bank

1302. PORTER, H.
Old private bankers of north Lincolnshire
pp.289–296: ill. in *The Lincolnshire magazine*, vol.2, 1934–36.
> Sheaths Bank and Smith, Ellison & Co.

1303.   **LEIGHTON-BOYCE, J.A.S.L.**
Smiths the bankers, 1658–1958
London: National Provincial Bank, 1958.   337p., genealogical table, 17p. of plates.
Includes index.
> pp.137–181: the Lincoln Bank, ie. Smith, Ellison & Brown.

1304.   **NATIONAL WESTMINSTER BANK**
Smith's Bank Branch, Lincoln, 1775–1975
[Lincoln]: [The Bank], [1975].   8p.: ill.

1305.   ——————
National Westminster Bank Limited, Castle Hill, Lincoln: [notes on the building]
[Lincoln]: [The Bank], [1979].   1 sheet: ill.
> Built 1543; Lincoln area office of the National Westminster, 1970–79; since 1979, Pemberton
> House owned by the Dean and Chapter.

1306.   **WINFIELD, Simon**
Lincoln Smith's, founded 1775
[Lincoln]: [The Author], [1983].   20 leaves, 3 leaves of plates.

Midland Bank

1307.   **TOLLIDAY, Martin**
Lincoln story
pp.674–675: ill. in *Midbank chronicle*, May, 1972.
> Concerns Lincoln Branch of the Midland Bank.

1308.   **MIDLAND BANK**
Midland Bank in Lincoln: 150 years of banking, 1833–1983
[Lincoln]: [The Bank], [1983].   [4]p.: ill.

Other Banks

1309.   **LINCOLNSHIRE DISTRICT BANK**
Prospectus of joint stock company, to be entitled the Lincolnshire District Bank
Lincoln: printed W. and B. Brooke, [c.1826/27].   3p.

SHOPS

General

1310.   **LAWRENCE, Rosemary**
Shopping in Lincoln
pp.21–23 in *Lincolnshire life*, vol.5, no.2, April-May, 1965.

1311.
Bailgate shopping: [LSG supplement, March 29, 1979]
Lincoln: Lincolnshire Chronicle, 1979.   ivp.: ill.

1312.
Shopping in Lincoln: [report of results of meetings for teachers and lecturers held at Bishop Grosseteste College, 1978–79]
[1979?].   132p.: ill., maps.
Typescript.
> Work arose out of discussion on the ways of introducing study of urban geography into schools.   See also *Work in Lincoln* above.

Booksellers and Stationers

1313.   **WOOD, William**
A Catalogue of large and valuable collection of antient and modern books, many of them new and elegantly bound: consisting of above five thousand volumes, in all branches of polite literature, arts and sciences, which will be sold very cheap
[Lincoln]: William Wood, [c.1762].   124p., [1] folded leaf of plates.

1314.   **ROSE AND DRURY**
Rose and Drury's catalogue of books
[Lincoln]: [Rose and Drury], [c.1773].   40p.

1315.
[Various cards, labels, forms]
Lincoln: printed J.W. Drury, 1805.
> Many of the items, which are in the Local Studies Collection of Lincoln Central Library, are printer's proofs.

1316.   **COLE, John**
A Catalogue of old books, with specimens, now on sale by John Cole
[Lincoln]: [John Cole]; London: sold by Balwin, Cradock, and Joy, 1817.   138p.

1317.   ————————
A Catalogue of standard books, made out on an entirely new plan, which are constantly on sale by John Cole, High Street, Lincoln
Lincoln: John Cole, 1817.   8p.

1318.   ————————
A Catalogue of standard books, &c., &c. constantly on sale by John Cole, bookseller and stationer, High-Street, Lincoln
Lincoln: John Cole, 1817.   12p.

1319.   **KEYWORTH, J.**
Keyworth's catalogue of old and new books
Lincoln: printed Keyworth, 1823.   106p.

1320.   **TURNER, John**
A Catalogue of the valuable stock-in-trade, printing presses & materials, household furniture, &c., which will be sold by auction...16th & 17th day of July, 1845, on the premises of Mr Charles Brogden, a bankrupt, on the Castle Hill, Lincoln
Lincoln: printed E. Keyworth, [1845].   14p.

1321.   **BROGDEN, T.J.N.**
[Terms for auctioneering of items and advert for stationery, October 20th]
Lincoln: printed T.J.N. Brogden, 184?.   1 sheet.

1322.   **DRURY, James**
[Request for patronage of printing, bookselling and stationery business from customers of his late brother]
Lincoln: printed James Drury, [1851?].   1 sheet.

1323.   **DRURY, Mrs. J.H.**
[Announcement of closure of business, February 11th, 1851]
[Lincoln]: [Drury], 1851.   1 sheet.

1324.   **DRURY, James**
[Announcement that has sold business to Mr. Lockyer, July, 1851]
[Lincoln]: [James Drury], [1851].   1 sheet.

1325.   **BYATT, Anthony**
Picture postcards and their publishers: an illustrated account identifying Britain's major postcard publishers, 1894 to 1939, and the great variety of cards they issued
Malvern: Golden Age Postcard Books, 1978.
    pp.238–239: J.W. Ruddock & Sons.

1326.   **CROFT, Eric**
A Postcard view of Lincolnshire
pp.34–35: ill. in *1981 picture postcard annual*, 1980.
    p.36: paragraph on J.W. Ruddock & Sons, postcard publishers of Lincoln.

1327.   **ELVIN, Laurence**
Jackson's of Lincoln: dyers, cleaners, launderers, 1791–1988
Lincoln: Jackson's Lincoln Laundry, 1988.   28p.: ill.
ISBN 0951392808

Cooperative Societies

1328.   **LINCOLN EQUITABLE COOPERATIVE AND INDUSTRIAL SOCIETY**
Rules of the Lincoln Equitable Cooperative and Industrial Society, Limited
Dewsbury: printed by J. Ward, 1875.   19p.

1329.   **CO-OPERATIVE CONGRESS**
Handbook of the twenty-third annual Co-operative Congress, to be held at Lincoln, on 18th, 19th, and 20th May, 1891
Lincoln: printed Akrill, Ruddock & Keyworth, 1891.   140p.: ill., folded map, [9] plates.
    pp.1–16: Lincoln Co-operative Society; pp.16–18: Lincoln Land and Building Society;
    pp.45–140: visitor's guide to Lincoln and its Cathedral Church, with a brief sketch of the
    neighbourhood.

1330.   **LINCOLN EQUITABLE COOPERATIVE AND INDUSTRIAL SOCIETY**
Rules of the Lincoln Equitable Cooperative and Industrial Society, Limited
Manchester: Cooperative Printing Society, 1895.   26p.

1331.   **McINNES, Duncan**
History of cooperation in Lincoln, 1861–1911
Manchester: Cooperative Wholesale Society, 1911.   135p.: ill.
Includes index.

1332.   **LINCOLN CO-OPERATIVE SOCIETY**
Rules of the Lincoln Co-operative Society, Limited
Manchester: Co-operative Society, 1927.   48p.

1333. WOMEN'S CO-OPERATIVE GUILD CONGRESS
Women's Co-operative Guild Congress, 1942, held at Lincoln, June 8th, 9th, 10th, 11th:
[programme of arrangements]
[Manchester]: [Co-operative Printing Society], 1942.   19p.: ill.
  pp.7–13: Lincoln.

1334. LINCOLN CO-OPERATIVE SOCIETY
Education programme and handbook, session 1955–6
[Lincoln]: [Lincoln Co-operative Society], [1955].   40p.

1335. BRUCKSHAW, Frank
A Century of achievement: the story of Lincoln Co-operative Society
by Frank Bruckshaw and Duncan McNab.
Manchester: Cooperative Press, [1961].   122p.: ill., 11p. of plates.

1336. JUDGE, K.
Lincoln Co-op, 1880–1961
[1961].   4p.: ill.
Typescript.

1337.
Co-operative House, Silver Street, Lincoln, opens 9.15am this Friday, October 2nd:
[*Lincoln weekend chronicle* special co-operative souvenir]
Lincoln: Lincolnshire Chronicle, 1970.   XXp.: ill.

1338. VICKERS, Bette
Co-op superstore special: [advertisement feature]
pp.7–14: ill. in *Lincolnshire chronicle*, Wednesday, August 9, 1978.

1339. LINCOLN CO-OPERATIVE SOCIETY
Birth of an idea: 125 years, Lincoln Co-operative Society: [LSG supplement]
Lincoln: LSG, [1986].   8p.: ill.

Pennell's

1340. PENNELL, Richard
A Descriptive catalogue of a selection of the best roses in cultivation: also an abridged list of some new and good hardy plants, trees, shrubs, fruits, &c., propagated for sale
Lincoln: printed W. and B. Brooke, [1847].   9p.

1341. ——————
A Catalogue of selected roses, hardy ornamental trees, flowering shrubs, evergreens, coniferae, fruits, forest trees, etc., cultivated and sold by Richard Pennell, for the autumn of 1850 and spring of 1851
Lincoln: printed W. and B. Brooke, 1850.   15p.

1342. MATHER, John
R. Pennell & Son...the history of this Lincoln nursery firm over the last 200 years and their contribution to the many clematis cultivars available today
pp.68–71: ill. in *The Garden*, vol.111, pt.2, February, 1986.

Other Shops

1343. WETHERALL, Benjamin
[Advertisement]
Lincoln: printed W. Wood, 1771.   1 sheet.

1344. BLYTH, H.
[Advertisement for services as grocer, tea dealer, tallow chandler, and hop merchant, 217, High Street, Lincoln, featuring 'sermon on malt']
[Lincoln]: [s.n.], [18??].   1 sheet: ill.

1345. TURNER, John
[Advertisement for service of grocer, tea dealer and tallow chandler]
[Lincoln]: [s.n.], [18??].   1 sheet: ill.
   Two issues with different woodcuts.

1346.
Otter & Wroot, chemists and druggists, Lincoln: [list of wares]
Lincoln: printed W. Brooke, [18??].   1 sheet.

1347.
The Paris Chocolate Company, London, have appointed for the sale of their chocolate, bonbons, &c., C.K. Tomlinson, chemist and druggist, no.292, High Street, Lincoln: [advertisement]
London: [s.n.], [18??]   [4]p.

1348.
Lincolnshire daguerreotype or photographic establishment on premises directly opposite St.Mark's Place, High-Street, Lincoln: [advertisement]
Lincoln: printed W. and B. Brooke, [18??].   1 sheet.

1349. WILKINSON, I.O.
Observations on the treatment of fevers by the use of alcoholic stimulants, with special remarks respecting the case of the late Mr G. Adams, and a description of the botanic or eclectic treatment of fever ...
Lincoln: printed I.O. Wilkinson at the Botanic Press, [1862]. 4p.
Accompanied by: *The Eclectic and Botanic Dispensary, 28, Steep Hill, Lincoln:* [prospectus], [4]p.

1350. HUNTER & HOBLING
[Advertisement]
Lincoln: printed J.W. Drury, [1805].   1 sheet.

1351. KIRK, F.
F. Kirk, hair-cutter & perfumer, opposite the butter-house, Lincoln: [advertisement in verse]
Lincoln: printed W. Brooke, [1826].   1 sheet.

1352. CASWELL, William
The Red Boot, cheap and fashionable boot and shoe mart, 279, High Street, Lincoln: [advertisement]
Lincoln: printed Robert Bulman, [1849].   1 sheet.

1353. NORTON, W.C.
[Announcement of retirement from business as confectioner and fruiterer and introduction of successor, Henry Graham, July 14th, 1849]
Lincoln: printed W. and B. Brooke, 1849.   1 sheet.

1354.   **SYMPSON, Elizabeth**
[Notice of dissolution of partnership between Elizabeth and Charles Sympson with advertisement for chemist]
Lincoln: printed T.J.N. Brogden, 1850.   1 sheet.

1355.
[Advertisement for Hubard Photographic Gallery, at Mrs Wallis's, Silver Street, near Broadgate]
Lincoln: printed James Drury, [189?].   1 sheet.

1356.   **THORNTON, L.T.**
Catalogue of highly important sale of new carriages, &c., Drill Hall, Lincoln: to be sold by auction by Messrs Richard Hall, Vickers & Shaw...on Thursday, March the 26th, 1896... carriages belonging to Mr L.T. Thornton, 166, High Street
Lincoln: printed Cousans, 1896.   15p.

1357.   ───────────
The Old coach factory, Lincoln: catalogue of all the valuable stock-in-trade...belonging to Mr L.T. Thornton, carriage builder, including the stock of new carriages...will be sold by Messrs Richard Hall, Vickers & Shaw, on...March 30th, 1897
Lincoln: printed James Williamson, [1897].   15p.

1358.
A Look at Lincoln
p.234 in *Musical opinion & music trade review*, no.315, December, 1903.
    Concerns music shops in Lincoln.

1359.
[In the High Court of Justice, King's Bench Division]: *Curtis and Mawer, Ltd. v. the mayor, aldermen and citizens of the city of Lincoln*
[Lincoln]: [s.n.], [1922].   36 leaves, [8]p.
    Legal case over responsibility for fire on premises.

1360.   **BOOTS THE CHEMIST**
Our wonder shops: Branch 31: Lincoln
pp.139–141: ill. in *The Bee*, February, 1927.
Continued: pp.187–188: ill., March, 1927 and pp.316–317: ill., June, 1927.

1361.
Concerning Lincoln's most historic cafe premises and the business of R.W. Stokes and Sons, Ltd.
[Lincoln]: [R.W. Stokes], [c.1958].   [4]p.
    Very brief mention; mainly about coffee and tea.

1362.
Spotlight on Lincoln
pp.1–3: ill. in *The New bond: the house journal of F.W. Woolworth & Co. Ltd.*, vol.19, no.5, October, 1960.
    Brief history of Woolworth's store built on site of the Saracen's Head.

1363.   **ELVIN, Laurence**
Bygone Lincoln
pp.4–8: ill. in *The Fireside magazine*, February, 1965.
    About Mawer & Collingham.

1364.   **GUDSBY, F. Leslie**
The Chemist's apprentice
pp.42–45: ill. in *Lincolnshire life*, vol.19, no.2, May, 1979.
> Describes pre-World War I apprenticeship at chemist's shop in the High Street where British Home Stores now stands.

1365.   **CURTIS'S OF LINCOLN**
Sausage event: A to Z of Curtis's sausages
[1980].   [2] leaves.
Typescript.

1366.   **SMITH, Sally**
Not so plain Jane
pp.92–93: ill. in *Farmers weekly*, July 23, 1982.
> About Jane Howard's shop in Bailgate.

1367.   **GRIFFIN, Dave**
Jeweller meets shopfitter
pp.46, 47, 52 in *Watchmaker, jeweller & silversmith*, vol.52, September, 1983.
> Describes the refitting of the Lincoln jewellers, John Smith, near the Stonebow. First part of a two-part case study.

1368.   ———————
Shopfitting: a case study
pp.37–39 in *Watchmaker, jeweller & silversmith*, vol.53, January, 1984.

1369.   **JOHNSTON, Jim**
The Chemist in the Baile
pp.26–27: ill. in *Lincolnshire life*, vol.24, no.9, December, 1984.
> Article based on inventory of John Wickham who died in 1730.

1370.   **ERICSON, August**
A Fisherman's tale
[Lincoln]: [The Author], [c.1986].   [8]p.: ill.
> Story of the Sign of the Fish shop on Sincil Street.

Markets

1371.
Market for fat cattle at Lincoln: [minutes of a meeting, 5th July, 1793]
[Lincoln]: [s.n.], 1793.   1 sheet.

1372.
The Cattle markets: [letter to the inhabitants of Lincoln, signed 'One of you']
Lincoln: printed T.J.N. Brogden, [18??].   1 sheet.

1373.
[Notice of dinner to commemorate establishment of Lincoln fat stock market, February 13, 1805]
Lincoln: printed J.W. Drury, 1805.   1 sheet.

1374.
Copy of a memorial intended to be presented to the quarterly meeting of the Lincoln Town Council on Tuesday, May the 5th, 1841: [letter requesting provision of corn exchange and corn market, near the Cornhill]
[Lincoln]: [s.n.], 1841.   1 sheet.

1375.   ANDREW, Wm.
Lincoln city markets: to the citizens and inhabitants of Lincoln
Lincoln: printed J.W. Drury, 1846.   [2]p.

1376.   ―――――
The Market question: to the inhabitants of Lincoln: [letter]
[Lincoln]: [The Author], [1846].   1 sheet.

1377.   ―――――
The Market Question: [letter to the inhabitants of Lincoln]
[Lincoln]: The Author, [1846?].   1 sheet.
    Claim that has no personal interest in sale of land near Cornhill.

1378.   BUNYAN, R.
*To the mayor, aldermen and burgesses of the city of Lincoln: the memorial of a body of
the tradesmen and other inhabitants of the city of Lincoln...as subscribers or
shareholders in a company...for the erection of a corn exchange and stallage
market...signed on behalf of the memorialist by R. Bunyan, Wm. Andrew*
[Lincoln]: [The Authors], [1846].   [2]p.
    'Copy of a memorial intended to be presented to the quarterly meeting of the Lincoln Town
    Council, on Tuesday, May the 5th, 1846'.

1379.   GRESHAM, Wm.
To the agriculturalists and cattle dealers attending the Lincoln markets: [letter, May 7th,
1846]
Lincoln: printed J. Stainton, 1846.   1 sheet.

1380.
The Market question: to the inhabitants of Lincoln: [letter signed 'Wide awake']
Lincoln: printed T.J.N. Brogden, 1846.   1 sheet.
    Questioning right of Corporation to spend public money on the plan.

1381.
[Poster about Lincoln October fair, September 23rd, 1847]
[Lincoln]: [s.n.], 1847.   1 sheet.

1382.
Lincoln new markets, near the Corn Hill: [announcement of opening, 18th October, 1847]
Lincoln: printed J.W. Drury, 1847.   1 sheet.

1383.
[Poster about wool market, 18th June, 1849]
Lincoln: printed W. Bellatti, 1849.   1 sheet.

1384.
Covered market, Above-hill Lincoln: [notice of continuation of adjourned meeting,
February 18th, 1850]
[Lincoln]: [s.n.], 1850.   1 sheet.

1385.   LINCOLN CORPORATION
*The Central Market: official opening by the Right Worshipful, the mayor of Lincoln, 18th
May, 1938*
[Lincoln]: [The Corporation], [1938].   [7]p.: ill.
    About new building with brief history of the old Lincoln markets.

1386.
[Transcription of minutes of meeting of Lincoln City Council concerning butter market, 25th September, 1736]
pp.35–37 in *The Lincolnshire historian*, no.1, summer, 1947.

1387.　**ELVIN, Laurence**
The Corn Exchange
pp.7–10: ill. in *The Fireside magazine*, June, 1967.

1388.　**WILKES, Peter**
Lincoln's central market
pp.16–17: ill. in *Lincolnshire life*, vol.25, no.11, February, 1986.

Early Closing Association

1389.
[Letter to the inhabitants of Lincoln, July 20, 1846]
[Lincoln]: [Lincoln Association for the Abridgement of the Hours of Business in All Trade], [1846].　1 sheet.

1390.　**LINCOLN EARLY CLOSING ASSOCIATION**
Report of the Lincoln Early Closing Association
Lincoln: printed Lincolnshire Advertiser, [1846/47].　[2]p.

1391.　**BOOLE, George**
The Right use of leisure: an address, delivered before the members of the Lincoln Early Closing Association, February 9th, 1847
London: J. Nisbet, 1847.　25p.

1392.　**LINCOLN EARLY CLOSING ASSOCIATION**
[Resolution of meetings of chemists and druggists and perfumers]
Lincoln: printed R. Bulman, 1847.　1 sheet.

1393.　——————————
Report of the Lincoln Early Closing Association meeting
Lincoln: printed Lincolnshire Times, 1847.　1 sheet.
Originally published: *Lincolnshire times*, February 23, 1847.

LEGAL AND OTHER SERVICES

1394.　**LINCOLN AND LINCOLNSHIRE FREEHOLD LAND SOCIETY**
The Lincoln and Lincolnshire Freehold Land Society
Lincoln: printed Lincolnshire Times, [1850?].　8p.
　　　Office at Grantham Place, Lincoln.

1395.　**LINCOLN AND LINCOLNSHIRE INSURANCE OFFICE**
Proposed Lincoln and Lincolnshire Insurance Office, May 18th, 1850
Lincoln: printed T.J.N. Brogden, 1850.　1 sheet.

1396.　**ANDREW, William**
A Letter to the shareholders of the Lincolnshire Fire Office
Lincoln: printed T.J.N. Brogden, [1854].　14p.

1397.
Taking a closer look at Lincoln
London: Prudential Assurance Company, [1977].   [9]p.: ill.
    Attracting custom for new offices on Brayford.

1398.   **DAVIES, Jeannette**
Andrew & Co., Lincoln solicitors: the first 150 years
by Jeannette Davies and Philip Race.
Lincoln: Andrew & Co., Solicitors, 1982.   42p.
    Includes material about Sir Francis Hill, senior partner in the firm.

1399.   **ANDREW & CO.**
Andrew & Co., Solicitors: [brochure]
[Lincoln]: [Andrew & Co., Solicitors], [1987].   [12]p.: ill.
    Includes brief history.

1400.   **LINCOLNSHIRE PROPERTY, BUILDING AND GENERAL FINANCE COMPANY**
Lincolnshire Property, Building and General Finance Company, Ltd.: [rules]
Lincoln: printed C. Akrill, [c.1870?].   8p.

1401.   **LINCOLNSHIRE GENERAL FINANCE COMPANY**
1876–1962: a brief account of the founding and growth of the Lincolnshire General Finance Company, Limited
[Lincoln]: [The Company], [1963].   [6]p.: ill.

INDUSTRY

General

1402.
[Notes on Lincoln firms]
pp.441–44[7] in *Proceedings of the Institution of Mechanical Engineers*, 1885.
    pp.441–442: Ruston sheaf iron works; pp.442–443: Robey's globe works; pp.443–444:
    Clarke's crank and forge works; p.444: Wellington foundry and new machine works; p.445:
    City iron and wire works; p.445: Britannia iron and wire works; pp.445–446: Bracebridge gas
    works; pp.446–447: Lincoln water works; p.447: sewage pumping station.

1403.   **INSTITUTION OF MECHANICAL ENGINEERS**
Lincoln meeting, 1920: notices of works open to the visit of the members
[London]: [The Institution], 1920.   51p.
    Includes: Corporation electric power station; tramway depot; tramways; refuse destructor;
    sewage works; waterworks; James Cook & Sons; Clarke's Crank and Forge Co.; Clayton &
    Shuttleworth; Wm. Foster & Co.; Robey & Co.; Ruston & Hornsby.

1404.   **ABERCONWAY, Lord**
The Basic industries of Great Britain: coal, iron, steel, engineering, ships: an historic and economic survey
London: Ernest Benn, 1927.   xii, 390p., [frontis].
Includes index.
    pp.83–90: engineering industry in Lincoln; Rustons; Clayton & Shuttleworth; Wm. Foster;
    Babcock & Wilcox.

1405. ARMSTRONG, J.W.
100 years of engineering in Lincoln
[1949]. 11 leaves.
Typescript.
   Discussion centred around products rather than particular firms.

1406. ALFORD, L.C.G.
The Development of industrial Lincoln; a lecture given to the Lincoln Historical
Association and the Lincoln Training College
[1950]. 15 leaves.
Typescript.
   Covers period form 1840s-1950s, but concentrates upon Rustons.

1407. BLOOMFIELD, G.T.
The Motor vehicle, cycle and aircraft industries of the East Midlands
pp.3–4, maps in *The East Midland geographer*, no.17, June, 1962.
   Lincoln mentioned passim.

1408.
From the files: an exhibition of business records arranged by the Lincolnshire Archives
Office and the Lincoln City Libraries, Central Library, Lincoln, 27th January–13th
February, 1965: [catalogue]
[1965]. 7p.
Typescript.
   Issued by the City of Lincoln Libraries, Museum and Art Gallery Committee.

1409. McCULLAGH, Patrick
The East Midlands: a regional study
London: Oxford University Press, 1969. 127p.: ill., maps.
For schools.
   pp.50–57: reasons for growth of industry in Lincoln.

1410. BIRCH, N.C.
An Industrial archaeology tour in Lincolnshire
[197?]. 8 leaves.
Typescript.
   Under aegis of Rugby College of Engineering Technology, Education Unit. pp.5–8: Lincoln.

1411.
Products manufactured in Lincoln
[1970]. [2]p.
Typescript.

1412.
Men, mills and machines: an exhibition of industrial archaeology in Lincolnshire
Lincoln: Lincoln City Museum, 1971. [12]p.
   Includes brief notes on some Lincoln industries.

1413. NICHOLLS, Lorna Mary
From agriculture to industry: the story of how Lincoln became an industrial city:
including the story of some of my own family and their connection with local industrial
firms
[1971]. 53p.
Typescript.
   Study done while at Bishop Grosseteste College.

1414.
Lincoln: 'city for engineering enterprise'
pp.7–8: ill. in *New locations*, September, 1973.

1415.　**HALLAM, Margaret Ann**
The Social & economic effect of the introduction of the steam-engineering industry into
Lincoln, 1850–1900
130 leaves: ill., maps.
Typescript.
Thesis [B.Ed. Hons.] – Kesteven College of Education, 1974.
Includes bibliography.
    Covers: the development of the industry; population changes in Lincoln and their relation to
    industrial change; housing and health; educational developments; religious provision, with
    particular reference to non-conformity.　Appendix includes photocopies of many of the source
    documents used.

1416.　**MILNER, C.V.A.**
The Agricultural engineering industry in Lincoln, 1840–1900
[1975].　38 leaves.
Typescript.
    Report from M.Sc. economics course which includes information on Clayton & Shuttleworth,
    Ruston and Robey.

1417.　**WILLS, Lesley**
The Industrial development of Lincoln, 1800–1900
72 leaves: ill.
Thesis [B.A. Hons.] – Sunderland Polytechnic, 1981.
    With particular reference to Rustons.

1418.　**WRIGHT, Neil R.**
Lincolnshire towns and industry, 1700–1914
Lincoln: History of Lincolnshire Committee, 1982.　xiv, 300p.: ill., [9]p. of plates.
(History of Lincolnshire, XI)
Includes index.
ISBN 0902668102
    Many references to Lincoln.

Clayton & Shuttleworth

1419.
To J. Shuttleworth, Esq., mayor of the city of Lincoln: [letter threatening him with
disobedience of men in his employ]
Lincoln: printed Doncaster, [18??].　1 sheet.

1420.
Messrs. Clayton and Shuttleworth's agricultural implement works
p.126 in *The Illustrated London news*, no.1551, vol. LV, August 7, 1869.

1421.
Stamp End works
pp.437–440 in *Transactions of the Institution of Mechanical Engineers*, August, 1885.
    Works belonging to Clayton & Shuttleworth.

1422.
[Article about Clayton & Shuttleworth]
p.210 in *Lincolnshire poacher*, vol.1, no.9, February, 1901.

1423.   **CLAYTON & SHUTTLEWORTH**
Lincoln works improvements in 1911
[Lincoln]: [Clayton & Shuttleworth], [1911].   [12]p.: ill.

1424.   **SMITH-CLAYTON FORGE**
An Anniversary
Lincoln: Smith-Clayton Forge, [1950].   [16]p.: ill.
  About the Forge itself.

1425.   **MUIR, Augustus**
75 years: a record of progress: Smith's stamping works, Coventry, Ltd.: Smith-Clayton Forge, Ltd., Lincoln
Coventry: Ribble Road Works, 1958.   104p., [14]p. of plates, [frontis].
  Clayton Forge was once part of Clayton and Shuttleworth; its name was changed in December, 1929.

1426.   **MARSHALL, J.R.**
Was exporting ever fun?
pp.54–55 in *Lincolnshire life*, vol.8, no.7, September, 1968.
  Describes the endeavours of Clayton Shuttleworth to promote overseas business.

1427.
A Traktorgyar tortenete, 1901–1945–IG
[edited by] Rozsa Gyula.
Budapest: Globus Nyomada, 1971.   143p.: ill.
Text in Hungarian.   Half-title: '70 eves a traktorgyar, Voros Csillag traktorgyar, 1971',
['70 years a traction-engine factory, Red Star..., 1971']
  This 'history of a traction engine factory' refers to the Hungarian branch of Clayton-Shuttleworth and mentions the founders, Nathaniel Clayton and Joseph Shuttleworth passim.

1428.   **COMMISSION ON INDUSTRIAL RELATIONS**
Report, no.15: Clayton Dewandre Company, Limited
London: HMSO, 1977.   48p.

1429.   **WILSON, Catherine M.**
Industrial archaeology notes, 1982
pp.113–117: ill. in *Lincolnshire history and archaeology*, vol.18, 1983.
  p.116: Stamp End iron works of Clayton & Shuttleworth.

1430.   **CLAYTON & SHUTTLEWORTH**
Notes on the dissolution of Clayton & Shuttleworth, Ltd., in 1924: details of location of records and drawings: brief details of the late Alfred Shuttleworth
[1924].
Ms.

Clayton & Shuttleworth Products

1431.
[Clayton & Shuttleworth exhibits]
pp.20–23: ill. in *The Exhibition catalogue of the International Exhibition*, 1862.

1432. **CLAYTON & SHUTTLEWORTH**
*The End of the Red Baron, Baron von Richtofen: presented to the workers in the aircraft
works as a souvenir of their participation in the construction of the 'Camel' B7270 by
Clayton & Shuttleworth*
Lincoln: Clayton & Shuttleworth, [1918].   [2]p.: ill.

1433. **ROBSON, Norton G.**
Some notes on the steam wagons of Clayton & Shuttleworth, Ltd., Lincoln
[19??].   [6] leaves: ill.
Typescript.

1434.
New third-class Pullman cars, L.B.& S.C.R.
pp.246–248 in *The Railway magazine*, October, 1921.
      Made by Clayton Wagons, Ltd.

1435.
The Harrogate Pullman car train: introduction of all-Pullman trains between London and
Leeds...
pp.113–118: ill. in *The Railway magazine*, August, 1923.
      Wagons made by Clayton's.

1436.
New Pullman cars for L.M.S. Caledonian section: three first-class dining cars and one
third-class buffet car, built by Clayton Wagons, Ltd., have recently been placed in service
in Scotland
pp.960–964: ill. in *The Railway gazette*, June 29, 1923.

1437. **CLAYTON WAGONS**
*The 'Clayton' driver's handbook: containing necessary instructions for driving, working
and maintaining the Clayton steam wagon*
Lincoln: Clayton Wagons, [1930s?].   [23]p.: ill.
Includes index.

1438. **ROBSON, Norton G.**
The British steam rail car, 1847–1948: [paper to be read before the Institution of
Locomotive Engineers, February 23rd, 1949]
[London]: [The Institution], [1949].   14 leaves.
      References to Clayton wagons.

1439. ——————
The Road vehicle registers of Clayton Wagons, Ltd., Lincoln, 1920–1930
compiled from original records by Norton G. Robson.
[1949].   [17] leaves: ill.
Typescript.

1440.
Heat transfer equipment: still tube heat exchangers
Lincoln: Clayton Dewandre, [1950].   Various pagings: ill.

1441. **MARSHALL, J.R.**
Is this the oldest of the county steamers?
pp.56–57: ill. in *Lincolnshire life*, vol.7, no.11, January, 1968.
      About Clayton & Shuttleworth steam thresher in Budapest.

1442.   **WALLS, John**
Clayton & Shuttleworth and Marshall aircraft production
Lincoln: Brayford Press, 1977.   18p.: ill.
(Control column publication)
    Third in the series detailing Lincolnshire's aircraft history.

Foster's

1443.   **FOSTER, William, & CO.**
*Illustrated catalogue of portable and fixed agricultural steam engines, thrashing
machines, portable & fixed corn mills, sawing machinery, &c.*
Nottingham: R. Allen, 1864.   21p.: ill.
    Includes items relating to 1865–66, but is difficult to tell which parts are integral from the form.

1444.   **BRACEBRIDGE HALL CLUB**
Rules of Bracebridge Hall Club
[Lincoln]: [William Foster], [c.1920].   22p.: ill.

1445.   **FOSTER, William, & CO.**
1856–1956: William Foster & Company, Limited, centenary celebration
Lincoln: William Foster, [1956].   7p.: ill.
    Brief firm history with menu and programme.

1446.   ————————
William Foster & Co., Ltd., 1856–1961: [notes]
1 sheet.
Typescript.

Robey's

1447.   **BELL, W.T.**
*Memorable ceremony at Lincoln works...golden wedding presentation to W.T. Bell...and
Mrs W.T. Bell*
Lincoln: [s.n.], [1942].   [5] leaves: ill.
Originally published: *Lincolnshire chronicle*, 29th August, 1942.

1448.   **ROBEY & CO.**
Robey of Lincoln, 1939–1945
Lincoln: Robey, [1945].   30p.: ill.
    Refers to souvenir booklet published in 1918.

1449.
*Lincoln works chief's anniversary: big celebration at Robey's: Mr and Mrs W.T. Bell's
diamond wedding*
[Lincoln]: [Robey], 1952.   12p., [27]p. of plates.

1450.   **BRUCE, J.M.**
The Robey products
pp.349–351: ill. in *Air pictorial: journal of the Air League*, November, 1961.

1451.   **ROBEY & CO.**
Robey and Co., Ltd.: [letter recommending sale of the company to Dunford & Elliott]
[3]p.
Typescript.

1452.   **ROBINSON, Guy**
Robey of Lincoln, Ltd.
pp.32–33: ill. in *Lincolnshire life*, vol.19, no.1, April, 1979.

Robey's Products

1453.   **WALLS, John**
Robey aircraft production
Lincoln: Aero Litho, 1974.   23p.: ill.
   Second booklet in the series documenting Lincolnshire's aircraft industry.

1454.   **SOUTHWORTH, P.J.M.**
Some early Robey steam engines
[Chesterfield]: The Author, 1986.   43p.: ill.
   Photographs with commentary.

1455.   **STEVENSON, Raymond**
Robey of Lincoln, Ltd.: points of the past, potential of the future
[19??].   22 leaves, [11] leaves of plates.
Typescript.

Ruston's

1456.   **RUSTON & HORNSBY**
The Training of an engineer
Lincoln; Grantham: Ruston & Hornsby, [19??].   38p.: ill.
(Publication, no.8714)

1457.   **RUSTON, PROCTOR & CO.**
A Training ground for engineers
[Lincoln]: [Ruston], [c.1911].   48p.: ill.
(Publication, no.3596)

1458.   ——————
The Progress of Ruston Proctor and Co., Ltd., Engineers, Lincoln, England: 1889–1911
[Lincoln]: [Ruston, Proctor], [1911].   64p.: ill.
   Chiefly illustrations.

1459.   **RUSTON & HORNSBY**
Beevor souvenir: January, 1950, souvenir of opening of new Beevor iron foundry...
[Lincoln]: [Ruston], [1950].   40p.: ill.
(Publication, no.9072)

1460.   ——————
Our part in the Great War: [album]
Lincoln: Ruston & Hornsby, 1919?.   123p.: ill.
Cover title.
   Photographs of products involved with war on land, protection of ships against mines and war in the air.

1461.   **RUSTON**
Visit of H.R.H. the Prince of Wales, K.G., to the Ruston excavator works, Lincoln
[Lincoln]: [Ruston], [1927?].   [16]p.: ill.

1462.   **EVANS, Arthur F.**
The History of the oil engine: a review in detail of the development of the oil engine, from the year 1860 to the beginning of the year 1930
London: Sampson Low, Marston, [1932?].   xiii, 318p., [76]p. of plates.
Includes index.
> Brief references to Ruston.

1463.   **HAMMOND, Rolt**
Ruston's in war, 1939–1945
[Lincoln]: [Ruston], [1946?].   77p.: ill.
> Describes how various Ruston products (generating sets, engines, tanks) contributed to the war effort.   Copious illustration.

1464.
Ruston souvenir: Royal Show, Lincoln, 1947
[Lincoln]: [Ruston & Hornsby], [1947].   33p.: ill.
(Publication, no.8873)
> Includes history and photographs of Lincoln.

1465.   **ALFORD, L.C.G.**
The History of Ruston & Hornsby, Limited, of Lincoln: a lecture given to the Lincoln Branch of the Workers Educational Association and other organizations
[1947].   15p.
Typescript.
> Some of the same information is repeated in the more general talk, dated 1950.

1466.   **RUSTON**
Rustons souvenir
Lincoln: [Ruston], [1950s?].   [4]p.: ill.
(Publication, no.9476)

1467.   **RUSTON & HORNSBY**
Lincoln and the works of Ruston & Hornsby, Ltd.
Lincoln: printed Doncaster, 1950?.   55p.: ill.
(Publication, no.8776)
> Short guide to the city, followed by brief guide to the firm, but most importantly giving specifications of products.

1468.   **RUSTON**
A Ruston survey of the development of power
Lincoln: Ruston, 1953.   44p.: ill.
(Publication, no.9323)
> Ruston coronation year souvenir, 1953.

1469.   **HAYNES, Walter**
History of Ruston & Hornsby, Limited, and the founders Joseph Ruston, Esq., 1857, and Richard Hornsby, Esq., 1815, Lincoln and Grantham
Lincoln: [The Author], 1954.   3 vols.: ill.

1470.   **WILLIAMSON, Harold J.**
Designed for digging: the first 75 years of Bucyrus-Erie Company
by Harold J. Williamson and Kenneth H. Myers, II.
Evanston, Ill.: Northwestern University Press, 1955.   384p.: ill., [frontis].
(Northwestern University studies in business history, vol.II)
Includes index.
> pp.249–266: Ruston-Bucyrus.

1471. **NEWSUM, Bernard**
One hundred years of good company
[Lincoln]: [Ruston & Hornsby], [1957].   272p.: ill., 42p. of plates.
Includes index.
> Anecdotal history concerned with personalities as well as industrial developments.

1472. **RUSTON CENTENARY CONGRESS**
Ruston Centenary Congress, Harrogate, 14–16 May, 1957: verbatim report
1957.   72 leaves.
Typescript.

1473. **RUSTON**
One hundred years of good company: the story of Ruston & Hornsby, Limited, by
*Bernard Newsum: **The history of Ruston & Hornsby, Limited**, by Walter Haynes:*
acknowledgement
[Lincoln]: [Ruston], [1957].   [2]p.

1474. ————————
1857...this was when it started: [leaflet]
Lincoln: Ruston, [1967].   [4]p.: ill.
> Brief history.

1475. **CARCHEDI, F.**
Development of the internal combustion engine by the Company (G.E.C.- E.E. Combine)
over 80 years
[19??].   12 leaves, [4] leaves of plates.
Typescript.
> General Electric Company and English Electric.

1476. **RUSTON DIESELS**
Vulcan's heritage: a brief history of the Vulcan site
Newton-le-Willows: Ruston, 1975?.   32p.: ill.
(Publication, no.RD020)
> Traces individual histories and subsequent merger of the Vulcan Foundry, English Electric Co.,
> Davey, Paxman & Co, and Rustons.   Copious illustration.

1477. **ANDERSON, George B.**
One hundred booming years: a history of Bucyrus-Erie Company, 1880–1980
South Milwaukee, Wis.: The Company, 1980.   303p.: ill.
Includes index.
ISBN 096041360X
> References to Ruston-Bucyrus.

1478. **BATES, Ralph**
Lincoln recollections
pp.31–32: ill. in *Lincolnshire life*, vol.21, no.1, April, 1981.
> Came to Lincoln in 1902 and started work at Rustons in 1907.

1479. **HOOLEY, Ray**
Ruston: the first 125 years
pp.7–12: ill. in *The Stationary engine*, issue 104, October, 1982.

1480. **RUSTON**
Ruston Gas Turbines, Ltd., New Products Division: open day, Saturday, 15th May, 1982
Lincoln: Ruston, [1982].   9p., plan.

1481. HOOLEY, Ray
Journey to Asia Minor: 1909: (letters from an outworker): using a selection of letters
written by a Ruston installation engineer, Ray Hooley gives us a glimpse of the trials and
tribulations of the engine hey-day
pp.6–10: ill. in *The Stationary engine*, January, 1984.
    Letters exchanged between Mr. G. Marcuse and the Company.

1482. JOIS, Jacqueline
The History of Ruston Gas Turbines in Lincoln: how social and economic conditions
affected its growth and how it adapted itself to them
55 leaves, maps.
Typescript.
Thesis [B.A. Hons.] – Humberside College of Higher Education, [19??].
Includes bibliography.

Ruston's Products

1483. RUSTON, PROCTOR & CO.
Illustrated catalogue: agricultural section, 1904–5
Lincoln: Ruston, Proctor, 1904.   127p.: ill.
(Publication, no.944)
    Includes thrashing machines, portable steam machines, steam tractors, etc.

1484.
The Locomotives of the Great Eastern Railway
p.203: ill. in *The Locomotive*, 15th November, 1909.
    'Johnson' class shunting engine made by Ruston, Proctor & Co.

1485. RUSTON, PROCTOR & CO.
*Steam traction engines constructed by Ruston, Proctor & Co. sheaf iron works, Lincoln,
England*
Lincoln: Akrill, Ruddock & Keyworth, [1912–14].   [14]p.: ill.

1486. RUSTON & HORNSBY
Ruston aircraft production: a souvenir of Ruston's 1000th aeroplane
Lincoln: Ruston & Hornsby, 1920?.   14p.: ill.
    Mainly colour paintings and photographs of factory workers and products.

1487. ——————
Some points on 'Ruston-Hornsby' 1923 cars 'sixteen' & 'twenty'
Lincoln: Ruston & Hornsby, 1923.   31p.: ill.

1488. ——————
Ruston-Hornsby cars: models, 1923
Lincoln: Ruston & Hornsby, [1923].   16p.: ill.

1489. BARNES, W.
Excavating machinery as represented by power shovels, drag lines & grabbing cranes
London: Ernest Benn, 1928.   247p.: ill.
Includes index.
    pp.10–12: the Dunbar and Ruston steam navvy; p.110: vertical multitubular type thermax
    boiler.

1490. ——————
Lincoln and excavating machinery
pp.369–375: ill. in *The Lincolnshire magazine*, vol.1, 1932–34.
   Rustons.

1491. **RUSTON, PROCTOR & CO.**
*Instructions and useful information specially compiled for the 110 HP Clerget engine
constructed under the license of Gwynnes, Ltd., London by Ruston, Proctor & Co., Ltd*
Lincoln: Ruston, [c.1940]. 37p.: ill.
(Publication, no.3701)

1492. **RUSTON & HORNSBY**
*Instructions and useful information specially written for the guidance of users of the
Ruston vertical airless injection oil engine, enclosed type*
Lincoln: Ruston & Hornsby, [1940s?]. 24p.: ill., 2p. of plans.
(Publication, no.4461)

1493. **RUSTON & HORNSBY**
Ruston long jib crane navvies: [prospectus]
Lincoln: Ruston & Hornsby, [1940s?]. 19p.: ill.
(Publication, no.4916)

1494. ——————
The Ruston shale cutter
Lincoln: Ruston & Hornsby, [1940s-1950s?]. 7p.: ill.
(Publication, no.5193)

1495. ——————
Ruston universal excavator, no.6: [prospectus]
Lincoln: Ruston & Hornsby, [1940s-1950s?]. 32p.: ill.
(Publication, no.5234)

1496. ——————
No.4 full circle universal Ruston: [prospectus]
Lincoln: Ruston & Hornsby, [1940s-1950s?]. 1 sheet: ill.
(Publication, no.5310)

1497. ——————
Power excavating for small jobs with a 'Ruston no.4': [catalogue]
Lincoln: Ruston & Hornsby, [1940s-1950s?]. 39p.: ill.
(Publication, no.5366)

1498. ——————
Specification of the Ruston no.135 excavator, dragline or shovel
Lincoln: Ruston & Hornsby, [1950s?]. 16p.: ill.
(Publication, no.5412)

1499. ——————
Specification of the Ruston steam, no.10 excavator
Lincoln: Ruston & Hornsby, [1950s?]. 15p.: ill.
(Publication, no.5428)

1500. ——————
The Importance of adaptability: [prospectus for Ruston, no.4]
Lincoln: Ruston & Hornsby, [1950s?]. 1 sheet: ill.
(Publication, no.5446)

1501. ──────────
Excavating machinery: [catalogue]
Lincoln: Ruston & Hornsby, [1950s?].   32p.: ill.
(Publication, no.5568)

1502. ──────────
Specification of the Ruston no.25 steam, quarry type shovel
Lincoln: Ruston & Hornsby, [1950s?].   8p.: ill.
(Publication, no.5569)

1503. ──────────
What Britain thinks of the Ruston no.4 full-circle excavator: [prospectus]
Lincoln: Ruston & Hornsby, [1950s?].   1 sheet.
(Publication, no.5581)

1504. ──────────
The Ruston no.20 crane navvy
Lincoln: Ruston & Hornsby, [1950s?].   23p.: ill.

1505. ──────────
Ruston no.15 excavator: [prospectus]
Lincoln: Ruston & Hornsby, [1950s?].   23p.: ill.

1506.   **WADE, A.H.**
Introduction to excavating practice
Revised ed.
Lincoln: Ruston-Bucyrus, 1957.   139p.
> 'A comprehensive reference book for the assistance of Ruston-Bucyrus sales engineers'.   Of
> interest because of publisher; only 2 passing references to Lincoln.

1507.
British diesel mines locomotives
London: Locomotive and Allied Manufacturers' Association of Great Britain, [Mines
Locomotive Group], 1959.   72p.: ill.
> Many illustrations of Ruston's machines.

1508.
British diesel engine catalogue
edited by D.S.D. Williams.   6th ed.
London: published for the British Internal Combustion Engine Manufacturers'
Association by Temple Press, 1965.   li, 253p.: ill.
Originally published: 1947; subsequent eds.: 1950; 1954; 1957; 1961.
> pp.220–237: Ruston & Hornsby products.

1509.   **RUSTON & HORNSBY**
A Ruston car comes home!
Lincoln: Ruston & Hornsby, [1967].   [4]p.: ill.
> About restoration of 1920 car; includes specifications.

1510.
The Ruston Hornsby
p.55: ill. in *Lincolnshire life*, vol.7, no.9, November, 1967.
> Ruston Hornsby motor car; article tells of restoration of some of the cars by the firm.

1511.   **TONKS, Eric S.**
Ruston & Hornsby locomotives
Greenford: Industrial Railway Society, 1974.   92p.: ill., map.
> 'In the 1960s one in every four industrial diesels in Britain was a Ruston'.

1512.   **WALLS, John**
Ruston aircraft production: a souvenir of Ruston's 1000th aeroplane
Lincoln: Aero Litho, 1974.   23p.: ill.
> First of a series documenting Lincolnshire's aircraft industry; during First World War the city
> was one of the largest aircraft production centres in the world.

1513.   **MOUNFIELD, N.M.**
The Development & design of Lincoln-built excavators
62 leaves: ill.
Typescript.
Thesis [Cert. Ed.] – Loughborough College of Education, 1975.
> Deals with Rustons.

1514.   **ROBINSON, W. Heath**
The Gentle art of advertising
London: Duckworth, 1979.   88p.: ill.
Reproduced from original undated [10]p. separate issue.
> pp.10–19: 'The gentle art of excavating', by Heath Robinson, issued by Ruston-Bucyrus Ltd.,
> Lincoln.   Characteristically amusing cartoon of dragline, drag-shovel, skimmer, grab crane and
> walking dragline.

1515.   **EDGINGTON, David**
Stationary engines for the enthusiast
compiled, edited & published by David Edgington & Charles Hudson.
[S.l.]: [The Authors], 1981.   [54] leaves: ill.
ISBN 0887833101
> 5p. on Ruston & Hornsby.

1516.   **GRIMSHAW, Peter N.**
Excavators
Poole: Blandford, 1985.   160p.: ill.
Includes index.
> References in the text to Ruston & Dunbar, Ruston & Hornsby, Ruston Proctor.

1517.   **RUSTON**
The Ruston range of industrial gas turbines
[Lincoln]: [Ruston], [c.1986].   1 folded sheet: ill.
(Publication, no.051)

1518.   **WORTHINGTON-WILLIAMS, Michael**
The Lincoln Imp: the story of the Ruston-Hornsby car
pp.33–38: ill. in *The Automobile*, January, 1987.

1519.   **SIMS, Brian J.**
Sixty famous engines
Perth: Vintage Tractor, 1988.   [48]p.: ill.
(Milestones series, no.6)
ISBN 0907742327
> [3]p. on Rustons.

Other Firms

1520.   **CHAMBERS, James**
[Open letter to prospective customers of his iron and brass foundry]
[Lincoln]: [The Author], 1821.   1 sheet.

1521.   **DAWSON, Frank**
Three generations: the beginning and end of a family company
Lincoln: James Dawson, [19??].   41p.: ill.

1522.   **HOUSE OF JEWSON**
The House of Jewson, 1836–1936
[Norwich?]: [House of Jewson], [1937].   22p., 13p. of plates.
> p.15: reference to new branch of the timber business opening in Lincoln in 1907. The premises
> were destroyed by fire in 1933 and later rebuilt.

1523.   **CLARKE, William, & SON**
A Century of progress, 1842 to 1942
Lincoln: William Clarke, [1942].   [11]p.: ill.
> History of firm of coal and coke merchants.

1524.   **GWYNNES PUMPS**
Land drainage pumps
Lincoln: Gwynnes Pumps, [1943?].   54p.: ill., map.
> Works moved from Hammersmith to Lincoln in 1927 to the premises of William Foster & Co.

1525.
The Magazine visits Lincoln
pp.32–37: ill. in *The Hovis magazine*, Christmas, 1949.
> Hovis company flour mill on the Brayford.

1526.   **GWYNNES PUMPS**
100 years of Gwynnes Pumps
London: Gwynnes Pumps, [1951?].   20p.: ill.
(Publication, no.783)

1527.   **SINGLETON, FLINT & CO.**
A Proud record of achievement, 1808–1958
Lincoln: Singleton, Flint, [1958].   [14]p.
Cover title: *150 years of outstanding service to agriculture.*
> History of firm making covers for stacked crops and brushes.

1528.   **HIND, C.J.**
Akroyd Stuart and the oil engines of Lincolnshire: [advance copy of paper to be presented
at a general meeting of the Association to be held at the Institute of Marine Engineers,
Thursday, 21st November, 1963]
[London]: [Diesel Engineers and Users Association], [1963].   6p., [5] leaves of plates.

1529.   **MILLER, R.A.**
A Geography thesis: an examination of the Lincoln brick works during the past 100 years
[1967].   [c.50]p.: ill., maps.
Ms.
> School project which examines geological basis for the industry, the Lincoln Brick Co. and
> concentrates upon Bracebridge and Waddington works.   Illustrations are hand-drawn plans
> and black and white photographs.

1530.
Wm. Wright and Son, Lincoln, Ltd.: builder's handbook, 1969
Cheltenham: Ed. J. Burrow, 1969.   64p.: ill.

1531.
A Century of Lincoln history on wheels
in *Lincolnshire echo*, Wednesday, October 6, 1976.
> History of motor car distributors Gilbert and Son, Ltd.

1532.
Recommended offer by Hill Samuel & Co., Limited on behalf of J.H. Fenner & Co.,
Holdings, Limited for the whole of the share capital of James Dawson & Son, Limited
[Lincoln]: [Directors of James Dawson & Son], [1978].   22p.

1533.
Craftsmen in brick and concrete
pp.20–25 in *Lincolnshire life*, vol.18, no.10, January, 1979.
> Mainly about the work of the building firm of Simons of Lincoln.

1534.   **DAVIES, Anita**
Simons of Lincoln
pp.20–21: ill. in *Lincolnshire life*, vol.26, no.7, October, 1986.

1535.   **ELVIN, Laurence**
Family enterprise: the story of some North Country organ builders
Lincoln: The Author, 1986.   172p.: ill., [24]p. of plates.
Includes index.
ISBN 0950004960
> Nicholson family of Rochdale set up a dynasty of Lincoln organ builders. Coverage of the firm
> of Cousans.   Biographical details of five Lincoln Cathedral organists: Skelton; Young;
> Bennett; Slater; Marshall.

1536.
Butterball, 1937–1987: 50 years in Lincoln
Lincoln: Beatrice Swift, 1987.   37, [5]p.: ill.

Steam Engines

1537.   **CLYMER, Floyd**
Floyd Clymer's album of historical steam traction engines
New York: Bonanza, 1949.   158p.: ill.
> Lincoln firms which feature in the plates include: Clayton & Shuttleworth; Wm. Foster;
> Robey; Ruston-Proctor.

1538.   **GILLFORD, F.W.**
The Traction engine
South Godstone: Oakwood, [1950s/1960s?].   36p.: ill.
(Locomotion papers, 8)

1539.   **CLARK, Ronald H.**
Steam-engine builders of Lincolnshire
Norwich: Goose, 1955.   xvi, 150p.: ill., [2] leaves of plates.
Includes index.
> pp.9–24: Clayton & Shuttleworth; pp.28–36: William Foster & Co.; pp.81–83: Penistan & Co.;
> pp.85–100: Robey & Co.; pp.100–111: Ruston & Hornsby; pp.111–113: B.D. Taplin & Co.

1540.   **KIDNER, R.W.**
The Steam lorry
Lingfield: Oakwood, 1956.   28p.: ill.
(Locomotion papers, 5)
Originally published: 1948.
> Mentions Clayton, Robey and Foster.

1541.   **WRIGHT, Philip A.**
Traction engines
London: A. & C. Black, 1959.   xiv, 89p., 25p. of plates.
Includes index.
> References to Clayton & Shuttleworth, Foster, Robey and Ruston.

1542.   **BEAUMONT, Anthony**
Traction engine prints: fifty rare items, with descriptions
Lingfield: Oakwood, [1960s?].   50p.: ill.
> Illustrations of a variety of heavy machinery, including some produced by Foster and Clayton
> & Shuttleworth.

1543.   **CLARK, Ronald H.**
The Development of the English traction engine
Norwich: Goose, 1960.   xxv, 390p.: ill.
Includes index.
> Many references to Lincoln firms.

1544.   **BEAUMONT, Anthony**
Traction engine pictures
London: Percival Marshall, [1961].   64p.: ill.
> Includes plates of machines produced by: Ruston & Proctor; Ruston & Hornsby; Clayton &
> Shuttleworth; Robey; and Foster.

1545.   ——————
Traction engine pictures
London: Percival Marshall, 1961.   64p.: ill.

1546.   ——————
Traction engines on parade
London: Percival Marshall, 1963.   [5]p., 58p. of plates.

1547.   **CLARK, Ronald H.**
The Development of the English steam wagon
Norwich: Goose, 1963.   xvii, 207, [31]p.: ill.
> p.71: Foster; pp.90–92: Clayton & Shuttleworth; pp.122–125: Robey.

1548.   **PICKLES, W.**
Showman's engines
Lingfield: Oakwood, [c.1962].   24p.: ill.
(Locomotion papers, 27)
> Clayton & Shuttleworth and Robey mentioned.

1549.
Traction engines at work
Lingfield: Oakwood, [c.1965].   [21]p.: ill.
> Includes some Foster's machines.

1550.   **DEITH, C.L.**
Steam on the farm
pp.12–13 in *Vintage steam*, vol.1, May, 1967.
> Mentions Ruston, Robey, Clayton & Shuttleworth and Foster machines at steam gathering, at
> Mawthorpe near Alford.

1551.
Leading dimensions and particulars of the Foster 7 n.h.p. class 'LR' showman's road
locomotive
pp.72–83, 116–118: ill. in *Steaming*, vol.12, no.1, [1968].

1552.   ALEXANDER, Ron
Traction engines in New Zealand
by Ron Alexander and Graham Radcliffe.
Aramolio, N.Z.: Steam Traction Society, 1969.   [46]p.: ill.
> Includes Clayton & Shuttleworth and Robey machines.

1553.   BEAUMONT, Anthony
Traction engines and steam vehicles in pictures
Newton Abbot: David & Charles, 1969.   112p.: ill.
Includes index.
ISBN 0715346660
> Includes Foster, Clayton & Shuttleworth, Robey and Ruston machines.

1554.   FINCH, Barry J.
A Rally of traction engines
London: Ian Allan, 1969.   128p.: ill.
ISBN 0711001227
> Includes pictures of Ruston, Foster and Clayton & Shuttleworth machines.

1555.   TRUE, John B.
The Traction engine register
compiled by John B. True and Brian K. Kinsey; edited by Brian Johnson.
Worthing: Worthing Historic Vehicle Group, 1969.   45p.: ill.
> Engines listed by manufacturer, giving number, date, name, type and location. Includes:
> Clayton & Shuttleworth; Foster; Robey; Ruston Proctor; Ruston; and Ruston Hornsby
> machines.

1556.   BEAUMONT, Anthony
A Gallery of old timers: 51 pictures of steam wagons, traction engines, fairground rides,
ploughing engines, rollers and other old-timers
Hemel Hempstead: Model & Allied, 1970.   [6]p., 50p. of plates.
> Includes: Foster, Ruston, Clayton & Shuttleworth steam engines.

1557.   ENDACOTT, D.L.
A Steam happening: authentic photographic record of engines and wagons in the
West-Country
Falmouth: J.H. Lake, [1970].   44p.: ill.
> Collection of plates, including machines manufactured by Foster, Robey and Ruston.

1558.   HUGHES, W.J.
A Century of traction engines: being an historical account of the rise and decline of an
industry whose benefits to mankind were and are incalculable
Newton Abbot: David & Charles, 1970.   ix, 262p.: ill.
Originally published: 1959.   Includes index.
ISBN 0715342304
> Many references to Clayton & Shuttleworth, with a few to Foster, Ruston and Robey.

1559.   JOY, David
Traction engines in the north
Clapham, via Lancaster: Dalesman, 1970.   96p.: ill.
Includes index.
> Includes: Clayton & Shuttleworth, Foster, Robey and Ruston machines.

1560. FINCH, Barry
Traction engines in review
with text by Jack Hampshire.
London: Ian Allan, 1971.   104p.: ill.
ISBN 0711002347
> Includes pictures of Foster, Robey, Clayton & Shuttleworth and Ruston machines.

1561.   JOHNSTONE, Brian
Steam traction engines, wagons and rollers in colour
London: Blandford, 1971.   180p.: ill.
ISBN 0713705477
> Foster, Clayton & Shuttleworth, Robey and Ruston machines.

1562.   BEAUMONT, Anthony
Traction engines past and present
Newton Abbot: David & Charles, 1974.   96p.: ill.
ISBN 0715363794

1563.   BLOOM, Alan
Your book of traction engines
London: Faber & Faber, 1975.   78p.: ill.
Includes index.
ISBN 0571104134
> Includes: Foster, Robey and Clayton & Shuttleworth machines.

1564.   WHITEHEAD, R.A.
A Century of steam-rolling
London: Ian Allan, 1975.   192p.: ill., [64]p. of plates.
Includes index.
ISBN 071100515X
> pp.73–74: Clayton & Shuttleworth; pp.86–88: Robey; pp.88–89: Ruston-Proctor.

1565.
The Steam engine.   1: Steam in industry and agriculture
Sutherland, Australia: South Pacific Electric Railway, 1976.   [44]p.: ill.
> Mainly photographs, including Clayton, Robey and Ruston machines.

1566.   WILKES, Peter
The Glory of steam
pp.36–38: ill. in *Lincolnshire life*, vol.17, no.9, December, 1977.
> Mentions Clayton & Shuttleworth, Hornsby & Son and Robey, but emphasis on county rather than the city.

1567.   BURKE, Brian
The Australian steam engine listing
compiled by Brian Burke and John Norris; edited by Robert Mills.
Sydney: New South Wales Steam Preservation Co-operative Society, 1978.   32p.: ill.
ISBN 0959585508
> Includes engines by Lincoln firms Clayton & Shuttleworth, Robey, Ruston and Foster.

1568.   BEAUMONT, Anthony
Steam on the road
London: Ian Allan, 1979.   96p.: ill.
ISBN 0711008949

1569.   **FINCH, Barry J.**
Traction engines in colour
London: Ian Allan, 1980.   112p.: ill.
ISBN 0711010323
>   pp.86–89: Ruston and Foster engines.

1570.   **WHITEHEAD, R.A.**
A Kaleideoscope of traction engines
London: Marshall, Harris & Baldwin, 1980.   [48] leaves: ill.
Includes index.
ISBN 0906116201
>   Contains references to Clayton & Shuttleworth, Foster, Robey and Ruston machines.

1571.   **HUTCHINSON, Ian K.**
Traction engine locomotives
Farnham: Road Locomotive Society, 1981.   64p.: ill.
>   pp.37–38: Clayton & Shuttleworth, Ruston and Robey machines.

1572.   **SAWFORD, Eric**
Preserved steam traction
Wellingborough: Patrick Stephens, 1985.   160p.: ill.
Includes index.
>   Contains references to Clayton & Shuttleworth, Foster, Robey and Ruston machines.

1573.   **BROOKS, Richard**
Lincolnshire built engines
by Richard Brooks and Martin Longdon; edited by Lesley Colsell.
Lincoln: Lincolnshire, Recreational Services, Museums, [1986].   40p.: ill.
ISBN 0861111273
>   Clayton & Shuttleworth, Wm. Foster and Ruston.

1574.   **CRAWLEY, John**
Steam rollers in focus
Turvey: John Crawley, 1986.   128p.: ill.
ISBN 0950854649
>   Contains pictures of Robey, Foster, Clayton & Shuttleworth and Ruston machines.

Tanks

1575.   **WILLIAMS-ELLIS, Clough**
The Tank Corps
by Clough Williams-Ellis and A. Williams-Ellis.
London: Country Life, 1919.   288p., map, [25] leaves of plates.

1576.   **ROYAL COMMISSION ON AWARDS TO INVENTORS**
*Minutes of proceedings before the Royal Commission on Awards to Inventors at
Lincoln's Inn Hall...on Tuesday, 7th October, 1919: claims in respect of tank inventions*
London: The Commission, 1919.   178p.

1577.   **STERN, Albert G.**
Tanks, 1914–1918: the log-book of a pioneer
London: Hodder and Stoughton, 1919.   xi, 297p.: ill., [45]p. of plates.
>   Mentions Foster & Co. and Tritton.

1578.   BROWNE, D.G.
The Tank in action
Edinburgh: William Blackwood, 1920.   517p., 15p. of plates.
Includes index.

1579.   FULLER, J.F.C.
Tanks in the Great War, 1914–1918
London: John Murray, 1920.   xxiv, 331p.: ill., [8]p. of plates.
Includes index.

1580.   TRITTON, William
A Short history of the tanks designed by Sir William Tritton and Major Wilson
[1920?].   7 leaves.
Typescript.

1581.   FOSTER, William, & CO.
The Tank: its birth and development
Lincoln: William Foster, [1920].   90p.: ill., [frontis].
>   Brief history of the firm, the development of the tank and some information about the firm's
>   products during peacetime.

1582.   SWINTON, Ernest D.
*Eyewitness: being personal reminiscences of certain phases of the Great War, including
the genesis of the tank*
London: Hodder & Stoughton, 1932.   321p., [8] leaves of plates.
>   Concentrates upon creation of the tank, but little at actual design level. Passing references to
>   Foster & Co. and Tritton, but mainly centres on debate at the War Office and Swinton's claim
>   that he was the 'originator'.

1583.   SUETER, Murray
The Evolution of the tank: a record of Royal Naval Air Service caterpillar experiments
London: Hutchinson, 1937.   352p., [10]p. of plates.
Includes index.
>   Much space devoted to discussion of the true origins of the idea and author's complaint that he
>   did not get the recognition he deserved.   However, many references to Foster & Co. and, in
>   particular, to Sir William Tritton.

1584.   HALSTEAD, Ivor
The Truth about our tanks
[London?]: Lindsay Drummond, [1942].   222p., maps, [16]p. of plates.
>   Opening chapter about inception assesses Tritton's contribution and mentions Foster & Co.,
>   but majority of book is account of the tanks' performance in action.

1585.   MURLAND, J.R.W.
The Royal Armoured Corps
London: Methuen, 1943.   106p.: ill., [8]p. of plates.
>   Covers invention of the tank and the contribution of Tritton.

1586.
*An Illustrated record of the development of the British armoured vehicle: tanks,
1915–1918, the First World War*
Bovington: Royal Armoured Corps Tanks Museum, [after 1956].   29p.: ill.

1587.   **FOLEY, John**
The Boilerplate war
London: Frederick Muller, 1963.   195p., [10]p. of plates.
Includes index.
(Star book)
ISBN 0352308842
>   Anecdotal history of the tank for the general reader rather than 'tank men'.   Contains opening
>   references to Foster & Co. and Sir William Tritton.

1588.   **ROGERS, H.C.B**
Tanks in battle
London: Seeley, Service, 1965.   240p., maps, [33] leaves of plates.
(Imperial Services library, vol.VIII)
Includes index.
>   Includes references to William Foster & Co.; pp.39–41, 63–67: references to Sir William
>   Tritton.   Plates include the 'Whippet' designed by Tritton.

1589.   **EBBRELL, John**
'The Devil is coming': fifty years ago the first fighting tanks thundered into action at the
Battle of the Somme: John Fletcher tells how the iron machines transformed the face of
warfare
pp.13–16: ill. in *Data journal*, October, 1966.

1590.   **COOPER, Bryan**
The Ironclads of Cambrai
London: Pan, 1967.   224p., maps, [4]p. of plates.
(British battle series)
Includes index.
ISBN 0330025791
>   The birth of the tank and Tritton's part mentioned.

1591.   **CHAMBERLAIN, Peter**
Tanks of World War I: British and German
by Peter Chamberlain and Chris Ellis.
London: Arms and Armour, 1969.   80p.: ill.
(Illustrated studies in twentieth century arms)
Includes bibliography.
>   Mentions Tritton and William Foster & Co.   Plates include: No.1 Lincoln Machine; Little
>   Willie; and Mother.

1592.   **CHADWICK, Kenneth**
The Royal Tank Regiment
edited by General Sir Brian Horrocks.
London: Leo Cooper, 1970.   157p.
ISBN 0850520207

1593.   **MACKSEY, Kenneth**
Tank: a history of the armoured fighting vehicle
by Kenneth Macksey and John H. Batchelor.
London: Macdonald, 1970.   160p.: ill.
Includes index.
>   Historical, technical and military aspects.   Contains references to Sir William Tritton, but no
>   great detail.

1594.
Purnell's history of the World Wars special: the tank story
edited by Andrew Kershaw
London: Phoebus, 1972.   [1650]p.: ill.
   pp.1638–1643: ill.: 'The tank story', by Kenneth Macksey.

1595.
The Tank story
edited by Andrew Kershaw.
London: Phoebus, 1973.   64p.: ill.
   Contains references to Tritton, Foster & Co. and Little Willie.

1596.   **FLETCHER, David**
British tanks of the Great War.   Part 1: Foster, Daimler and Holt
by David Fletcher and Dick Harley.
pp.2–9: ill. in *Tankette*, vol.15, no.1, 1978.

1597.   ——————
British tanks of the Great War.   Part 2: Tritton trench crossers
by David Fletcher and Dick Harley.
pp.8–[9]: ill. in *Tankette*, vol.15, no.2, 1978.

1598.   ——————
British tanks of the Great War.   Part 3: Big wheel machines
by David Fletcher & Dick Harley.
pp.7–11: ill. in *Tankette*, vol.15, no.3, 1978.
   Contains references to Foster & Co.

1599.   **FISK, Roy**
Abe and the tanks: [short story]
pp.32–33: ill. in *Lincolnshire life*, vol.20, no.11, February, 1981.

1600.   **KIRCHOFF, Mark**
Origins of the tank
20 leaves: ill.
Special history course project – University of Minnesota, 1981.
   Covers contribution of Foster & Co. and William Tritton.

1601.
Water carrier for Mesopotamia
p.39: ill. in *Lincolnshire life*, vol.20, no.12, March, 1981.
   About development of the tank, with coverage of Fosters and Sir William Tritton.   Article
   draws attention to BBC TV programme entitled 'Arrival of the water carrier for Mesopotamia'.

1602.   **FLETCHER, David**
Landships: British tanks in the First World War
London: HMSO, 1984.   60p.: ill.
Includes index.
ISBN 0112904092
   Contains references to Tritton.

1603.
'Flirt' home to a heroine's welcome
ill. in *Soldier*, 23rd April, 1984.
   Refers to 1917 British Mark IV 'Flirt' tank restored in Lincoln.

1604.   **HOOLEY, Ray**
The Story of 'Flirt', a Mk.IV fighting tank of the 6 Tank Battalion
[1985].   [15] leaves.
Typescript.
> Includes reminiscences of people involved with the tank.

1605.   **BARRINGTON, P.K.**
Lincoln's pride
pp.126–127: ill. in *Tank*, [December, 1985?].
> About Flirt 2.

1606.   **DRYDEN, R.E.**
The Lincoln Tank Group
pp.50–51: ill. in *Stand to!: the journal of the Western Front Association*, no.14, summer, 1985.

1607.   **HOOLEY, Ray**
From the Hornsby-Akroyd oil engine evolved the chain tractor...the acknowledged forerunner to the tank: Ray Hooley tells how the engine came into being and he acquired a WW1 tank for a small Lincoln museum
pp.4–6: ill. in *Stationary engine*, February, 1985.

1608.   **BARTHOLOMEW, E.**
First World War tanks
Princes Risborough: Shire, 1986.   32p.: ill.
(Shire album, 172)
Includes bibliography.
> Fosters and Tritton mentioned.

1609.   **SMITHERS, A.J.**
A New Excalibur: the development of the tank, 1909–1939
London: Leo Cooper in association with Secker & Warburg, 1986.   262p.: ill.
Includes evaluative bibliography and index.
> Copiously illustrated with detailed and balanced account in the text.   References are mainly to Tritton personally, but some to Foster & Co.

1610.   **WILSON, A. Gordon**
Walter Wilson: a portrait of an inventor
edited by Rodney Dale.
London: Duckworth, 1986.   173p.
ISBN 0715621270
> Mentions Tritton and the tank.

1611.   **TURNER, John T.**
'Nellie': the history of Churchill's Lincoln-built trenching machine
Lincoln: Society for Lincolnshire History and Archaeology, 1988.   82p.: ill.
(Occasional papers in Lincolnshire history and archaeology)

Road Vehicles

1612.
Lincoln Elk motorcycles for 1920
Lincoln: J. Kirby, [1920].   [10]p.: ill.

1613. **BROWN, Roger G.**
The Car makers of Lincolnshire
pp.20–26: ill. in *Lincolnshire life*, vol.19, no.3, June, 1979.
Concerns Lincoln firms of R.M. Wright and Ruston-Hornsby.

1614. ——————
The Story of the Lincoln Elk motorcycle
pp.20–22: ill. in *Lincolnshire life*, vol.25, no.12, March, 1986.
Manufactured by James Kirby.

Aircraft

1615. **WALLS, John**
The Lincoln aircraft industry. Part one
pp.36–41: ill. in *Lincolnshire life*, vol.12, no.2, April, 1972.
Includes: Ruston; Robey; Clayton & Shuttleworth.

1616. ——————
The Lincolnshire aviation industry. Part II
pp.32–36: ill. in *Lincolnshire life*, vol.14, no.12, February, 1975.
Deals with post-World War I period.

Other Industrial Products

1617. **LIVENS, F.H.**
Some Lincolnshire oil-engines
pp.673–707: ill., [1]p. of plates in *Excerpt minutes of proceedings of the meetings of the Institution of Mechanical Engineers in Lincoln*, 1920.

1618. **TRITTON, William**
The Origin of the thrashing machine
Lincoln: William Foster, [c.1920]. 16p.: ill.
(Publication, 735)
Originally published: in *The Lincolnshire magazine*.
Mentions Ruston, Clayton and Foster.

1619. **ARMITAGE, C.V.**
Lincolnshire industries: the pump maker
pp.305–311: ill. in *The Lincolnshire magazine*, vol.1, 1932–34.
References to Lincoln-based firms.

1620. **HIND, C.J.**
Akroyd Stuart and the oil engines of Lincolnshire
London: Diesel Engineers and Users Association, 1964. x, 21, xviip.: ill.
Includes: Hornsby-Akroyd; Robey; Clayton-Babcock; Ruston Proctor; Ruston & Hornsby.

1621. **BONNETT, Harold**
Saga of the steam plough
Newton Abbot: David & Charles, 1972. 208p., [18]p. of plates.
Originally published: 1965.
ISBN 0715357425
Includes references to Clayton & Shuttleworth, Robey and Ruston.

EMPLOYMENT AND CAREERS

1622.   **CAMERON, Alice**
An Unemployment centre
London: Archbishop of York's Committee on Unemployment, [1934].   16p.
(Challenge to Christians)
    Based on experience with the People's Service Club at Lincoln.

1623.   **LINCOLN, Juvenile Advisory Committee**
Annual report, 1934
[1934].   11p.
Typescript.
    Contains assessment of employment prospects in various sectors: engineering, agriculture, etc.,
and also concerned with further education.

1624.   **LINCOLN YOUTH EMPLOYMENT SERVICE**
City of Lincoln careers guide
Worcester: Worcester Press, [1965?].   59p.: ill.

POLITICS

1625.
Triumph of liberal principles: a report of the speeches delivered at the public dinner at the City Arms Hotel, Lincoln, on Friday, October 17, 1834, on the occasion of presenting to Sir William Amcotts Ingilby, Bt., M.P., two splendid jugs as a tribute of affectionate regard from the people of Lincolnshire for his patriotic service as their representative....
Stamford: printed John Drakard, [1834].   24p.

1626.   **LUCY, Henry W.**
A Diary of two Parliaments
London: Cassell, 1886.   2 vols.
   Vol.1, p.193: account of Seely's annual speech; p.281: Seely as new Member.

1627.   **MADDISON, A.R.**
Lincolnshire and Lincoln M.P.s
pp.195–197 in *LN&Q*, vol.4, no.31, 1895.

1628.
[Article about Charles Roberts as Liberal candidate for Lincoln in general election]
p.107 in *Lincolnshire poacher*, vol.1, no.5, September, 1900.

1629.
[Article about Seely as Unionist candidate for Lincoln in general election]
p.106: ill. in *Lincolnshire poacher*, vol.1, no.5, September, 1900.

1630.   **McKISACK, May**
The Parliamentary representation of the English boroughs during the Middle Ages
London: Oxford University Press, 1932.   xii, 180p.
(Oxford historical series)
Includes index of persons and places.
   Brief references to Lincoln passim.

1631.
Lincoln city elections, 1322 and 15th century: [extracts from P.R.O. material contributed by J. Bean King]
p.75 in *LN&Q*, vol.23, no.4, 1935.

1632.   **WELBY, Alfred C.E.**
Lincoln city poll, 1547
p.31 in *LN&Q*, vol.24, no.2, 1936.

1633.
Lincoln for the people
Lincoln: Lincoln Communist Party, 1945.   23p.

1634.   **NEALE, J.E.**
Elizabeth I and her Parliaments, 1559–1581
London: Jonathan Cape, 1953.   2 vols.
Includes index.
>   Vol.2: many references to Robert Monson.

1635.   **ASKHAM, Francis**
The Gay Delavals
London: Jonathan Cape, 1955.   256p.: ill., [8]p. of plates.
>   pp.199–200: Lincoln election of 1790 which cost Fenton Cawthorne £2,500 to win.

1636.   **NEALE, J.E.**
The Elizabethan House of Commons
Revised ed.
Harmondsworth: Penguin, 1963.   444p., 4p. of plates.
Originally published: 1949.
>   pp.48, 96: Lincoln city elections.

1637.   **NAMIER, Lewis Bernstein**
The House of Commons, 1754–1790
Lewis Namier and John Brooke.
London: published for the History of Parliament Trust by HMSO, 1964.   3 vols.
(History of Parliament)
>   Vol.1: introductory survey; pp.327–328: Lincoln;   Vol.2, p.209: John Chaplin; p.216: Thomas Clarges; p.418: Fenton Cawthorne;   Vol.3, p.62: George Augusta Lumley Saunderson; p.63: Richard Lumley Savile; p.151: George Monson; pp.438–439: Coningsby and Humphrey Sibthorp; pp.417–418: Thomas Scrope; pp.589–590: Robert Vyner.

1638.   **PELLING, Henry**
Social geography of British elections, 1885–1910
>   pp.204–228: East Midlands region; pp.212–213: Lincoln city.   Includes references to Joseph Ruston and the firm of Ruston.

1639.   **SEDGWICK, Romney**
The House of Commons, 1715–1754
London: published for the History of Parliament Trust by HMSO, 1970.   2 vols.
(History of Parliament)
>   General information on Lincoln with biographical entries for M.P.s: John Tyrwhitt; John de la Fountain Tyrwhitt; Charles Monson; John Monson; Charles Hall; Coningsby Sibthorp; Richard Grantham.

1640.   **OLNEY, R.J.**
Lincolnshire politics, 1832–1885
Oxford: Oxford University Press, 1973.   xii, 284p., maps.
Includes index.
>   Ph.D. thesis with same title submitted to University of Oxford, 1970.

1641.   **PRICE, Christopher**
Spotlight on local politics: the Squire of Lincoln
p.174 in *New statesman*, vol.86, no.2212, 10 August, 1973.
>   Covers Dick Taverne, identity of the Labour party and the problems of Lincoln: Roman remains versus industry.

1642.   **TAVERNE, Dick**
My day
p.31: ill. in *Vogue*, March 1st, 1973.

1643.   **HASLER, P.W.**
The House of Commons, 1558–1603
London: published for the History of Parliament Trust by HMSO, 1981.   3 vols.
(History of Parliament)

> General information on Lincoln and biographical entries for M.P.s: George Anton; Francis Bullingham; Robert Farrar; John Joye (Joyce); Thomas Fairfax; Peter Eure (Evers); Charles Dymoke; Thomas Grantham II; Anthony Thorold; Robert Monson; Thomas Wilson; John Wecome; Stephen Thymbleby; John Savile II.

1644.   **BINDOFF, S.T.**
The House of Commons, 1509–1559
London: published for the History of Parliament Trust by Secker & Warburg, 1982.   3 vols.
(History of Parliament)

> General information about Lincoln and biographical entries for M.P.s: William and Robert Alanson; Richard Clerke; John Halton; Thomas Grantham; Vincent Grantham; Robert Dighton; Anthony Missenden; Robert Farrar (Ferrers); Francis Kempe; Thomas Moigne; George St.Pole; William Yates; William Rotherham.

1645.   **CARLISLE, Kenneth**
Kenneth Carlisle, M.P.: mid-term report, 1982
Lincoln: The Author, 1982.   [4]p.: ill.

1646.   **HENNING, Basil Duke**
The House of Commons, 1660–1690
Lincoln: published for the History of Parliament Trust by Secker & Warburg, 1983.   3 vols.
(History of Parliament)

> General information on Lincoln and biographical entries for M.P.s: Robert Bolles; Edward Hussey; Thomas Hussey; John Monson; Henry Monson; Thomas Meres; Christopher Nevile.

1647.   **THORNE, R.G.**
The House of Commons, 1790–1820
London: published for the History of Parliament Trust by Secker & Warburg, 1986.   5 vols.
(History of Parliament)

> General information about Lincoln and biographical entries for M.P.s: John Fenton Cawthorne; Richard Ellison; John Nicholas Fazakerley; Ralph Bernal; Robert Hobart; William Monson; George Rawdon; Humphrey Sibthorp; Coningsby Waldo Sibthorp; John Savile (2nd Earl of Mexborough); Henry Sullivan.   The completion of the continuous coverage of the period 1386–1832 to be provided by the History of Parliament series is expected within the next 15 years.

1648.   **DENT, Sally**
The Political geography of Lincoln in 1841
71 leaves: ill.
Thesis [B.A.] – University of Liverpool, 1986.

POLLBOOKS

1649.
An Alphabetical list of the free-men who voted at the election holden at Lincoln, on Thursday and Friday, the 26th and 27th of March, 1761, for the two representatives in Parliament for the city of Lincoln
Lincoln: printed and sold by W. Wood, [1761].   30p.

1650.
A Correct alphabetical list...Saturday, 19th of March, 1768...
Lincoln: printed and sold by W. Wood, [1768].   30p.

1651.
An Alphabetical list...on Wednesday, the 12th of October, 1774...
Lincoln: printed and sold W. Wood, [1774].   31p.

1652.
An Alphabetical list of the free-men who voted at the election holden at Lincoln, on Wednesday, the 12th of October, 1774, for the two representatives in Parliament for the city of Lincoln
Lincoln: printed and sold by W. Wood, [1774].   31p.

1653.
A Correct alphabetical list of the freemen who voted at the election holden at Lincoln, on Wednesday, the 13th of September, 1780, for the two representatives in Parliament for the city of Lincoln
Lincoln: printed W. Wood, [1780].   30p.

1654.
An Alphabetical list...Wednesday, the thirteenth of September, 1780, for the two representatives in Parliament for the said city
Lincoln: printed and sold by Mary Rose, [1780].   27p.

1655.
An Alphabetical list of the freemen who voted at the election holden at the Guildhall of the city of Lincoln, on Saturday, the nineteenth of June, 1790, for the two representatives in Parliament for the said city
Lincoln: printed & sold J. W. Drury, [1790].   32p.

1656.
An Alphabetical list...on Saturday, the nineteenth of June, 1790, for...
2nd ed., corrected.
Lincoln: printed and sold by J.W. Drury, [1790].   40p.

1657.
An Alphabetical list of the freemen who voted at the election holden at the Guildhall of the city of Lincoln, on Saturday, the first of November...1806...for two representatives for the said city
Lincoln: J.W. Drury, [1806].   34p.

1658.
An Alphabetical list of the freemen who voted at the election holden at the Guildhall of the city of Lincoln, on Saturday, the first of November in the year of our Lord, 1806...for two representatives in Parliament for the said city
Lincoln: printed J.W. Drury, [1806].   32p.

175

1659.
An Alphabetical list of the freemen who voted at the election of two representatives in Parliament for the city of Lincoln, June 17, 1818
Lincoln: Drury, 1818. 36p.

1660.
The Poll for two Members of Parliament...on Wednesday and Thursday, March 8th and 9th, 1820, from the book of the returning officers, arranged in alphabetical order: with the addresses, bills, &c...
Lincoln: printed for Drury, 1820. 47p.

1661.
The Poll for two Members of Parliament to represent the city of Lincoln: taken on Thursday and Friday, the eighth and ninth days of June, 1826...with all the speeches, addresses, papers, &c.
Lincoln: printed and sold by Drury, 1826. 98p.

1662.
The Poll for two Members of Parliament...on Thursday and Friday, the eighth and ninth days of June, 1826...
Lincoln: Drury, 1826. 86p.

1663.
The Poll for two Members of Parliament...on Monday and Tuesday, the tenth and eleventh days of December, 1832...containing the complete register of persons entitled to vote
Lincoln: E.B. Drury, 1833. 74p.

1664.
The Poll for two Members of Parliament...on Tuesday and Wednesday, the 6th and 7th of January, 1835
[Lincoln]: [Keyworth], 1835. 24p.

1665.
The Poll for two Members of Parliament to represent the city of Lincoln, taken on Monday, 24th July, 1837
Lincoln: printed and sold E.B. Drury, 1837. 87p.

1666.
Lincoln city election, July 24, 1837
Lincoln: E.B. Drury, 1837. 87p.

1667.
The Poll books for Members in Parliament to represent the city of Lincoln, July, 1837
Lincoln: printed T.J.N. Brogden, [1837]. 28p.

1668.
The Free and independent electors who recorded their votes in favour of William R. Collett, Esq., M.P., on Tuesday, June 29, 1841, when he was returned to Parliament as representative of the city of Lincoln
London: printed John Oliver, [1841]. 22p.

1669.
A List of the freemen and electors of the city of Lincoln, alphabetically arranged, taken from the books of the returning officer, July 29th, 1841
Lincoln: Charles Brogden, 1841. 30p.

1670.
*A Correct list of the poll, as taken on Tuesday, the 29th day of June, 1841, for two
Members to serve in Parliament for the city of Lincoln*
Lincoln: printed and sold by J. Stainton, 1841.   27p.

1671.
Poll book: 1841: a list of the freemen and electors of the city of Lincoln...July 29th, 1841
Lincoln: Charles Brogden, 1841.   30p.

1672.
*A Correct list of the poll, as taken on Thursday, the 29th day of July, 1847, for two
Members to serve in Parliament, for the city of Lincoln: also the addresses, squibs, &c.,
issued during the contest*
Lincoln: printed and sold by J. Stainton, [1847].   32, xxip.

1673.
*List of freemen and electors, as they voted in the different stations and booths, for two
Members of Parliament to represent the city of Lincoln...on Thursday, 29th July, 1847*
Lincoln: printed by J.W. Drury, 1847.   36p.

1674.
*A Correct list of the poll, as taken on Thursday, the 29th day of July, 1847, for two
Members to serve in Parliament...also the addresses, squibs, &c., issued during the
contest*
Lincoln: printed and sold by J. Stainton, [1847].   32, xxp.

1675.
*Lincoln city election: the poll book for a Member in Parliament to represent the city of
Lincoln, March, 1848*
Lincoln: printed Robert Bulman, 1848.   52p.

1676.
*Lincoln city election: the poll book for two Members in Parliament to represent the city
of Lincoln, July, MDCCCLII*
Lincoln: Charles Akrill, 1852.   24, [33]p.

1677.
*Lincoln city election: the poll book for two Members in Parliament to represent the city
of Lincoln, March, MDCCLVII*
Lincoln: C. Akrill, 1857.   57p.

1678.
Lincoln city election: the poll-book for two Members in Parliament...March, 1857
Lincoln: C. Akrill, 1857.   57p.

1679.
*The Poll book for a Member in Parliament to represent the city of Lincoln, February,
1862*
Lincoln: printed Edward R. Cousans, 1859.   58p.

1680.
Lincoln city election: the poll book...April, 1859
Lincoln: Chas. Akrill, 1859.   57p.

1681.
Lincoln city election: the poll book for a Member in Parliament to represent the city of Lincoln, February, 1862
Lincoln: C. Akrill, 1862.   49p.

1682.
The Poll book for two Members in Parliament to represent the city of Lincoln
Lincoln: Chas. Akrill, 1865.   60p.
Also published in an issue of 61p.

1683.
Register of electors: [1908/09–   ]
[Lincoln]: [Lincoln Corporation], [1908–   ].   Various pagings.

INDIVIDUAL ELECTIONS

1684.
[A List of the names of] persons who fail'd in their promise to vote for Robert [Cracroft], Esq., at the late election for the city of Lincoln, which at [once will] shew the just expectation he had of being chose by a great [majority]
[Lincoln]: [s.n.], [1754].   1 sheet.
   Missing words supplied in ink.

1685.
To the worthy freemen of Lincoln: [letter]
[Lincoln]: [Friends of Mr Scrope], [1761].   7p.
   Includes letter from Coningsby Sibthorp, with satiric annotations.

1686.   **SIBTHORP, Mr**
[Letter concerning election, October 6, 1774]
[Lincoln]: [s.n.], [1774].   1 sheet.

1687.   **LUMLEY, Lord**
[Open letter concerning election, September 12, 1780]
[Lincoln]: [s.n.], [1780].   1 sheet.

1688.
[Election communication about Mr Savile, March 26, 1784]
[Lincoln]: [s.n.], [1784].   1 sheet.

1689.   **VYNER, Robert**
[Letter, March 31, 1784]
Lincoln: printed Rose and Drury, 1784.   1 sheet.

1690.   —————————
[Letter, April 2, 1784]
Lincoln: printed Rose and Drury, 1784.   1 sheet.

1691.
[Election communication, April 14, 1784]
Lincoln: printed Rose and Drury, 1784.   1 sheet.

1692.
[Election communication, April 18, 1784]
[Lincoln]: [s.n.], [1784].   1 sheet.

1693.   **RAWDON, George**
[Letter, April 10th, 1790]
[Lincoln]: [s.n.], [1790].   1 sheet.

1694.   _____
[Notice about payment for voters, 24th June, 1790]
[Lincoln]: [s.n.], [1790].   1 sheet.

1695.   _____
[Letter, June 26th, 1790]
[Lincoln]: [s.n.], [1790].   1 sheet.

1696.
Rawdon and liberty for ever: [song to tune of the Warwickshire lad]
Lincoln: printed Brooke, [1790?].   1 sheet.

1697.
*An Address to the inhabitants of Lincoln by John Candlebags, alias John Boilmilk, alias
J.S___h*: [poem]
[Lincoln]: [s.n.], [1794].   1 sheet.

1698.   **ELLISON, Richard**
[Letter, 14th May, 1796]
[Lincoln]: [s.n.], [1796].   1 sheet.

1699.   **RAWDON, George**
[Letter, 14th May, 1796]
[Lincoln]: [s.n.], [1796].   1 sheet.

1700.   **ELLISON, Richard**
[Letter, May 21st, 1796]
[Lincoln]: [s.n.], [1796].   1 sheet.

1701.   _____
[Letter, May 21st, 1796]
[Lincoln]: [s.n.], [1796].   1 sheet.
    Not duplicate of the above.

1702.   **RAWDON, George**
[Letter, May 27th, 1796]
[Lincoln]: [s.n.], [1796].   1 sheet.

1703.   **ELLISON, Richard**
[Letter, May 28, 1796]
Sudbrooke Holme: [The Author], [1796].   1 sheet.

1704.
*Jim Crow exhibition: a grand masquerade will take place at the City Arms Hotel,
sometime next week, which will be attended by various choice political jumpers*: [squib]
[Lincoln]: [s.n.], [18??].   1 sheet.

1705.
[Squib about loss of various birds]
[Lincoln]: [s.n.], [18??].   1 sheet.

1706.
Colonel Sibthorp: [article from the *Boston herald*, Tuesday, May 28]
Boston: printed William Henry Adams, [18??].   1 sheet.

1707.
[Letter signed 'One of the popular side']
Lincoln: printed E.B. Drury, [18??].   1 sheet.

1708.
[Letter signed 'An Englishman', in support of Sibthorp and Ellis]
Lincoln: printed T.O. Brumby, [18??].   1 sheet.

1709.
Great novelty! : [squib in form of poster advertising grand menagerie]
Boston: printed C.F. Barber, [18??].   1 sheet.

1710.
Christian electors of the city of Lincoln: address, no.1
[Lincoln]: [s.n.], [18??].   1 sheet.

1711.
Greater than the 'great' (Blue) 'novelty'!!! : [squib in form of poster for auction of various animals]
Lincoln: printed T.O. Brumby, [18??].   1 sheet.

1712.
[Squib in form of series of riddles]
[Lincoln]: [s.n.], [18??].   1 sheet.

1713.
Grand novelty: [spoof in form of advertisement for exhibition of various animals]
Lincoln: printed T.J.N. Brogden, [18??].   1 sheet.

1714.
[Letter signed 'A brother elector', with excerpt from *A Midsummer night's dream*, featuring Bulwer as Bottom]
Lincoln: printed T.J.N. Brogden, [18??].   1 sheet.

1715.
[Letter signed 'A freeman and an elector']
[Lincoln]: [s.n.], [18??].   1 sheet.
     Against Liberals and Municipal Corporation Reform Bill.

1716.   **WILKINSON, John S.**
[Letter denying that Rudgard insulted Heneage]
John S. Wilkinson, R. Hunt, M. Penistan, D. Mortimer.
[Lincoln]: [s.n.], [18??].   1 sheet.
     Originally published: in *Lincolnshire times*, March 24.

1717.
A Chapter of accidents: [political spoof in form of chapter from Bible]
Lincoln: printed S. Thorpe, [18??].   1 sheet.
     Concerns Viscount Melbourne.

1718.   **SIBTHORP, Humphrey**
[Letter, April 9th, 1800]
Lincoln: printed John Smith, 1800.   1 sheet.

1719. —————
[Letter, April 12, 1800]
[Lincoln]: [s.n.], [1800]. 1 sheet.

1720. —————
[Letter, June 21, 1802]
Lincoln: printed J.W. Drury, 1802. 1 sheet.

1721. **ELLISON, Richard**
[Letter, 21st June, 1802]
Lincoln: printed J.W. Drury, 1802. 1 sheet.

1722. —————
[Letter, June 30th, 1802]
Lincoln: printed J.W. Drury, 1802. 1 sheet.

1723. **SIBTHORP, Humphrey**
[Letter, June 30, 1802]
Lincoln: printed Smith, 1802. 1 sheet.

1724. **ELLISON, Richard**
[Letter, 7th July, 1802]
Lincoln: printed J.W. Drury, 1802. 1 sheet.

1725. **SIBTHORP, H.W.**
[Letter, October 18, 1806]
Lincoln: printed J.W. Drury, 1806. 1 sheet.

1726.
[Election announcement, October 20, 1806]
Lincoln: printed J.W. Drury, 1806. 1 sheet.

1727. **ELLISON, Richard**
[Letter, October 20, 1806]
Lincoln: printed J.W. Drury, 1806. 1 sheet.

1728.
[Letter signed 'An independent freeman', October 21, 1806]
Lincoln: printed Smith, 1806. 1 sheet.

1729. **MONSON, W.**
[Letter, October 23, 1806]
Lincoln: printed J.W. Drury, 1806. 1 sheet.

1730. **SULLIVAN, John**
[Letter, October 24th, 1806]
Lincoln: printed J.W. Drury, 1806. 1 sheet.

1731.
Monson: [poem, October 25th, 1806]
Lincoln: printed Smith, 1806. 1 sheet.

1732. **MONSON, W.**
[Letter, October 25, 1806]
Lincoln: printed Smith, 1806. 1 sheet.

1733.   **SULLIVAN, John**
[Letter, October 26th, 1806]
Lincoln: printed J.W. Drury, 1806.   1 sheet.

1734.   **MONSON W.**
[Letter, Tuesday, October 28, 1806]
Lincoln: printed Smith, 1806.   1 sheet.

1735.   —————————
[Letter, October 29, 1806]
Lincoln: printed Smith, 1806.   1 sheet.

1736.
Facts: [poem about Colonel Monson, October 31, 1806]
Lincoln: printed Brooke, 1806.   1 sheet.

1737.   **MONSON, W.**
[Summons to meeting, October 31, 1806]
Lincoln: printed Smith, 1806.   1 sheet.

1738.   **ELLISON, Richard**
[Letter, November 1, 1806]
Lincoln: printed Smith, 1806.   1 sheet.

1739.   **MONSON, W.**
[Letter, November 1, 1806]
Lincoln: printed Smith, 1806.   1 sheet.

1740.   —————————
[Letter, April 30, 1807]
Lincoln: printed Smith, 1807.   1 sheet.

1741.   —————————
[Letter, May 5, 1807]
Lincoln: printed J.W. Drury, 1807.   1 sheet.

1742.
[Notice about subscriptions for support of Richard Ellison, May 15, 1807]
Lincoln: printed J.W. Drury, 1807.   1 sheet.

1743.   **ELLISON, Richard**
[Letter about election for representation of county, May 16, 1807]
Lincoln: printed J.W. Drury, 1807.   1 sheet.

1744.   **ATKINSON, Michael**
[Letter, December 18, 1807]
Lincoln: printed Smith, 1807.   1 sheet.

1745.   **MEXBOROUGH, Lord**
[Letter, December 22, 1807]
Lincoln: printed Smith, 1807.   1 sheet.

1746.
Queries & answers: [squib against Earl of Mexborough]
Lincoln: printed A. Stark, [1807?].   1 sheet.

1747.
Lincoln election: [minutes of meeting, January 2nd, 1808]
Lincoln: printed A. Stark, 1808.   1 sheet.

1748.
Lincoln election: [pro Harcourt, January 2, 1808]
Lincoln: printed A. Stark, 1808.   1 sheet.

1749.   **HARCOURT, G.W.R.**
[Letter, January 2nd, 1808]
London: printed G. Spilsbury, 1808.   1 sheet.

1750.   ——————
[Letter, January 3, 1808]
Lincoln: printed J.W. Drury, 1808.   1 sheet.

1751.   ——————
[Letter, January 3, 1808]
Lincoln: printed A. Stark, 1808.   1 sheet.

1752.   ——————
[Letter, January 5th, 1808]
Lincoln: printed J.W. Drury, 1808.   1 sheet.

1753.   ——————
[Letter, January 10th, 1808]
Lincoln: printed W. Brooke, 1808.   1 sheet.

1754.
[Letters from Mexborough to independent electors of city of Lincoln and from Col.
Harcourt to the Earl of Mexborough, January, 1808]
Lincoln: printed W. Brooke, 1808.   1 sheet.

1755.
The Cause of virtue: [pro Harcourt song]
Lincoln: printed W. Brooke, [1808].   1 sheet.

1756.
*To the worthy and independent freemen of the city of Lincoln: a fair and impartial
comparison between the present candidates, the Earl of Mexborough and Colonel
Harcourt*: [letter]
Lincoln: printed J.W. Drury, [1808].   1 sheet.

1757.
[Pro Harcourt song to the tune of Hearts of oak]
Lincoln: printed A. Stark, [1808].   1 sheet.

1758.   **ELLISON, Richard**
[Election notice, September 30th, 1812]
Lincoln: printed Drury, 1812.   1 sheet.

1759.   **FAZAKERLEY, J.N.**
[Letter, September 30, 1812]
Lincoln: printed Brooke, 1812.   1 sheet.

1760.   ——————
[Letter, October 1, 1812]
Lincoln: printed W. Brooke, 1812.   1 sheet.

1761.   **ELLISON, Richard**
[Letter, October 2nd, 1812]
Lincoln: Drury, 1812.   1 sheet.

1762. **SULLIVAN, John**
[Letter suggesting that his nephew Sir Henry Sullivan should stand, October 2, 1812]
Lincoln: printed J. Wilkinson, 1812.   1 sheet.

1763.
[Letter about delay in delivery of writ for the city of Lincoln and Fazakerley's promise to investigate should he be elected, 3rd October, 1812]
Lincoln: printed Drury, 1812.   1 sheet.

1764.
[Statements by Col. Ellison's committee following his resignation, October 5, 1812]
[Lincoln]: [s.n.], [1812].   1 sheet.

1765. **MEXBOROUGH, Lord**
[Letter, October 5, 1812]
Lincoln: printed W. Brooke, 1812.   1 sheet.

1766. **FAZAKERLEY, J.W.**
[Letter, October 9, 1812]
Lincoln: printed W. Brooke, 1812.   1 sheet.

1767. **ELLIS, Henry**
[Letter, October, 1812]
Lincoln: printed Drury, 1812.   1 sheet.

1768.
Lincoln election: [May 18, 1814]
Lincoln: printed Drury, 1814.   1 sheet.

1769. **ELLISON, Richard**
[Letter, May 18th, 1814]
Lincoln: printed Drury, 1814.   1 sheet.

1770.
Lincoln election: [about selection of candidates, May 19, 1814]
Lincoln: printed Drury, 1814.   1 sheet.

1771. **SIBTHORP, Coningsby**
[Letter, May 20th, 1814]
Lincoln: printed Drury, 1814.   1 sheet.

1772. ───────────
[Letter, May 21, 1814]
[Lincoln]: [s.n.], [1814].   1 sheet.

1773.
[Account of meeting, June 20th, 1818]
Lincoln: printed Drury, 1818.   1 sheet.

1774.
City chronicles, A.D. 1818: [to the tune The House that Jack built]
[Lincoln]: [s.n.], [1818].   1 sheet.

1775.
Sketch of the election booth in Lincolnshire, 1819
[London]: ordered by the House of Commons to be printed, 1819.   1 sheet: ill.
　　Situated in Lincoln Prison.

1776.
[Letter from 'An old stager', March 3, 1820]
Lincoln: printed Drury, 1820. 1 sheet.

1777.
Lincoln election: [resolutions of a meeting of the friends of Robert Smith, Esq., at the Rein-deer Inn, on Saturday, the fourth of March, 1820]
Lincoln: printed Drury, 1820. 1 sheet.

1778.
Lincoln election: [resolution at meeting of the friends of Robert Smith, 4th March, 1820]
Lincoln: printed Smith, 1820. 1 sheet.

1779.
[Letter from 'A freeman', March 4th, 1820]
Lincoln: printed W. Brooke, 1820. 1 sheet.

1780.   **DAVENPORT, E.D.**
[Letter, 6th March, 1820]
Lincoln: printed Drury, 1820. 2 sheets.

1781.
[Letter from 'A sincere well-wisher to the case of freedom and independence', March 6th, 1820]
Lincoln: printed W. Brooke, 1820. 1 sheet.

1782.
[Letter from Robert Smith's committee, 6th March, 1820]
Lincoln: printed Drury, 1820. 1 sheet.

1783.   **SMITH, Robert**
[Letter, 6/7th March, 1820]
Lincoln: printed Drury, 1820. 1 sheet.

1784.   ——————
[Letter, March 1820]
Lincoln: printed Drury, 1820. 1 sheet.

1785.   **DAVENPORT, E.D.**
[Letter, 8th March, 1820]
Lincoln: printed J. Smith, 1820. 1 sheet.

1786.
[Election squib, 8th March, 1820]
Lincoln: printed W. Brooke, 1820. 1 sheet.
    Mock auction of 'a small number of curious animals of the camelion species...[whose] mutation of colour commonly takes place at general elections'.

1787.   **SIBTHORP, C.W.**
[Letter, March 8th, 1820]
Lincoln: printed Drury, 1820. 1 sheet.

1788.
[Letter from Mr. Smith's committee, March 9, 1820]
Lincoln: printed Drury, 1820. 1 sheet.

1789.   **SIBTHORP, C.W.**
[Letter, March 9th, 1820]
Lincoln: printed Drury, 1820.   1 sheet.

1790.   **SMITH, Robert**
[Letter, March 11th, 1820]
Lincoln: printed Drury, 1820.   1 sheet.

1791.   —————
A Report of the speech of Robert Smith, Esq., delivered at the Rein-deer Inn in Lincoln, on Tuesday, April 11, 1820, at the dinner given to celebrate his return to Parliament for that city...to which is added a list of the subscribers to the fund
Lincoln: printed and sold by W. Brooke, 1820.   20p.
> Also account of election, sketch of Smith's public life and list of subscribers to the election fund.

1792.   **WILLIAMS, John**
[Letter, March 11th, 1822]
Lincoln: printed W. Brooke, 1822.   1 sheet.

1793.
[Letter signed 'A brother freeman', March 13, 1822]
Lincoln: printed W. Bradbury, 1822.   1 sheet.

1794.
Mr Williams' election: [summons to meeting, March 13, 1822]
Lincoln: printed Bradbury, 1822.   1 sheet.

1795.
[Request not to promise votes, March 16th, 1822]
Lincoln: printed Keyworth, 1822.   1 sheet.

1796.
Mr Williams' committee...: [summons to meeting, March 16, 1822]
Lincoln: printed J. Smith, 1822.   1 sheet.

1797.
[Letter signed 'An independent freeman', March 18th, 1822]
Lincoln: printed W. Brooke, 1822.   1 sheet.

1798.
[Letter signed 'A brother freeman', March 18th, 1822]
Lincoln: printed Keyworth, 1822.   1 sheet.

1799.
[Letter signed 'A freeman', 18th March, 1822]
Lincoln: printed W. Bradbury, 1822.   1 sheet.

1800.
[Resolutions of meeting in support of Col. Ellison, 19th March, 1822]
Lincoln: printed Jane Drury, 1822.   1 sheet.

1801.   **ELLISON, R.**
[Letter, 19th March, 1822]
Lincoln: printed W. Bradbury, 1822.   1 sheet.

1802.   **WILLIAMS, John**
[Letter, 19th March, 1822]
Lincoln: printed Drury, 1822.   1 sheet.

1803.
[Letter signed 'One of the mob', 20th March, 1822]
Lincoln: printed W. Brooke, 1822.   1 sheet.

1804.
[Letter signed 'No foreigner', March 20th, 1822]
Lincoln: printed Keyworth, 1822.   1 sheet.

1805.   **WILLIAMS, John**
[Letter, March 21st, 1822]
Lincoln: printed W. Brooke, 1822.   1 sheet.

1806.
Rare news for the Pinks: [squib, March 22, 1822]
Lincoln: printed John Smith, 1822.   1 sheet.

1807.   **WILLIAMS, John**
[Letter, March 23, 1822]
Lincoln: printed J. Smith, 1822.   1 sheet.

1808.   ——————
[Letter, March 25th, 1822]
Lincoln: printed W. Brooke, 1822.   1 sheet.

1809.
Song: [in support of Williams]
Lincoln: printed W. Brooke, [1822?].   1 sheet.

1810.
Extension of the elective franchise: [petition, March 30th, 1826]
Lincoln: printed J.W. Drury, 1826.   1 sheet.

1811.
Extension of the elective franchise: [resolutions of meeting at Rein-deer Inn, Lincoln,
April 3rd, 1826]
Lincoln: printed W. Brooke, 1826.   1 sheet.

1812.   **SMITH, Robert**
[Letter announcing that standing down, April 29th, 1826]
[Lincoln]: [s.n.], [1826].   1 sheet.

1813.   **FAZAKERLEY, J.N.**
[Letter, May 1st, 1826]
Lincoln: printed Hall, 1826.   1 sheet.

1814.   **SIBTHORP, Charles De Laet Waldo**
[Letter, 31st May, 1826]
Lincoln: printed J.W. Drury, 1826.   1 sheet.

1815.
[Letter signed 'An independent freeman', 1st June, 1826]
Lincoln: printed Keyworth, 1826.   1 sheet.

1816.
The Third man: [letter informing freemen that T.G. Corbett will stand as candidate, 1st June, 1826]
Lincoln: printed Drury, 1826.   1 sheet.

1817.   **CORBETT, Thomas George**
[Letter, 2nd June, 1826]
Lincoln: printed Drury, 1826.   1 sheet.

1818.   **FAZAKERLEY, J.N.**
[Letter, June 2nd, 1826]
Lincoln: printed W. Brooke, 1826.   1 sheet.

1819.   **SIBTHORP, Charles De Laet Waldo**
[Letter, 2nd June, 1826]
Lincoln: printed Drury, 1826.   1 sheet.

1820.
Run away! : [squib offering reward, 3rd June, 1826]
Lincoln: printed Keyworth, 1826.   1 sheet.

1821.   **FAZAKERLEY, J.N.**
[Letter, June 3rd, 1826]
Lincoln: printed J.W. Drury, 1826.   1 sheet.

1822.   **SIBTHORP, Charles De Laet Waldo**
[Letter, 3rd June, 1826]
Lincoln: printed J.W. Drury, 1826.   1 sheet.

1823.
[Letter signed 'A freeman', 5th June, 1826]
Lincoln: printed Keyworth, 1826.   1 sheet.

1824.
[Squib giving political definitions, 5th June, 1826]
Lincoln: printed Keyworth, 1826.   1 sheet.

1825.   **FAZAKERLEY, J.N.**
[Letter, June 5th, 1826]
Lincoln: printed Hall, 1826.   1 sheet.

1826.
[Squib against Sibthorp and Corbett, 6th June, 1826]
Lincoln: printed Keyworth, 1826.   1 sheet.

1827.
Caution, beware false witness: [signed 'Another freeman', June 6th, 1826]
Lincoln: printed W. Brooke, 1826.   1 sheet.

1828.   **SIBTHORP, Charles De Laet Waldo**
[Letter, June 6th, 1826]
Lincoln: printed Keyworth, 1826.   1 sheet.

1829.   **CORBETT, Thomas George**
[Letter, 7th June, 1826]
Lincoln: printed Drury, 1826.   1 sheet.

1830.
[Letter signed 'A third freeman', June 7th, 1826]
Lincoln: printed Keyworth, 1826.   1 sheet.

1831.
[Squib in form of poster announcing 'found...', 7th June, 1826]
Lincoln: printed Keyworth, 1826.   1 sheet.

1832.
The Blues: [instructions to voters, 8th June, 1826]
Lincoln: printed Drury, 1826.   1 sheet.

1833.   **FAZAKERLEY, J.N.**
[Letter, June 8th]
Lincoln: printed Hall, [1826?].   1 sheet.

1834.   **SIBTHORP, Charles De Laet Waldo**
[Letter, 8th June, 1826]
Lincoln: printed J.W. Drury, 1826.   1 sheet.

1835.
To the worthy and independent friends of Col. Sibthorp: [letter, June 9th, 1826]
Lincoln: printed Keyworth, 1826.   1 sheet.

1836.
[Letter signed 'Libertatis amicus', 9th June, 1826]
Lincoln: printed Keyworth, 1826.   1 sheet.

1837.   **FAZAKERLEY, J.N.**
[Letter, 10th June, 1826]
Lincoln: printed Drury, 1826.   1 sheet.

1838.
[Poster in support of Fazakerley]
Lincoln: printed J. Smith, [1826].   1 sheet.

1839.
Young Corbett, a new song
Lincoln: printed Drury, [1826].   1 sheet.

1840.
A New song, 1826: [to an old tune]
Lincoln: printed Drury, 1826.   1 sheet.

1841.   **BULWER, E.L.**
Speech of E.L.Bulwer, Esq., nomination day of Lincoln election, July 22
Lincoln: printed E.B. Drury, [183?].   1 sheet.

1842.   **MEXBOROUGH, Lord**
[Letter, July 12th, 1830]
[Lincoln]: [s.n.], [1830].   1 sheet.

1843.   **SIBTHORP, Charles De Laet Waldo**
[Letter, 12th July, 1830]
[Lincoln]: [s.n.], [1830].   1 sheet.

1844.
[Resolution of meeting calling upon Montague John Cholmeley to stand as candidate, July 19, 1830]
[Lincoln]: [s.n.], [1830].   1 sheet.

1845.   **MEXBOROUGH, Lord**
[Letter, July 22nd, 1830]
Lincoln: printed W. Brooke, 1830.   1 sheet.

1846.   **SIBTHORP, Charles De Laet Waldo**
[Letter, 22nd July, 1830]
[Lincoln]: [s.n.], [1830].   1 sheet.

1847.
[Notice to reserve votes because of imminent appearance of the 'third man', July 23rd, 1830]
[Lincoln]: [s.n.], [1830].   1 sheet.

1848.   **MEXBOROUGH, Lord**
[Letter, July 23rd, 1830]
Lincoln: printed W. Brooke, 1830.   1 sheet.

1849.
To the worthy and independent Blues: [letter, July 24, 1830]
[Lincoln]: [s.n.], [1830].   1 sheet.

1850.   **FISHER, Wm.**
[Letter about charge of breaking windows, July 24th, 1830]
[Lincoln]: [s.n.], [1830].   1 sheet.

1851.   **MASON, Richard**
[Letter to John Fardell about breaking of window by William Fisher, 24th July, 1830]
[Lincoln]: [s.n.], [1830].   1 sheet.

1852.   **SIBTHORP, Charles De Laet Waldo**
[Letter, July 31st, 1830]
[Lincoln]: [s.n.], [1830].   1 sheet.

1853.   —————
Lincoln county election: [letter, August 9th, 1830]
[Lincoln]: [s.n.], [1830].   1 sheet.

1854.
To Christian Non-conformists: [letter signed 'A Non-conformist']
[Lincoln]: [s.n.], [1830].   1 sheet.

1855.
[Letter signed 'An occupier']
[Lincoln]: [s.n.], [1830].   1 sheet.

1856.
Address of the rejected from the borough of Whitby: [copy of letters to electors of Whitby from C.B. Phipps; designed to spike his candidacy for Lincoln]
[Lincoln]: [s.n.], [1830].   1 sheet.

1857.
Sibthorp: the true friend of liberty: [verse]
Lincoln: printed T.O. Brumby, [1830?].   1 sheet.

1858.
A New song
Lincoln: printed T.O. Brumby, [1830?].   1 sheet.

1859.
New song
Lincoln: printed R.E. Leary, [1830?].   1 sheet.

1860.   **FARDELL, John George**
[Correspondence, election lists and bills relating to 1830 election]
[1830].   [c.30] leaves.
Ms.; printed material.

1861.
Reform: [letter to the independent freemen of the city of Lincoln, residing in Boston,
April 23rd, 1831]
Boston: printed John Noble, 1831.   1 sheet.

1862.   **FARDELL, John**
[Letter, April 23, 1831]
Lincoln: printed J.W. Drury, 1831.   1 sheet.

1863.
[Letter signed 'A freeman', April 25]
Lincoln: printed J. Stainton, [1831?].   1 sheet.

1864.
[Letter signed 'A freeman', April 25, 1831]
Lincoln: printed W. Brooke, 1831.   1 sheet.

1865.   **HENEAGE, G.F.**
[Letter, April 25, 1831]
[Lincoln]: [s.n.], [1831].   1 sheet.

1866.
[Letter signed 'A reformer', April 26th, 1831]
Lincoln: printed E.B. Drury, 1831.   1 sheet.

1867.
Caution: [letter signed 'The son of a freeman', April 26th, 1831]
Lincoln: printed Keyworth, 1831.   1 sheet.

1868.   **SIBTHORP, Charles De Laet Waldo**
[Letter, 26th April, 1831]
Lincoln: printed J.W. Drury, 1831.   1 sheet.

1869.
[Letter signed 'A brother freeman', April 27th, 1831]
Lincoln: printed J.W. Drury, 1831.   1 sheet.

1870.   **FAZAKERLEY, J.N.**
[Letter, 27th April, 1831]
Lincoln: printed E.B. Drury, 1831.   1 sheet.

1871.   **HALL, Gage John**
[Letter, April 27th, 1831]
Lincoln: printed W. Brooke, 1831.   1 sheet.

1872.   **SIBTHORP, Charles De Laet Waldo**
[Letter, 27th April, 1831]
Lincoln: printed T.O. Brumby, 1831.   1 sheet.

1873.
Election dirge: [poem, April 28th]
Lincoln: printed R.E. Leary, [1831?].   1 sheet.

1874.
[Letter signed 'A citizen of Lincoln', April 28th, 1831]
Lincoln: printed J.W. Drury, 1831.   1 sheet.

1875.   **SIBTHORP, Charles De Laet Waldo**
[Letter, 30th April, 1831]
Lincoln: printed J.W. Drury, 1831.   1 sheet.

1876.
Prophetic mirror: signs and portentous events relative to Lincoln: [election squib signed
'Veteranus', April/May, 1831]
[Lincoln]: [printed E.B. Drury], [1831].   1 sheet.

1877.   **FAZAKERLEY, J.N.**
[Letter, June 12, 1832]
Lincoln: printed W. Brooke, 1831.   1 sheet.

1878.   **SIBTHORP, Humphrey Waldo**
[Letter in support of brother, June 15th, 1832]
Lincoln: printed W. Brooke, 1831.   1 sheet.

1879.
[Letter to mayor requesting meeting to discuss reform, September 17th, 1831]
Lincoln: printed J.W. Drury, 1831.   1 sheet.

1880.
*Admirable consistency!: of Col. Sibthorp's supporter!: extract from Mr Alderman Steel's
speech, at a reform meeting...on Saturday, 15th of October, 1831*
Lincoln: printed R.E. Leary, 1831.   1 sheet.

1881.
[Letter signed 'A citizen']
Lincoln: printed J.W. Drury, [1831?].   1 sheet.

1882.
[Letter signed 'A freeman that wishes to save his country']
Lincoln: printed E.B. Drury, [1831?].

1883.
Bow-wow! : [poem]
Lincoln: printed E.B. Drury, [1831?].   1 sheet.

1884.
[Letter signed 'A freeman']
Lincoln: printed E.B. Drury, [1831?].   1 sheet.

1885.
[Poster, May 14, 1832]
Lincoln: printed E.B. Drury, 1832.   1 sheet.

1886.
[Letter against Sibthorp, June 6th, 1832]
Lincoln: printed W. Brooke, 1832.   1 sheet.

1887.
[Notice about punishment of wrong-doers during election, June 6th, 1832]
Lincoln: printed E.B. Drury, 1832.   1 sheet.

1888.   **HENEAGE, G.F.**
[Letter, June 6th, 1832]
Lincoln: printed W. Brooke, 1832.   1 sheet.

1889.   **BULWER, Edward Lytton**
[Letter, June 8th, 1832]
Lincoln: printed E.B. Drury, 1832.   1 sheet.

1890.   —————————
[Letter, June 12th, 1832]
Lincoln: printed E.B. Drury, 1832.   1 sheet.

1891.   **FAZAKERLEY, J.N.**
[Letter in support of Bulwer, June 12, 1832]
[Lincoln]: [s.n.], [1832].   1 sheet.

1892.   **SIBTHORP, Humphrey Waldo**
[Letter on behalf of brother, June 12th, 1832]
Lincoln: printed T.O. Brumby, 1832.   1 sheet.

1893.
[Announcement of publication of proceedings of election, June 13, 1832]
Lincoln: printed E.B. Drury, 1832.   1 sheet.

1894.   **HENEAGE, G.F.**
[Letter, June 13th, 1832]
Lincoln: printed R.E. Leary, 1832.   1 sheet.

1895.   **SIBTHORP, Charles De Laet Waldo**
[Letter, June 13, 1832]
Lincoln: printed T.O. Brumby, 1832.   1 sheet.

1896.
[Letter signed 'An elector', June 14th, 1832]
Lincoln: printed W. Brooke, 1832.   1 sheet.

1897.
[Letter signed 'An elector', June 14th, 1832]
Lincoln: printed W. Brooke, 1832.   1 sheet.

1898.   **HENEAGE, G.F.**
[Letter, June 14th, 1832]
[Lincoln]: [s.n.], [1832].   1 sheet.
    Contains printing error, giving 'Haeneage'

1899.   —————————
[Letter, June 14th, 1832]
Lincoln: printed Keyworth, 1832.   1 sheet.

1900.
[Letter with exhortation not to forget during election time 'that a dreadful scourge is hanging over us', June 16th, 1832]
Lincoln: printed J. Stainton, 1832.   1 sheet.

1901.
A Specimen of Colonel Sibthorp as a law maker: [June 16th, 1832]
Lincoln: printed E.B. Drury, 1832.   1 sheet.

1902.
[Letter, June 16th, 1832]
Lincoln: printed T.O. Brumby, 1832.   1 sheet.
    Against 'A Specimen of Col. Sibthorp as a law maker', printed by E.B. Drury.

1903.
[Notice from mayor about 'necessity of abstaining from tumult' during election canvass, June 16th, 1832]
Lincoln: printed J.W. Drury, 1832.   1 sheet.

1904.
Freemen and citizens: beware you are not deceived by sham profession, take care you are not blind to your true interest and served up to table like 'Rabbits smothered in onions': [June 16, 1832]
Lincoln: printed R.E. Leary, 1832.   1 sheet.

1905.
[Letter with the exhortation not to forget religion during election, June 16th, 1832]
Lincoln: printed J. Stainton, 1832.   1 sheet.

1906.
[Letter, June 16th, 1832]
Lincoln: printed R.E. Leary, 1832.   1 sheet.

1907.
[Notice that E.L. Bulwer to meet reformers, June 16th, 1832]
Lincoln: printed E.B. Drury, 1832.   1 sheet.

1908.   **WRIGLESWORTH, William**
[Notice about law and order from the mayor, June 16th, 1832]
Lincoln: printed J.W. Drury, 1832.   1 sheet.

1909.   **HENEAGE, G.F.**
[Letter, June 18, 1832]
Lincoln: printed E.B. Drury, 1832.   1 sheet.

1910.   **BULWER, Edward Lytton**
[Letter, June 19th, 1832]
Lincoln: printed E.B. Drury, 1832.   1 sheet.

1911.   **SIBTHORP, Charles De Laet Waldo**
[Letter, 19th June, 1832]
Lincoln: printed T.O. Brumby, 1832.   1 sheet.

1912.
[Election squib, June 20th, 1832]
Lincoln: printed Leary, 1832.   1 sheet.

1913.
[Notices of Free and Easys, July 2nd, July 10th, November 22nd, December 12, 1832]
Lincoln: printed E.B. Drury, 1832.   4 sheets.

1914.
[Letter about Sibthorp and reform signed 'A freeman', 5th July, 1832]
Lincoln: printed T.O. Brumby, 1832.   1 sheet.

1915.
[Notice of meeting of reformers, July 17, 1832]
Lincoln: printed E.B. Drury, 1832.   1 sheet.

1916.   **BULWER, Edward Lytton**
[Letter, July 21, 1832]
Lincoln: printed E.B. Drury, 1832.   1 sheet.

1917.
Consistency!: [letter signed 'A lover of truth', August 6, 1832]
Lincoln: printed E.B. Drury, 1832.   1 sheet.
    Follows address signed 'A lover of consistency', printed at Boston.

1918.
[Notice of Free & Easy held by reformers, August 6, 1832]
Lincoln: printed E.B. Drury, 1832.   1 sheet.

1919.
[Notices of Free and Easys held by reformers, August 11th, 20th, 25th, 1832]
Lincoln: printed E.B. Drury, 1832.   3 sheets.

1920.
[Notice of reformers' Free and Easy, September 1st, 1832]
Lincoln: printed E.B. Drury, 1832.   1 sheet.

1921.
Colonel Sibthorp's speech in the House of Commons, on Tuesday, September 6, on the passing of the Reform Bill, copied from The Times of that day
Lincoln: printed E.B. Drury, [1832].   1 sheet.
    Speech is punctuated by laughter.

1922.
[Reformers' Free and Easy, September 17th]
Lincoln: printed E.B. Drury, [1832].   1 sheet.

1923.
[Reformers' Free and Easy, September 25th, 1832]
Lincoln: E.B. Drury, 1832.   1 sheet.

1924.
Report of the speeches delivered by E.L. Bulwer...Sir W.A. Ingilby...the Hon. C.A. Pelham...Sir M.J. Cholmeley...Edward Heneage...at the great meeting of the Lincoln Blue Free and Easy, held in...the Monson's Arms Inn on...Sept. 27, 1832
Stamford: printed John Drakard, [1832].   24p.

1925.
Lincoln Great Reform Festival: [notice about public dinner, October 26, 1832]
Lincoln: printed E.B. Drury, 1832.   1 sheet.

1926. ANTI-SLAVERY SOCIETY
[Letter, June 13, 1832]
Lincoln: printed W. Brooke, 1832. 1 sheet.

1927.
Lincoln Grand Reform Festival: report of the speeches of the Right Hon. Lord Yarborough [and others]...delivered at the above Festival, at the City Arms Hotel, Lincoln, on Thursday, the 8th of November, 1832
Stamford: printed by John Drakard, [1832]. 36p.

1928.
[Notice of meeting to celebrate passing of Reform Bill, November 13, 1832]
Lincoln: printed E.B. Drury, 1832. 1 sheet.

1929.
[Notice of reward by Col. Sibthorp for information about the stone-thrower who injured him, November 15, 1832]
Lincoln: printed T.O. Brumby, 1832. 1 sheet.

1930.
Reform Festival: [poster, November 20th, 1832]
Lincoln: printed E.B. Drury, 1832. 1 sheet.

1931.
[Poster about Reform Festival, November 24, 1832]
Lincoln: printed Keyworth, 1832. 1 sheet.

1932.
[Notice of reformers' Free and Easy, November 26th, 1832]
Lincoln: printed E.B. Drury, 1832. 1 sheet.

1933.
Theatre, Lincoln: [notice to supporters of Col. Sibthorp, November 27th, 1832]
Lincoln: printed W. Brooke, 1832. 1 sheet.

1934.
[Poster, November 28, 1832]
Lincoln: printed E.B. Drury, 1832. 1 sheet.

1935.
[Notice of Free and Easy with Col. Sibthorp, November 30th, 1832]
Lincoln: printed T.O. Brumby, 1832. 1 sheet.

1936. HENEAGE, Edward
[Letter in support of brother, 1 December, 1832]
Lincoln: printed R.E. Leary, 1832. 1 sheet.

1937. SIBTHORP, Charles De Laet Waldo
[Letter, 1st December, 1832]
[Lincoln]: [s.n.], [1832]. 1 sheet.

1938.
[Notice of meeting of friends of Col. Sibthorp, December 3rd, 1832]
Lincoln: printed T.O. Brumby, 1832. 1 sheet.

1939.
[Letter signed 'A freeman', December 3rd, 1832]
Lincoln: printed W. Brooke, 1832. 1 sheet.

1940.   **HITCHINS, James**
[Letter, December 3rd, 1832]
Lincoln: printed Keyworth, 1832.   1 sheet.

1941.   **SIBTHORP, Charles De Laet Waldo**
[Letter, 3rd December, 1832]
Lincoln: printed T.O. Brumby, 1832.   1 sheet.

1942.
*Paul Pry presents his compliments to Colonel Sibthorp and, if he does not intrude, begs
leave to put a few questions to him...*: [December 4th, 1832]
Lincoln: printed W. Brooke, 1832.   1 sheet.

1943.
[Election squib, December 4, 1832]
Lincoln: printed T.O. Brumby, 1832.   1 sheet.

1944.   **BROWN, George**
Sibthorp's charity: [letter to Humphrey Sibthorp, December 5, 1832]
Lincoln: printed E.B. Drury, 1832.   1 sheet.

1945.   **LINCOLN CORPORATION**
[Warning about violence during elections, December 5th, 1832]
Lincoln: printed W. Brooke, [1832].   1 sheet.

1946.
[Squib in form of advertisement for bull, 5th December, 1832]
[Lincoln]: [s.n.], [1832].   1 sheet.

1947.   **SIBTHORP, Charles De Laet Waldo**
[Letter, 5th December, 1832]
Lincoln: printed Leary, 1832.   1 sheet.

1948.   **BULWER, Edward Lytton**
[Letter, December 6, 1832]
Lincoln: printed T.O. Brumby, 1832.   1 sheet.

1949.   _____
[Letter, December 6, 1832]
Lincoln: printed E.B. Drury, 1832.   1 sheet.

1950.
[Letter signed 'An inhabitant', Thursday, December 6th]
Lincoln: printed R.E. Leary, [1832?].   1 sheet.

1951.   **SIBTHORP, Charles De Laet Waldo**
[Letter, 6th December, 1832]
Lincoln: printed W. Brooke, 1832.   1 sheet.

1952.   **SIBTHORP, Humphrey Waldo**
[Letter on behalf of brother, 7th December, 1832]
Lincoln: printed T.O. Brumby, 1832.   1 sheet.

1953.   **SIBTHORP, Charles De Laet Waldo**
[Letter, December 7th, 1832]
Lincoln: printed T.O. Brumby, 1832.   1 sheet.

1954.
Speech of Mr Bulwer, at Lincoln on the day of nomination, Saturday, December 8th, 1832
Lincoln: printed R.E. Leary, 1832. 1 sheet.

1955. **HENEAGE, G.F.**
[Letter, 8th December, 1832]
Lincoln: printed R.E. Leary, 1832. 1 sheet.

1956. **SIBTHORP, Charles De Laet Waldo**
[Letter, December 10th, 1832]
[Lincoln]: [s.n.], [1832]. 1 sheet.

1957.
[Results of the poll, December 11, 1832]
Lincoln: printed E.B. Drury, 1832. 1 sheet.

1958. **SIBTHORP, Charles De Laet Waldo**
[Letter, December 11th, 1832]
Lincoln: printed T.O. Brumby, 1832. 1 sheet.

1959. **HENEAGE, G.F.**
[Letter, 12th December, 1832]
Lincoln: printed R.E. Leary, 1832. 1 sheet.

1960. **BULWER, Edward Lytton**
[Letter, December 13, 1832]
Lincoln: printed Brooke, 1832. 1 sheet.

1961.
Exposure of the shifty conduct of Mr. Bulwer's electoral committee: [December 13, 1832]
Lincoln: printed T.O. Brumby, 1832. 1 sheet.

1962. **LINCOLN CORPORATION**
[Notice of election]
Lincoln: printed W. Brooke, [1832]. 1 sheet.

1963.
To the ten pound householders of Lincoln: [letter signed 'A ten pound householder']
Lincoln: printed E.B. Drury, [1832?]. 1 sheet.

1964.
[Letter signed 'Liber']
Lincoln: printed T.O. Brumby, [1832?]. 1 sheet.

1965.
To the truly conscientious and honest reformers of Lincoln: [letter signed 'One of the working classes']
Lincoln: printed E.B. Drury, [1832?]. 1 sheet.

1966.
A Word to the electors of England in general, and to those of the city of Lincoln in particular: [letter signed 'An Englishman who ardently wishes the peace, prosperity and happiness of his native land']
Lincoln: printed E.B. Drury, [1832?]. 1 sheet.

1967.
On legislative enactments for the observance of the Sabbath: [letter signed 'A Nonconformist']
Lincoln: printed E.B. Drury, [1832?].   1 sheet.

1968.
Reform Festival: [squib poster giving order of procession]
Lincoln: printed Keyworth, [1832?].   1 sheet.

1969.
[Notice of reformers' dinner]
Lincoln: printed E.B. Drury, [1832].   1 sheet.

1970.
[Letter]
Lincoln: printed E.B. Drury, [1832].   1 sheet.

1971.
Tory taxation unmasked: [exhortation to vote for Heneage and Bulwer]
[Lincoln]: [s.n.], [1832].   1 sheet.

1972.
[Poster denouncing John Goodworth as a turncoat]
[Lincoln]: [s.n.], [1832].   1 sheet.

1973.
[Letter about slavery]
Lincoln: printed J.W. Drury, [1832].   1 sheet.

1974.
The Last dying words and confession of poor unfortunate turncoat at Washingborough
Lincoln: printed R.E. Leary, [1832].   1 sheet.

1975.
[Election squib pro Heneage and Bulwer, anti Sibthorp]
Boston: printed C.F. Barber, [1832].   1 sheet.

1976.
[Letter signed 'One of the working classes']
Lincoln: printed E.B. Drury, [1832].   1 sheet.

1977.
The Ape of the Bulwer Island: [poem]
Lincoln: printed Leary, [1832].   1 sheet.

1978.
[Election squib: mock auction]
Lincoln: printed T.O. Brumby, [1832].   1 sheet.

1979.
Thanks to Paul Pry, or The Grey list reformed: [anti Bulwer and Heneage squib]
Lincoln: printed J.W. Drury, [1832].   1 sheet.

1980.
[Poem pro Heneage and Bulwer and against Sibthorp]
[Lincoln]: [s.n.], [1832].   1 sheet.

1981.
Colonel Wodehouse's opinion of reformers
Lincoln: printed Brumby, [1832]. 1 sheet.

1982.
[Letter]
Lincoln: printed E.B. Drury, [1832]. 1 sheet.

1983.
To the bondmen of Lincoln: [election squib signed 'A thorough Tory']
Lincoln: printed W. Brooke, [1832?]. 1 sheet.

1984.
A New song
Lincoln: printed T.O. Brumby, [1832]. 1 sheet.

1985.
[New song to the tune Derry Down]
Lincoln: printed Leary, [1832]. 1 sheet.

1986.
Report of the speeches delivered at the great meeting of the Lincoln Blue Free and Easy
to welcome Sir Wm. Ingilby, Bart., held in the banquetting room of the City Arms
Hotel...together with the subsequent proceedings in the case of Amos Gilbert, a convict...
Stamford: printed John Drakard, [1832]. 35p.
Originally published: in Drakard's *Stamford news*.
   Includes a speech by E.B. Drury.

1987.   **SIBTHORP, Charles De Laet Waldo**
[Letter]
Lincoln: printed J.W. Drury, [1832?]. 1 sheet.

1988.
Taxes! taxes! taxes!
Lincoln: printed W. Brooke, [1832]. 1 sheet.

1989.
Paul Pry, in the fulfilment of his duties, has pryed into the Bill issued by the Pink Party,
headed Taxes! Taxes! Taxes! and he pronounces Fudge! Fudge! Fudge!
Lincoln: printed Keyworth, [1832]. 1 sheet.

1990.   **YARBOROUGH, Lord**
[Letter to Mr. Hitchins about Reform Bill]
Lincoln: printed E.B. Drury, [1832]. 1 sheet.

1991.   **SIBTHORP, Charles De Laet Waldo**
[Letter, May 6, 1833]
[Lincoln]: [s.n.], [1833]. 1 sheet.

1992.   _____
'Facts are stubborn things': [letter, May 16, 1833]
[Lincoln]: [s.n.], [1833]. 1 sheet.

1993.
[Letter signed 'A citizen of Lincoln']
[Lincoln]: [s.n.], [1833]. 1 sheet.

1994.
Thanks to Paul Pry, or The Grey list reformed
[Lincoln]: [s.n.], [1832]. 1 sheet.
  Abridged form.

1995. **BULWER, Edward Lytton**
[Letter, December 1, 1834]
Lincoln: printed W. and B. Brooke, 1834. 1 sheet.

1996.
[Letter signed 'One of the other side', December 4th, 1834]
[Lincoln]: [s.n.], [1834]. 1 sheet.

1997.
[Letter signed 'A voter', December 10, 1834]
Lincoln: printed Keyworth, 1834. 1 sheet.
  Against letter signed 'One of the other side'.

1998. **SIBTHORP, Charles De Laet Waldo**
[Letter, December 8, 1834]
Lincoln: printed T.O. Brumby, 1834. 1 sheet.

1999.
To the truly independent electors of Lincoln: [letter signed 'A voter', December 10, 1834]
Lincoln: printed Keyworth, 1834. 1 sheet.

2000.
[Letter, December 12th, 1834]
Lincoln: printed W. and B. Brooke, 1834. 1 sheet.

2001. **HENEAGE, G.F.**
[Letter, December 12th, 1834]
Lincoln: printed W. and B. Brooke, 1834. 1 sheet.

2002.
[Letter signed 'A fearless elector', December 16, 1834]
Lincoln: printed J. Stainton, 1834. 1 sheet.

2003. **NORTHHOUSE, W.S.**
[Letter, December 18th, 1834]
Lincoln: printed at the Lincoln Gazette, 1834. 1 sheet.

2004.
[Letter, December 22, 1834]
Lincoln: printed W. and B. Brooke, 1834. 1 sheet.

2005. **BULWER, Edward Lytton**
[Letter, December 22, 1834]
Lincoln: W. and B. Brooke, 1834. 1 sheet.

2006.
[Letter signed 'One of the gentry', December 24, 1834]
[Lincoln]: [s.n.], [1834]. 1 sheet.

2007.
[Letter signed 'One of the gentry', December 26, 1834]
[Lincoln]: [s.n.], [1834]. 1 sheet.

2008.
[Letter signed 'One of the gentry', December 29, 1834]
Lincoln: printed W. and B. Brooke, 1834.   1 sheet.

2009.
[Squib letter signed 'A Blue rat', December 30, 1834]
Lincoln: printed E.B. Drury, 1834.   1 sheet.

2010.
*The Disclaimer and declaration unanimously agreed to at a public meeting,
held at the Town Hall...30th December, 1834*
Lincoln: printed J. Stainton, 1834.   1 sheet.
    Against intimidation or retaliation.

2011.
[Letter signed 'A brother freeman']
[Lincoln]: [s.n.], [1834?].   1 sheet.

2012.
[Reply to paper subscribed by 'One of the other side']
[Lincoln]: [s.n.], [1834?].   1 sheet.

2013.
[Letter signed 'One of the popular side']
Lincoln: printed E.B. Drury, [1834–35?].   1 sheet.

2014.
*The Devil not so black as he is painted [and] On a certain little decorated figure
near the Stonebow*: [verse]
[Lincoln]: [s.n.], [1834].   1 sheet.

2015.
To the bondmen of Lincoln: [squib letter signed 'A thorough Tory']
Lincoln: printed W. Brooke, [1834?].   1 sheet.

2016.
Lost...the confidence of the electors of Lincoln: [squib]
[Lincoln]: [s.n.], [1834].   1 sheet.

2017.
[Letter signed 'A Christian dissenter']
Lincoln: printed T.O. Brumby, [1834].   1 sheet.

2018.
[Letter signed 'An elector of the Bail']
Lincoln: printed T.O. Brumby, [1834?].   1 sheet.

2019.
[Letter signed 'Another elector of the Bail']
Lincoln: printed T.O. Brumby, [1834?].   1 sheet.

2020.
[Poster about Poor Law with exhortation to vote for Sibthorp on the grounds that he
opposed the Bill]
[Lincoln]: [s.n.], [1834?].   1 sheet.

2021.
Caution to innholders, &c., &c.: [letter signed 'The landlord's ghost']
[Lincoln]: [s.n.], [1834?].   1 sheet.

2022.   **LIBERAL SOCIETY**
To the freemen and electors of Lincoln who call themselves, or are called, Pink: [letter]
Lincoln: printed J. Stainton, [1834?].   1 sheet.

2023.
[Letter signed 'One of the gentry', January 1, 1835]
Lincoln: printed W. and B. Brooke, 1835.   1 sheet.

2024.   **CHAPLIN, Charles**
[Letter to A. Boucherett, January 9th, 1835]
[Lincoln]: [s.n.], [1835].   1 sheet.

2025.   **SIBTHORP, Charles De Laet Waldo**
[Letter, January 9th, 1835]
Lincoln: printed T.O. Brumby, 1835.   1 sheet.

2026.   **BULWER, Edward Lytton**
[Letter, January 10th, 1835]
Lincoln: printed Keyworth, 1835.   1 sheet.

2027.
[Letter signed 'A freeman and an elector', September 2nd, 1835]
Lincoln: printed T.J.N. Brogden, 1835.   1 sheet.

2028.
To the freemen & electors of the city of Lincoln: to all whom it may concern, whether Pinks or Blues, Liberals or Conservatives: [letter signed 'A Conservative but no bigot', September 3rd, 1835]
Lincoln: printed T.O. Brumby, 1835.   1 sheet.

2029.   **BROGDEN, T.J.N.**
To Mr. W.S. Northhouse: [letter refuting the charge that he is the 'tool of the Conservatives', November 17th, 1835]
Lincoln: printed T.J.N. Brogden, 1835.   1 sheet.

2030.
[Letter signed 'Scipio']
Lincoln: printed E.B. Drury, [1835].   1 sheet.

2031.
[Letter signed 'A freeman & elector']
Lincoln: printed T.J.N. Brogden, [1835].   1 sheet.

2032.
[Letter signed 'A brother elector of the Bail']
Lincoln: printed T.O. Brumby, [1835].   1 sheet.

2033.
[Letter signed 'An occupier']
Lincoln: printed T.J.N. Brogden, [1835].   1 sheet.

2034.
[Letter signed 'Nemo']
Lincoln: printed E.B. Drury, [1835].   1 sheet.

2035.
Questions and queries respectfully submitted to the electors of Lincoln: [letter signed 'A ten pound householder']
Lincoln: printed E.B. Drury, 1835.   1 sheet.

2036.
[Letter signed 'T. Nettleship', January 2nd, 1836]
Lincoln: printed J.W. Drury, 1836.   1 sheet.

2037.
Bulwer & Co. ... to the opponents of military flogging: [letter]
Lincoln: printed T.J.N. Brogden, [1836].   1 sheet.

2038.   **BULWER, E.L.**
[Letter, May 16th, 1837]
Lincoln: printed E.B. Drury, 1837.   1 sheet.

2039.   ——————
[Letter, June 11, 1837]
Lincoln: printed E.B. Drury, 1837.   1 sheet.

2040.   **CHURCHILL, Charles Henry**
[Letter, July 11th, 1837]
[Lincoln]: [s.n.], [1837].   1 sheet.

2041.   **BROMHEAD, E.ff.**
[Resolutions of meeting of Lincoln Conservative and Guardian Society, June 26, 1837]
Lincoln: printed T.J.N. Brogden, 1837.   1 sheet.

2042.   **ELLIS, Henry**
[Letter, June 26th, 1837]
Lincoln: printed T.J.N. Brogden, 1837.   1 sheet.

2043.   **BULWER, E.L.**
[Letter, June 27, 1837]
Lincoln: printed E.B. Drury, 1837.   1 sheet.

2044.   **CHURCHILL, Charles Henry**
[Letter, June 27, 1837]
Lincoln: printed E.B. Drury, 1837.   1 sheet.

2045.   **ELLIS, Henry**
[Letter, June 28, 1837]
Lincoln: printed T.O. Brumby, 1837.   1 sheet.

2046.
To the religious public: [letter signed 'An admirer of John Wesley', July 1st, 1837]
Lincoln: printed T.O. Brumby, 1837.   1 sheet.
   Author is probably the Reverend Mr Sack.

2047.
Agreement of coalition...E.B. Lytton and Charles Henry Churchill: [3rd July, 1837]
Lincoln: printed T.O. Brumby, 1837.   1 sheet.
   Serious or spoof ?.

2048.
To the Rev. Mr Sack: [letter signed 'A Wesleyan', July 4th, 1837]
Lincoln: printed J. Stainton, 1837.   1 sheet.

2049.
[Letter signed 'An independent elector', July 7th, 1837]
Lincoln: printed T.O. Brumby, 1837.   1 sheet.

2050.
Passing notes on the election: no.1: [signed 'Poz', July 12, 1837]
[Lincoln]: [s.n.], [1837].   1 sheet.

2051.
Bulwer pipes, Churchill pays, who wins?: [signed 'Paul Pry', 13th July, 1837]
[Lincoln]: [s.n.], [1837].   1 sheet.

2052.
[Letter, July 20, 1837]
Lincoln: printed T.O. Brumby, 1837.   1 sheet.

2053.   **SIBTHORP, Charles De Laet Waldo**
[Letter, July 26th, 1837]
Lincoln: printed T.J.N. Brogden, 1837.   1 sheet.

2054.
*Remarks on the late election for the city of Lincoln, taken from the **Lincoln standard**,
August 2nd, 1837*
Lincoln: printed T.J.N. Brogden, 1837.   1 sheet.

2055.   **ELLIS, Henry**
[Letter in support of Sir Henry Sullivan, October 5]
[Lincoln]: [s.n.], [1837?].   1 sheet.

2056.
Shameless intimidation: [request for information about threats, October 31st, 1837]
Lincoln: printed T.J.N. Brogden, 1837.   1 sheet.

2057.
To the Conservative freemen and electors of the city of Lincoln: [letter signed 'An
elector']
[Lincoln]: [s.n.], [1837].   1 sheet.

2058.
Wiggitt Wack-wife Bulmer's lament: [verse]
[Lincoln]: [s.n.], [1837].   1 sheet.

2059.
*Radical procession: Blues attend the glorious procession which is to escort E.L. Bulwer,
Esq. and Colonel Churchill out of the city, after their defeat at the poll*
[Lincoln]: [s.n.], [1837].   1 sheet.

2060.
[Letter pro Sibthorp and Ellis]
[Lincoln]: [s.n.], [1837?].   1 sheet.

2061.
*Colonel Churchill's speech delivered at a meeting of the Liberal constituency of Lincoln,
December 26, 1838*
Lincoln: printed James Drury, 1838.   1 sheet.

2062.
To farmers, graziers, cowkeepers, higglers, coalporters, to be sold by auction by Judas T.J.N. Renegade: [spoof lampooning T.J.N. Brogden]
[Lincoln]: [s.n.], [1838].   1 sheet.

2063.
A Lover of Toryism: [election squib in form of playbill]
Lincoln: printed Sarah Thorpe, 1838.   1 sheet.

2064.   **CHURCHILL, Charles Henry**
[Letter, January 7th, 1839]
Lincoln: printed J. Stainton, 1839.   1 sheet.

2065.   **SIBTHORP, Charles De Laet Waldo**
[Letter, January 8, 1839]
London: printed William Stevens, 1839.   1 sheet.

2066.
[Letter signed 'A member of the Pitt Club', from the *Lincoln standard* of Wednesday, January 23rd, 1839]
Lincoln: printed T.J.N. Brogden, 1839.   1 sheet.

2067.   **BULWER, Edward Lytton**
[Letter, February 6th, 1839]
Lincoln: printed James Drury, 1839.   1 sheet.

2068.   **BROMHEAD, Jno. N.**
[Letter, 21st May, 1839]
Jno. N. & E.A. Bromhead.
[Lincoln]: [s.n.], [1839].   1 sheet.

2069.   **BROMHEAD, E.ff.**
[Letter in support of W.R. Collett, May 25, 1839]
Lincoln: printed T.O. Brumby, 1839.   1 sheet.

2070.   **BROMHEAD, Jno. N.**
[Letter, May 25th, 1839]
Jno. N. & E.A. Bromhead.
[Lincoln]: [s.n.], [1839].   1 sheet.

2071.   **BULWER, Edward Lytton**
[Letter, May 25th, 1839]
[Lincoln]: [s.n.], [1839].   1 sheet.

2072.   **RUDGARD, John**
[Letter, May 25th, 1839]
Lincoln: printed J. Stainton, 1839.

2073.   **SIBTHORP, Charles De Laet Waldo**
[Letter, 25th May, 1839]
Lincoln: printed T.O. Brumby, 1839.   1 sheet.

2074.   **RAWLINS, William**
[Letter announcing meeting of friends of W.R. Collett, May 27th, 1839]
[Lincoln]: [s.n.], [1839].   1 sheet.

2075.   **COLLETT, W.R.**
[Letter and announcement of meeting, May 28th, 1839]
Lincoln: printed T.O. Brumby, 1839.   1 sheet.

2076.   ——————
[Letter, May 29th, 1839]
[Lincoln]: [s.n.], [1839].   1 sheet.

2077.   ——————
[Letter, May 29th, 1839]
Lincoln: printed T.J.N. Brogden, 1839.   1 sheet.

2078.   ——————
[Letter, June 6th, 1839]
Lincoln: printed T.J.N. Brogden, 1839.   1 sheet.

2079.
On elections
by an elector.
Lincoln: printed W. and B. Brooke, [1839?].   1 sheet.

2080.   **WALKER, 'Gridiron'**
[Letter]
Lincoln: printed T.J.N. Brogden, 1839.   1 sheet.

2081.
'The Original citizen', hashed up by 'a whipper-snapper of the press'
[Lincoln]: [s.n.], [184?].   1 sheet.
Originally published: in *Free trade and radical Lincolnshire advertiser*, June 19th.
    About Seely.

2082.
[Letter signed 'One of the people']
[Lincoln]: [s.n.], [184?].   1 sheet.
    Mentions Seely.

2083.   **SEELY, Charles**
[Letter, December 19th, 1840]
Lincoln: printed James Drury, 1840.   1 sheet.

2084.   **BULWER, Edward Lytton**
[Letter, December 21st, 1840]
Lincoln: printed James Drury, 1840.   1 sheet.

2085.
From the Roman Catholic calendar of the lives of the saints: [election squib]
Lincoln: printed R.E. Leary, [1840s/1850s?].   1 sheet.

2086.
[Letter signed 'A freeman']
[Lincoln]: [s.n.], [1840s?].   1 sheet.
    Mentions Seely.

2087
[Letter signed 'A freeman', May 31st, 1847]
Lincoln: printed J. Stainton, 1841.   1 sheet.

2088.   **BULWER, Edward Lytton**
[Letter, June 15th, 1841]
[Lincoln]: [s.n.], [1841].   1 sheet.

2089.
[Letter signed 'An elector of the Bail', 17th June, 1841]
Lincoln: printed T.O. Brumby, 1841.   1 sheet.

2090.
Blue consternation and all in confusion: [signed 'A voter', June 17, 1841]
Lincoln: printed T.O. Brumby, 1841.   1 sheet.

2091.
[Letter signed 'An elector', June 21st, 1841]
Lincoln: printed James Drury, 1841.   1 sheet.

2092.
Lost, or taken away by force: [election squib, June 22nd, 1841]
Lincoln: printed James Drury, 1841.   1 sheet.

2093.
Lincoln: a close borough!: [signed 'Another elector', June 22nd, 1841]
Lincoln: printed T.O. Brumby, 1841.   1 sheet.

2094.
[Letter signed 'A placeman', 23rd June, 1841]
Lincoln: printed W. and B. Brooke, 1841.   1 sheet.

2095.
To the placemen of Lincoln: [letter signed 'One of the gentry', 24th June, 1841]
Lincoln: printed W. and B. Brooke, 1841.   1 sheet.

2096.   **SIBTHORP, Charles De Laet Waldo**
[Letter, June 24, 1841]
Lincoln: printed T.O. Brumby, 1841.   1 sheet.

2097.
A Second letter of a place man of Lincoln to one of the gentry: [26th June, 1841]
Lincoln: printed W. and B. Brooke, 1841.   1 sheet.

2098.   **SIBTHORP, Charles De Laet Waldo**
[Letter, July 2, 1841]
[Lincoln]: [s.n.], [1841].   1 sheet.

2099.   **WORSLEY, Lord**
Speech delivered in the Castle Yard, Lincoln, at the nomination, on Monday, July 5, 1841
Lincoln: printed and sold by James Drury, [1841].   16p.
     Originally published: in *Lincoln gazette*.

2100.   **SIBTHORP, Charles De Laet Waldo**
[Letter, 13th July, 1841]
[Lincoln]: [s.n.], [1841].   1 sheet.

2101.
Plain questions easily answered by plain men: [signed 'A Lincoln elector']
Lincoln: printed T.O. Brumby, [1841].   1 sheet.

2102.
[Letter signed 'One of you', in support of Sibthorp and Collett]
Lincoln: printed Charles Brogden, [1841?].   1 sheet.

2103.
The Pieman's lament: [poem]
Lincoln: printed Brogden, [1841?].   1 sheet.
   A parody on the American song 'De Boatmen dance'.   About Seely and Jones.

2104.
Will Parry!: [poem]
Lincoln: printed R.E. Leary, [1841?].   1 sheet.

2105.
A Lamentation of the Right Honorable Simon Pure: [election squib]
Lincoln: printed E.B. Drury, [1841?].   1 sheet.

2106.
Blue gammon!: [election squib]
Lincoln: printed T.O. Brumby, [1841].   1 sheet.

2107.
[Election squib]
Lincoln: printed T.O. Brumby, [1841].   1 sheet.

2108.
A Scene from a forthcoming play, entitled Lincoln election, or The citizen candidate: [squib]
Lincoln: printed John Hall, [1841].   1 sheet.
   Seely is one of the protagonists.

2109.
[Letter pro Sibthorp and Collett]
Lincoln: printed Charles Brogden, [1841].   1 sheet.

2110.
[Letter signed 'A freeman']
Lincoln: printed T.O. Brumby, [1841].   1 sheet.

2111.
The Military: [letter in support of Seely signed 'An elector']
[Lincoln]: [s.n.], [1841?].   1 sheet.

2112.
The Protestant electors of the city of Lincoln: [letter signed 'A Wesleyan']
[Lincoln]: [s.n.], [1841?].   1 sheet.
   Sibthorp and Seely mentioned.

2113.
Lincoln city election: [letter signed 'A member of the committee']
[Lincoln]: [s.n.], [1841?].   1 sheet.
   Refers to Mr. Collett's election committee.

2114.
Men of Lincoln: [letter pro Sibthorp and Collett signed 'One of you']
[Lincoln]: [s.n.], [1841?].   1 sheet.

2115.
A Dream: [poem about Sibthorp and Collett signed 'Sam Slick']
Lincoln: printed C. Brogden, [1841].   1 sheet.

2116.
Lincoln Races, 1841: [election squib]
Lincoln: printed Charles Brogden, 1841.   1 sheet.

2117.   **SEELY, Charles**
Mr Seely's speech delivered at the City Assembly Rooms, on the 9th of November, 1842, at a meeting...to celebrate municipal reform
Lincoln: printed J. Stainton, 1842.   1 sheet.

2118.
[Letter signed 'A voter', June 17th, 1843]
Lincoln: printed C. Keyworth, 1843.   1 sheet.

2119.   **COLLETT, S. Russell**
[Letter, May 18, 1844]
Lincoln: printed Drury, 1844.   1 sheet.

2120.   **SIBTHORP, Charles De Laet Waldo**
[Letter, February 3rd, 1845]
Lincoln: printed T.J.N. Brogden, 1845.   1 sheet.

2121.
Politics in Lincoln: [letter signed 'Anti humbug']
[Lincoln]: [s.n.], [1845].   1 sheet.
Originally published: in *Lincolnshire herald*, Tuesday, February 4, 1845.

2122.
[Letter to Mr Charles Seely signed 'An old Liberal', February 7, 1845]
[Lincoln]: printed T.J.N. Brogden, 1845.   1 sheet.

2123.
Theatricals extraordinary: [Lincoln election squib, Drury Lane, March 27th, 1845]
[Lincoln]: [s.n.], [1845].   1 sheet.

2124.
[Letter, June 21st, 1845]
Lincoln: printed T.J.N. Brogden, 1845.   1 sheet.

2125.
[Poster, July 1, 1845]
Lincoln: printed J. Hall, 1845.   1 sheet.

2126.
Mr Charles Seely and Mr Henry Welbourne Jones: two citizen candidates!: [letter signed 'Civis', September 15, 1845]
Lincoln: [s.n.], [1845].   1 sheet.

2127.   **BROMHEAD, Edmund A.**
[Letter, December 15, 1845]
Lincoln: printed T.J.N. Brogden, 1845.   1 sheet.

2128. **MARSHALL, Henry**
[Letter in support of Welbourne Jones, December 20, 1845]
[Lincoln]: [s.n.], [1845]. 1 sheet.

2129.
[Letter signed 'An elector' against Rudgard and Williams, who were canvassing for Bulwer Lytton]
Lincoln: printed J. Stainton, [1845]. 1 sheet.
    Originally published: in *Boston herald*, January 7th, 1845.

2130.
[Letter signed 'Whig of the old school']
Lincoln: printed J. Stainton, [1845?]. 1 sheet.

2131.
Report of the Radical Free & Easy held at the Magpies' Inn, Lincoln
Lincoln: printed G.J. Lockyer, [1845?]. 1 sheet.

2132.
[Letter signed 'One of the people']
Lincoln: printed Charles Brogden, [1845?]. 1 sheet.

2133.
The Beaten man: [poem]
[Lincoln]: [s.n.], [1845]. 1 sheet.

2134.
[Notice of meeting]
Lincoln: printed John Hall, [1845]. 1 sheet.

2135.
Seely and Jones for ever!: a new song
Lincoln: printed J. Hall, [1845?]. 1 sheet.

2136.
Great novelty!!: [election squib in form of programme of entertainments]
[Lincoln]: [s.n.], [1845?]. 1 sheet.
    Welbourne Jones and Seely mentioned.

2137.
Public notice: [election squib signed 'The ghost of that red cow', including spoof letter to Seely from Jones, June 16th, 1846]
Lincoln: printed T.J.N. Brogden, 1846. 1 sheet.

2138.
[Letter signed 'One of the requisitionists', September 7th, 1846]
[Lincoln]: [s.n.], [1846]. 1 sheet.

2139.
[Spoof letter signed 'Charles Seely', January, 1847]
[Lincoln]: [s.n.], [1847]. 1 sheet.

2140.
[Resolutions of a meeting to support candidacy of Lytton, 28th May, 1847]
[Lincoln]: [s.n.], [1847]. 1 sheet.

2141.
[Letter signed 'A freeman', May 31st, 1847]
Lincoln: printed J. Stainton, 1847.   1 sheet.

2142.
[Notice of meeting and list of resolutions to be proposed, June 2nd, 1847]
Lincoln: printed J. Stainton, 1847.   1 sheet.

2143.
[Letter signed 'A Protestant elector', June 2, 1847]
[Lincoln]: [s.n.], [1847].   1 sheet.

2144.
[Letter signed 'A hater of humbug', 3rd June, 1847]
[Lincoln]: [s.n.], [1847].   1 sheet.

2145.
City election: reformers of Lincoln
[Lincoln]: [s.n.], [1847].   1 sheet.
    Originally published: in *Lincolnshire advertiser*, 4th June, 1847.

2146.
City elections: [letter to the reformers of Lincoln signed 'A reformer', June 7th, 1847]
[Lincoln]: [s.n.], [1847].   1 sheet.

2147.
The Holy alliance: [letter to the electors of Lincoln signed 'A hater of tyrants and slave drivers', June 7th, 1847]
Lincoln: printed J. Stainton, 1847.   1 sheet.

2148.
[Letter to Mr Charles Seely signed 'An old Liberal', June 8th, 1847]
Lincoln: printed T.J.N. Brogden, 1847.   1 sheet.

2149.   **COLLETT, W.R.**
[Letter, June 10, 1847]
Lincoln: printed Charles Brogden, 1847.   1 sheet.

2150.
[Letter against Seely signed 'A freeman', July 15th, 1847]
[Lincoln]: [s.n.], [1847].   1 sheet.

2151.
[Letter signed 'A Wesleyan', June 15th, 1847]
Lincoln: printed T.J.N. Brogden, 1847.   1 sheet.

2152.
Night scene at the Queen: [election squib, June 16th, 1847]
Lincoln: printed R.E. Leary, 1847.   1 sheet.

2153.
[Letter signed 'A Protestant elector', June 16, 1847]
Lincoln: printed T.O. Brumby, 1847.   1 sheet.

2154.
[Resolutions of public meeting, 18th June, 1847]
Lincoln: printed T.O. Brumby, 1847.   [2]p.

2155.　**HITCHINS, Jas.**
Election: [letter, June 18th, 1847]
[Lincoln]: [s.n.], [1847].　1 sheet.

2156.
City election: [resolutions of a meeting in support of Sibthorp and Collett, 21st June, 1847]
[Lincoln]: [s.n.], [1847].　1 sheet.

2157.
To the Liberal electors of Lincoln: [letter signed 'A real dark Blue', June 22nd, 1847]
[Lincoln]: [s.n.], [1847].　1 sheet.

2158.
To Mr C. Ward: [letter signed 'A voter for the Colonel', June 25th, 1847]
[Lincoln]: [s.n.], [1847].　1 sheet.

2159.　**LYTTON, E. Bulwer**
[Letter, June 26th, 1847]
[Lincoln]: [s.n.], [1847].　1 sheet.

2160.　**COLLETT, W.R.**
[Letter, June 28th, 1847]
Lincoln: printed T.J.N. Brogden, 1847.　1 sheet.

2161.　**SEELY, Charles**
[Letter, June 28th, 1847]
Lincoln: printed J.W. Drury, 1847.　1 sheet.

2162.
Rare sport: [squib about plumper catchers, June 30th, 1847]
[Lincoln]: [s.n.], [1847].　1 sheet.
　　　Contains ink additions giving real names.

2163.　**SIBTHORP, Charles De Laet Waldo**
[Letter, June 30, 1847]
London: printed Shaw, 1847.　1 sheet.

2164.　——————
[Letter, June, 1847]
London: printed Shaw, 1847.　1 sheet.
Different issue.

2165.
City election: [resolutions of public meeting, June, 1847]
Lincoln: printed W. Doncaster, 1847.　1 sheet.

2166.　**SIBTHORP, Charles De Laet Waldo**
[Letter, June, 1847]
Lincoln: printed T.O. Brumby, 1847.　1 sheet.

2167.
[Letter signed 'An elector', July 1st, 1847]
Lincoln: printed Charles Brogden, 1847.　1 sheet.

2168.
[Letter signed 'Anti-mendax', July 2nd, 1847]
[Lincoln]: [s.n.], [1847].　1 sheet.

2169.   COLLETT, W.R.
[Letter, July 8th, 1847]
Lincoln: printed T.J.N. Brogden, 1847.   1 sheet.

2170.   SWAN, Robert
[Letter, 13th July, 1847]
Lincoln: printed T.O. Brumby, 1847.   1 sheet.
    Swan was chairman of committee for managing Mr Collett's election.

2171.   COULDWELL, Charles
[Letter to Mr Charles Seely, July 22nd, 1847]
Lincoln: printed T.J.N. Brogden, 1847.   1 sheet.

2172.
Lincoln election, extracted from the Examiner newspaper of July 24, 1847
Lincoln: printed W. and B. Brooke, 1847.   1 sheet.

2173.   COLLETT, W.R.
[Letter, July 26th, 1847]
[Lincoln]: [s.n.], [1847].   1 sheet.

2174.
Lincoln election: [July 26th, 1847]
Lincoln: printed W. Bellatti, 1847.   1 sheet.

2175.
Who are the traitors?: [July 26, 1847]
Lincoln: printed W. Bellatti, 1847.   1 sheet.

2176.   SIBTHORP, Humphrey Waldo
[Letter, July 26th]
Lincoln: printed J.W. Drury, [1847?].   1 sheet.

2177.   SIBTHORP, Charles De Laet Waldo
[Letter, 26th July, 1847]
[Lincoln]: [s.n.], [1847].   1 sheet.

2178.
The Traitors unmasked: [July 27, 1847]
Lincoln: printed James Drury, 1847.   1 sheet.

2179.
[Letter signed 'A true Blue', July 28th, 1847]
Lincoln: printed W. Bellatti, 1847.   1 sheet.

2180.   SIBTHORP, Humphrey W.
[Letter, July 28, 1847]
Lincoln: printed J.W. Drury, 1847.   1 sheet.

2181.
Unseat deceit: [letter to the editor of the *Lincolnshire advertiser* signed 'An old Lincoln Liberal', December 15, 1847]
[Lincoln]: printed John Hall, 1847.   1 sheet.

2182.   LILBURN, Richard
[Letter to Mr T.M. Keyworth, December 24th, 1847]
Lincoln: printed John Hall, 1847.   1 sheet.

2183.
Seely and Jones for ever!: a new song
[Lincoln]: [s.n.], [1847].   1 sheet.

2184.
A Parody on an auld song: [signed 'A. McFreeman']
[Lincoln]: [s.n.], [1847].   1 sheet.
    About Charles Seely.

2185.
[Spoof letter signed 'Charles Seely' with imprint 'Alderman Bullfungus at Blunderbuss
Newspaper Office']
[Lincoln]: [s.n.], [1847].   1 sheet.

2186.
Another scene from a forthcoming play, entitled Lincoln election, or The citizen candidate
[Lincoln]: [s.n.], [1847].   1 sheet.

2187.
Lincoln election: a grave remonstrance to the hater of tyrants and slave drivers: [signed
'The poisoned plum cake's ghost']
Lincoln: printed T.J.N. Brogden, [1847].   1 sheet.

2188.
The Original citizen candidate
Lincoln: printed T.J.N. Brogden, [1847].   1 sheet.
Originally published: in *The Free trade and radical Lincolnshire advertiser*, June 19th,
[1847?]

2189.
[Letter signed 'Mickey Free']
Lincoln: printed T.J.N. Brogden, [1847?].   1 sheet.

2190.
Song of the reformers
Lincoln: printed John Hall, [1847?].   1 sheet.

2191.
[Letter signed 'A member of the committee']
Lincoln: printed T.J.N. Brogden, [1847].   1 sheet.

2192.
[Letter signed 'A teacher in the school for grown children']
Lincoln: printed J. Stainton, [1847?].   1 sheet.

2193.
[Letter signed 'An elector']
Lincoln: printed T.J.N. Brogden, [1847?].   1 sheet.

2194.
City of Lincoln: a close borough!
[Lincoln]: [s.n.], [1847?].   1 sheet.
    About Sibthorp, Lytton, Seely and Collett.

2195.
[Letter signed 'One of yourselves']
[Lincoln]: [s.n.], [1847].   1 sheet.
    Lytton and Seely mentioned.

2196.
[Poster]
Lincoln: printed John Hall, 1847. 1 sheet.

2197.
[Letter signed 'A lover of justice']
Lincoln: printed R. Bulman, [1847?]. 1 sheet.

2198.
The Blue Devil's canvass: [poem]
[Lincoln]: [s.n.], [1847]. 1 sheet.

2199.
[Letter signed 'One of yourselves']
Lincoln: printed J. Stainton, [1847?]. 1 sheet.

2200.   **POLLARD, W.**
Separation of church & state impolitic & injurious: [letter]
Lincoln: printed W. Bellatti, [1847]. 1 sheet.
       In support of Bulwer Lytton.

2201.
[Letter, 11th March, 1848]
Lincoln: printed John Hall, 1848. 1 sheet.

2202.   **HOBHOUSE, Thomas B.**
[Letter, March 11th, 1848]
Lincoln: printed J. Stainton, 1848. 1 sheet.

2203.   **LYTTON, Edward Bulwer**
[Letter, March 11, 1848]
Lincoln: printed James Drury, 1848. 1 sheet.

2204.   ───────────
[Letter, March 14, 1848]
[Lincoln]: [s.n.], [1848]. 1 sheet.

2205.
An Address: [signed 'The operative stone masons', March 15th, 1848]
Lincoln: printed R.E. Leary, 1848. 1 sheet.
       In support of trade unions.

2206.   **HUMFREY, L.C.**
[Letter, March 15, 1848]
Lincoln: printed W. Doncaster, 1848. 1 sheet.

2207.   **SIBTHORP, Humphrey W.**
[Letter denying that gave £300 towards expenses of election petition against Seely, March 16th, 1848]
[Lincoln]: [s.n.], [1848]. 1 sheet.

2208.
Lincoln city election
Lincoln: printed T.J.N. Brogden, 1848. 1 sheet.
Originally published: in *Lincolnshire chronicle*, March 24th, 1848.

2209.
[Advertisement for edition of *Nottingham journal* which will carry report of committee appointed by House of Commons to inquire into validity of the return of Charles Seely]
Lincoln: printed J.W. Drury, [1848?].   1 sheet.

2210.
City election proceedings
Lincoln: printed W. Bellatti, 1848.   1 sheet.
Originally published: in *Lincolnshire times*, April 4th, 1848.

2211.   **HALL, John**
[Letter to Anti-mendax, August 15, 1849]
Lincoln: printed John Hall, 1849.   1 sheet.

2212.   **MOORE, Henry**
To the thinking, working men of Lincoln: [letter, January 22nd, 1850]
Brigg: printed Cressey, 1850.   1 sheet.

2213.
[Letter signed 'A citizen elector', February 26, 1851]
Lincoln: printed W. Bellatti, 1851.   1 sheet.

2214.   **SIBTHORP, Charles De Laet Waldo**
[Letter, March 10th, 1852]
[Lincoln]: [s.n.], [1852].   1 sheet.

2215.   **SEELY, Charles**
[Letter, 13th March, 1852]
[Lincoln]: [s.n.], [1852].   1 sheet.

2216.   **SIBTHORP, Charles De Laet Waldo**
[Letter, March 22nd, 1852]
[Lincoln]: [s.n.], [1852].   1 sheet.

2217.
[Election squib in form of lost/reward poster, 25th March, 1852]
[Lincoln]: [s.n.], [1852].   1 sheet.

2218.   **LYTTON, Edward Bulwer**
[Letter, March 25th, 1852]
[Lincoln]: [s.n.], [1852].   1 sheet.

2219.
[Resolutions of meeting of Conservatives held at Spread Eagle Inn, March 27th, 1852]
[Lincoln]: [s.n.], [1852].   1 sheet.

2220.
No dictation!: [notice of public meeting of 'the friends of freedom of election', March 27th, 1852]
[Lincoln]: [s.n.], [1852].   1 sheet.

2221.   **TURNER, Montague Meryweather**
[Letter, March 27th, 1852]
[Lincoln]: [s.n.], [1852].   1 sheet.

2222.   **BULWER, H.L.**
[Letter, 31st March, 1852]
[Lincoln]: [s.n.], [1852].   1 sheet.

2223.   **SIBTHORP, Humphrey W.**
[Letter, March 31st, 1852]
[Lincoln]: [s.n.], [1852].   1 sheet.

2224.   **TURNER, Montague Meryweather**
[Letter, March 31, 1852]
[Lincoln]: [s.n.], [1852].   1 sheet.

2225.
[Letters between Richard Mason and Sir Henry Lytton Bulwer about the candidacy for Lincoln, March, 1852]
[Lincoln]: [s.n.], [1852].   1 sheet.

2226.   **HENEAGE, G. Fieschi**
[Letter, April 1st, 1852]
[Lincoln]: [s.n.], [1852].   1 sheet.

2227.
[Squib in form of advertisement for lecture 'on the art and uses of blackguardism', April 2nd, 1852]
[Lincoln]: [s.n.], [1852].   1 sheet.

2228.
To Mr Charles Seely and his free trade allies: [letter, April 2, 1852]
[Lincoln]: [s.n.], [1852].   1 sheet.

2229.   **TURNER, Montague Meryweather**
[Letter, April 5th, 1852]
[Lincoln]: [s.n.], [1852].   1 sheet.

2230.   **SIBTHORP, Charles De Laet Waldo**
[Letter, April 10th, 1852]
[Lincoln]: [s.n.], [1852].   1 sheet.

2231.
To the Protestant electors of the city of Lincoln: [letter signed 'A Protestant', July 2nd, 1852]
[Lincoln]: [s.n.], [1852].   1 sheet.

2232.
[Letter signed 'A freeman', July 2nd, 1852]
[Lincoln]: [s.n.], [1852].   1 sheet.

2233.   **HENEAGE, G.F.**
[Letter, July 3rd, 1852]
[Lincoln]: [s.n.], [1852].   1 sheet.

2234.
[Poster requesting friends of Colonel Sibthorp to be at the nomination, July 5th, 1852]
Lincoln: printed T.J.N. Brogden, 1852.   1 sheet.

2235.
[Poster about preservation of peace during poll, July 6th, 1852]
Lincoln: printed W. and B. Brooke, 1852.   1 sheet.

2236.   **SIBTHORP, Charles De Laet Waldo**
[Letter with state of poll, July 8th, 1852]
Lincoln: printed T.O. Brumby, 1852.   1 sheet.

2237.   **COLLETT, W.R.**
[Letter]
[Lincoln]: [s.n.], [1852].   1 sheet.

2238.
To Mr Chas. Seely, Esq., ex-M.P.: [letter signed 'Anti-Seelyite']
[Lincoln]: [s.n.], [1852].   1 sheet.

2239.
[Poster pro Seely and anti Henry Bulwer Lytton]
[Lincoln]: [s.n.], [1852].   1 sheet.

2240.
The Military: [letter signed 'An elector']
Lincoln: printed Charles Akrill, [1852].   1 sheet.

2241.   **SEELY, Charles**
[Letter, December 15th, 1855]
Lincoln: printed Chas. Akrill, 1855.   1 sheet.

2242.   **SIBTHORP, Gervase T.W.**
[Letter, 15th December, 1855]
Lincoln: printed Edward R. Cousans, 1855.   1 sheet.

2243.   **CARLINE, Richard**
[Letter announcing death of Col. Sibthorp and the candidacy of Gervase Sibthorp]
[Lincoln]: [s.n.], [1856].   1 sheet.

2244.
[Letter from election committee about possibility of Sir Henry Lytton Bulwer standing as candidate]
[Lincoln]: [s.n.], [1856?].   1 sheet.

2245.   **SIBTHORP, G.T. Waldo**
[Letter, March 14th, 1857]
Lincoln: printed T.O. Brumby, 1857.   1 sheet.

2246.
[Poster, giving date of poll, 24th March, 1857]
Lincoln: printed W. and B. Brooke, 1857.   1 sheet.

2247.
[Letter signed 'An on-looker', March 24th, 1857]
Lincoln: printed Edward R. Cousans, 1857.   1 sheet.

2248.   **SIBTHORP, G.T. Waldo**
[Letter, March 25th, 1857]
Lincoln: printed R. Loder, 1857.   1 sheet.

2249.   **HENEAGE, G.F.**
[Letter, March 26th, 1857]
Lincoln: printed T.O. Brumby, 1857.   1 sheet.

2250.   **SIBTHORP, G.T. Waldo**
[Letter, March 30th, 1857]
Lincoln: printed Edward R. Cousans, 1857.   1 sheet.

2251.
[Letter to J. Hinde Palmer signed 'An elector']
Lincoln: printed R. Loder, [1857].   1 sheet.

2252.   SHUTTLEWORTH, Joseph
[Letter in support of J. Hinde Palmer]
[Lincoln]: [s.n.], [1857].   1 sheet.

2253.
[Election squib, April 27th, 1859]
Lincoln: printed R.E. Leary, 1859.   1 sheet: ill.

2254.   SIBTHORP, G.T. Waldo
[Letter, 14th April, 1859]
Lincoln: printed Thomas Oxley, T.O. Brumby, 1859.   1 sheet.

2255.
Chick! chick! chick!: [election squib in form of letter addressed to Major Sibthorp by
'Molly Muggins', April 18th, 1859]
Lincoln: printed J. Ellett Brogden, 1859.   1 sheet.

2256.   SIBTHORP, G.T. Waldo
[Letter, 2nd May, 1859]
Lincoln: printed Loder, 1859.   1 sheet.

2257.
Great attraction: [election squib]
[Lincoln]: [s.n.], [1859].   1 sheet.

2258.
[Election squib in form of theatre poster]
Lincoln: printed Loder, [1859?].   1 sheet.

2259.   SEELY, Charles
[Letter, October 18th, 1861]
Lincoln: printed Charles Akrill, 1861.   1 sheet.

2260.
The Sunday question to the electors of Lincoln: [October 29th, 1861]
Lincoln: printed R.E. Leary, 1861.   1 sheet.

2261.   SEELY, Charles
Speech of Mr Charles Seely at the nomination, on Saturday, November 9, 1861
Lincoln: printed J. Ellett Brogden, 1861.   1 sheet.

2262.
[Letter, November 11th, 1861]
Lincoln: printed R.E. Leary, 1861.   1 sheet.

2263.
[Political cartoon]
Lincoln: printed R.E. Leary, [1861?].   1 sheet: ill.

2264.
The New 'perfect cure' : a radical song
[Lincoln]: [s.n.], [1862].   1 sheet.

2265.
[Letter signed 'An elector', May 27th, 1865]
Lincoln: printed J.E. Brogden, 1865. 1 sheet.
Originally published: in *Lincoln standard*, May 30th, 1865.

2266. **HENEAGE, G.F.**
[Letter, November 16, 1868]
Lincoln: printed J.E. Brogden, 1868. 1 sheet.

2267. **PALMER, J. Hinde**
[Letter, 16th November, 1868]
Lincoln: printed Charles Keyworth, 1868. 1 sheet.

2268. **MARSHALL, William**
[Letter with copy of defamatory letter, October 22nd, 1870]
Lincoln: printed Edward R. Cousans, 1870. 1 sheet.

2269.
Flying visit to Lincoln of England's Grand Old Traitor!
[Lincoln]: [s.n.], [1870]. 1 sheet.

2270.
Lincoln city election, February 2nd, 1874: result of poll
Lincoln: printed S. Ward, 1874. 1 sheet.

2271. **CHAPLIN, Edward**
[Letter, February 3rd, 1874]
Lincoln: printed T.O. Brumby, 1874. 1 sheet.

2272. **SEELY, Charles**
[Letter, February 3rd, 1874]
Lincoln: printed Pacy and Ouzman, 1874. 1 sheet.

2273. **PALMER, John Hinde**
Report of the presentation of an address to Mr John Hinde Palmer, Q.C., late M.P. for Lincoln, at a meeting held in the Corn Exchange, on the 27th October, 1874
Lincoln: printed Charles Akrill, 1874. 16p.

2274. **CHAPLIN, Edward**
[Letter, 9th March, 1880]
[Lincoln]: [s.n.], [1880]. 1 sheet.

2275.
[Letter canvassing for Col. Chaplin, 9th March, 1880]
[Lincoln]: [s.n.], [1880]. 1 sheet.

2276. **SEELY, Charles**
[Letter, March 31st, 1880]
Lincoln: printed Samuel Ward, 1880. 1 sheet.

2277. ―――――――
[Letter, May 5th, 1885]
Lincoln: printed Henry E. Cousans, 1885. 1 sheet.

2278. ―――――――
[Letter, 28th June, 1895]
Lincoln: M.A. Doncaster, 1895. 1 sheet.

221

2279. ───────────
[Letter, 12th July, 1904]
Lincoln: Gazette and Echo, 1904.   [3]p.

2280. ───────────
Reprint of speech delivered by C.H. Seely, Esq., M.P., at the Corn Exchange, Lincoln, on the 30th September, 1904
Lincoln: printed Gazette and Echo, [1904].   19p.

MUNICIPAL HISTORY

2281.
[Paragraph on Charter of the city of Lincoln]
in *The London gazette*, Thursday, January 8–Monday, January 12, 1684.

2282. **MADOX, Thomas**
Firma burgi, or An historical essay concerning the cities, towns and buroughs of England, taken from records
London: printed by William Bowyer, 1726.   [24], 297, [28]p.
Includes index.
> Includes various brief references to Lincoln; the information is often contained in notes.

2283. **OLDFIELD, T.H.B.**
An Entire and complete history, political and personal, of the boroughs of Great Britain: to which is prefixed an original sketch of constitutional rights, from the earliest period until the present time...
London: printed for G. Riley, 1792.   3 vols.
> Vol.2, pp.206–211: Lincoln.

2284. **LONG, George**
The Summary and observations which conclude the report of Messrs Long & Buckle, the commissioners of enquiry into the state of the Lincoln Corporation
Lincoln: printed E.B. Drury, [183?].   1 sheet.
> Originally published: in the Parliamentary report on the city of Lincoln.

2285. **ROSS, John**
Civitas Lincolnia: from its municipal and other records
Lincoln: Edward Ralph Cousans, 1870.   118p.

2286. **LINCOLN CORPORATION**
City of Lincoln and county of the same city: [leaflet]
[Lincoln]: [The Corporation], [19??].   1 folded sheet: ill.
> Derivation of the name of the city, with mayoralty seal and arms.

2287. **BIRCH, Walter de Gray**
City of Lincoln: catalogue of the royal Charters and other documents belonging to the Corporation of Lincoln, preserved in the Muniment Room of the Corporation offices
pp.88–95 in *LN&Q*, vol.10, no.3, 1908.
Continued: pp.107–118, vol.10, no.4; pp.150–156, vol.10, no.5, 1909; pp.218–223, vol.10, no.7; pp.250–255, vol.10, no.8; pp.19–26, vol.11, no.1, 1910; pp.62–64, vol.11, no.2; pp.94–96, vol.11, no.3; pp.123–128, vol.11, no.4.

2288. **HILL, J.W.F.**
Notes on some aspects of the legal and constitutional history of the city of Lincoln
pp.177–232 in *AAS reports and papers*, vol.37, 1923–25.
> Covers the Corporation, Gilds, etc.

2289.
Lincoln municipal activities: [scrapbook of newspaper articles]
[1927].   [51]p.
> Includes: water; gas; electricity; roads; transport; emergency services; health service; housing;
> education; parks and cemeteries; commons; markets; libraries, museums and art gallery;
> Technical college; and finance.   Comprises series of 16 articles with photographs of council
> members reponsible for each section.

2290.
Provisions for the government of the city of Lincoln, circa 1300
translated by Samuel Lyon.
pp.25–30 in *LN&Q*, vol.20, no.2, 1928–29.
> Includes preface by J.W.F. Hill.   Lyon was town clerk in 1785.

2291.   **HILL, J.W.F.**
*The Tercentenary of the grant of the Charter of Charles I, 18 December, 1628–18
December, 1928*
Lincoln: Lincoln Corporation, 1928.   [3]p.: ill.

2292.   **LINDSEY COUNTY COUNCIL**
*The Lindsey County Council and the Assessment Committee and the Rating Authority for
the city of Lincoln: description of Lindsey County Council Hall and offices, with
description of Lincoln Corporation offices*
[Lincoln]: [The Council], [1933].   4 leaves.
Accompanies: 10p. photograph album.
> Includes: facade from Newland main entrance; facade from south-east; facade from
> south-west; north frontage and entrance; west facade; north frontage showing caretaker's lodge
> and old St Martin's Church; north frontage from north-east showing north entrance gateway.

2293.   **THOMAS, J.H.**
*Town government in the sixteenth century: based chiefly on the records of the following
provincial towns: Cambridge, Chester, Ipswich, Leicester, Lincoln, Manchester,
Northampton...*
London: George Allen & Unwin, 1933.   188p., [4] leaves of plates.
Includes index.
> Lincoln mentioned passim.

2294.   **TAIT, James**
The Medieval English borough: studies on its origins and constitutional history
Manchester: Manchester University Press, 1936.   xx, 371p.
(Publications of the University of Manchester, CCXLV.   Historical series, LXX)
Includes index.
> References to Lincoln passim.

2295.   **HILL, J.W.F.**
The Corporation of Lincoln
Lincoln: Architectural and Archaeological Society, [1940s-1950s?].   56p.
> Concerns the legal and constitutional history of the city of Lincoln.

2296.   **LINCOLN CORPORATION**
*Local government re-organisation in England: statement on behalf of Lincoln City
Council*
Lincoln: The Corporation, 1971.   8p.

2297.   **MEREWETHER, H.A.**
The History of the boroughs and municipal corporations of the United Kingdom, from
the earliest to the present time
by H.A. Merewether and A.J. Stephens.
Brighton: Harvester Press, 1972.   3 vols.
Originally published: 1835.
  pp.268–270: Lincoln; other references passim.

2298.
'74 Lincolnshire reorganisation: election special bulletin, no.4, April, 1973
Lincoln: Holland, Kesteven and Lindsey County Council and Lincoln City Council,
1973.   [4]p.: ill., map.

2299.   **JOHNSON, C.P.C.**
No government democracy in days of old
ill. in *Lincolnshire echo*, Friday, December 30, 1977.
  Local government from medieval period to municipal reform in 1830s.

MUNICIPAL OFFICES

2300.
Chronological table of the high sheriffs of the county of Lincoln, and of the knights of the
shire, citizens and burgesses in Parliament within the same, from the earliest accounts to
the present time
London: printed for Joseph White, 1779.   iv, 55p.

2301.
Names of the mayors, bailiffs, sheriffs and chamberlains of the city of Lincoln,
since...1313...with a concise abridgement of the city Charter...a compendious account of
the city and town...the whole forming a complete history of Lincoln
Lincoln: printed and sold by J.W. Drury, [1787?].   125p.

2302.
Instructions to presiding deputy sheriff
Lincoln: printed W. and B. Brooke, [18??].   [2]p.

2303.
Election of a coroner: [notice]
Lincoln: printed W. Brooke, 1827.   1 sheet.
  Ms. additions suggest that was used as a template for later notice.

2304.   **HADDERSLEY, C.R.**
[Letter relating to election of coroner, January 11th, 1831]
Lincoln: printed T.O. Brumby, 1831.   1 sheet.

2305.
[Resolutions of a meeting of the magistrates and grand jury at March Assizes, held at
Lincoln Castle, relating to the office of high sheriff, 9 March, 1831]
London: printed James & Luke Hansard, [1831].   7p.

2306.   **CARLINE, Richard**
[Notebook kept during his time as chamberlain, 1832–33, and later as sheriff, 1834–35]
[1832–35].   [35] leaves.
Ms.

> Includes accounts of Leet Jury, St Thomas' Day, Christmas Day, Easter Day, Holyrood Day
> during Carline's time both as chamberlain and then as sheriff.   Also for the period 1834–35,
> St Michael's Day, the appointment of constables and elections.

2307.
[Lincolnshire: resolutions and correspondence relating to the office of high sheriff, 8
February, 1832]
London: printed James and Luke Hansard, 1832.   7p.

2308.   **HOLGATE, Chas. Henry**
[Letter applying for post of coroner]
Lincoln: printed T.O. Brumby, 1838.   1 sheet.

2309.
Election of coroner: [result, April 2, 1839]
Lincoln: printed W. and B. Brooke, 1839.   1 sheet.

2310.
[Lists of magistrates, overseers of the poor, surveyors of the highways, parochial
constables, Lincoln police constables]
Lincoln: printed W. Peck, 1846–47.   2 sheets.

2311.
[Lists of magistrates, overseers of the poor...]
Lincoln: printed W. Peck, 1847–48.   2 sheets.

2312.
[Lists of magistrates, overseers of the poor...]
Lincoln: printed Charles Akrill, 1855–56.   2 sheets.

2313.
Presentation to the ex-mayor of Lincoln, Edwin Pratt, Esq., April 7th, 1892
[Lincoln]: [printed Williamson], [1892].   11p.
> Originally published: in *Lincoln gazette*.

2314.
The First mayor, sheriff & under sheriff of Lincoln of the 20th century
pp.166–168: ill. in *Lincolnshire poacher*, vol.1, no.8, 1901.
> Refers to C.W. Pennell, F.H. Livens and M.H. Footman.

2315.
*Citie of Lincolne and county of ye same citie: to wyt: crying Chrystemes in ye 15th
century*: [Christmas, 1908/New Year, 1909 greetings from the high constable of Lincoln]
[Lincoln]: [Lincoln Corporation], [1908].   [3]p.
> Refers to custom performed by the City Waits.

2316.
Sept-centenary of election of first mayor of Lincoln
Lincoln: [Lincoln Corporation], 1909.   [3]p.
> Christmas/New Year greetings card from mayor and mayoress, giving brief history based on
> Charters and pipe rolls.

2317.
Sept-centenary of election of first mayor of Lincoln [and] quin-centenary of Charter by King Henry IV, 21st November, 1409, and of election of first sheriffs of Lincoln...presented for use in the...city of Lincoln...
Lincoln: printed Ruddock, 1910.   1 sheet: ill.
   Intended to be displayed on the wall in various Departments of the Corporation.

2318.   **HILL, J.W.F.**
Three lists of the mayors, bailiffs and sheriffs of the city of Lincoln
pp.217–256 in *AAS reports and papers*, vol.39, no.2, 1929.

2319.   **FANE, R.W.R.**
A List of the high sheriffs of Lincolnshire, 1154–1935
[Lincoln]: [s.n.], [1939].   29, [11]p.
Includes index.

2320.   **KING, John Bean**
A List of the mayors, sheriffs, chamberlains, recorders and town clerks of the city of Lincoln
[1945].   104, [16]p.
Ms.
   Pages have been inserted covering recent years, including some newspaper photographs.

2321.   **LINCOLN CORPORATION**
City of Lincoln mayoral souvenir, 1966–7
[Lincoln]: [The Corporation], [1967].   [5]p.: ill.
   Gives information on office of mayor.

CIVIC INSIGNIA

2322.   **JEWITT, Llewellyn**
The Corporation plate insignia of office of the cities and towns of England and Wales
edited and completed with large additions by W.H. St John Hope.
London: Bemrose, 1895.   2 vols.
   Vol.2, pp.71–78: Lincoln.

2323.   **WILLIAMS, J.G.**
The City of Lincoln: the mayor's ring
pp.97–102, [2] leaves of plates in *LN&Q*, vol.6, no.48, 1900.

2324.   _____
[Paper on the three state swords of the city of Lincoln]
pp.18–32, [1] leaf of plates in *Proceedings of the Society of Antiquaries*, vol.XIX, December 12, 1901.

2325.   _____
City of Lincoln civic insignia: the swords
pp.193–203, [1] leaf of plates in *LN&Q*, vol.6, no.51, 1901.

2326.   _____
City of Lincoln civic insignia: the maces
pp.129–135, [2] leaves of plates in *LN&Q*, vol.6, no.49, 1901.

2327. ——————
Lincoln civic insignia: the King Richard II sword
pp.65–71, [1] leaf of plates in *LN&Q*, vol.7, no.55, 1902.

2328. ——————
Lincoln civic insignia: the King Richard II sword, continued
pp.97–106, [1] leaf of plates in *LN&Q*, vol.7, no.56, 1902.

2329. ——————
Lincoln civic insignia: the Charles I, or third, sword
pp.65–72, [1] leaf of plates in *LN&Q*, vol.8, no.63, 1904.

2330. ——————
Lincoln civic insignia: the Charles I, or third, sword, continued
pp.97–117, [1] leaf of plates in *LN&Q*, vol.8, no.64, 1904.

2331. ——————
Lincoln civic insignia: the Charles I, or third, sword, continued
pp.129–155, [1] leaf of plates in *LN&Q*, vol.8, no.65, 1905.

2332. ——————
Lincoln civic insignia: the Charles I, or third, sword, continued
pp.161–185, [1] leaf of plates in *LN&Q*, vol.8, no.66, 1905.

2333. **KERR, W.J.B.**
The Puzzling inscription on the third state sword of the city of Lincoln
pp.241–243 in *LN&Q*, vol.12, no.8, 1913.

2334. **WILLIAMS, J.G.**
The Insignia of the city of Lincoln
pp.181–199: ill. in *The Journal of the British Archaeological Association*, new series,
vol.XXVII, pt.2, December, 1921.

2335. **HILL, J.W.F.**
The City of Lincoln insignia
pp.177–183 in *The Lincolnshire magazine*, vol.1, 1932–34.

2336. ——————
The City of Lincoln insignia
Lincoln: Lincolnshire Publishing Company, 1964. [14]p.: ill.
Originally published: 1950.

2337. **SWAIN, Marilyn**
The World of antiques: city of Lincoln collection of silver. 1: civic insignia
p.7: ill. in *Lincolnshire life*, vol.24, no.12, March, 1985.

2338. ——————
The World of antiques: city of Lincoln collection of silver. 2: civic plate
p.7: ill. in *Lincolnshire life*, vol.25, no.1, April, 1985.

2339. **SULLIVAN, B.**
Some notes on the city of Lincoln's great mace
[1987]. [2] leaves.
Typescript.

FREEMEN

2340.
The Oath of a free-man of the city of Lincoln
[Lincoln]: [W. Wood], [17??].   1 sheet.

2341.
[Meeting for admissions to freedom of the city, October 27, 1806]
Lincoln: printed J.W. Drury, 1806.   1 sheet.

2342.   **PINK, W.D.**
Lincoln poor freemen
pp.232–233 in *LN&Q*, vol.2, no.8, 1891.

2343.
Presentation of the honorary freedom of the city to the Royal Air Force station
Waddington, Saturday, the 25th day of April, 1959
Lincoln: [Lincoln Corporation], [1959].   6p.: ill.

2344.   **WARD, Harry**
Freemen in England
[Epsom]: [The Author], 1967.   [43]p.
    pp.57–58 Lincoln.

2345.
The Ceremony of the presentation of the honorary freedom of the city to Sir Charles
Bruce Locker Tennyson, the Theatre Royal, Clasketgate, Lincoln, Saturday, the 9th day
of May, 1970
Lincoln: Lincoln Corporation, 1970.   1 folded sheet: ill.

2346.   **GILD OF FREEMEN OF THE CITY OF LINCOLN**
Rules
[Lincoln]: [The Gild], [1973].   [14]p.

2347.
Roll of honorary freemen of the city, 1891–1974
[1974].   [6]p.
Typescript.

MUNICIPAL ELECTIONS

2348.
The Pious petition of lawyer Noodle: [verse]
[Lincoln]: [s.n.], [18??].   1 sheet.

2349.
Extension of the elective franchise: [account of meeting, April 3, 1826]
Lincoln: printed W. Brooke, 1826.   1 sheet.

2350.
People of Lincoln: [letter about government signed 'Lincolniensis']
[Lincoln]: [s.n.], [1832?].   1 sheet.

2351.
Thomas & John: [dialogue about election of town council]
Lincoln: printed Keyworth, [1832?].   1 sheet.

2352.   **NORTHHOUSE, W.S.**
Hints to municipal electors: a test for candidates, with directions, and the clauses in the Corporation Reform Act connected with the election of councillors
London: Joseph Thomas, [1832?].   12p.

2353.   **HITCHINS, James**
To the public: [letter giving explanation of property deal and allegations of bribery, December, 1833]
Lincoln: printed James Hitchins, 1833.   [4]p.

2354.
Corporation Reform Bill: to the inhabitants of Lincoln: [letter signed 'An elector of the Bail']
Lincoln: printed Brogden, [1835?].   4p.

2355.
[Letter against Municipal Reform Bill signed 'Anti-Jacobin', July 2nd, 1835]
Lincoln: printed T.J.N. Brogden, 1835.   1 sheet.

2356.
[Letter about municipal elections]
Lincoln: printed E.B. Drury, 1835.   1 sheet.
Originally published: in *Municipal corporation reformer*, July 11, 1835.

2357.
[Letter about Municipal Corporation Reform Bill signed 'A Conservative but no bigot', September 3rd, 1835]
Lincoln: printed T.O. Brumby, 1835.   1 sheet.

2358.
To the burgesses under the new Municipal Reform Act: [letter signed 'A friend to good order', 30th November, 1835]
Lincoln: printed T.O. Brumby, 1835.   1 sheet.

2359.   **LINCOLN CONSERVATIVE AND GUARDIAN SOCIETY**
Municipal elections: [resolutions of the ordinary meeting of the Lincoln Conservative and Guardian Society...10th December, 1835]
Lincoln: printed T.J.N. Brogden, 1835.   1 sheet.

2360.
Municipal reform: [petition, December 19, 1835]
Lincoln: printed E.B. Drury, 1835.   1 sheet.

2361.   **HITCHINS, James**
[Letter to the municipal electors, December 22, 1835]
[Lincoln]: [s.n.], [1835].   1 sheet.

2362.
[Account of meeting of the Friends to Conservatism, December 22nd, 1835]
Lincoln: printed T.J.N. Brogden, 1835.   1 sheet.

2363.
Doings of the old Corporation starchamber as exhibited at the Guildhall, twenty-second of December, 1835: [squib]
Lincoln: printed J. Stainton, 1835.   1 sheet.

2364.
[Letter about the Municipal Corporation Reform Bill signed 'The Liberal Society']
[Lincoln]: [s.n.], [1835?].   1 sheet.

2365.
A List of the names of the persons elected councillors for the city of Lincoln...26th December, 1835
Lincoln: printed W. and B. Brooke, 1835.   1 sheet.

2366.
Lincoln's first municipal election, 1835: [results]
Lincoln: printed E.B. Drury, 1835.   1 sheet.

2367.
To the inhabitants of Lincoln: [letter making charges of self interest, in decision of Corporation about reletting – as opposed to selling – the City Arms Hotel, March 4th, 1837]
Lincoln: printed J. Stainton, 1837.   1 sheet.

2368.
[Letter against Robert Swan signed 'A hater of tyrants and slave drivers']
[Lincoln]: [s.n.], [1838?].   1 sheet.

2369.   **HAYES, George**
[Notice of revision of lists of voters, 15th September, 1839]
Lincoln: printed James Drury, 1839.   1 sheet.

2370.   **CALDER, G.**
[Letter, September 2nd, 1842]
Lincoln: printed W. and B. Brooke, 1842.   1 sheet.

2371.
[Notice of election of a councillor, 14th June, 1843]
Lincoln: printed R.E. Leary, 1843.   1 sheet.

2372.
List of persons entitled to vote in the election of Members for the city of Lincoln, in respect of property occupied within the parish of Saint Margaret...31st July, 1843
Lincoln: printed W. and B. Brooke, 1843.   1 sheet.

2373.   **SWAN, Robert**
[Letter, September 27th, 1843]
Robert Swan, Henry Williams, William Marshall.
Lincoln: printed T.O. Brumby, 1843.   1 sheet.

2374.
[Poster warning against disturbing the peace during the municipal election, 1st November, 1843]
Lincoln: printed R.E. Leary, 1843.   1 sheet.

2375.
Election of auditors: [notice and instructions, February 23rd, 1844]
Lincoln: printed T.O. Brumby, 1844.   1 sheet.

2376.
[Notice about admission to the register of voters, 15th July, 1844]
Lincoln: printed T.O. Brumby, 1844. 1 sheet.

2377.
List of persons entitled to vote in the election of Members for the city of Lincoln, in
respect of property occupied within the parish of Saint Peter-at-Arches...July 31st, 1844
Lincoln: printed W. and B. Brooke, 1844. 1 sheet.

2378.
List of persons objected to...August 31st, 1844
Lincoln: printed W. and B. Brooke, 1844. 1 sheet.

2379.
List of claimants...August 31st, 1844
Lincoln: printed W. and B. Brooke, 1844. 1 sheet.

2380.
[Notice of election of auditors and assessors, February 24th, 1845]
Lincoln: printed John Hall, 1845. 1 sheet.

2381.
The Mayor & Corporation: [letter to the burgesses of Lincoln signed 'One of the 1500!!
who treated the mayor with "contumely" ', April 11th, 1845]
Lincoln: printed T.J.N. Brogden, 1845. 1 sheet.

2382.
List of persons entitled to vote...parish of Saint Paul...31st July, 1845: [no.3]
Lincoln: printed W. and B. Brooke, 1845. 1 sheet.

2383.
List of persons objected to...28th August, 1845
Lincoln: printed W. and B. Brooke, 1845. 1 sheet.

2384.
Claimant: 28th day August, 1845: the following person claims to have his name inserted
in the list of persons entitled to vote in the election of members for the city of Lincoln
Lincoln: printed W. and B. Brooke, 1845. 1 sheet.

2385.
List of citizens of the city of Lincoln, in the parish of Saint Paul...September 3rd, 1845
Lincoln: printed W. and B. Brooke, 1845. 1 sheet.

2386.   **CARLINE, Richard**
[Letter, December 15th, 1845]
Lincoln: printed T.O. Brumby, 1845. 1 sheet.

2387.
The List of citizens of the city of Lincoln, in the parish of St Mary-le-Wigford
Lincoln: printed W. and B. Brooke, [1845?]. 1 sheet.

2388.
The List of citizens of the city of Lincoln, in the parish of St Peter-at-Arches
Lincoln: printed W. and B. Brooke, [1845?]. 1 sheet.

2389.
[Notice about admission to register of voters, 8 July, 1846]
Lincoln: printed W. Peck, 1846. 1 sheet.

2390.
List of persons entitled to vote...parish of Saint Peter-at-Arches...July 31, 1846
Lincoln: printed W. and B. Brooke, 1846. 1 sheet.

2391.
[Poster about revision of the burgess' lists, no.536, 22 September, 1846]
Lincoln: printed W. Peck, 1846. 1 sheet.

2392.
[Notice of election of auditors and assessors, February 24th, 1847]
Lincoln: printed T.J.N. Brogden, 1847. 1 sheet.

2393.
List of claimants to be published by the overseers, August 28th, 1847
Lincoln: printed W. and B. Brooke, 1847. 1 sheet.

2394.
Lists of claimants objected to, 28th August, 1847: [no.8]
Lincoln: printed W. and B. Brooke, 1847. 1 sheet.

2395.   **PONSONBY, Frank**
[Notice about revision of lists of voters, 30th September, 1847]
Lincoln: printed James Drury, 1847. 1 sheet.

2396.
[Notice of election of councillors, 23rd October, 1847]
Lincoln: printed T.J.N. Brogden, 1847. 1 sheet.

2397.
Shade of Thomas Michael Keyworth, Esq.: [poem]
[Lincoln]: [s.n.], [1847?]. 1 sheet.

2398.   **LILBURN, Richard**
To James Hitchins, fishmonger, &c.: [letter, February 7th, 1848]
[Lincoln]: [s.n.], [1848]. 1 sheet.

2399.   **STEPHENSON, John**
To the burgesses of the middle ward: [letter, September 4th, 1848]
Lincoln: printed T.J.N. Brogden, 1848. 1 sheet.

2400.   **WARD, Charles**
To the burgesses of the upper ward: [letter, September 4th, 1848]
Lincoln: printed for W. Peck, 1848. 1 sheet.

2401.
To the burgesses of the middle ward: [letter signed 'A working man', October 31st, 1848]
[Lincoln]: [s.n.], [1848]. 1 sheet.

2402.
[Notice about admission to register of voters, 9th July, 1849]
Lincoln: printed W. Bellatti, 1849. 1 sheet.

2403.   **ALLINSON, Charles**
To the electors of the middle ward: [letter, September 24th, 1849]
Lincoln: printed T.J.N. Brogden, 1849. 1 sheet.

2404.   **HAYES, George**
[Notice of court to revise lists of voters, 15th September, 1849]
Lincoln: printed James Drury, 1849. 1 sheet.

2405.
Revision of the burgess' lists: [18th September, 1849]
Lincoln: printed W. Bellatti, 1849. 1 sheet.

2406. **CALDER, Geo.**
To the electors of the middle ward: [letter, September 24th, 1849]
[Lincoln]: [s.n.], [1849]. 1 sheet.

2407. **WILKINSON, J.S.**
To the electors of the middle ward: [letter, September 24th, 1849]
Lincoln: printed at the Times, 1849. 1 sheet.

2408. **ANDREW, William**
To the municipal electors of the lower ward: [letter, 27th September, 1849]
William Andrew, Henry Moss.
Lincoln: printed James Drury, 1849. 1 sheet.

2409.
[Notice of election of councillors, 25th October, 1849]
Lincoln: printed W. Bellatti, 1849. 1 sheet.

2410.
Brogden [on] barristers!: [squib]
Lincoln: printed Charles Loder, [185?]. 1 sheet.

2411. **SAYLES, F.A.**
To the municipal electors of the lower ward: [letter, June 1st, 1850]
Lincoln: printed at the Times, 1850. 1 sheet.

2412. **ANDREW, William**
To the municipal electors of Lincoln: [letter, 3rd June, 1850]
Lincoln: printed T.J.N. Brogden, 1850. 1 sheet.

2413. **FISHER, Wm.**
To the municipal electors of Lincoln: [letter, 3rd June, 1850]
Lincoln: printed T.J.N. Brogden, 1850. 1 sheet.

2414. **NORTON, W.C.**
To the electors of the upper ward: [letter, October 5th, 1850]
W.C. Norton, L.G. Hall.
Lincoln: printed T.J.N. Brogden, 1850. 1 sheet.

2415.
To the electors of the middle ward: [spoof letter signed 'John Ruston', October 8th, 1850]
[Lincoln]: [s.n.], [1850]. 1 sheet.

2416.
Lilbum's royal menageries will be exhibited for one night only: [election squib]
[Lincoln]: [s.n.], [1850]. 1 sheet.

2417.
To the electors of the upper ward: [letter in support of Wm. Parry]
Lincoln: printed W. Bellatti, [1850?]. 1 sheet.

2418.
List of citizens of the city of Lincoln, in the parish of Saint Swithin
Lincoln: printed Brogden, 1850. 6 sheets.

2419.
Municipal electors of the Bridge ward in the city of Lincoln: [spoof? letter signed 'Bully Smith', 21st October, 1851]
Lincoln: printed T.O. Brumby, 1851.   1 sheet.

2420.   **BELLATTI, William Henry**
[Letter refuting charges made against him by James Hitchins in handbill called *The Bane and the antidote*, December 11th, 1851]
[Lincoln]: [The Author], [1851].

2421.   **BROGDEN, T.J.N.**
To the electors of the upper ward: [letter, September 30, 1854]
Lincoln: printed T.J.N. Brogden, 1854.   1 sheet.

2422.   **CLAYTON, Nathaniel**
To the municipal electors of the middle ward: [letter, October 2nd, 1854]
Lincoln: printed Charles Akrill, 1854.   1 sheet.

2423.   **WARD, Charles**
To the burgesses of the upper ward, October 2nd, 1854: [letter]
Lincoln: printed W. Peck, 1854.   1 sheet.

2424.   **TUXFORD, W.**
To the independent municipal electors of the middle ward: [letter, September 17th, 1855]
Lincoln: printed R.E. Leary, 1855.   1 sheet.

2425.
To the electors of the upper ward: [letter, October 15th, 1855]
[Lincoln]: [s.n.], [1855].   1 sheet.

2426.
To the electors of the upper ward: [letter, October 15th, 1855]
Lincoln: printed R.E. Leary, 1855.   1 sheet.

2427.
To the electors of the upper ward: [letter signed 'An elector', October 16th, 1855]
Lincoln: printed R.E. Leary, 1855.   1 sheet.

2428.
To Messrs Clayton, Shuttleworth & Co.: [letter signed 'The foundrymen', October 29th, 1855]
Lincoln: printed W. Doncaster, 1855.   1 sheet.
   Requesting right to vote freely.

2429.   **PARRY, William**
To the electors of the upper ward: [letter, October 30th, 1855]
Lincoln: printed R.E. Leary, 1855.   1 sheet.

2430.
The Lincoln meeting, November 1st, 1855: [election squib in form of race programme]
Lincoln: printed R.E. Leary, 1855.   1 sheet.

2431.
Lincoln autumn meeting, 1855...Council Stakes: [election squib in form of race programme]
Lincoln: printed Doncaster, 1855.   1 sheet.

2432.
Encroachments of corporations: [letter signed 'An ejected parish leaseholder']
Lincoln: printed Charles Akrill, [1855?].   1 sheet.

2433.
The Lower ward donkey race: [poem]
[Lincoln]: [s.n.], [1855].   1 sheet.

2434.
To the electors of the lower ward: [letter signed 'A father of eight children']
Lincoln: printed Charles Akrill, [1855?].   1 sheet.

2435.   **WARD, Charles**
To the burgesses of the upper ward: [letter, September 23rd, 1857]
Lincoln: printed W. Peck, 1857.   1 sheet.

2436.
City of Lincoln municipal elections: [notice of date of poll, 12th October, 1858]
Lincoln: printed J. Ellett Brogden, 1858.   1 sheet.

2437.
Hypocracy!!: a farce.   Scene 1: a brewery scene; 2: the Corn Exchange
Lincoln: printed J. Ellett Brogden, [186?].   1 sheet.
    Features members of Council: Carline; Marshall; Hebb; Harrison; Chambers.

2438.
To the municipal electors of the city of Lincoln: [letter signed 'A Conservative',
November 12th, 1860]
Lincoln: printed R. Loder, 1860.   1 sheet.

2439.   **NORTON, John**
To the municipal electors of the lower ward: [letter, June, 1861]
[Lincoln]: [s.n.], [1861].   1 sheet.

2440.   **BORLAND, Adam**
Brown v. Borland: [letter to the electors of the lower ward, October 28th, 1862]
Lincoln: printed C. Keyworth, 1862.   1 sheet.

2441.
Electors awake, salute the happy morn: [poem]
[Lincoln]: [s.n.], [1862].   1 sheet.

2442.
From the Roman Catholic calendar of the lives of the saints: [election squib]
Lincoln: printed R.E. Leary, [1862].   1 sheet.

2443.   **ASHLEY, William**
To the municipal electors of the lower ward: [letter, October 28, 1867]
Lincoln: printed Edward R. Cousans, 1867.   1 sheet.

2444.   **SIMPSON, Thos.**
To the municipal electors of the lower ward: [letter, October 28, 1867]
Lincoln: printed Edward Cousans, 1867.   1 sheet.

2445.
[Spoof advertisement for book published by E.B. Drury]
Lincoln: printed T.J.N. Brogden, [1868?].   1 sheet.

2446.
To the mortal remains of a Cornhill barber: [spoof funeral card]
[Lincoln]: [s.n.], [1868].   1 sheet.

2447.
[Notice of meeting at the Guildhall]
Lincoln: printed Charles Keyworth, [1868?].   1 sheet.

2448.
[Letter signed 'A hard-working citizen']
Lincoln: printed T.J.N. Brogden, [1868?].   1 sheet.

2449.
[Election squib in form of auction catalogue]
Lincoln: printed R.E. Leary, [1868?].   1 sheet.

2450.
[Election squib in form of playbill]
Lincoln: printed John Smith, [1868?].   1 sheet.

2451.   **MARSHALL, William**
[Letter with copy of handbill by political enemy, October 22nd, 1870]
Lincoln: printed Edward R. Cousans, 1870.   1 sheet.

2452.   **HUGHES, Charles Leadbitter**
Municipal election, 1873: [letter from the mayor of Lincoln to his constituents and fellow citizens]
Lincoln: printed Akrill, 1873.   1 sheet.

2453.   **CLARK, F.J.**
Municipal election, 1877: [letter to the electors of the lower ward, October 15, 1877]
Lincoln: printed Samuel Ward, 1877.   1 sheet.

2454.   **CLOSE, Henry Stanley**
To the municipal electors of the middle ward: [letter, October 2nd, 1879]
Henry Stanley Close, William B. Danby.
Lincoln: printed C.F. Doncaster, 1879.   1 sheet.

2455.   **HALL, Richard**
Municipal elections, 1880: [letter, 22nd October, 1880]
Richard Hall, Sharpley Bainbridge, R.J. Ward.
Lincoln: printed W.A. Pacy, 1880.   1 sheet.

2456.   **KERANS, F. Harold**
To the electors of Lincoln & Bracebridge: [letter, June 17th, 1886]
Lincoln: printed Pacy and Trevatt, 1886.   1 sheet.

2457.   ————————
To the electors of the city of Lincoln and Bracebridge: [letter, 5th July, 1886]
Lincoln: printed James Williamson, 1886.   1 sheet.

2458.   **BENSON, J.W.**
Municipal election, 1894: lower ward: [letter]
Lincoln: printed Keyworth, 1894.   1 sheet.

2459.
[Boundary Act, 1837]: Lincoln: report upon the proposed municipal boundary and
division into wards of the city of Lincoln
[4]p.: ill., [1] leaf of maps in *Report on municipal corporation boundaries, England and
Wales. Part II*, [1837?].

2460.
Report of the boundary commissioners for England and Wales, 1868
London: Boundary Commission, 1868.   xiv, 478p.

2461.
Report of the boundary commissioners for England and Wales, 1885: [supplementary
report]
London: Boundary Commission, 1885.   3 vols.

2462.   **LINCOLN CORPORATION**
*City of Lincoln: representation to the minister of health, under section 54 of the Local
Government Act, 1888, as to the alteration of the boundary for the city and county
borough and the county of the same city*
[Lincoln]: [The Corporation], 1919.   ii, 48 leaves, 1 leaf of maps.

2463.   —————————
Ministry of health enquiry, at the Guildhall, Lincoln, 7th January, 1920...proposed
extension of Lincoln city boundaries to include Bracebridge, Boultham and portions of
Bracebridge Heath, North Hykeham and Skellingthorpe
[1920].   [138] leaves.
Typescript.

2464.
[Statutory instruments, 1958, no.1175: local government, England and Wales]: *Alteration
of areas: the Lincoln–parts of Kesteven and city of Lincoln (boundaries) order*
[London]: [HMSO], [1958].   13p.
  Extension of city boundary to incorporate Skellingthorpe Aerodrome and adjoining land.

2465.   **LOCAL GOVERNMENT COMMISSION FOR ENGLAND**
*Report and proposals for the Lincolnshire and East Anglia general review area,
presented to the minister of housing and local government, April, 1965*
London: HMSO, 1965.   142p.
  pp.19–29: Lincoln.   Local government boundaries revision affecting town planning.

2466.   —————————
Maps A–F
London: HMSO, 1965.
  Map D: Lincoln.

2467.
[Statutory instruments, 1967, no.88: local government, England and Wales]: *Alteration of
areas: the Lincoln order, 1967*
London: HMSO, 1967.   26p., [1]p. of maps.

2468.
[Local government, England and Wales]: *Changes in local government areas: the
Lincoln and North Kesteven areas order, 1982*
London: HMSO, 1982.   4p., map.

PARISH VALUATIONS

2469.
Particulars and valuation of the parish of...in the city of Lincoln, made under...an Act of
the 9th year of the reign of His Majesty King George the Fourth for paving, lighting,
watching and improving the city of Lincoln...1828
[1828].   88 leaves.
Ms.
> Manuscript to be found at Lincoln Central Library.   Covers parishes of: St John; St Nicholas;
> St Paul-in-the-Bail; St Peter-in-Eastgate; St Margaret; St Mary Magdalene-in-the-Bail;
> St Michael-on-the-Mount; St Martin; St Peter-at-Arches; St Swithin; St Benedict;
> St Mary-le-Wigford; St Mark; St Peter-at-Gowts; St Botolph.

2470.
*Valuation of the parish of... in the city of Lincoln, made under the direction of the
commisioners for paving, lighting, watching and improving the city of Lincoln, and the
Bail and Close of Lincoln...1828*
[Lincoln]: [s.n.], [1828].   Various pagings.
> Includes: St Benedict; St Swithin; St Nicholas; St Botolph; St John the Baptist; St Mark;
> St Martin; St Mary Magdalene; St Peter-at-Gowts; St Michael-on-the-Mount;
> St Peter-in-Eastgate; St Margaret; St Mary-le-Wigford.

BYELAWS

2471.
*Reports from commissioners on municipal corporations in England and Wales: report on
the city of Lincoln*
London: printed James & Luke G. Hansard, [1832].   27p.

2472.
Local Government Act, 1858: [opinion of counsel, Wm. Cunningham Glen about the
adoption of the Act, 20th October, 1865]
[Lincoln]: [Lincoln Corporation], [1865].   1 sheet.

2473.
Lincoln Corporation Act, 1915, ch.lxxvii: 5 & 6 Geo.5
London: printed by Eyre and Spottiswoode for Frederick Atterbury, 1915.   95p.
Spine title.

2474.
Lincoln Corporation [Act]: 5 & 6 George V.   Session, 1914–1915
London: Solicitors' Law Stationery Society, 1915.   99p.

2475.   LINCOLN CORPORATION
City of Lincoln Corporation, Lincoln: preliminary survey report
P.E. Consulting Group, Ltd.
[1967].   13 leaves.
Typescript.
> '..organization and methods appraisal'.

2476. ——————
City and county of the city of Lincoln: survey report, 19th December, 1967
Urwick, Orr & Partners, Ltd. [for Lincoln Corporation].
[1967].   20, 7 leaves.
Typescript.

2477.   **HORSNELL, J.S.**
Chief executive and town clerk: interim report
Lincoln: Lincoln Corporation, 1970.   5 leaves.
Cover title: *Interim report of chief executive.*

2478. ——————
Committee structure: report
by the chief executive.
[1971].   47 leaves.
Typescript.

COMMONS

2479.
Orders and agreements made and agreed upon between the mayor, sheriffs, citizens and commonalty of the city of Lincoln of the one part, and the inhabitants of the town of Canwick, with a general consent, the 21st December, in the 27th year of the reign of Queen Elizabeth, by virtue of Her Majesty's commission
Lincoln: printed Rose and Drury, [179?].   1 sheet.

2480.
Inclosure of Lincoln fields, &c.: [notice of meeting, September 11th, 1799]
Lincoln: printed Drury, 1799.   1 sheet.

2481.
Meeting of the proprietors of estates and persons having right of common and other interests within the open and common fields, meadows, pastures, uninclosed lands and liberties thereof, held at the Reindeer Inn... September, 1799: [resolutions]
[Lincoln]: [s.n.], [1799].   1 sheet.

2482.
[Notice of meeting about enclosure of acre of land at back of the race stand so can be used as 'place of public entertainment and recreation' when no races taking place, July 10th]
[Lincoln]: [Lincoln Corporation], [18??].   1 sheet.

2483.
City of Lincoln: report of the committee on commons, roads, bridges, conduits, &c.
Lincoln: printed Keyworth, 1836.

2484.
The South Common: the opinions of Mr Lush, barrister at law, on the authority of the turnpike trustees to divide the common by fencing off the new road, March 8, 1842
Lincoln: printed T.O. Brumby, 1842.   1 sheet.

2485.
[Notice about adjourned meeting about the commons, 4th January, 1847]
Lincoln: printed T.J.N. Brogden, 1847.   1 sheet.

2486.
*Commons: the committee appointed...to take into consideration the present state of the
several commons, and the rights of depasturing the same, and to report their opinion
whether some appropriation more advantageous...might not be made...*
[Lincoln]: [Lincoln Corporation], [1847].   [3]p.

2487.   **LILBURN, Richard**
[Letter about commons, January 25th, 1847]
Lincoln: printed Charles Brogden, 1847.   1 sheet.

2488.
[Notice of meeting about commons, 31st May, 1847]
Lincoln: printed J. Hall, 1847.   1 sheet.

2489.
[Notice of meeting of freemen about Holmes and Leys Commons, 10th September, 1847]
Lincoln: printed James Drury, 1847.   1 sheet.

2490.
[Notice about rights upon public commons, 16th October, 1847]
Lincoln: printed T.O. Brumby, 1847.   1 sheet.

2491.
[Notice of meeting for distribution of money by Great Northern and Midland Railway
Companies, 28th June, 1852]
Lincoln: printed W. and B. Brooke, 1852.   1 sheet.
    In connection with Holmes Common.

2492.
Proclamation from the Queen: [squib concerned with the sale of the freemen's commons,
21st September, 1855]
Lincoln: printed J. Lockyer, 1855.   1 sheet.

2493.
Orders in council, October 10th, 1855: [account of meeting]
Lincoln: printed G.J. Lockyer, 1855.   1 sheet.
    Concerns removal of William Rudgard from the council and the disposal of the commons.

2494.
Notice! sale postponed: [spoof auction bill about commons, October 25th, 1855]
Lincoln: printed G.J. Lockyer, 1855.   1 sheet.

2495.
*Canwick Common: scheme proposed to be adopted with reference to the appropriation
of the money arising from the sale of part of the Canwick Common to the Lincoln Burial
Board and the Great Northern Railway Company*
Lincoln: printed R. Leary, 1867.   8p.

2496.
Public notice: [about official opening of the Arboretum]
Lincoln: Robert E. Leary, [1872].   1 sheet.

2497.
Opening of the Lincoln Arboretum: the order of procession: [August 22, 1872]
Lincoln: printed Robert E. Leary, 1872. 1 sheet.

2498.
[Programme of events during opening of the Arboretum]
Lincoln: printed Robert E. Leary, [1872]. 1 sheet.
    Includes Corporation being greeted by 50 fairies.

2499. **LINCOLN CORPORATION**
Byelaws with respect to the pleasure grounds and open spaces in the said city, made by
the Council, 11th October, 1937, confirmed by the minister of health, 26th November,
1937, operative as from 1st January, 1938
Lincoln: The Corporation, 1937. 11p.

2500. **HOSKINS, W.G.**
The Common lands of England and Wales
by W.G. Hoskins and L. Dudley Stamp.
London: Collins, 1963. xvii, 366p.
(New naturalist: a survey of British natural history, 45)
    pp.114–115: Lincoln commons and the Lincoln Corporation Act of 1915.

2501. **ELVIN, Laurence**
Bygone Lincoln: the Temple Gardens
pp.6–10: ill. in *The Fireside magazine*, September, 1965.

2502. **LINCOLN, Planning and Architecture Committee**
City of Lincoln: a draft plan for the commons
[1972]. 15 leaves, [3] leaves of plans.
Typescript.

2503. **ROBINSON, David N.**
Poachings: Lincoln's Arboretum
p.41 in *Lincolnshire life*, vol.16, no.11, January, 1977.

2504.
[Lincoln City Council Act, 1985, Eliz.II, chapter xxxviii]: *An Act to...make further*
provision with regard to the commons and fairs of the city, the seizing of stray horses, the
prevention of flooding and for the maintenance of the omnibus undertaking...
London: HMSO, 1985. ii, 14, [9]p.
    Includes correspondence with Lincoln Commons Horse Association and the subsequent
    amendment of the Bill.

STREET LIGHTING

2505.
Heads of the intended bill for paving the foot-ways of certain streets within the city of
Lincoln: for cleansing, lighting and watching the said city: and for removing and
preventing nuisances, annoyances and encroachments therein
[Lincoln]: [s.n.], [17??]. [4]p.

2506.
[Anno triesimo primo Georgii III Regis cap.LXXX]: *An Act for paving the footways of certain streets within the city of Lincoln: for cleaning, lighting and watching the said streets...and for removing and preventing nuisances...*
London: printed Charles Eyre and Andrew Strachan, 1791.   pp.2791–2843.

2507.
Act for paving the footways of certain streets within the city of Lincoln: and for other purposes therein mentioned: [notice of implementation, July 12, 1791]
[Lincoln]: [Lincoln Corporation], [1791].   1 sheet.

2508.
[An Act for paving the footways...for cleansing, lighting and watching... request for compliance, November 30, 1811]
Lincoln: printed Drury, 1811.   1 sheet.

2509.
[9 Geo.IV.   Sess. 1828]: *An Act for paving, lighting, watching and improving the city of Lincoln and the Bail and Close of Lincoln, in the county of Lincoln: and for regulating the police therein*
Lincoln: printed E.B. Drury, 1828.   98p.

2510.
[9 Geo.IV.   Sess. 1828]: *An Act for paving, lighting, watching and improving the city of Lincoln and the Bail and Close of Lincoln, in the county of Lincoln: and for regulating the police therein*
[London]: [s.n.], [1828].   103p.

2511.
[9 Geo.IV.   Sess. 1828]: *Abstract of an Act for paving, lighting, watching, and improving the city of Lincoln and the Bail and Close of Lincoln, in the county of Lincoln: and for regulating the police therein*
Lincoln: printed Robert Ely Leary, [1828].   40, [4]p.
Includes index.

2512.   **CHARLESWORTH, E.P.**
Report made in pursuance of an order passed by the commissioners of lighting and paving, on the 10th day of March, 1832, for the purpose of surveying the city, Bail and Close of Lincoln, and ascertaining what footpaths and gutters are required...
E.P. Charlesworth, Matthew Sewell, John Brown.
[Lincoln]: [Lincoln Corporation], [1832].   3p.
Alphabetical list of roads where improvements needed and what work to be done.

2513.   **BETHAM, Edward**
Particulars and valuation of the parishes of Lincoln; made in the year 1828...under the direction of the commissioners for paving, lighting, watching and improving the city of Lincoln...
by Edw. Betham and Edw. J. Wilson.
Lincoln: printed by E.B. Drury, 1833.   [c.80] leaves.
Under each parish gives proprietors' names, description of premises, occupiers' names, annual value, value of houses under £6 p.a.

2514.
A Scale for lighting the public lamps in the city, Bail & Close of Lincoln, from September 23rd to December 31st, 1833
Lincoln: [Lincoln Corporation], 1833.   1 sheet.
_____   January 1st to April 30th, 1834.
_____   1835.
_____   1836.
_____   1838.
_____   January 1st to May 15th, 1847.

2515.
City of Lincoln, 1836: report of the committee on commons, roads, bridges, conduits, &c.: report of the watch committee: first report of the finance committee
Lincoln: printed Keyworth, [1836].   24p.

2516.
Manure: [invitation to tender for job of sweeping & cleansing the streets, November 8th, 1836]
Lincoln: printed T.J.N. Brogden, 1836.   1 sheet.

2517.
Notice: Lighting and Paving Act: unless the footways, for the proper state of which you are liable under this Act, shall be hereafter well and sufficiently cleansed, an information will be lodged against you without further notice, 1st February, 1836
Lincoln: printed J. Stainton, 1836.   1 sheet.

2518.   **LINCOLN CORPORATION**
To bricklayers and paviours: [invitation to tender for job of making barrel tunnel from the Butchery...by order W.A. Nicholson, city surveyor, May 10th, 1838]
Lincoln: printed W. and B. Brooke, 1838.   1 sheet.

2519.
Abstract of the receipts and expenditure of the commissioners for lighting, paving and improving the city, Bail and Close of Lincoln, from July 1st, 1844, to July 1st, 1845
Lincoln: printed R.E. Leary, 1844.   1 sheet.

2520.
Enquiries before Arnold Taylor, Esq., H.M. inspector, concerning a petition from the Lincoln Local Government Board for the repeal of parts of the Lincoln Lighting and Paving Act, 1828, held in the Guildhall...June 11, 1866
[1866].   75 leaves.
Ms., based upon shorthand notes.

2521.   **LINCOLN, Urban Sanitary Authority**
Byelaws...with respect to new streets and buildings
Lincoln: Lincoln Corporation, 1901.   60p.

OTHER MUNICIPAL FUNCTIONS

2522.
[Anno vicesimo quarto Georgii II Regis]: *An Act for the more speedy and easy recovery of small debts within the city of Lincoln...*
London: printed by Thomas Baskett, 1751.   pp.387–398.

2523.
[Notice concerning payment of rent for shops in the Butchery, 25th May, 1786]
Lincoln: printed Rose and Drury, 1786.   1 sheet.

2524.
[Resolutions of meeting of general quarter sessions of the peace about Sunday observance]
[Lincoln]: [s.n.], [1792].   1 sheet.

2525.   **HAYWARD, Wm.**
[Refutation of report that floor of Assembly Room in dangerous condition, July 3, 1802]
Lincoln: printed J.W. Drury, 1802.   1 sheet.

2526.
[Form for assize of bread, 180_]
Lincoln: printed J.W. Drury, [1805].   1 sheet.

2527.
[Notice requiring butchers to bring skins to be stamped, January 11, 1805]
Lincoln: printed J.W. Drury, 1805.   1 sheet.

2528.
City of Lincoln and county thereof: [fines for all short weights and measures '...by order of the Leet Jury...July 11, 1805']
Lincoln: printed J.W. Drury, 1805.   1 sheet.

2529.
Winchester measures: an account of the quantities and prices of corn and oatmeal from the return received...: [form]
[Lincoln]: [J.W. Drury], [1805].   1 sheet.

2530.
[Request for meeting to consider petitioning Parliament against the renewal of the Insolvent Debtors Act, May 11th, 1819]
Lincoln: printed W. Brooke, 1819.   1 sheet.

2531.
A Petition against the General Registry Bill, of which the following is a copy, and now lying for signature at Mr Drury's, the Post-Office, Lincoln
Lincoln: printed J.W. Drury, [1820?, 1826?].   1 sheet.

2532.
[3 Geo.IV.   Sess. 1822]: *An Act to enable the justices of the peace for the divisions of Lindsey, Kesteven and Holland, in the county of Lincoln, to take down the present County Hall for the said county and to erect a convenient hall instead...*
[London]: [printed Dyson & Jones], 1822.   12p.
        Situated in Castle Yard.

2533.
[Letter to the mayor requesting meeting to discuss licensing of hawkers and pedlars, 5th June, 1822]
Lincoln: printed W. Brooke, 1822.   1 sheet.

2534.
To the mayor, sheriffs, citizens and commonalty of the city of Lincoln: the memorial of the undersigned lessees and holders of property within the city of Lincoln, for terms of years granted by the Corporation
Lincoln: printed W. Brooke, 1826.   [2]p.

2535.
Lincoln district of the parts of Lindsey, in the county of Lincoln: rules and regulations made by the magistrates for the preservation of the peace and protection of property
Lincoln: printed J.W. Drury, [1830]. 2p.

2536.
Suppression of vagrancy: [division of the Bail and Close of Lincoln, with the wapentakes of Aslace and Lawress and part of the wapentake of Well, 10th February, 1832]
[Lincoln]: [Lincoln Corporation], 1832. 1 sheet.

2537.
Notice: [on the implementation of the Weights and Measures Act, October 12, 1835]
Lincoln: printed E.B. Drury, 1835. 1 sheet.

2538.   **LONGSTAFF, F.J.**
Lincoln new court, for the recovery of debts under £20: [letter suggesting establishment, July 24th, 1840]
F.J. Longstaff and G.W. Hebb.
Lincoln: printed W. and B. Brooke, 1843. 1 sheet.

2539.
[Notice about letting of the Butchery or Shambles of the city of Lincoln, 10th August, 1847]
Lincoln: printed T.J.N. Brogden, 1847. 1 sheet.

2540.
Nuisances: [notice of implementation of Nuisances Removal and Disease Prevention Act, 1848, 23rd October, 1848]
Lincoln: printed W. Doncaster, 1848. 1 sheet.

2541.
Caution against the sale of unwholesome meat or fish: [poster, August 24th, 1849]
Lincoln: printed W. Bellatti, 1849. 1 sheet.

2542.
[Notice about re-opening and restoring of footpaths, August 15th, 1849]
Lincoln: printed W. Bellatti, 1849. 1 sheet.

2543.
Caution! nuisances: [poster giving notice of fines, August 23rd, 1849]
Lincoln: printed W. Bellatti, 1849. 1 sheet.

2544.   **LINCOLN, Urban Sanitary Authority**
Byelaws...with respect to the tents, vans, sheds and similar structures for human habitation
Lincoln: Lincoln Corporation, 1877. 10p.

2545.   ─────────────
City of Lincoln: byelaws...with respect to common lodging houses
Lincoln: Lincoln Corporation, 1882. 12p.

2546.   **LINCOLN CORPORATION**
Local Government Superannuation Acts, 1937–1953, and benefits regulations, 1954
Lincoln: [The Corporation], [1954]. 10p.

2547.
Lincoln Crematorium: service of dedication, Thursday, 14th November, 1968
[Lincoln]: [Lincoln Corporation], 1968.   [4] leaves: ill., plan.
> Includes information about building.

2548.   **LINCOLN CITY COUNCIL**
Traffic regulations in the city: a summary of the proposed amendments and additions of the Lincoln City Council
Lincoln: The Council, 1975.   15p., [2]p. of maps.

PLANNING

2549.   **LINCOLN CORPORATION**
The Eminently desirable building site of St Peter-at-Arches Lincoln: [prospectus]
[Lincoln]: [The Corporation], [1935].   [3]p., map.

2550.   **ATKINSON, Robert**
City of Lincoln: report on town planning, 1934–1939
[after 1940].   74 leaves.
Typescript.
> From the library of Sir Francis Hill.

2551.   **LINCOLN CORPORATION**
City of Lincoln: Town and Country Planning Act, 1947: report of the survey, 1951: the analysis
[1951?].   70 leaves: ill., [8] leaves of maps.
Typescript.

2552.   _____
Town and Country Planning Act, 1947: report of the survey, 1951: the analysis
[1951?].   66 leaves, 6 maps.
Typescript.

2553.   _____
The City of Lincoln Skewbridge compulsory purchase order, 1952
Lincoln: The Corporation, 1952.   39p.

2554.   _____
[Public Health Act, 1925 and Restriction of Ribbon Development Act, 1935]: *Bye-law: parking spaces*
[Lincoln]: The Corporation, [1956].   [2]p.

2555.
The Future of Lincoln
[Nottingham]: [Nottingham, Derby & Lincoln Society of Architects], 1961.   22p.

2556.   **LINCOLN CORPORATION**
A Development policy and guide lines plan for the Birchwood area, Lincoln
Lincoln: The Corporation, 1967.   10p.: ill.
> Produced by Planning Department and City Architect's Department.

2557.   **JACKSON, Percy**
Lincoln central area planning policy principles: report of the city planning officer to the Town Planning Committee, Thursday, 23rd November, 1967, as approved by the City Council, 12th December, 1967.
Lincoln: Lincoln Corporation, 1967.   17 leaves, map.

2558.   **MINISTRY OF HOUSING AND LOCAL GOVERNMENT**
City of Lincoln: revised provisional list of buildings of architectural or historical interest for consideration in connection with the provisions of section 32 of the Town and Country Planning Act, 1962.
[1968].   55 leaves.
Typescript.
    Based on survey completed in 1968; supercedes list of 1947.

2559.   **LINCOLN, Planning Department**
Development plan studies.   3: shopping.
Lincoln: The Department, 1968.   47 leaves.

2560.   ───────
Lincoln planning information handbook
London: Pyramid, [1968].   44p.: ill., map.

2561.   **LINCOLN, Planning & Architecture Committee**
Office development: 'The Park'
1969.   8 leaves, map.
Typescript.
Map on inside cover.

2562.   **LINCOLN, Department of Planning and Property**
Birchwood local plan: draft written statement
Lincoln: The Department, [197?].   47p.: map.

2563.   **LINCOLN, Planning & Architecture Committee**
Flaxengate area planning brief
1971.   3 leaves, [2] leaves of plans.
Typescript.

2564.   ───────
Lincoln central area
[1971].   [14]p.: ill.
Typescript.
Cover title: *Centre 71: Lincoln central area redevelopment.*

2565.   **JACKSON, Percy**
Population: [revised]
Lincoln: Lincoln, Town Planning Department, [1971].   15, xiip., [1] leaf of maps.

2566.   **LINCOLN COUNTY BOROUGH COUNCIL**
Applications for planning permission, listed building consent and confirmation of a compulsory purchase order in connection with a proposed central area redevelopment scheme of the city
1972.   116p.
Typescript.
    Preceded by 8p. letter from Department of the Environment, East Midlands region, summarizing the inspector's findings and refusing permission.

2567.   LINCOLN, Department of Planning and Architecture
City of Lincoln: a draft plan for the commons.
Lincoln: The Department, 1972.   15, [7] leaves, [2] leaves of maps.

2568.   LINCOLN, Planning & Architecture Committee
City of Lincoln, Brayford North: draft planning brief
1973.   10 leaves, [1] leaf of plans.
Typescript.

2569.   ——————
Draft action area plan: Newark Road and planning brief for Boundary Street
1973.   8, ip., [3] leaves of maps.
Typescript.

2570.   LINCOLN CORPORATION
The Sincil Street area: the future
Lincoln: The Corporation, 1973.   7p.

2571.   LINCOLN CIVIC TRUST
*Feasibility study by the Environmental Committee for the Lincoln Civic Trust for
landscaping Waterside North*
[Lincoln]: The Trust, [1974].   4 leaves, [1] folded plan.

2572.   LINCOLN, Department of Planning and Architecture
Birchwood: draft district plan: public consultation
Lincoln: The Department, 1975.   37p.

2573.   ——————
The Lincoln commons: a plan for their future development
Lincoln: The Department, 1975.   19p.: ill., maps.

2574.   ——————
A Plan for Birchwood: discussion document
Lincoln: The Department, 1976.   15p., maps.

2575.   ——————
Hartsholme Country Park: discussion document
Lincoln: The Department, 1976.   6, ivp., 4p. of maps.

2576.   ——————
Land to the south of Doddington Road: a policy statement
Lincoln: The Department, 1976.   20p., map.

2577.   ——————
Nettleham Glebe: development design brief
Lincoln: The Department, 1976.   30p., maps.

2578.   ——————
Sincil Street and markets area: a discussion document
Lincoln: The Department, 1976.   21p., maps.

2579.   ——————
Westgate: policy
Lincoln: The Department, 1976.   [24]p.: ill., maps.
    Includes 3p. history of the area by Christina Colyer.

2580. ―――――――
Doddington Park: draft supplementary planning guidance
Lincoln: The Department, 1977. 15p., maps, plans.

2581. ―――――――
Hartsholme Country Park: proposals
Lincoln: The Department, 1977. 19p., [6]p. of maps.

2582. **LINCOLN, Planning & Architecture Committee**
Land to the south of Doddington Road: industrial design guide
Lincoln City Council in association with North Kesteven Council.
Lincoln: The Council, 1977. 11, ii, ip., : ill., plans.

2583. **LINCOLN, Department of Planning and Architecture**
Lincoln's approach roads: roads from the north
Lincoln: The Department, 1977. 28p.: ill., maps.

2584. ―――――――
Sincil Street and markets area: planning guidance
Lincoln: The Department, 1977. 3p., [1]p. of maps.

2585. ―――――――
Site of Belle Vue House, Belle Vue Road: developer's guide
Lincoln: The Department, 1978. 3p., [1]p. of maps.

2586. ―――――――
Birchwood neighbourhood centre: supplementary planning guidance
Lincoln: The Department, 1978. 5p., [4]p. of maps.

2587. ―――――――
Boundary Street area: planning policy
Lincoln: The Department, 1978. 6p., [2]p. of maps.

2588. ―――――――
Brayford Wharf North: draft planning brief
Lincoln: The Department, 1978. 10p., [1] leaf of plans.

2589. ―――――――
Clasket Gate to Lower West Gate district plan: issues and options
Lincoln: The Department, 1978. iv, 31p., [6]p. of maps.

2590. ―――――――
Clasket Gate to Lower West Gate district plan: report of survey
Lincoln: The Department, 1978. 37p., [2]p. of maps.

2591. ―――――――
Doddington Park phase 3: housing area design guide
Lincoln: The Department, 1978. 5p., [3]p. of plans.

2592. ―――――――
Land to the south of Doddington Road: industrial design guide
Lincoln: The Department, 1978. 11p.: ill.

2593. ―――――――
Proposals for the Sobraon area
Lincoln: The Department, 1978. [3]p., maps.

2594. ───────────
Sobraon area: draft planning proposals
Lincoln: The Department, 1978.   4p., [1]p. of maps.

2595.   **LINCOLNSHIRE COUNTY COUNCIL, Planning Department**
Lincolnshire: population.   Vol.1 : 1979
[Lincoln]: The Council, 1979.
Cover title: *A digest of population characteristics and trends in Lincolnshire.*
    Includes Lincoln statistics.

2596.   **LINCOLN, Department of Planning and Architecture**
Blenheim Road and Woodstock Street area: developer's guide
Lincoln: The Department, 1979.   [2]p., [1]p. of maps.

2597.   **LINCOLN CITY COUNCIL**
City of Lincoln planning information handbook
London: Pyramid, [1979?].   52p.: ill., maps.

2598.   **LINCOLN, Department of Planning and Architecture**
Clasket Gate to Lower West Gate district plan: proposals
Lincoln: The Department, 1979.   11p., [3]p. of maps.

2599.
Lincoln Corn Exchange
pp.32–33: ill. in *Lincolnshire life*, vol.19, no.3, June, 1979.
    About redevelopment of the area.

2600.   **LINCOLN, Department of Planning and Architecture**
Published planning policies in Lincoln
Lincoln: The Department, 1979.   7p.

2601.   **SELLORS, M.R.**
The Lincoln area: a background paper to the Lincolnshire structure plan
M.R. Sellors, county planning officer.
Lincoln: Lincolnshire County Council, 1979.   101p.: ill., maps.

2602.   **LINCOLN, Department of Planning and Architecture**
Clasket Gate to Lower West Gate district plan: final draft for public comment
Lincoln: The Department, 1980.   24p., [2]p. of maps.

2603.   ───────────
Land north-west of Nettleham Road: developer's design brief
Lincoln: The Department, 1981.   [10]p.: ill., maps.

2604.   **LINCOLN, Planning & Architecture Committee**
Bailgate planning brief
Lincoln: Lincoln City Council, [1982].   6p., [1]p. of plans.

2605.   **LINCOLN, Department of Planning and Architecture**
Nettleham Glebe: development design brief
Lincoln: The Department, 1982.   [8]p., 1p. of maps.

2606.   **LINCOLN CITY COUNCIL**
Planning advice to applicants.   Note 3: Shop fronts and advertisements: policy guidelines
Lincoln: The Council, [1982?].   [7]p.: ill.

2607.   **LINCOLN, Planning & Architecture Committee**
Birchwood footpaths design guidance
Lincoln: Lincoln City Council, 1983.   6p.: ill., plans.

2608.   _____
Design guidance for land adjoining proposed Tritton Road-Ropewalk link
Lincoln: The Committee, 1983.   [3]p., map.

2609.   _____
North eastern periphery district plan: report of publicity
Lincoln: Lincoln City Council, 1983.   36p.
     Statement of the public consultations.

2610.   _____
St Mark's Station: planning guidance
Lincoln: The Department, 1983.   [5]p., maps.

2611.   **LINCOLNSHIRE COUNTY COUNCIL**
Cathedral area relief project
Lincoln: The Council, [1984].   8p.: ill., 1 folded map.

2612.   **LINCOLN CITY COUNCIL**
City of Lincoln planning information handbook
Wallington: Home Publishing, [1984?].   40p.: ill., maps.

2613.   **LINCOLN, Planning & Property Department**
Beevor Street: area 3: design brief
Lincoln: Lincoln City Council, 1985   [4]p., plan.

2614.   _____
Birchwood local plan: draft written statement
Lincoln: Lincoln City Council, 1985.   46p.: ill., maps, plans.

2615.   _____
Clasket Gate to Lower West Gate local plan: [written statement and proposals map]
Lincoln: Lincoln City Council, 1985.   29p., 1p. of maps.

2616.   **LINCOLN, Planning & Architecture Committee**
Developers' design brief: Garmston House, former Grand Cinema, 262–263, High Street,
Lincoln and premises fronting onto St Martin's Lane
1985.   12p., [3]p. of plans.
Typescript.

2617.   _____
Developers' design brief: Grantham Street/Flaxengate, Lincoln
1985.   6p., [1]p. of maps.
Typescript.

2618.   _____
*Planning advice to applicants.   Note 4: Shop fronts and advertisements: design
guidance for Bailgate, Steep Hill and upper part of High Street*
Lincoln: Lincoln City Council, 1985.   7p., map.

2619.   _____
Planning advice to applicants.   Note 5: Guest house/bed & breakfast accommodation in
residential areas
1985.   4p.
Typescript.

2620.   _____
Birchwood local plan: draft written statement
Lincoln: The Department, 1986.   47p., maps, plans.

2621.   **LINCOLN, Planning & Property Department**
Skewbridge local plan
Lincoln: The Department, 1986.   4 leaves, [1]p. of maps.

2622.   **LINCOLN, Planning & Architecture Committee**
Planning advice to applicants.   Note 6: Security grilles and shutters
1987.   3p.
Typescript.

2623.   _____
Planning advice.   Note 7: Flats and houses in multiple occupation
1987.   9p.
Typescript.

HOUSING

2624.   **LINCOLN CORPORATION**
Opening of the Wyatt Bequest Homes by the Right Worshipful, the mayor of Lincoln...6th April, 1927
Lincoln: printed J.W. Ruddock, 1927.   [4]p.: ill.

2625.
A Notable experiment in slum clearance in Lincoln, 1928–1929
Lincoln: printed Lincolnshire Publishing, [1929].   [7]p.: ill.
     Work of the Voluntary Slum Clearance Committee.

2626.   **LINCOLN CORPORATION**
[Housing Act, 1930, 1935, 1936, 1937]: *Official representation*
Lincoln: The Corporation, 1930–37.   Various pagings.

2627.   **LINCOLN, Housing & Town Planning Committee**
[Housing Act, 1930]: Official representation...Waterside South and Sincil St.
[1930].   [33] leaves: ill.
Typescript.

2628.   _____
[Housing Act, 1930]: Official representation in connection with Witham St., Corporation Lane, City Court, Thorngate, Jackson's Court, Bell's Passage, Sparrow Lane and Waterside North
[1931].   41 leaves: ill.
Typescript.

2629.   _____
[Housing Act, 1930]: Official representation in connection with...Norman St..., Pelham St..., Waterside South
[1933].   Various pagings.
Typescript.

2630. _____
[Housing Act, 1930]: Official representation in connection with Mint Lane...Danes
Terrace...Danesgate...Grantham St...Occupation Rd.
[1934]. Various pagings.
Typescript.

2631. _____
[Housing Act, 1930]: Official representation...
[1934]. Various pagings.
Typescript.

2632. _____
[Housing Act, 1930]: Official representation in connection with...High Street...Mill Lane,
Princess St., Sincil St., Waterside North
[1935]. 136p.
Typescript.

2633.
*Civic survey & housing exhibition, the Usher Art Gallery, Lincoln, Saturday, 23rd
September to Sunday, 1st October, 1944*: [programme]
[Lincoln]: [Lincoln Corporation], 1944. [4]p.: ill.

2634.   **LINCOLN CORPORATION**
Official opening of 'Shuttleworth House', a seventeen storey block of flats at Stamp End
by the Right Worshipful, the mayor of Lincoln...17th March, 1966
[1966]. [5]p.: ill., plan.
Typescript.

2635.   **HARTLEY, Owen A.**
Housing policy in four Lincolnshire towns, 1919–1959
Typescript.
Thesis [Ph.D.] – University of Oxford, 1969.
    pp.1–9: abstract; pp.149–213: Lincoln.

ACCOUNTS

2636.   **LINCOLN CORPORATION**
*Abstract of the receipts and expenditure of the Corporation of Lincoln, from the 1st
September, 1844, to the 1st September, 1845*
Lincoln: printed T.O. Brumby, 1845. [13]p.

2637. _____
*Abstract of the receipts and expenditure of the Corporation of Lincoln, from 1st
September, 1845, to the 1st September, 1846*
Lincoln: printed T.J.N. Brogden, 1846.

2638. _____
Copy of report of finance committee
Lincoln: printed T.O. Brumby, [pre 1847]. 1 sheet.

2639. _____
*Abstract of the receipts and expenditure of the Corporation of Lincoln, from 1st
September, 1846 to 1st September, 1847*
Lincoln: printed T.J.N. Brogden, 1847.

2640.
[Notice about settlement of corporation accounts, August 10, 1847]
Lincoln: printed W. Peck, 1847.   1 sheet.

2641.   **LINCOLN CORPORATION**
*Abstract of the receipts and expenditure of the Corporation of Lincoln, from 1st
September, 1849, to 1st September, 1850*
Lincoln: R. Bulman, 1850.

2642.   ─────────────
*Abstract of the receipts and expenditure of the Corporation of Lincoln, from 1st
September, 1850, to 1st September, 1851*
Lincoln: G.J. Lockyer, 1851.

2643.   ─────────────
Abstract of the audited accounts: [1883–1908].
Lincoln: The Corporation, 1884–1908.   2 vols.

2644.   ─────────────
*Abstract of the audited accounts... of the city of Lincoln, from the 25th March, 1888, to
26th March, 1889*
Lincoln: printed Charles Keyworth, 1889.   12p.

2645.   ─────────────
Summonses and accounts: [1891–1949]
Lincoln: The Corporation, 1891–1949.   Various pagings.

2646.   ─────────────
Lincoln Corporation epitome: [1913–56]
Lincoln: The Corporation, 1913–56.   Various pagings.

2647.   ─────────────
Estimates for the borough rate, year ending 31st March, 1921–23
Lincoln: The Corporation, 1920–22.   Various pagings.

2648.   ─────────────
City of Lincoln annual reports: [1921–1930]
Lincoln: The Corporation, 1921–56.   Various pagings.

2649.   ─────────────
Estimates for the general district rate and water rate: [1921, 1923, 1927]
Lincoln: The Corporation, 1921–27.   Various pagings.

2650.   ─────────────
Estimates for the general rate and water rate: [1931, 1936]
Lincoln: The Corporation, 1931–36.   Various pagings.

2651.   ─────────────
Estimates for the general rate and capital estimates, year ending: [1966, 1969]
Lincoln: The Corporation, 1966–69.   Various pagings.

2652.   ─────────────
Survey of city and county of the city of Lincoln
P.A. Management Consultants.
[1967].   39, [20] leaves.
Typescript.
     Organisation and methods survey designed to improve the efficiency of local authorities.

2653. —————
Rate estimates, 1969–1970, and capital expenditure programme, 1969–1974
Lincoln: The Corporation, 1969. 175p.

2654. —————
Rate estimates, 1970–1971, and capital expenditure programme, 1969–1974, presented
to the City Council at a meeting on Wednesday, 25th February, 1970
Lincoln: The Corporation, 1970. 132p.: ill.

2655. —————
Rate estimates and capital projects: [1971–85]
[1971–85]. 3 vols.
Typescript.

2656. —————
Abstract of the treasurer's accounts: [1971–74].
Lincoln: The Corporation, 1971–74. 3 vols.
    Vol.3 contains 16p. reproduction of: *Abstract of receipts & expenditure of the Corporation of*
    Lincoln, from the 1st September, 1865, to the 1st September, 1866.

2657. —————
Transport undertaking accounts for the year ended 31st March, 1973
Lincoln: The Corporation, [1973]. 7p.: ill.

2658. **LINCOLN CITY COUNCIL**
City of Lincoln finances: abstract of accounts for the year ended...: [1974–80]
Lincoln: The Council, 1974–80. Various pagings.

2659. **AFFLECK, G.G.**
Lincoln area transportation strategy: report to transportation committee
[Lincoln]: [Lincolnshire County Council], [1975]. 50p.: ill.

2660. **LINCOLN CITY COUNCIL**
Annual report and accounts: [1980, 1980/81, 1982]: *Abstract of accounts and financial*
statistics: [1982, 1983]: *Statement of accounts and financial statistics*: [1983, 1983/84,
1985]
Lincoln: The Council, 1980–85. Various pagings.

2661. —————
Direct labour: annual report and accounts: [1982, 1983/84, 1985]
Lincoln: The Council, 1982–85. Various pagings.

2662. —————
Annual report: [1982, 1983–85, 1986]
Lincoln: The Council, 1982–86. Various pagings.
    Presented in newspaper format.

2663. —————
Budget and capital programme: [1985, 1986/87, 1988]
Lincoln: Council, Policy and Resources Committee, 1985–87. Various pagings.

2664.   LINCOLN, Burial Board
Burial ground of the parish of Saint Margaret, provided under the Burials beyond the
Metropolis Act, and the statutes incorporated therewith: regulations of the Burial Board,
and fees and payments to be received for interments, tombs, monuments...
Lincoln: printed W. and B. Brooke, 1856.   8p.

2665.   LINCOLN, Housing Committee
The Municipal tenants' handbook: compendium of useful information for tenants of the
housing estates of the city of Lincoln
Gloucester: British Publishing, [1930s?].   32p.: ill.

2666.   LINCOLN CORPORATION
Official handbook of Lincoln Civic Week, September 22nd to 29th, 1935
Lincoln: The Corporation, 1935.   72p.: ill.

2667.   ⸺⸺⸺⸺
City of Lincoln: standing orders for the regulation of the proceedings and business of the
Council and its committees, as adopted...1937
Lincoln: The Corporation, 1937.   28p.

2668.   ⸺⸺⸺⸺
City of Lincoln: standing orders and reference and delegation to committees
Lincoln: The Corporation, 1949.   48p.

2669.   ⸺⸺⸺⸺
City of Lincoln: year book and diary of the Council, with the members of the Council,
committees, officers, magistrates, etc.
Lincoln: The Corporation, 1949–71.   Various pagings.

2670.   ⸺⸺⸺⸺
City of Lincoln standing orders, reference and delegation to committees, financial
regulations, delegation to officers
Lincoln: The Corporation, [1972].   64p.

2671.   CITY INFORMATION OFFICE
Information for new residents
Lincoln: The Office, [1973].   5p.

2672.
Twinning: Deutsch-Britische Partnerschaften
compiled and edited by Rolf Breitenstein...[et al].
London: Oswald Wolff, 1974.   164p.: ill.
Includes index.
    pp.13–15: Lincoln and Neustadt an der Weinstrasse; transcript of a BBC 'Look North'
    interview of 3rd July, 1974, between reporter John Burns and Robin Rushton, publicity officer
    to the Corporation of Lincoln.   Devoted to a description of the gift of vines which were
    planted in the grounds of the Old Bishop's Palace, forming Britain's most northerly vineyard.

2673.   CITY INFORMATION OFFICE
Information for new residents
Lincoln: The Office, [1979].   10p., map.
Map on inside cover.

MILITARY HISTORY

MILITIA

2674.
[Resolutions of a meeting of the committee appointed...to consider...a printed paper...intituled *Heads of a plan for raising Corps*].
[Lincoln]: [s.n.], 1782.   1 sheet.

2675.
Minutes of a meeting...to consider...establishing a fund...for the purpose of giving bounties...to a certain number of sea-men and land-men...who shall enter into His Majesty's service..., 18th February, 1793
[Lincoln]: [s.n.], [1793].   1 sheet.

2676.
[Notice of meeting about defence of landed property, April 28th, 1794]
[Lincoln]: [s.n.], [1794].   1 sheet.

2677.
At a general meeting...held at the Castle of Lincoln...seventh day of June, 1794...to take into consideration the best means of carrying into effect the plans...for the internal defence of this county...
[Lincoln]: [s.n.], [1794].   3p.

2678.
County-Hall in the Castle of Lincoln, June 7th, 1794, at a meeting of the general committee of expenditure, chosen and appointed at a general county meeting held this day: [resolutions]
[Lincoln]: [s.n.], [1794].   3p.
    Formation of bodies of cavalry.

2679.
[Notice of meeting to discuss raising a subscription for internal defence of the city and county of Lincoln, 9th June, 1794]
[Lincoln]: [s.n.], [1794].   1 sheet.

2680.
[Notice that books for signatures in support of plans for the internal defence of the city to be at town-clerk's office, June 17, 1794]
[Lincoln]: [s.n.], [1794].

2681.
[Minutes of a meeting held to consider internal defence, Tuesday, the 17th day of June, 1794]
Lincoln: [s.n.], [1794].   [2]p.

2682.
City of Lincoln and the vicinity thereof: [resolutions of meeting to discuss subscriptions for internal defence, 17th June, 1794]
[Lincoln]: [s.n.], [1794].   [2]p.

2683.
[Notice that books for enrolment of volunteers are in town-clerk's office, June 17th, 1794]
[Lincoln]: [s.n.], [1794].   1 sheet.

2684.
City and county of the city of Lincoln and vicinity thereof: [notice of formation of Corps of volunteer cavalry, February 28, 1797]
[Lincoln]: [s.n.], [1797].   1 sheet.

2685.
At a meeting held at the Guildhall in the city of Lincoln, on Thursday, the 2nd day of March, 1797, in pursuance of public notice, to consider of the propriety of forming a force for the protection of the country and for the defence of the kingdom
[Lincoln]: [s.n.], [1797].   2p.

2686.
City and county of the city of Lincoln and vicinity thereof, at a numerous meeting held at the Guildhall...Saturday, the fourth of March, 1797...for the purpose of considering the propriety of raising a volunteer Corps of cavalry...
[Lincoln]: [s.n.], [1797].   1 sheet.

2687.
City and county of the city of Lincoln and vicinity thereof: at a meeting of the gentlemen enrolled to form a volunteer Corps of cavalry, held at the Guildhall...Thursday, the ninth day of March, 1797
[Lincoln]: [s.n.], [1797].   1 sheet.

2688.
City and county of the city of Lincoln, and the vicinity thereof: at a meeting of the gentlemen enrolled to form a volunteer Corps of cavalry, held at the Guildhall of the said city of Lincoln...: [Thursday, March 16, 1797]
[Lincoln]: [s.n.], [1797].   2p.

2689.
Guild Hall, Thursday, May 10th, 1798: at a meeting of the inhabitants of the city, Bail and Close of Lincoln, who subscribed their names to the declaration of the public meeting held on Tuesday last for the purpose of forming an association under the plan proposed by Mr. Dundas's letter....
[Lincoln]: [s.n.], [1798].   1 sheet.

2690.
Guildhall, Lincoln, May 12th, 1798: at the adjourned meeting of the Armed Association of Lincoln Volunteer Infantry, held pursuant to the resolution at the public meeting of yesterday
Lincoln: [s.n.], [1798].   1 sheet.

2691.
At a meeting of the inhabitants of the city, Bail and Close of Lincoln, held at the Guildhall of the said city, on Friday, the 11th day of May, 1798, to consider the propriety of forming military associations, at this important crisis...
Lincoln: [s.n.], [1798].   2p.

2692.
Supplementary militia: [order to make list of men aged 18–45 in each parish]
[Lincoln]: [s.n.], [1799].   1 sheet.

2693.
[Notice of requirement to make list of young men eligible to serve in militia, 13th
November, 1799]
[Lincoln]: [s.n.], [1799].   1 sheet.

2694.
*At a meeting of the persons who are desirous of forming a Corps of cavalry for the
'general defence of Great Britain', held at the Guildhall..the eighth day of August, 1803*
Lincoln: printed J.W. Drury, 1803.   2p.

2695.
*At an adjourned meeting of the committee for appropriating and managing the
subscription for the purposes of the volunteer Corps within the city of Lincoln...15th of
August, 1803*
Lincoln: printed W. Brooke, 1803.   3p.

2696.
*Guildhall, Lincoln, 20th December, 1806: at a general meeting of the city, Bail and
Close of Lincoln...it was unanimously resolved that it would be proper to raise a fund, by
voluntary subscription*
Lincoln: printed J.W. Drury, [1806].   1 sheet.

2697.
[Notice of meeting about further subscription for support of the volunteer infantry]
Lincoln: printed J.W. Drury, 1806.   1 sheet.

2698.
*Guildhall...June 7, 1809: at a meeting of the inhabitants of the city, Bail and Close of
Lincoln, and of the four towns of Waddington, Branston, Canwick and Bracebridge,
convened by public advertisement*
Lincoln: printed J.W. Drury, 1809.
     Resolution to keep up volunteer Corps.

2699.
St Peter's-at-Arches militia: [notice of meeting, January 22, 1846]
[Lincoln]: [s.n.], [1846].   1 sheet.

2700.
Militia club: parish of St Peter-at-Arches: [rules]
Lincoln: printed W. and B. Brooke, [1846?].   [2] sheets.

2701.   **NEAVE, David**
Anti-militia riots in Lincolnshire, 1757 and 1796
pp.21–27 in *Lincolnshire history and archaeology*, vol.11, 1976.

2702.
[Resolutions of meeting to discuss raising of Corps of light-horse to be called the Loyal
Lincoln Yeomanry, 27th August, 1794]
[Lincoln]: [s.n.], [1794].   1 sheet.

2703.
*The True lover's parting, or Honest John the farmer turned gentleman who enlisted in
the Lincolnshire volunteers on Christmas Eve, 1793*
[Lincoln]: [s.n.], [1794].   1 sheet: ill.
    'Then saluting each other he bid her good by/ And marched up to Lincoln where the regiment
    does lie.'

2704.   **ROYAL NORTH BRITISH DRAGOONS**
Deserted, from Nottingham, on the 29th of January, 1805, John Winger
Lincoln: printed J.W. Drury, 1805.   1 sheet.

2705.   ——————
[Notice for reward for apprehension of deserter]
Lincoln: printed J.W. Drury, [1805].   1 sheet.

2706.
Captain Smith's company: [list of volunteers]
Lincoln: [J.W. Drury], [1805?].   1 sheet.

2707.   **RAMSAY, W.**
[Letter to Colonel William Monson re inscription of word Hindoostan on colours of 76th
Regiment in India, 24th October, 1806]
Lincoln: printed Smith, 1806.   1 sheet.

2708.
North Lincolnshire Yeomanry cavalry: regimental orders, 4th May, 1833
Hull: printed William Stephenson, 1833.   16p.
    Quarters in Lincoln from May 18th to May 25th.

2709.
*Historical record of the eighty-first regiment, or Loyal Lincoln Volunteers: containing an
account of the formation of the regiment in 1793 and of its subsequent services to 1872*
Gibraltar: Twenty-eighth Regimental Press, 1872.   256p., [3] leaves of plates.

2710.
The Lincolnshire Regiment: battle honours borne on the colours
London: HMSO, [c.1903].   12p.
    Depot headquarters at Lincoln.

2711.
*The Ceremony of trooping the colour by the 2nd Bt. the Lincolnshire Regt., to
commemorate the 250th anniversary of the raising of the Regiment, June 20th, 1685*
Lincoln: The Regiment, 1935.   [12]p.: ill., [2] leaves of plates.
    Took place at the barracks in Lincoln.

2712.   **WOODWARD, Gordon Hardcore**
Joining the Lincolnshire Regiment, 1926
pp.42–43: ill. in *Lincolnshire life*, vol.21, no.1, April, 1981.
    Joined up in Lincoln.

2713.   **HUTSON, Stan**
Saturday night soldiers
pp.28–30, 49: ill. in *Lincolnshire life*, vol.25, no.7, October, 1985.
    About the 60th Field Regiment based at the Lincoln barracks.

AIR FORCE

2714.   **HUNT, Leslie**
Wings over Lincolnshire
pp.50–53: ill. in *Lincolnshire life*, vol.7, no.9, November, 1967.
    About No.503 (County of Lincoln) Squadron.   Recruiting office opened in Saltergate in
    January, 1927.

2715.   **JONES, Paddy**
The Waddington story
pp.42–46: ill. in *Lincolnshire life*, vol.8, no.5, July, 1968.
    RAF base which became affiliated to the city of Lincoln in 1947, under the municipal liaison
    scheme.

2716.   **HANCOCK, T.N.**
Bomber county: a history of the Royal Air Force in Lincolnshire
Lincoln: Lincolnshire Library Service, 1978.   142p.: ill., folded map.
Includes index.
ISBN 0861111001
    Brief references to the city.

2717.
Lads line-up for Lincoln squadron of ATC
p.xv in *Wings '79*: [an LSG supplement]
Lincoln: LSG, 1979.

2718.   **TAYLOR, Raymond**
Reunion in Lincoln
p.32: ill. in *Lincolnshire life*, vol.20, no.6, September, 1980.
    35 year reunion of RAF personnel who served in Burma, held in Lincoln, May, 1980.

2719.   **INGHAM, M.J.**
A Guide to the Air Force memorials of Lincolnshire
Nettleham: Beckside Design, 1987.   36p.: ill.
ISBN 0951210807
    p.21: Lincoln Cathedral and Lincoln County Hospital.

CIVIL DEFENCE

2720.
The New Volunteer Drill Hall at Lincoln
p.12 in *Lincolnshire chronicle*, May 3rd, 1890.

2721.   CHIEF CONSTABLE OF LINCOLN
Lincoln and the Lighting Order
Lincoln: issued by the Chief Constable of Lincoln, [1915].   1 sheet.

2722.
The Story of No.11 Group, Royal Observer Corps
edited by J. Newton.
Lincoln: [The Editor], 1946.   120p.: ill.
    pp.10–13: the early days of Lincoln centre.

2723.   LINCOLN CIVIL DEFENCE CORPS
Guide to the welfare section
[1960].   [5]p.
Typescript.

2724.   KETTERINGHAM, John
Royal Observer Corps in Lincolnshire
pp.42–44: ill. in *Lincolnshire life*, vol.20, no.6, September, 1980.
    Group Headquarters were in Lincoln.

2725.   LINCOLN CITY COUNCIL
Lincoln and nuclear weapons
Lincoln: The Council, [after 1982].   [6]p.: ill.

WAR MEMORIALS

2726.
In memoriam: a family record of Lincoln's part in the Great War sacrifice
Lincoln: Lincoln Review, [1918].   50p.: ill.
Cover title: *A Record of the Lincoln boys who laid down their lives in the Great War,
1914–18.*

2727.   LINCOLN CORPORATION
*City of Lincoln war memorial: official souvenir and programme of the unveiling
ceremony, Wednesday, October 25th, 1922*
[Lincoln]: [The Corporation], [1922].   32p.: ill.

2728.
[Official information leaflets at time of Second World War: especially concerning
evacuation, billeting, air raid precautions and fire prevention]
[S.l.]: [s.n.], [194?].

2729.   LINCOLN, Civil Defence Division
The Civil defence bulletin: [issue no.4, June, 1952].
[Lincoln]: [The Division], [1952].

WELFARE

POOR RELIEF IN LINCOLN

2730.
An Act for the better relief and employment of the poor of the several parishes within the city of Lincoln, and county...and of the parish of St Margaret...14th May, 1796: 36 Geo.III ch.II.
London: printed by George Eyre and Andrew Strahan, 1796. 52p.

2731.
An Act for vesting absolutely one third part of three crofts of land...for the benefit of the poor of the parishes of Saint Swithin and Saint Peter-in-Eastgate in the city of Lincoln...
[Lincoln]: [s.n.], [1780]. 10p.

2732.
A House of industry: [proposal for building general work house in city, March 16, 1790]
Lincoln: printed Brooke, 1790. 1 sheet.

2733. **LINCOLN CORPORATION**
Heads of the intended Bill for the relief and maintenance of the poor of the several parishes within the city of Lincoln, as prepared in the year 1791
[Lincoln]: [The Corporation], [1791]. [4]p.

2734.
[Resolutions of meeting of the committee of the subscribers to the fund for the purchase of corn, 18th July, 1795]
[Lincoln]: [s.n.], [1795]. 1 sheet.

2735.
City of Lincoln: [resolutions at a general meeting of the inhabitants of the city of Lincoln...the 7th day of December, 1795...to consider the propriety of an application to Parliament for an Act for the relief and general regulation of the poor
[Lincoln]: [s.n.], [1795]. 1 sheet.

2736.
[Resolutions of meeting of inhabitants of the city, Bail and Close of Lincoln to discuss measures to conserve flour and to raise a subscription for poor relief, 28th July, 1795]
[Lincoln]: [s.n.], [1795]. 1 sheet.

2737.
[36 Geo.III, 1796]: *An Act for the better relief and employment of the poor of the several parishes within the city of Lincoln, and the county of the same city...*
[London]: [s.n.], [1796]. 63p.

264

2738.
[Notice of special meeting of guardians of the poor and the directors of the House of Industry...consideration of tbe propriety of petitioning for repeal of Act of Incorporation of the year 1796: 9th May, 1820]
Lincoln: printed W. Brooke, 1796.   1 sheet.

2739.
Bye-laws, rules and ordinances, made by virtue of the powers granted by an Act for the better relief and employment of the poor of the several parishes within the city of Lincoln, and county of the same city, and of the parish of Saint Margaret...
Lincoln: printed Drury, 1797.   31p.

2740.
[Resolutions of meeting to discuss subscription for poor relief, 7th December, 1799]
Lincoln: printed Drury, 1799.   1 sheet.

2741.
City, Bail and Close of Lincoln: minutes of a general meeting of the subscribers towards the relief of the poor, held at the Guildhall, on Thursday, the 26th of December, 1799, to consider the mode of applying the fund already subscribed
Lincoln: printed W. Brooke, [1799].   [3]p.

2742.   **LINCOLN UNION**
Library of the Lincoln Union Workhouse: rules
Lincoln: printed W. and B. Brooke, [18??].   1 sheet.

2743.
Voting paper for the parish of Saint Martin: [for guardians]
Lincoln: printed W. and B. Brooke, [18??].   1 sheet.

2744.
An Act for the better relief and employment of the poor of the several parishes within the city of Lincoln...: [copy of a clause in the Act of Parliament under which the Lincoln House of Industry was established]
Lincoln: printed J.W. Drury, 1802.   1 sheet.

2745.   **BENEVOLENT SOCIETY**
The Nature, design & rules of the Benevolent Society instituted at Lincoln, February 1st, 1803, for the relief of the industrious poor of all denominations, in time of sickness or accidental distress
Lincoln: printed by W. Brooke, 1803.   10p.

2746.   **LINCOLN HOUSE OF INDUSTRY**
State of the Lincoln House of Industry from the first Wednesday in June, 1803, to the first Wednesday in June, 1804
Lincoln: printed J.W. Drury, 1804.   1 sheet.

2747.
[A Meeting for consideration of subscription to be distributed amongst the poor, October 17, 1809]
Lincoln: printed J.W. Drury, 1809.   1 sheet.

2748.   **LINCOLN CORPORATION**
Bye-laws, rules & ordinances made by virtue of the powers granted by an Act of Parliament intitled An Act for the better relief and employment of the poor of the several parishes within the city of Lincoln...
Lincoln: printed W. Brooke, 1809.   31p.

2749.
[Resolutions of a meeting to set up National Society for the Education of the Poor in Lincoln, January 23, 1812]
Lincoln: printed Drury, 1812.   1 sheet.

2750.
[Resolutions of a meeting to consider subscription for relief of the poor, 25th January, 1814]
Lincoln: printed Drury, 1814.   1 sheet.

2751.
[Soliciting subscriptions for purchase of coal for the poor, January 27th, 1814]
Lincoln: printed W. Brooke, 1814.   1 sheet.

2752.
To the gentlemen composing the committees for the distribution of the late subscription for relieving the poor of the city, Bail and Close of Lincoln: [letter signed 'A friend to the poor', February 1st, 1814]
[Lincoln]: [s.n.], [1814].   1 sheet.

2753.   **LINCOLN HOUSE OF INDUSTRY**
State of the Lincoln House of Industry, from the first Wednesday in June, 1814, to the first Wednesday in June, 1815: [18th annual report]
Lincoln: printed Marrat, 1815.   1 sheet.

2754.
Extracted from the returns made to Parliament in compliance with an Act passed in the 55th Geo.III: [table giving details of poor relief in the city]
Lincoln: printed Drury, [1815].   1 sheet.

2755.
Abstract of returns of charitable donations, &c., 1787–1788, so far as relates to the county of Lincoln
London: House of Commons, 1816.   p.669: ill.
Cover title.   Running title: *Abstract of returns of charitable donations (county of Lincoln) for benefit of poor persons: 26 Geo.III, 1786.*
    pp.734–738: city of Lincoln.

2756.
A List of the persons who receive permanent relief from the directors of the Lincoln House of Industry, residing out of the said House, out of the poor rates received of the several incorporated parishes within the city of Lincoln...
Lincoln: printed by Drury, 1819.   8p.

2757.
Lincoln House of Industry: [notice of meeting, 15th July, 1820]
Lincoln: printed W. Brooke, 1820.   1 sheet.

2758.
[Resolutions of a special assembly of the guardians of the poor, 15th June, 1820]
Lincoln: printed Drury, 1820.   1 sheet.

2759.
[Resolutions of a special assembly of the guardians of the poor, 18th May, 1820]
Lincoln: printed W. Brooke, 1820.   1 sheet.

2760.
[Resolutions of meeting of the guardians of the poor for electing guardian auditors of the accounts of the Lincoln House of Industry, 4th May, 1820]
Lincoln: printed W. Brooke, 1820. 1 sheet.

2761.
[Resolutions of a special meeting, 20th July, 1820]
Lincoln: printed W. Brooke, 1820. 1 sheet.

2762.
An Account of the subscription made by the inhabitants of the parish of St Mary Magdalen, in January, 1820, for the relief of the poor and the establishment of a nightly watch
Lincoln: printed W. Brooke, 1820. 1 sheet.

2763.
[1 & 2 Georgii IV, cap.XLIX]: *An Act for the better relief and employment of the poor of the several parishes within the city of Lincoln, and county of the same city...7th May, 1821*
London: printed George Eyre and Andrew Strahan, 1821. pp.1541–1556.

2764.
Lincoln House of Industry: [notice of special meeting, 23rd November, 1821]
Lincoln: printed W. Brooke, 1821. 1 sheet.

2765.
[Notice of meeting in the parish of St Martin to grant rate to overseers of the poor, June 28th, 1821]
Lincoln: printed W. Brooke, 1821. 1 sheet.

2766.
[Notice of meeting of parish of Saint Swithin to reduce poor rates, September 15, 1821]
Lincoln: printed W. Brooke, 1821. 1 sheet.

2767.
[Notice of meeting in Saint Swithin's parish to reduce the poor rates, September 24th, 1821]
Lincoln: printed Brooke, 1821. 1 sheet.

2768.
[Letter about relief of poor in Ireland, June 22, 1822]
Lincoln: printed W. Brooke, 1822. 1 sheet.

2769.
To the inhabitants of the city, Bail & Close of Lincoln, and their vicinity: [letter raising subscriptions for the poor in Ireland, June 22, 1822]
Lincoln: printed W. Brooke, 1822. 1 sheet.

2770. LINCOLN HOUSE OF INDUSTRY
State of the accounts of the Lincoln House of Industry, from the first Wednesday in June, 1825, to the first Wednesday in June, 1826
Lincoln: printed W. Brooke, 1826. 16p.
_____ printed Keyworth, 1827–28.
_____ printed R.E. Leary, 1829.
_____ printed J.W. Drury, 1830.
_____ printed R.E. Leary, 1831–33.
_____ printed J.W. Drury, 1834.
_____ printed Brogden, 1835–36.

2771.
Public meeting for the relief of the distresses in the manufacturing districts, May 24th, 1826
Lincoln: printed W. Brooke, 1826. 1 sheet.

2772.
Subscription for the relief of the distressed manufacturers: [31st day of May, 1826]
Lincoln: printed W. Brooke, 1826. 1 sheet.

2773.
A Statement on parish workhouses, in order to induce the public, particularly the inhabitants of St Martin's in the city of Lincoln, to bestowe more consideration on this important subject...the propriety of taking the poor out of the incorporated workhouse
Lincoln: printed E.B. Drury, 1827. 14p.

2774.
Report on the administration of the Poor Laws, and the management of the poor, in the county of Lincoln
[S.l.]: [Commissioners of the Poor Laws], [183?]. pp.131a–149a.
Accompanies: *First report from the commissioners of the Poor Laws.*
  pp.131a–133a: Lincoln.

2775.
To the directors of Lincoln House of industry: [letter signed 'A ratepayer', December 7th, 1833]
Lincoln: printed E.B. Drury, 1833. 1 sheet.

2776.
Register of burials in the burial ground of the workhouse, 1828–37
[1837?]. [4]p.
Typescript.

2777.
To the Worshipful mayor of Lincoln: [letter about raising a subscription for the poor, 4th January, 1837]
Lincoln: printed J.W. Drury, 1837. 1 sheet.

2778.
[List of subscribers for the poor, 6th June, 1837]
Lincoln: printed J.W. Drury, 1837. 1 sheet.

2779. LINCOLN UNION
Extract from the quarterly abstract, shewing the number of paupers relieved and the amount of money expended, for the quarter ending 25th December, 1838: also shewing the balances due to and from the several parishes on the 25th December, 1838: [table]
Lincoln: printed W. and B. Brooke, 1839. 1 sheet.

2780. —————————
Extract from the quarterly abstract...ending 25th March, 1839
Lincoln: printed W. and B. Brooke, 1839. 1 sheet.

2781. —————————
Register of baptisms, 1827–1841
[184?]. 8p.
Typescript.
> Gives date, name, parents, parents' abode and occupation.

2782. —————————
Extract from the quarterly abstract...ending 25th December, 1839
Lincoln: printed W. and B. Brooke, 1840. 1 sheet.

2783. —————————
Extract from the quarterly abstract...ending 25th September, 1844
Lincoln: printed W. and B. Brooke, 1844. 1 sheet.

2784.
[Resolutions of a meeting for raising subscription for the relief of the poor, 10th March, 1845]
Lincoln: printed John Hall, 1845. 1 sheet.

2785.
[Letter to the mayor requesting meeting to consider the condition of the poor, 18th December, 1846]
Lincoln: printed W. Peck, 1846. 1 sheet.

2786.
List of recipients of the Lincoln city charities, as paid at the Christmas quarter pay day, 1846, with the ages of recipients and the sums paid to each
Lincoln: printed James Drury, 1846. 1 sheet.

2787.   **LINCOLN, General Relief Committee**
Necessitous poor: third distribution
[Lincoln]: [Lincoln Corporation], [1847]. [4]p.
> Ticket system whereby poor paid half price unless they were 'really destitute'.

2788.   **CURTIS, Geo.**
[Letter to guardians of the Lincoln Union applying for job as relieving officer, August 23rd, 1851]
[Lincoln]: [s.n.], [1851]. 1 sheet.

2789.   **LINCOLN UNION**
Parochial lists of in-door & out-door paupers relieved in the several parishes in the Union, for the half-year ending 29th September, 1880
Lincoln: printed Chas. Keyworth, [1880]. 41p.
Includes index.
> pp.3–7: city of Lincoln parishes.

2790.   **PADLEY, G.E.B.**
To the guardians of the poor of the Lincoln Union: [letter]
Welton-by-Lincoln: The Author, 1899. [3]p.
> Application for appointment as registrar of births.

2791.   **COSSEY, Frank**
A Study of the treatment of the poor in the eighteenth century
[19??].   23, ii leaves.
Typescript.
Includes bibliography.
> Exemplified by Lincoln records of the period: overseer's accounts for the parishes of St Mary
> Magdalene, St Benedict, St Botolph and St Peter-at-Arches.   Work done in connection with
> W.E.A.

2792.   **LINCOLN UNION**
Confirming order for the amalgamation of parishes, county borough of Lincoln
London: printed Eyre and Spottiswoode, 1907.   12p.

2793.   **MILTON, E.R.**
Lincoln's House of Industry: early days of Lincoln Workhouse
Lincoln: Lincoln Teachers' Centre, Resource Service, [1948?].   8p.
(Lincoln Teachers' Centre, Resource Service archive, 1)
Originally published: in *Lincolnshire chronicle*, 28 August, 4 September and 11
September, 1948.

2794.
Charities Act, 1960: review of local charities for the poor and the sick poor in the county
borough of Lincoln
[196?].   11, [9]p.
Typescript.

2795.
Directory of voluntary and caring organizations
Lincoln: Lincoln Area Volunteer Bureau, 1984.   42p.
Includes index.
> Accompanied by *Volunteer*: [leaflet].

NAMED CHARITIES AND ORGANISATIONS

2796.   **CLERICAL FUND**
*Rules of an institution called the Clerical Fund...for the relief of certain necessitous
clergymen in the county of Lincoln*
Revised and corrected.
Lincoln: printed Drury, 1820.

2797.   ─────────────
*The Annual state of the subscriptions to a Fund for the relief of certain necessitous
clergymen, widows and orphans of clergymen in the county of Lincoln, for the year
ending June 24th, 1829*
[Lincoln]: [s.n.], [1829].   [2]p.

2798.   ─────────────
*The Annual state of the subscriptions to a fund for the relief of certain necessitous
clergymen, widows and orphans of clergymen, in the county of Lincoln, for the year
ending June 24th, 1831*
[Lincoln]: [s.n.], [1831].
Also published: 1832–39.

2799. ——————————
*The Annual state of the subscriptions to a fund for the relief of certain necessitous
clergymen, widows and orphans of clergymen, in the county of Lincoln, for the year
ending midsummer, 1840*
[Lincoln]: [s.n.], [1840].   16p.
Also published: 1841–42; 1844; 1846–48; 1850; 1856.

2800. ——————————
*Rules of an institution called the Clerical Fund, established in the year 1797, for the
relief of certain necessitous clergymen, widows and orphans of clergymen, in the county
of Lincoln*
Lincoln: printed W. and B. Brooke, 1841.   9p.

2801. ——————————
Annual reports, 1870, 1873–77, 1879–91
[Lincoln]: [s.n.], [1870–91].   Various pagings.

2802.   **CLOTHING CLUB OF THE BAIL AND NEWPORT**
Rules for the Clothing Club of the Bail and Newport
Lincoln: printed W. and B. Brooke, [18??].   1 sheet.

2803.   **LINCOLN DORCAS CHARITY**
Lincoln Dorcas Charity: rules for the regulation of this charity
Lincoln: printed W. Brooke, [18??].   1 sheet.

2804. ——————————
*Rules for the regulation of this charity [and] statement of the Dorcas Charity accounts,
January 20th, 1818*
Lincoln: printed W. Brooke, 1818.   1 sheet.

2805.   **ST ANNE'S BEDEHOUSES**
Regulations and bye-laws relating to St Anne's Bedehouses, Lincoln, June 19th, 1848
[Lincoln]: [The Bedehouses], [1848].   1 sheet.

2806. ——————————
Form of consecrating of the Chapel of St Anne's, at the Bede Houses, Lincoln
Lincoln: printed G.J. Lockyer, [18??].   14p.

2807.
*Charity Commission: in the matter of the charity known as St Anne's Bedehouses, in the
city of Lincoln, founded by indenture dated 13th August, 1847...*: [scheme including
appointment of trustees]
London: HMSO, 1928.   10p.

2808.
*Attorney-General v. Slack: scheme for the management and regulation of the church
lands charity in the parish of St Peter-at-Gowts, Lincoln, and the application of the
income thereof, directed by the Court of Chancery*
London: C. Roworth, 1854.   21p.
    Concerns the use of funds to establish a school house in the parish.

2809.
*Answer to Mr Christopher Hodgson's letter to His Grace, the Archbiship of Canterbury,
on the present regulations for the distribution and management of the funds of Queen
Anne's Bounty*
Lincoln Church Association for the Augmentation of Poor Livings.
London: Simpkin, Marshall, 1866.   40p.

2810.   **LADIES NURSING FUND**
Ladies Nursing Fund: report
Lincoln: Brookes & Vibert, [1868].   7p.

2811.
[Newscuttings from *Lincolnshire echo*, 1914–15, relating to Prince of Wales Relief Fund, Lincoln]
[Lincoln]: [Lincolnshire Echo], [1914–15].   1 portfolio.

2812.
In the matter of the charity called St Giles Hospital, in the former city of Lincoln, founded by indenture dated the 15th December, 1564: and in the matter of the Charities Act, 1960: [scheme]
[London]: [Charity Commissioners for England and Wales], 1964. 3, 3p.

2813.   **LINCOLN AND DISTRICT MARRIAGE GUIDANCE COUNCIL**
Eighth annual report of the executive committee, 1969–1970
Lincoln: The Council, 1970.   [8]p.

2814.   **LINCOLN AND DISTRICT CITIZENS ADVICE BUREAU**
Annual report, 1971–72
Lincoln: The Bureau, [1973].   11p.

2815.   ──────────
Citizens' Advice Bureau, Lincoln & District: annual report: [1977–78]
[Lincoln]: [The Bureau], [1979].

2816.   **MURRAY, Flora A.R.**
Lindsey & Holland Rural Community Council, 1927–1974
[Lincoln]: [The Council], [1974].   19p.
    HQ in Lincoln.

2817.
The Shaftesbury Society Housing Association: opening ceremony at Ashley Court, Lincoln, Friday, 4th July, 1986
Lincoln: Shaftesbury Society, 1986.   4 leaves.

THE ELDERLY

2818.   **LINCOLN, Welfare Committee**
[National Assistance Act, 1948]: *Welfare services available to elderly and handicapped people in Lincoln*
[Lincoln]: [The Committee], [c.1950].   1 folded sheet.

2819.
CLACE magazine
[Lincoln]: [City of Lincoln Association for the Care of the Elderly], [196?].

2820.
What can we do for Grandma or Grandad, Uncle Arthur or Cousin Mildred ?: [appeal for Ashby Court Residential and Day Care Centre]
Lincoln: City of Lincoln Association for the Care of the Elderly, [196?].   9p.

2821.
The City of Lincoln campaign to help the aged, 1965–66: our seven year plan
[City of Lincoln Association for the Care of the Elderly].
[1965].   [5] leaves, [3] folded plans.
Typescript.

2822.
Our city
[Lincoln]: [City of Lincoln Association for the Care of the Elderly], [c.1965].   [10]p.: ill.

2823.
[Leaflet giving details of projects]
[Lincoln]: [CLACE], [1966].   [4]p.
   CLACE = City of Lincoln Association for the Care of the Elderly.

2824.
Open day for Fosse House, Saturday, 31st December, 1966
Lincoln: Lincoln, Welfare Committee, 1966.   [3]p.
   Details about residential homes for the elderly.

2825.
The Day Centre, Park Street, Lincoln: official opening...Tuesday, 27th October, 1970:
[programme]
Lincoln: City of Lincoln Association for the Care of the Elderly, 1970.   [8]p.

2826.
R.E.A.C.T.: care in the community, 24 hour protection, peace of mind
Lincoln: Lincoln City Council, [after 1974].   [18]p.: ill.
   R.E.A.C.T.= Responsive Emergency Alarm Control Terminal.

2827.   **HYDE, Alison**
Lincoln gets carried away
pp.558–559: ill. in *Health and social service journal*, vol.94, 19th May, 1984.
   About ambulance service operating from St George's Geriatric Day Hospital.

THE YOUNG

2828.
[Notice about illegality of employing climbing boys under the age of 21, April 15th,
1843]
Lincoln: printed W. and B. Brooke, 1843.   1 sheet.

2829.   **LINCOLN, Juvenile Advisory Committee**
Annual report, 1933
[1933].   15p.
Typescript.

2830.
*A Study in juvenile delinquency: who has offended? : a study of juvenile delinquency in
Lincoln made by a Workers' Educational Association tutorial class of the Oxford
University tutorial classes joint committee*
London: W.E.A., [1944].   23p.

2831.
Report of the enquiry into child welfare in the city of Lincoln...at the request of the
Lindsey and Holland Rural Community Council, in preparation for the Harrogate
Conference on Social Work, April 19th-23rd, 1950
Lincoln Standing Conference of Women's Organisations.
[1949?]. 16p.
Typescript.

2832.
Youth action: a directory of voluntary service
Lincoln: Lincoln Teachers' Centre, [1973]. [31] leaves.

UNEMPLOYMENT

2833. CAMERON, A.M.
Civilisation and the unemployed
London: Student Christian Movement Press, 1934. 152p.
Ch.6–7: the Lincoln experiment, 1927–33. Deals with setting up of a workshop in Lincoln,
but aim is to give example of basic approach; little detail about Lincoln as such.

2834.
Time to spare
edited F. Greene.
[Manchester]: [BBC], [1935].
Experiences of unemployed people. pp.96–101: 'Time to spare', by W. O'Neill, a metal
turner from Lincoln, about People's Service Club.

THE DISABLED

2835. MULTIPLE SCLEROSIS SOCIETY, Lincoln and District Branch
Multiple Sclerosis Society: newsletter
[Lincoln?]: [The Branch], [19??].

2836. LINCOLN DIOCESAN MISSION IN AID OF THE DEAF AND DUMB
29th report, 1924
Lincoln: printed Lincolnshire Chronicle, 1924. 11p.

2837. LINCOLN ASSOCIATED PHYSICALLY HANDICAPPED SOCIETY
Year book, 1972
Lincoln: The Society, 1972. 36p.: ill.
Information about number of Lincoln based charities.

2838. LINCOLN AND DISTRICT SPASTICS ASSOCIATION
Year book, 1977
Lincoln: The Association, [1977]. 40p.: ill.

2839. ——————
*The Lincoln & District Spastics Society year book and the Lincolnshire Steam
Spectacular: souvenir programme*
Lincoln: The Society, [1980]. 36p.
  pp.20–23: list of engines, including Clayton & Shuttleworth, Foster, and Robey machines.

2840. **INVALID CHILDREN'S AID ASSOCIATION**
Invalid Children's Aid Association: year book, 1981–82
Lincoln ed.
London: The Association, [1981]. 36p.: ill.
  Differentiated from other editions by fact that advertising is local and address of Lincoln
  organiser is given.

2841. **LINCOLN & DISTRICT MENCAP SOCIETY**
Lincoln & District Mencap Society: year book, 1986
[Lincoln?]: [The Society], [1986].

WOMEN

2842. **LYING-IN CHARITY**
Lincoln City Lying-in Charity: rules for the regulation of this charity
Lincoln: printed W. and B. Brooke, [1805?]. [3]p.
  Charity established in 1805.

2843. ——————
[Notice of meeting of subscribers to Lying-in Charity at Lincoln, January 21, 1805]: *To
consider the following rules*
Lincoln: printed J.W. Drury, 1805. 1 sheet.

2844. ——————
*Regulations for conducting the county of Lincoln Lying-in Charity for the relief of poor
married women*
Lincoln: printed W. Brooke, [after 1805]. 1 sheet.

2845. ——————
Rules for conducting the Lying-in Charity, for the relief of poor married women
Lincoln: printed W. Brooke, [after 1805]. 1 sheet.

2846. ——————
*A Short account of a charity, established at Lincoln, in the year 1805, for the benefit of
poor married lying-in women, and for the instruction of girls in reading and plain work:
the rules...and abstract of...accounts, and a list of the subscribers*
Lincoln: printed W. Brooke and sold by him, 1810. 24p.

2847. ——————
County of Lincoln Lying-in Charity for the relief of poor married women
Lincoln: printed W. and B. Brooke, [184?]. 2p.

2848.
Prostitution & prostitutes versus humanity: [letter to William Andrew, Esq., 11th May,
1847]
Lincoln: printed T.J.N. Brogden, 1847. [2]p.
  Questioning Corporation policy of prosecuting such offenders and calling for the establishment
  of a refuge.

2849.
[Penitent females' home: letter announcing stone-laying ceremony, 22 April, 1850]
[Lincoln]: [s.n.], [1850].   1 sheet.

2850.
[Penitent females' home: details of procession prior to stone-laying, 2nd May, 1850]
Lincoln: printed W. and B. Brooke, 1850.   1 sheet.

2851.
[Letter suggesting that ministers preach sermons of behalf of the penitent females' home, 11th June, 1850]
[Lincoln]: [s.n.], [1850].   1 sheet.

2852.   **PENITENT FEMALES' HOME**
Lincoln and Lincolnshire Penitent Females' Home: (second annual report)
Lincoln: printed W. and B. Brooke, 1849.   19p.

2853.   **PERKINS, J.A.**
Unmarried mothers and the Poor Law in Lincolnshire, 1800–1850
pp.21–33 in *Lincolnshire history and archaeology*, vol.20, 1985.
    Some coverage of Lincoln House of Industry.

EDUCATION

2854. DIOCESAN BOARD OF EDUCATION
Rules of the Diocesan Board of Education, for the county of Lincoln, provisionally settled at a meeting on the 18th September, 1839, and to be finally settled at the general meeting on the 24th October, 1839
Lincoln: printed T.O. Brumby, 1839.   12p.

2855. ————————
Rules of the Board of Education for the diocese of Lincoln adopted at a meeting of the Board...April 18th, 1884...
Lincoln: printed H.E. Cousans, [1884].   6p.
   Very general rules.

2856. FISHER, R. Elizabeth
Chancellor Leeke's role as an educator in the city of Lincoln, 1877–1900
[19??].   19, [9] leaves.
Typescript.

2857. PETERS, Nina
Education in the city of Lincoln between 1830 and 1870
[19??].   37 leaves.
Typescript.

2858.
Secondary education in Lincoln: report by the chief education officer to the Education Committee on the present system of secondary education and possible schemes for the reorganization...with a view to eliminating selection...
[19??].   27 leaves: ill.
Typescript.

2859. LINCOLN CORPORATION
Scheme for the constitution of an Education Committee under section 17 of the Education Act, 1902
Lincoln: The Corporation, 1903.   [3]p.
(Circular, 17)

2860. LINCOLN, Education Committee
Standing orders made by the Education Committee of the city of Lincoln, for the regulation of their proceedings and business
Lincoln: printed Keyworth, 1905.   12p.

2861.
School attendance bye-laws
Lincoln: printed Keyworth, 1907.   3p.
(Form 17 S.A.)

2862.   LINCOLN, Education Committee
Estimates for the year ending 31st March, 1936
Lincoln: The Committee, 1935.   15p.

2863.
The Headmistress speaks: [essays]
London: Kegan Paul, Trench, Trubner, 1937.   277p.
     pp.195–209: 'Differentness', by L.E. Savill, headmistress of High School for Girls, Lincoln.

2864.   LINCOLN, Education Committee
Education Week handbook
Lincoln: The Committee, 1938.   92p.: ill.
     Took place 2–8 October, 1938.

2865.
Lincoln Education Week, 2–8 October: [photograph album]
[Lincoln]: [s.n.], [1938].
     Includes: central exhibition at the Usher Art Gallery; plays at St.Giles Senior School; and
     classrooms at Sincil Bank.

2866.   SUTCLIFFE, A.
Selection for secondary education without a written examination
by A. Sutcliffe and J.W. Canham.
London: John Murray, 1945.   88p.: ill.
     First author was headmaster of the City School and the second, Science master. Book draws
     upon experience of awarding special places in Lincoln.   Same authors also wrote *Experiments
     in homework and physical education.*

2867.
Educational facilities in Lincolnshire
Bristol: British Isles, [195?].   20p.: ill.
     p.14: St.George's School, Riseholme Grange, Lincoln; p.15: the Lincoln Commercial School.

2868.   LINCOLN, Education Committee
*Programme of events in Lincoln during Commonwealth Technical Training Week, 27th
May, 1961–4th June, 1961*
Lincoln: printed Keyworth & Fry, [1961].   15p.
     Produced in association with Lincoln Junior Chamber of Commerce and the Lincoln Youth
     Council.

2869.   ⸺⸺⸺
*Programme of events in Lincoln during Commonwealth Technical Training Week, 27th
May, 1961–4th June, 1961*
Lincoln: The Committee, 1961.   15p.

2870.   MADDISON, John
A History of education in Lincoln
46 leaves: ill.
Ms.
Long essay – Kesteven Training College, 1961.
     Includes: *Lincoln Diocesan Training College*: [prospectus], 1955, 7p.: ill.   No guide to
     sources or bibliographic detail.

2871.   STERRY, M.A.
Elementary education in Lincoln, 1870–1903
384 leaves.
Typescript.
Thesis [Ph.D.] – University of Nottingham, [c.1971].

2872.
The Prospect for the village school: papers of a seminar
by Roy Nash, Sheila Addison, Alan Sigsworth and Roy Whitaker.
Lincoln: Bishop Grosseteste College, Centre for the Study of Rural Society, 1977.   24p.
>   Does not concentrate upon Lincoln and Lincolnshire in particular; Lincolnshire was the host
>   county.

2873.   **LINCOLN, Education Department**
Lincoln city education: records of the former Education Department of Lincoln City
Council, deposited by the Lincolnshire division of the County Education Service on 22
October, 1976
[1977].   24 leaves.
Typescript.
>   Contains material in the Lincolnshire Archives Office: non-current records of individual
>   schools; legal and financial records; records of governors of the grammar schools; papers of
>   Canon E.T. Leeke.   Items less than 30 years old may not be consulted.

2874.   **LAMMING, John David**
Education in Lincoln, 1800–1902
425p.
Thesis [Ph.D.] – University of Leeds, 1979.

2875.   **ACTON, Ray**
L.E.A.P.: a successful launch into historical aids
by Ray Acton and Tim Hall.
pp.8–11: ill. in *Teaching history*, no.38, February, 1984.
>   Lincolnshire Educational Aids Project based in Lincoln.

2876.   **LAMONT, Adrian Christopher**
Elementary education in Lincoln, 1903 to 1933
vi, 86 leaves: ill.
Typescript.
Thesis [Master of Education] – University of Nottingham, 1984.
>   Discusses role of the established Church in the provision of elementary education.

SCHOOLS

2877.   **GEORGE, William**
*Sermon preach'd at the Parish-Church of St Peter's-at-Arches in the city of Lincoln,
September 18, 1752, at the triennial meeting of the subscribers to the charity-schools in
the said city*
Lincoln: printed W. Wood, 1752.   25p.

2878.
Establishment for young ladies: [prospectus for Miss Bains's school]
[Lincoln]: [s.n.], [18??].   1 sheet.

2879.
Preparatory school: [prospectus of school run by Miss Adcock and Mrs Wm. Newton]
[Lincoln]: [s.n.], [18??].   1 sheet.

2880.
St Peter-at-Gowts Infant School: [programme of events to celebrate stone laying]
Lincoln: printed Keyworth, [18??].   1 sheet.

2881.   **ACKRILL, J.**
J. Ackrill respectfully informs the inhabitants of Lincoln and its vicinity that he intends opening...a day school
Lincoln: printed W. and B. Brooke, [18??].   1 sheet.

2882.   **BRITISH SCHOOLS**
British Schools, Mint-Lane, Lincoln: [prospectus for boys' school and girls' school]
Lincoln: printed W. and B. Brooke, [18??].   1 sheet.

2883.   **ERMINE INFANTS SCHOOL**
Ermine Infants School: [prospectus]
Lincoln: [The School], [18??].   7 leaves.

2884.   **LADIES' SCHOOL**
Ladies' School, Portland Place, Saint Mary's, Lincoln: [prospectus of school run by Miss E. Moulton]
Lincoln: printed W. and B. Brooke, [18??].   1 sheet.

2885.   **LINCOLN FREE GRAMMAR SCHOOL**
Lincoln Free Grammar School: [prospectus]
[Lincoln]: [s.n.], [18??].   1 sheet.

2886.   **MRS. CAPP'S SEMINARY**
Terms of Mrs. Capp's Seminary, Lincoln
Lincoln: printed W. and B. Brooke, [18??].   1 sheet.

2887.   **NUTTER, C.C.**
[Prospectus for school for young gentlemen]
[Lincoln]: [s.n.], [18??].   1 sheet.

2888.   **ROOME, Mrs.**
[Notice about school in Cornhill]
[Lincoln]: [s.n.], [18??].   1 sheet.

2889.   **DRURY, Miss**
Miss Drury's School for Young Ladies: terms per annum
Lincoln: printed Drury, 1805.   1 sheet.

2890.
Report of the Lincoln School in union with the National Society for the Education of the Poor in the Principles of the Established Church
Lincoln: printed Drury, [1819].   3p.
Also published: 1820; 1821.

2891.
Boarding school for young gentlemen, Potter Gate, Minster Yard, Lincoln, conducted by George Boole
[Lincoln]: [s.n.], [183?].   1 sheet.

2892.
At a public meeting held at the Guildhall in the city of Lincoln...: [resolution to establish infant school]
Lincoln: [s.n.], [1831?].   [2]p.

2893. LINCOLN INFANTS' SCHOOL SOCIETY
Annual statement of the Lincoln Infants' School Society
Lincoln: printed J.W. Drury, 1832. 10p.
  Instituted in 1831.

2894. ──────────
Lincoln Infants' School Society: [list of subscribers and abstract of accounts, September 29th, 1832 to September 18th, 1833]
Lincoln: printed Brooke, 1833. 1 sheet.

2895. LINCOLN NATIONAL SCHOOL
Lincoln National School: annual report: [1831]
Lincoln: printed J.W. Drury, 1832. 8p.

2896. CLASSICAL, COMMERCIAL & MATHEMATICAL ACADEMY
Classical, Commercial & Mathematical Academy, High-Street, Lincoln: [prospectus]
Lincoln: printed W. and B. Brooke, [1833]. 1 sheet.
  Classical, Commercial & Mathematical Academy run by George Boole.

2897. KING, Miss
[Prospectus for school]
Lincoln: printed W. and B. Brooke, 1834. 1 sheet.

2898.
Lincoln Grammar School, 1836: statement of the Corporation visitors
Lincoln: printed Keyworth, 1836. 8p.

2899. LINCOLN SCHOOL
The Annual report of the Lincoln School, founded in the year 1813, in union with the National Society for the Education of the Poor in the Principles of the Established Church
Lincoln: printed E.B. Drury, 1827. 8p.
────── printed Brooke, 1829.
────── printed Keyworth, 1830.
────── printed J.W. Drury, 1832.

2900. LINCOLN INFANTS' SCHOOL SOCIETY
Lincoln Infants' School Society: [list of subscribers and abstract of accounts...1835–36]
Lincoln: printed Brooke, 1836. 1 sheet.

2901. WADDINGTON ACADEMY
Waddington Academy, near Lincoln, conducted by Geo. Boole: [prospectus, December 24, 1839]
Lincoln: printed W. and B. Brooke, 1839. 1 sheet.

2902. LINCOLN VICTORIA INFANT SCHOOL
Rules of the Lincoln Victoria Infant School
Lincoln: printed W. and B. Brooke, [184?]. 4p.

2903. LAMPRAY, J.
[Prospectus for school run by Rev. J. Lampray, April, 1840]
Lincoln: printed W. and B. Brooke, 1840. 1 sheet.

2904. LINCOLN NATIONAL SCHOOLS
Rules of the Lincoln National Schools
Revised.
Lincoln: printed W. and B. Brooke, 1843. 16p.
  'Public schools for the purpose of promoting the education of such poor children as shall be chosen...'.

2905.
The Grammar School, Lincoln: [2 bound vols. of lists, 1858–1875]
[Lincoln]: [s.n.], [1875?].   Various pagings.

2906.   LINCOLN RAGGED SCHOOL
The Twenty-fourth annual report of the Lincoln Ragged School...from Nov. 1st, 1875, to October, 1876
Lincoln: printed Chas. Akrill, 1877.   15p.
Also published: 1878–79.

2907.
[Charity Commission]: *In the matter of the Hospital of Jesus Christ, otherwise known as Christ's Hospital, in the city of Lincoln, and all the endowments thereof, or attached thereto...*
[London]: [The Commission], 1883.   15p.

2908.   LINCOLN GRAMMAR SCHOOL
Lincoln Grammar School, December 21st, 1891: order of service for opening of new wing
Lincoln: printed James Williamson, [1891].   4p.

2909.   LINCOLN HIGHER GRADE AND CONTINUATION DAY SCHOOL
Lincoln Higher Grade and Continuation Day School: session 1894–5: [prospectus]
[Lincoln]: The School, [1894].   [4]p.

2910.
Lincoln Elementary Schools: programme of a grand bazaar in aid of the above schools, to be opened by Her Grace, the Duchess of Portland, on November 20th, 1895, at 2pm and by Mrs Charles Hilton Seely, on November 21st, 1895...
Lincoln: printed Keyworth, [1895].   [3]p.

2911.
Bishop King School, Lincoln: [notes on the school's history]
[19??].   3 leaves.
Typescript.

2912.
St Joseph's: its history
[19??].   [3]p.
Typescript.

2913.   GARTON, Charles*
Lincoln School, 1090 to 1300: a draft history
[1980].   215 leaves.
Typescript.

2914.   ─────────
Lincoln School, 1300–1500: a draft history
[1981].   216–482 leaves: ill.
Typescript.

2915.   ─────────
Lincoln School, 1500–1585: a draft history
[1983].   483–953 leaves.
Typescript.

* Corrigendum: this entry and the four following entries have inadvertently been misfiled and should, in fact, be located on chronological grounds after entry 2997.

2916. —————————
Lincoln School, 1585–1683: a draft history
[1985].   954–1317 leaves.
Typescript.

2917. —————————
Lincoln School, 1683–1800: a draft history
[1988].   1318–1630 leaves.
Typescript.

2918.   **LAMMING, J.D.**
The Lincoln Blue Coat School
[19??].   115 leaves.
Typescript.
> pp.57–109: appendices, containing photocopies of primary sources such as the ordinances, letters from the governors to the Charity Commission, etc.   Also includes short biography of Richard Smith.

2919.   **LINCOLNSHIRE COUNTY COUNCIL, Education Committee**
Lincoln division: [list of schools]
[19??].   [10] leaves.
Typescript.

2920.   **SOUTH PARK HIGH SCHOOL**
South Park High School magazine
[Lincoln]: [The School], [19??].

2921.   **ST MARY'S SCHOOL**
St Mary's School, Lincoln: [prospectus]
Lincoln: [The School], [19??].   8p.: ill., map.
> Contains enclosure giving list of governors, staff and activities.

2922.   **ST JOSEPH'S CONVENT BOARDING AND DAY SCHOOL**
St Joseph's Convent Boarding and Day School: prospectus
[Lincoln?]: [The School], [19??].   Various pagings: ill.
Includes: *St Joseph's nursery class*: [prospectus], 4p.; and list of uniform requirements, 5p.
> From September, 1983: known as St Joseph's School; run by Educational Charitable Trust rather than the Sisters of Providence.

2923.   **WILCOCK, Jennifer**
The Development of nursery education in Lincoln
[19??].   6p.
Typescript.

2924.
Schemes for the endowment & management of the Lincoln Grammar School, appointed by orders in Council, dated the 23rd day of August, 1883, and the 11th day of January, 1900
Lincoln: printed James Williamson, 1900.   32p.
> Amendments are shown in red type

2925.   **CENTRAL COUNCIL FOR VOLUNTARY SCHOOLS**
The Seventh year book of the Central Council for Voluntary Schools in Lincoln, year ending 31st December, 1905
Lincoln: W.K. Morton, 1905.   [10]p.

2926. LINCOLN GRAMMAR SCHOOL
Lincoln Grammar School
[Lincoln]: [The School], [1906]. [8]p., 10 plates.

2927.
Lincoln Grammar School, 1090–1906
pp.524–525 in *Journal of education: a monthly record and review*, no.445, vol.38 (new series, 28), August 1, 1906.

2928. BELL, W.J.
Monks Road County Primary School: [notes on the history until 1906]
[1906?].   3 leaves.
Typescript.
Accompanies: Speech of the mayor, Councillor W.J. Bell, [6] leaves; Notes on the buildings, [2] leaves.

2929. LINCOLN SCHOOL
Lincoln School prospectus
Lincoln: printed J.W. Ruddock, [1909].   31p.: ill.

2930.
City of Lincoln: Municipal Technical Day School for Boys
Lincoln: printed Keyworth, 1909.   35p.: ill.

2931. HUNT, Alfred
A Few notes concerning the founder of Lincoln Christ's Hospital, Richard Smith, 1533–1602
[Lincoln]: [s.n.], [191?].   [4]p.
   Demand that Welton and Potterhanworth should benefit according to Smith's intentions.

2932.
Scheme made by the Board of Education under the Charitable Trusts Acts, 1853 to 1894, for the alteration of the scheme regulating the Foundation of Christ's Hospital at Lincoln
London: HMSO, 1911.   17p.: ill.

2933. HUNT, Alfred
Notes for a history of Lincoln Christ's Hospital and the interest therein of the parish of Welton
Lincoln: printed W.K. Morton, [1911?].   19p.

2934. HIGH SCHOOL FOR GIRLS
High School for Girls, Lincoln: [prospectus]
[Lincoln]: [The School], [c.1914].   18p.: ill.

2935. OLD HOLTONIANS
Holtonians' reunion, Monday, April 13th, 1914, at Rosemary Lane School, Lincoln: souvenir programme
[Lincoln]: [Old Holtonians], [1914].   [14]p.: ill.
   John Holton was headmaster for 43 years.

2936.
South Park Open-Air School: special report, year ending October, 1914
Lincoln: Lincoln, Education Committee, 1914.   60p.: ill.

2937. LINCOLN OLD BLUE COAT BOYS' ASSOCIATION
Object & rules of the Lincoln Old Blue Coat Boys' Association
[Lincoln]: [The Association], [c.1918].   7p.

2938.   **CITY SCHOOL**
The Pioneer: the magazine of the City School, Lincoln
[Lincoln]: [The School], [1920s/1930s?].

2939.
South Park Secondary School for Girls to be opened on Thursday, 11th May, 1922, at 2.30pm...programme of opening ceremony
[Lincoln]: [Lincoln, Education Committee], [1922].   [10]p.: ill.

2940.   **HUNT, Alfred**
The Foundation of Lincoln Christ's Hospital: a brief outline of Welton and Potterhanworth's interest therein and a few notes concerning the founder of Lincoln Christ's Hospital, Dr. Richard Smith, with genealogy
Lincoln: printed Keyworth, [1923].   18p.: ill.

2941.
Scheme made by the Board of Education under the Charitable Trusts Acts, 1853 to 1894, of the alteration of the scheme regulating the Foundation of Christ's Hospital at Lincoln
London: HMSO, 1924.   2p.

2942.
Scheme made by the Board of Education under the Charitable Trusts Acts, 1853 to 1894, for the alteration of the schemes regulating the Lincoln Grammar School
London: HMSO, 1925.   2p.

2943.   **SOUTH PARK HIGH SCHOOL**
[Prospectus]
[Lincoln]: [The School], [193?].   16p.

2944.
Scheme made by the Board of Education under the Charitable Trusts Acts, 1853 to 1925, in the matter of the Lincoln North District Old National School
London: HMSO, 1931.   2p.

2945.   **YOUNG, C.E.**
A History of Lincoln School
pp.342–347: ill. in *The Lincolnshire magazine*, vol.1, 1932–34.

2946.
St Giles Council Senior School, Lincoln, to be opened...20th September, 1933
Lincoln: Lincoln, Education Committee, 1933.   [3]p.: ill.

2947.   **COLLIS, A.E.**
History of the City School
[1934].   13, [7] leaves: ill.
Typescript.
    Includes copies of: *Report on music*, from inspection, 1916; *School report*, 1902; extract from prospectus, 1930; sketch of Monks Road building and plaque to A.E. Collis; and *Lincolnshire echo* article about the discovery of typescript.

2948.   **DALTON, R.F.**
Witton Dalton, last headmaster of Christ's Hospital, Lincoln, and his times
pp.67–72: ill. in *The Lincolnshire magazine*, vol.3, 1936–38.

2949.   **GOY, W.H.**
Reminiscences: the Lincoln Blue-Coat School
pp.19, 22–23: ill. in *The Lincolnshire magazine*, vol.3, 1936–38.

2950.   LINCOLN SCHOOL
Schola Lincolniensis: opening of new buildings, 20th January, 1937
Lincoln: printed J.W. Ruddock, 1937.   7p.: ill.

2951.
*South Park High School for Girls, Lincoln: the new buildings to be opened by H.A.S.
Wortley...14th October, 1938*
[Lincoln]: [Lincoln, Education Committee], [1938].   15p.: ill.
   Original date for opening by the Earl of Stanhope was set for October 7th.

2952.   LINCOLN CHRIST'S HOSPITAL GIRLS' HIGH SCHOOL
Lincoln Christ's Hospital Girls' High School, 1893–1943
[Lincoln]: [The School], [1943].   12p., [5] leaves of plates.

2953.   CITY SCHOOL
The City School, Lincoln: jubilee, 1896–1946
[Lincoln]: [The School], [1946].   80p., [6] leaves of plates.
Also published: including *Book of remembrance, 1939–45*, with 77p. of plates.
   Articles on various aspects of school life.   One of forewords by J.W.F. Hill, mayor and old
   boy of the School.

2954.   LENYGON, James
Last ten Blue Coat boys
in *Lincolnshire chronicle*, 17 December, 1949.

2955.   ──────────
Best schoolmaster in the world: old Blue Coat boy's tribute to last head
in *Lincolnshire chronicle*, 31 December, 1949.

2956.   ──────────
City Blue Coat School: reduced income: beginning of the end
p.6: ill. in *Lincolnshire chronicle*, Saturday, 14 January, 1950.

2957.
Features in local administration: selection for grammar schools: the Lincoln method
pp.367–370 in *Education: the official organ of the Association of Education Committees*,
vol.XCIX, no.2563, Friday, March 7, 1952.

2958.   SUTCLIFFE, A.
Feature in local administration: the 'house' system in the Hartsholme Infant School,
Lincoln
pp.171–175: ill. in *Education: the official organ of the Association of Education
Committees*, vol.CIII, no.2662, Friday, January 29, 1954.

2959.   CITY SCHOOL
School exhibition, 1959
[Lincoln]: [The School], [1959].   1 folded sheet.

2960.   LINCOLN SCHOOL
Lincoln School: [prospectus]
[Lincoln]: [The School], [1959].   [3]p.

2961.   ──────────
Lincoln School: [prospectus]
[Lincoln]: [The School], [mid 1960s?].   [4]p.

2962.   **BARKER, Jean**
Survey of training and employment based on information supplied by school-leavers of
Christ's Hospital Girls' High School, Lincoln, 1959–1964
Jean Barker, Jean Reeves.
[after 1964].   32 leaves: ill.
Typescript.
   Assessment of effectiveness of careers advisory service.

2963.   **BISHOP KING SCHOOL**
Bishop King Church of England Secondary School: [prospectus]
[Lincoln]: [The School], [c.1964].   [3]p.

2964.
*City and county of the city of Lincoln, Education Committee: official opening of the
Birchwood Infant School...on Thursday, 16th December, 1965*
Lincoln: printed Keyworth & Fry, 1965.   [11]p.: ill.

2965.   **CITY SCHOOL**
City School, Lincoln: school exhibition, 1965
[Lincoln]: [The School], [1965].   1 folded sheet.

2966.   **LINCOLN HIGH SCHOOL OLD GIRLS' HOUSING ASSOCIATION**
Notice of annual general meeting, report of the management committee and accounts for
the year ended 31st December, 1965
[Lincoln]: The Association, 1966.   8p.
Typescript.
_____   1967, [7]p.
_____   1974, [7]p.

2967.   **LINCOLN, Education Committee**
Second report by the chief education officer to the Education Committee on the
re-organisation of secondary education in Lincoln
1966.   23p.: ill.
Typescript.

2968.   _____
The Organization of secondary education in Lincoln: third report
[1966].   11 leaves.
Typescript.

2969.
St Christopher's School: [opening ceremony]
[Lincoln]: [Lincoln, Education Committee], [1966].   [12]p.: ill.

2970.   **WATTS, A.G.**
Method.   2: Christ's Hospital Girls' High School, Lincoln
pp.28–33 in *The Journal of the Careers Research and Advisory Centre*, vol.2, no.1, 1966.
   Method of giving career advice.

2971.   **BOOTHROYD, Basil**
Father of the man
pp.394–396 in *Punch*, September 18, 1968.
   Experiences in Lincoln at Choir School.

2972.
Manor Leas Infant School: programme of official opening...on Wednesday, 10th July, 1968
[Lincoln]: Lincoln, Education Committee, 1968.   [3]p., plan.

2973.
The City School: programme of official opening to be performed by Alderman Sir Francis Hill..on Friday, 17th September, 1968
Lincoln: Lincoln, Education Committee, 1969.   [8]p.: ill.
Ill. on inside covers.

2974.
Birchwood Middle School: programme of official opening...Tuesday, 25th March, 1969
Lincoln: Lincoln, Education Committee, 1969.   [3]p., plan.
   Includes description of buildings.

2975.
Manor Leas Middle School: programme of official opening...on Tuesday, 15th July, 1969
Lincoln: Lincoln, Education Committee, 1969.   [3]p., plan.

2976.
Bracebridge Infant School: programme of official opening to be performed by the mayor of Lincoln...Friday, 3rd July, 1970...
Lincoln: Lincoln, Education Committee, [1970].   [3]p., plan.

2977.   **LINCOLN EDUCATION AUTHORITY**
[Changes of character of a number of Lincoln schools]
Lincoln: printed Keyworth & Fry, 1971.   1 sheet.

2978.
St.Francis School, Lincoln
Lincoln: Lincoln, Education Committee, [1971].   [20]p.: ill.

2979.
Yarborough High School: official opening, Saturday, March 27th, 1971
[Lincoln]: [Lincoln, Education Committee], [1971].   [8]p.: ill.

2980.   **CLARKE, John**
John Clarke's orationes et declamationes habitae in schola Lincolniensi: speech day proceedings in an English School, 1624 and 1625
edited with introduction, translation and notes by Charles Garton.
Buffalo, N.Y.: State University of New York, Department of Classics, 1972.   203p.: ill.
(Arethusa monographs, IV)
Includes index.   Parallel Latin and English text.
   Includes 2 photographs of Greyfriars and reproduction of the Lincoln School speeches as printed in *Formulae oratoriae*, 1632.   Book is dedicated to Sir Francis Hill.

2981.   **LINCOLN CHRIST'S HOSPITAL SCHOOL**
Lincoln Christ's Hospital School appeal
[Lincoln]: [The School], [1972].   [4]p., plan.

2982.   **GOWENLOCK, Donald**
St Faith's School, 1873–1973
[1973?].   25p., [2]p of plates.
Typescript.

2983.
St Giles Nursery School new building: programme of official opening...2nd April, 1973
Lincoln: Lincoln, Education Committee, 1973.   [3]p.: ill.

2984.   **LINCOLN CHRIST'S HOSPITAL GIRLS' HIGH SCHOOL**
A Book of memories: Lincoln Christ's Hospital Girls' High School, 1893–1974
Lincoln: The School, 1974.   34p.

2985.   **ST.FAITH'S SCHOOL**
*St Faith's Church of England Controlled First School: programme of official opening
ceremony...on Saturday, 1 February, 1975*
[Lincoln]: [The School], [1975].   [7]p.
    Includes brief history.

2986.   **GARTON, Charles**
How Usher Beverley took his leave of this world
pp.190–198 in *Didaskalos: the journal of the Joint Association of Classical Teachers,*
vol.5, no.2, 1976.
    Was usher at Lincoln school under headmaster John Clarke and was also vicar of Cherry
    Willingham.

2987.   **ST HUGH'S SCHOOL**
St Hugh's Catholic First School, 1874–1976: [prospectus]
[compiled by the staff].
Lincoln: [Lincoln, Education Committee], [1976].   15p.: ill.

2988.   **CUNNINGHAM, Catherine L.**
Christ's Hospital Foundation in Lincoln
[153] leaves: ill., maps.
Typescript.
Thesis [B.Ed.] - University of Warwick, 1977.
    Photocopies of pictures of various sites and buildings throughout history of school; and of
    newspaper cuttings.   Appendix consists of copies of primary material, such as prospectuses,
    commissioners' reports, etc.

2989.   **JOHNSON, C.P.C.**
Coping with 100 in one class...
p.5: ill. in *Lincolnshire echo*, Tuesday, December 20, 1977.

2990.   ——————
Early days in the county's schools
ill. in *Lincolnshire echo*, Tuesday, December 6, 1977.
    About grammar schools.

2991.   ——————
University and charity schools
ill. in *Lincolnshire echo*, Tuesday, December 13, 1977.

2992.   **LINCOLN CHRIST'S HOSPITAL SCHOOL**
Lincoln Christ's Hospital School: [prospectus]
[Lincoln]: [The School], 1977.   12p., 4p. of plates.
    Gives a brief history and description of the buildings.

2993.   **OLD CHRIST'S HOSPITAL LINCOLNIANS**
Old Christ's Hospital Lincolnians magazine
No.8, November, 1978.
[Lincoln]: [Old Christ's Hospital Lincolnians], [1978].

2994.   ST GILES SCHOOLS
The St Giles Schools, Lincoln: St Giles Nursery School, St Giles First School, Myle Cross Middle School: [prospectus]
[Lincoln]: The Schools, [1978?].   15p.: ill.

2995.
Lincoln Ancaster High School: [an appraisal carried out in October, 1979]
Lincoln: Lincolnshire County Council, Education Committee, 1979.   80p.: ill., map.

2996.   FISK, Roy
Abe and the Blue-Coat School: [short story]
pp.40–41 in *Lincolnshire life*, vol.20, no.6, September, 1980.

2997.
Lincoln St Christopher's School: [an appraisal carried out in April, 1980]
Lincoln: Lincolnshire County Council, Education Committee, 1980.   16p.

2998.   SIR FRANCIS HILL MIDDLE SCHOOL
Sir Francis Hill Middle School: [prospectus]
[Lincoln]: The School, [1981].   5p.

2999.
Yarborough High School prospectus: [1981/82]
Lincoln: Lincolnshire County Council, Education Committee, 1981.   14p.: ill.

3000.   CATHEDRAL SCHOOL
The Cathedral School, Lincoln: prospectus
Lincoln: The School, [1983].   12p.: ill., map.

3001.   DEPARTMENT OF EDUCATION AND SCIENCE
Report by H.M. inspectors on St Peter and St Paul Roman Catholic Voluntary Aided High School, Lincoln
Stanmore: DES, 1984.   9p.
   Short inspection as part of national monitoring of secondary education.

3002.   ——————
Report by H.M. inspectors on St.Faith's Voluntary Controlled First School, Lincoln
Stanmore: DES, 1984.   16p.

3003.   LINCOLN, Housing and Estates Department
List of schools in Lincoln with effect from 1st September, 1984
[1984].   5p.
Typescript.

3004.   COBB, Rachel J.
A Study into the history of the Lincoln Cathedral Choir School
37 leaves, 4 leaves of plates.
Typescript.
Thesis [B.Ed.] – University of London, 1985.

3005. **JACOB, Lyon**
[Announcement of willingness to teach Hebrew]
Lincoln: printed W. and B. Brooke, [18??].   1 sheet.

3006. **LEEKE, E.T.**
[Letter to Bishop of Lincoln regarding evening schools in the city]
[Lincoln]: [s.n.], [18??].   [2] leaves.

3007. **THORPE, Miss**
[Notice about water colour and pencil drawing tuition]
[Lincoln]: [s.n.], [18??].   1 sheet.

3008. **WARWICK, Dr.**
[Notice of lecture on chemical science and syllabus]
[Lincoln]: [s.n.], [18??].   [3]p.

3009. **WEISS, Martin**
[Letter announcing intention to teach French and German in place of Signor Matheo]
[Lincoln]: [s.n.], [18??].   1 sheet.

3010. **D'ALBRIONE, Signor**
[Advertisement for lessons in French, Italian and Spanish, August 13th, 1833]
Lincoln: printed Brooke, 1833.   1 sheet.

3011. **SLATTERIE, Mr.**
[Notice of lectures on elocution]
Lincoln: printed T.J.N. Brogden, 1835.   1 sheet.

3012. **LEARY, William**
A Survey of adult education in the city of Lincoln
[19??].   44 leaves.
Typescript.
Includes bibliography.

3013. **VARLEY, Joan**
The Rev. William Mantle
[19??].   [6] leaves.
Typescript.
    Life and interest in night schools.

3014.
Lincoln Pupil-Teacher Centre: first annual report, year ended December 31st, 1899
Lincoln: printed Keyworth, [1900].   9, [3]p.
Also published: 1901, 18p.

3015. **WORKERS' EDUCATIONAL ASSOCIATION, Lincoln and District Branch**
Workers' Educational Association, Lincoln and District Branch: [annual report]
[Lincoln]: [The Branch], [191?–   ].   Various pagings.

3016. ─────────────
*38th annual report of the Workers' Educational Association, Lincoln and District
Branch...May, 1948-April, 1949*
[Lincoln]: [The Branch], [1949].

3017.
Adult Training Centre, Long Leys Road: official opening, Thursday, 22nd July, 1965...
Lincoln: Lincoln, Health Department, 1965.   [3] leaves, plans.

3018.   **WORKERS' EDUCATIONAL ASSOCIATION, Lincoln and District Branch**
Hear here: [student magazine, 1966/67–1968/69]
Typescript.
   1966/67 issue was 2nd.

3019.   **ALLAWAY, A. John**
Challenge and response: WEA East Midland District, 1919–1969
Nottingham: Workers Educational Association, 1969.   131p.
Includes index.
   Lincoln mentioned passim: Adult Education Centre; LEA; Peoples' Service Club; WEA
   Branch.

3020.   **LINCOLN TEACHERS CENTRE**
Lincoln Teachers Centre, spring '73
[Lincoln]: [The Centre], [1973].

3021.   **TOLLEY, B.H.**
The People's scientific university: science education in the East Midlands, 1860–1890
pp.116–131 in *Midlands history*, vol.VII, 1982.
   Various references to classes in Lincoln.

Bishop Grosseteste College

3022.   **BISHOP GROSSETESTE COLLEGE**
Bishop Grosseteste College of Education: [prospectus]
[Lincoln]: [The College], [c.1968/69].   20p.: ill.

3023.
A Short history of Bishop Grosseteste College, Lincoln
pp.44–46: ill. in *Lincolnshire life*, vol.10, no.10, December, 1970.

3024.   **BISHOP GROSSETESTE COLLEGE**
Bishop Grosseteste College, Lincoln: [prospectus]
[Lincoln]: [The College], [1976].   36p.: ill.

3025.   _____
Bishop Grosseteste College, Centre for Rural Studies: [prospectus]
[Lincoln]: [The College], [c.1976/77].   [4]p.

3026.   _____
Bishop Grosseteste College of Education, Lincoln: Diploma of Higher Education:
[prospectus]
[Lincoln]: [The College], [1976].   [5]p.: ill.

3027.   **RICHARDSON, Joy**
Bishop Grosseteste College
pp.26–30: ill. in *Lincolnshire life*, vol.22, no.7, October, 1982.

3028.   **CHAPPELL, Helen**
Lessons for tomorrow's teachers: Helen Chappell talks to a group of student teachers on
the threshold of their careers
pp.35, 37: ill. in *The Observer magazine*, 7th September, 1986.
   Features students from Bishop Grosseteste College.

Theological College

3029.
Memorial presented by the principal of Lincoln Training School, at the request of the diocesan inspectors and secretaries to a committee of the Diocesan Board appointed to consider the question of enlargement of the present accommodation in the institution
Lincoln: printed James Williamson, [1873].   16p.

3030.   **RAGG, Lonsdale**
Training schools of the English clergy.   IX: Scholae Cancellari Lincolniensis
pp.917–926: ill. in *The Treasury*, [19??].

3031.   **DIOCESAN ARCHITECTURAL SOCIETY**
Report
p.vii in *AAS reports and papers*, vol.29, 1907–08.
    Lincoln Scholae Cancellari Chapel.

3032.   **LINCOLN THEOLOGICAL COLLEGE**
Lincoln Theological College magazine
Vol.1, no.1, Trinity, 1920–vol.11, no.40, Michaelmas, 1930.
[Lincoln]: [The College], [1920–30].   11 vols.

3033.   ——————
Lincoln Diocesan Training College magazine
[Lincoln]: [The College], [1949, 1957].

3034.   **ZEBEDEE, D.J.H.**
Lincoln Diocesan Training College, 1862–1962
Lincoln: The College, [1962].   143p., 6 leaves of plates.

3035.   **LINCOLN THEOLOGICAL COLLEGE**
Lincoln Theological College: [prospectus]
[Lincoln]: [The College], [1965].   [4]p.: ill., map.
Also published: 1976, 14p.: ill.

3036.
A History of Lincoln Theological College, 1874–1974
Lincoln: printed Keyworth & Fry, 1974.   39p., 8p. of plates.

Art, Science and Technical Colleges

3037.
The Lincoln School of Art
pp.525–526: ill. in *The Illustrated London news*, no.1289, vol.XLV, Saturday, November 26, 1864.
    Includes engraving of the room in Silver Street housing the public exhibition of Lincoln School of Art.

3038.
Catalogue of pictures and works of art, exhibited at the School of Art, Lincoln
Lincoln: printed W. Doncaster, 1867.   23p.
    Encloses 2 newspaper articles on 'The Lincoln art treasures exhibition'.

3039.   **LINCOLN SCHOOL OF SCIENCE AND ART**
Conditions and particulars for competition
[Lincoln]: [The School], [188?].   2 sheets.

3040. —————
Science and Art School: syllabus of science, art and technical classes, Lincoln, session 1895–96
[Lincoln]: [The School], [1895]. 18p.

3041. **LINCOLN SCHOOL OF ART, Committee**
Lincoln School of Art: [list of subscribers]
[Lincoln]: [The Committee], [1884]. 2 sheets.

3042. —————
A Brief history of the Lincoln School of Art: [draft]
[19??]. [25] leaves.
Typescript; Ms.

3043. **LINCOLN SCHOOL OF ART**
Lincoln School of Art: prospectus, 1954–55
Lincoln: The School, 1954. 8p.
Also published: 1955–56.

3044. **LINCOLN CENTRAL SCIENCE CLASSES**
Programme of the Lincoln Central Science Classes, 1884–5
[Lincoln]: [The Classes], [1884]. [4]p.

3045. —————
Programme of the Lincoln Central Science Classes, 1885–1886
Lincoln: printed Akrill, Ruddock & Keyworth, 1885. [7]p.

3046. **LINCOLN SCHOOL OF SCIENCE**
Syllabus of the Lincoln School of Science, 1887–8
Lincoln: printed Henry E. Cousans, 1887. 20p.

3047. —————
Lincoln School of Science: [prospectus, 1889–90]
[Lincoln]: [The School], [1889]. [3]p.

3048. —————
Lincoln School of Science, Monks Road, Lincoln, session 1889–90: [prospectus]
[Lincoln]: [The School], [1889]. [3]p.

3049. —————
Lincoln School of Science: report of committee of conference of committees for science and technical work in Lincoln
[Lincoln]: [Lincoln School of Science], [1892]. 3 sheets.

3050. **LINCOLN SCHOOL OF CARPENTRY**
Lincoln School of Carpentry: report and balance sheet for 1893
[Lincoln]: [The School], [1893]. [4]p.: ill.

3051. **COLLIS, A.E.**
Proposed scheme for the Lincoln Organised Science School: memorandum
[Lincoln]: [s.n.], [1894?]. [3]p.

3052. **LINCOLN ORGANISED SCIENCE SCHOOL**
Lincoln Organised Science School: advanced course, Science and Art School, Monks' Road, session 1895–6: [prospectus]
[Lincoln]: [The School], [1895]. [4]p.

3053. **MUNICIPAL TECHNICAL SCHOOL**
Municipal Technical School: prospectus of classes for session 1909–10
Lincoln: printed Keyworth, [1909].   74p.: ill., 8 leaves of plates.

3054.
The Technical College, Lincoln: to be opened...13th July, 1932
[Lincoln]: [Lincoln Education Authority], [1932].   8p., [2] leaves of plates.

3055. **LINCOLN TECHNICAL COLLEGE**
Lincoln Technical College: Departments of Engineering and Building and Science:
[prospectus for session 1954–55]
Lincoln: The College, 1954.   40p.

3056. ───────────
Lincoln Technical College: Departments of Commerce and Domestic Science:
[prospectus for session 1954–55]
Lincoln: The College, 1954.   24p.

3057.
*Official opening of the new extension of the Lincoln Technical College...on Thursday, 1st
June, 1961, at 3pm.*: [programme]
Lincoln: printed Keyworth & Fry, 1961.   [7]p.

3058. **LINCOLN TECHNICAL COLLEGE**
*Lincoln Technical College: outline of courses of study issued in conjuction with
Commonwealth Technical Training Week, 29th May to 4th June, 1961*
Lincoln: The College, 1961.   8p.

3059. ───────────
Lincoln Technical College prospectus, 1963–64
[Lincoln]: [The College], [1963].   78p.: ill.

3060. **LINCOLN COLLEGE OF TECHNOLOGY**
Lincoln College of Technology, 1981–82: [prospectus]
[Lincoln]: [The College], [1981].   188p.

3061.
Lincoln College of Technology centenary, 1886–1986: [an LSG supplement]
Lincoln: LSG, 1986.   XIIp.

3062. **LINCOLN COLLEGE OF ART**
Lincoln College of Art: [information sheets]
[19??].   [18] leaves.
    Information on staff and courses.

Proposed University of Lincolnshire

3063.
Report of proceedings of a meeting called by the Right Worshipful mayor of Lincoln at
Lincoln School, on 11th October, 1963, to consider the establishment of a university at
Lincoln
[1963].   [27]p.
Typescript.

3064.
Minutes of the proceedings of the conference called by the Right Worshipful mayor of
Lincoln, on Saturday, the 18th January, 1964, at the Lincoln Technical College...at
11a.m., in connection with the establishment of the University of Lincolnshire
[1964]. [5]p.
Typescript.

3065.
Minutes of the first meeting of the steering committee, 28th November, 1964
[1964]. 3p.
Typescript.

3066. YAGER, R.S.
University of Lincolnshire
p.31 in *Lincolnshire life*, vol.4, no.1, February, 1964.

3067.
Proposed University of Lincolnshire: steering committee, 1st May, 1965: [minutes]
[1965]. 7p.
Typescript.

SUNDAY SCHOOLS

3068.
An Address to parents
Lincoln: printed Brooke, [1791]. 4p.
    About Sunday schools.

3069.
*Rules of the Sunday School, at Lincoln, established and principally conducted by the
Methodists*
Lincoln: printed by W. Brooke, 1812. 8p.

3070.
The Third report of the Skellingthorpe Sunday-School, 1826
Lincoln: printed W. Brooke, 1826. 4p.

3071. DIOCESE OF LINCOLN
*Examination of pupil teachers, monitors and Sunday school teachers in religious
knowledge, January 20th, 1900: class list*
Lincoln: James Williamson, [1900]. 11p.
    Some of those mentioned are from Lincoln parishes.

3072. LINCOLN SUNDAY SCHOOL UNION
*Souvenir programme of the diamond jubilee celebrations of the Lincoln Sunday School
Union, November 20th, 21st and 22nd, 1909, with a short history of the Lincoln Sunday
School Union*
Lincoln: printed Critch, [1909]. [16]p.: ill.

CRIME AND PUNISHMENT

3073.
[Notice recommending quiet behaviour following arguments between inhabitants and soldiers, July 22, 1794]
[Lincoln]: [Lincoln Corporation], [1794].   1 sheet.

3074.   LINCOLN, Watch Committee
Lincoln Corporation: report of the Watch Committee
Lincoln: [The Committee], 1836.   17p.

3075.
Damnable practices of three Lincoln-shire witches, Joane Flower, and her two daughters, Margret and Phillipa Flower...who for the same were executed at Lincolne, the 11 March last
[London]: printed by G. Eld for John Barnes, 1610.
Also published: pp.96–103 in *A Pepysian garland*, 1922.

3076.
The Bloody Papist, or A true relation of the horrid and barbarous murder committed by one Ro. Sherburn of Kyme in Lincolnshire, a notorious Papist, upon his wife, whom in an inhumane manner he murder'd in her bed, for which he is now a prisoner in Lincoln Gaol
London: printed George Larkin, 1683.   [2]p.

3077.   ECHARD, Laurence
The Hainousness of injustice done under the pretence of equity: in a sermon preach'd in the Cathedral Church of Lincoln, before the Honourable Baron Turton, at the Assizes holden for that county, on Monday, the eighth of August, 1698
London: printed for M. Wotton, 1698.   20p.
    Author Prebend of Lincoln Cathedral and Chaplain to the Bishop.

3078.
A True and genuine confession: with a short account of the life and behaviour of that wicked and barbarous murderer, John Keele...
[Lincoln]: [s.n.], [1731].   8p.: ill.
    Title-page verso: '...the text of an excellent sermon preached by the Rev. Mr. York, before the prisoners at the Castle Chapel in Lincoln, on Sunday, March 12, 1731.'   Trial was held at Lent Assizes in County Hall, Lincoln, and Keele was condemned to be gibbeted alive for the murder of his wife and child.

3079.
The Remarkable trial of Philip Hooton, auctioneer, late of the parish of Sutton St Edmunds, in the county of Lincoln, who was executed at Lincoln, on Monday, the 6th of March, 1769...for the cruel murder of Mr Samuel Stockton...
5th ed.
Lincoln: printed and sold by Drury, [1769].   40p.

3080.
The Authentic lives and trials of the four unfortunate men who this day [i.e. Friday, March 19, 1784] suffered death upon Lincoln gallows: Thomas Wood, Richard Downing and William Davison for house-breaking, and Richard Bull for sheep-stealing
Lincoln: printed and sold opposite the Bank, [1784].   1 sheet.

3081.
A Full and circumstantial narrative of the life and trial of John Wilson, who suffered death yesterday upon Lincoln gallows, for the bloody and cruel murder of William Mason of Deeping Fen, in the said county
Lincoln: printed and sold Drury, [1788].   24p.

3082.
The Trial of William Burder, for the murder of William Harrington at Spittlegate, near Grantham, on the 12th of January, 1791, before the Honourable Sir Nash Grose, at Lincoln, on Wednesday, 9th March following
Grantham: printed W. Allen, 1791.   24p.

3083.
The Lives, trials and behaviour at the place of execution of the two unfortunate men who suffered death this day upon Lincoln gallows: William Campwell for forgery, and John Betts for horse-stealing
Lincoln: printed by Drury, 1791.   1 sheet: ill.

3084.
The Life and trial of the unfortunate Spence Broughton, who suffered death at Tyburn, near York, on Saturday, the 14th day of April, 1792, for robbing the Rotherham mail...
3rd ed.
Lincoln: printed and sold by J.W. Drury, [1792].   20p.: ill.

3085.
God's revenge against murder, or Divine justice exemplified in the trial and condemnation of those wicked and cruel brothers, Thomas and Isaac Hallam for the bloody and inhuman murder of Mr Wright of Market Raisin, and Thomas Gardiner, the Lincoln postboy, in January 1732–3, for which wicked actions they were tried at the late Lent Assizes at Lincoln....
Lincoln: printed J.W. Drury, 1794.   24p.

3086.
A Dreadful and horrid murder committed by Jas. Raithby, a labourer, on the bodies of Mr Thomas Hall and his nephew, & Mary Grant, his housekeeper, at Threddlethorpe, in Lincolnshire, with a copy of verses
[S.l.]: printed Pitts, [18??].   1 sheet: ill.
    Committed to Castle at Lincoln.

3087.
[Notice of reward for information about burglary, October 22, 1805]
Lincoln: printed J.W. Drury, 1805.   1 sheet.

3088.
[Notice announcing reward for discovery of felons responsible for theft of hams and bacon from Saracen's-Head Inn Yard, August 5, 1805]
Lincoln: printed J.W. Drury, 1805.   1 sheet.

3089.   **TEMPERLY, Thomas**
The Last dying speech and confession of Thomas Temperly, who was executed at Lincoln, on the 12th of March, 1806, for the murder of Mary Kirkman
South Shields: printed J. Paxton, [1806].   1 sheet.
    He was also a native of Lincoln.

3090. ——————
The Last dying speech and confession of Thomas Temperley, who was executed at
Lincoln, on the 12th of March, 1806, for the murder of Mary Kirkman
Newcastle: printed M. Angus, [1806?]. 1 sheet.

3091. SOUTH CLIFF ASSOCIATION
Rules and orders of the South Cliff Association
Lincoln: printed J.W. Drury, 1808. [11] leaves, [4]p.
Cover title.
> 'Instituted in the year, 1808, for the prosecution of all persons who shall be guilty of felonies,
> thefts, crimes or misdemeanors, on or against the persons or property of the members'.

3092.
[Notice of reward in connection with burglary of house of Mr Hadnah Yates, draper and
taylor of city, November 3, 1812]
Lincoln: printed A. Wilkinson, 1812. 1 sheet.

3093. ASSOCIATION FOR THE PROSECUTION OF FELONS
Rules of the Association for the Prosecution of Felons, in the city of Lincoln and county
of the same city
Lincoln: printed W. Marrat, 1816. 12p.

3094.
The Execution and full account of the trial of Elizabeth Warriner, for the unnatural
murder of her son-in-law on the twenty-seventh of November last
Lincoln: printed Drury, [1817?]. 1 sheet.

3095.
An Account of Elizabeth Whiting, who was executed at Lincoln, Saturday, March 15,
1817, for the murder of her child
Lincoln: printed W. Brooke, [1817]. 1 sheet.

3096.
A Right, true and full account of the unfortunate malefactors executed this day, March
27, on Cobb's Tower, at Lincoln
Lincoln: printed Drury, [1818]. 1 sheet.

3097. ASSOCIATION FOR THE PROSECUTION OF FELONS
The Articles & resolutions of the new Lincoln Association for the Prosecution of Felons
within the city of Lincoln and county thereof
Lincoln: printed William Brooke, 1821. 16p.

3098.
The True history of Joseph Birkett, malefactor, aged 35, executed at Lincoln, on Friday,
the 2nd of August, 1822, for highway robbery
Lincoln: printed [Jane?] Drury, [1822]. 1 sheet.

3099.
Horrid murders!: the confession and dying declaration of John Jones, who was executed
at Lincoln, on the 24th of April, 1822, for the murder of his wife, six childen and two
servants
Bishopwearmouth: printed G. Garbutt, [1822]. 1 sheet.

3100.
*The Last dying words, speech and confession of Elizabeth Warriner, who was convicted
at the last Lincoln Assizes, for the horrid murder of her step-son, J. Warriner, by poison,
and who was executed at the city of Lincoln...8th day of April, 1822*
Edinburgh: reprinted for Wm. Baillie, [1822?]. 1 sheet.
    Date of execution is corrected in pencil to July 26, 1817.

3101.
*The Last and true dying account! of Wm. Arden, Jno. Doughty and Benj. Candler, who
were hanged at Lincoln gallows on Friday, March 21, 1823, for committing horrid crimes*
Lincoln: printed Drury, [1823]. 1 sheet: ill.

3102.
*Particulars of the remarkable trial and awful execution of Hannah Scott, who was
executed at Lincoln, on Monday last, for the horrid murder of her bastard child*
Gateshead: reprinted by Stephenson, [1824]. 1 sheet.

3103.
*An Account of the life, trial and execution of John Smith, who was executed at Lincoln on
Monday, April 5th, 1824, for the murder of Sarah Arrowsmith, who was pregnant with
child to him at that time*
Stockton: printed J. Appleton, [1824]. 1 sheet: ill.

3104.   ASSOCIATION FOR THE PROSECUTION OF FELONS
*Rules of the Association for the Prosecution of Felons in the city, Bail and Close of
Lincoln, and the villages within twelve miles thereof*
Revised.
Lincoln: printed Brooke, [1826]. 16p.

3105.
*Copy of verses: John Clarke, Timothy Brammer and Thomas Strong, who were executed
on Friday, the 19th of March, 1830*
Lincoln: printed R.E. Leary, 1830. 1 sheet.

3106.
*The Trial, confession & execution of Richard Cooling and Thomas Motley, for arson at
Lusby: executed at Lincoln, July 29, 1831*
Lincoln: printed Keyworth, [1831]. 1 sheet: ill.

3107.
*Particulars of the trial and execution of John Greenwood, who was executed at Lincoln,
on Friday, the 18th of March, 1831, for burglary at Theddlethorpe*
Lincoln: printed Keyworth, [1831]. 1 sheet: ill.

3108.
*Particulars of the trial and execution of Michael Lundy, who was executed on the drop at
Lincoln, on Saturday, March 12, 1831, for the wilful murder of Thomas Sewards, his
father in law*
Lincoln: printed T.O. Brumby, [1831]. 1 sheet: ill.

3109.
*Some account of the two stack burners of Lincolnshire, Richard Cooling and Thomas
Mottley, who were hanged at Lincoln, on Friday, the 29th July, 1831, for fire-raising at
Lusby*
Lincoln: printed E.B. Drury, [1831]. 1 sheet.

3110.
Trial and execution of William Hall, for the murder of Edward Button, at Grimsby: executed at Lincoln, July 22, 1831
Lincoln: printed Keyworth, 1831.   1 sheet: ill.

3111.
*Particulars of the trial and execution of Thomas Knapton, aged 17, late of Gainsbro',
mariner, who was executed on the new drop, at Lincoln, on Friday, the 26th day of July,
1833, for a rape committed on the body of Frances Elstone, aged 19, on Sunday, the 30th
of June last, on the high-road between Gainsbro' and Kirton*
Lincoln: printed T.O. Brumby, [1833].   1 sheet: ill.

3112.
*A Full, true and particular account of William Taylor, the unfortunate man who was
executed on the new drop at Lincoln, on Monday, the 18th March, 1833, for the wilful
murder of William Burbank, on the road from Sleaford to Boston...*
Lincoln: printed Leary, 1833.   1 sheet.

3113.
*A Correct account of all the executions that have taken place at Lincoln, from 1722 to the
present time*
Lincoln: printed for W. Peck, [1833?].   1 sheet.

3114.   **ASSOCIATION FOR THE PROSECUTION OF FELONS**
Lincoln new Association for the Prosecution of Felons: [announcement of annual dinner
and list of subscribers, March 24th, 1834]
Lincoln: printed J.W. Drury, 1834.   1 sheet.

3115.
*An Account of all the executions that have taken place at Lincoln, from the year 1722 up
to the present time, 1835*
Lincoln: printed Keyworth, [1835].   [4]p.

3116.
*An Account of the dreadful murders of Wm. Marshall and D.E. Hutchinson, at Kirton in
Lindsey, on Monday, December 12th, 1836, to which is added the trial of Dimpsey, the
supposed murderer, at Lincoln March Assizes, 1837*
Lincoln: printed Thorpe, [1837].   16p.

3117.
*A Sorrowful lamentation over those two unfortunate men, David Booth, aged 32, and
John Parish, aged 48, now under sentence of death, in Lincoln Castle*: [verse]
Lincoln: printed W. Brooke, [184?].   1 sheet: ill.

3118.
*Prospectus of a proposed association called the Lincoln Mutual Assurance and
Protection Society from felonious and malicious injuries to persons and property*
Lincoln: James Drury, 1842.   2p.

3119.
[Notice about meeting to promote the abolition of the punishment of death, April 23rd,
1847]
Lincoln: printed R. Bulman, 1847.   1 sheet.

3120.
An Account of the trial, conviction and condemnation of M. Ann Milner, at Lincoln Assizes, July 20th, 1847, for the murder of Hannah Jickells at Barnetby-le-Wold
Lincoln: printed R.E. Leary, 1847.   1 sheet.

3121.
The Trial and confession of Joseph Travis for the murder of Mr Copeman, at Kirton, December 19th, 1847
Lincoln: printed R.E. Leary, 1847.   1 sheet.

3122.
Burglary: £5 reward: [notice, March 27th, 1851]
Lincoln: printed T.J.N. Brogden, 1851.   1 sheet.

3123.
An Account of the life, trial, condemnation and execution of Henry Carey & Wm. Picket who were executed at Lincoln, on Friday, August 5th, 1859, for the murder of William Stevenson, at Sibsey, on the 17th March last
Lincoln: printed R.E. Leary, 1859.   1 sheet: ill.

3124.
A Narrative of the bloudy murders committed by Sir John Fites, alias Fitz, 1605...to which is added the revelation of two horrible murders done in Lincolnshire, made known in 1604
edited by J.O. Halliwell.
London: printed for private circulation by J.E. Halliwell, 1860.   viii, 55p.
    Concerns Thomas Cash and John Dillworth, who were both executed at Lincoln.

3125.   **HUGGINS, Geoffrey**
Witchcraft and the Christian Church
[1970].   32 leaves.
Typescript.
        pp.19–20: Flower sisters, who were executed at Lincoln, in 1618.

3126.   **HUGGETT, Renee**
Daughters of Cain: the story of nine women executed since Edith Thompson, in 1923
Renee Huggett and Paul Berry.
Bath: Cedric Chivers, 1971.
Originally published: 195?.
        pp.75–116: Ethel Lillie Major.

3127.   **WILSON, Patrick**
Murderess: a study of the women executed in Britain since 1843
London: Michael Joseph, 1971.   318p.
ISBN 0718108590
        Includes: Eliza Joyce; Catherine Wilson; Priscilla Biggadike; Mary Leffey; and Ethel Lillie Major; all of whom were executed at Lincoln.

3128.   **HARRISON, Cyril**
Some Lincolnshire highway men
p.27 in *Lincolnshire life*, vol.18, no.3, June, 1978.
        Mentions Lincoln Assizes and Lincoln Castle.

LAW COURTS

3129.   **DYER, James**
An Exact abridgment in English of all the reports of that learned and reverend judge, Sir
James Dyer, Knight, and sometime Lord Chief Justice of the Common Pleas
composed by Sir Thomas Ireland.
London: printed for Matthew Walbancke and John Place, 1651.   295, [56]p.

3130.
A Calendar of the felon prisoners, confined in His Majesty's gaol, the Castle of Lincoln,
in and for the county of Lincoln, at the Assizes holden on Saturday, the 6th day of March,
1784...
[Lincoln]: [s.n.], [1784].   1 sheet.

3131.
[Resolutions of general quarter sessions of the peace...14th day of July, 1798]
[Lincoln]: [s.n.], [1798].   1 sheet.

3132.
A Calendar of the felon prisoners, in His Majesty's gaol, the Castle of Lincoln, in and for
the county of Lincoln, at the Assizes to be holden on Saturday, the 31st of July, 1802
Lincoln: printed Smith, 1802.   1 sheet.

3133.
A Calendar of the prisoners, confined in His Majesty's gaol, the Castle of Lincoln, in and
for the county of Lincoln, at the Assizes holden on Saturday, the 9th of March, 1805, and
the following five days
Lincoln: printed J.W. Drury, 1805.   1 sheet.

3134.
A Calendar of the prisoners, confined in His Majesty's gaol, the Castle of Lincoln, in and
for the county of Lincoln, at the Assizes holden on Saturday, the 27th of July, 1805, and
the following days
Lincoln: printed J.W. Drury, 1805.   1 sheet.

3135.
*Coroner's precept to summon a jury, 180_*
[Lincoln]: [printed J.W. Drury], [1805].   1 sheet.

3136.
The Crown calendar for the Lincolnshire Lent Assizes, holden at the Castle of Lincoln,
on Saturday, the 8th day of March, 1823
Lincoln: printed J.W. Drury, 1823.   1 sheet.

3137.
The Crown calendar for the Lincolnshire Summer Assizes
Lincoln: printed J.W. Drury, 1827.   1 sheet.

3138.
Sentences of the prisoners tried at the Lincolnshire Lent Assizes, holden at the Castle of
Lincoln, on Saturday, 14th March, 1829
Lincoln: printed J.W. Drury, 1829.   1 sheet.

3139.
Sentences of the prisoners for the Lincolnshire Summer Assizes
Lincoln: printed Keyworth, 1829.   1 sheet.

3140.
*The Crown calendar for the Lincolnshire Lent Assizes, holden at the Castle of Lincoln,
on Saturday, the fifth of March, 1831...*
Lincoln: printed Keyworth, 1831.   1 sheet.

3141.
*Sentences of the prisoners for the Lincolnshire Lent Assizes, holden at the Castle of
Lincoln, on Saturday, the fifth day of March, 1831...*
Lincoln: printed Keyworth, 1831.   1 sheet.

3142.
*The Crown calendar for the Lincolnshire Summer Assizes, to be holden at the Castle of
Lincoln, in and for the county of Lincoln, on Saturday, the sixteenth day of July, 1831...*
Lincoln: printed Keyworth, 1831.   1 sheet.

3143.
City of Lincoln and county of the same city: the crown calendar for the Lent Assizes, 1832
[Lincoln]: [s.n.], [1832].   1 sheet.

3144.
The Liberty of the Bail of Lincoln, parcel of the Duchy of Lancaster: [request to let Leet
Jury enter any premises, November 7, 1836]
Lincoln: printed T.J.N. Brogden, 1836.   1 sheet.

3145.
A Sheet of the trials at Lincoln Summer Assizes, 1838: [account of proceedings]
Lincoln: printed James Drury, 1838.   1 sheet.

3146.
*Sentences of the prisoners at the Lincolnshire Lent Assizes, holden at the Castle of
Lincoln, on Saturday, the 9th day of March, 1838*
Lincoln: printed Keyworth, 1838.   1 sheet.

3147.
Circuits of the judges: Lincoln and Oxford Assizes
pp.164–166: ill. in *The Illustrated London news*, March 15, 1845.
    Route and description of processions.

3148.
*Sentences for the Lincolnshire Lent Assizes, holden at the Castle of Lincoln, in and for
the county of Lincoln, on Saturday, the 6th day of March, 1847*
Lincoln: printed R.E. Leary, 1847.   1 sheet.

3149.
*The Crown sentences for the Lincolnshire Lent Assizes, holden at the Castle of Lincoln,
in and for the county of Lincoln, on Saturday, the ninth day of March, 1850*
Lincoln: printed R.E. Leary, 1850.   1 sheet.

3150.
*The Crown sentences for the Lincolnshire Lent Assizes, holden at the Castle of Lincoln,
in and for the county of Lincoln, on Wednesday, the 5th day of March, 1851*
Lincoln: printed R.E. Leary, 1851.   1 sheet.

3151.
A Calendar of prisoners for trial at the general quarter sessions of the peace, to be holden at the Sessions House in the city of Lincoln...April, 1854–April, 1877
[S.l.]: [s.n.], [1854–77]. 75 sheets.
> Gives: name of prisoner; age; occupation; name of committing magistrate; date of warrant; date when taken into custody; nature of offence; name of official before whom tried, with jury's verdict and sentence added in Ms.

3152.
Lincoln City Summer Assizes, Thursday, July 22nd, 1858...Green v. Greetham
Lincoln: W. Doncaster, 1858. 28p.
> Libel case.

3153.
Crown sentences for the Lincolnshire Summer Assizes, holden at Lincoln, on Saturday, the 23rd of July, 1859
Lincoln: printed R.E. Leary, 1859. 1 sheet.

3154. **WALTON, Robert**
Random recollections of the Midland Circuit
London: printed for the author, 1869. xi, 227p.
> pp.28–35: Lincoln.

3155. ─────────────
Random recollections of the Midland Circuit
London: The Author, 1873. x, 180p.
> pp.69–102: Lincoln anecdote.

3156.
[A Series of records, in English, illustrative of the history of Lincolnshire anterior to A.D. 1400. Vol.1]
[translated and edited by William Boyd].
[Horncastle]: [W.K. Morton], [1880s?]. 96p.
Published in limited edition of 250 copies. Lacks title-page.
> Roll of the Pleas and Assizes taken at Lincoln, 1218–19.

3157.
The Earliest Lincolnshire Assize rolls, A.D. 1202–1209
edited by Doris M. Stenton.
Lincoln: Lincoln Record Society, 1926. lxxxii, 357p.
(Lincoln Record Society, 22)
Includes index.

3158.
Records of some sessions of the peace in Lincolnshire, 1360–1375
edited by Rosamond Sillem.
Lincoln: Lincoln Record Society, 1936. xcii, 325p.
(Lincoln Record Society, 30)
Includes index.

3159.
Rolls of the Justices in Eyre, being the rolls of Pleas and Assizes for Yorkshire in 3 Henry III, 1218–19
edited by Doris Mary Stenton.
London: Quaritch, 1937. lvi, 577p.
(Publications of the Selden Society, vol.56)
Includes index.
> Includes a number of references to Lincoln.

3160.
A Lincolnshire Assize roll for 1298: (P.R.O. Assize roll, no.505)
edited by Walter Sinclair Thomson.
Lincoln: Lincoln Record Society, 1944. cxxvii, 305p.
(Lincoln Record Society, 36)
Includes index.

3161.   **WARD, Arthur**
Stuff and silk
Ramsey: Gansey, 1950?. 229p.: ill.
> pp.126–156: Lincoln is included in his reminiscences of the Midland Circuit.

3162.
Records of some sessions of the peace in Lincolnshire, 1381–1396.   Vol.I: The parts of Kesteven and the parts of Holland
edited by Elisabeth Kimball.
Lincoln: Lincoln Record Society, 1955. lxvi, 110p.
(Lincoln Record Society, 49)

3163.
Select cases in the Court of King's Bench under Edward II
edited by G.O. Sayles.
London: Quaritch, 1957. 193p.
(Publications of the Selden Society, vol.74)
Includes index of names and places.   Parallel Latin text with English translation.
> Lincoln mentioned passim.

3164.
Records of some sessions of the peace in Lincolnshire, 1381–1396.   Vol.II: The parts of Lindsey
edited by Elisabeth Kimball.
Lincoln: Lincoln Record Society, 1962. xi, 331p.
(Lincoln Record Society, 56)
Includes index.
> Many references to city.

3165.
Records of some sessions of the peace in the city of Lincoln, 1351–1354, and the borough of Stamford, 1351
edited by Elisabeth G. Kimball.
Lincoln: Lincoln Record Society, 1971. xxx, 67p., [frontis].
(Lincoln Record Society, 65)
Includes index.

3166.   **NIELD, Basil**
Farewell to the Assizes: the sixty-one towns
London: Garnstone, 1972. ix, 279p.: ill.
> pp.76–80: Lincoln.

POLICE

3167.
Night watch [and] day police, Saturday, Sept. 13th, 1834–Mon., 1st June, 1935: [rota]
[Lincoln]: [Brumby], 1834.   c.240p.
Printed list with Ms. additions.

3168.   LINCOLN, Chief Constable
To the chairman & members of the Watch Committee: annual report with respect to
crime in the city]
[19??].   14 leaves.
Typescript.

3169.   ——————
Ninth annual report, 1910.
1910.   14 leaves.
Typescript.

3170.   ——————
Annual report of the Chief Constable, 1966
1966.   31, [8]p.: ill.
Typescript.

PRISONS

3171.   GARMSTON, John
*A Sermon preach'd at the Guild-hall in the city of Lincoln, June the 19th, 1715, to the
prisoners confin'd for debt in the city-prison*
London: printed for John Knight, 1715.   23p.
   Author was master of the Free School in Lincoln.

3172.
The Case of Edward Cooper, a prisoner in Lincoln Castle
Lincoln: printed W. Brooke, 1792.   16p.

3173.
*Escape: escaped from Lincoln Castle in the night of Friday, the 13th of September...the
two following prisoners: James Skelton...James Nicholls*
[Lincoln]: [printed J.W. Drury], 1805.   1 sheet.

3174.   NIELD, James
[Letter to Dr. Lettsom regarding conditions in Lincoln Castle prison]
pp.196–199 in *The Gentleman's magazine*, March, 1805.

3175.   ——————
Lincoln Castle gaol and Lincoln City and County Gaol
p.328 in *Account of prisons for debtors in England, Scotland & Wales*, [after 1805?].

3176.
*The Report of the commissioners appointed to enquire into the condition and treatment of
prisoners confined to Lincoln Castle: and the conduct and management of the said prison*
[London]: [Luke Hansard], [1812].   193p., 2 folded plans.

3177.   **LINCOLN COUNTY GAOL**
Lincoln County Gaol: [rules and orders]
Lincoln: printed J.W. Drury, 1812.   8p.

3178.
Lincoln Castle, 14th August, 1812: [notice of meeting of commission to enquire into prison conditions]
Lincoln: printed J. Smith, 1812.   1 sheet.

3179.   **LINCOLN COUNTY GAOL**
Rules for the government of the County Gaol and Castle of Lincoln
Lincoln: printed J.W. Drury, 1826.   14p.

3180.   ─────────────
Rules for the government of the County Gaol and Castle of Lincoln: made and established in a court of gaol sessions, held at Lincoln, on the 5th day of January, 1827...
London: printed Luke Hansard, 1827.   56p., 4 plans.
Includes index.
   Plans by William Webb.

3181.
[2 Will.IV.   Sess.1831]: *An Act to enable the Justices of the Peace for the three divisions of the county of Lincoln to purchase the site of Lincoln Castle: and to empower the court of gaol sessions.... to maintain and support the Judges' House, County Hall and Courts of Assize...*
[London]: [printed Jones & Walmisley], [1831].   33p.

3182.   **SMIRKE, Robert**
Reports...on the state of Lincoln Castle, ordered by the court of gaol sessions to be printed, 1st January, 1835
Robert Smirke and Edward James Willson.
Lincoln: printed T.J.N. Brogden, 1835.   13p., plan.
   Includes lithograph plan of the Castle and adjoining premises.

3183.   **LINCOLN CITY GAOL**
City of Lincoln Gaol rules
Lincoln: printed W. and B. Brooke, [1837].   16p.

3184.   **LINCOLN COUNTY GAOL**
Rules and regulations for the government of the County Gaol and Castle of Lincoln, adopted and established at a court of gaol sessions, held on the fifth day of October, 1843...
Lincoln: printed W. and B. Brooke, 1844.   56, [7]p.
Includes index.

3185.
Specification of works to be done in re-building the County Gaol, Lincoln
Nicholson and Goddard, architects.
Lincoln: printed W. and B. Brooke, 1845.   Various pagings.
   Includes specifications for work of: plasterer; digger; bricklayer; smith and ironfounder; carpenter and joiner; stone mason; slater; plumber; and glazier.

3186.   **BURTON, Frederick**
[Letter about fever in the Gaol, 8th September, 1849]
[Lincoln]: [s.n.], [1849].   1 sheet.

3187.
Statutory and supplementary regulations for the government of the City Gaol
Lincoln: printed Chas. Akrill, 1866.   83p.
Includes index.

3188.   **BAMFORD, Samuel**
Bamford's passages in the life of a radical and early days
edited by Henry Dunckeley.
London: T. Fisher Unwin, 1893.   2 vols.
    pp.308–338: Lincoln prison.

3189.   **PECKOVER, Emily**
The Old prison in Lincoln Castle
p.264: ill. in *Architectural review*, September–October, 1955.

3190.   **JOHNSON, Barbara**
Lincoln Castle prison, 1786–1878
[1960s/1970s?].   6p.
Typescript.

3191.   **BROCKWAY, Fenner**
An 'Old boy' goes back
pp.19, 21: ill. in *Daily telegraph weekend*: [colour supplement], no.90, June 17, 1966.
    Conscientious objector imprisoned in Lincoln Gaol during the First World War.

3192.   **CHAMBERS, M.W.**
Ten shillings or seven days
[Nottingham]: [The Author], [1941].   8p.
    Account of week spent in Lincoln Gaol for having driving licence overdue.

3193.   **HOWARD, John**
The State of the prisons
Bicentennial ed.
Abingdon: Professional Books, 1977.   vii, 489, [22]p.
Originally published: 1777.   Includes index.
ISBN 0903486415
    pp.295–300: County Gaol, Lincoln Castle; pp.303–305: Lincoln City Gaol.

3194.   **WRIGHT, John**
John Howard's visits to Lincolnshire
pp.32–33: ill. in *Lincolnshire life*, vol.16, no.12, February, 1977.
    Concerns the philanthropist's visits to the Castle County Gaol and the Stonebow City Gaol.

3195.   **COWLIN, Dorothy**
A Prisoner's castle is his home
pp.26–27 in *Lincolnshire life*, vol.18, no.3, June, 1978.
    Based on Samuel Bamford's account of his imprisonment.

3196.   **DEPARTMENT OF EDUCATION AND SCIENCE**
Report by H.M. inspectors on Education Department, H.M. Prison, Lincoln
Stanmore: DES, 1984.   20p.

PUBLIC HEALTH

3197.   LINCOLN BOARD OF HEALTH
[Report, November 19, 1831]
Lincoln: printed W. Brooke, 1831.   1 sheet.

3198.   ⸺
[Report]
Lincoln: printed E.B. Drury, [1831?].   1 sheet.

3199.
[Notice of day of thanksgiving and prayer for immunity from cholera, September 17, 1849]
Lincoln: printed W. Bellatti, 1849.   1 sheet.

3200.   LINCOLN, Local Government Board
A Summary of receipts and disbursements on account of the Public Health Act, 1848, and the Local Government Act, 1858, from the 1st September, 1871, to the 31st August, 1872
H.K. Hebb, clerk to the Board, Thurstan G. Dale, treasurer.
Lincoln: C. Keyworth, 1872.   14p.

3201.   LINCOLN INSTITUTION FOR NURSES
Memorial to the late Mrs Bromhead
[Lincoln]: [s.n.], [1886].   [3]p.

3202.   ⸺
Regulations for nurses
[Lincoln]: [The Institution], 189?.   2 sheets.

3203.
Catalogue and general programme of health exhibition held at Lincoln, August 3rd to 19th, 1899, in connection with the Provincial Conference of the Sanitary Inspectors Association
Lincoln: Exhibition Committee, [1899].   129p., plan.

3204.
Lincoln health exhibition, August 3rd to 19th, 1899: [lectures]
Lincoln: Exhibition Committee, 1899.   [46]p.

3205.   LINCOLN, Urban Sanitary Authority
Regulations made by the mayor, aldermen & citizens of the city of Lincoln, acting by the council as the Urban Sanitary Authority, with respect to dairies, cowsheds and milkshops in the city of Lincoln
Lincoln: Lincoln Corporation, 1900.   12p.

3206.   REECE, D.J.
Dr. D.J. Reece's report to the Local Government Board on the epidemic of enteric fever in the city of Lincoln, 1904–5
London: HMSO, 1906.   57p.: ill., map.
(Reports of medical inspectors of the Local Government Board, no.226)

3207.
[Album of photographs: First World War]
[1914–18]. 29p.
> Photographs taken when Lincoln Christ's Hospital School, Wragby Rd., was used as military hospital, the Fourth Northern General Hospital.

3208.
[Scrapbook, covering period 1914–1918]
[1914–18]. 59p.
> Items about the Fourth Northern General Hospital: newspaper articles; tickets; letters. All well-documented.

3209.   **MINISTRY OF HEALTH**
[10 & 11 Geo.5. Ministry of Health provisional order confirmation, Lincoln extension, Act, 1920, ch.CCVII]: *An Act to confirm a provisional order of the Minster of Health relating to Lincoln*
London: HMSO, 1920. 26p.

3210.   ─────────────
[10 & 11 Geo.5. Ministry of Health provisional order, Lincoln extension]: *A Bill intituled an Act to confirm a provisional order...*
London: HMSO, 1920. 27p.

3211.   **LINCOLN, Medical Officer of Health**
Report by the medical officer of health on the administration of the Health Services
[193?].   61 leaves.
Typescript.
> Includes printed 51x38cm tree diagram, showing the suggested scheme of the whole of the medical services under the Council.

3212.   **LINCOLN CORPORATION**
Report by the town clerk to the Highways Committee upon the Public Health Act, 1936
[1936?].   29 leaves.
Typescript.

3213.   ─────────────
Report by the town clerk to the Maternity and Child Welfare Committee upon the Public Health Act, 1936
[1936].   5 leaves.
Typescript.

3214.   ─────────────
Report by the town clerk to the Health and Hospital Committee upon the Public Health Act, 1936
[1936?].   30 leaves.
Typescript.

3215.   **BERY, M.L.**
Thirty-ninth annual report on medical inspection of school children: [year ended 31st December, 1946]
Lincoln: Lincoln, Education Committee, [1947].   11p.

3216.	NATIONAL HEALTH SERVICE, Executive Council of the City of Lincoln
Dental, medical, maternity and pharmaceutical services: lists of dentists, doctors, chemists, etc...
[1948].	[12] leaves.
Typescript.
> Includes supplement for opthalmic services: lists of opthalmic medical practitioners, opthalmic opticians and dispensing opticians, [4] leaves.

3217.	LINCOLN, City Health Department
Lincoln clean air: information handbook
London: Pyramid, [c.1962].	16p.: ill.

3218.	─────────────
[Clean Air Act, 1956]: Lincoln no.1 smoke control area
1962.	[2] sheets: plan.
Typescript.

3219.
Pocket phones lighten G.P.'s burden
pp.4–5: ill. in *Pulse*, July 19, 1969.
> Scheme in Lincoln to help general practitioners.

3220.	BROMHEAD NURSING HOME
Progress report, 1982
[Lincoln]: [The Home], [1982].
> Private health care.

LINCOLN TYPHOID EPIDEMIC

3221.
The Lincoln typhoid epidemic, 1904–5: teacher's notes
[19??].	14 leaves.
> Photocopies of photographs, newspaper articles, etc.

3222.
Lincoln typhoid epidemic: [folder of miscellaneous material relating to the 1904–5 outbreak]
[19??].	1 portfolio.
> Photocopies of newspaper articles, etc.

3223.	HALLGARTH, W.E.R.
The Lincoln typhoid epidemic
pp.34–35: ill. in *Lincolnshire life*, vol.19, no.1, April, 1979.

3224.	BRISCOE, Keith
Typhoid in Lincoln, 1904–1905
prepared by Keith Briscoe, J.S. English, Elizabeth A. Melrose.
Lincoln: Bishop Grosseteste College and Lincolnshire Library Service, [1981].	76p.: ill., maps + 24 slides + 1 audio cassette.

3225.	MORTON, G.F.
Lincoln typhoid outbreak, 1905
pp.24–25: ill. in *Lincolnshire life*, vol.25, no.1, April, 1985.

3226.   **BRAY, Christopher**
The Enemy in our midst: the story of Lincoln's typhoid epidemic, 1905
by Christopher Bray, Kirsty Grantham and Ann Wright.
Lincoln: K.M. Associates, 1987.   38p.: ill., 1 folded map.
ISBN 0951268007

SANITATION

3227.
City of Lincoln: the sanitary question: [signed 'In medio tutissimus ibis', May 22nd,
1850]
Lincoln: printed T.J.N. Brogden, 1850.   1 sheet.

3228.   **LINCOLN, Urban Sanitary Authority**
*Byelaws...with respect to the cleansing of footways and pavements and cleansing of
privies, ashpits and cesspools*
Lincoln: Lincoln Corporation, 1877.   18p.

3229.   ——————
*City of Lincoln: byelaws made by the mayor, aldermen and citizens of the city of Lincoln,
acting by the council, as the Urban Sanitary Authority, with respect to nuisances*
Lincoln: Lincoln Corporation, 1877.   10p.

3230.   ——————
*City of Lincoln: sewerage: house connections: regulations as to house drains and the
mode of connecting drains of private property with the public sewers*
Lincoln: Lincoln Corporation, 1881.   14p.

3231.   ——————
[Public Health Act, 1875]: *Urban Sanitary Authority meetings, Jan. 6, 1891 to Nov. 6,
1894*
Lincoln: Lincoln Corporation, 1891–94.   Various pagings.
Spine title: *City of Lincoln epitomes.*
> Includes proceedings of: Lighting, Building and Improvements Committee; Highways and
> Paving Committee; Waterworks Committee; Sanitary Committee.

3232.   **LINCOLN, Water Supply Committee**
*City of Lincoln: Public Health Act, 1875: report...to consider...the different sources of
supply of water for the city: and as to whether any other and better sources of supply can
be obtained*
Lincoln: printed Keyworth, 1892.   12p.
> Considerations of a special committee appointed by the council, based upon report by Mr de
> Rance.   Appendix includes letters from Mr de Rance answering queries.

3233.   **SANITARY INSPECTORS ASSOCIATION**
Visit to the city of Lincoln: annual provincial conference: [proceedings]
in *The Sanitary inspectors journal: a monthly journal of public health*, new series, vol.5,
nos.3–4, August–September, 1899.
> Covers: official reception; Corporation luncheon; the Health Exhibition; paper by Mr Hebb,
> '1866 to 1899: thirty-three years' work in Lincoln, under the Public Health Acts'; annual
> provincial dinner; visit to the sewage works.   Mr Hebb was former clerk to the Urban Sanitary
> Committee.

MEDICAL OFFICERS' REPORTS

3234.   **HARRISON, Charles**
Annual report of Dr. C. Harrison, for the year ending 31st December, 1876
[Lincoln]: [s.n.], [1877].   11p.

3235.   ―――――――――
Report of C. Harrison, Esq., M.D., medical officer of health and public analyst for the city of Lincoln, respecting the water supply of the city
Lincoln: printed Charles Keyworth, 1885.   [6]p.: ill., [4] maps.

3236.   **BERY, M.L.**
Annual report on medical inspection of school children: [1933–1950]
Lincoln: Lincoln, Education Committee, 1933–50.   Various pagings.
   Comprises 26th–43rd annual reports.

314

HOSPITALS

LINCOLN COUNTY HOSPITAL

3237.
Statutes and constitutions for the government of an infirmary or hospital, to be established at Lincoln, for the sick and lame poor in that county and city
Lincoln: printed for the benefit of the hospital, 1745.   54p.

3238.   **LINCOLN COUNTY HOSPITAL**
Rules and orders of the County Hospital at Lincoln for the relief of the sick and lame poor
Lincoln: printed by S. Simmons, 1782.   27p.

3239.   ───────
State of Lincoln County Hospital, from June 24th, 1791 to June 24th, 1792
Lincoln: printed W. Brooke, 1792.   4p.
(No.XXIII)
>   Contains engraving of building.

3240.
[List of people with right to recommend patients to the Lincoln County Hospital]
Lincoln: printed W. and B. Brooke, [18??].   1 sheet.

3241.   **LINCOLN COUNTY HOSPITAL**
Rules of the County Hospital at Lincoln
Revised and corrected.
Lincoln: printed William Brooke, 1819.   25p.

3242.   ───────
Rules of the County Hospital at Lincoln, as revised and corrected in the year 1819
Lincoln: printed William Brooke, 1819.   25p.

3243.   ───────
State of the Lincoln County Hospital, from June 24, 1819 to June 24, 1820, inclusive:
[51st annual report]
Lincoln: printed W. Brooke, [1820].   8p.

3244.
Prayers for the use of Lincoln County Hospital
Lincoln: printed by William Brooke, 1824.   18p.

3245.   **NICHOLSON, John**
State of the Lincoln County Hospital
Lincoln: Samuel J. Burch, [1845].   [3]p.
>   Letter originally published: in *Stamford mercury*, republished by Samuel J. Burch for the
>   attention of the governors.

3246. LINCOLN COUNTY HOSPITAL
State of the Lincoln County Hospital, from December 25th, 1845 to December 25th, 1846, inclusive: [77th annual report]
Lincoln: printed W. and B. Brooke, [1846]. 32p.

3247. ——————————
State of the County Hospital at Lincoln, 1848: seventy-ninth annual report
Lincoln: W. and B. Brooke, printers, 1848.
    Lists annual subscribers, benefactors and legacies with accounts and statistics.

3248. ——————————
State of the County Hospital at Lincoln, 1849; eightieth annual report
Lincoln: W. and B. Brooke, printers, 1849.

3249.
Lincoln County Hospital: [letter about meeting, 8th February, 1850]
[S.l.]: [s.n.], 1850. 1 sheet.

3250.
Lincoln County Hospital: [letter from G. Waldo Sibthorp about meeting to discuss dismissal/ reinstatement of matron, February, 1850]
[Lincoln]: [s.n.], [1850]. 1 sheet.

3251. LINCOLN COUNTY HOSPITAL
State of the Lincoln County Hospital, from December 31st, 1870 to December 31st, 1871: the one hundred & second report
Lincoln: printed C. Keyworth, [1871]. 60p.

3252.
Order of service for the laying of the first stone of the new Lincoln County Hospital, on July 27, 1876
Lincoln: James Williamson, 1876. 8p.

3253. SYMPSON, Thomas
A Short account of the old and of the new Lincoln County Hospitals
Lincoln: printed James Williamson, 1878. 63p., plans, 2 leaves of plates.
    'a description of the old Lincoln County Hospital...especially of the various causes productive of insalubrity in its wards...and of the attempt to remove the causes of its unwholesomeness'.

3254.
Lincoln new County Hospital
pp.747–748: ill. in *The Builder*, July 5, 1879.
    Description of building with ground plan.

3255. WATKINS & SCORER
[Letter refuting anonymous charges about excessive cost of building the new Dispensary]
[Lincoln]: [Watkins & Scorer], [1881]. 7p.
    Accompanies: table of architect's charges, 1 sheet.

3256.
Order of proceedings at the laying of the foundation-stone of the new building at the Lincoln County Hospital, by Joseph Ruston, Esq....donor of the new building, on Saturday, June 20, 1891...
Lincoln: printed Akrill, Ruddock & Keyworth, 1891. [3]p.

3257.
Lincoln County Hospital: order of proceedings on the occasion of the opening of the Children's Ward and the new buildings given by Joseph Ruston, Esq., Tuesday, June 7th, 1892, at 2.30pm
Lincoln: printed Akrill, Ruddock & Keyworth, [1892].   7p.

3258.   **WATKINS, W., & SON**
Lincoln County Hospital: the architects and Mr Charles Brook: [correspondence]
[Lincoln]: [W. Watkins], [1903].   4 sheets.
Originally published: in *Lincoln leader*, 1903.
      Demand for withdrawal of remarks made at quarterly meeting of the Hospital governors.

3259.
Lincolnshire Yeomanry Memorial: unveiling ceremony, Friday, April 7th, 1922
[Lincoln]: [s.n.], [1922].   [16]p.: ill.
      New X-ray Department and Pathological Laboratory as memorial to the Lincolnshire Yeomanry.

3260.   **MOORE, Arthur**
The History and development of the County Hospital system
pp.268–271: ill. in *The Lincolnshire magazine*, vol.2, 1934–36.

3261.   **LINCOLN COUNTY HOSPITAL**
Nursing at Lincoln County Hospital
Lincoln: The Hospital, [1940s?].   22p.: ill.

3262.
Lincoln County Hospital, Hospital Library: order of proceedings of the official opening, 21 November, 1963 at 3pm
[Lincoln]: [Lincoln No.1 Hospital Management Committee and Lincoln City Libraries], [1964].   [4]p.

3263.   **BOORER, David**
Libraries for nurses.   2: Lincoln County Hospital
pp.505–507: ill. in *Nursing times*, vol.62, no.15, 15 April, 1966.

3264.   **BURGESS, David G.**
Lincoln Medical Library
pp.289–293 in *Postgraduate medical journal*, vol.42, May, 1966.

3265.
Opening by Her Royal Highness the Princess Margaret...of the Maternity Wing of the Lincoln County Hospital, Wednesday, 4th December, 1968
[Lincoln]: Sheffield Regional Hospital Board, Lincoln No.1 Hospital Management Committee, 1968.   [8]p., [frontis].

3266.   **MARTINEAU, H.D.**
Hospital hospitality
pp.30–33: ill. in *Lincolnshire life*, vol.15, no.3, May, 1975.
      Recounts stay in the Eye Ward of Lincoln County Hospital.

3267.   **BROOK, Florence Foster**
Nursing in many fields
London: Johnson, 1977.   126p.
      pp.68–92: describes her recollections of working at Lincoln County Hospital in 1929; not very favourable, but based upon personalities rather than locality.

3268.   TRENT REGIONAL HEALTH AUTHORITY
The Way ahead: phase one
[Nottingham]: [The Authority], [c.1978].   1 folded sheet: ill.
Describes first phase of building project.

3269.
County Hospital, Lincoln, 1878–1978
pp.30–32: ill. in *Lincolnshire life*, vol.18, no.11, February, 1979.

3270.   INGHAM, M.J.
1769: County Hospital, Lincoln: Sewell Road, 1878–1978
[Lincoln]: [Lincolnshire Area Health Authority], 1979.   20p.: ill., 4p. of plans.
Opened in 1769, moved to Drury Lane in 1777 and current site in 1878.

3271.
Lincoln Hospitals radio
[1980].   1 sheet.
Typescript.

3272.   LINCOLN COUNTY HOSPITAL
People who care for your health: [leaflet]
[Lincoln]: [The Hospital], [1986].   1 folded sheet: ill.
Details about extension.

LINCOLN LUNATIC ASYLUM

3273.   LINCOLN LUNATIC ASYLUM
*Rules for the government of the Lincoln Lunatic Asylum, prepared for the consideration
of the governors by the committee appointed to revise the rules*
Lincoln: printed by E.B. Drury, [18??].   14p.

3274.   _____
*Lincoln Lunatic Asylum: attendants' daily return of the names and state of the patients
under their respective charge*: [table]
[Lincoln]: [s.n.], [18??].   1 sheet.

3275.   HETT, William
The Lunatic restored or comforted: a sermon
Lincoln: printed and sold by William Hett, [18??].   23p.
Profit to go to the Lunatic Asylum.

3276.   LINCOLN LUNATIC ASYLUM
Lincolnshire County Pauper Lunatic Asylum: south elevation and ground plan
[Lincoln]: [s.n.], [18??].   1 sheet.
Scale: 1 inch = 1 foot.

3277.   _____
[Table for recording nature of coercion, restraint or severity]
[Lincoln]: [s.n.], [18??].   1 sheet.

3278.   _____
Lincoln Lunatic Asylum: [letter requesting donations for establishment of institution and
giving list of benefactors, May 13th, 1807]
[Lincoln]: [s.n.], [1807].   [2]p.

3279. ⸻

Lincoln Lunatic Asylum: [list of benefactors and plea for more funds]
Lincoln: printed W. Brooke, 1817. 4p.

3280. ⸻

Rules for the Lunatic Asylum at Lincoln, as settled and arranged at a public meeting of the subscribers holden at the County Hospital, Nov. 4, 1819
Lincoln: printed William Brooke, 1819. 20p.

3281. ⸻

The First report of the Lincoln Lunatic Asylum
Lincoln: printed W. Brooke, 1822. [4]p.: ill.
⸻ third report, 1825.
    Includes list of annual subscribers and benefactors by donation.

3282. ⸻

Lincoln Lunatic Asylum: [annual report]
Lincoln: printed W. Brooke, [after 1822]. 3p.

3283. **CHARLESWORTH, E.P.**

Remarks on the treatment of the insane and the management of lunatic asylums: being the substance of a return from the Lincoln Lunatic Asylum, to the circular of His Majesty's secretary of state
London: C. & J. Rivington, 1828. 39p., folded plan.
    Text is in question-and-answer form and gives detailed statistics about cases and the Asylum itself.

3284. **LINCOLN LUNATIC ASYLUM**

At a general board of governors: [minutes of a meeting held 31st Oct., 1828]
Lincoln: The Asylum, 1828. [4]p.
    Includes a report to the board by Dr. E.P. Charlesworth upon which it was decided to implement his ideas about restraint and inspection.

3285. ⸻

State of the Lincoln Lunatic Asylum, with a plan of the building grounds and of the alterations in progress: 4th report
Lincoln: J.W. Drury, 1828. 12, [2]p., plan.

3286. **HALLIDAY, Andrew**

A Letter to Lord Robert Seymour: with a report of the number of lunatics and idiots in England and Wales
London: Thomas and George Underwood, 1829. 88p.
    pp.23–24: Lincoln.

3287. **LINCOLN LUNATIC ASYLUM**

State of the Lincoln Lunatic Asylum, 1829
Lincoln: printed E.B. Drury, 1829. 16p., [1] folded leaf of plates.
Accompanies: *Minutes of a general board of governors, Oct. 13th, 1828*, 4p.
⸻ 1833, printed J.W. Drury.
⸻ 1834, printed E.B. Drury.

3288. ⸻

Abstract of the deed of conveyance to the Rev. George Gordon and Charles Mainwaring, Esq., of the piece of land whereon the Lincoln Lunatic Asylum is built
Lincoln: printed E.B. Drury, [183?]. 4p.

3289. LINCOLN LUNATIC ASYLUM
Lincoln Lunatic Asylum: [instructions to governors acting as visitor]
[Lincoln]: [s.n.], [183?].   1 sheet.

3290. _____
Lincoln Lunatic Asylum: instructions for the admission of patients
Lincoln: W. and B. Brooke, [1830s/1840s].   3p.

3291. _____
Lincoln Lunatic Asylum: instruction for the admission of patients: [with admission form]
[Lincoln]: [s.n.], [1830s/1840s].   3p.

3292. _____
Lincoln Lunatic Asylum: state of the patients' accounts: [table]
[Lincoln]: [s.n.], [1830s/1840s].   1 sheet.

3293. _____
State of the Lincoln Lunatic Asylum: [1830, 1831, 1838, 1839, 1840]
Lincoln: [s.n.], [1830–41].   Various pagings.

3294. _____
Sixth report of the Lincoln Lunatic Asylum
Lincoln: printed M. Keyworth, 1830.   16p.
_____ seventh, 1831.

3295. _____
Orders and regulations made at the weekly and general boards of the Lincoln Lunatic Asylum, from September 3, 1820, to March 8, 1830
Lincoln: printed M. Keyworth, [1830].   11p.

3296. _____
Proceedings of the general quarterly board of the Lincoln Lunatic Asylum, held on October 13, 1830, with the official papers
Lincoln: printed E.B. Drury, 1830.   64p.
Accompanies: *State of the Lincoln Lunatic Asylum*: [for 1839, 1841, 1852, 1871].

3297. _____
Proceedings of the general quarterly board of the Lincoln Lunatic Asylum, held on October 13, 1830, with the official papers
Lincoln: printed E.B. Drury, 1830.   64p.
Accompanies: *State of the Lincoln Lunatic Asylum*: [for 1849].
  Newspaper cutting attached to front flyleaf: letter from Sir E.H. Bromhead to the editor of *The Lancet*, 'On the disuse of instruments of restraint in lunacy...in the Lincoln Lunatic Asylum'. Post 1843?.

3298. _____
State of the Lincoln Lunatic Asylum, 1832
Lincoln: Brooke, 1832.   16p.

3299. _____
State of the Lincoln Lunatic Asylum, 1833
Lincoln: printed J.W. Drury, 1833.   16p.

3300. _____
State of the Lincoln Lunatic Asylum, 1834
Lincoln: printed E.B. Drury, 1834.   16p.

3301.   **HILL, Robert G.**
[Letter requesting to be considered for post of house-surgeon at the Lincoln Lunatic Asylum, May, 1835]
[Lincoln?]: [s.n.], [1835].   1 sheet.

3302.   **LINCOLN LUNATIC ASYLUM**
Lincoln Lunatic Asylum: [circular asking for donations to develop female side of the Asylum]
Lincoln: [Officers of the Lincoln Lunatic Asylum], 1836.   [3]p.

3303.   ——————
Lincoln Lunatic Asylum: [request for funds for extending female side, with list of benefactors, October, 1836]
[Lincoln]: [s.n.], [1836].   1 sheet.

3304.   **HILL, Robert Gardiner**
[Application for post of superintendent house surgeon and apothecary of the Royal Lunatic Asylum at Glasgow]
Lincoln: printed W. and B. Brooke, [1838].   [3]p.
    Includes extracts from annual reports of Lincoln Lunatic Asylum as well as testimonials.

3305.   ——————
Total abolition of personal restraint in the treatment of the insane: a lecture on the management of lunatic asylums...delivered at the Mechanics Institution, Lincoln...1838, ...with statistical tables
London: Simpkin, Marshall, [1839].   112, [32]p.: ill.
    Appendices give detailed information relating to Lincoln Lunatic Asylum: classification of disease for purposes of restraint, types of restraint, rates of mortality.

3306.   **LINCOLN LUNATIC ASYLUM**
Lincoln Lunatic Asylum: [invoice, with rules]
Lincoln: printed W. and B. Brooke, [184?].   [3]p.

3307.   **COOKSON, W.D.**
Evidence of the non-restraint system of the Lincoln Lunatic Asylum, extracted from the minute book
Lincoln: printed W. and B. Brooke, 1841.   43p.

3308.   **LINCOLN LUNATIC ASYLUM**
State of the Lincoln Lunatic Asylum, 1841
Lincoln: [s.n.], [1841].

3309.   ——————
Rules of the Lincoln Lunatic Asylum, instituted MDCCCXIV
Lincoln: printed J. Stainton, 1841.   32p.

3310.   ——————
State of the Lincoln Lunatic Asylum, 1842
Lincoln: [s.n.], [1842].

3311.   ——————
Proceedings of the Lincoln Lunatic Asylum, relative to classification, inspection and other matters bearing upon the subject of restraint
Lincoln: printed W. and B. Brooke, [1843].   27p.
    'Being chiefly Appendix A of Mr R.G. Hill's publication on the *Total abolition of personal restraint in the treatment of the insane.*'

3312. ——————
State of the Lincoln Lunatic Asylum, 1844
Lincoln: [s.n.], [1844].

3313. ——————
State of the Lincoln Lunatic Asylum, 1845–1852
[Lincoln]: [s.n.], [1845–52].   Various pagings.

3314. ——————
State of the Lincoln Lunatic Asylum, 1846
Lincoln: printed W. and B. Brooke, 1846.   52p., plan.

3315. ——————
State of the Lincoln Lunatic Asylum, 1847
Lincoln: [s.n.], [1847].

3316. ——————
*Proceedings of the Lincoln Lunatic Asylum: and communications with Her Majesty's
commissioners in lunacy, with an appendix containing extracts from the various reports...*
London: Longman, 1847.   iii, 93p.

3317. ——————
*Proceedings of the Lincoln Lunatic Asylum: and communications with Her Majesty's
commissioners in lunacy, with an appendix...illustrating the medical and general
economy of the establishment*
Lincoln: W. and B. Brooke, printers, 1847.   93p.
    Intended to refute criticisms made by two of the commissioners in lunacy.

3318. ——————
State of the Lincoln Lunatic Asylum, 1848
Lincoln: [s.n.], [1848].

3319. ——————
State of the Lincoln Lunatic Asylum: 25th report
Lincoln: printed by W. and B. Brooke, 1849.   xxxiv, 61p., plan.
Accompanies: *Proceedings...., 1830.

3320. ——————
State of the Lincoln Lunatic Asylum, 1845–49
[Lincoln]: [s.n.], [1850?].   Various pagings, plans.

3321.   **PIERCE, W.M.**
To the governors of the Lincoln Lunatic Asylum: [letter]
Lincoln: printed W. and B. Brooke, 1851.   6p.
    About claims of Hill that he did not receive full credit for the policy of non-restraint introduced
    at the Asylum.

3322.   **LINCOLN LUNATIC ASYLUM**
Rules of the Lincoln Lunatic Hospital
Lincoln: printed W. and B. Brooke, 1857.   18p.
    Revised, 1856.

3323.   **CLARK, James**
*A Memoir of John Conolly, M.D., D.C.L., comprising a sketch of the treatment of the
insane in Europe and America*
London: John Murray, 1869.   xii, 298p., [frontis].
    Contains references to Lincoln Lunatic Asylum and the work of Charlesworth and Hill.

3324.   **LINCOLN LUNATIC ASYLUM**
Regulations for the government of the Lincoln Lunatic Hospital
Lincoln: printed James Williamson, 1870.   28p.

3325.   ──────────
Rules of the Lincoln Lunatic Hospital
Revised.
Lincoln: printed James Williamson, 1876.   18p.

3326.   ──────────
State of the Lincoln Lunatic Hospital: [1878, 79, 82, 83]
Lincoln: printed James Williamson, 1878–83.   Various pagings.

3327.   ──────────
State of the Lincoln Lunatic Hospital, from January 1st to December 31st, 1880, inclusive
Lincoln: printed James Williamson, [1880].   28p.: ill.

3328.   **LINCOLN No.2 HOSPITAL MANAGEMENT COMMITTEE**
Lincoln No.2 Hospital Management Committee, Sheffield Regional Hospital Board: handbook, 1957
[Lincoln]: [The Committee], [1957].   20p.
    Bracebridge Heath Hospital and the Lawn Hospital.

3329.   **LINCOLN HEATH HOSPITAL MANAGEMENT COMMITTEE**
A Booklet to mark the one hundred and fiftieth anniversary of the Lawn Hospital, Lincoln
[Lincoln]: The Committee, [1969].   20p., 2p. of plates.
    Plates: the hospital reproduced from the first report of 1822 and statue of Edward Parker
    Charlesworth.

3330.   **WALK, Alexander**
Lincoln and non-restraint
pp.481–495 in *The British journal of psychiatry*, vol.117, no.540, November, 1970.
    Work of Gardiner Hill and E.P. Charlesworth at the Lincoln Lunatic Asylum and its influence
    upon John Conolly who was responsible for the policy being generally accepted.

3331.   **GRANVILLE, A.B.**
Spas of England and principal sea-bathing places.   Vol.2: The Midlands and South
Bath: Adams & Dart, 1971.   ix, 640p.: ill.
Originally published: 1841.   Includes index.
    pp.82–103: Lincoln; mainly concerned with the Lunatic Asylum, with an assessment of the
    theories and practices of Drs. Hill and Charlesworth, and the spring at Monkswell.

LINCOLN GENERAL DISPENSARY

3332.
[Letter to mayor requesting meeting to discuss establishment of a General Dispensary, January 11th, 1826]
Lincoln: printed W. Brooke, 1826.   1 sheet.

3333.
[Resolution of meeting to discuss establishment of a General Dispensary, February 6th, 1826]
Lincoln: printed W. Brooke, 1826.   1 sheet.

3334.   **LINCOLN GENERAL DISPENSARY**
Laws of the General Dispensary at Lincoln
Lincoln: printed J.W. Drury, 1826.   10p.

3335.   —————————
Lincoln General Dispensary: [resolutions of general meeting of the governors, February 11th]
Lincoln: printed W. Brooke, [after 1826].   1 sheet.

3336.   **SMITH, Robert William**
[Application for post of apothecary to the Lincoln Dispensary: with testimonials]
[Lincoln]: [s.n.], [after 1826].   [6]p.

3337.   —————————
The Second annual report of the Lincoln General Dispensary
Lincoln: printed E.B. Drury, 1828.   12p.
—————————   third, 1829.

3338.   **HILL, Robert Gardiner**
[Application for post of apothecary to the Lincoln General Dispensary: testimonials]
Lincoln: printed W. and B. Brooke, [1834].   [3]p.

3339.   **LINCOLN GENERAL DISPENSARY**
General Dispensary: [appeal for more money, 1st December, 1840]
Lincoln: printed W. and B. Brooke, 1840.   1 sheet.

3340.   —————————
Lincoln Dispensary: [request for annual subscribers, April, 1851]
[Lincoln]: [s.n.], [1851].   1 sheet.

OTHER HOSPITALS

3341.
Scheme for the management and regulation of the Mere Hospital, within the liberty of the city of Lincoln, and the application of the income thereof, approved by the Court of Chancery, by order, dated 16th January, 1858
London: printed by C. Roworth, 1858.   19p.

3342.
St John's Hospital, Lincoln: [notes on history]
[19??].   6 leaves.
Typescript.

3343.   **FALLA, W.A.S.**
St John's Hospital, Lincoln
[Lincoln]: [The Hospital], [1966].   [18]p.: ill.

3344.
Opening of the City Hospital for the treatment of infectious diseases, Long Leys Road, Wednesday, 2nd November, 1904
Lincoln: Lincoln Corporation, [1904].   14p., [frontis].

3345.   FOURTH NORTHERN GENERAL HOSPITAL
The Magazine: the monthly record of the 4th Northern General Hospital, Lincoln
Vol.1, no.1, October, 1916-vol.1, no.12, September, 1917.
Lincoln: [The Hospital], [1916].   Various pagings.
Ceased publication with no.12.

3346.   BRACEBRIDGE HEATH HOSPITAL
Bracebridge Heath Hospital, Lincolnshire: report for the year ending 31st December, 1945, and statement of accounts to 31st March, 1946
[Lincoln]: [The Hospital], [1946].   29p.: ill.

3347.   FALLA, W.A.S.
Bracebridge Heath Hospital centenary, 1852–1952
[Lincoln]: [Lincoln No.2 Hospital Management Committee], [1952].   20p.

3348.   LAWN HOSPITAL
The Lawn, Lincoln, registered hospital for mental & nervous diseases: annual report, 1944–47
Lincoln: printed Doncaster, 1944–47.   Various pagings.

3349.   LINCOLN No.2 HOSPITAL MANAGEMENT COMMITTEE
Bracebridge Heath Hospital, near Lincoln, and The Lawn Hospital, Lincoln: reports of the Hospital Management Committee, 1948–57, and statement of accounts for year ended...
[Lincoln]: [The Committee], [1948–58].   Various pagings.
>Incorporates former annual reports of individual institutions.   On the take-over under the National Health Service Act, 1946, The Lawn became essentially for paying patients, while Bracebridge Heath was the larger county mental hospital.

3350.   MELTON, Beatrice Louise
Short history & guide of The Lawn Hospital
Lincoln: The Author, 1969?.   24p.: ill.
>Name of 'The Lawn' given in 1884.   Author responsible for article in *Lincolnshire life* about Rev. Dr. Francis Wilde and Dr. Willis.

3351.   FRIENDS OF LINCOLN HOSPITALS ASSOCIATION
Report on the activities of the Friends of Lincoln Hospitals Association: [1956]
Lincoln: printed Elpeeko, [1957].   [4]p.

3352.   ⸻
Annual report
[after 1960].   Various pagings.
Typescript.

LIBRARIES

3353.
The Public Libraries (England) Acts, 1855 to 1890: [result of poll as to whether should be adopted, 23rd January, 1892]
Lincoln: printed Charles Keyworth, 1892.   1 sheet.

3354.
Opening of the City of Lincoln Public Library, 19th October, 1895: plan of luncheon tables
[Lincoln]: [s.n.], [1895].   1 sheet.

3355.   **LINCOLN PUBLIC LIBRARY**
Supplement to the catalogue of books in the Lending and Reference Departments and key to the indicator for works of fiction
Lincoln: The Library, 1898.   60p.

3356.   **LINCOLN, Libraries, Museum and Art Gallery Committee**
Review
[Lincoln]: [The Committee?], [19??].

3357.   **LINCOLN PUBLIC LIBRARY**
Author-list of books in the Lending Department suitable for boys and girls
Lincoln: The Library, 1903.   35p.

3358.   **LINCOLN PUBLIC LIBRARY, Committee**
Annual report of the committee for the year ended...
Lincoln: The Library, 1905–14.   Various pagings.

3359.   **CORNS, A.R.**
City of Lincoln Public Library: catalogue of the books in the Lending Department
Lincoln: Lincoln Public Library, 1909.   xi, 415p.
   First catalogue of Library published: 1895; 2 supplements: 1898, 1902.

3360.
[Notice of meeting to discuss site for Carnegie Library]
Lincoln: printed W.H. Leary, [1910].   1 sheet.

3361.
Bracebridge Branch Library, opened 26th January, 1946, by H.M. Cashmore, F.L.A., city librarian of Birmingham
[Lincoln]: [Lincoln, Public Libraries], [1946].   7p.: ill.
   Details about first branch library in the city of Lincoln.

3362.
Centenary year report on the Public Library
[Lincoln]: [Lincoln, Libraries, Museum and Art Gallery Committee], [1950].   8p.

3363.   **BAKER, F.T.**
[Notes on Lincoln City Libraries, 1892–1914]
[1960s?].   [14] leaves.
Ms.

3364.
Ermine Branch Library and Ravendale Clinic: [programme of opening ceremony]
[Lincoln]: [Lincoln Corporation], [1962].   [10]p.: ill.

3365.   **GOODHEAD, Freda E.**
The City library viewpoint: [in symposium on 'The library and the teenager']
pp.106–109 in *The Assistant librarian*, vol.56, no.6, June, 1963.
     Especially Ermine Branch.

3366.
County commentary: Tennyson Research Centre opens in Lincoln
pp.62–63: ill. in *Lincolnshire life*, vol.4, no.4, August/September, 1964.

3367.
Lincoln City Libraries, 1914–1964
Lincoln: Lincoln, Libraries, Museum and Art Gallery Committee, [1964].   16p.: ill.

3368.
Opening of the Tennyson Research Centre, Lincoln City Library
[Lincoln]: [printed Keyworth & Fry], [1964].   [7]p.: ill.

3369.
Round and about: an occasional newsletter for members of the Lincoln City Libraries
Group Loads Service
No.1, December, 1965–
[Lincoln]: [s.n.], [1965–   ].

3370.   **LINCOLNSHIRE COUNTY LIBRARY SERVICE**
County Library Headquarters, Brayford House, Lucy Tower Street, Lincoln: programme
of official opening...Tuesday, 30th March, 1971
[Lincoln]: [The Library Service], [1971].   [4]p.: ill.

3371.   **CAMPBELL, Nancie**
Tennyson in Lincoln: a catalogue of the collections in the Research Centre
Lincoln: Tennyson Research Centre, City Library, 1971–73.   2 vols.
ISBN 0901058034

3372.   **LINDSEY AND HOLLAND COUNTY LIBRARY**
Lincolnshire collection: [pamphlet]
[Lincoln]: [The Library], [c.1973].   [4]p.: ill.

3373.
Sources for library history: East Midlands
pp.29–38 in *Library history*, vol.6, no.2, 1982.
     pp.33–34: Lincolnshire.

3374.   **FELLOWS, Richard A.**
Sir Reginald Blomfield: an Edwardian architect
London: A. Zwemmer, 1985.   182p.: ill.
(Architects in perspective)
ISBN 0302005900
     Architect responsible for the Central Library.

ARCHIVES

3375.　MAJOR, Kathleen
The Diocesan Record Office
pp.12–17 in *AAS reports and papers*, new series, vol.3, 1939–40.

3376.　LINCOLN DIOCESAN RECORD OFFICE
[Reports from 1 October, 1945–30th June, 1948]
[1945–48].　Various pagings.
Typescript.
> Covers last four months' independent existence of the Record Office.

3377.　VARLEY, Joan
Local archives in Great Britain.　VI: The Lincolnshire Archives Committee
pp.5–16 in *Archives*, no.6, Michaelmas, 1951.

3378.　LINCOLNSHIRE ARCHIVES COMMITTEE
Index: archivists' reports, 1948–58 [and] 1958–1968
Lincoln: The Committee, 1961–75.　2 vols.

3379.　FINCH, Mary
Five years of the Lincolnshire Archives Office, 1958–63
pp.29–37 in *The Lincolnshire historian*, vol.2, no.11, [1963].

3380.　VARLEY, Joan
The Lincolnshire Archives Office
pp.1–13 in *Bulletin of local history (East Midlands region)*, 1970.

3381.　HILL, J.W.F.
From Canon Foster to the Lincolnshire Archives Office
pp.71–73 in *Lincolnshire history and archaeology*, vol.13, 1978.

3382.　FINCH, Mary
The Common chronicle: Lincolnshire's archival heritage
pp.24–26: ill. in *Lincolnshire life*, vol.23, no.4, July, 1983.
> Coverage of work of C.W. Foster, Lincolnshire archival material and its housing.

MUSEUMS

3383.
A Museum for Lincoln: a want
the editors of *Lincolnshire notes & queries.*
pp.74–76 in *LN&Q*, vol.3, no.2, 1892.

3384.   CASWELL, C.J.
A Museum for Lincoln
pp.242–243 in *LN&Q*, vol.3, no.24, 1893.
> Scheme involving use of Newport Arch as entrance to the museum and the repositioning of the Stonebow to act as an entrance to the grounds.

3385.   WOODRUFFE-PEACOCK, Adrian
A County museum for Lincolnshire
pp.164–170 in *LN&Q*, vol.4, no.30, 1895.

3386.   FRANKLIN, Henry
Lincoln Castle as a county folk museum? : ideal setting for 'modern' bygones: suggested new use for old prison buildings
Lincoln: Lincolnshire Chronicle, [1942].   7p.: ill.
Originally published: in *Lincolnshire chronicle*, 25 April, 1942.

3387.   ELWES, J.
'Lincolnshire past, present & future' conference: [programme]
Lincoln: Lincolnshire Past, Present & Future Committee, [1963].   25p.
> Biographical sketches of speakers, including John Betjeman.   Subjects include: foundation of a folk museum in Lincoln; Lincoln School of Art; Russell Flint Exhibition at the Usher Gallery.

CITY AND COUNTY MUSEUM

3388.   ROYAL ARCHAEOLOGICAL INSTITUTE
Catalogue of antiquities, exhibited in the museum formed during the annual meeting of the Archaeological Institute, held at Lincoln, in July, 1848
30p., [13] leaves in *Proceedings of the Archaeological Institute, at the annual meeting at Lincoln*, 1848.

3389.
Museum catalogue
Lincoln: printed W. and B. Brooke, [c.1899].   pp.75–94.

3390.   SYMPSON, E. Mansel
The Greyfriars' Museum, Lincoln
p.49 in *LN&Q*, vol.9, no.70, 1906.

329

3391.   **BLATHWAYT, F.L.**
Owls and hawks of Lincolnshire, with special reference to the collection in the City and
County Museum, Lincoln
Lincoln: The Museum, 1909.   13p.: ill.
(Lincoln City and County Museum publications, no.6)

3392.   **BAKER, F.T.**
Museums and the local historian
pp.21–25 in *The Lincolnshire historian*, no.1, summer, 1947.
    County Museum in Lincoln.

3393.   **SMITH, John Hermaine**
The Armeria: a fireside chat on arms and armour, containing notes and a catalogue of
the exhibits in the City Museum
Lincoln: printed J.W. Ruddock, [1951].   64p.: ill.

3394.
Greyfriars, Lincoln, the City & County Museum, Lincoln: an illustrated guide to the
building
Lincoln: Lincoln, Libraries, Museum and Art Gallery Committee, [c.1955].   8p.: ill.

3395.   **LINCOLN CITY AND COUNTY MUSEUM**
A Brief outline of the collections
Lincoln: The Museum, 1968.   1 folded sheet: ill.

MUSEUM OF LINCOLNSHIRE LIFE

3396.   **MUSEUM OF LINCOLNSHIRE LIFE**
[Pamphlet]
[Lincoln]: [The Museum], [c.1970?].   1 folded card: ill.

3397.
The Museum of Lincolnshire Life
pp.32–35: ill. in *Lincolnshire life*, vol.16, no.1, March, 1976.

3398.   **WILSON, C.M.**
Museum of Lincolnshire Life history trail
Lincoln: Lincolnshire Museums, 1977.   [6]p.: ill.

3399.   **STEMP, Robin**
Women's costume in England, 1825–1900
Lincoln: Lincolnshire Museums, 1978.   25p.: ill.
(Museum of Lincolnshire Life occasional paper, no.1)
    Detailed drawings of costumes in the collection at the Museum, with accession numbers.

3400.   _____
Women's costume in England, 1900–1930
Lincoln: Lincolnshire Museums, [1978].
(Museum of Lincolnshire Life occasional paper, no.2)

3401.   **WILSON, Catherine M.**
From small beginnings: the story of the Museum of Lincolnshire Life
pp.138–139: ill. in *A Prospect of Lincolnshire*, 1984.

3402.   **WILKES, Peter**
The Museum of Lincolnshire Life
pp.34–35: ill. in *Lincolnshire life*, vol.26, no.3, June, 1986.

NATIONAL CYCLE MUSEUM

3403.   **FAIRHEAD, Linda**
National Cycle Museum
pp.30–31: ill. in *Lincolnshire life*, vol.25, no.3, June, 1985.

ART GALLERY

3404.   **WILLIAMSON, G.C**
The Ward Usher collection at Lincoln
pp.169–174: ill. in *The Connoisseur*, vol.V, no.19, March, 1903.
    Article about the collector's special interest in watches, miniatures and china.

3405.
The Royal visit to Lincoln: the Prince of Wales to open the Usher Gallery next
week...details of the arrangements: story of the Usher bequest, photos of the gallery
pp.13–20: ill. in *Lincolnshire chronicle*, Saturday, 21 May, 1927.

3406.
Souvenir and official programme of the opening of the Usher Art Gallery, Lincoln, by
H.R.H. the Prince of Wales, May 25th, 1927
[Lincoln]: [Lincoln Corporation], 1927.   [64]p.: ill.
    Gives detailed description of the building and portraits of eminent people associated with it; for
example, the architect, Blomfield.

3407.
Extension to the Usher Art Gallery...opened on 11th November, 1959
[Lincoln]: [Lincoln, Libraries, Museum and Art Gallery Committee], [1959].   [3]p.

3408.
Opening of the Tennyson Room at the Usher Art Gallery by Lord David Cecil, C.H., on
29th October, 1960
Lincoln: Lincoln, Libraries, Museum and Art Gallery Committee, 1960.   [3]p.

3409.
An Introduction to the Usher Gallery and Curtois Wing, Lindum Road, Lincoln
Lincoln: Lincoln, Libraries, Museum and Art Gallery Committee, 1968.   1 folded sheet.

3410.   **WOOD, Richard H.**
The Founding of the Usher Gallery, Lincoln
Lincoln: Lincolnshire Museums, 1979.   6p.: ill.
(Lincolnshire Museums information sheet.   Fine and decorative art series, 1)

3411.   **SWAIN, Marilyn**
The World of antiques: James Ward Usher and the Usher Gallery
p.5: ill. in *Lincolnshire life*, vol.23, no.10, February, 1984.

GUIDES

3412.   **USHER GALLERY**
Usher Art Gallery
[Lincoln]: [The Gallery], [1946].   [2]p.

3413. ─────────────
Usher Gallery, Lindum Road, Lincoln
[Lincoln]: [The Gallery], [1976].   1 folded sheet: ill.

COLLECTIONS AND EXHIBITIONS

3414.   **DAVIS, Alec**
Lincoln's historic watches
pp.380–383: ill. in *Horological journal*, November, 1939.
> About James Ward Usher's collection and the catalogue that he wrote.

3415.   **USHER GALLERY**
Festival exhibition of church plate & vestments, 27th June to end of August, 1951
Lincoln: printed J.W. Ruddock, 1951.   37p., 13p. of plates.
Includes index.
> Items from Lincoln Cathedral, Museum and St.Mark's.

3416.   ─────────────
Coronation year, 1953: special exhibition: Lincoln illustrated, 30th May to 5th July:
[guide to exhibition]
Lincoln: [The Gallery], 1953.   5p.
> Covers: pictures and prints; archaeology; historical documents; Royal Lincolnshire Regiment; engineering.

3417.   ─────────────
The Collection of the late Sir Francis Hill, 1899–1980: an exhibition of paintings, watercolours, prints and coins bequeathed to the Usher Gallery, 7 November–13 December, 1981
Lincoln: Lincolnshire Museums, 1981.   27p.: ill.

3418.   **SWAIN, Marilyn**
The World of antiques
p.5: ill. in *Lincolnshire life*, vol.22, no.9, December, 1982.

3419.   ─────────────
The World of antiques: Usher collection.   1: miniatures
p.5: ill. in *Lincolnshire life*, vol.23, no.11, February, 1984.

3420.   ─────────────
The World of antiques: Usher collection.   2: enamels
p.7: ill. in *Lincolnshire life*, vol.23, no.11, February, 1984.

3421.   ─────────────
The World of antiques: Usher collection.   3: chinese porcelain
p.15: ill. in *Lincolnshire life*, vol.24, no.1, April, 1984.

3422.   ─────────────
The World of antiques: Usher collection.   5: Sevres porcelain
p.7: ill. in *Lincolnshire life*, vol.24, no.3, June, 1984.

3423.   ─────────────
The World of antiques: Usher collection.   6: Chelsea porcelain
p.7: ill. in *Lincolnshire life*, vol.24, no.4, July, 1984.

3424. —————————

The World of antiques: Usher collection.   7: Worcester porcelain
p.7: ill. in *Lincolnshire life*, vol.24, no.5, August, 1984.

3425. —————————

The World of antiques: Usher collection.   8: Derby porcelain
p.7: ill. in *Lincolnshire life*, vol.24, no.6, September, 1984.

3426. —————————

The World of antiques: Usher collection.   9: watches
p.7: ill. in *Lincolnshire life*, vol.24, no.7, October, 1984.

3427. —————————

The World of antiques: Usher collection.   10: silver
p.7: ill. in *Lincolnshire life*, vol.24, no.8, November, 1984.

3428.   MILLER, Gary
*The Tree: a return to grace: an exhibition and publication to celebrate a
commission...for the Usher Gallery, Lincoln*
Lincoln: Lincolnshire County Council, 1987.   31p.: ill.
ISBN 086111132X

PUBLIC UTILITIES

SEWERS

3429. MOORE, J.
To the commissioners of the Court of Sewers for the county of Lincoln, the city of Lincoln and county of the same city, and part of the county of Nottingham
[Lincoln]: [s.n.], [1831]. [2]p.
> Letter complaining about conduct of Robert Swan in resigning post and informing a relative of the vacancy 2 days before anybody else.

3430.
Clerkship of the Sewers: a nice job, and a pretty pair of Lincoln lawyers
Lincoln: printed R.E. Leary, [1831]. 4p.
> Satiric comment on the Robert Swan affair.

3431.
Commission of Sewers, 8 January, 1831, within the limits of the county of Lincoln, city of Lincoln and county of the said city, and part of the county of Nottingham, or in the borders or confines of the same
Lincoln: printed E.B. Drury, [1831]. 21p.

3432. GILES, Geo.
Report made to the Sanitary Committee of the Corporation of Lincoln on a general underground sewerage of the city and an estimate of the probable cost of effecting the same...
Lincoln: printed W. Bellatti, 1849. 51, xip.
> Includes large proposed plan for the sewerage of the city dated 1840.

3433. ANGLIAN WATER AUTHORITY, Lincoln Sewage Division
Canwick Sewage Treatment works: open day, Sunday, 26th September, 1976
[Lincoln]: [The Division], [1976]. 1 folded sheet.
> Details of sewage treatment in Lincoln.

DRAINAGE

3434.
Copy report of the Town Council of the city of Lincoln, deputed to visit Croydon and Worthing for the purpose of viewing the works of drainage and irrigation adopted in those places
Lincoln: printed R.E. Leary, 1865. 15p.

3435.   **MIDDLETON, David**
Drainage of the city of Lincoln: prize essay
Lincoln: C. Loder, Standard, 1866.   22p.
> pp.7–14: essay; pp.14–20: report of quarterly meeting of Town Council, 9th May, 1865, at
> which result of competition announced.

3436.
How shall we drain the city?: a letter
Lincoln: Cousans and Gale, 1867.   8p.
Originally published: in *Lincolnshire chronicle*, March 2nd, 1867.

3437.   **UPPER WITHAM INTERNAL DRAINAGE BOARD**
Boultham Pumping Station: opening ceremony...on Tuesday, 28th April, 1953
[1953].   [3], 14 leaves: ill., 1 plan.
Typescript.

3438.   **EYLES, J.F.**
C.2176: Sincil Dyke, Lincoln
pp.20–23: ill. in *AM: the house journal of A. Monk & Co., Ltd*, spring, 1963.
> Describes contract work carried out by the firm.

3439.   **GORE, Derek**
The Lincolnshire Car Dyke: a field survey
Derek Gore, Jane Greenhalgh, Christopher Smith.
Nottingham: University of Nottingham, Department of Classical and Archaeological
Studies, 1970.   17, [3] leaves: ill.

3440.   **UPPER WITHAM INTERNAL DRAINAGE BOARD**
Brief history of drainage and description of major pumping schemes, 1958–1973
Lincoln: The Board, [1973].   30p.: ill.

3441.   ──────────────
A Brief history, 1933 to 1983
[Lincoln]: [The Board], [1983].   27p.: ill., 1 folded map.

FLOODS

3442.
The Floods, December, 1876–January, 1877
in *Lincoln, Rutland and Stamford mercury*, January 5th, 12th, 1877.

3443.   **LINCOLN, Floods Sub-committee**
*City of Lincoln: report of the Floods Sub-committee to the mayor and Corporation of the
city of Lincoln*
Lincoln: Lincoln Corporation, 1914.   16p., map.
> Contains revised map of the city of Lincoln, with Bracebridge, Boultham & Canwick (scale 10
> inches to 1 mile), showing streets flooded in 1910.   Includes notes on waterways: the Witham;
> the Fossdyke; and Sincil Bank.

3444.
Lincoln flood relief scheme
pp.661–662: ill. in *Civil engineering*, vol.51, no.600, June, 1956.

3445.   **PAYNTING, Tony**
Anglia plugs Lincoln floods for £10M
pp.8–10: ill., maps in *Surveyor*, 30 September, 1982.
    Drainage scheme by Anglian Water Authority.

3446.   **ANGLIAN WATER AUTHORITY, Lincoln Division**
River Witham system scheme: Lincoln flood alleviation
Lincoln: The Division, 1984.   17p.: ill., maps.

3447.
Telemetry system aids fight to avert flooding
pp.215, 217 in *Water services*, vol.90, pt.1083, May, 1986.
    Surveillance carried out by Anglian Water Authority, Lincoln Division.   Not much about
    Lincoln, though does mention flooding problem there.

WATER SUPPLY

3448.
[9 & 10 Vict.]: *An Act for better supplying with water the inhabitants of the city of Lincoln, and certain parishes and places adjacent thereto, in the county of Lincoln*
London: printed George Eyre and William Spottiswoode, [18??].   pp.2005–2031.

3449.
Lincoln proposed water works: [notice of meeting, 6th November, 1845]
Lincoln: printed John Hall, 1845.   1 sheet.

3450.   **LINCOLN WATER WORKS**
Report of the engineer, T. Hawksley, 7th November, 1845
Lincoln: printed T.J.N. Brogden, 1845.   1 sheet.

3451.   ─────────────
Abstract of the receipts and expenditure of the capital and revenue accounts, together with the report of the directors, submitted to the annual meeting of proprietors on 26th June, 1850
Lincoln: printed W. and B. Brooke, [1850].   8p.

3452.   **RANCE, Chas. E. de**
Water supply: report: [to the Waterworks Committee of the Lincoln Corporation]
Lincoln: printed M.A. Doncaster, 1891.   21p.: ill.
    Search for a water supply for the city; analysis of the situation and various proposals.

3453.   **HULL, Edward**
Lincoln water supply, 1898: report: [to the Waterworks Committee of the Corporation, on underground sources of supply]
Lincoln: printed M.A. Doncaster, 1898.   8p.
    Investigation of possibilities of adding to current supplies from other sources.

3454.   **GRIFFITH, Percy**
Lincoln water supply, 1899: report: [to the Waterworks Committee of the Corporation of Lincoln, on proposed boring at Boultham]
Lincoln: printed Doncaster, 1899.   12p.: ill., 1 plan.
    Includes: 1p. supplementary report of 9th January, 1900.

3455.
Memoirs of the Geological Survey, England and Wales: the water supply of Lincolnshire from underground sources: with records of sinkings and borings
edited by Horace B. Woodward.
London: HMSO, 1904.   vi, 229p.: ill., 1 folded map.
Includes index.
> pp.125–131: Lincoln.

3456.   **HILL, G.H., & SON**
Lincoln water supply, 1905: a report: [to the chairman and members of the Waterworks Committee, Lincoln]
Lincoln: printed Doncaster, 1905.   3p.
> pp.17–18: accountant's statement of approximate cost of Hill's proposal.

3457.   **GRIFFITH, Percy**
Lincoln water supply: report...on boring operations
Lincoln: printed Doncaster, 1905.   4p.
> Report on progress at Boultham since the delay caused by losing the boring tool.

3458.   **HOUSTON & McGOWEN**
Report..on their treatment of the water...
Messrs. Houston & McGowen.
Lincoln: printed Doncaster, 1905.   8p.

3459.   **WHITTAKER, William**
Lincoln water supply, 1905: report: [to the special committee of the Council of the city of Lincoln: water supply, on underground sources of supply]
Lincoln: printed Doncaster, 1905.   11p.

3460.
[6 Edw.7.   Local Government Board's Provisional Orders Confirmation (no.11) Act, 1906, ch.CXXIII]: *An Act to confirm certain provisional orders of the Local Government Board relating to Lincoln and Uttoxeter*
London: printed by Eyre and Spottiswoode for Rowland Bailey, [1906].   14p.
> Provisional order for altering the Lincoln Waterworks Act, 1871 and the Local Government Board's provisional order confirmation (Aberavon, &c) Act, 1880.

3461.   **LINCOLN WATER WORKS**
Report by the waterworks engineer on the future supply of water to the city and district
Lincoln: Lincoln Corporation, 1907.   31 leaves: ill.

3462.   **GRIFFITH, Percy**
Corporation of Lincoln water supply: report: [to...committee on water supply about Boultham boring]
London: Metchim, 1907.   7p.
> The water was stagnant so deeper drilling recommended.

3463.   **HULL, Edward**
Lincoln water supply, 1907: report: [to the Waterworks Committee of the Corporation]
Lincoln: printed W.K. Morton, 1907.   8p.: ill, 1 plan.
> Relates to stagnancy of Boultham boring.

3464.
Lincoln Corporation Bill: [minutes of evidence before select committee on private bills, Friday, 13th March, 1908]
London: printed Geo. Kelly, 1908.   pp.47–100.
> Concerns Lincoln Corporation [Water] Bill.

3465.
Lincoln Corporation Bill: [minutes of evidence before select committee on private bills, Monday, 16th March, 1908]
London: printed Geo. Kelly, 1908.   pp.103–145.

3466.
Lincoln Corporation Bill: [minutes of evidence before select committee on private bills, Friday, 20th March, 1908]
London: Geo. Kelly, 1908.   pp.231–238.

3467.
[8 Edw.7, ch.xxxiii]: *Lincoln Corporation Act, 1908, water, &c: an Act to confer further powers upon the Corporation of Lincoln with respect to their water undertaking...*
London: Eyre and Spottiswoode for Rowland Bailey, 1908.   70p.

3468.   **LOCAL GOVERNMENT BOARD**
[8 Edw.VII, session 1908]: *Report of the Local Government Board on the Lincoln Corporation Bill, 1908*
[London]: [The Board], [1908].   9p.

3469.
Inauguration of the new water supply...3rd & 4th October, 1911: programme of opening proceedings...also an account, in brief, of Lincoln's municipal enterprises during the last half-century
Lincoln: Gazette & Echo, 1911.   43p.: ill.
> Municipal enterprises include: the Arboretum; waterworks; markets; fairs; abattoirs; drainage and sewerage; highways; fire-brigade; gas works; library; electricity; tramways; education; museum; City Hospital; finance.

3470.
Lincoln's new water
[Lincoln]: [s.n.], [1911].   [4]p.: ill.
Supplements: *Lincoln gazette and times*, Saturday, October 7th, 1911.
> Account of the Elkesley scheme.

3471.
Duty tests made by the British Engine, Boiler and Electrical Insurance Co., Ltd., of a pumping station installed at Elkesley near Retford for the city of Lincoln...constructed by Ashton Frost & Co...
[Blackburn]: [Ashton Frost], 1913.   43p.: ill.

3472.   **HOROBIN, Charles**
The Water supply of Lincoln: to be read June 9th, 1921 [at] the Institution of Water Engineers
[S.l.]: [s.n.], [1921].   13p.
> Gives brief history of Roman and mediaeval water supply, but most of paper is concerned with the early twentieth century.

3473.
Lincoln water supply
Lincoln: Lincoln Corporation, 1935.   [8]p.
> Issued during Civic Week, 1935, in connection with the centenary of local government.

3474.
Centenary of the city of Lincoln water undertaking, 1846: June 1946: [brochure]
Lincoln: [Lincoln Corporation], [1946].   30p.: ill.
> Gives historical background of water supply from Roman times until the 1846 Act 'for better supplying with water...the city of Lincoln' and then the problems in implementing it, with passing reference to the 1904–05 typhoid epidemic.

3475.   LINCOLN AND DISTRICT WATER BOARD
Water engineer and manager's report to the Water Committee, for the year ended 31st March....1952–1958
Lincoln: The Board, [1952–58].   Various pagings.

3476.
[Statutory instruments, 1962, no.1956]: *Water, England and Wales: the Lincoln and District Water Board (Grove) order, 1962*
London: HMSO, 1962.   [2]p.

3477.
[Statutory instruments, 1963, no.1549]: *Water, England and Wales: the Lincoln and District Water Board (Elkesley) order, 1963*
London: HMSO, 1963.   [2]p.

3478.
[Statutory instruments, 1963, no.1621]: *Water, England and Wales: the Lincoln and District Water Board (byelaws) order, 1963*
London: HMSO, 1963.   1 sheet.

3479.
Why we should add fluoride to Lincoln's water
by a Lincoln doctor.
Lincoln: Lincoln Medical & Dental Committees, [c.1965].   [4]p.

3480.   LINCOLN AND DISTRICT WATER BOARD
Annual report and accounts, for year ended 31st March...: [1965]
[Lincoln]: The Board, 1965.

3481.
[Statutory instruments, 1968, no.1616]: *Water supply, England and Wales: the Lincoln and District Water Board (general powers) order, 1968*
London: HMSO, 1968.   [3]p.

3482.   ROBINSON, David N.
Poachings
pp.17, 19: ill. in *Lincolnshire life*, vol.12, no.1, March, 1972.
> Includes item on Lincoln water supply.

3483.   LEWIS, M.J.T.
The Rolt memorial lecture, 1983: our debt to Roman engineering: the water supply of Lincoln to the present day
pp.57–73: ill., maps in *Industrial archaeology review*, vol VII, pt.1, 1984.

ELECTRICITY

3484.   LINCOLN, Electricity Works
Terms of supply, regulations for wiring and general information
Lincoln: The Works, 1898.   20p.

3485.
Lincoln Corporation electric supply works
pp.636–639: ill. in *The Electrician*, March 3, 1899.

3486.
St Swithin's Power Station
[1957].   [12]p.
Typescript.

3487.   SHERIFF, Tom
How power came to Lincoln
p.5 in *New St Swithin magazine*, no.1, February, 1975.

GAS

3488.
[9 Geo.IV, sess. 1828]: *An Act for lighting with gas the city of Lincoln, and the Bail and Close of Lincoln, in the county of Lincoln*
[Lincoln]: [R. Mason, C. Hayward], [1828].   52p.

3489.
Caution relating to the gas works: [12th October, 1830]
Lincoln: printed E.B. Drury, 1830.   1 sheet.

3490.   LINCOLN GASLIGHT AND COKE COMPANY
Statement of account for one year, from 31st December, 1830 to 31st December, 1831
[Lincoln]: The Company, [1831].   1 sheet.

3491.   —————————
Statement of account...1831–1832
[Lincoln]: The Company, [1832].   1 sheet.

3492.   —————————
[Book of contracts for years 1832–46]
[1832–46].   [c.200] leaves.
   Contracts are between the Gaslight Company and shopkeepers for the supply of gas.

3493.   —————————
Statement of account...1838–1839
[Lincoln]: The Company, [1839].   1 sheet.

3494.   TOYNBEE, Robert
[Letter calling meeting about establishment of new company to supply gas 'on more favorable terms', October 15th, 1849]
[Lincoln]: [s.n.], [1849].   1 sheet.

3495.
[36 & 37 Vict.,   Lincoln Gaslight and Coke Company Act, 1873, ch.cxx]: *An Act to enable the Lincoln Gaslight...Co. to execute new works: to extend their limits of supply : to enable them to raise money...*
London: printed by George Eyre and Andrew Spottiswoode, 1873.   10p.

3496.
[43 & 44 Vict.,   Lincoln Gaslight and Coke Company Act, 1886, ch.lxxvi]: *An Act to enable the Lincoln Gaslight...Co. to raise additional capital: and for other purposes, 19th July, 1880*
London: printed George Edward Eyre and William Spottiswoode, 1880.   [9]p.

3497.   LINCOLN, Gas Department
Gas: the dependable clean heat fuel
Oldham: J. Allan Hanson, 1936.   20p.: ill.
   Includes brief local history of gas.

3498. ─────────────
Official inauguration of the new carbonising plant, Wednesday, 2nd October, 1946
[Lincoln]: The Department, 1946.   39p.: ill.
   Refers to the Bracebridge Carbonising Plant.

3499.   EAST MIDLANDS GAS BOARD, Lincolnshire Division
Bracebridge Gasworks, Lincoln
[Lincoln]: [The Division], 1954.   16p.: ill.
Cover title.
   Commemorating visit of the Institution of Gas Engineers, Eastern Section, 8th April, 1954.

3500. ─────────────
Bracebridge Works: open day, 21st July, 1962: [notes]
[1962].   5 leaves.
Typescript.

3501.   ROBERTS, D.E.
The Lincoln gas undertaking, 1828–1949
Leicester: East Midlands Gas, 1981.   46p.: ill.
(East Midland gas undertakings, 5)
Includes bibliography.
ISBN 0950633941
   Lincoln Gaslight and Coke Company Act was passed on 9th May, 1828, and the company passed into public ownership in May, 1949.

POST OFFICE

3502.
Lincoln and Grimsby time bill: [form]
[Lincoln]: [printed J.W. Drury], [1805].   1 sheet.

3503.
[Notice about payment of post horse duty, June 24, 1818]
Lincoln: printed Smith, 1818.   1 sheet.

3504.
[Notice about collection and delivery, 5th April, 1822]
Lincoln: printed Drury, 1822.   1 sheet.

3505.
[Notice of public meeting about alterations in Post Office duties, October 8th, 1849]
[Lincoln]: [s.n.], [1849].   1 sheet.

3506.
[Notice about memorial against changes which is available for signatures, October 11th, 1849]
Lincoln: printed James Drury, 1849.   1 sheet.

3507.   **LINCOLN PHILATELIC SOCIETY**
Exhibition of postage stamps and postal history, 6 to 24 October, 1971...: [catalogue]
Lincoln: Usher Gallery, 1971.   17p.
    Gives brief accounts of history of club and Lincolnshire postal history.

3508.   **BAKER, W.**
Lincoln postal history
[1976].   113 leaves: ill.
Typescript.
    Includes: photographs; postmarks; newscuttings.

REFUSE

3509.   **PRATT, Edwin**
City of Lincoln: town's refuse, its destruction and its uses: a short 'paper' read at an informal meeting of the Lincoln Corporation, on the 22nd April, 1904
Lincoln: The Corporation, 1904.   12p., 2 leaves of plates.

EMERGENCY SERVICES

3510.   **LINCOLN FIRE BRIGADE**
Annual report: [January 1st–December 31st, 1963–67; 1969–70]
Lincoln: The Fire Brigade, 1963–70.   Various pagings.

3511.   ─────────────
Official opening of new headquarters, South Park Avenue, on June 27th, 1964
[Lincoln]: [The Fire Brigade], [1964].   [8]p.: ill.
    Description of building.

ABATTOIR

3512.   **LINCOLN, Urban Sanitary Authority**
Byelaws...with respect to the slaughter-houses
Lincoln: Lincoln Corporation, 1877.   18p.

3513.
Opening of city abattoir, Greetwell Hollow, by James Hoy, Esq., parliamentary secretary,
Ministry of Agriculture, Fisheries and Food, Wednesday, 26th April, 1967
[1967].   [3]p.
Typescript.
    About new abattoir and the Monks Road abattoir.

TELEPHONES

3514.
Inaugural civic visit by the Right Worshipful the mayor of Lincoln...on Wednesday, 22nd
April, 1959
[1959].   4p.: ill.
Typescript.

3515.   BRITISH TELECOM
The Lincoln connection: annual review, 1983/84
[Lincoln?]: B.T.N.E., 1983.   18p.: ill.
Cover title.

PLANNING AND THE ENVIRONMENT

3516.   LINCOLN CIVIC TRUST
[The Companies Act, 1948]: *Memorandum of Association of Lincoln Civic Trust, Limited [and] Articles of Association of Lincoln Civic Trust, Limited*
Lincoln: The Trust, [1953].   23p.

3517.   ——————————
Lincoln Civic Trust, Limited, inaugural meeting...11th November, 1953 [and] Lincoln Civic Trust nominations for the officers and council
[1953].   2 sheets.
Typescript.

3518.   ——————————
Lincoln: [pamphlet]
Lincoln: The Trust, [1953?].   7p.: ill.
    Pamphlet recommending the foundation of the Trust and setting out aims.   Includes picture of restoration of the Cardinal's Hat.

3519.   ——————————
Annual report, 1954–
[Lincoln]: [The Trust], [1954–   ].   Various pagings.

3520.
Schedule of ancient monuments and buildings
[S.l.]: [s.n.], [after 1954].   1 sheet.
Originally published: in *Annual report* of the Lincoln Civic Trust.

3521.   ——————————
[Prospectus]
Lincoln: The Trust, [196?].   [3]p.

3522.
The Bail: report by Restoration and Preservation Sub-committee: [of Lincoln Civic Trust]
[196?].   [2] leaves.
Typescript.

3523.
Bailgate, Lincoln: [notes]
Restoration and Preservation Sub-committee, Lincoln Civic Trust.
[1960s/1970s].   [8] leaves.
Typescript.

3524.   LINCOLN CIVIC TRUST
Imprimis: a quarterly report on what Lincoln Civic Trust is doing, with unofficial opinions on some of the things it might do
No.1, September, 1963–
[Lincoln]: [The Trust], [1963–   ].   Various pagings.

3525.
Survey of the East Gate: [for the Lincoln Civic Trust]
undertaken by students of Lincoln Technical College.
[1966].   [c.80]p.
Ms.
> Survey of about 43 buildings, including those in James Street and East Bight.

3526.
Buildings' survey within the city of Lincoln, undertaken for the Civic Trust, 1966
compiled by students of Lincoln Technical College.
[1966].   51p.: ill.
Ms.
> Survey of 25 buildings, each judged either worthy or unworthy of preservation on basis of 18
> points.

3527.   **BANWELL, H.**
The Problems facing Lincoln: [address to annual meeting of Lincoln Civic Trust, 24th
May, 1967]
[1967].   7p.
Typescript.
> In particular, threat of motor cars.

3528.   **LINCOLN CIVIC AWARD TRUSTEES**
Lincoln Civic award
[Lincoln]: [The Trustees], [1967].   2 sheets.
Also published: 1970,   1 folded sheet: ill.
> About the award.

3529.   **LINCOLN CIVIC TRUST**
Lincoln Civic Trust appeal fund
Lincoln: The Trust, [1967?].   [8]p.: ill.

3530.   **LINCOLN, Department of Planning and Architecture**
City of Lincoln: conservation area.   No.1: The historic core
Lincoln: Lincoln Corporation, 1968.   16, viip., map, [9]p. of plates.

3531.   **LINCOLN CIVIC TRUST**
Bailgate, Lincoln: notes
[1968].   [11] leaves.
Typescript.

3532.   _____
Lincoln Civic Trust appeal fund
[Lincoln]: [The Trust], [1969].   [8]p.: ill.

3533.   _____
A Report on the feasibility of a fund raising programme presented to the executive
committee, Friday, 23rd May, 1969
carried out by Maurice Hawker.
[1969].   7, [1] leaves.
Typescript.

3534.   **ROBINSON, David N.**
Poachings
p.29 in *Lincolnshire life*, vol.8, no.11, January, 1969.
> Column includes item: 'Historic core', Lincoln conservation area, no.1.

3535.
Feasibility study by the Environment Committee of the Lincoln Civic Trust for
landscaping Waterside North, Lincoln
[197?].   4 leaves, [1] folded plan.
Typescript.

3536.
The Future of Lincoln is your concern
Lincoln: Nottingham, Derby & Lincoln Society of Architects, [197?].   1 folded sheet: ill.

3537.   **LINCOLN, Department of Planning and Architecture**
*A Town scheme of grants for the repair and restoration of historic buildings in the city of
Lincoln*
Lincoln: Lincoln Corporation, 1970.   12p.: ill., map.

3538.   **LINCOLN CORPORATION**
Lincoln conservation area
Lincoln: The Corporation, 1971.   [2]p.

3539.   **LINCOLN CIVIC TRUST**
Lincoln Civic Trust in action: news sheet
No.1, July, 1972–   .
[Lincoln]: [The Trust], [1972–   ].

3540.
*The Erosion of history: archaeology and planning in towns: a study of historic towns
affected by modern development in England, Wales and Scotland*
edited by Carolyn M. Heighway.
London: Council for British Archaeology, Urban Research Committee, 1972.   vii,
126p.: maps, plans.
    Lincoln mentioned in lists of towns with Roman and Saxon remains under threat from modern
    development, but no particular detail.

3541.
The Sincil Street area: a discussion document on its future
prepared by the Lincoln Society.
[Lincoln]: The Society, 1974.   [18] leaves: ill.

3542.   **AMERY, Colin**
The Rape of Britain
Colin Amery and Dan Cruikshank.
London: Elek, 1975.   192p.: ill.
ISBN 0236309439
    pp.117–120: Lincoln, showing evidence of destruction of historic buildings. Focusses upon
    effect of proposed ring roads.

3543.
Planning problems in historic cities & towns: 7th–10th April, 1975: [conference
proceedings]
Lincoln: [Lincoln, Department of Planning and Architecture], 1975.   56p., [9]p. of plates.
ISBN 0902092049
    pp.101–114: 'Archaeology in Lincoln', by C. Colyer.

3544.   **ANDERSON, J.S.**
Lincoln's older buildings: a guide to their repair and maintenance
Lincoln: Lincoln, Department of Planning and Architecture, 1976.   20p.: ill.

3545.   BAKER, F.T.
Lincoln Civic Trust Queen's jubilee year project: the restoration of Ellis' Mill, Mill Road, Lincoln
pp.3–5: ill. in Lincoln Civic Trust *Annual report*, 1977.
> Follow-up reports: p.9, *Annual report*, 1978; and pp.8–9, *Annual report*, 1980.

3546.   LINCOLN, Department of Planning and Architecture
Conservation grants in Lincoln
Lincoln: The Department, 1979.   11p.: ill., maps.

3547.   LINCOLN CIVIC TRUST
St.Mary's Guildhall, Lincoln: restoration appeal: [leaflet]
Lincoln: The Trust, [1983].   1 folded sheet: ill.

3548.   SAYER, Michael
Conserving the great medieval towns of England.   2: Lincoln, the cliff top Cathedral city
pp.20–23, 35: ill. in *Period home*, vol.3, pt.6, April–May, 1983.

3549.   ANDERSON, John
Spirit of the place
pp.26–28: ill. in *Heritage outlook*, March–April, 1984.
> Walk round city with emphasis on conservation and town planning.

3550.   JONES, M.J.
Lincoln: archaeology and redevelopment
pp.2–9: ill. in *Popular archaeology*, vol.7, pt.1, February, 1986.

CULTURAL LIFE

3551. **LINCOLN SOCIETY OF ARTS**
Thirteenth annual report & statement of accounts, session 1962–63
Lincoln: printed Doncaster, 1963.   [6]p.

3552. **LINCOLN COUNCIL OF CULTURAL ORGANISATIONS**
Directory of members, 1964
[1964].   [11]p.
Typescript.

3553. **LINCOLN SOCIETY OF ARTS**
Fifteenth annual report & statement of accounts, season 1964–65
[Lincoln]: [The Society], [1965].   [6]p.
_____ seventeenth, 1966–67.

3554. **FOX, Clive**
Beyond local boundaries: the Lincolnshire Association for the Arts
pp.500, 502: ill. in *Country life*, March 7, 1974.
    Association often exhibits in Usher Art Gallery.

3555. **MASEFIELD, Patrick**
A Downhill struggle: an independent report on the arts in Lincoln, with proposals for their development
Lincoln: Lincolnshire County Council, 1985.   176p.: ill., maps.
Cover title.
    Paints a very gloomy picture of arts deprivation in the region, concentrating attention upon the city.   Report was commissioned by Lincoln County Council and Lincolnshire and Humberside Arts.

DRAMA

3556.
[Collection of posters and play-bills]
[1740–1840].
    Includes over 1100 items held at the Lincoln Central Library.

3557.
At the New Theatre in the King's Arms Yard, Lincoln: on Thursday, the 30th of October, 1766, will be perform'd the oratorio of Acis and Galatea: set to music by Mr Handel...
Lincoln: printed J. Rose, 1766.   14p.

3558.   **D., H.**
[Letter to Mr Urban about the list of properties for the play about Tobit performed in Lincoln in Elizabethan times]
pp.481–482 in *The Gentlemen's magazine*, vol.57, 1787.
Includes amongst many other ambitious sets 'the cyty of Jerusalem, with towers and pinnacles' and 'the cyty of Ninevah', both of which were kept in St Swithin's Church.

3559.   **ROBERTSON, Thomas**
[5 letters written to James Winston with account of the Lincoln circuit]
[Lincoln]: [s.n.], [1803–05].   [23]p.

3560.   **COOPER, Francis J.**
[Theatre Royal, Lincoln: miscellaneous notes, papers and plans contained in box file]
[S.l.]: [s.n.], [19??].   1 portfolio.
At Lincoln Central Library.

3561.   **COLEMAN, John**
Fifty years of an actor's life
London: Hutchinson, 1904.   727p., [16]p. of plates.
pp.608–617: 'At Sheffield and Lincoln'.

3562.   **BULLOCH, John Malcolm**
Dame Madge Kendal's Robertson ancestors
pp.398–400 in *Notes and queries*, December 3rd, 1932.
Continued: pp.418–420, December 10th; pp.434–437, December 17th.
Last part in particular devoted to James Shaftoe Robertson and Thomas Shaftoe Robertson.

3563.   **RADION CINEMA**
Souvenir programmme, March 27th, 1939
[Lincoln]: [The Cinema], [1939].   [9]p.

3564.   **MANDER, Raymond**
'Maria Marten': an early version
by Raymond Mander and Joe Mitchenson.
pp.38–39 in *Theatre notebook*, vol.2, no.2, January–March, 1948.
Article based on playbill of performance at Lincoln Theatre, in 1830.

3565.   **LOEWENBERG, Alfred**
The Theatre of the British Isles excluding London: a bibliography
[London]: [Society for Theatre Research], [1950].
p.42: Lincolnshire and Lincoln.

3566.   **LINCOLN THEATRE ROYAL**
Progress report, 1955–1957
[Lincoln]: [The Theatre], [1957].   [5]p.

3567.   _____
Plays and players, 1955–1958
[Lincoln]: [The Theatre], [1958].   23p.
Includes index.

3568.
The Lincoln Theatre record, 1958–1959: a souvenir booklet
[Lincoln]: [Lincoln Theatre Club], [1959].   10p., [1] leaf of plates.
Lists productions, with index of plays and players.

3569.
The Lincoln Theatre record, 1959–1960
[Lincoln]: [Lincoln Theatre Club], [1960].   17p.

3570.   **CLEMENTSON, Diana W.**
The Theatre Royal, Lincoln
74p.: ill., maps, folded plans.
Thesis [B.Ed.] – Training College, Lincoln, [1961?].

3571.   **GARDENER, Kate**
Live theatre in Lincolnshire
p.15 in *Lincolnshire life*, vol.2, no.1, spring, 1962.
    About the Lincoln Theatre Company.

3572.   **CRAIG, Hardin**
Mystery plays at Lincoln: further research needed
pp.37–41 in *The Lincolnshire historian*, vol.II, no.11, 1963.

3573.   **HILL, Roland**
Theatre in the provinces.   20: Lincoln Theatre partnership
pp.27–29: ill. in *Theatre world*, January, 1963.
    Lincoln Theatre Royal and touring company.

3574.   **LILLICRAP, C.A.**
The Repertory theatre in Lincolnshire
[4]p. in *Lincolnshire past, present and future*, 1963.

3575.   **CAMERON, Kenneth**
The N-town plays at Lincoln
by Kenneth Cameron and Stanley J. Kahrl.
8p. in *Theatre notebook*, vol.20, no.2, winter, 1965/66.

3576.   **BROWNE, E. Martin**
The Mysteries: made from the Lincoln cycle of mystery plays: [play]
Acting ed.
London: Samuel French, 1966.   49p.
    Adaptation and abridgement of the cycle of plays written about 1425, made for a production at
    Coventry Cathedral.

3577.   **JOHNSTON, Alexandra**
Medieval drama in England, 1966
[1967].   14, 99 leaves.
Typescript.
    Production of the N-cycle at Grantham with 99 leaves of text of drama.

3578.   **LINCOLN THEATRE ROYAL**
PSSSST: the magazine of the Lincoln Theatre Royal.
Vol.1, 1969–   .
[Lincoln]: [The Theatre], [1969–   ].   Various pagings.
    Issued three times a year.

3579.   **KAHRL, Stanley**
The Theatre in medieval Lincoln
pp.1–8 in *PSSSST*, vol.1, 1969.

3580.
Lincoln Theatre Company and Lincolnshire young people present Youth Project '69: the Lincoln cycle of mystery plays...Saturday, 23rd August, 1969: [programme]
[Lincoln]: [The Theatre Company], 1969.   [12]p.
> Includes notes on the production by Clare Venables and Rhys McConnochie; and 'Medieval drama in Lincoln', by Stanley J. Kahrl, a shortened version of article appearing in *PSSSST*.

3581.
The Living Cathedral: Lincoln Theatre Company's Youth Project, 1970: [programme]
Lincoln: The Theatre Company, 1970.   16p.: ill.

3582.
Lincoln theatre: report by chief executive
[1971].   pp.175–198.
Typescript.
> Records decision of Lincolnshire County Council to opt for renovation of Theatre Royal rather than the building of a new theatre at the Brayford.

3583.
New theatre project: feasibility study report: [for Lincoln Theatre Association, Ltd.]
Newbury: Maurice Hawker, [1971].   12, [15] leaves: ill., 1 map.

3584.   **LINCOLNSHIRE NEW THEATRE TRUST**
Lincolnshire New Theatre: a progress report
Lincoln: The Trust, 1971.   8 leaves, [4] leaves of plates.

3585.   ―――――――――
The Chairman's first annual report
Lincoln: The Trust, 1973.   14p.: ill.

3586.   **WARWICK, Lou**
Theatre un-royal, or 'They called them comedians': a history of the Theatre, sometime Royal, Marefair, Northampton, 1806–84 and 1887
Northampton: The Author, 1973.   279p.: ill.
> pp.25–64: the Lincoln Company.

3587.   ―――――――――
Drama that smelled, or 'Early drama in Northampton and hereabouts'
Northampton: The Author, 1975.   231p.
> pp.187–196: the Lincoln Company; Thomas Shaftoe Robertson and Robert Henry Franklin.

3588.   **HEMINGWAY, G.Y.**
The Robertson family and the Lincoln & Nottingham theatrical circuit
[1976].   [82] leaves.
Typescript.

3589.   **HARE, Arnold**
George Frederick Cooke's early years in the theatre
pp.12–21 in *Theatre notebook*, vol.31, no.1, 1977.
> Evidence from theatre playbills in Lincoln Central Library that he was appearing in the 1770s.

3590.
Lincoln cycle of mystery plays, 1981: 22nd June–4th July
p.39: ill. in *Lincolnshire life*, vol.21, no.3, June, 1981.

3591.   **MEREDITH, Peter**
Acting medieval plays
Peter Meredith, Willam Tydeman, Keith Ramsay.
Lincoln: Honywood Press, 1985.   56p.: ill.
(Lincoln Cathedral publications)
>   Pamphlet of background talks from 1981 production of Lincoln mystery cycle; pp.47–54:
>   article on Lincoln mystery plays, by Keith Ramsay, producer.

3592.
Lincoln mystery plays
pp.25–28: ill. in *Lincolnshire life*, vol.25, no.4, July, 1985.

CHORAL SOCIETIES

3593.   **LINCOLN MUSICAL SOCIETY**
Rules of the Lincoln Musical Society
Lincoln: printed E.B. Drury, [1832].   4p.

3594.   **LINCOLN CHORAL SOCIETY**
*Accounts of Lincoln Choral Society for their second year, commencing April 18th, 1835,
ending April 18th, 1836*
Lincoln: printed T.J.N. Brogden, 1836.   [3]p.

3595.
Caution
Lincoln: printed E.B. Drury, [1836].   1 sheet.
>   Concerns Lincoln Choral Society.

3596.
To the public: counter-caution
Lincoln: printed T.J.N. Brogden, [1836].   1 sheet.

3597.   **KEALEY, Joseph**
[Statement refuting handbill entitled *Counter-caution*, stating that Mr Cooper had been
appointed treasurer to the Choral Society, September 20th, 1836]
Lincoln: printed E.B. Drury, 1836.   1 sheet.

3598.   **LINCOLN CHORAL SOCIETY**
[Resolutions of a meeting of Lincoln Choral Society, September 21st, 1836]
Lincoln: printed E.B. Drury, 1836.   1 sheet.

3599.   **NORTH, William**
[Letter about the post of treasurer, September 27th, 1836]
Lincoln: printed T.J.N. Brogden, 1836.   1 sheet.

3600.   **LINCOLN CHORAL SOCIETY**
Accounts...1836–1837
Lincoln: printed T.J.N. Brogden, 1837.   1 sheet.

3601.   ──────────
*Accounts of the Lincoln Choral Society, for their third year, commencing May, 1836, and
ending May, 1837*
Lincoln: printed W. and B. Brooke, [1837].   3p.

3602.   ——————
Accounts...1837–1838
Lincoln: printed T.J.N. Brogden, 1838.   1 sheet.

3603.
[Minutes and scrapbook of newspaper cuttings, programmes, etc., copies of letters]
[1921–33].   c.100 leaves.
Ms.
   Carefully annotated, documenting the range of the Lincoln Musical Society's activities.

3604.   **LINCOLN MUSICAL SOCIETY**
[Committee register, 1930–34; minutes, 1931–34; 5 items of correspondence, 1931–35]
[1930–35].   1 vol. (loose-leaf).
Typescript; Ms.
   Includes: *Constitution and rules*, revised May 1st, 1931.

3605.
[Scrapbook of items relating to Lincoln Musical Society]
[1933].   12 leaves.

3606.   **LINCOLN MUSICAL SOCIETY**
Constitution and rules
Further revision.
[1973].   3, 7 leaves.
Typescript.

ORGANS AND ORGANISTS

3607.
Lincoln triennial festival, Thursday, June 21st: specification of the organ specially erected for the occasion by Cousans, Sons & Co., Lincoln
[Lincoln]: [Cousans], [19??].   1 sheet.

3608.
Specification of the organ built by the John Compton Organ Company, in St Swithin's Church, Lincoln
[prepared by] Rushworth & Dreaper, Ltd.
[19??].
Typescript.

3609.   **ST MARTIN'S CHURCH**
Specification of the new 3 manual organ
[Lincoln]: [The Church], [1902].   [3]p.
   Includes list of subscribers.

3610.   ——————
St Martin's new organ: [statement of account]
[Lincoln]: [The Church], 1902.   [2]p.

3611.
Description of the new organ built for St Paul's Church, Lincoln: [specifications]
[Lincoln]: [Cousans], [c.1910].   2 sheets: ill.

3612.
Description of organ erected in the Silver Street United Methodist Church, Lincoln, by Cousans, Sons & Co., Lincoln
[Lincoln]: [Cousans], [c.1911?].   1 sheet: ill.

3613.   **ELVIN, Laurence**
Wesley Chapel, Lincoln: its organs and organists
pp.80–82: ill. in *The Choir*, April, 1931.

3614.   _____
The New organ at St Giles' Church, Lincoln
pp.269–271: ill. in *The Lincolnshire magazine*, vol.3, 1936–38.

3615.   _____
The Organ at the Church of the Holy Cross, Lincoln
pp.45–46, 48 in *The Choir*, May-June, 1943.

3616.   _____
The Organ at the church of St Giles, Lincoln
pp.235–236 in *Musical opinion*, April, 1944.

3617.   _____
The Organ in Newland Congregational Church, Lincoln
pp.487, 489–490: ill. in *Musical opinion*, May, 1956.

3618.
Church of England Chapel, Lincoln Prison: specification of the organ built in 1958, by Cousans (Lincoln), Ltd.
[Lincoln]: [Cousans], [1958].   1 sheet.

3619.   **ELVIN, Laurence**
The Passing of a historic Methodist Church: its organ
pp.170–173: ill. in *The Choir*, vol.52, no.9, September, 1961.
　　Refers to Wesley Chapel.

3620.
Organ recital by Conrad Eden...Thursday, 17th October, 1963: [programme]
Lincoln: printed W.J. Harrison, [1963].   [3]p.
　　Includes specifications of the Newland Congregational Church organ.

3621.   **ELVIN, Laurence**
St Catherine's Methodist Church, Lincoln
pp.215–218: ill. in *The Choir*, vol.55, no.11, November, 1964.
　　About the organ.

3622.   _____
Organs and organ building in Lincoln and Nottingham
pp.729, 731 in *Musical opinion*, vol.87, no.1044, September, 1964.

3623.   **MONKS ROAD METHODIST CHURCH**
Dedication of organ, Saturday, October 9th, 1965
[Lincoln]: [The Church], [1965].   [3]p.
　　Includes specifications of the Monks Road Methodist Church organ.

3624.   **MARSHALL, Philip**
The Organs and organists of Lincoln Cathedral
P.M.
Lincoln: printed Keyworth & Fry, [1969].   1 sheet: ill.
　　With specifications and list of organists.

3625.   **ELVIN, Laurence**
The Very small organ
pp.95–97, 99, 101 in *Musical opinion*, [197?].
  p.99: Cousans of Lincoln.

3626.
The Organ: [of Newland Congregational Church: specifications]
Lincoln: Cousans, 1971.   [2]p.: ill.

3627.   **CRAMPTON, E.C.**
East Anglian safari
pp.24–32: ill., map in *Cinema organ*, vol.XX, no.96, December, 1972.
  pp.30–32: about organ from Ritz Cinema, then in private ownership in Spalding.

3628.   **ELVIN, Laurence**
The Restoration of a Victorian organ
pp.593, 595 in *Musical opinion*, vol.95, no.1139, August, 1972.
  Organ at Newland Congregational Church.

3629.   **CRAMPTON, E.C.**
East Anglian safari: [continued]
pp.8–11: ill. in *Cinema organ*, vol.XXI, no.97, March, 1973.
  p.8: ex-Savoy Cinema organ.

3630.   ──────────
The Melody lingers on...being a history of organs installed in Lincolnshire cinemas
pp.6–12: ill. in *Cinema organ*, vol.XXII, no.102, June, 1974.
  p.10: Lincoln.

3631.   **ELVIN, Laurence**
A Great Victorian: the 75th anniversary of Father Willis's death, 11th February, 1901
pp.293–295: ill. in *Musical opinion*, March, 1976.
  Henry Willis built the organ in Lincoln Cathedral.

3632.   ──────────
The Organists of Lincoln Cathedral, 1794–1986
Lincoln: The Author, 1986.   [14]p.: ill.
ISBN 0950004979

SUBSCRIPTION AND SOCIETY LIBRARIES

3633.
To the ladies and gentlemen of the city and neighbourhood of Lincoln: [proposal to institute a circulating library]
Lincoln: printed S. Simmons, [c.1786].   3p.

3634.
Rules of a society, recently formed in Lincoln, for promoting useful knowledge: with a catalogue of the books belonging to the society
Lincoln: printed by W. Brooke, 1812.   10p.

3635.   FALSTAFF NEWS ROOM
City of Lincoln: Falstaff News Room, established October 10th, 1829: at a meeting of the subscribers held in the News Room, on Wednesday, 1st June, 1831: [resolutions]
Lincoln: printed R.E. Leary, 1831.   4p.

3636.   CITY NEWS ROOM
[List of papers taken in the City News Room, April 9th, 1835]
Lincoln: printed W. and B. Brooke, 1835.   1 sheet.

3637.
Proprietary subscription news room and reading room, near the Guild-hall, Lincoln: [prospectus]
Lincoln: printed E.B. Drury, [1835].   1 sheet.

3638.   RAILWAY EXPRESS NEWS ROOM
Railway Express News Room, 263, High Street: [list of newspapers taken, December 24, 1846]
[Lincoln]: [s.n.], [1846].   1 sheet.

3639.   CITY NEWS ROOM
Reading for the million: 30 different newspapers taken in, at the old City News Room, 259, High Street, Lincoln
Lincoln: printed R. Bulman, [1849].   1 sheet.

3640.
Free news & reading room, Lincoln, established 1869: rules and regulations
[Lincoln]: [s.n.], [1869].   1 sheet.

3641.   CORNS, A.R.
Lincolnshire libraries and literature
pp.xli–xlv, [1]p. of plates in *Book auction records*, vol.7, 1909–10.
   Traces history of libraries, printing and booksellers catalogues in the city.

3642.   MELROSE, Elisabeth Anne
Three 18th-century Lincoln libraries
pp.40–48: ill. in *Lincolnshire history and archaeology*, vol.19, 1983.
   Covers: Lincoln Book Society; Lincoln Subscription Library; Drewry's Circulating Library.

3643.   BROOKE'S CIRCULATING LIBRARY
A Catalogue of Brooke's Circulating Library, Lincoln, comprising two thousand volumes in history, biography, voyages, travels, arts and sciences, divinity, poetry, plays and miscellaneous literature
[Lincoln]: printed W. Brooke, 1801.   122p.

3644.   DREWRY'S CIRCULATING LIBRARY
Catalogue of Joshua Drewry's Circulating Library, at his shop adjoining the Stone-bow, in the High-Street, Lincoln
[Lincoln]: [Drewry], [1794].   [32], [15]p.

3645.   LINCOLN & NOTTINGHAM ARCHITECTURAL SOCIETY
Catalogue of books in the library of the Lincoln & Nottingham Architectural Society
Lincoln: printed James Williamson, [c.1889].   8p.

3646.   LINCOLN LIBRARY
Rules and laws of the Lincoln Library, instituted January 1st, 1814
Lincoln: printed Drury, [1814].   18p.

3647. BETHAM, E.
Lincoln Library: [at the general meeting held on the 5th of January, 1820: report of the committee]
Lincoln: printed Drury, [1820]. 3p.
  Reply to anonymous statement criticizing 3 successive committees.

3648.
[List of members of new library]
[Lincoln]: [s.n.], [1822]. 1 sheet.

3649. LINCOLN LIBRARY
Rules and laws of the Lincoln Library
Lincoln: printed J.W. Drury, [1828]. 8p.

3650. ───────
Lincoln Library regulations
Lincoln: printed J.W. Drury, [c.1828]. 15p.

3651. ───────
Catalogue of the Lincoln Library with the rules and regulations, a list of the names of the proprietors and an alphabetical index to the names of the authors
Lincoln: The Library, [1834?]. 165p.
  Supplements for 1840–42 bound at back.

3652. ───────
Supplement to the catalogue of the Lincoln Library with the rules and regulations, a list of the proprietors, corrected to MDCCCXLV, and alphabetical indexes to the authors and principal subjects
Lincoln: The Library, 1845. 369p.

3653. ───────
[Notice about temporary closure for painting, July 23rd, 1850]
[Lincoln]: The Library, [1850]. 1 sheet.

3654. ───────
Catalogue of the Lincoln Library: with the rules & regulations and an alphabetical index to the names of authors
Lincoln: The Library, 1867. 128p.

3655.
We, the undersigned, request that the Worshipful the mayor will be pleased to convene a public meeting of such persons within the city, Bail and Close of Lincoln, and the vicinity, as wish to promote the establishment of a permanent Stock Library...
Lincoln: printed Drury, 1813. 1 sheet.

3656. LINCOLN STOCK LIBRARY
[List of subscribers to fund for retirement of Miss Bunch as sub-librarian]
[Lincoln]: The Library, [after 1814]. 1 sheet.

3657.
Documents extracted from the books of record and papers lying upon the table of the Stock Library, in the city of Lincoln: followed by observations partly suggested by these documents and partly derived form other sources of information
a friend to religion.
[Lincoln]: [s.n.], [1819]. 2p.

3658. LINCOLN STOCK LIBRARY
Laws for the regulation of the Lincoln Stock Library
[Lincoln]: [s.n.], [1882]. 4p.

3659.
Testimonial fund to Miss Bessie Birkett, librarian of the Stock Library: list of subscribers
and particulars of investment of fund
trustees of the testimonial fund.
[1894]. [5]p.
Ms.

3660. SYMPSON, E. Mansel
The Lincoln Stock Library
pp.97–106, [1] leaf of plates in *LN&Q*, vol.12, no.4, 1912.

3661. LINCOLN SUBSCRIPTION LIBRARY
Laws, regulations, &c., of the subscription library established at Lincoln, July, 1786,
with a list of the president, &c...and the committee for the ensuing year
Lincoln: printed S. Simmons, [1786?]. 11p.

3662. ──────────
[Prospectus]
Lincoln: printed A. Stark, [c.1814]. [2]p.

3663. LINCOLNSHIRE INCORPORATED LAW SOCIETY
Catalogue of the library of the Lincolnshire Incorporated Law Society, 1912
Lincoln: printed W.K. Morton, [1912]. 59p.
    Library situated in St.Edmund's Chambers, Silver Street.

3664. ──────────
Catalogue of the library of the Lincolnshire Incorporated Law Society, 1923
Lincoln: The Society, 1923. 72p.

3665. ──────────
Library catalogue, 1934
Lincoln: The Society, [1934]. 74p.

3666. MECHANICS' INSTITUTION LIBRARY
Catalogue of the Lincoln and Lincolnshire Mechanics' Institution Library
Lincoln: printed M. Keyworth, 1834. 34p.
    Arranged by class of book and then alphabetically.

3667. ──────────
Catalogue of the Lincoln and Lincolnshire Mechanics' Institution Library, established
October 31, 1833
Lincoln: printed W. and B. Brooke, [1838?]. 70, ivp.

3668. ──────────
Appendix to the catalogue of the Lincoln and Lincolnshire Mechanics' Institution
Library, containing the titles of books added 1839–1843
Lincoln: printed James Drury, 1843. 28, iip.
Includes index.

3669.
[Resolution to establish medical library in Lincoln, 25th June, 1825]
[Lincoln]: [s.n.], [1825]. 1 sheet.

3670.
[Resolution of meeting about formation of medical library or book society, September 17th, 1825]
[Lincoln]: [s.n.], [1825].   1 sheet.

3671.   **NEW PERMANENT LIBRARY**
Rules of the New Permanent Library established at Lincoln, May 31, 1822
Lincoln: printed W. Brooke, [1822?].   4p.

3672.   ——————
Catalogue of the New Permanent Library, established at Lincoln, May 31, 1822
Lincoln: printed W. Brooke, 1827.   16p.
Supplement: printed R.E. Leary, [c.1830].

3673.   **NEW SUBSCRIPTION LIBRARY**
Rules and catalogue of the New Subscription Library
Lincoln: printed W. Brooke, 1827.   6, 16, 2p.
Supplement: printed 1830 by Leary.

3674.   **ST MARTIN'S PAROCHIAL LENDING LIBRARY**
Rules for the regulation of St Martin's Parochial Lending Library
[Lincoln]: [s.n.], [1822].   12p.

3675.   **THOMAS COOPER MEMORIAL CHAPEL**
Catalogue of books
[Lincoln]: [The Chapel], [19??].   18p.

3676.   **LUCAS, S.T.**
The Wickham collection
[197?].   5 leaves.
Typescript.
     Concerns removal of the Wickham library from the Cathedral to the Sibthorp Library of
     Bishop Grosseteste College.

LITERARY AND PROFESSIONAL SOCIETIES

3677.
Rules and regulations for the subscription assemblies at the City Assembly Rooms, September 29, 1808
Lincoln: printed J.W. Drury, 1808.   1 sheet.

3678.
[Resolutions of a meeting about Lincoln County Assembly Rooms, July 19th, 1825]
[Lincoln]: [s.n.], [1825].   1 sheet.

3679.
Report of the proceedings at the fourth Shakespearian dinner, held at the City Arms Hotel, Lincoln, Tuesday, Nov. 2, 1835
Lincoln: Gazette Office, 1835.   16p.
Originally published: in *Lincoln gazette*.

3680.   **F.L.A.R.E.**
Newsletter
[197?].
Typescript.

3681.   ——————
[Prospectus]
Lincoln: F.L.A.R.E., [1977].   1 sheet.

3682.   ——————
Catalogue: educational materials produced by F.L.A.R.E. and the F.L.A.R.E. Education
Group
[1980].   7p.
Typescript.

3683.   **FRIENDS OF LINCOLN LIBRARIES, MUSEUM AND ART GALLERY**
[Prospectus]
[Lincoln]: [The Friends], [1971].   1 folded card: ill.

3684.   **JESSOP, Charles P.V.**
Lincoln Astronomical Society: [chronology]
[197?].   36p.
Typescript.

3685.   **LINCOLN DIOCESAN ARCHITECTURAL SOCIETY**
Thirty-fifth report
pp.lxxv–lxxvi in *AAS reports and papers*, vol.14, 1877–78.

3686.   **LINCOLN LADIES' BOOK SOCIETY**
[Rules and list of members]
Lincoln: printed W. Brooke, [184?].   1 sheet.

3687.   **LINCOLN LITERARY SOCIETY**
The Rules of the Lincoln Literary Society, established February, 1829
Lincoln: printed by W. Brooke, 1829.   8p.

3688.   **LINCOLN RECORD SOCIETY**
Annual report, 1910/11–
[Lincoln]: [The Society], [1911–   ].   Various pagings.

3689.   ——————
The Lincoln Record Society: [list of publications]
Lincoln: The Society, 1934.   [4]p.

3690.   ——————
Report for the year, 1932–33
Lincoln: The Society, 1934.   [4]p.

3691.   **LINCOLN SOCIETY OF ARTS**
Annual report
8th, 1957–58.
[Lincoln]: [The Society], [1958].

3692.   **LINCOLN YOUNG MEN'S MUTUAL IMPROVEMENT SOCIETY**
Rules of the Lincoln Young Men's Mutual Improvement Society
Lincoln: printed C. Akrill, [1850?].   [6]p.
    Established: July, 1850.

3693.   **LINCOLNSHIRE MEDICAL BENEVOLENT SOCIETY**
*Laws of the Lincolnshire Medical Benevolent Society, with a list of the officers,
benefactors and subscribers*
Lincoln: printed E.B. Drury, 1831.   16p.

3694.   **BRIGGS, Allan H.**
The Lincolnshire Medical Benevolent Society: [address delivered at the 150th anniversary
celebration dinner, Woodhall Spa, 23rd September, 1954]
Lincoln: printed J.W. Ruddock, [1954].   16p.
    Includes account of the treatment of a Mr Headley at the Lawn.   Dr. Charlesworth was
    treasurer of the Society for 19 years.

3695.   **LINCOLNSHIRE SOCIETY FOR THE ENCOURAGEMENT OF
ECCLESIASTICAL ARCHITECTURE**
*Lincolnshire Society for the Encouragement of Ecclesiastical Architecture: 2nd report,
1845–1849*
[Lincoln]: [The Society], [1849].

3696.   **HILL, J.W.F.**
Early days of a society
pp.57–63 in *Lincolnshire history and archaeology*, no.1, 1966.
    History of Lincoln Society for the Encouragement of Ecclesiastical Antiquities, which became
    the Lincoln Diocesan Architectural Society and subsequently the Architectural Society for the
    Counties of Lincoln and Nottingham.

3697.   **LINCOLNSHIRE TOPOGRAPHICAL SOCIETY**
Rules of the Lincolnshire Topographical Society
Lincoln: printed W. and B. Brooke, 1841.   10p.

3698.   ————————
First report of the Lincolnshire Topographical Society, with a list of members
Lincoln: printed W. and B. Brooke, 1841.   12p.

3699.
Procedure adopted for the Lindum Parliament
Lincoln: printed Akrill, Ruddock & Keyworth, [19??].   9p.
    Debating society which met in the Church Institute once a fortnight.

3700.   **LOCAL HISTORY SOCIETY**
Annual report, 1949/50–
[Lincoln?]: [The Society], [1950–   ].   Various pagings.
    Since 1965/66 incorporating the Lincolnshire Architectural and Archaeological Society.

3701.   **BECKWITH, Ian**
The Lincolnshire Local History Society
by Ian Beckwith and David Robinson.
p.22 in *Lincolnshire life*, vol.8, no.5, July, 1968.

3702.   **LONDON LINCOLNSHIRE SOCIETY**
Annual report
16th, 1900–01
[London?]: [The Society], [1901].
————————   18th, 1902.

3703.
[Letter to the mayor about the establishment of a Mechanics' Institution, October 29,
1833]
Lincoln: printed W. Brooke, 1833.   1 sheet.

3704.
[Resolutions of a meeting to establish a Mechanics' Institution in Lincoln, 31st October, 1833]
Lincoln: printed E.B. Drury, 1833.   1 sheet.

3705.   **MECHANICS' INSTITUTION**
[Notice of public meeting, December 14th, 1833]
Lincoln: printed Keyworth, 1833.   1 sheet.

3706.
[Lincoln & Lincolnshire Mechanics' Institution: election of the committee]
Lincoln: printed E.B. Drury, [after 1833].   3p.

3707.   **MECHANICS' INSTITUTION**
Origin and rules of the Lincoln and Lincolnshire Mechanics' Institution
Lincoln: printed J.W. Drury, [1833].   50p.

3708.   ─────────
Proceedings at the first lecture to the Lincoln and Lincolnshire Mechanics' Institution, on Tuesday, April 22nd, 1834
Lincoln: printed Brooke, [1834].   4p.

3709.   ─────────
[Notice of conversation meeting, October 30th, 1834]
[Lincoln]: [s.n.], [1834].   1 sheet.

3710.   ─────────
Syllabus of a course of lectures on anatomy
Lincoln: printed W. and B. Brooke, 1834.   1 sheet.

3711.   ─────────
[Notice of conversation meeting, January 23, 1835]
Lincoln: printed E.B. Drury, 1835.   1 sheet.

3712.   ─────────
[Notice of meeting, November 20th, 1835]
Lincoln: printed E.B. Drury, 1835.   1 sheet.

3713.   ─────────
Abstract of accounts, November 1, 1836 to October 31, 1837
Lincoln: printed T.O. Brumby, 1837.   1 sheet.

3714.   ─────────
[List of names for election of annual and quarterly members]
Lincoln: printed E.B. Drury, [1837?].   [4]p.

3715.   ─────────
Report...1837
Lincoln: printed T.O. Brumby, 1837.

3716.   ─────────
The Seventh anniversary of the Lincoln Mechanics' Institution [and] abstract of accounts, Nov. 1st, 1838 to October 31st, 1839
Lincoln: printed at the Lincoln Gazette, 1839.   1 sheet.

3717. ———————
Seventh annual meeting, Thursday, December 3rd, 1840
Lincoln: [s.n.], [1840].   1 sheet.
Originally published: in *Lincoln gazette.*

3718. ———————
[Notice of lectures]
Lincoln: printed W. and B. Brooke, 1840.   1 sheet.

3719. ———————
[List of names for election of committee]
Lincoln: printed T.O. Brumby, 1841.   1 sheet.

3720. ———————
Eighth anniversary of the Lincoln & Lincolnshire Mechanics' Institution
Lincoln: printed W. and B. Brooke, [1841].   4p.

3721. ———————
[Notice of lectures, March 17th, 1842]
Lincoln: printed W. and B. Brooke, 1842.   1 sheet.

3722. ———————
[Notice of lectures, June 3rd, 1842]
Lincoln: printed W. and B. Brooke, 1842.   1 sheet.

3723. ———————
[Notice of lectures, June, 1842]
Lincoln: printed James Drury, 1842.   1 sheet.

3724. ———————
[Notice of lectures, November, 1842]
Lincoln: printed W. and B. Brooke, 1842.   1 sheet.

3725. ———————
[List of names for election of committee]
Lincoln: printed C. Keyworth, 1842.   1 sheet.

3726. ———————
Origin and rules of the Lincoln and Lincolnshire Mechanics' Institution
Lincoln: printed J.W. Drury, [1843?].   pp.35–50.

3727. ———————
[List of names for election of committee]
Lincoln: printed T.O. Brumby, 1844.   1 sheet.

3728. ———————
[List of names for election of committee]
Lincoln: printed E. Keyworth, 1845.   1 sheet.

3729. ———————
[Notice of lecture, October 27th, 1847]
Lincoln: printed W. Bellatti, 1847.   1 sheet.

3730. ———————
[Notice about special meeting, November 2nd, 1848]
Lincoln: printed James Drury, 1848.   1 sheet.

3731. —————————
Fifteenth anniversary of the Lincoln & Lincolnshire Mechanics' Institution, 1848:
[annual report]
[Lincoln]: The Institution, 1848.   4p.
————————   16th, 1849.
————————   17th, 1850.

3732. —————————
[Notice of lecture, February, 1849]
Lincoln: printed J. Stainton, 1849.   1 sheet.

3733. —————————
[Notice of annual soiree, April 10th, 1849]
Lincoln: printed W. and B. Brooke, 1849.   1 sheet.

3734. —————————
[Notice of meeting, September 7th, 1849]
Lincoln: printed R. Bulman, 1849.   1 sheet.

3735. —————————
[Notice of lectures, January, 1850]
Lincoln: printed W. Doncaster, 1850.   1 sheet.

3736. —————————
[Plan for new building and letter from president]
[Lincoln]: The Institution, [1861].   [4]p., plan.

3737.
[Notice of meeting to discuss establishment of a Mendicity Society, December 2nd, 1831]
Lincoln: printed J.W. Drury, 1831.   1 sheet.

3738.   **P & C CLUB**
The P & C Club, Lincoln: minute book
[1923].   2 vols.
Ms.

3739.
[Notice of meeting to discuss formation of a Philosophical and Scientific Institution,
January 13th, 1841]
[Lincoln]: [s.n.], [1841].   1 sheet.

3740.   **BARNES, Patricia M.**
The Pipe Roll Society and the Lincoln Record Society: an association of mutual benefit:
[paper read at annual general meeting of L.R.S., 1983]
pp.37–39 in *Lincolnshire history and archaeology*, vol.19, 1984.
      Mentions C.W. Foster, Frank and Doris Stenton.

3741.   **SOCIETY FOR LINCOLNSHIRE HISTORY AND ARCHAEOLOGY**
Newsletter, 1974–
[Lincoln]: [The Society], [1974–   ].   Various pagings.

3742.
[Letter to mayor requesting meeting to discuss establishment of benefit societies, June 1, 1805]
Lincoln: printed J.W. Drury, 1805.   1 sheet.

3743.
[Resolutions of meetings to discuss establishment of benefit societies or clubs, June 7th, 1805]
Lincoln: printed J.W. Drury, 1805.   1 sheet.

3744.   SOCIETY FOR THE ENCOURAGEMENT OF BENEFIT SOCIETIES
Rules: [July 18, 1805]
Lincoln: printed J.W. Drury, 1805.   1 sheet

3745.
Rules to be observed and kept by all and every one of the members of a Friendly Society, instituted by a number of honorary members and a committee of the Society for Encouraging Benefit Clubs in Lincoln...and to be held at the...sign of the Black-Bull..
Lincoln: printed J.W. Drury, [1806].   1 sheet.

3746.   LINCOLN FEMALE FRIENDLY SOCIETY
Rules of the Lincoln Female Friendly Society: proposed and unanimously adopted at a special general meeting held February 3, 1817
Lincoln: printed W. Brooke, 1817.   22p.

3747.   FRIENDLY UNION SOCIETY
Rules to be observed, performed and kept, by all and every the members of the Friendly Union Society, held at the house of Mr William Taylor, the sign of the Black Horse, in the Close of Lincoln, which commenced the seventh day of December, in the year of our Lord one thousand eight hundred and sixteen
Lincoln: printed by J. Hall, [1817].   13p.

3748.   BENEVOLENT SOCIETY
Benevolent Society, Lincoln, instituted in the year 1803: a sermon will be preached at the Methodist Chapel, Lincoln, on Sunday, the 4th of January, 1818...
Lincoln: printed Brooke, [1818].   3p.
    Leaflet publicizing sermon in aid of the Society giving aims and soliciting patronage.

3749.
The Tradesman's Union Society, for sick, lame and infirm members, to be held at the house of Luke Wood, the Marquis of Granby, in the city of Lincoln
Lincoln: printed W. Brooke, 1824.   19p.
Includes index.

3750.   LINCOLN GUARDIAN SOCIETY
The Lincoln Guardian Society, for the protection of trade: [rules]
Lincoln: printed E.B. Drury, 1827.   16p.

3751.
Lincoln: [address to draw the attention of the educated and opulent classes in Lincoln and its neighbourhood to this important and interesting subject]
Lincoln: printed W. Brooke, [1828].   4p.
    Calls for establishment of a Friendly Society in Lincoln.

3752.   **LINCOLN GENERAL FRIENDLY INSTITUTION**
Rules and assurance tables of the Lincoln General Friendly Institution
Lincoln: printed W. Brooke, 1829.   32p.

3753.   —————
Advantages of the Lincoln General Friendly Institution
Lincoln: printed J. Stainton, [183?].   4p.

3754.   —————
[Accounts]
Lincoln: W. Brooke, [1830].   4p.

3755.   **GOOD NAZARENE FRIENDLY SOCIETY**
*Rules of the Good Nazarene Friendly Society, held at the...Crown Inn, in Butchery-Street,
in the city of Lincoln, established January 3, 1766, altered and amended at a general
meeting...31st May, 1830, according to the statute of 10 Geo.IV, cap.56*
Lincoln: printed W. Brooke, 1830.   20p.
Includes index.

2756.   **SOCIETY OF SOCIAL FRIENDS**
*Society of Social Friends, held at the Black Horse, Lincoln, in a commodious room, stiled
the cabin of comfort: rules and regulations*
Lincoln: printed Keyworth, [1830?].   1 sheet.

3757.   **BROMHEAD, Edward ffrench**
*Instructions for establishing friendly institutions upon the improved principle, and in
conformity with the Act: with the prospectus, proceedings, application to the barrister,
enrolment, tables, forms, book-keeping, the Lincoln rules...*
4th ed.
London: W. Simpkin and R. Marshall, 1831.   43p.: ill.

3758.   **LINCOLN PRINTERS' AND BOOKBINDERS' SOCIETY**
Rules and regulations of the Lincoln Printers' and Bookbinders' Society
Lincoln: printed E.B. Drury, 1831.   7p.

3759.   **LINCOLN GENERAL FRIENDLY INSTITUTION**
[Anniversary programme]
Lincoln: printed E.B. Drury, 1832.   1 sheet.
—————   1833.

3760.   **BOND OF UNITY FRIENDLY SOCIETY**
*Rules of the Bond of Unity Friendly Society, held at the house known by the sign of the
Green Dragon Inn, Water-side in the city of Lincoln*
Lincoln: printed M. Keyworth, 1832.   16p.

3761.   **LINCOLN GENERAL FRIENDLY INSTITUTION**
Abstract of the accounts of the Lincoln General Friendly Institution: [1833/34–1839/40]
[Lincoln]: [The Institution], [1833–40].
—————   1843/44–1844/45.

3762.   **LINCOLN CONSERVATIVE AND GUARDIAN SOCIETY**
[Notice of meeting, 10th July, 1835]
Lincoln: printed T.J.N. Brogden, 1835.   1 sheet.

3763.   —————
Declaration of the principles and rules of the Lincoln Conservative and Guardian Society
Lincoln: printed T.J.N. Brogden, 1835.   8p.

3764.
To Mr W.S. Northhouse
a member of the Lincoln Conservative and Guardian Society.
Lincoln: T.J.N. Brogden, 1835. 4p.
Retaliation following attack on the Society made by Northhouse in the paper.

3765. **LINCOLN FEMALE FRIENDLY SOCIETY**
Abstract of the accounts of the Lincoln Female Friendly Society from June 8th, 1835 to May 23rd, 1836
Lincoln: printed W. and B. Brooke, 1836. 1 sheet.
_____ 4th June, 1838 to 20th May, 1839.
_____ 27th May, 1844 to 12th May, 1845.

3766. **INDEPENDENT ORDER OF ODD FELLOWS OF THE MANCHESTER UNITY FRIENDLY SOCIETY, Lincoln District**
Laws & regulations of the Lincoln District of the Independent Order of Odd Fellows of the Manchester Unity, instituted at Lincoln, May 16th, 1836
Lincoln: printed P.G. Leary, [1845]. 26p.

3767. **BENEVOLENT SOCIETY**
[Notice of sermons and list of subscriptions, December, 1837]
Lincoln: printed T.O. Brumby, 1837. 1 sheet.

3768. **INDEPENDENT ORDER OF ODD FELLOWS OF THE MANCHESTER UNITY FRIENDLY SOCIETY, Lincoln District**
Laws of the widows' and orphans' fund of the Lincoln District, Manchester Unity, of the Independent Order of Odd Fellows, July, 1839
Lincoln: printed J. Stainton, 1840. 7p.

3769. **DANBY, John William**
Articles of agreement and rules and regulations of the Lincoln Horse Association
Lincoln: printed W. and B. Brooke, 1842. 13p.

3770. **LINCOLN GLEE CLUB**
Rules and regulations of the Lincoln Glee Club, held at the County Assembly Rooms
Lincoln: printed W. and B. Brooke, 1842. 8p.

3771. _____
[Open letter about dining at County Assembly Rooms, Wed., 3rd May, 1843]
[Lincoln]: [The Club], [1843]. 1 sheet.

3772. **ANCIENT FORESTERS OF COURT NEWPORT, NO.1313**
Rules and regulations of the Ancient Foresters of Court Newport, no.1313, held at the Ivy Tavern, Lincoln
Lincoln: printed T.J.N. Brogden, 1844. 17p.

3773.
[Letter under auspices of the Independent Order of Odd Fellows of the Manchester Unity warning members against a letter signed 'A brother of both the orders', October 9th, 1847]
Lincoln: printed R.E. Leary, 1847. 1 sheet.

3774. **LINCOLN BENEFIT BUILDING SOCIETY**
Rules of the Lincoln Benefit Building Society
Lincoln: printed by W. Bellatti, [1847]. 19, [5]p.

3775.   LINCOLN TOTAL ABSTINENCE SOCIETY
[Notice of lectures]
Lincoln: printed R. Bulman, 1849.   1 sheet.

3776.   LINCOLN HORTICULTURAL SOCIETY
Formation of the Lincoln Horticultural Society
Lincoln: printed W. Bellatti, [1850].   8p.

3777.   LINCOLN TEMPERANCE SOCIETY
Annual report of the Lincoln Temperance Society
Lincoln: printed by C. Akrill, [1857].   8p.

3778.   STURDY, William
Buds of the mind: [verse]
Lincoln: printed J.E. Brogden, 1859.   59p.
       pp.18–19: poem, entitled 'Lincoln Benevolent Society'.

3779.   INDEPENDENT ORDER OF ODD FELLOWS OF THE MANCHESTER UNITY FRIENDLY SOCIETY, Lincoln District
Manchester Unity, Independent Order of Odd Fellows: [programme of events in celebration of the anniversaries of the various lodges in Lincoln of Odd Fellows]
Lincoln: printed Charles Keyworth, 1862.   1 sheet.

3780.   LINCOLN CLUB
Rules of the Lincoln Club
Lincoln: printed Edward R. Cousans, 1862.   8p.

3781.   FARMERS' GLORY LODGE
Rules for the government of the Farmers' Glory Lodge, of the Lincoln District of the Independent Order of Odd Fellows of the Manchester Unity Friendly Society
Lincoln: printed C. Keyworth, 1865.   10p.

3782.   INDEPENDENT ORDER OF ODD FELLOWS OF THE MANCHESTER UNITY FRIENDLY SOCIETY, Lincoln District
Laws & regulation of the Lincoln District of the Independent Order of Odd Fellows of the Manchester Unity
Lincoln: printed Charles Keyworth, 1869.   26p.

3783.   LINCOLNSHIRE AUTOMOBILE CLUB
Rules, list of members and diary
[Lincoln?]: [The Club], [19??].   Various pagings.
Issued annually.
       HQ at Saracen's Head, Lincoln.

3784.   LINCOLN & LINCOLNSHIRE CANINE SOCIETY
First great dog show, Saturday, March 10th, 1906, in the Corn Exchange, Lincoln: [programme]
Lincoln: printed Critch, 1906.   16p.: ill.

3785.   LINCOLN CITIZENS' LEAGUE
Lincoln Citizens' League: general meeting, Albion Hotel, Friday, 17th October, 1924
Lincoln: printed J.W. Ruddock, [1924].   15p.

3786.   LINCOLN ENGINEERING SOCIETY
Annual report and proceedings for 1933
[Lincoln]: [The Society], [1933].   98, [20]p.

3787. **LINCOLN & DISTRICT MASTER BUILDERS' ASSOCIATION**
Rules of Association
Lincoln: printed Lincolnshire Chronicle, [194?].   50p.

3788. **KIRKE WHITE BOYS' CLUB**
1899–1949: golden jubilee, 20th–26th November, 1949
[Lincoln]: [The Club], 1949.   15p.: ill.

3789. **LINCOLN AND DISTRICT Y.M.C.A.**
New building scheme: appeal target 15,000
Lincoln: Appeal Committee of the Lincoln Y.M.C.A, [1967].   [7]p.: ill., plans.

3790.
19th Lincoln (Bracebridge) Scout Group: official opening of the Group headquarters,
Manby Street, Saturday, 9th May, 1970...
[1970].   [11]p.
Typescript.

3791. **LINCOLNSHIRE VINTAGE VEHICLE SOCIETY**
Progress fron Lincoln
[1971].   13 leaves, plan.
Typescript.

3792.
Organisations in Lincoln, 1973: a list of clubs, societies, trade, community & religious
organisations in the Lincoln area
compiled by the staff of the Central Reference Library, Lincoln.
Lincoln: Lincolnshire Library Service, 1973.

3793. **LINCOLN MODEL RAILWAY AND WARGAMING SOCIETY**
Prospectus
Lincoln: The Society, 1973.   [2]p.

3794. **LINCOLN LIBERAL CLUB**
Lincoln Liberal Club centenary, 1874–1974
[Lincoln]: [The Club], [1974].   46p.: ill.
  Notes on history by F.T. Baker.

3795.
Old Contemptibles Association, Lincoln Branch, jubilee year, 1914–1974
[1974].   28p.
Typescript.

3796. **LINCOLN SOCIETY OF MAGICIANS**
Jubilee magic presented by Lincoln Society of Magicians: [programme]
[1977].   [4]p.
Typescript.

3797. **LINCOLN AND DISTRICT Y.M.C.A.**
Annual report: [110th, 1978–79; 111th, 1979–80]
[Lincoln]: [Lincoln Y.M.C.A.], [1979–80].   2 vols.

3798. **LINCOLN LIBERAL CLUB**
Report of the directors, for the year ended 31st December, 1979, and balance sheet &
accounts
[Lincoln]: [The Club], [1979].   [4]p.: ill.

3799.   BIRCHWOOD COMMUNITY ASSOCIATION
Constitution
[1980].   2 sheets.
Typescript.

3800.   LINCOLN AND DISTRICT Y.M.C.A.
New direction: 113th annual report of Lincoln Young Men's Christian Association
[Lincoln]: [Lincoln Y.M.C.A.], [1982].

3801.   BAKER, F.T.
Rotary Club of Lincoln diamond jubilee, 1922–1982
Lincoln: Lincoln Rotary Club, 1982.   18p.

FREEMASONRY

3802.   CHAPTER OF CONCORD
Itnotgaotu: bye-laws of the Chapter of Concord, Royal Arch Masons, no.374, Lincoln
[Lincoln]: The Lodge, [18??].   1 sheet.

3803.   PROVINCIAL GRAND LODGE
The Order of procession of the Provincial Grand Lodge of Free Masons for the county of Lincoln, held at the lodge-rooms in the city of Lincoln, April 21, 1820: [with hymns sung]
Lincoln: printed W. Brooke, 1820.   [2]p.

3804.   WITHAM LODGE, No.374
Witham Lodge, no.374, of freemasons: [notices of meetings, January 15th, 1848 and January 20th, 1849]
[Lincoln]: [The Lodge], [1849].

3805.   OLIVER, G.
An Account of the centenary of the Witham Lodge, no.374, holden in the city of Lincoln, June 9th, 1842...including a narrative of the circumstances attending the author's removal from the deputy grand mastership of the province
London: R. Spencer, 1862.   68p.

3806.   DIXON, William
A History of freemasonry in Lincolnshire: being a record of all extinct and existing lodges, chapters, &c: century of the working of Provincial Grand Lodge and the Witham Lodge, together with biographical notices of provincial grand masters...
Lincoln: James Williamson, 1894.   xv, 365p.
Includes index.

SPORT

3807.
The City Sports Centre: [prospectus]
[Lincoln]: [Lincoln Corporation], 1973.   1 folded sheet: ill., plan.

3808.
Jeux sans frontieres, Lincoln, England, 23 August, 1978: [programme]
Lincoln: printed J.W. Ruddock, 1978.   31p.: ill., [1]p. of plans.

3809.   DRURY, Ray
Lincoln Flying Imps
pp.38–39: ill. in *Lincolnshire life*, vol.17, no.7, October, 1977.
About Lincoln Aeromodellers Club .

3810.   LINCOLN AND DISTRICT ANGLING ASSOCIATION
Lincoln and District Angling Association: year 1975
Lincoln: The Association, 1975.   60p., plans.

3811.   LINCOLN BOAT CLUB
The Charter
[Lincoln]: The Club, [1968].
Includes brief historical notes on history of Club.

3812.
Lincoln Canoe Club
[1972].   1 sheet.
Typescript.

3813.   HAIGH, Melvyn
Lincoln Canoe Club: twenty five years, 1957–82
compiled by Melvyn Haigh, Tony Lund, Laurence Oliver.
Lincoln: The Club, 1982.   68p.: ill.

3814.
Lincoln and what happened there
pp.971–979 in *The Caravan*, vol.18, no.7, July, 1950.
Rally of Caravan Club held on West Common.

3815.
Lincoln was the largest rally ever
pp.959–966: ill. in *The Caravan*, vol.18, no.7, July, 1950.

3816.
[Cricket in Lincoln and surrounding area, 1853–c.1880: newspaper cuttings]
[1853–1880].   1 scrapbook and 1 envelope of cuttings.
Typescript.

3817.   LINCOLN CRICKET AND FOOTBALL CLUB
Athletic sports: [programme]
[Lincoln]: [The Club], [1883].   [8]p.

3818.   LINCOLN AND DISTRICT AMATEUR CRICKET ASSOCIATION
Official handbook: [seasons 1910–13]
Lincoln: Gazette and Echo, 1910–13.   Various pagings.
Rules and list of fixtures.

3819.
Cricket scoring book: [matches between Ruston's and opponents, 1914–29, recorded in
Lincolnshire echo, the 'favourite' cricket scoring book]
[1914–29].   [58]p.
Ms.

3820.   ST GEORGE'S HOSPITAL CRICKET CLUB
25 years, 1959–84, silver jubilee
Lincoln: The Club, [1984].   [16]p.: ill.

3821.   VELO CLUB, LINCOLN
The Lincoln grand prix and the West Common junior race, Sunday, 21 May, 1978:
[programme]
[Lincoln]: [The Club], [1978].   [12]p., maps.

3822.   ——————
West Common junior road race, Sunday, May 20th, 1979
[Lincoln]: [The Club], [1979].   [13]p.: ill., map.

3823.
Study of disused railways in England and Wales: potential cycle routes: Lincoln lines: a study for the Department of Transport
John Grimshaw and Associates.
London: The Department, 1982.   36p.: ill., maps.
(Annex, no.22)

3824.   LINCOLN CITY FOOTBALL CLUB
Report of the proceedings at the fifth annual general meeting of the members of the Lincoln Football Club
[Lincoln]: [The Club], [1866].   1 sheet.

3825.   GROSSE, G. Harold
Lincoln City Football Club, 1884–1933
pp.299–301: ill. in *The Lincolnshire magazine*, vol.1, 1932–34.

3826.   DIX, Benny
Cock o' the North: an account of Lincoln City F.C.'s career in the northern section
Lincoln: printed Hedley Slack, [1933].
    Northern section began in 1921.

3827.   SAWYER, John J.
Down the years with Lincoln City
Lincoln: [The Author], [1954].   52p.
    History of the Imps, 1883–1953.

3828.
*The Red Imps, 1975/76 : **Lincolnshire chronicle**: a soccer special*: [15th August, 1975]
Lincoln: Lincolnshire Chronicle, 1975.   12p.: ill.

3829.
Into the third with the Imps: [LSG supplement, August, 1976]
Lincoln: LSG, 1976.   20p.: ill.

3830.   LINCOLN CITY FOOTBALL CLUB
Lincoln City Football Club promotion book
[Lincoln]: [The Club], [1976].   [28]p.: ill.

3831.   ——————
Official year book, 1975/76
[Lincoln]: [The Club], [1976].   [30]p.: ill.
    Includes section on Smith-Clayton Forge, Ltd., sponsors.

3832.
Kick-off: [LSG supplement]
Lincoln: LSG, 1977.

3833.   **NANNESTAD, Ian**
The Changing patterns of leisure in Lincoln, 1860–1900, with particular reference to the growth of football
48 leaves.
Typescript.
Thesis [B.A. Hons.] – University of Birmingham, 1977.

3834.
Lincoln City F.C.: an LSG supplement
Lincoln: LSG, 1978.   16p.: ill.

3835.
Kick off: [LSG supplement]
Lincoln: LSG, 1979.   16p.: ill.

3836.   **LINCOLN CITY FOOTBALL CLUB**
Official fixture list, 1980/81
[Lincoln]: The Club, [1980].   [14]p.

3837.   **LAMMING, Douglas**
The Imps of 1931–32
pp.24–25: ill. in *Lincolnshire life*, vol.23, no.1, April, 1983.
   Covers time when the Imps won Football League Division 3 (North) Championship.

3838.   **LINCOLN CITY FOOTBALL CLUB**
Centenary souvenir: centenary year, 1883–1983
Lincoln: The Club and LSG, 1983.   51p.: ill.

3839.
Bygones: soccer in Lincolnshire: [*Lincolnshire echo* special edition]
Lincoln: Lincolnshire Echo, 1986.   28p.: ill.

3840.   **MOULSON, Con**
The History of the Southcliffe and Canwick Golf Club, Ltd.
[19??].   33 leaves.
Typescript.

3841.
Show of fox-hounds at Lincoln
pp.125–126: ill. in *The Illustrated London news*, no.1551, vol.LV, August 7, 1869.

3842.
Account of the formation of the Skellingthorpe decoy
[1880].   3 leaves.
Ms.

3843.   **PADLEY, J.S.**
Plan and survey of Lincoln race course, including the rise and falls...
[Lincoln]: [Lincoln Corporation], [18??].   1 sheet of plans.

3844.
Lincoln races, 1805: [programme]
Lincoln: printed J.W. Drury, 1805.   1 sheet.

3845.
Lincoln West-Common, 1805: [notice that those driving carriages over seeded part of race course will be prosecuted]
[Lincoln]: [s.n.], [1805].   1 sheet.

3846.
Lincoln West Common: [notice about prosecution of those damaging race course, August 20, 1805]
Lincoln: printed J.W. Drury, 1805.   1 sheet.

3847.
Lincoln races, 1820: [programme]
Lincoln: printed Drury, 1820.   1 sheet.

3848.
Lincoln races, 1824: second day
[Lincoln]: [Clerk of the Course], [1824].   1 sheet.
  About Witham Sweepstake.

3849.
Lincoln race course: [explanation of proposals to erect permanent grand-stand, February 28th, 1825]
Lincoln: printed W. Brooke, 1825.   1 sheet.

3850.
A Correct account of the dreadful riot which took place on Lincoln Race Course in the afternoon and evening of Friday, September 30th, 1831, with other matters connected therewith
Lincoln: printed R.E. Leary, 1831.   1 sheet.

3851.
Lincoln races, 1840: [programme, September 23rd]
Lincoln: printed W. and B. Brooke, 1840.   1 sheet.

3852.
Lincoln races, 1849: [programme, March 7th]
Lincoln: printed W. and B. Brooke, 1849.   1 sheet.

3853.
Lincoln races, 1849: [programme, August 9th]
Lincoln: printed W. and B. Brooke, 1849.   1 sheet.

3854.
Lincoln articles prior to meeting 13th, 15th, 16th March, 1948, and Lincoln summer meetings 21st & 22nd July, 1948: [scrapbook of newspaper cuttings relating to horse racing at Lincoln]
[1948].   43p.: ill.
Typescript.

3855.
Lincoln races: [official race card for the spring meeting, March 19th, 1949]
Lincoln: Clerk of the Course for Lincoln Corporation, 1949.   18p.: ill.

3856.
Lincolnshire Handicap centenary, 1849–1949: with an historical survey of Lincoln races for the past 352 years
edited by George Bonney.
Lincoln: Lincoln, Races Committee, [1949].   [15]p.: ill.

3857.
Carholme chronicle: specially published by the Lincolnshire chronicle for the 'Save the Races' campaign: Lincolnshire Handicap meeting, March 16–18, 1964
Lincoln: Lincolnshire Chronicle, 1964. 4p.: ill.

3858.
Lincoln races, spring meeting, Tuesday, March 16th, 1964: official race card
Lincoln: Clerk of the Course for the Lincoln Corporation, 1964.   16p.
_____   March 17th,   13p.
_____   March 18th,   13p.

3859.
Some notes on the history of Lincoln races
[1964].   [4]p.: ill.
Typescript.
Originally published: in *The Fireside magazine.*

3860.   **FISK, Roy**
Abe and the Lincolnshire Handicap
pp.36–37: ill. in *Lincolnshire life,* vol.20, no.12, March, 1981.

3861.
Proposed public covered baths: notice of poll of citizens
Lincoln: Lincoln Corporation, [1896].   1 sheet.

3862.   **SWALLOW, S.C.**
The Lincoln amateur swimming club, 1901–1977
Lincoln: [The Author], 1978.   48p.

3863.   _____
A History of swimming in Lincoln
[1984].   262, [21]p.: ill.
Typescript.

3864.
Lincoln Vulcan Swimming Club history: past, present and future
[1986].   [8]p.
Typescript.

3865.   **LINCOLN AND DISTRICT TABLE TENNIS LEAGUE**
Handbook for season, 1975–1976
[Lincoln]: [The League], [1975].   30p.

3866.   _____
Handbook for season, 1979–1980
Lincoln: printed Herbert Lill, [1979].   30p.

3867.
Hoyle's twenty-four rules for whist in verse...with Bob Short's abridgement of Hoyles's Game of whist: and laws of the game
by a Lincoln amateur.
Lincoln: printed W. Brooke, 1830.   16p.

RESTAURANTS AND INNS

3868.   **EXLEY, C.L.**
List of Lincoln inns
[19??].   22p.
Typescript.
Spine title.
> Gives name, address and landlord.

3869.   **APPLEYARD, Simon**
'Life' looks at 2 Lincolnshire hotels: The Eastgate, Lincoln; The Kingsway, Cleethorpes
pp.22–27: ill. in *Lincolnshire life*, vol.5, no.3, June–July, 1965.

3870.   **STEPHENSON, Amanda**
'Life' visits The Chalet at Lincoln
pp.24–25, 28: ill. in *Lincolnshire life*, vol.5, no.5, November–December, 1965.

3871.   **TRUST HOUSE HOTELS**
£30,000 hotel in precincts of Lincoln Cathedral opens 4th May, 1965: [press release about Eastgate Hotel]
[1965].   [7] leaves.
Typescript.

3872.   **FAULDS, Ian**
Lincolnshire inns revisited.   No.2: The Green Dragon at Lincoln
pp.50–51 in *Lincolnshire life*, vol.12, no.11, January, 1973.

3873.   **JARVIS, A. Clifford**
Old Lincolnshire inns: The White Hart, Lincoln
pp.40–43: ill. in *Lincolnshire life,* vol.14, no.7, September, 1974.

3874.   **KENT, Elizabeth**
Country cuisine
London: Sidgwick and Jackson, 1980.
> Mentions White's Restaurant in Lincoln.

3875.   **CHARTRES, John**
Lincoln's inns
pp.16–19: ill. in *The Historian*, no.1, autumn, 1983.
> Luttrell psalter contains an illustration of Constantinople.   Article argues that the picture is based on city of Lincoln and suggests that the city's inns are denoted by barley sheaves and ale bush shown around church.

ECCLESIASTICAL

3876.
Declaration of the laity of the Church of England, city, Bail and Close of Lincoln and the neighbourhood, to the Worshipful the mayor of the city of Lincoln, February 19th, 1834
Lincoln: printed J.W. Drury, 1834.   1 sheet.

3877.   PARKER, John Henry
An Introduction to the study of Gothic architecture
Oxford; London: The Author, 1849.   240p.: ill.
    pp.33–34: early Norman churches at Lincoln, especially St Peter-at-Gowts.

3878.   MADDISON, A.R.
The Transcripts in the Bishop of Lincoln's Registry
pp.159–166 in *AAS reports and papers*, vol.XVI, pt.II, 1882.
    Argument for having parish registers transcribed and sent to London rather than sending the originals.   Author describes personal experience of studying Mss. and restoring them.

3879.   VENABLES, Edmund
Bishop Antony Beekes' register of the Prebendaries of Lincoln, 1333 and 1334
pp.469–475 in *The Archaeological journal*, vol.XLII, [1885?].

3880.
Lincoln episcopal records in the time of Thomas Cooper, S.T.P., Bishop of Lincoln, A.D. 1571 to A.D. 1584
edited by C.W. Foster.
Lincoln: Lincoln Record Society, 1912.   xxiv, 447p., [frontis].
(Lincoln Record Society, 2)
Includes index.
    Includes references to Lincoln.

3881.
Rotuli Hugonis de Welles, Episcopi Lincolniensis, A.D. MCCIX–MCCXXXV
edited by W.P.W. Phillimore.
Lincoln: Lincoln Record Society, 1912.   xxvii, 304p.
(Lincoln Record Society, 3)
Includes index.   Text in Latin.
    Includes many references to Lincoln.

3882.
Rotuli Hugonis de Welles, Episcopi Lincolniensis, A.D. MCCIX–MCCXXXV.   Vol.II
edited by W.P.W. Phillimore.
Lincoln: Lincoln Record Society, 1913.   347p.
(Lincoln Record Society, 6)

3883.
Speculum dioeceseos Lincolniensis sub Episcopis Gul. Wake et Edm. Gibson, A.D. 1705–1723. Part 1: Archdeaconries of Lincoln & Stow
Lincoln: Lincoln Record Society, 1913. xxiv, 210p., [frontis].
(Lincoln Record Society, 4)
Includes index.

3884.
Rotuli Roberti Grosseteste, Episcopi Lincolniensis, A.D. MCCXXXV–MCCLIII, necnon Rotulis Henrici de Lexington, Episcopi Lincolniensis, A.D. MCCLIV–MCCLIX
edited by F.N. Davis.
Lincoln: Lincoln Record Society, 1914. xii, 557p.
(Lincoln Record Society, 11)
Includes index.

3885.
Rotuli Hugonis de Welles, Episcopi Lincolniensis, A.D. MCCIX–MCCXXXV. Vol.III
edited by F.N. Davis.
Lincoln: Lincoln Record Society, 1914. 235p.
(Lincoln Record Society, 9)
Includes index.

3886.
The Chantry certificates for Lincoln and Lincolnshire, returned in 1548 under the Act of Parliament of 1 Edward VI
edited by C.W. Foster and A. Hamilton Thompson.
pp.183–294 in *AAS reports and papers*, vol.36, 1921–22.
    pp.198–206: Tattershall Chantry; St Bennet Chantry; Dalderby Chantry; St Margaret's Blyton Chantry; Guild of St Anne.

3887.
Rotuli Ricardi Gravesend, Episcopi Lincolniensis, A.D. MCCLVIII–MCCLXXIX
edited by F.N. Davis.
Lincoln: Lincoln Record Society, 1925. xliv, 405p.
(Lincoln Record Society, 20)
Includes index.

3888.
The State of the Church in the reigns of Elizabeth and James I, as illustrated by documents relating to the diocese of Lincoln. Vol.1
edited by C.W. Foster.
Lincoln: Lincoln Record Society, 1926. cxlviii, 562p.
(Lincoln Record Society, 23)

3889. **FOSTER, C.W.**
The Lincoln episcopal registers, being the substance of an address delivered to the Canterbury and York Society
pp.155–168b in *AAS reports and papers*, vol.41, 1932–33.

3890. **MAJOR, Kathleen**
The Lincoln diocesan records
pp.39–66 in *Transactions of the Royal Historical Society*, 4th series, vol.22, 1940.

3891. ————————
Lincoln diocesan records as sources for the genealogist: a lecture delivered to the Society of Genealogists on May 24th, 1941
pp.158–171 in *The Genealogists' magazine*, September, 1941.

3892.
*The Rolls and register of Bishop Oliver Sutton, 1280–1299. Vol.I: Institutions to
benefices and confirmations of heads of religious houses in the archdeaconry of Lincoln*
edited by Rosalind M.T. Hill.
Lincoln: Lincoln Record Society, 1948. xxvii, 295p.
(Lincoln Record Society, 39)

3893.   **HILL, Rosalind**
Bishop Sutton and his archives: a study in the keeping of records in the thirteenth century
pp.43–53 in *The Journal of ecclesiastical history*, vol.I, 1950.
    Registrar was John de Scalleby.

3894.
The Rolls and register of Bishop Oliver Sutton, 1280–1299. Vol.II
edited by Rosalind M.T. Hill.
Lincoln: Lincoln Record Society, 1950. xix, 205p.
(Lincoln Record Society, 43)
Includes index.

3895.   **MAJOR, Kathleen**
*A Handlist of the records of the Bishop of Lincoln and of the Archdeacons of Lincoln and
Stow*
London: Oxford University Press, 1953. 122p.
Includes index.
    Includes some references to the city and institutions of the city.

3896.   **WILLIAMSON, Dorothy M.**
Sede vacante records of the diocese of Lincoln
pp.13–20 in *Society of Local Archivists bulletin*, no.12, October, 1953.

3897.
*The Rolls and register of Bishop Oliver Sutton, 1280–1299. Vol.III: Memoranda, May
19, 1290–May 18, 1292*
edited by Rosalind M.T. Hill.
Lincoln: Lincoln Record Society, 1954. lxxxvi, 250p.
(Lincoln Record Society, 48)
Includes index.

3898.
The Rolls and register of Bishop Oliver Sutton, 1280–1299. Vol.IV
edited by Rosalind M.T. Hill.
Lincoln: Lincoln Record Society, 1958. viii, 221p.

3899.
*The State of the ex-religious and former chantry priests in the diocese of Lincoln,
1547–1574, from returns in the Exchequer*
edited by G.A.J. Hodgett.
Lincoln: Lincoln Record Society, 1959. xxii, 181p.
(Lincoln Record Society, 53)

3900.   **LE NEVE, John**
Fasti Ecclesiae Anglicanae, 1300–1541. I: Lincoln diocese
compiled by H.P.F. King.
London: Athlone, 1962. xi, 143p.
    Contains names of clergy within city.

3901.
The Register of Bishop Philip Repingdon, 1405–1419. Vol.I: Memoranda, 1405–1411
edited by Margaret Archer.
Lincoln: Lincoln Record Society, 1963. li, 209p.
(Lincoln Record Society, 57)

3902.
The Register of Bishop Philip Repingdon, 1405–1419. Vol.II: Memoranda, 1411–1414
edited by Margaret Archer.
Lincoln: Lincoln Record Society, 1963. pp.211–441.
(Lincoln Record Society, 58)
Includes index.

3903.
The Rolls and register of Bishop Oliver Sutton, 1280–1299. Vol.V
edited by Rosalind M.T. Hill.
Lincoln: Lincoln Record Society, 1965. vii, 255p.
(Lincoln Record Society, 60)
Includes index.

3904.
An Episcopal court book for the diocese of Lincoln, 1514–1520
edited by Margaret Bowker.
Lincoln: Lincoln Record Society, 1967. xxxii, 161p.
(Lincoln Record Society, 61)
Includes index.

3905.
The Rolls and register of Bishop Oliver Sutton, 1280–1299. Vol.VI: Memoranda, May 19, 1297–September 12, 1299
edited by Rosalind M.T. Hill.
Lincoln: Lincoln Record Society, 1969. ix, 236p.
(Lincoln Record Society, 64)
Includes index.

3906.   **SMITH, David**
The Rolls of Hugh of Wells, Bishop of Lincoln, 1209–35
pp.155–195 in *Bulletin of the Institute of Historical Research*, vol.XLV, no.112, November, 1972.

3907.
The Rolls and register of Bishop Oliver Sutton. Vol.VII: Ordinances, May 19, 1290–September 19, 1299
edited by Rosalind M.T. Hill.
Lincoln: Lincoln Record Society, 1975. xv, 192p.
(Lincoln Record Society, 69)
Includes index.

3908.   **LE NEVE, John**
Fasti Ecclesiae Anglicanae, 1066–1300.   III: Lincoln
compiled by Diana M. Greenway.
London: University of London, Institute of Historical Research, 1977. xxvi, 195p.
Includes index.
    Contains names of clergy of the city.

3909.
Lincolnshire returns of the census of religious worship, 1851
edited by R.A. Ambler.
Lincoln: Lincoln Record Society, 1979. xcv, 317p.
(Lincoln Record Society, 72)

3910.
The Register of Bishop Philip Repingdon, 1405–1419. Vol.III: Memoranda, 1414–1419
edited by Margaret Archer.
Lincoln: Lincoln Record Society, 1982. 327p.
(Lincoln Record Society, 74)
Includes index.

3911.
The Register of Richard Fleming, Bishop of Lincoln, 1420–31. Vol.1
edited by N.H. Bennett.
York: Canterbury and York Society, 1984. viii, 149p.
(Canterbury and York Society, 73)
Includes index.

3912.
The Rolls and register of Bishop Oliver Sutton. Vol.VIII: Institutions, collations and sequestrations, all archdeaconries, except Lincoln and Northampton
edited by Rosalind M.T. Hill.
Lincoln: Lincoln Record Society, 1986. xii, 256p.
(Lincoln Record Society, 76)
ISBN 0901503401

DIOCESAN HISTORY

3913.
Lincoln diocese
[London?]: [s.n.], [1728]. pp.137–192
    p.152: city of Lincoln.

3914.
A Dialogue: Clericus and Laicus on the Eucharist
Lincoln: Brookes & Vibert, [18??]. 11p.

3915. **MASSINGBERD, F.C.**
A Real diocesan synod as the remedy for present difficulties: a letter to the Lord Bishop of Lincoln
London: Longmans, Green, 1868. 50p.

3916. **HEBB, H.K.**
Lincoln Cathedral: a complaint made to the Archbishop of Canterbury respecting breaches of the rubric during the communion service and His Grace's decision thereon
Lincoln: printed James Williamson, [1886]. 24p.
    Complaint brought by Hebb against Venables because he 'stood in front of the altar' during part of the communion service.

3917.   JEUNE, F.H.
Lincoln Cathedral: case as to the mode of conducting the ante-communion service laid before F.H. Jeune and his opinion thereon
Lincoln: printed James Williamson, [1886].   16p.

3918.   CLEMENTS, Jacob
Church courts: an address at the annual conference of archdeacons and rural deans of the diocese, held at Lincoln, July 30th, 1889
Lincoln: James Williamson, [1889].   18p.

3919.   VENABLES, Edmund
Lincoln
by Edmund Venables and George G. Perry.
London: SPCK, 1897.   371p.
(Diocesan histories)
Includes index.

3920.   MOOR, C.
Roman Cardinals at Lincoln
24p. in *AAS reports and papers*, [19??].

3921.   VENABLES, Edmund
An Incident in the episcopate of Bishop John of Buckingham, 1393–1395
by the Precentor of Lincoln.
7p. in *AAS reports and papers*, [19??].
    Feud between the Dean and the Canons.

3922.
A Subsidy collected in the diocese of Lincoln in 1526
edited by H. Salter.
Oxford: Blackwell, 1909.   348p.
    Transcribed from Ms. in Muniment Room of the Cathedral.   The document throws light on the adminstration of Cardinal Wolsey and lists names of clergy by place.   Lincoln and Lincolnshire are, of course, included, but the diocese stretched as far as Northamptonshire and Oxfordshire.

3923.   SYMPSON, E. Mansel
The Church plates of the diocese of Lincoln
pp.213–222, 10 leaves of plates in *The Archaeological journal*, 2nd series, vol.XVII, no.3, 1910.
    Includes items by Lincoln silversmiths.

3924.   CRONIN, H.S.
Wycliffe's canonry at Lincoln
pp.564–569 in *The English historical review*, October, 1920.

3925.   COURTNEY, Janet E.
Recollected in tranquillity
London: Heinemann, 1926.   279p., [6] leaves of plates.
    p.83: 'Lincoln in the seventies', reminiscences, mainly about the clergy.

3926.   NIJHOFF, S. Gravenhage-Martinus
Nederlandsche uitgaven, door Michael Honywood in ons Land gekocht, midden 17e eeuw, en thans nog te Lincoln bewaard
pp.131–148, [1] leaf of plates in *Het Boek*, [1932?].
    Includes bibliography of the Cathedral Library, by W.H. Kynaston.

3927.   MOOR, C.
The See of Lincoln
pp.121–126 in *AAS reports and papers*, new series, vol.1, 1936–37.
    Removal of capital of the diocese from Dorchester to Lincoln.

3928.   MAJOR, Kathleen
The Finances of the Dean and Chapter of Lincoln from the twelfth to the fourteenth
century: a preliminary survey
pp.149–167 in *The Journal of ecclesiastical history*, vol.V, no.2, October, 1954.
    Reference to financial dealings between Dean and Chapter and city of Lincoln.

3929.   MORTON, William
The Book of William Morton, almoner of Peterborough Monastery, 1448–1467
transcribed and annotated by W.T. Mellors; edited by P.I. King.
Oxford: Oxford University Press for the Northamptonshire Record Society, 1954.
197p., 1 leaf of plates.
(Publications of the Northamptonshire Record Society, vol.XVI)
Includes glossary and indexes of places/persons and subjects.
        References to Lincoln (Lincolnia, Lyncolnia) and its Bishops: William Alnwick; Richard
        Flemyng; and William Gray.

3930.   BOWKER, Margaret
The Secular clergy in the diocese of Lincoln, 1495–1520
Cambridge: Cambridge University Press, 1968.   253p.
(Cambridge studies in medieval life and thought.   New series, vol.XIII)
Includes bibliography and index.

3931.   SMITH, David M.
The Administration of Hugh of Wells, Bishop of Lincoln, 1209–1235
405 leaves.
Typescript.
Thesis [Ph.D.] – University of Nottingham, 1970.
Includes bibliography.

3932.   OWEN, Dorothy M.
Church and society in medieval Lincolnshire
Lincoln: History of Lincolnshire Committee, 1971.   170p., maps, VIII plates.
(History of Lincolnshire, V)
Includes index.
ISBN 0902668048
        Majority of Lincoln references to Bishops and Cathedral, but also to hospitals, friaries and
        other parishes.

3933.   PUROLA, Laurine
Bishop John Williams and the diocese of Lincoln, 1632–1641
339p.
Typescript.
Thesis [Ph.D.] – New Brunswick Rutgers, State University of New Jersey, 1981.
Includes bibliography.

3934.   SWABY, J.E.
Ecclesiastical and religious life in Lincolnshire, 1640–1660
315 leaves, [1] leaf map.
Typescript.
Thesis [Ph.D.] – University of Leicester, 1982.
Includes bibliography.

CHAPTER RECORDS

3935.
Chapter acts of the Cathedral Church of St Mary of Lincoln, A.D. 1520–1536
edited by R.E.G. Cole.
Lincoln: Lincoln Record Society, 1915. xii, 238p.
(Lincoln Record Society, 12)
 References to the Close and other churches in the city.

3936.
Chapter acts of the Cathedral Church of St Mary of Lincoln, A.D. 1536–1547
edited by R.E.G. Cole.
Lincoln: Lincoln Record Society, 1917. xxv, 223p.
(Lincoln Record Society, 13)

3937.
Chapter acts of the Cathedral Church of St Mary of Lincoln, A.D. 1547–1559
edited by R.E.G. Cole.
Lincoln: Lincoln Record Society, 1920. xxxv, 206p.
(Lincoln Record Society, 15)

3938.
Calendars of administrations on the Consistory Court of Lincoln, A.D. 1540–1659
edited by C.W. Foster.
Lincoln: Lincoln Record Society, 1921. xi, 410p.
(Lincoln Record Society, 16)
Includes index.

3939.
The Registrum antiquissimum of the Cathedral Church of Lincoln. Vol.I
edited by C.W. Foster.
Lincoln: Lincoln Record Society, 1931. lxxi, 351p., maps, XXIII plates.
(Lincoln Record Society, 27)
Includes index.
 pp.277–295: Thorngate Castle and the Condet family; pp.267–276: episcopal residences at
 Lincoln; also many references in the text.

3940.
The Registrum antiquissimum of the Cathedral Church of Lincoln. Vol.II
edited by C.W. Foster.
Lincoln: Lincoln Record Society, 1933. xlviii, 403p., XX plates.
(Lincoln Record Society, 28)
Includes index.

3941.
The Registrum antiquissimum of the Cathedral Church of Lincoln. Vol.III
edited by C.W. Foster.
Lincoln: Lincoln Record Society, 1935. xl, 487p., IX plates.
(Lincoln Record Society, 30)
Includes index.

3942.
The Registrum antiquissimum of the Cathedral Church of Lincoln. Vol.IV
edited by C.W. Foster and Kathleen Major.
Lincoln: Lincoln Record Society, 1937.   xxxix, 344p., XVIII plates., [frontis].
(Lincoln Record Society, 32)
Includes index.

3943.
The Registrum antiquissimum of the Cathedral Church of Lincoln: facsimiles of charters in volumes V and VI
Lincoln: Lincoln Record Society, 1945.   XX plates.
(Lincoln Record Society, 42)

3944.
The Registrum antiquissimum of the Cathedral Church of Lincoln. Vol.V
edited by Kathleen Major.
Lincoln: Lincoln Record Society, 1946.   xxviii, 249p.
(Lincoln Record Society, 40)

3945.
The Registrum antiquissimum of the Cathedral Church of Lincoln. Vol.VI
edited by Kathleen Major.
Lincoln: Lincoln Record Society, 1950.   xxv, 230p.
(Lincoln Record Society, 41)
Includes index.

3946.
The Registrum antiquissimum of the Cathedral Church of Lincoln. Vol.VII
edited by Kathleen Major.
Lincoln: Lincoln Record Society, 1953.   xxvii, 284p.
(Lincoln Record Society, 43)
Includes index.

3947.
The Registrum antiquissimum of the Cathedral Church of Lincoln. Vol.VIII
edited by Kathleen Major.
Lincoln: Lincoln Record Society, 1958.   xx, 258p.
(Lincoln Record Society, 51)
Includes index.
    Concerned entirely with city of Lincoln.

3948.
The Registrum antiquissimum of the Cathedral Church of Lincoln. Vol.IX
edited by Kathleen Major.
Lincoln: Lincoln Record Society, 1968.   xxxii, 329p., [frontis].
(Lincoln Record Society, 62)
Includes index.
    Particularly rich in references to the city of Lincoln.

3949.
The Registrum antiquissimum of the Cathedral Church of Lincoln. Vol.X
edited by Kathleen Major.
Lincoln: Lincoln Record Society, 1973.   lxx, 378p.
(Lincoln Record Society, 67)
Includes index.
    Covers parishes around Cathedral: St Peter-in-Eastgate; St Margaret-in-Pottergate; St Andrew and Holy Trinity on the Hill; St Mary Magdalene.

3950.
The Registrum antiquissimum of the Cathedral Church of Lincoln: facsimiles of charters in vols.VIII, IX and X
Lincoln: Lincoln Record Society, [1973].   vi, XXVIII leaves of plates.
(Lincoln Record Society, 68)

CATHEDRAL

3951.
An Historical account of the antiquities in the Cathedral Church of St Mary, Lincoln
Lincoln: printed and sold by W. Wood, 1771. 55p.

3952.
Desiderata curiosa, or A collection of divers, scarce and curious pieces relating chiefly to matters of English history, consisting of choice tracts, memoirs, letters, wills, epitaphs, &c.
transcribed by Francis Peck.
London: Thomas Evans, 1779. xvii, 581p.
pp.294–323: Liber VIII, number 1, 'The History and antiquities of the Cathedral Church of the Blessed Virgin S.Mary at Lincoln', collected by Robert Sanderson.

3953.   MADDISON, A.R.
A Short account of the Vicars Choral, poor clerks, organists and Vicars of Lincoln Cathedral, from the 12th century to the accession of Edward 6th
London: [The Author?], 1878.   iii, 95p.

3954.   _____
The Vice-chancellorship of Lincoln Cathedral: a letter addressed to the Right Reverend Christopher, Lord Bishop of Lincoln
[Lincoln]: [The Author], [1879?]. 8p.
Condemning appointment to post of one not a member of the Vicars Choral as 'gross violation of six centuries of precedents'.

3955.   PERRY, George G.
Some episcopal visitations of Lincoln Cathedral
by the Rev. Prebendary Perry.
20p. in *The Archaeological journal*, vol.XXXVIII, no.149, 1881.

3956.   HILL, J.W.F.
The Western spires of Lincoln Minster and their threatened removal in 1726
[S.l.]: [s.n.], [19??]. 17p.

3957.   SHULL, Virginia
Clerical drama in Lincoln Cathedral, 1318 to 1561
pp.946–966 in *Publications of the Modern Language Association of America*, new series, vol.LII, 1937.
Includes references to Christopher Wordsworth's *Notes on medieval services in England*, 1898, which contains section devoted to Lincoln customs.

3958.   MAJOR, Kathleen
The Office of Chapter clerk at Lincoln in the Middle Ages
pp.163–188 in *Medieval studies presented to Rose Graham*, 1950.

3959. EXLEY, C.L.
The Leet, or Manorial, Court of the Cathedral Church of Lincoln
pp.307–314 in *The Lincolnshire historian*, no.8, [1951?].

3960. READ, E. Anne
A Checklist of books, catalogues and periodical articles relating to the Cathedral Libraries of England
Oxford: Oxford Bibliographical Society, 1970.   vii, 59p.
(Occasional publication, no.6)
   pp.30–32: Lincoln.

3961.
Lincoln: a living Cathedral: an anthology of the people who work and worship in the Cathedral Church of the Blessed Virgin Mary of Lincoln
Lincoln: Dean and Chapter of Lincoln Cathedral, 1972.   36p.: ill.

3962. SPENCE, Keith
Cathedral craftsmanship at Lincoln
pp.486–487: ill. in *Country life*, vol.CLIV, no.3974, August 23, 1973.

3963. PRUETT, John H.
Career patterns among the clergy of Lincoln Cathedral, 1660–1750
pp.204–216 in *Church history*, vol.44, 1975.

3964.
Cathedrals, abbeys and churches of England and Wales: descriptive, historical, pictorial
edited by T.G. Bonney.
London: Cassell, 1978.
   pp.77–90: Lincoln, by Edmund Venables.

3965. PRICE, Anne
A Special occasion
pp.1474–1476: ill. in *Country life*, October 25, 1979.
   Fashion show in the Cathedral to raise money for restoration.

3966. LINNELL, Naomi
The Catalogues of Lincoln Cathedral Library
pp.1–9 in *Library history*, vol.7, no.1, 1985.

3967. CUNNINGHAM, J.A.
St Hugh of Lincoln: the iconography of St Hugh of Lincoln: an exhibition of photographs: [catalogue]
Lincoln: Honywood Press, 1986.   14p.

3968. VARAH, George Hugh
The Cathedral Church of the Blessed Virgin Mary: the Cathedral stone
[Lincoln]: The Author, 1987.   32p.: ill., plans.
Cover title: *Lincoln Cathedral stone.*

RELIGIOUS HOUSES

3969.   COOKSON, W.D.
On the Hospital of the Holy Innocents, called Le Malardri, at Lincoln: with some account of ancient customs and usages touching leprosy
pp.29–66, [1] leaf of plans in *A Selection of papers relative to the county of Lincoln*, 1843.

3970.   OLIVER, George
An Account of the religious houses, formerly situated on the eastern side of the River Witham: being the substance of certain papers read before the Lincoln Topographical Society, in the year 1842
London: R. Spencer, 1846.   xviii, 187p.
>   pp.81–97: 'Contest between the Abbot of Kirkstead and the mayor of Lincoln', which concerns a dispute about use of dock by Lincoln merchants.

3971.
Charter of Hugh of Bayeux to the Church and Canons of St Mary of Torrington, temp. Henry II
communicated by the Rev. E. Venables.
pp.183–189 in *The Archaeological journal*, vol.XXXIII, [1880?].
>   Outlines connection with Robert De Chesney, 4th Bishop of Lincoln, who founded the Gilbertine Priory of St Catherine, Lincoln.

3972.   PALMER, C.F.R.
The Friar-preachers, or Blackfriars, of Lincoln
pp.10–14 in *The Reliquary: quarterly archaeological journal and review*, no.97, vol.XXV, July, 1884.

3973.   SYMPSON, G. Mansel
The Monasteries, friaries and hospitals of Lincoln
pp.169–172 in *LN&Q*, vol.2, no.6, 1891.
>   Concerns Hospitals of St Giles and of the Holy Innocents.

3974.   _____
The Monasteries, friaries and hospitals of Lincoln, continued
pp.210–213 in *LN&Q*, vol.2, no.7, 1891.
>   Concerns St Katherine's Priory.

3975.   _____
The Monasteries, friaries and hospitals of Lincoln, continued
pp.235–239 in *LN&Q*, vol.2, no.8, 1891.
>   Concerns St Katherine's Priory.

3976.   FAIRBANK, F.R.
The Leper Hospital of the Holy Innocents, Lincoln
pp.55–56 in *LN&Q*, vol.4, no.26, 1894.

3977.   BOND, Henry
The Grey friars at Lincoln
Lincoln: Keyworth, 1899.   pp.25–34.
Originally published: in *Catalogue of the Health Exhibition, Lincoln*, 1899.

3978.   GRAHAM, Rose
S.Gilbert of Sempringham and the Gilbertines: a history of the only English monastic order
London: Elliot Stock, 1901.   240p., [12] leaves of plates.
> Includes many references to Lincoln: Bishops; citizens; Hospital of the Holy Sepulchre; Priory of St Katherine.

3979.   COLE, R.E.G.
The Priory of St.Katherine-without-Lincoln, of the order of St Gilbert of Sempringham
pp.264–336, [1] leaf of plates in *AAS reports and papers*, vol.27, 1903–04.

3980.   CLAY, Rotha Mary
The Mediaeval hospitals of England
London: Methuen, 1909.   xxii, 357p., XXX leaves of plates.
Includes index.
> Includes: Holy Innocents; St Giles; St Katherine; St Sepulchre.

3981.
Visitations of religious houses in the diocese of Lincoln. Vol.1: Injunctions and other documents from the registers of Richard Flemyng and William Gray, Bishops of Lincoln, A.D. 1420 to A.D. 1436
edited by A. Hamilton Thompson.
Lincoln: Lincoln Record Society, 1914.   xxxi, 318p.
(Lincoln Record Society, 7)
Includes index.   Parallel Latin text and English translation.

3982.   PENNY, James Alpass
Notes on the monasteries and other religious institutions near the River Witham, from Lincoln to the sea
Horncastle: W.K. Morton, 1918.   152p.
Includes index.
> Includes: St Katherine's Priory outside Lincoln; the Malandry or Hospital of the Holy Innocents; Hospital of St Giles outside Lincoln; the Franciscans; Dominicans; Carmelite friars; Augustinian friars; Monks Abbey.

3983.
Transcripts of charters relating to the Gilbertine houses of Sixle, Ormsby, Catley, Bullington and Alvingham
edited, with a translation, from the King's Remembrancer's memoranda rolls nos.183, 185 and 187 by F.M. Stenton.
Lincoln: Lincoln Record Society, 1922.   xxxvi, 113, 113, 167p.
(Lincoln Record Society, 18)
Includes index.
> Includes references to witnesses from Lincoln.

3984.   WELBY, Alfred
The Hospital of the Holy Innocents, Lincoln, 1316–36
pp.89–91 in *LN&Q*, vol.20, no.6, 1928–29.

3985.   BRADLEY, Edith
The Story of the English abbeys told in counties.   Vol.II: The eastern counties
London: Robert Hale, 1939.   x, 236p.
Includes index.
> p.22: Priory of St Mary Magdalene; pp.57–58: Priory of St Katherine outside Lincoln.

3986.　**SPENCE, H.D.M.**
Cloister life in the days of Coeur de Lion
with illustrations by Herbert Railton and A. Quinton.
London: Ibister, 1962.　203p.: ill.
　　pp.3–27: Hugh of Lincoln.

3987.　**BOYTON, Peggy**
The Malandry: [short story]
pp.42–43: ill. in *Lincolnshire life*, vol.19, no.8, November, 1979.
　　Features Hugh of Avalon and a scribe who becomes a leper.

3988.　**MIDMER, Roy**
English mediaeval monasteries, 1066–1540: a summary
London: Heinemann, 1979.　viii, 385p.
Includes index.
ISBN 0434465356
　　pp.198–201: Lincoln.

3989.　**WHITE, Andrew**
Lincoln's mediaeval friaries
Lincoln: Lincolnshire Museums, 1979.　4p.: ill., map.
(Lincolnshire Museums information sheet.　Archaeology series, no.7)

PARISH RECORDS

3990.
The Parish registers of St.Margaret, in the Close of Lincoln, 1538–1837
edited by C.W. Foster.
Lincoln: Lincoln Record Society, 1915.　xv, 184p., [frontis].
(Publications of the Lincoln Record Society, Parish Registers Section, 2)
Includes index.

3991.
*The Parish registers of St Peter-at-Gowts in the city of Lincoln: baptisms, 1540–1837,
burials, 1538–1837, marriages, 1826–1837*
edited by Reginald C. Dudding.
Lincoln: Lincoln Record Society, 1923.　xvi, 142p.
(Publications of the Lincoln Record Society, Parish Registers Section, 8)

3992.
The Parish registers of the city of Lincoln: marriages, A.D. 1538–1754
edited by C.W. Foster.
Lincoln: Lincoln Record Society, 1925.　xiii, 290p.
(Publications of the Lincoln Record Society, Parish Registers Section, 9)
Includes index.

3993.　**USHER GALLERY**
Exhibition of parochial records held in the Usher Art Gallery, Lincoln, 14th June–2nd
July, 1939
[1939].　44 leaves.
Typescript.
　　Includes some items from Lincoln.

3994.   LINCOLNSHIRE ARCHIVES OFFICE
Deposited parish registers: [list]
Lincoln: The Office, 1985.   13 leaves.
   p.8: Lincoln.

INDIVIDUAL PARISHES

3995.
List of churches and chapels, built, rebuilt, or enlarged in the diocese of Lincoln since 1840
Lincoln: printed James Williamson, 1875.   51p.
   p.13: city of Lincoln churches.

3996.   VENABLES, Edmund
Church building in Lincoln a hundred years ago
by Rev. Precentor of Lincoln.
pp.102–105 in *Lincoln diocesan magazine*, no.3, December, 1886.

3997.
A List and brief description of the churches of Lincoln previous to the period of the Reformation
pp.326–354 in *AAS reports and papers*, vol.19, 1887–88.

3998.   BROCK, E.P. Loftus
The Churches of the city of Lincoln: [paper read before the meeting of the British Archaeological Society at Lincoln, on Wednesday, 31st July, 1889]
pp.135–137 in *Lincoln diocesan magazine*, vol.VII, no.65, September, 1891.
Continued: pp.147–149, vol.VII, no.66, October, 1891.

3999.   VENABLES, Edmund
Divine service in the parish churches of Lincoln in the first half of the eighteenth century
E.V.
pp.55–57 in *Lincoln diocesan magazine*, vol.VIII, no.72, April, 1892.
   Concerns religious observance in the city, based on Ms. returns in the episcopal Registry.

4000.
The Lincoln Church House magazine
Vol.7, October, 1901–vol.11, November, 1906.
Lincoln: Keyworth, 1901–06.   Various pagings.
Issued monthly.
   Lincoln Central Library wanting nos.: 112, January, 1905; 122, November, 1905; 129, June, 1906; 131–133, August–October, 1906.   In addition, Lincolnshire Archives Office has vol.5, nos. 53, 57, 58, 60, February–September, 1900; vol.6, no. 62, November, 1900.

4001.   HOLLES, Gervase
Lincolnshire church notes made by Gervase Holles, A.D. 1634 to A.D. 1642
edited by R.E.G. Cole.
Lincoln: Lincoln Record Society, 1911.   xiii, 281p., [frontis].
(Lincoln Record Society, 1)
   pp.52–68: Bishop's Palace; St Swithin's; St Michael's; St Martin's; St Peter-in-Eastgate; Cathedral.

4002.   COLE, R.E.G.
Observations on Gervase Holles' Lincolnshire notes, A.D. 1634–1642, Lincoln
pp.378–420, [4] leaves of plates in *AAS reports and papers*, vol.31, 1911–12.
>   Includes: Bishop's Palace; St Swithin's; St Botolph's; St Mark's; St Benedict's;
>   St Mary-le-Wigford; St Michael's-on-the-Mount; St Martin's; St Peter-in-Eastgate; the
>   Cathedral.

4003.   BROWN, G. Baldwin
The Arts in early England
New and revised ed.
London: John Murray, 1926.   5 vols.
>   Vols.I and II, relating to life in Saxon England and its architecture, have references to
>   individual churches in Lincoln.

4004.
Lincoln churches, Bishop's Commission
pp.39–45: ill. in *The National monuments review*, vol.1, [1928?].
Originally published: in *Lincolnshire echo*, March 2, 1928.
>   Inquiry into proposed merger of St Peter-at-Arches and St Benedict with St Martin's and
>   St Mary-le-Wigford.

4005.   MONSON, William John
*Lincolnshire church notes made by William John Monson, F.S.A., afterward sixth Lord
Monson of Burton, 1828–1840*
edited by his grandson John, ninth Lord Monson.
Lincoln: Lincoln Record Society, 1936.   xx, 474p., map, [frontis].
(Lincoln Record Society, 31)
Includes index.

4006.   BONNEY, H.K.
*Bonney's church notes: being notes on the churches in the archdeaconry of Lincoln,
1845–1848*
edited by N.S. Harding.
Lincoln: Keyworth, 1937.   xiv, 290p.: ill.
>   pp.1–4: deanery of Christianity, i.e. Lincoln.

4007.   LINCOLNSHIRE OLD CHURCHES TRUST
Annual report, 1953–
[Lincoln]: [The Trust], [1953–   ].   Various pagings.

4008.
*The Parishes and churches of Lincoln: report of a commission appointed by the Lincoln
Diocesan Pastoral Reorganisation Committee*
Lincoln: Lincoln Diocesan Board of Finance, 1958.   31p., plans.

4009.
Lincoln City Centre Group Ministry
[1981].   [4]p.
Typescript.

4010.   BEAUMONT, J.
All Saints Church, Lincoln, 1904–64: [jubilee brochure]
Lincoln: printed J.W. Ruddock, 1964.   [11]p.: ill.

4011.   BETTS, A.P.
All Saints Church, Bracebridge, Lincoln: historical guide
[Lincoln]: [The Church], [1979].   8p.: ill.

4012.
The Restoration and enlargement of the Parish Church of All Saints, Bracebridge
[drawn by] J. Pearson, architect.
Lincoln: Pickering Litho, [187?]. 1 sheet of plans.

4013. CHURCH OF THE HOLY CROSS
The Opening and dedication of Holy Cross, Boultham, new church hall by the Lord Bishop of Lincoln...Tuesday, June 20th, 1967, at 7.30pm
[Lincoln]: [The Church], [1967]. 4p.
Includes short history.

4014. DALBY, Victor Ivor
A Short history of the parish of Boultham
Lincoln: Bargate, 1969. 18p.: ill.

4015. CHURCH OF OUR LADY OF LINCOLN
Our Lady of Lincoln: Christian stewardship campaign, 1965
[Lincoln]: [The Church], [1965]. [9]p.: ill.
Includes pictures of the church.

4016. TRUMAN, J.E.
Church of St Andrew, Lincoln: a record of its growth and development, 1870 to 1910
Lincoln: Keyworth, printer, 1910. 18p., 2 leaves of plates.

4017. SURRY, Nigel
The Becke brass at St Benedict's, Lincoln
pp.265–267: ill. in *Transactions of the Monumental Brass Society*, [19??].
John Becke was former mayor of the city; three of his sons were sheriff and one was mayor twice.

4018.
[Memorandum raising funds for preservation of St Benedict's Church]
[Lincoln]: [s.n.], [1929]. [4]p.: ill.
Campaign by Lincoln Churches Defence Committee, Lincolnshire Architectural and Archaeological Society and Society for the Protection of Ancient Buildings.

4019.
The Churches of St Benedict and St Mary-le-Wigford, Lincoln
Lincoln: Vicar and Churchwardens, [194?]. 7p.: ill.

4020. ST.BENEDICT'S APPEAL FUND
Saint Benedict's Church, Lincoln, to be the Lincoln Diocesan Mothers' Union Centre: [pamphlet]
Lincoln: The Fund, [1969?]. [3]p.

4021. PARKER, J.W.
Saint Benedict's Church, Lincoln
[Lincoln]: [Lincoln Diocese Mothers' Union], [1976]. 19p.: ill.

4022. HAWTHORN, Jean
St Benedict's and 'Old Kate'
p.51: ill. in *Lincolnshire life*, vol.19, no.6, September, 1979.

4023. RAMSAY, A.C.
St Botolph's, Lincoln: church extension: [letter]
A.C. Ramsay, J.A. MacKonochie, John Thurman.
p.160, [2] leaves of plates in *Lincoln diocesan magazine*, vol.VI, no.54, October, 1890.
Contains plates and plans by W. Scorer for new church of St Katherine and All Saints.

4024.   **LINCOLN DIOCESAN ARCHITECTURAL SOCIETY**
[Report]
p.vii in *AAS reports and papers*, vol.27, 1903–04.
> Concerns new pulpit at St Botolph's Church, Lincoln.

4025.
Church history: St Botolph's Church, Lincoln
[Ramsgate]: [Church Publishers], [1967].   8p.

4026.   **LINCOLN DIOCESAN ARCHITECTURAL SOCIETY**
[Report]
pp.ix–x in *AAS reports and papers*, vol.23, 1895–96.
> Concerns St Faith's and Far Newland.

4027.   **ST FAITH'S CHURCH**
The Windows of S.Faith's: being descriptive of the saints and holy scenes commemorated in the windows of S.Faith's Church, Lincoln
[Lincoln]: [The Church], [19??].   8p.
Cover title.
> 'Sold for the benefit of St Faith's Schools'.

4028.
The Story of a great adventure
Lincoln: printed Keyworth, [193?].   16p.: ill.
> Materials from St Peter-at-Arches used to build St Giles.

4029.
A Brief outline of the history of S.Giles's parish, Lincoln
Lincoln: printed Keyworth, 1947.   19p.: ill., plan.

4030.
St Giles's Church, Lincoln
p.98 in *The Ringing world*, no.3016, vol.LXV, Friday, February 7, 1969.
Ill. on front cover.
> About bells which were removed from St Peter-at-Arches.

4031.   **KETTERINGHAM, John R.**
The Church that moved: the parish and church of Saint Giles, Lincoln
Lincoln: [The Author], [197?].   16p.: ill.

4032.   ——————
The Church that moved: 50th birthday of St Giles, Lincoln
pp.40–41: ill. in *Lincolnshire life*, vol.26, no.3, June, 1986.

4033.   **SYMPSON, E. Mansel**
St John the Evangelist's Church, Lincoln
pp.65–66, [1] leaf of plates in *LN&Q*, vol.13, no.3, 1914.

4034.   **SHAW, Carolyn**
A Brief history of the Church of St John the Evangelist, Bracebridge Heath, Lincoln
[Lincoln]: [The Church], 1983.   [12]p.: ill.

4035.   **CHURCH OF ST JOHN, ERMINE**
Lincoln's church of tomorrow: [progress report and statement of needs, June, 1963]
[Lincoln]: [The Church], [1963].   3p.: ill.

4036.   WILLDERN, A.R.
[Press cuttings and notes relating to St Mark's Church]
[1950].   [45] leaves.
Typescript; Ms.

4037.   RODWELL, Warwick
The Archaeology of the English church: the study of historic churches and churchyards
London: Batsford, 1981.   192p.: ill.
Includes index.
ISBN 0713425903
    In addition to Cathedral, references to St Mark's and St Paul-in-the-Bail.

4038.   ST.MARTIN'S CHURCH
St.Martin's parish, Lincoln: [appeal for fund to support curate in parish]
[Lincoln]: [The Church], 1865.   [3]p.

4039.   —————
Proposed new parish church for St Martin's, Lincoln: [minutes of meeting and
subscriptions list]
[Lincoln]: [The Church], 1867.   [3]p.

4040.   LINCOLN DIOCESAN ARCHITECTURAL SOCIETY
[Report]
pp.lxxxii, lxxxv in *AAS reports and papers*, vol.11, 1872–73.
    Concerns: St Martin's; St Mary-le-Wigford; St Mark's.

4041.   EXLEY, C.L.
St Martin's church plate: [notes]
[19??].   [5] leaves: ill.
Typescript; Ms.

4042.
[Folder of material relating to St Martin's Church]
[19??].   1 portfolio.
Typescript.
    Photographs and list of memorials; also photographs of St Faith's Church.

4043.   ST MARTIN'S CHURCH
The Late debt upon St Martin's Church: the result of the urgent appeal
[Lincoln]: [The Church], [1901].   [4]p.

4044.   —————
The Result of the urgent appeal, dated November 1st, 1900
[Lincoln]: [The Church], 1901.   [4]p.

4045.
St Martin's Church, Lincoln: some account of the churches which used to stand in the
present parish of St Martin
4p. in *St Martin's parish magazine*, October, 1906.

4046.   LINCOLN DIOCESAN ARCHITECTURAL SOCIETY
[Report]
pp.lxvi–lxvii in *AAS reports and papers*, vol.31, 1911–12.
    Concerns St Martin's Church and Mission Church of St Katherine and All Saints.

4047. ST MARTIN'S CHURCH
St Martin's Church, Lincoln: handbook of the grand bazaar, 'The Lure of the Orient'
held in the Drill Hall, Broadgate, Tuesday, 13th November, 1928 and four following days
[Lincoln]: [The Church], [1928].   64p.: ill.
  Includes history of parish, with information on the Church, old parish room, new building and
  account of churches which used to stand in the parish of St Martin.

4048.   ——————————
St Martin's, Lincoln, parish magazine
January, 1937–April, 1951.
[Lincoln]: [The Church], [1937–51].

4049.
Unequal partners
p.12 in *The Church times*, November 22, 1968.
  Commenting on appeal of St Martin's PCC against scheme of demolition of Church; appeal
  was dismissed.

4050.   HEALEY, Kenneth
The Lincoln judgement: was PCC consulted?
p.8 in *The Church times*, November 29, 1968.

4051.
The Preces, responses, apostles' creed, &c., &c., as used in the Church of St Mary
Magdalene, Lincoln: [music]
Lincoln: Brookes and Vibert, [184?].   14p.

4052.
An Account of the history of the Parish Church of Saint Mary Magdalen in the city of
Lincoln, together with extracts from the earlier parish registers...amplification of an
address
[1943].   13, 15p.
Typescript.

4053.   SHARPE, Edmund
An Account of the churches visited during the Lincoln excursion of the Architectural
Association, August 22nd–August 27th, 1870
London: E. & F.N. Spon, 1871.   152p.: ill., 65 plates.
  Much about Cathedral; also St Mary-le-Wigford, St Benedict and St Peter-at-Gowts.

4054.   WORDSWORTH, J.
Anglo-Saxon dedicatory inscription on the tower of St Mary-le-Wigford Church in
Lincoln, over the Roman epitaph of Sacer, son of Bruscus
pp.16–17, [1] leaf of plates in *AAS reports and papers*, vol.15, 1879–80.

4055.   HAMMERSLEY, John
Historical sketch of the Church of St Mary-le-Wigford with St Mark, with notes about
St Benedict's Church, also in this parish
[19??].   16p.
Typescript.

4056.   S., J.A.
Two ancient churches in Lincoln
pp.19–21: ill. in *AAS reports and papers*, [19??].
  Refers to St Mary-le-Wigford and St Peter-at-Gowts.

4057.   **MARSTRAND, Vilhelm**
The Old inscription from St Mary-le-Wigford in Lincoln
[1938].   56 leaves.
Typescript.

4058.   **CHURCH OF ST MARY-LE-WIGFORD**
Church of St Mary-le-Wigford: [for the information and use of visitors]
[Lincoln]: [The Church], [1938].   [3]p.

4059.   **THOMPSON, A. Hamilton**
The Churches of St Mary-le-Wigford, St Benedict and St Peter-at-Gowts, Lincoln
pp.162–166, plans in *The Archaeological journal*, vol.CIII, 1946.

4060.   **CHURCH OF ST MARY-LE-WIGFORD**
*The Gates: the magazine of the parish of S.Mary-below-hill, Lincoln, with which is
incorporated The Window*
No.13, January, 1954–no.60, December, 1957.
[Lincoln]: [The Church], [1954–57].
     St Mary-below-hill commonly known as St Mary-le-Wigford.

4061.   **TAYLOR, H.M.**
Why should we study the Anglo-Saxons?: [the Rede lecture, 1966]
Cambridge: Cambridge University Press, 1966.   49p.: ill.
     pp.30, 32: Anglo-Saxon towers of St Mary-le-Wigford and St Peter-at-Gowts.

4062.   **FISHER, E.A.**
Anglo-Saxon towers: an architectural and historical study
Newton Abbot: David & Charles, 1969.   208p.: ill., maps.
Includes index.
ISBN 0715344722.
     Many brief references; p.269: St Mary-le-Wigford and St Peter-at-Gowts.

4063.   **TAYLOR, Harold M.**
St Mary-le-Wigford
pp.87–88 in *Royal Archaeological Institute: programme of the summer meeting at
Lincoln*, 1974.

4064.   **HAMMERSLEY, John**
St Mary-le-Wigford, Lincoln
pp.24–26: ill. in *Lincolnshire life*, vol.17, no.4, July, 1977.

4065.   **KERR, Nigel**
A Guide to Anglo-Saxon sites
Nigel and Mary Kerr.
London: Granada, 1982.   207p.: ill.
ISBN 0246117753
     pp.118–121: St Mary-le-Wigford and St Peter-at-Gowts.

4066.
St Mary-le-Wigford with St Mark, Lincoln
Lincoln: printed Lincolnshire Publishing, [1986].   [3]p.
     Brief history.

4067.   **MADDISON, A.R.**
Extracts from the register of St Michael-on-the-Mount, Lincoln, 1575–1651
pp.41–43 in *LN&Q*, vol.8, no.62, 1904.

4068.
[Notice of meeting to discuss building of new church in parish of St Nicholas, Newport, 7th May, 1838]
Lincoln: printed T.J.N. Brogden, 1838. 1 sheet.

4069. **PELTOR, L.F.**
The Ancient suburb of Newport and the parishes of St Nicholas and St John Baptist
Lincoln: printed W.J. Harrison, [1937?]. [11]p., [2] leaves of plates.

4070. **VENABLES, Edmund**
The Destroyed churches of St Paul and St Martin, in the city of Lincoln
pp.208–216 in *AAS reports and papers*, vol.13, 1875–76.

4071. **MILTON, E.R.**
The Church and parish of St Paul-in-the-Bail
Lincoln: printed Keyworth, 1946. 43p., [2] leaves of plates.

4072. **SOCIETY FOR THE PROTECTION OF ANCIENT BUILDINGS**
Annual report of the committee...June, 1928: [51st]
London: The Society, 1928. 137p., [36]p. of plates.
   Includes paragraph on St Peter-at-Arches and St Benedict's, with plates.

4073. **EXLEY, C.L.**
St Peter-at-Arches, Lincoln
pp.314–317: ill. in *The Lincolnshire magazine*, vol.1, 1932–34.

4074. **SHARPE, Edmund**
An Account of the churches visited during the Lincoln excursion of the Architectural Association, August 22nd–August 27th, 1870
London: E. & F.N. Spon, 1871. 152p., 65 leaves of plates.
   pp.15–13: Cathedral; p.53: St Peter-at-Gowts and St Benedict.

4075. **JEANS, G.E.**
Inscription in St Peter-at-Gowts, Lincoln
p.109 in *LN&Q*, vol.1, no.4, 1888.

4076. **THOMPSON, A. Hamilton**
Saxon churches in Lincolnshire
pp.53–80, [2] plates in *Memorials of old Lincolnshire*, 1911.
   Brief references to St Peter-at-Gowts, St Mary-le-Wigford and Bracebridge All Saints.

4077. **TOWNROE, J.W.**
St Peter-at-Gowts Parish Church: history and notes
[Lincoln]: [The Church], [1930]. [4]p.

4078. **HOULDEN, G.**
Notes on the parish and Parish Church of St Peter-at-Gowts, Lincoln
[Lincoln]: [The Church], [1953]. 16p.: ill.

4079. **BATES, David W.**
The Parish of St Peter-at-Gowts and St Andrew, Lincoln
[Lincoln]: [Church of St Peter-at-Gowts], [1971]. [7]p.

4080. **TAYLOR, Harold M.**
St Peter-at-Gowts
pp.88–90 in *Royal Archaeological Institute: programme of the summer meeting at Lincoln*, 1974.

4081.   BAKER, David Jordan
St Peter-at-Gowts Church: [guide]
Lincoln: The Church, 1985.   12p.: ill.
Based on earlier work compiled in 1953; completely rewritten.

4082.
An Account of the pews: [at St Peter-at-Gowts]
[1931].   [4] leaves: ill.
Typescript.
Original appropriation, 1724, and present occupiers, 1798.   Photographs taken in 1931 from
original sheets.

4083.   NELSON, Thomas Sherlock
Saint Peter-at-Pleas (ad Placita), Lincoln
[Lincoln]: [The Author], [1896].   4p.
Gives lists of rectors of St Peter-at-Pleas, St Peter-at-Arches, St Benedict, with history of how
they became the parish of St Peter-at-Arches with St Benedict.

4084.
*Subscription from the parochial associations of St Peter-in-Eastgate and St Margaret,
Lincoln, in aid of the Society for the Propagation of the Gospel in Foreign Parts, for the
year 1847*
Lincoln: printed T.O. Brumby, 1847.   1 sheet.

4085.
*Order of service to be used on laying the foundation stone of the new church of the united
parishes of Saint Peter-in-Eastgate & Saint Margaret, Lincoln, on the feast of Saint
Michael and All Angels*
Lincoln: printed Edward R. Cousans, 1869.   8p.

4086.   CHURCHES OF ST PETER-IN-EASTGATE AND ST MARGARET'S
S.Peter's-in-Eastgate & S.Margaret's parish magazine
No.1, 1893–no.12, 1893.
[Lincoln]: [The Churches], [1893].

4087.   COLE, R.E.G.
Tomb of Master Peter Efford, in St Peter-in-Eastgate Church
pp.210–212 in *LN&Q*, vol.13, no.7, 1915.

4088.   LINCOLN DIOCESAN ARCHITECTURAL SOCIETY
[Report]
pp.lxxiii, lxxxvi in *AAS reports and papers*, vol.32, 1913–14.
Concerns St Peter-in-Eastgate and St Swithin's.

4089.
*The Form and manner of the dedication of a new aisle and furniture in the Church of
Saint Peter-in-Eastgate by the Lord Bishop of Lincoln, on Thursday, 2nd July, 1914,
within the octave of St Peter's Day*
Lincoln: printed Keyworth, [1914].   8p.

4090.
The Churches of St Peter-in-Eastgate and St Giles, Lincoln: calendar & blotter, 1931
Leeds: Standard Publishing, [1931].   [18]p.: ill., 1p. of plates.
Includes: 'A second-rate story', by A. Malcolm Cook, about the laying of the boundary of
St Margaret's parish in the early 19th century because of dissatisfaction with rates
assessment.   St Peter-in-Eastgate parish was united with that of St Margaret.

4091.   **COOK, A. Malcolm**
A Glimpse of the parish of S.Peter-in-Eastgate
[Lincoln]: [Church of St Peter-in-Eastgate], [1932?].   15p.: ill.
    'To be sold for the benefit of the Parish Room Building Fund'.

4092.
Peter's progress: the story of the Church of St Peter-in-Eastgate, Lincoln
[1970].   36p.
Typescript.
    Centenary history.

4093.
Order of service to be used on laying the foundation stone of the new Parish Church of St Swithin, in Lincoln, on Monday, in Easter Week, 1869
Lincoln: printed Jas. Williamson, [1869].   9p.

4094.   **VENABLES, Edmund**
The History and description of St Swithin's Church Lincoln
pp.22–32 in *AAS reports and papers*, vol.19, 1887–88.

4095.   **CHURCHES OF ST SWITHIN & ST ANDREW**
Teacher and fisherman: church magazine, March, 1967
[Lincoln]: [The Churches], 1967.   [12]p.
    Includes article on the history of St Andrew's Church, 1878–1967, by a member of the
    congregation.

CHURCH DEDICATIONS

4096.   **VENABLES, Edmund**
The Dedications of the churches of Lincolnshire as illustrating the history of the county
by the Rev. Precentor Venables.
pp.1–26 in *AAS reports and papers*, vol.26, 1881–82.

4097.   **KAYE, David**
Church dedications in Lincolnshire
129 leaves, [6] leaves of maps.
Typescript.
Thesis [M.A.] – University of Leicester, 1979.
    Information about Lincoln churches passim; arranged by dedication rather than geographically.

4098.   _____
The Open road...saintly links: St Swithin
pp.16–20: ill. in *Lincolnshire life*, vol.22, no.4, July, 1982.
    Includes the Lincoln St Swithin's.

BELLS

4099.   NORTH, Thomas
The Church bells of the county and city of Lincoln: their founders, inscriptions, traditions and peculiar uses: with a brief history of church bells in Lincolnshire: chiefly from original and contemporaneous records
Leicester: printed for the author by Samuel Clarke, 1882.   xxi, 780p.: ill., 28 leaves of plates.
Includes index.
> p.58: Lincoln bellfoundry; Cathedral bells and those of: St Andrew; St Benedict; St Margaret; St Mark; St Martin; St Mary-le-Wigford; St Mary Magdalene; St Michael; St Nicolas; St Paul; St Peter-at-Arches; St Peter-at-Gowts; St Peter-in-Eastgate; St Swithin; the Guildhall. Arranged by place, giving details of size, founders and inscriptions.

4100.
Lincoln Cathedral: bells & ringers: notes collected from various sources by a vice-president of the Lincoln Diocesan Guild of Church Bell Ringers
[Lincoln]: [The Guild], [1927].   [8]p.

4101.   PAUL, G.
The Cathedral Church of the Blessed Virgin Mary, Lincoln
p.318 in *The Ringing world*, no.3027, vol.LXV, Friday, April 25, 1969.
Ill. on front cover.
> Concerns Cathedral bells.

4102.   KETTERINGHAM, John
The Bells and ringers of Lincoln Cathedral
pp.684–685 in *The Ringing world*, August 19, 1983.

4103.   —————
More on the bells and ringers of Lincoln Cathedral
pp.300–302: ill. in *The Ringing world*, April 5, 1985.

4104.   —————
The Bells and ringers of Lincoln Cathedral: Great Tom
pp.453–455: ill. in *The Ringing world*, May 24, 1985.

4105.   —————
Lincoln Cathedral: a history of the bells, bellringers and bellringing
Lincoln: The Author, 1987.   80p.: ill.
> pp.30–37: the Lincoln bell founders.

MONUMENTAL INSCRIPTIONS

4106.
Lincoln Cathedral: an exact copy of all the ancient monumental inscriptions there, as they stood in 1641
collected by Robert Sanderson
London: Simpkin, Marshall, 1851.   ix, 52p.

4107.   **MADDISON, A.R.**
Inscriptions in St Martin's churchyard, Lincoln [and] St Margaret's churchyard
pp.157–160 in *LN&Q*, vol.9, no.73, 1907.

4108.
St Swithin's old graveyard, Saltergate, Lincoln: [list of inscriptions on gravestones]
Messrs. Watkins, Coombes & Partners.
[1954].   48 leaves.
Typescript.

4109.
Proposed improvement, Newport Church Lane: schedule of inscriptions of gravestones
affected by the scheme
[196?].   [2] leaves, plan.
Typescript.
      Includes [1]p. Ms. notes, by F.T. Baker.

4110.
Lincoln St Paul: memorial descriptions
[1969].   [10] leaves.
Typescript.

4111.
List of inscriptions on tombstones in St Mark's churchyard
made by students of the Lincoln Technical College.
[197?].   [3] leaves, [1] folded map.
Typescript.

4112.
Monumental inscriptions, 1707–1981: [from St Helen's Church, Boultham]
[1981].   [27] leaves.
Typescript.

4113.   **GREENHILL, Frank Allen**
Monumental incised slabs in the county of Lincoln
Newport Pagnall: Francis Coales Charitable Foundation, 1986.   xxx, 144p., 56p. of
plates.
ISBN 0951007602
      Arranged by place.   Lincoln: Cathedral; Churches of St Benedict; St Botolph; St Giles;
      St Mark; St Mary-le-Wigford; St Paul; St Peter-at-Gowts; St Swithin; Lincoln County and City
      Museum; and Trust for Lincoln Archaeology.

CHURCH MUSIC

4114.
*A Collection of old and modern anthems as they are now performed in the Cathedral
Church of the Blessed Virgin Mary in Lincoln....*
Lincoln: printed by W. Wood, 1775.   175p.

4115.
*A Selection of hymns and psalms, as sung in the Church of Saint Peter's-at-Arches, in the
city of Lincoln*
Lincoln: printed and sold by Drury, 1817.   23p.

4116.
A Collection of hymns and psalms for public worship in general use at the parish
churches of the city of Lincoln and the neighbouring villages
Lincoln: printed J.W. Drury, [1830s?].   99p.

4117.
A Collection of psalms and hymns for public worship: now used at all the parish
churches of the city of Lincoln and in general use in the neighbouring villages
Lincoln: printed T.J.N. Brogden, 1836.   177p.

4118.
A Collection of psalms and hymns for public worship, now used at all the parish
churches of the city of Lincoln: and in general use in the neighbouring villages
2nd ed.
Lincoln: T.J.N. Brogden, 1837.   177p.
Includes index.

4119.
A Collection of psalms and hymns...now used at all the parish churches of the city of
Lincoln, with but one exception
5th ed.
Lincoln: T.J.N. Brogden, 1840.   177p.

4120.
A Collection of psalms and hymns for public worship: now used at all the parish
churches of the city of Lincoln
7th ed.
Lincoln: T.J.N. Brogden, 1842.   177p.
    Printed on blue paper.

4121.
A Collection of psalms and hymns for public worship: now used at all the parish
churches of the city of Lincoln
Lincoln: T.J.N. Brogden, 1845.   178p.

4122.
A Collection of psalms and hymns for public worship, with a supplement
Lincoln: W. and B. Brooke, 1852.   256, [16]p.

4123.   **MARSHALL, Philip**
In laudem sancti Hugonis: music for Saint Hugh: [vocal score with piano accompaniment]
Lincoln: Lincoln Cathedral Reproductions, 1980.   66p.
    New work written by the then organist of the Cathedral to celebrate the 700th anniversary of
    the consecration of the Angel Choir in honour of St Hugh.

RELIGIOUS SOCIETIES

4124.   **SOCIETY FOR PROMOTING CHRISTIAN KNOWLEDGE, Lincoln**
Committee
[Minutes of a meeting of the Lincoln Committee of the Society for Promoting Christian
Knowledge]
Lincoln: printed Drury, 1811.   [2]p.

4125.   CHURCH MISSIONARY SOCIETY
At a meeting of the subscribers and friends of the Church Missionary Society, held in the Guildhall in Lincoln, on Thursday, the 30th July, 1818: [minutes]
Lincoln: printed Drury, [1818].   3p.

4126.
Lincoln depository for tracts calculated to counteract infidel and blasphemous publications
[Lincoln]: [s.n.], [1820].   3p.
    Fundraising for collection of SPCK tracts to be based at the National School.

4127.   LINCOLN AUXILIARY BIBLE SOCIETY
The Seventh report of the Lincoln Auxiliary Bible Society, 1822–23, with the laws and regulations of the institution, the resolutions of the seventh annual general meeting and a list of subscribers and benefactors
Lincoln: printed by William Brooke, 1823.   24p.

4128.   LINCOLN CHURCH MISSIONARY ASSOCIATION
Statement for the eleventh year
Lincoln: printed Brooke, 1829.   4p.
_____   twelfth, 1830.
_____   thirteenth, 1831.

4129.   SOCIETY FOR PROMOTING CHRISTIAN KNOWLEDGE, Lincoln Committee
The First annual report of the Lincoln District Committee, comprehending a circuit of twelve miles round Lincoln
Lincoln: printed M. Keyworth, 1829.   10p.
_____   third, 1831, 12p.
_____   fourth, 1832, 12p.
_____   tenth, 1838, 12p.

4130.   LINCOLN RELIGIOUS TRACT COMMITTEE
Statement of the accounts of the Lincoln Religious Tract Committee, April 1st, 1840 to March 31st, 1841
Lincoln: printed W. and B. Brooke, 1841.   1 sheet.

4131.   CHURCH MISSIONARY SOCIETY, Lincoln Association
Church Missionary Society jubilee
Lincoln: The Association, 1848.   [3]p.

4132.   SOCIETY FOR THE PROPAGATION OF THE GOSPEL IN FOREIGN PARTS
Diocese of Lincoln: district and parochial associations with the remittances made to the Society in the year 1848
[London]: [The Society], [1848].   20p.
_____   1851, 28p.

4133.   LINCOLN COUNCIL OF CHURCHES
Directory of members
[Lincoln]: [The Council], [19??].

4134.   THOMPSON, Joseph S.
The Story of Ashton's Court Mission
[1962].   28p.
Typescript.

ROMAN CATHOLIC CHURCH

4135.
[Letter to the mayor requesting meeting to discuss 'the recent usurpation of spiritual authority and territorial jurisdiction in this country by the Pope of Rome', November 4th, 1850]
Lincoln: printed R. Bulman, 1850.   1 sheet.

4136.   HOLDEN, John
Address of the Catholics of Lincoln to all the inhabitants of the city...signed on behalf of the Catholic congregation of Lincoln, John Holden, November 25th, 1850
Lincoln: printed at the Times, 1850.   1 sheet.

4137.
To the Roman Catholics in Lincoln: [counter-statement to letter signed 'John Holden', in form of reproduction of letter from Beaumont to Lord Zetland]
Lincoln: printed T.J.N. Brogden, [1850].   1 sheet.

4138.
The English Catholic nonjurors of 1715: being a summary of the register of their estates, with genealogical and other notes and an appendix of unpublished documents in the Public Record Office
edited by Edgar E. Estcourt and John Orlebar Payne.
London: Burns & Oates, [1885].   xvii, 394p.
Includes index.
 pp.160–167: Lincoln.

4139.   BENNETT, Brian
The Catholic Church in Lincoln
Lincoln: Bennett, 1982.   32p., 8p. of plates.
 Covers the period from the 4th century A.D. until the present, but the later history is 'in outline only'.   Started life as a history of St Hugh's in particular.

NON-CONFORMITY

4140.   WALKER, John
An Attempt towards recovering an account of the numbers and sufferings of the clergy of the Church of England, heads of colleges, fellows, scholars, &c., who were sequester'd, harras'd, &c., in the late times of the grand rebellion...
London: printed by W.S. for J. Nicholson, 1714.   436p.
 pp.43–47: Lincoln.

4141.   CALAMY, Edmund
The Nonconformist's memorial: being an account of the ministers who were ejected or silenced after the Restoration, particularly by the Act of Uniformity, which took place on...Aug. 24, 1662
abridged and corrected by Samuel Palmer.   2nd ed.
London: Alexr. Hogg, 1777–78.   2 vols.
Originally published: 1775.
 pp.139–170: Lincolnshire.

4142.   **PROCTOR, John**
A Letter to the public, in consequence of a letter addressed to Mr John Proctor of Nettleham by the Rev. William Hett, minister of that parish
Lincoln: printed J.W. Drury, 1793.   8p.

4143.   **HETT, W.**
Antinomianism unmasked, a tragi-comedy...being a full and direct answer to an appeal to the publick by John Proctor, farmer
Lincoln: printed W. Brooke, 1793.   38p.

4144.   **PROCTOR, John**
*A Vindication of scripture truths, in reply to **Antinomianism unmasked, a tragi-comedy**, by the Rev. W. Hett, M.A., with a poem on prejudice: not a ghost, but a true portrait of the soul under its baleful influence...*
Lincoln: printed for the author, and sold by Drury, 1793.   32p.

4145.
The Case of Mr Israel Worsley, dissenting minister at Lincoln, accused of religious infidelity by one of his congregation: containing the accusation, the defence and the opinions thereupon...
Lincoln: W. Brooke, 1808.   55p.
     The accuser was W. Brooke.

4146.   **HETT, William**
Letters respecting the restrictions laid upon dissenting teachers, the qualifications required of them and the privileges granted to them, written and sent to the Right Honourable Lord ABCDEFGHIJKLMNOPQRSTUVWXYZ
London: printed for F.C. and J. Rivington, 1810.   71p.

4147.   **MAWER, William**
A Reply to several letters on the privileges, &c., of dissenters: written and sent to the Right Hon. Lord ABC &c., by the Rev. W. Hett, Prebendary of Lincoln, in two letters addressed to that gentleman
Lincoln: printed for the author by A. Stark and sold by E. Baron, 1810.   40p.

4148.
The Counterbalance, or Reasons why I am a dissenter
Lincoln: printed E.B. Drury, [182?].   12p.

4149.
Dissent justified by the dissimilarity between established churches and the churches formed by the apostles
Lincoln: printed E.B. Drury, [182?].   8p.

4150.
The Case of the English dissenters: respectfully submitted by the dissenters of the city of Lincoln to the consideration of their fellow-citizens of the national Church...for their restoration to equal rights in the community
Lincoln: printed W. Brooke, 1827.   16p.

4151.   **BYRON, B.**
Report of a sermon, preached at the Independent Chapel, Lincoln, on Sunday evening, June the 21st, 1829...as taken in shorthand by Robinson Taylor
Lincoln: printed by E.B. Drury, 1829.   33p.

4152. ─────────
Farewell sermon, preached at the Independent Chapel, Lincoln, on Sunday evening, June 21st, 1829
Lincoln: printed by R.E. Leary, 1829.   8p.

4153.
Non-conformist and Catholic churches listed in Lincolnshire directories from 1826–1856: [list]
[19??].   [2] leaves.
Typescript.

4154.   **PLUMB, J.**
Early Nonconformity in Lincolnshire
3 vols.
Typescript.
Thesis [M.A.] – University of Sheffield, [19??].
    Lincoln mentioned passim.

4155.
Official handbook of the 'Old Lincoln' bazaar held in connection with St Catherine's Wesleyan Church...November 23rd, 24th & 25th, 1904
Lincoln: printed J.W. Ruddock, 1904.   36p.
    Includes history of Church as well as brief guide to the landmarks of Lincoln.

4156.
The Seconde parte of a register, being a calendar of manuscripts under that title intended for publication by the Puritans about 1593, and now in Dr. Williams' Library, London
edited by Albert Peel.
Cambridge: Cambridge University Press, 1915.   2 vols.
Includes index.
    Lists ministers thrown out of livings.   Some references to Lincoln.

4157.   **MATTHEWS, A.G.**
Calamy revised: being a revision of Edmund Calamy's account of the ministers and others ejected and silenced, 1660–2
Oxford: Clarendon Press, 1934.   lxxiii, 603p.
Includes index.
    Supplement to original rather than new ed.   Alphabetical biographical entries, with index locorum as well as general index.

4158.   **HILL, J.W.F.**
Early Non-conformity in Lincoln
[Lincoln]: [Newland Congregational Church], 1936.   19p.

4159.   **MELLONE, S.H.**
Early Non-conformity in Lincoln, anterior to the rise of the Methodist movement
pp.262–263 in *The Lincolnshire magazine*, vol.3, 1936–38.

4160.   **HILL, J.W.F.**
The Beginnings of Puritanism in a country town
pp.40–49 in *Congregational Historical Society transactions*, vol.XVIII, no.2, November, 1957.

4161.
A Short introduction to St Andrew's Presbyterian Church, Lincoln
[1964].   1 sheet.
Typescript.

4162. **HADLEY, Jo**
The Growth of Non-conformity in Lincoln, 1760–1851
36 leaves.
Typescript.
Thesis [Certificate of local history] – Bishop Grosseteste College, [c.1978].
Includes bibliography.

4163. **WEBSTER, W.F.**
Protestation returns, 1641/2: Lincolnshire
Nottingham: [The Author], 1984.   x, 142p., 1 folded map.
Includes index.
ISBN 095051621X
 pp.38–43: Lincoln.

4164. **LINCOLNSHIRE ARCHIVES OFFICE**
Deposited non parochial registers: [list]
[Lincoln]: [The Office], [1985].   [5] leaves.
 Includes: Wesleyan Methodist; Primitive Methodist; Free Methodist; Congregational;
 workhouse registers.

Baptist

4165.
*The Prisoner against the Prelate, or A dialogue between the common gaol and Cathedral
of Lincoln: wherein the true faith and Church of Christ are briefly discovered &
vindicated...*
written by a prisoner of the baptised churches in Lincolnshire.
[S.l.]: [s.n.], [c.1662].   80p.
 The argument for full immersion rather than sprinkling, i.e. vindication of the Baptist cause by
 proving that Cathedral practices are aligned with those of Rome. In the form of a dialogue
 between 'Jayle' and 'Cathedral'.

4166. **RUDYARD, Thomas**
*The Anabaptist preacher unmask'd, in a further discovery of his lying wonder out of
Lincolnshire: as also the news from Richard Hobbs, an Anabaptist preacher in Dover,
examined....*
by T.R.
[London]: [s.n.], 1672.   19p.
 Some references to Lincoln happenings, but mostly Panton.

4167. **BYRON, Benjamin**
*An Admonition against injurious extremes occasioned by the recent agitation of the
baptismal regeneration, and antipaedobaptist controversies, in this city*
Lincoln: printed for the author by W. Brooke, 1828.   47p.

4168. **CRAPS, John**
*The Immersion of believers a Christian duty and not an injurious extreme, or Strictures
on the Rev. B. Byron's Admonition*
Lincoln: printed and sold by W. Brooke, 1828.   91p.

4169. ─────────────
*Cautionary observations against the unscriptural and pernicious doctrine of baptismal
regeneration: occasioned by a paper on that subject recently published and circulated in
the city of Lincoln: respectfully submitted to... the Church of England*
Lincoln: printed for the author by J.W. Drury, 1828.   43p.

4170. LINTON, W.S.
The History of the General Baptist Church, in Lincoln, now known as the Thomas Cooper Memorial Baptist Church
compiled from various documents and records by W.S. Linton.
[1911].   [36] leaves.
Typescript.

4171. BURRAGE, Champlin
The Early English dissenters in the light of recent research, 1550–1641
Cambridge: Cambridge University Press, 1912.   2 vols.
Some references to Anabaptists at Lincoln and many references to John Smyth.

4172. UNDERWOOD, A.C.
A History of the English Baptists
London: Baptist Union, 1947.   286p., [frontis].
Includes index.
Contains references to John Smyth and Thomas Cooper.

4173.
These five and twenty years: being a brief history of the Thomas Cooper Memorial Church, St Benedict Square, Lincoln, 1923–1948
[Lincoln]: printed Elpeeko, [1948].   65p.: ill., [frontis].

4174. HIMBURY, D. Mervyn
British Baptists: a short history
London: Carey Kingsgate, 1962.   144p.
Includes bibliography.
Ch.4: Lincolnshire Association of General Baptists.

4175. STICKLER, H.E.
Mint Street Baptist Church: a short history written for the bi-centenary, 1767–1967
[1967].   10p.
Typescript.
Cover title: Mint Street Baptist Church Lincoln.

4176.
Of interest to Baptist pilgrims
[Leicester]: [East Midland Baptist Association], [c.1970].   [3]p.
Includes brief biographical note on John Smyth.

4177. MONKS ROAD BAPTIST CHURCH
Monks Road Baptist Church, Lincoln: handbook
4th ed.
[1970].   [9]p.
Typescript.
Originally issued: 1967; subsequent eds.: 1968; and 1969.

4178. BRENCHER, John F.
T.C.M.: a report on Thomas Cooper Memorial Church
pp.4–5: ill. in *Fellowship*, vol.2, no.12, November–December, 1980.

Methodist

4179.
The Lord's day plan of the preachers called primitive Methodists
[Lincoln]: [s.n.], [1821].   [2]p.

4180.   **WATMOUGH, A.**
A History of Methodism in the neighbourhood and city of Lincoln, including a sketch of early Methodism in the county of Lincoln
Lincoln: printed by R.E. Leary, 1829.   iii, 155p.

4181.   **COOPER, Thomas**
To the Rev. William Smith, Wesleyan minister, Lincoln: [letter, August 25th, 1835]
Lincoln: printed W. and B. Brooke, 1835.   1 sheet.

4182.   **NORRISS, William**
Wesleyan agitators and Puritan dissenters: [account of meeting at Corn Exchange to hear statements of Everett, Dun and Griffith, expelled Wesleyan ministers, January 1st, 1850]
Lincoln: printed T.J.N. Brogden, 1850.   1 sheet.

4183.   **BARRATT, George**
Recollections of Methodism and Methodists in the city of Lincoln: with cursory remarks on some places and persons in the surrounding circuits...
Lincoln: Charles Akrill, 1866.   94p.
    As title suggests, very much personal reminiscence.

4184.   **UNITED FREE METHODIST CHURCHES**
Plan of services of the Saxon Street circuit, Lincoln, 1885–6
[Lincoln]: [The Churches], [1885].   1 sheet.

4185.
The Home messenger: a magazine for Lincoln Methodists
Vol.IX, no.1, January, 1900–vol.XI, no.12, December, 1902.
[Lincoln]: [s.n.], [1900–02].

4186.
Lincoln High Street circuit plan and directory, Sept. quarter, 1924
Lincoln: printed H. Slack, 1924.   1 folded sheet.

4187.   **NEESHAM, R.**
An Examination of Mr W. Mawer's reply to the Reverend Mr Hett's letters respecting dissenting teachers: containing a scriptural repudiation of the Methodistic pretensions to supernatural illumination
Lincoln: printed W. Brooke, 1810.   48p.

4188.   **DRAPER, J.C.**
An Essay on family devotion
Lincoln: W. Brooke, 1812.   67p.
    Addressed to 'the preachers and leaders in the Lincoln circuit'.

4189.
An Appeal to Christians on behalf of the Methodist missions: with the resolutions unanimously passed at a meeting held at Lincoln, July 10, 1816, for the formation of an Auxiliary Methodist Missionary Society for the Lincoln District
Lincoln: printed by W. Brooke, 1816.   8p.

4190.
*The Report of the Wesleyan Methodist Sunday Schools, in the city of Lincoln, 1822: with
a list of annual subscribers*
Epworth: T.O. Brumby, 1823.   9p.

4191.   **AUXILIARY METHODIST MISSIONARY SOCIETY FOR THE LINCOLN
DISTRICT**
*The Eighth report of the committee of the Methodist Missionary Auxiliary Society for the
Lincoln District: with the resolutions of the eighth annual meeting and a list of the
contributions*
Lincoln: printed W. Brooke, 1825.   28p.

4192.   _____
*The Sixteenth annual report of the Auxiliary Methodist Missionary Society for the
Lincoln District, 1832*
Lincoln: printed E.B. Drury, [1832].   4p.

4193.   _____
*The Seventeenth annual report of the Auxiliary Methodist Missionary Society for the
Lincoln District*
Lincoln: printed E.B. Drury, 1833.   23p.

4194.
Contributions to the Wesleyan missionary fund, for the year 1832: Lincoln circuit
[Lincoln]: [s.n.], [1832].   pp.3–21.

4195.   **COOPER, Thomas**
To the Rev. William Smith, Wesleyan minister, Lincoln: [letter, August 25th]
3rd ed.
Lincoln: printed W. and B. Brooke, 1835.   4p.
　　Vituperative series of letters aiming to draw attention to what Cooper saw as the shortcomings
　　of the Methodists.

4196.   _____
A Second letter to the Rev. William Smith, Wesleyan minister, Lincoln: [September 1st]
Lincoln: printed W. and B. Brooke, 1835.   4p.

4197.   _____
A Third letter to the Rev. William Smith, Wesleyan minister, Lincoln: [September 9th]
Lincoln: printed W. and B. Brooke, 1835.   4p.

4198.   _____
A Fourth letter to the Rev. William Smith, Wesleyan minister, Lincoln: [September 15th]
Lincoln: printed W. and B. Brooke, 1835.   4p.

4199.   _____
To XXXXX: [November 1st]
Lincoln: T.J.N. Brogden, 1835.   4p.

4200.   _____
Postscript: to XXXXX: [November 21st]
[Lincoln]: [T.J.N. Brogden], 1835.   [2]p.

4201.
*Circuits of the following counties, viz. Lincolnshire, Nottinghamshire, Derbyshire,
Leicestershire, Warwickshire, Northamptonshire and Rutlandshire*
Lincoln: W. and B. Brooke, [184?].
　　pp.306–312: Lincoln.

4202. **BAGGE, James**
Newport Church: correspondence submitted to the notice of the subscribers towards a gallery in the above church for the accommodation of Sunday School children
Lincoln: printed W. and B. Brooke, 1840.   24p.

4203. **AUXILIARY METHODIST MISSIONARY SOCIETY FOR THE LINCOLN DISTRICT**
The Twenty-sixth annual report of the Auxiliary Methodist Missionary Society for the Lincoln District
_____ 28th
_____ 30th
_____ 31st
_____ 32nd
[Lincoln]: [s.n.], [1842–48].   5 vols.

4204.
Regulations of the United Free Methodist Churches in the Lincoln circuit, passed at a special general meeting of the churches, held in Lincoln, February 7th, 1860
Lincoln: printed Charles Akrill, 1860.   12p.

4205. **LINCOLN WESLEY CHAPEL**
Lincoln Wesley Chapel, Clasketgate: jubilee celebration: programme of the grand bazaar
[Lincoln]: [The Chapel], [1861?].   40p.
    pp.27–40: 'Annals of Lincoln-circuit Methodism', compiled by the Rev. Edward Workman.

4206. **WORDSWORTH, Christopher**
A Pastoral to the Wesleyan Methodists in the diocese of Lincoln
by the Bishop of Lincoln.   3rd ed.
Lincoln: printed James Williamson, 1873.   xiv, 19, vip.

4207. _____
Irenicum Wesleyanum, or Proposal for union with Wesleyan Methodists
by the Bishop of Lincoln.
Lincoln: printed James Williamson, 1876.   15p.

4208. **UNITED METHODIST FREE CHURCH**
United Methodist Free Church, Silver Street, Lincoln: annual report & abstract of trust accounts, for the year ending Sept. 30th...: [1894, 1895].
Lincoln: printed Keyworth, 1894–95.   [4]p.

4209. **BAILGATE METHODIST CHURCH**
Year book
[Lincoln]: [The Church], [19??].

4210. **KIRKHAM, W.**
Pulpit preparation
[Lincoln?]: [s.n.], [1901].   8p.
    Paper given at a meeting of the Lincoln Wesley local preachers.

4211.
Wesley Guild, 1904–5, Lincoln St Catherine's Branch
Lincoln: Leader, 1904.   [8]p.

4212. **WESLEYAN METHODIST CONFERENCE**
Wesleyan Methodist Conference, Lincoln: official handbook
[Lincoln]: [printed Ruddock], [1909].   96p.: ill.

4213.   **UNITED METHODIST CHURCH, SAXON ST.**
Trust accounts from Sept. 1st, 1909, to Aug. 31st, 1910
[Lincoln]: [The Church], [1910].   [2]p.

4214.   —————————
46th anniversary celebrations, Sunday, October 29th, 1911
[Lincoln]: [The Church], [1911].   [4]p.

4215.
Austrian village bazaar, St Catherine's, Lincoln
Lincoln: Lincoln Printing Company, [1913?].   40p.: ill.

4216.
'The Orient': a great missionary exhibition, in the Drill Hall, Lincoln, February 12th to 22nd, 1913, promoted by the Wesleyan Churches in the Lincoln district
[Lincoln]: [printed H. Slack], [1913].   48p.: ill.
    p.17: 'Lincoln and the foreign field'.

4217.
A Souvenir: Hannah Memorial Wesleyan Church, 1875–1925
Lincoln: printed Critch, [1925].   [7]p.: ill.

4218.   **WESLEYAN METHODIST CONFERENCE**
Official handbook of the 182nd conference held at Wesley Chapel, Lincoln, 15 to 28 July, 1925
Lincoln: J.W. Ruddock, 1925.   xvi, 144p.: ill., 1 map.
Cover title: *Wesleyan Methodist Conference, 1925, Lincoln.*
    Contains individual articles on Methodism in Lincoln and its history, including 'The older free
    churches in Lincoln', by J.W.F. Hill.

4219.   **ST CATHERINE'S WESLEYAN CHURCH**
Handbook of jubilee celebrations, 1881–1931
[Lincoln]: [The Church], 1931.   [8]p.: ill.

4220.   **HANNAH MEMORIAL CHAPEL**
Year book and blotter, 1932
[Lincoln]: [The Chapel], [1932].   [8]p.: ill.

4221.
St Giles new Methodist School-Chapel, Addison Drive, Lincoln: foundation stone-laying ceremony and service of thanksgiving, Wednesday, 23rd March, 1932
Lincoln: J.W. Ruddock, [1932].   [5]p., [frontis].

4222.   **SELBY, Wilfrid E.**
One hundred years, 1836–1936: the story of Wesley Chapel, Lincoln, compiled from the records of the church and recollections of its members
Lincoln: J.W. Ruddock, [1936?].   75p., 12p. of plates.

4223.
Adventure...achievement! 1818–1944: [souvenir of the thanksgiving meeting held on September 30th, 1944, to mark the clearance of the debt on the Portland Place Memorial Methodist Church, Lincoln]
Lincoln: printed Hedley Stack, [1944].   [15]p., [frontis].

4224.   **WEST PARADE METHODIST CHURCH**
The Methodist Church, West Parade, Lincoln: jubilee celebrations, 1907–1957
[Lincoln]: [The Church], [1957].   [6]p.: ill.
    Includes brief history.

4225.   **ERMINE ESTATE WEST METHODIST CHURCH**
Ermine Estate West Methodist Church: [fund raising prospectus]
[Lincoln]: [The Church], [1960].   [3]p., plan.

4226.   **LEARY, William**
The Story of Wesley Chapel and the Rosemary Lane Wesleyan day schools
Lincoln: J.W. Ruddock, 1961.   23p., 4p. of plates.
    The Chapel was closed in 1961.

4227.
Opening and dedication of new church: the Methodist Church, Monks Road, Lincoln
Lincoln: [Monks Road Society], 1962.   [4]p.

4228.   **BAILGATE METHODIST CHURCH**
Newsletter, Aug/Sept., 1964
[Lincoln]: [The Church], [1964].

4229.   **ELVIN, Laurence**
The Rev. John Hannah, D.D.
pp.10–12, [1]p. of plates in *The Home of the Wesleys*, October, 1964.

4230.
Lincoln South circuit: proposed new Methodist Church
[Lincoln]: [Birchwood Methodist Church Building Fund Appeal], [1964].   [3]p., plan.

4231.   **DOLBY, George W.**
The Architectural expression of Methodism: the first hundred years
London: Epworth, 1964.   x, 195p.
    pp.149–151: the Wesley Chapel, Lincoln.

4232.   **ELVIN, Laurence**
Bygone Lincoln: Hannah Memorial Methodist Church
pp.8–11: ill. in *The Fireside magazine*, March, 1965.

4233.   ————————
One hundred years, 1864–1964.
pp.8–12 in *The Epworth witness*, vol.1, no.4, spring, 1965.
    Covers: United Methodist Chapel, Silver St.; St Peter's Wesleyan Chapel in Alfred St.

4234.   **METHODIST LOCAL PREACHERS' MUTUAL AID ASSOCIATION**
*Order of services and general arrangements for the 116th aggregate meeting, Lincoln,
1965*
[S.l.]: [The Association], [1965].   59p.: ill.
    pp.11–12: 'A survey of Methodism in Lincoln', by W. Leary.

4235.   **CLIFTON, Enid M.**
Old Lincolnshire plans.   1: The plan of the Wesleyan Methodist preachers in the Lincoln
circuit, 1835
pp.11–12 in *The Epworth witness*, vol.1, no.6, spring, 1966.

4236.   **BIRCHWOOD METHODIST CHURCH**
Opening of the new Methodist Church, Birchwood, Lincoln and souvenir brochure
[Lincoln]: [The Church], [1966].   [6]p.: ill.

4237.   **ELVIN, Laurence**
Newark Road Methodist Church, Lincoln
pp.13–14 in *The Epworth witness*, vol.1, no.3, spring, 1967.

4238. CLIFTON, Enid M.
The First Methodist Chapel in Lincoln
pp.13–14 in *The Epworth witness*, vol.1, no.9, autumn, 1967.

4239. ELVIN, Laurence
Portland Street Methodist Church, Lincoln, 1884–1965.   1: some historical notes
pp.12–13 in *The Epworth witness*, vol.1, no.11, autumn, 1968.

4240. JACKSON, MR
Portland Street Methodist Church, Lincoln, 1884–1965.   2: some reminiscences
pp.13–15 in *The Epworth witness*, vol.1, no.11, autumn, 1968.

4241. LINCOLN CENTRAL CIRCUIT
Lincoln Central Circuit proposed new Methodist Church for Bracebridge Heath
[Lincoln]: [The Circuit], [c.1968].   [3]p., plan.

4242. BRACEBRIDGE METHODIST CHURCH
Dedication of new church buildings: souvenir booklet
[Lincoln]: [The Church], [1969].   10p.

4243. LEARY, William
Methodism in the city of Lincoln, from its origin in the eighteenth century to the present
Lincoln: The Author, 1969.   79p.: ill.
Issued in a limited run of 500 copies.   Includes bibliography.

4244. BAXTER, J.A.
Portland Place Memorial Chapel, Lincoln.
pp.92–93 in *The Epworth witness*, vol.2, no.6, autumn, 1973.

4245. ELVIN, Laurence
Silver Street United Methodist Chapel, Lincoln.
pp.95–96 in *The Epworth witness*, vol.2, no.6, autumn, 1973.

4246. LYONS, N.J.L.
John Wesley and Lincolnshire: a reassessment.
p.106 in *The Epworth witness*, vol.2, no.7, spring, 1974.
'Wesley avoided Cathedral cities for obvious reasons, and only retrospective casuistry could
ever allow Lincoln itself to claim him'.

4247. ELVIN, Laurence
The Wesleyan Methodist Conference at Lincoln, 1909.
pp.108–110 in *The Epworth witness*, vol.2, no.7, spring, 1974.

4248. MONKS ROAD METHODIST CHURCH
The Monks Road Methodist Church, Lincoln: 1914–1974: diamond jubilee celebrations
[Lincoln]: [The Church], [1974].   [8]p.: ill.

4249. CENTRAL METHODIST CHURCH
*1874–5 to 1974–5: the centenary of the H.& P.P. lines: the centenary brochure of
Central Methodist Church, High Street, Lincoln*
[Lincoln]: [The Church], 1975.   [12]p.
Cover title.

4250. LEARY, William
Lincolnshire Methodist material in archives, 1975: [list]
[1975].   [46] leaves.
Typescript.
Covers items in Lincolnshire County Archives.   [4] leaves: Lincoln.

4251. —————————
Centenary history of Bailgate Methodist Church, Lincoln, 1880–1980
Lincoln: Brayford, 1979. [20]p.: ill.

4252. —————————
Collection of Methodist preaching plans for Lincolnshire, deposited at the Archives
Office, Lincoln Castle, 1979: [list]
[1979]. [20] leaves.
Typescript.
　　[3] leaves: Lincoln.

4253. **JOHNSON, C.P.C.**
Bailgate beginnings: some notes on the early history of our church
Lincoln: published for the Bailgate Development Fund, 1983. 12p.

4254. **REEVE, Mary**
Moorland Park Methodist Church, Lincoln and its neighbourhood: a brief history
Lincoln: [The Author], 1984?. 7p., map.

4255. **ANDERSON, C.L.**
A Reminder of days gone by
p.188 in *Journal of the Lincolnshire Methodist History Society*, vol.3, no.9, spring, 1986.
　　Memories of Wesley Circuit Bazaar of 1910.

4256. **LEARY, William**
Lincolnshire Methodism: celebrating 250 years
Buckingham: Barracuda, 1988. 136p.: ill.
Includes index.
　　Many references to Lincoln.

Congregationalist

4257. **BARKER, J.T.**
*Congregationalism in Lincolnshire: a paper presented to the Lincolnshire Association of
Independent Ministers and Churches*
London: Judd and Glass, 1860. 60p.
　　pp.41–43: Zion Chapel; Newland Chapel; High St. Chapel; St Peter-at-Gowts.

4258. **NEWLAND CONGREGATIONAL CHURCH**
Manual for 1868
Lincoln: printed by C. Akrill, [1868]. 82p.

4259.
Lincoln Congregational magazine
[Lincoln]: [s.n.], [188?–　].

4260. **WILLIAMSON, J.**
*Parting words, being two sermons preached in Newland Church, Lincoln, on June 21st,
1885, on the occasion of his relinquishing the pastorate of the Church*
Lincoln: printed Akrill, Ruddock & Keyworth, [1885]. 19p.
　　Second sermon concerns his ministry at Newland Church.

4261.
The Monks Road stone-laying
pp.148–149 in *Lincoln Congregational magazine*, August, 1898.

4262.
Opening of Monks Road District Church
pp.45–46 in *Lincoln Congregational magazine*, March, 1899.

4263.
Opening and dedication of the new church at South Bar, Thursday, September 18th, 1902
pp.195–196 in *The Congregational church magazine*, October, 1902.

4264.   **NEWLAND CONGREGATIONAL CHURCH**
Manual of the Newland Congregational Church, Lincoln
Lincoln: printed Lincolnshire Chronicle, 1927.   28p.

4265.   **WATSON, William H.**
South Bar Congregational Church, Lincoln: diamond jubilee souvenir, 1876–1936
Lincoln: printed Harrison, [1936].   12p.: ill.

4266.   **NEWLAND CONGREGATIONAL CHURCH**
Diamond jubilee celebrations, 4th October to 11th October, 1936, marking the sixtieth
anniversary of the present church building on 30th May, 1876
[1936].   24p.: ill.
Typescript.
> Includes history of the Church.

4267.   **WATSON, William H.**
Newland Congregational Church, Lincoln; diamond jubilee celebrations,
1876–1936...marking the sixtieth opening of the present church building...
Lincoln: Newland Congregational Church, [1936].   24p.: ill.
> Short sketch of the history concentrating upon the careers of the incumbents.

4268.   **NEWLAND CONGREGATIONAL CHURCH**
An Introduction to Newland Congregational Church, Lincoln
[Lincoln]: [The Church], [c.1950].   [10]p., map.

4269.   **FAR NEWLAND CONGREGATIONAL CHURCH**
Centenary celebrations, 1864–1964
[Lincoln]: [The Church], [1964].   [3]p.

4270.   **NEWLAND CONGREGATIONAL CHURCH**
Newland Congregational Church: statement of general account, for the year ended 31st
December, 1969
[1969].   4 leaves.
Typescript.

4271.   **NEWLAND UNITED REFORMED CHURCH**
Statement of general account for the year ended...
[Lincoln]: [The Church], [197?–   ].

4272.   **UNITED REFORMED CHURCH OF LINCOLN**
Easter, 1974: [magazine]
[Lincoln]: [The Church], [1974].

4273.   **GODFREY, Frank**
[Reminiscences of Newland Congregational Church, Lincoln]
[1974].   10 leaves.
Ms.
> Covering period since 1929.

4274.
[Notes on effect that formation of United Reformed Church will have]
[1974].   [2] leaves.
Typescript.

4275.   **HILL, J.W.F.**
Newland Congregational Church, 1820–1974; a history
Lincoln: M.A. Mahon, 1979.   36p., 8p. of plates.
Contains an appendix covering the period 1974–1979.
> In 1972 the Congregational and Presbyterian denominations became the United Reformed
> Church.

Unitarian

4276.
*The Petition of the Unitarian Protestant dissenters of Lincoln, and other friends to
religious liberty*
[Lincoln]: [s.n.], [18??].   1 sheet.

4277.
*A Letter addressed to the Rev. John Grundy, containing strictures upon a sermon
delivered by him before an assembly of Unitarian minsters at the Unitarian Chapel, in
Lincoln, June 29, 1808*
Manchester: printed C. Wheeler, 1810.   64p.

4278.   **HAWKES, James**
*A Sermon occasioned by the death of our late venerable sovereign, George III, delivered
at the Unitarian Chapel, Lincoln, February 6th, 1820*
Lincoln: printed and sold by W. Brooke, 1820.   14p.

4279.   **WARREN, John Crosby**
From Puritanism to Unitarianism at Lincoln
pp.1–31, [2] leaves of plates in *Transactions of the Unitarian Historical Society*, vol.II,
pt.1, December, 1919.

4280.   **TAYLER, J. Lionel**
*A Little corner of London, Newington Green, with its history and tradition of a
Non-conformist meeting house*
Lincoln: J.W. Ruddock, 1925.   79p., [8] leaves of plates.
> Author was minister of Lincoln Unitarian Chapel.

4281.   **BOLAM, C. Gordon**
*Three hundred years, 1662–1962: the story of the churches forming the North Midland
Presbyterian and Unitarian Association*
[Nottingham]: [The Association], [1962].   55p., [4] leaves of plates.
> pp.37–39: High Street Chapel, Lincoln.

4282.
The History of the Lincoln Unitarian congregation and Chapel
[1962].   [4]p.
Typescript.

4283.   **WOODALL, R.D.**
Midland Unitarianism and its story, 1662–1962
Sutton Coldfield: Norman A. Tector, [1962].   51p.: ill.
> Lincoln mentioned briefly a few times.

4284.   STOREY, John A.
Lincoln Unitarian Chapel, 1725–1975: [notes]
[1975].   [2]p.
Typescript.

Ecumenism

4285.   BREMNER, W.J.
Lincoln's friendly spirit
pp.63–64: ill. in *The Congregational monthly*, June, 1954.
>   Comments on relations between Anglicans, especially the Cathedral, and Non-conformists.

4286.   BARKER, Frank
Ecumenical movements of real significance on a modern housing estate
pp.4–5 in *The Congregational monthly*, February, 1965.
>   On the Ermine Estate.

4287.
Roman Catholic mass in Lincoln Cathedral
pp.26–27: ill. in *Lincolnshire life*, vol.18, no.2, May, 1978.

4288.   CARLEY, Austin
The Lincoln-Bruges link
pp.33, 37: ill. in *Lincolnshire life*, vol.24, no.11, February, 1985.
>   Mentions LINK, an Anglo-Catholic entente, and centres on Canon Devaux, president of the
>   Groot Seminary in Bruges who is a Canon of Lincoln Cathedral.

BIOGRAPHICAL

4289.   FOSS, Edward
The Judges of England, with sketches of their lives and miscellaneous notices connected with the courts of Westminster from the time of the Conquest
London: Longman, Brown, Green and Longmans, 1848–64.   9 vols.
> Covers period 1066–1864, giving biographical notices of clerics: Bishops, Precentors, treasurers, etc., including those of Lincoln.

4290.   SIMPSON, Justin
Obituary and records for the counties of Lincoln, Rutland & Northampton, from the commencement of the present century to the end of 1859
Stamford: William R. Newcomb, 1861.   x, 482p.
Includes index.
> Useful biographical source but unfortunately no access by place.   Also records antiquarian discoveries.

4291.   WATKINS, Morgan G.
The Worthies of Lincolnshire
London: Elliot Stock, 1885.   40p.
> Alphabetical arrangement.

4292.   PRESS, C.A. Manning
Lincolnshire leaders: social and political
London: Jarrold, 1894.   142p.: ill.
> Subjects include: Heanage; Chaplin; Ellison; Joseph Ruston.

4293.   GASKELL, Ernest
Lincolnshire leaders: social and political
London: Queenhithe, [c.1908].   [c.140] leaves, [c.110] plates.
Issued for 'private circulation'.
> Includes biographical sketches of many people connected with city, including: Monson; Heneage; Chaplin; Ellison; Maddison; Sibthorp; Foster.

4294.   WEST, John E.
Cathedral organists
London: Novello, 1899.
> pp.46–50: Lincoln.

4295.   MEDCALF, J.
Lincolnshire in history and Lincolnshire worthies
London: Ward, Lock, 1903.   252p., [24]p. of plates.
Reprinted with additions from: *Lincolnshire poacher.*

4296.
Who's who in Lincolnshire
Limited ed.
Worcester: Ebenezer Baylis, 1935.   240p.

4297.   **OWEN, Dorothy M.**
Lincolnshire women in history
pp.31–45 in *The Lincolnshire historian*, vol.II, no.6, 1959.
  Includes some Lincoln women.

4298.   **GARTON, Charles**
The Cambridge connection of old Lincolnshire schools: a checklist
pp.3–27 in *History of Education Society bulletin*, no.20, autumn, 1977.
    pp.5–8: Lincoln.   Information extracted mainly from *Alumni Cantabrigiensis*.

4299.   **BORMAN, William**
The Life of the ingenious agricultural labourer, James Anderton, the founder and builder of the model of Lincoln Cathedral...together with St Stephen's, Hull, and St Botolph's, Lincoln, with a short sketch of Lincoln Cathedral
Newcastle-on-Tyne: printed J. Beall, 1868.   12p.: ill.

4300.   **HARGREAVES, J.G.**
A Wonderful building
pp.526–542 in *The Gentleman's magazine*, 1870.
    About a model of Lincoln Cathedral made by J. Anderton from cork and exhibited at the Great
    Exhibition of 1862.   A model of St Botolph's was also constructed.

4301.
Exhibition of arts: [advertising poster]
Guildford: Biddle, [1884].   1 sheet: ill.
    About models of Cathedral and St Botolph's built by Anderton.

4302.   **FRISWELL, J.H.**
The Frederick Andrew Home, West Malling, Kent: Frederick Andrew: the man: recollections of one who knew him
Lincoln: printed J.W. Ruddock, 1937.   10p.: ill.

4303.
The Lincolnshire tragedy: passages in the life of the fair gospeller, Mistress Anne Askew recounted by the unworthie pen of Nicholas Moldwarp, B.A., and now set forth by the author of 'Mary Powell'
London: Richard Bentley, 1866.   296p.

4304.   **SIDNEY, Philip**
A New light on Anne Askewe
p.288 in *The Gentleman's magazine*, September, 1903.

4305.   **WILKES, Peter**
Anne Askew...Lincolnshire's martyr
pp.40–42: ill. in *Lincolnshire life*, vol.10, no.1, March, 1970.
    Martyred in 1546 at the age of 25.

4306.
Priestly golden jubilee: Church of St Hugh, Lincoln: the Right Reverend Monsignor E.H. Atkinson, V.G., Prot. Apost., 1926–1976
[Lincoln]: [The Church], [1976].   [13]p.: ill.

4307.   **BAILEY, James Thomas**
Data re James Thomas Bailey, F.Coll.H., M.R.S.T.
[1953].   [4] leaves.
Typescript.

4308.
Mr Geo. Bainbridge, J.P.: death of a Lincoln leader of commerce: [obituary]
in *Lincoln leader*, February 19th, 1916.

4309.
The Collection of Sharpley Bainbridge, Esq., J.P., Lincoln
pp.223–239, 272–275: ill. in *The Art journal*, new series, August, 1898.
    Bainbridge was a merchant in city.

4310.   **BIRKS, Tony**
The Art of the modern potter
London: Country Life, 1967.   160p.: ill.
pp.62–76: work of Gordon Baldwin, born in Lincoln in 1932 and trained initially at
Lincoln School of Art.

4311.   **ESCREET, J.M.**
The Life of Edna Lyall (Ada Ellen Bayley)
London: Longmans, Green, 1904.   266p., [2] leaves of plates.
    pp.24–34: Lincoln.

4312.   **BEE, John**
A Bee-line on organs
pp.40–41: ill. in *Lincolnshire life*, vol.21, no.5, August, 1981.
    Born in Lincoln, 1895.

4313.   **BEE, Janet**
The Honeysuckle and the Bee: the story of a musician
[Worcester]: [The Author], 1985.   52p.: ill., [20]p. of plates.
    Concerns John Bee.

4314.   **BENNETT, A.C.**
Brief notes relating to the late Dr. George J. Bennett, organist of Lincoln Minster
[1930].   6 leaves.
Ms.

4315.
Bennett of Lincoln: [obituary]
pp.896–897: ill. in *Musical times*, October 1, 1930.

4316.   **BENSON, Arthur Christopher**
The Life of Edward White Benson, sometime Archbishop of Canterbury
London: Macmillan, 1900.   644, 851p., [30] plates.
Includes index.
    Extensive coverage of time in Lincoln.

4317.   **BAKER, James**
The Life of Sir Thomas Bernard, baronet
London: John Murray, 1819.   xiii, 190p., [frontis].
    Born in Lincoln, 1750, but little other material on the city.

4318.   **BEST, Henry**
*Four years in France, or Narrative of an English family's residence there during that
period: preceded by some account of the conversion of the author to the Catholic faith*
London: Henry Colburn, 1826.   443p.
    Best was born in Lincoln and both his father and grandfather were Prebendaries of the
    Cathedral.   Although some detail about Cathedral services and encounters with Catholic
    neighbours are given, majority of the book is about France.

4319.
An Address given by the Very Reverend N.S. Rathbone, Dean of Hereford, at a memorial
service for Canon P.B.G. Binnall held in Lincoln Cathedral, on 10 December, 1980
pp.5–6 in *Lincolnshire history and archaeology*, vol.17, 1982.

4320.
Presentation of testimonials to Professor Boole
in *Lincolnshire chronicle*, 28 December, 1849.

4321.
[Obituary of George Boole]
in *The Illustrated London news*, 21st January, 1865.

4322.
[Announcement of subscription for a memorial to George Boole]
[Lincoln]: [s.n.], [1865].   1 folded sheet.

4323.
The Boole memorial: [request for further subscriptions]
[Lincoln]: [s.n.], [1865].   [2]p.

4324.   **H., R.**
George Boole, F.R.S.: an essay biographical and expository
43p. in *British quarterly review*, no.LXXXVII, July 2, 1866.
    Includes section subheaded 'Life at Lincoln'.

4325.   **BOOLE, Mary Everest**
Home-side of a scientific mind
pp.105–114 in *The University magazine*, January, 1878.
Continued: pp.173–183, February, 1878; pp.326–336, March, 1878; pp.454–460; April,
1878.
    Discursive memoir of her husband but little specifically about Lincoln.

4326.   **KNEALE, William**
Boole and the revival of logic
pp.149–175 in *Mind*, new series, vol.LVII, no.226, April, 1948.
    pp.149–158: biographical details.

4327.
Centenary of the celebration of the laws of thought by George Boole
pp.63–130 in *Proceedings of the Royal Irish Academy*, vol.57, no.6, 1955.

4328.
George Boole as student and teacher by some of his friends and pupils
edited by Rush Rhees.
pp.74–78 in *Proceedings of the Royal Irish Academy*, vol.57, no.6, 1955.

4329.   **HACKETT, Felix E.**
The Method of George Boole
pp.79–87 in *Proceedings of the Royal Irish Academy*, vol.57, no.6, 1955.
    Mainly about work, but some biographical details.

4330.   **TAYLOR, Geoffrey**
George Boole, 1815–1864
pp.66–73 in *Proceedings of the Royal Irish Academy*, vol.57, no.6, 1955.
    Written by Boole's grandson.

4331. ⸻
George Boole, F.R.S., 1815–1864
pp.44–52, [1] leaf of plates in *Notes and records of the Royal Society of London*, vol.12, no.1, August, 1956.

4332. **KNEALE, W.**
Boole and the algebra of logic
pp.53–63 in *Notes and records of the Royal Society of London*, vol.12, no.1, August, 1956.
Several pages of biographical material.

4333.
Boole centenary celebrations, 1964: catalogue of manuscripts, books and personalia associated with George Boole...exhibited at the Central Library, Lincoln, 7th-21st November, 1964
issued by the Lincoln City Libraries, Museum and Art Gallery Committee.
[1964]. 8p.
Typescript.

4334.
Boole centenary celebrations, 7 November, 1964: at the City School, Lincoln: [programme and brief biography]
Lincoln: Mathematical Association, Lincolnshire Branch and Lincolnshire Local History Society, 1964. [4]p.: ill.

4335. **ELVIN, Laurence**
George Boole, LLD., F.R.S., 1815–1864: [a talk given to Lincoln Rotary Club, on Monday, 2nd November, 1964]
[1964]. 9 leaves.
Typescript.

4336. **GRIDGEMAN, N.T.**
In praise of Boole
pp.655–657: ill. in *The New scientist*, vol.24, no.420, 3 December, 1964.

4337. **ROBINSON, David**
Poachings: George Boole
p.60 in *Lincolnshire life*, vol.4, no.6, December/January, 1964/65.

4338. **SUMNER, W.L.**
Scientists, inventors and technologists: scientists
pp.507–513 in *Nottingham and its region*, 1966.
p.508: George Boole.

4339. **ROLLETT, A.P.**
Class consciousness: [presidential address to the Mathematical Association at the annual general meeting in London, April 17, 1968]
pp.219–241 in *The Mathematical gazette*, vol.LII, no.381, October, 1968.
Refers to George Boole's theories on education, as found in lecture given by him in 1848.

4340. **MacHALE, Desmond**
George Boole: his life and work
Dublin: Boole Press, 1985. 304p.: ill.
Includes index.

4341.   GARTON, Charles
A Fifteenth century headmaster's library
pp.29–38: ill. in *Lincolnshire history and archaeology*, vol.15, 1980.
Concerns John Bracebridge, headmaster of the Lincoln School.

4342.
[Obituary of William Brooke]
in *Stamford mercury*, 27th December, 1872.
Lincoln bookseller.

4343.   BUTLER, William John
Life and letters of William John Butler, late Dean of Lincoln and sometime Vicar of Wantage
London: Macmillan, 1897.   xi, 401p., [frontis].
Includes index.
Butler was Dean of Lincoln.

4344.   FELLOWES, Edmund H.
William Byrd: a short account of his life and work
Oxford: Clarendon Press, 1923.   123p.
Concentrates upon music rather than the man.

4345.   SHAW, Watkins
William Byrd of Lincoln
pp.52–59, [1] leaf of plates in *Music & letters*, vol.48, no.1, January, 1967.

4346.   SHARP, Geoffrey
Master of music, and of compromise: William Byrd
pp.4–6 in *Church music*, vol.2, no.23, February, 1968.

4347.   FELLOWES, Edmund H.
English cathedral music
revised by J.A. Westrup.   5th ed.
London: Methuen, 1969.   xi, 283p.
Originally published: 1941.   Includes index.
ISBN 0416148506
pp.62–76: William Byrd.

4348.   HOLST, Imogen
Byrd
London: Faber and Faber, 1972.   79p., [8]p. of plates.
(The Great composers)
ISBN 0571098134
pp.21–24: Byrd in Lincoln. For children.

4349.   SHARP, Geoffrey B.
Byrd & Victoria
Sevenoaks: Novello, 1974.   20p.
(Novello short biographies)

4350.   REESE, Gustave
The New Grove high renaissance masters: Josquin, Palestrina, Lassus, Byrd, Victoria
by Gustave Reese and others.
London: Macmillan, 1984.   330p.
Originally published: in *The New Grove dictionary of music and musicians*, 1980.
ISBN 0333382374
Includes: 'William Byrd', by Joseph Kerman; pp.231–236: early life, including Lincoln.

4351.   ELVIN, Laurence
Lincolnshire worthies: William Byrd.   1: His life
pp.160–162: ill. in *The Lincolnshire magazine.*

4352.   GARDINER, A.G.
Prophets, priests and kings
London: Alston Rivers, 1908.   332p., [40] leaves of plates.
    pp.227–234: Henry Chaplin.

4353.   LONDONDERRY, Marchioness of
Henry Chaplin: a memoir
prepared by his daughter, the Marchioness of Londonderry.
London: Macmillan, 1926.   x, 347p., [22] leaves of plates.

4354.   BLYTH, Henry
The Pocket Venus: a Victorian scandal
London: Weidenfeld and Nicolson, 1966.   301p., [16]p. of plates.
    Concerns Henry Chaplin.

4355.
Memorial to the late Edward Parker Charlesworth: [resolutions of meeting and list of subscribers]
[Lincoln]: [printed W. and B. Brooke], [1853].   [3]p.

4356.   MELTON, B.L.
Dr. Edward Parker Charlesworth, M.D.
in *The Lawn magazine*, 1st October, 1966.

4357.   CLARKE, Charles
Sixty years in Upper Canada, with autobiographical recollections
Toronto: William Briggs, 1908.   vi, 321p., [10] leaves of plates.
    Born in Lincoln, 1826, lived in the Stonebow, received education from Thomas Cooper and
    subsequently George Boole.   Also chapter on politics in Lincoln.

4358.   MORGAN, Roy
A Bloody con?: the 'quack medicine' that sold all round the world
pp.10–11: ill. in *Finders keepers*, vol.2, no.1, March, 1982.
    Francis Jonathan Clarke and his blood mixture.

4359.   GARTON, Charles
John Clarke's *Querela apologetica*
pp.261–281 in *Humanistica Lovaniensia: journal of neo-Latin studies*, vol.XXV, 1976.
    pp.261–265: about Clarke himself.

4360.
Death of N. Clayton, Esq., J.P.: [obituary notice]
in *Lincolnshire chronicle*, 26 December, 1890.

4361.
A Poet's autobiography: [review of the life of Thomas Cooper]
pp.373–376 in *Chambers' journal*, 15 June, 1872.

4362.   COOPER, Thomas
Thoughts at fourscore and earlier: a medley
London: Hodder and Stoughton, 1885.   380p., [frontis].

4363.
Commemoration of Thomas Cooper's eighty-second birthday, celebrated in the Millstone Lane Hall, Leicester, 24th March, 1887
[Leicester]: [s.n.], [1887]. 15p.
Biographical notes followed by poems.

4364. **PEERS, Robert**
Thomas Cooper: the Leicester Chartist
pp.239–252 in *Journal of adult education: a half yearly review issued by the British Institute of Adult Education*, vol.V, no.3, October, 1931.

4365. **CONKLIN, Robert J.**
Thomas Cooper, the Chartist, 1805–1892
Manilla: University of the Philippines Press, 1935. 482p.
Submitted as Ph.D. thesis for Columbia University in 1935.

4366. **COLE, G.D.H.**
Chartist portraits
London: Macmillan, 1941. 377p.
Includes bibliography and index.
pp.187–217: Thomas Cooper.

4367. **JAMES, W.L.G.**
Two Lincolnshire writers: a study of the lives and work [of] Thomas Cooper, 1805–1892, and Thomas Miller, 1807–1874
pp.14–23 in *The Lincolnshire historian*, vol.II, no.10, 1963.

4368. **COLLINS, Philip**
Thomas Cooper, the Chartist: Byron and the 'poets of the poor'
Nottingham: University of Nottingham, 1969. 24p.
Text of the Byron lecture, 1969.

4369. **COOPER, Thomas**
The Life of Thomas Cooper
Leicester: Leicester University Press, 1971. 31, viii, 400p., [frontis].
(The Victorian library)
Originally published: 1872. Another ed.: 1876, including short postscript and different frontispiece.

4370. **HUNDLEBY, H.R.**
Thomas Cooper, the Chartist poet and Christian preacher
[198?]. 8p.
Typescript.

4371. **ROBERT, Stephen**
Thomas Cooper: radical and poet, c.1830–1860
395 leaves. 2 vols.
Typescript.
Thesis [M.Litt.] – University of Birmingham, 1986.
Includes bibliography.

4372.
[Biographical article about John Crabtree]
pp.278–279: ill. in *Lincolnshire poacher*, vol.1, no.12, May, 1901.
Manager of G.N. & G.E. Joint Railway.

4373.
Two Lincoln worthies: Robert Craven and Abraham Morrice
pp.54–57 in *Journal of the Friends Historical Society*, vol.XXIV, 1927.
Some of the details are provided by J.W.F. Hill.

4374.　CROFT, William
[Autobiographical article]
pp.118–119, [1]p. of plates in *Lincolnshire poacher*, vol.1, no.6, November, 1900.
Canon at St.Hugh's Roman Catholic Church.

4375.　DE WINT, Harriet
A Short memoir of Peter De Wint and William Hilton, R.A.
London: printed Harrison, [185?].　32p.

4376.　COOPER, F.J.
Hilton House, Lincoln: a question of fashion in art
pp.390–394 in *The Lincolnshire historian*, no.11, [1953].
About De Wint and Hilton.

4377.　REDGRAVE, Gilbert R.
David Cox and Peter De Wint
London: Sampson Low, Marston, Searle & Rivington, 1891.　120p., [15] leaves of plates.
(Illustrated biographies of the great artists)

4378.　HOLME, Charles
Masters of English landscape painting: J.S. Cotman, David Cox, Peter De Wint
London: 'The Studio', 1903.　[48]p., [134]p. of plates.
Includes an essay on De Wint by Walter Shaw Sparrow and 39p. of plates.

4379.　ELVIN, Laurence
Lincolnshire worthies: Peter De Wint
pp.191–196: ill. in *Lincolnshire magazine*, vol.3, 1936–38.

4380.　HILL, J.W.F.
Peter De Wint: a footnote about his Lincoln home and the Castle ditch
pp.235–236 in *Lincolnshire magazine*, vol.3, 1936–38.

4381.　HARMSWORTH, Geoffrey
Peter De Wint and Lincoln
pp.245–250: ill. in *Apollo*, vol.XXI, no.155, November, 1937.
Author was responsible for Peter De Wint exhibition held at Usher Gallery, 1937.

4382.　LINCOLN, Libraries, Museum and Art Gallery Committee
Catalogue of the Peter De Wint collection
Lincoln: The Committee, 1947.　40p.: ill.
Holdings of the Usher Art Gallery.

4383.　DALTON, John
Painters and place.　6: Peter De Wint
pp.164–172: ill. in *The Countryman*, spring, 1962.

4384.　DAVIS, Frank
The Very English art of painting in watercolour
pp.24–25: ill. in *The Illustrated London news*, February 12, 1966.
Exhibition of De Wint at Reading Museum and Art Gallery.

4385.
Loan exhibition of paintings and drawings by P. De Wint in aid of Lincoln Cathedral Fabric Maintenance Fund
London: Thos. Agneu, 1966.   35p., [16] leaves of plates.

4386.   HERRMAN, Luke
The Timeliness of Peter De Wint
pp.232–233: ill. in *Country life*, February 3, 1966.

4387.   SMITH, M.L.
List of works by Peter De Wint, 1784–1849, in the Usher Gallery, Lincoln, January, 1970
[1970].   [8] leaves.
Typescript.

4388.   USHER GALLERY
Peter De Wint, 1784–1849: the Usher Gallery, Lincoln: [catalogue]
Lincoln: The Gallery, [1971?].   24p.: ill.

4389.   THOMAS, Denis
One long, glorious summer
pp.40–41, 43–44: ill. in *In Britain*, June, 1978.
    About Peter De Wint and Lincoln.

4390.   SCRASE, David
Drawings & watercolours by Peter De Wint: a loan exhibition inaugurated at the Fitzwilliam Museum, Cambridge
selected and catalogued by David Scrase.
Cambridge: Cambridge University Press, 1979.   xxv, 52p., 70, viiip. of plates.

4391.   THOMAS, Denis
Drawings and watercolours by Peter De Wint
pp.70–71: ill. in *The Connoisseur*, September, 1979.
    Drawing attention to exhibition at Fitzwilliam Museum at Cambridge.

4392.   SMITH, Hammond
Peter De Wint, 1784–1849
London: F. Lewis, 1982.   195p.: ill.
Includes index.
ISBN 0853170576
    Extensive appendices enumerating collections, sales, etc.

4393.   DAWSON, Derek
Peter De Wint
pp.28–30: ill. in *Lincolnshire life*, vol.24, no.8, November, 1984.

4394.
Peter De Wint, 1784–1849: a bicentenary exhibition, 24 November, 1984–12 January, 1985: [catalogue]
Hanley: Stoke on Trent City Museum and Art Gallery, 1985.   73p.: ill.
ISBN 0905080319

4395.
Clifford Landseer Exley, 4th January, 1874–8th January, 1957: [obituary]
pp.49–50 in *The Lincolnshire historian*, vol.II, no.4, 1957.

4396.
Letters from John Wallace to Madam Whichcot, and Some correspondence of John Fardell, deputy registrar, 1802–1805
letters edited by C.M. Lloyd; correspondence edited by Mary E. Finch.
Lincoln: Lincoln Record Society, 1973.   74p., [frontis].
(Lincoln Record Society, 66)
Includes index.
> Fardell correspondence of interest in connection with the city of Lincoln.

4397.   **STENTON, Doris Mary**
Charles Wilmer Foster, 3rd June, 1866–29th October, 1935: [obituary]
pp.215–218: ill. in *The Lincolnshire magazine*, vol.2, 1934–36.

4398.   ——————
Eminent local historians.   1: Canon C.W. Foster of Timberland, Lincolnshire, 1866–1935
pp.157–162 in *The Amateur historian*, vol.6, no.5, autumn, 1964.
> Founder of Lincoln Record Society.

4399.   **MAJOR, Kathleen**
Canon Charles Wilmer Foster, M.A. Hon., D.Litt. (Oxon), F.S.A.: a pioneer archivist and editor of records
pp.42–49: ill. in *Archives*, vol.XVIII, no.77, 1987.

4400.   **DEACON, Margaret B.**
G. Herbert Fowler, 1861–1940: the forgotten oceanographer
pp.261–296: ill. in *Notes and records of the Royal Society of London*, vol.38, pt.2, March, 1984.
> Founder of Bedfordshire Historical Record Society, who was born in Lincoln and was the son of the headmaster of Lincoln Grammar School.

4401.   **FOWLER, William**
The Correspondence of William Fowler of Winterton, in the county of Lincoln
edited by Joseph Thomas Fowler.
[Durham]: [privately printed], 1907.   772p.
Includes index.
> Minor references to Lincoln throughout the text.

4402.
Memorial to the late Thomas Charles Fry, Dean of Lincoln
Lincoln: [Lincoln Cathedral Restoration Fund], 1930.   3p.
> Includes receipts and payments of the Fund, 1922–29.

4403.   **WINTERBOTTOM, Derek O.**
Doctor Fry: a study of Thomas Charles Fry, headmaster of Berkhamsted School, 1888–1910, Dean of Lincoln, 1910–1930
Berkhamsted: [The Author], 1977.   56p.: ill., [frontis].

4404.   **RICHARDSON, Eric**
John of Gaunt's tree
pp.26–28: ill. in *Lincolnshire life*, vol.15, no.3, May, 1975.
> Lincoln is mentioned, especially in the context of Henry Beaufort, son of John of Gaunt and Katherine Swynford, who became Bishop of Lincoln.

4405.   **GARTON, Charles**
Boswell and Dr. Gordon
pp.63–64 in *Durham University journal*, new series, vol.XV, no.2.
> Account of Boswell's visit to Lincoln and his meeting with Dr. Gordon whom he mistakenly took for the Chancellor.

4406.   **HALL, B.C.**
Round the world in ninety years
Lincoln: [The Author], [19??].   150p.: ill.

4407.   **HALL, Richard**
Mr Richard Hall, J.P.: [biographical article]
pp.124–126: ill. in *Lincolnshire poacher*, vol.1, no.10, March, 1901.
    Secretary of the Lawn Hospital.

4408.   **RAYNER, Brother**
A Busy life: Wor. Bro. Richard Hall, P.M. of the Witham Lodge, no.297, Lincoln...an appreciation
[Bros. Rayner and Lilly].
Lincoln: printed M.A. Doncaster, 1907.   68, 21p., [frontis].
    Appendix provides verbatim proceedings of meeting at which the volume was presented.

4409.   **GATES, Samuel**
The Substance of a sermon, preached on the occasion of the death of Mr John Hannah, on Sunday, September 28th, 1800, at the Methodist Chapel in the city of Lincoln
Lincoln: printed and sold W. Brooke, 1800.   16p.

4410.   **JOBSON, Frederick J.**
The Beloved disciple: a sermon preached in Wesley-Chapel, Lincoln, January 26th, 1868, on the death of the Rev. John Hannah, D.D., with a biographical sketch of the deceased
London: printed Hayman, 1848.   viii, 139p.

4411.   **OVERTON, J.H.**
John Hannah: a clerical study
London: Rivingtons, 1890.   283p., [frontis].
    Born in Lincoln, 1818.

4412.   **GRAY, J.**
John Edward Harris, 1910–1968, elected F.R.S., 1956
pp.99–108 in *Biographical memoirs of the Royal Society*, vol.15, 1969.
    Born in Lincoln, attended Rosemary Lane Elementary School and City School. Became Professor of Zoology at Bristol.

4413.   **HETT, Marjorie J.F.**
A Family history
Horncastle: W.K. Morton, 1934.   139, [5]p., [10] leaves of plates.
    pp.17–25: William Hett, Priest Vicar of Lincoln, 1786–1833.

4414.
New portrait of Sir Francis Hill
pp.26–27 in *Lincolnshire life*, vol.16, no.2, April, 1976.
    Reproduction of the portrait by Leonard Boden which hangs in the Great Hall at the University of Nottingham.

4415.
Tributes to Sir Francis Hill, C.B.E.: [on his retirement as chairman of the Association of Municipal Corporations]
pp.632, 634–635, 637, [port.] in *The Municipal review*, vol.37, no.443, November, 1966.

4416.   **JONES, G.W.**
Lincoln: the past with the present
pp.194–196: ill. in *The Municipal review*, vol.46, no.550, October, 1975.
    Sir Francis Hill and the publication of *Victorian Lincoln*.

4417.   CARTER, H.B.
Sir Joseph Banks: the cryptic Georgian
pp.53–62: ill. in *Lincolnshire history and archaeology*, vol.16, 1981.
> Lecture in memory of Sir Francis Hill, delivered to the Society for Lincolnshire History and Archaeology, on 1 November, 1980, which gives a little biographical information about him.

4418.   WILLIAMS, Heather
[Thesis]
1 vol.
Thesis [Ph.D.] – University of Nottingham, [19??].
> pp.205–212: William Hilton.

4419.   GARLAND, Austin
Lincolnshire worthies.   No.2: William Hilton, R.A.
pp.161–165: ill. in *The Lincolnshire magazine*, vol.1, 1932–34.

4420.   HINE, J.E.
Days gone by: being an account of past years chiefly in central Africa
London: John Murray, 1924.   313p., map, [11]p. of plates.
> pp.62–64: theological training at Lincoln in 1886.

4421.
Two Lincolnshire artists: Lance Holtby, Norman Wright: a retrospective exhibition held in the Usher Gallery, Lincoln, 2nd to 30th May, 1970
[Lincoln]: [The Gallery], [1970].   1 folded card.
> Both at Lincoln School of Art.

4422.   SRAWLEY, J.H.
Michael Honywood: Dean of Lincoln, 1660–81, a story of the English Church in critical times
Lincoln: Friends of Lincoln Cathedral, 1950.   24p., [2] leaves of plates.
(Lincoln Minster pamphlets, 5)
Reprinted with corrections: 1981,   28p.: ill., with additional photographs.

4423.   WILLIAMS, Joan
Michael Honywood, 1596–1681: an exhibition in the Medieval Library of Lincoln Cathedral, May–October, 1981: [biographical notes and catalogue]
[Lincoln]: [The Cathedral], 1981.   10p.

4424.   MANNERS, Emily
Emily Hooton: first Quaker woman preacher, 1600–1672
London: Headley, 1914.   vii, 95p., [3] leaves of plates.
(Journal of the Friends Historical Society supplement, 12)
Includes index.
> pp.13–16: prisoner in Lincoln Castle and other references.

4425.   HOUGHTON, Harry
Operation Portland: the autobiography of a spy
London: Rupert Hart-Davis, 1972.   164p.
ISBN 0246105488
> Born in Lincoln.

4426.   HUNT, Frederick
And truly serve: memoirs of Frederick Hunt, sheriff of Lincoln, 1959–60, high constable, 1960–61
[1980].   52 leaves.
Typescript.

4427.
[Biographical details about John Irving]
in *Australian dictionary of biography, vol.2, 1788–1850.*
> Lincoln-born surgeon.

4428.   EVERITT, James
The Polemic divine, or Memoirs of the life, writings and opinions of the Rev. Daniel Isaac
London: Hamilton, Adams, 1839.   xx, 481p., [frontis].
> Wesleyan who set up school in Lincoln in 1799.   Account of this, pp.13–29.

4429.   HESSELL, Graham S.
Diana Jay: fashion designer
pp.36–37: ill. in *Lincolnshire life*, vol.18, no.1, April, 1978.
> Real name Diana McMahon; born in Lincoln and educated at South Park High School and 1
> year at Lincoln College of Art.

4430.   GREGORY, Benjamin
*The Life of Frederick James Jobson, D.D.,...with the funeral memorials of Dr. Osborn
and Dr. Pope and ten original sermons, printed from Dr. Jobson's own manuscripts*
sermons edited by Elizabeth Jobson.
London: T. Woolmer, 1884.   328p., [frontis].
> Memoir originally published: *Wesleyan-Methodist magazine*, February, March, April, 1881.
> Parents moved to Lincoln when child, articled to study architecture under E.J. Willson.
> Friend of Thomas Cooper.

4431.   JONES, J.D.
Three score years and ten: the autobiography of J.D. Jones
London: Hodder and Stoughton, 1940.   327p., [frontis].
> pp.34–65: Minister at Newland, 1889–98.

4432.   PORRITT, Arthur
J.D. Jones of Bournemouth
by Arthur Porrit [and others].
London: Independent Press, 1942.   340p., [7]p. of plates.
Includes index.

4433.   GOULDING, R.W.
Sir Richard Kaye, Bart., D.C.L., Dean of Lincoln
17p., [3] leaves of plates in 80th and 81st *Reports of the Architectural and
Archaeological Society in the county of Lincoln.*

4434.   CLAY, Rotha Mary
Samuel Hieronymus Grimm of Burgdorf in Switzerland
London: Faber and Faber, [1939].   xxx, 111p., 76p. of plates.
> pp.92–93: friendship with Dr. Richard Kaye, Dean of Lincoln, who was responsible for
> recording discoveries of Little St.Hugh and Bishop Hugh.

4435.   KEYWORTH, Leonard James
Lance-Corporal Leonard James Keyworth, V.C.
[2]p.: ill. in *The Link: the magazine of the City School Lincoln Association*, no.23,
autumn, 1985.

4436.   TUNER, S. Blois
Memorials of Sir Edward Lake, Chancellor of Lincoln, relative to his loyal services and
interview with Charles I after the Battle of Edgehill, from original evidence
pp.190–196 in *Memoirs illustrative of the history and antiquities of the county and city of
Lincoln*, 1850.

4437.   **LAMB, Charles**
The Essays of Elia; Last essays of Elia; Popular fallacies
London: Thomas Nelson, [18??].   iv, 448p.
> pp.216–223: 'Poor relations'.   Father's roots in Lincoln; references to 'above boys' and 'below boys'.

4438.   **LIDGETT, Thomas L.**
The Life of Thomas L. Lidgett, one of Lincolnshire's best known men as written by himself.
Lincoln: W.K. Morton, [1908].   54p., [frontis].
> Jeweller with shop in the High Street.

4439.   **LODGE, George**
George Lodge: artist, naturalist
edited by John Savory.
London: Croom Helm, 1986.   118p.: ill.
ISBN 0709933665
> Attended Lincoln School of Art.

4440.   **LOGSDAIL, William**
A Lincolnshire artist: William Logsdail
pp.39–44 in *Old Lincolnshire*, vol.1, 1885.
> Born in Lincoln, 1859, son of Lincoln Cathedral verger.   Attended Lincoln School of Art.

4441.   **COOPER, Francis J.**
William Logsdail of Lincoln, 1859–1944: memorial exhibition, 1952
Lincoln: Lincoln, Libraries, Museum and Art Gallery Committee, 1952.   19p.: ill.

4442.
The Study of medieval records: essays in honour of Kathleen Major
edited by D.A. Bullough and R.L. Storey.
Oxford: Clarendon Press, 1971.   327p., 4 plates, [frontis].
> pp.v–x: 'An appreciation', by Anne Whiteman.

4443.
[Biographical article about William Mansell]
p.26, [1]p.: ill. in *Lincolnshire poacher*, vol.2, no.14, July, 1901.
> Chief Constable of Lincolnshire.

4444.
From director to conductor
p.441: ill. in *Gramophone*, September, 1978.
> Article about Sir Neville Marriner and the Academy of St Martin-in-the-Fields.

4445.   **MARTIN, Jonathan**
The Life of Jonathan Martin of Darlington, tanner
written by himself.   3rd ed.
Lincoln: printed and sold for the author by R.E. Leary, 1828.   50p.: ill.
> Account of being attacked by a landlady in Lincoln.

4446.   **WALLIS, Lena**
Life and letters of Caroline Martyn
London: Labour Leader, 1898.   93p.
> Fabian; born in Lincoln, 1867, and lived there until age of 19.

4447.   MOZLEY, T.
Reminiscences chiefly of towns, villages and schools
London: Longmans, Green, 1885.   2 vols.
> Resident of Gainsborough.   pp.124–130: musings on nature of job of a Subdean, especially Subdean Bayley of Lincoln Cathedral.

4448.   BOOLE, George
An Address on the genius and discoveries of Sir Isaac Newton...Thursday, Feb. 5, 1835 at the Lincoln and Lincolnshire Mechanics' Institution...on the presentation of a marble bust of that philosopher by the Right Honourable Lord Yarborough
Lincoln: printed at the Gazette, 1835.   23p.

4449.   DAWES, Frank
William Norris of Lincoln
pp.738–741 in *The Musical times*, no.1565, vol.114, July, 1973.
> Master of the choristers in 1690.

4450.   OSBALDESTON, George
Squire Osbaldeston: his autobiography
edited, with commentary, by E.D. Cuming.
London: Bodley Head, 1926.   260p., [74]p. of plates.
Includes index.
> Connections with the Burton Hunt.

4451.   BIRD, W.H.B.
Osbert the sheriff
pp.188–216 in *The Genealogist*, new series, XXXII.
> Sheriff of Lincolnshire, 1096–1114 and Yorkshire, 1110–14, who had a Lincoln residence.

4452.   PACY, Joseph
The Reminiscences of a gauger: imperial taxation, past and present, compared
Newark: Tomlinsons and Whiles, 1873.   xi, 127p.
> Apprenticed to gunsmith in Lincoln but few details.

4453.   BINNALL, Peter B.
Lincolnshire worthies.   No.9: J.S. Padley
pp.28–29: ill. in *Lincolnshire life*, vol.20, no.6, September, 1980.
> Padley was an engineer and surveyor who worked upon fen drainage.

4454.   RUDD, Niall
T.E. Page: schoolmaster extraordinary
Bristol: Bristol Classical Press, 1981.   69p.: ill.
ISBN 0906515637
> Editor of the Classics with family connections with Lincoln.

4455.   BEST, Henry Digby
Conversations of Paley
communicated by the author of *Four years in France.*
pp.1–21 in *The New monthly magazine*, vol.XIX, no.LXXIII, January, 1827.
> Includes some Lincoln anecdotes featuring the Subdean of Lincoln.

4456.   CLARKE, M.L.
Paley: evidences for the man
London: SPCK, 1974.   viii, 161p.

4457.   LeMALHIEU, D.L.
The Mind of William Paley, a philosopher and his age
Lincoln, Neb.: University of Nebraska, 1976.   215p., [frontis].

4458.
[Biographical entry for Francis Cranmer Penrose]
pp.102–103 in *Dictionary of national biography*.

4459.   POOL, William
Death of an extraordinary man
[Lincoln]: published for Samuel Pool by Harry Fole, [c.1856].   1 sheet.
Originally published: *Lincolnshire chronicle*, September 12, 1856.
   Subject was inventor of an iron boat and improved paddles of steam engines.

4460.   MOULTON, S.H.
A Memorial of the late Mary Proudlove of the city of Lincoln
Lincoln: printed R. Bulman, 1851.   47p.
   Methodist, born in Hykeham, 1774.

4461.   FERREY, Benjamin
Recollections of A.N. Welby Pugin and his father, Augustus Pugin, with notices of their works
London: Edward Stanford, 1861.   xv, 473p.: ill., [8] plates.
   pp.45–47: account of Mrs Pugin getting locked in Lincoln Cathedral.

4462.
Lincolnshire life tunes in to the 'Quiet Man of Music': Steve Race
pp.44–45: ill. in *Lincolnshire life*, vol.6, no.3, May, 1966.

4463.   RACE, Steve
Musician at large
London: Eyre Methuen, 1979.   223p., [8]p. of plates.
ISBN 0413397408

4464.   OLLE, James G.
Henry Rond, 1871–1917, first city librarian of Lincoln
[1968].   [2] leaves.
Typescript.

4465.   ——————
A Librarian of no importance
pp.291–298 in *Library review*, vol.22, no.6, summer, 1970.
   About Henry Rond.

4466.   RUDDOCK, L.I.N.
The Diary of a day in the life of a Toc Emma merchant
by O.C. 'Gut'.
Lincoln: J.W. Ruddock, [1921?].   12p.

4467.
Captain J.S. Ruston: [biographical article]
pp.238–239 in *Lincolnshire poacher*.

4468.
[Obituary of Joseph Ruston]
in *Lincolnshire echo*, June 11th, 1897.

4469. PLATT, Catherine
Joseph Ruston, 1835–1897: a captain of industry
[1980]. 8 leaves.
Typescript.

4470. BUTTERY, Robert W.
Joseph Ruston, Victorian entrepreneur
[1988]. 19 leaves, [4] leaves of plates.
Typescript.
    'A'-level history project at De Aston School.

4471. SAMSON, Thomas
The Case of Thomas Samson, Gent.: setting forth the horrible persecution and oppression he has undergone, only appearing in the service of his King and countrey
[London]: [s.n.], [1698]. 16p.
    Includes petitions by Samson who was post-master of Lincoln branch.

4472.
An Appreciation of Lucie Evelyn Savill, O.B.E., M.A., headmistress, Lincoln Christ's Hospital Girls' High School, 1910–1943
by some of her old girls, former colleagues and friends.
Lincoln: Lincoln High School Old Girls' Association, 1971. 31p., [4]p. of plates, [frontis].

4473. KENSCHAFT, Patricia C.
Charlotte Angas Scott, 1858–1931
pp.98–110 in *The College mathematics journal*, vol.18, no.2, March, 1987.
    First British woman to receive doctorate. Her father, Caleb Scott, was Pastor of the Congregational Church in Lincoln and married Eliza Ann Exley. Charlotte was born in Lincoln but moved to Manchester at the age of seven.

4474. WRIGHT, Samuel
Memoir of the Rev. Thomas Scott
by Samuel Wright of Lincoln.
London: Jarrold, 1862. 12p.

4475.
Lincoln's benefactor passes: death of Mr Alfred Shuttleworth: [obituary]
in *Lincoln leader*, 28th November, 1925.

4476.
Death of Joseph Shuttleworth, Esq.: [obituary]
in *Lincolnshire chronicle*, February 2, 1883.

4477.
A Group of Parliamentary oddities: [Colonel Sibthorp]
pp.462–465 in *Fraser's magazine*, October, 1847.

4478.
Ode of Sibthorp, by the Poet Laureate: [April 26, 1845]
pp.220–221: ill. in *Ballads and contributions to **Punch**, 1842–50.*

4479. SYKES, Christopher
Colonel Sibthorp: a festival centenary
pp.14–20: ill. in *History today*, May, 1951.

4480. ALTICK, Richard D.
'Our gallant Colonel' in *Punch* and Parliament
pp.424–445: ill. in *Bulletin of the New York Public Library*, September, 1965.

4481. DAY, Peter
The Eccentric Conservative
pp.24, 41: ill. in *Isis*, no.1500, 11 November, 1965.
  About Colonel Sibthorp.

4482. MELTON, B.L.
He humiliated the Queen...but it was Lincoln that paid the price
pp.48–49 in *Lincolnshire life*, vol.8, no.5, July, 1968.
  About the Sibthorp family and especially the eccentricities of Charles De Laet Waldo Sibthorp.

4483. MORRIS, R.J.B.
Honest: but an outrageous opponent of reading for the masses
pp.574–575 in *Library Association record*, vol.79, no.10, October, 1977.
  Another of Colonel Sibthorp's crusades.

4484. KIME, Winston
Lincolnshire worthies.   No.24: Colonel Charles Sibthorp
pp.24–26: ill. in *Lincolnshire life*, vol.21, no.7, October, 1981.

4485. SHARMAN, Frank A.
Colonel Sibthorp: the Don Quixote of railways
pp.47–51 in *Journal of the Railway and Canal Historical Society*, vol.27, no.4, March, 1982.

4486. BRUCE, M.R.
John Sibthorp
pp.353–362 in *Taxon*, vol.19, no.3, June, 1970.
  Professor of Botany at Oxford who attended Lincoln School.

4487. BIBER, G.E.
Catholicity v. Sibthorp, or Some help to answer the question whether the Rev. R.W. Sibthorp, B.D., is now or ever was a Catholic?: in a series of letters addressed to him
London: F.G.F. and J. Rivington, 1842.   50, 55, 58, 55, 61p.

4488. FOWLER, J.
Richard Waldo Sibthorp: a biography, told chiefly in his own correspondence
London: W. Skeffington, 1880.   xvi, 392p., [frontis].

4489. STANCLIFFE, H.E.
Richard Waldo Sibthorp, 1792–1879: pious founder of St Anne's Bedehouses, Lincoln, the commemoration of the centenary of whose foundation falls this year, on July 26th in *Lincoln diocesan magazine*, August, 1948.

4490. G., G.A.
The Twenty-ninth president of the Lincolnshire Naturalists' Union: Arthur Smith, F.L.S.
pp.89–90, [1] leaf of plates in *Transactions of Lincolnshire Naturalists' Union*, 1934?.

4491. BURGESS, Walter H.
John Smith, the Se-Baptist, Thomas Helwys and the first Baptist Church in England, with fresh light upon the pilgrim fathers' church
London: James Clarke, 1911.   363, 32p.
  pp.45–62: time as preacher to the city of Lincoln, though more concerned with theology than external circumstances.

4492.   **LEARY, William**
Four Lincolnshire Methodists
[1979].   21 leaves.
Typescript.
    Includes John Smith, 1820–99.

4493.   **HUNT, Alfred**
A Few notes concerning the founder of Lincoln Christ's Hospital, of the old Blue Coat
School, Richard Smith, 1530–1602
pp.243–246, 1 folded genealogical table in *AAS reports and papers*, vol.35, 1919–20.

4494.   **NAYLOR, Kate**
Richard Smith, M.D., the founder of Christ's Hospital, Lincoln
Lincoln: Governors of the Foundation of Lincoln Christ's Hospital, 1951.   69p.: ill.,
plans, [4] leaves of plates.

4495.   **SMITH, John**
In loving remembrance of Walter Smith, of Lincoln
by his father.
Lincoln: The Author, [1870].   39p.

4496.
William Smith: one of the famous Smiths in history
[Lincoln]: [Lincoln Cathedral], [1972].   1 sheet: ill.

4497.   **SMYTH, John**
The Works of John Smyth, fellow of Christ's College, 1594–8
with notes and biography by W.T. Whitley.
Tercentenary ed.
Cambridge: Cambridge University Press, 1915.   2 vols.
    pp.xxxix–xlvii: Lincoln.

4498.   **BAKKER, Johannes**
John Smyth: de stichter van het Baptisme
[Utrecht]: H. Veenman & Zonen N.V. Wageningen, 1964.   204p., [2]p. of plates.
    Smyth in Lincoln in 1600 at St Peter-at-Arches and St Peter-at-Pleas.

4499.
[Biographical article about John Edward Spain]
pp.10–13: ill. in *Lincolnshire poacher*, vol.2, no.13, 1901.
    Attended Lincoln School of Art and subsequently apprenticed to William Scorer.

4500.   **MAJOR, Kathleen**
Doris Mary Stenton, 1894–1971
12p., [port.] in *Proceedings of the British Academy*, vol.LIII, 1972.

4501.   **STENTON, Doris Mary**
Frank Merry Stenton
pp.315–423, [port.] in *Proceedings of the British Academy*, vol.LIV, [1973?]
    Friendship with Canon Foster and involvement with Lincoln Record Society.

4502.   **STIRLING, Robert L.**
[Transcript of taped interview with Robert Stirling who became planning officer to
Lindsey County Council]
[1987].   [9] leaves.
Typescript.
    In 1924 became articled clerk to Lincoln City Engineer and eventually himself became
    Lincoln's Chief Assistant Engineer.

4503.
A Great and glorious victory: [account of Battle of Trafalgar with paragraph on John Sykes of Lincoln who fought by Nelson's side at battle of Cape St Vincent on Valentine's Day in 1797]
Lincoln: printed J.W. Drury, 1805.   1 sheet.

4504.   **TAYLER, J. Lionel**
The Story of a life
by the late J. Lionel Tayler.
London: Williams and Norgate, 1931.   411p., [48] leaves of plates.
    Minister of Unitarian congregation in Lincoln in 1923.

4505.   ——————
New England and new America and other writings of the late J. Lionel Tayler, with memoir and tributes
edited by F.H. Haywood.
London: Williams & Norgate, 1933.   333p., [frontis].

4506.   **LOOKER, Samuel J.**
Portrait of a great man: John Lionel Tayler, 1874–1930
London: J. Lionel Tayler Trustees, 1939.   46p.

4507.   **TAYLER, John Lionel**
Unitarianism: essays and addresses
edited with a biographical and critical study of the author by Samuel J. Looker.
London: J. Lionel Tayler Trustees, 1939.

4508.
Alderman Thomas Francis Taylor, J.P.: [biographical notes]
[1974].   4 leaves.
Typescript.
    Former mayor of Lincoln who was presented with the freedom of the city in 1974.

4509.
[Unveiling of the statue of Tennyson near the Cathedral, July 15th, 1905]
[Lincoln]: [s.n.], [1905].   1 sheet.

4510.
Death of Sir William Tritton, tank pioneer of 1914–18 war: [obituary]
ill. in *Lincolnshire chronicle*, 28 September, 1946.

4511.   **RIGBY, W.**
The Man who made tanks
pp.42–43: ill. in *Lincolnshire life*, vol.8, no.1, March, 1968.
    About Sir William Tritton and Foster's.

4512.   **TAYLOR, E.A.**
Reminiscences of James Ward Usher
[1921].   [3] leaves.
Typescript.

4513.   **ELVIN, Laurence**
About James Ward Usher of Lincoln
pp.5–8 in *The Fireside magazine*, no.3, vol.1, December, 1963.

4514.   BOURNE, John
James Ward Usher, 1845–1921: a story of the art collector and philanthropist who immortalized the Lincoln Imp
pp.36–40: ill. in *Lincolnshire life*, vol.10, no.6, August, 1970.

4515.   PERKINS, Ilona
James Ward Usher: the man behind the monument
pp.24–27: ill. in *Lincolnshire life*, vol.17, no.2, May, 1977.

4516.
The Precentor of Lincoln: [obituary of Edmund Venables]
pp.51–54 in *Lincoln diocesan magazine*, April, 1895.

4517.   WICKHAM, Edward C.
Lincoln Cathedral choir: sermon after Precentor Venables' death
[Lincoln?]: [s.n.], [1895].   7p.

4518.   T., M.L.
Was Archdeacon Wakeford impersonated?
London: John Bale, 1922.   16p.

4519.   WAKEFORD, John
Not peace but a sword: a biography
Biggin Hill: The Author, [c.1926?].   39p., [frontis].
     Mainly consists of letters in support of his good name.

4520.   TREHERNE, John
Dangerous precincts: the mystery of the Wakeford case
London: Jonathon Cape, 1987.   192p.: ill., [14]p. of plates.
     Wakeford was Prebendary of the Cathedral in 1912.

4521.   KETTERINGHAM, John
John Walden of Lincoln
p.6: ill. in *The Ringing world*, 4 January, 1985.
     92 year old bellringer at Lincoln Cathedral.

4522.
[Folder of information about William Tom Warrener, including list of paintings and news cuttings about exhibition mounted in 1940s in Usher Gallery]
[19??].   1 portfolio.

4523.   HOULT, Kenneth
The Life and work of the painter, William Warrener
pp.37–41 in *Lincolnshire writers*, summer/autumn, 1970.

4524.
William Tom Warrener, 1861–1934, 'l'Anglais au Moulin Rouge' : July 13th–September 8th, 1974: [exhibition catalogue]
Lincoln: Usher Gallery, 1974.   [14]p., [4]p. of plates.

4525.   PERKINS, I.
Poachings: Warrener masterpiece remains in Lincoln
pp.44–45: ill. in *Lincolnshire life*, vol.17, no.5, August, 1977.
     Gives brief resume of career of Tom Warrener, 1861–1934.

4526.   **SCORER, H.S.**
Some lesser-known architects of the nineteenth century
pp.839–850: ill. in *Journal of the Royal Society for the Encouragement of Arts,
Manufactures and Commerce*, vol.CXIX, no.5184, November, 1971.
>   About William Watkins who came to work in Lincoln in 1859.

4527.   **JACKSON, Thomas**
Memoirs of the life and writings of the Rev. Richard Watson
London: John Mason, 1834.   xv, 667p., [frontis].
>   Moved to Lincoln when 8 years old and educated at Lincoln Grammar School.

4528.   **WATSON, Richard**
The Works of the Rev. Richard Watson
London: John Mason, 1834–37.   12 vols.
>   Vol.1: memoirs of the life and writings of the Rev. Richard Watson, by Thomas Jackson.

4529.   ——————
Sermons and outlines [with] his character and writings by James Dixon
edited with a biographical sketch by William Willan.
London: Hamilton, Adams, [1865].   351p.

4530.   **STEVENSON, G.J.**
Methodist worthies
London: T.C. Jack, 1884.   2 vols.
>   pp.238–248: Richard Watson.

4531.   **RAGG, Lonsdale**
*A Memoir of Edward Charles Wickham: Dean of Lincoln, formerly headmaster of
Wellington College*
London: Edward Arnold, 1911.   xii, 236p., [5] leaves of plates.
>   pp.120–156: Lincoln, 1894–1910.

4532.
[Biographical article about J.G. Williams when mayor]
pp.7–9: ill. in *Lincolnshire poacher*, vol.1, no.1, May, 1900.

4533.   **BLOOMFIELD, David**
The 'Mad doctor' of Lincolnshire
with biographical notes by B.L. Melton.
pp.28–30: ill. in *Lincolnshire life*, vol.6, no.5, July, 1966.
>   About the Reverend Dr. Francis Willis, born in Lincoln in 1718, son of one of the Vicars of
>   Lincoln Cathedral.   He was physician to the Lincoln Hospital and was involved in its
>   establishment.

4534.   **MELTON, B.L.**
Notable Lincolnshire personages: Rev. Doctor Francis Willis and his sons
in *The Lawn magazine*, 1st June, 1966.

4535.   **MacALPINE, Ida**
George III and the mad-business
by Ida MacAlpine & Richard Hunter.
London: Penguin, 1969.   xv, 407p.: ill., [frontis].
ISBN 0713901063
>   pp.269–276: Dr. Francis Willis.

4536.
[Obituary of E.J. Willson]
in *Lincoln, Rutland and Stamford mercury*, Friday, September 15th, 1854.

4537.
[Biographical entry of E.J. Willson]
pp.678–679 in *Biographical dictionary of English architects, 1660–1840*, 1954.

4538.   FINCH, Mary
Edward James Willson of Lincoln: architect and antiquary
pp.42–43: ill. in *Lincolnshire life*, vol.26, no.9, December, 1986.

4539.   ⸺⸺⸺
Edward James Willson, estate architect, Hainton, 1833–54: [notes for a visit of the
Society for Lincolnshire History and Archaeology to Hainton, 6 September, 1986]
[Lincoln]: [s.n.], [1986].   4 leaves, map.

4540.
Edward James Willson appeal: [leaflet]
Lincoln: Society for Lincolnshire History and Archaeology, [c.1986].   1 folded sheet: ill.
   Gives biographical information.

4541.   KELSH, Thomas
*'Personal recollections' of the Right Reverend Robert William Willson, D.D., first Bishop
of Hobart Town, with a portrait of His Lordship, and an introduction on the state of
religion in Tasmania prior to the year 1844*
Hobart: Davies, 1882.   xiv, 157p., [frontis].
   Born in Lincoln, 1794, younger brother of E.J. Willson.

4542.
[Biographical entry of Robert William Willson]
pp.491–493 in *Dictionary of Australian biography*, vol.II, 1949.

4543.   W., J.T.
An Appreciation: [of Ken Wood]
p.9 in *Lincolnshire history and archaeology*, vol.17, 1982.
   Prominent member of the Society for Lincolnshire History and Archaeology.

4544.   WOODWARD, Reg
Boy on a hill: memories of childhood and youth in Lincoln between the wars
[Grantham]: [The Author], 1984.   [95]p.: ill.
ISBN 0950958603

4545.   WORDSWORTH, Charles
*Annals of my early life, 1806–1846, with occasional compositions in Latin and English
verse*
London: Longmans, Green, 1891.   xvi, 420p.
Includes index.
   Some references to brother Christopher, Bishop of Lincoln.

4546.   WORDSWORTH, Elizabeth
Glimpses of the past
London: A.R. Mowbray, 1912.   218p., [8] leaves of plates.

BIOGRAPHICAL

4547. BATTISCOMBE, Georgina
Reluctant pioneer: a life of Elizabeth Wordsworth
London: Constable, 1978. 320p., [12]p. of plates.
ISBN 0094612005
> Daughter of Bishop of Lincoln and friend of the Benson family.

4548. WOODWARD, C.S.
Susanna Wordsworth: head of Greyladies, 1900–1911
pp.508–514: ill. in *The Treasury*, [1911?].
> Lived in Pottergate for 15 years.

4549.
Mr Hugh Wyatt, J.P.: [biographical article while mayor]
pp.74–75, [1]p. of plates in *Lincolnshire poacher*, vol.1, no.4, August 31, 1900.

4550. BUMPUS, J.S.
A Veteran church musician: [obituary of J.M. Young]
in *The Church review*, March 11–18, 1897.
> Young was Cathedral organist.

BISHOPS

4551. HEARN, Thomas
Chronicon sive annales Prioratus de Dunstaple, una cum excerptis e chartulario eiusdem Prioratus
Thomas Hearnius.
Oxford: at the Sheldonian Theatre, 1733. ciii, 919p.
Includes index. Text in Latin.
> Many references to Bishops of Lincoln.

4552. PERRY, George Gresley
Biographical notices of the Bishops of Lincoln from Remigius to Wordsworth
by George Gresley Perry and John Henry Overton.
Lincoln: George Gale, 1900. 389p.
Facsimile published: by University Microfilms, 1972.
> The book was prepared for publication but due to the death of the publisher was not finished. The extant copy is made up from sheets retained by one of the printers and is in the Lincoln Cathedral Library.

4553. SCHALBY, John de
The Book of John de Schalby, Canon of Lincoln, 1299–1333, concerning the Bishops of Lincoln and their acts
translated with an introduction and notes by J.H. Srawley.
Lincoln: Friends of Lincoln Cathedral, 1949. 30p.
(Lincoln Minster pamphlets, no.2)

4554.
Portraits of Bishops of Lincoln from the Bishop's House, Eastgate, Lincoln: exhibited by courtesy of the Right Reverend Kenneth Riches, D.D., Lord Bishop of Lincoln...Usher Art Gallery Lincoln, February 17th to March 31st, 1962
Lincoln: Lincoln, Libraries, Museum and Art Gallery Committee, 1962. [22]p.
> Notes by A.M. Cook.

445

4555.   **PERRY, George G.**
Mediaeval Bishops of Lincoln: William Alnwick, 1436–1440
pp.83–86 in *Lincoln diocesan magazine*, vol.VII, no.62, June, 1891.

4556.   **VENABLES, Edmund**
Post-Reformation Bishops of Lincoln: Bishop Thomas Barlow
pp.36–38 in *Lincoln diocesan magazine*, vol.VI, no.47, March, 1890.
Continued: pp.52–54 in vol.VI, no.48, April, 1890.

4557.   **PERRY, George G.**
Mediaeval Bishops of Lincoln: Henry Beaufort, 1398–1405
pp.179–180 in *Lincoln diocesan magazine*, vol.V, no.44, December, 1889.

4558.   —————————
Mediaeval Bishops of Lincoln: Thomas Bek, 1342–7, John Gynwell, 1347–62
pp.70–73 in *Lincoln diocesan magazine*, vol.V, no.37, May, 1889.

4559.   **RUSSELL, George W.E.**
The Household of faith: portraits and essays
London: Hodder and Stoughton, 1902.   425p.
     p.158: Archbishop Benson; pp.216–223: Edward King.

4560.   **PERRY, George G.**
Mediaeval Bishops of Lincoln: John Bokingham, 1363–1398
pp.309–311 in *Lincoln diocesan magazine*, vol.V, no.39, July, 1889.

4561.   **McHARDY, A.K.**
The Early ecclesiastical career of John Buckingham
pp.3–11 in *Lincolnshire history and archaeology*, vol.8, 1973.

4562.   —————————
The Promotion of John Buckingham to the see of Lincoln
pp.127–135 in *The Journal of ecclesiastical history*, vol.XXVI, no.2, April, 1975.

4563.   —————————
John Buckingham and Thomas Beauchamp, Earl of Warwick
pp.48–52 in *Nottingham medieval studies*, vol.XIX, 1975.

4564.   **VENABLES, Edmund**
Bishops of Lincoln: Nicholas Bullingham
pp.67–69 in *Lincoln diocesan magazine*, vol.VII, no.59, March, 1891.

4565.   **PERRY, George G.**
Mediaeval Bishops of Lincoln: Henry Burghersh, 1320–1340
pp.179–182 in *Lincoln diocesan magazine*, vol.III, no.24, April, 1888.

4566.   —————————
Mediaeval Bishops of Lincoln: John Chedworth, 1451–1471
pp.115–120 in *Lincoln diocesan magazine*, vol.VIII, no.76, August, 1892.

4567.   —————————
Mediaeval Bishops of Lincoln: John de Dalderby, 1300–1320
pp.67–69 in *Lincoln diocesan magazine*, vol.III, no.17, September, 1887.
Continued: pp.83–85 in vol.III, no.18, October, 1887.

4568.   **COLE, R.E.G.**
Proceedings relative to the canonization of John de Dalderby
pp.243–276, [3] leaves of plates in *AAS reports and papers*, vol.33, 1915–16.

4569. **PERRY, George G.**
Mediaeval Bishops of Lincoln: Richard Flemyng, 1420–1431
pp.99–101 in *Lincoln diocesan magazine*, vol.V, no.51, July, 1890.
Continued: pp.115–117 in vol.VI, no.52, August, 1890.

4570. **OVERTON, J.H.**
Bishops of Lincoln: Dr. Fuller
by Canon Overton.
pp.309–311 in *Lincoln diocesan magazine*, vol.IV, no.32, December, 1888.
Continued: pp.4–5 in vol.IV, no.33, January, 1889.

4571. **VENABLES, Edmund**
Bishops of Lincoln: James Gardiner
pp.131–134 in *Lincoln diocesan magazine*, vol.VI, no.53, September, 1890.

4572. **ELLIS, Henry**
Account of the seal of Geoffrey, Bishop of Lincoln, natural son of King Henry the
Second: [in a letter from Henry Ellis... to the Right Honorable the Earl of Aberdeen,
president]
pp.31–33: ill. in *Antiquaries*, 1823.

4573. **PERRY, George G.**
Mediaeval Bishops of Lincoln: Richard de Gravesend, 1258–1279
by Canon Perry.
pp.50–52 in *Lincoln diocesan magazine*, no.5, September, 1886.
Continued: pp.82–84 in no.7, November, 1886.

4574. _____
Mediaeval Bishops of Lincoln: William Grey, 1431–1436
pp.3–6 in *Lincoln diocesan magazine*, vol.VII, no.57, January, 1891.

4575. **PEGGE, Samuel**
*Memoirs of the life of Roger De Weseham, Dean of Lincoln, Bishop of Coventry and
Lichfield, and principal favourite of Robert Grosseteste, Bishop of Lincoln...*
London: printed for J. Whiston and B. White, 1761.   60p.

4576. _____
*The Life of Robert Grosseteste, the celebrated Bishop of Lincoln...with an account of the
Bishop's works*
London: printed John Nichols, 1793.   385p., [1] leaf of plates.
Includes index.

4577. **BOOLE, George**
Philosophical remains of Bishop Grosseteste
pp.139–144 in *Memoirs illustrative of the history and antiquities of the county and city of
Lincoln*, 1850.
> About Grosseteste's work *Libellus Lincolniensis de phisicis lineis, angulis, et figuris, per quas
> omens acciones naturales complentur*, published in Nuremburg, 1503.

4578. **GROSSETESTE, Robert**
Roberti Grosseteste, Episcopi quondam Lincolniensis: epistolae
edited by Henry Richards Luard.
London: Longman, Green, Longman and Roberts, 1861.   467, 12p., [frontis].
Includes index of correspondents.   Text in Latin.

4579. PERRY, George G.
The Life and times of Robert Grosseteste
London: SPCK, 1871.   304p., [frontis].

4580. FELTEN, Joseph
Robert Grosseteste, Bischoff von Lincoln: ein Beitrag zur Kirchen- und Culturgeschichte des dreizehnten Jahrhunderts
Freiburg im Breisgau: Herder, 1887.   112p.

4581. COWAN, W.
Pre-Reformation worthies
London: Elliot Stock, 1897.   vii, 193p.
      pp.3–33: Grosseteste.

4582. STEVENSON, Francis Seymour
Robert Grosseteste, Bishop of Lincoln: a contribution to the religious, political and intellectual history of the thirteenth century
London: Macmillan, 1899.   xvi, 348p.

4583. BOULTER, B.C.
Robert Grosseteste: the defender of our liberties
London: SPCK, 1936.   151p., [4] leaves of plates.

4584. POWICKE, Maurice
Robert Grosseteste: Bishop of Lincoln
pp.482–507 in *Bulletin of the John Rylands Library*, vol.35, no.2, March, 1953.

4585. SRAWLEY, J.H.
Robert Grosseteste: Bishop of Lincoln, 1235–1253
Lincoln: Friends of Lincoln Cathedral, 1953.   36p., [frontis].
(Lincoln Minster pamphlets, 17)

4586.
Robert Grosseteste: scholar and Bishop: essays in commemoration of the seventh century of his death
edited by D.A. Callus.
Oxford: Clarendon Press, 1955.   xxv, 263p., [2] leaves of plates.
      Includes appendix by J.W.F. Hill.

4587. GARTON, Charles
Bishop Grosseteste and table manners
pp.38–40: ill. in *Lincolnshire life*, vol.21, no.2, May, 1981.
      Discusses authorship of the poem 'Stans puer ad mensam' and gives a translation of the poem
      itself.

4588. MANTELLO, F.A.C.
Bishop Robert Grosseteste and his Cathedral Chapter: an edition of the Chapter's objections to episcopal visitations
pp.367–378 in *Medieval studies*, vol.47, 1985.

4589. SOUTHERN, R.W.
Robert Grosseteste: the growth of an English mind in medieval Europe
Oxford: Clarendon Press, 1986.   xii, 337p.

4590. COLE, R.E.G.
Proceedings relative to the canonization of Robert Grosseteste, Bishop of Lincoln
pp.1–34, [2] leaves of plates in *AAS reports and papers*, vol.33, 1915–16.

4591. HILL, J.W.F.
The Tomb of Robert Grosseteste, with an account of its opening in 1792
pp.246–250, [1] leaf of plates in *Studies in honour of Robert Grosseteste.*

4592. HICKS, Edward Lee
The Life and letters of Edward Lee Hicks, Bishop of Lincoln, 1910–1919
edited by J.H. Fowler.
London: Christophers, 1922.   310p., [frontis].

4593. HEADLAM, Maurice
Bishop and friend: Nugent Hicks, sixty-fourth Bishop of Lincoln
London: Macdonald, [1944].   158p., [8]p. of plates.

4594. HICKS, Kathleen Nugent
From rock to tower: memories with reflections
2nd ed., revised and reset.
London: Macdonald, 1948.   288p.
Originally published: 1947.
    Memories of Nugent Hicks.

4595. MORGAN, E.C.
Statue of St.Hugh, Lincoln Cathedral
pp.81–83: ill. in *The London and Dublin orthodox journal of useful knowledge and Catholic intelligencer*, vol.XIII, no.319, Saturday, August 7, 1841.

4596.
Metrical life of St Hugh, Bishop of Lincoln
edited by J.F. Dimock.
Lincoln: printed W. and B. Brooke, 1860.   xxiv, 54p.
Verse in Latin.
    Printed from Ms. copies in the British Museum and the Bodleian.

4597.
Magna vita S.Hugonis, Episcopi Lincolniensis: from manuscripts in the Bodleian Library, Oxford, and the Imperial Library, Paris
edited by James F. Dimock.
London: Longman, Green, Longman, Roberts, and Green, 1864.   lxviii, 416, 15p.
(Rerum Britannicarum Medii Aevi scriptores)

4598. PERRY, George G.
The Life of St Hugh of Avalon, Bishop of Lincoln, with some account of his predecessors in the see of Lincoln
London: John Murray, 1879.   xii, 372p., [frontis].

4599. COX, J. Charles
The Solemn funerall of Hugh, Bishoppe of Lincolne: [transcript of account of the funeral by St John Gwyllym]
pp.156–157 in *Old Lincolnshire*, vol.1, 1885.
    Taken from bound Ms. vol. in Lichfield Cathedral Library.

4600.
View de Saint Hughes Chartreux, Eveque de Lincoln, 1140–1200
par un religieux de la Grande Chartreuse.
Montreuil: Typographie Notre-Dame des Pres, 1890.   xvi, 578p., [11] leaves of plates.
Text in French.

4601.   **WILLSON, T.J.**
The Tomb of St Hugh at Lincoln
pp.104–108, [1] leaf of plans in *The Archaeological journal*, June, 1894.

4602.
The Life of St Hugh of Lincoln
translated from the French Carthusian life and edited with large additions by Herbert
Thurston.
London: Burns & Oates, 1898.   xxvi, 650p., [frontis].
Includes index.

4603.
St Hugh of Lincoln, 1140–1200
London: Catholic Truth Society, [19??].   32p.
(Biographical series)

4604.
*St Hugh's day at Lincoln, A.D.1900: the sermons preached in the Minster: with a life of
St Hugh*
edited by H.R. Bramley.
Lincoln: Clifford Thomas, [1900].   137p., [frontis].

4605.   **MARSON, Charles**
Hugh, Bishop of Lincoln: a short story of one of the makers of mediaeval England
London: Edward Arnold, 1901.   xi, 159p., [frontis].

4606.   **FORBES, F.A.**
St Hugh of Lincoln
London: R. & T. Washbourne, 1917.   125p., [4] leaves of plates.
(Standard-bearers of the faith)

4607.   **SETH-SMITH, E.K.**
St Hugh of Lincoln, 1140–1200
London: SPCK, 1923.   32p.
(Little books on religion, 12)

4608.   **WOOLLEY, Reginald Maxwell**
St Hugh of Lincoln
London: SPCK, 1927.   xi, 214p., [frontis].

4609.   **CLAYTON, Joseph**
St Hugh of Lincoln: a biography
London: Burns, Oates & Washbourne, 1931.   xxi, 237p.

4610.   **EGAN, A.**
St Hugh: 'the Hammer of Kings'
pp.45–47 in *Lincolnshire poacher*, vol.3, no.1, winter, 1955.

4611.   **FROUDE, James Anthony**
*Saint Hugh of Lincoln: James Anthony Froude's study of 'A Bishop of the twelfth
century'*
with an introduction by Maurice Powicke.
Lincoln: Friends of Lincoln Cathedral, 1959.   32p., [2]p. of plates.
(Lincoln Minster pamphlets.   Second series, 1)

4612.   CHAUNDLER, Christine
St Hugh of Lincoln
London: A.R. Mowbray, 1961.   15p.
(Great saints library, 7)
    'Simply written lives for Christian reading'.

4613.   FENTON, Philip C.
Hugh of Lincoln: the Hammer of Kings
pp.768–776: ill. in *History today*, vol.XII, no.11, November, 1962.
Also published: *Lincolnshire life*, vol.3, nos.2 and 3, 1963.

4614.
The Life of St Hugh of Lincoln
edited by Decima L. Douie and Dom Hugh Farmer.
London: Thomas Nelson, 1962.   2 vols.

4615.   HAYES, Ernest H.
Yarns on Christian torchbearers
by Ernest H. Hayes and Lilian E. Cox.   8th ed.
Wallington: Religious Education Press, 1967.   96p.
Originally published: 1941.
    pp.13–22: Hugh of Lincoln.   For children.

4616.   BINNALL, P.B.G.
Saint Hugh, the master builder
pp.183–186 in *Lincoln diocesan magazine*, December, 1970.

4617.   SPURREL, Mark
*Saint Hugh: a worship drama by Mark Spurrel in Boston Parish Church on Thursday,
15th June...and at Lincoln Cathedral on Tuesday, 20th June...: [programme]*
[Boston?]: [s.n.], [1972].   [7]p.

4618.   BRUCE-MITFORD, Rupert
The Chapter House vestibule graves at Lincoln and the body of St.Hugh of Avalon
pp.127–140, [10]p. of plates in *Tribute to an antiquary: essays presented to Marc Fitch
by some friends*, 1976.

4619.   DUKE, Ducie
Saint Hugh of Avalon
pp.32–33: ill. in *Lincolnshire life*, vol.20, no.7, October, 1980.

4620.   FARMER, David Hugh
Saint Hugh of Lincoln
London: Darton, Longman and Todd, 1985.   117p., map, [4]p. of plates.
Includes index.
ISBN 0232516413

4621.   GIRALDUS CAMBRENSIS
The Life of St Hugh of Avalon, Bishop of Lincoln, 1186–1200
edited and translated by Richard M. Loomis.
New York: Garland, 1985.   lxv, 132, 132p.
(Garland library of medieval literature.   Series A, 31)

4622.   FARMER, D.H.
*St Hugh of Lincoln: an exhibition to commemorate the eighth centenary of his
consecration as Bishop of Lincoln in 1186*: [catalogue]
Oxford: Bodleian Library, 1986.   36p.: ill.
ISBN 1851240047

4623.   **GARTON, Charles**
The Metrical life of St Hugh of Lincoln: the Latin text with introduction, translation and notes
Lincoln: Honywood Press, 1986.   90p.
Text in Latin and English.

4624.   **GORDON, Eric**
St Hugh & Eynsham Abbey: the story of Hugh's election as Bishop of Lincoln at Eynsham Abbey, A.D. 1186
Eynsham: Eynsham History Group, 1986.   11p.: ill.
(Occasional paper, no.3)

4625.
St Hugh of Lincoln: lectures delivered at Oxford and Lincoln to celebrate the eighth centenary of St Hugh's consecration as Bishop of Lincoln
edited by Henry Mayer-Harting.
Oxford: Clarendon Press, 1987.   viii, 130p.: ill.
> Includes essays by: Henrietta Leyser; David M. Smith; Karl J. Leyser; David H. Farmer; David A. Stocker.

4626.   **COLE, R.E.G.**
The Body of St Hugh
by R.E.G. Cole and J.O. Johnston.
26p., [4] leaves of plates in *AAS reports and papers*, [19??].

4627.   **VENABLES, Edmund**
The Shrine and head of St Hugh of Lincoln
by the Rev. Precentor Venables.
21p. in *AAS reports and papers*,   [18??]

4628.   **FOSKETT, R.**
John Kaye and the diocese of Lincoln
342p.
Thesis [Ph.D.] – University of Nottingham, 1957.

4629.   **HANCHARD, J.**
A Sketch of the life of Bishop King, with portrait: a manual for churchmen
London: John Kensit, 1886.   24p., [frontis].
> Equates ritualism in the church with Roman Catholic practices and criticises the Bishop on these grounds.

4630.
Prosecution of the Bishop of Lincoln: [list of guarantors]
[Lincoln]: [s.n.], [1889].   [3]p.
> Fund for paying defence costs.

4631.   **KING, Edward**
[Letter of resignation, March 2nd, 1910]
[Lincoln]: [The Author], 1910.   1 sheet.

4632.   **BROOKE, C.E.**
Personal reminiscences of Bishop King
pp.4–9: ill. in *The Treasury*, April, 1910.

4633.   **LONDON, Bishop of**
The Late Bishop of Lincoln: written in the train on the way back from his funeral
pp.1–4: ill., [1] leaf of plates in *The Treasury*, April, 1910.

4634. ROGERS, Frederick
Impressions of a labour leader
pp.9–12: ill. in *The Treasury*, April, 1910.
    About Edward King.

4635. RANDOLPH, Berkeley William
Edward King: Bishop of Lincoln
London: Wells Gardner, Darton, 1911. 47p.
(Little biographies, 12)

4636. RUSSELL, George W.E.
Edward King, sixtieth Bishop of Lincoln: a memoir
London: Smith, Elder, 1912. 359p., [frontis].

4637. HOLLAND, Henry Scott
A Bundle of memories
London: Wells Gardner, [1915]. vii, 321p.
    pp.48–61: Edward King.

4638. RANDOLPH, B.W.
The Mind and work of Bishop King
by B.W. Randolph and J.W. Townroe.
London: A.R. Mowbray, 1918. viii, 262p., 25 leaves of plates.

4639.
Edward King, Bishop of Lincoln
London: Catholic Literature Association, [c.1932]. 20p.
(Heroes of the Catholic revival, 13)

4640. HUTCHINSON, F.W.
Reminiscences of a Lincolnshire parson
Ely: W. Jefferson, 1951. 82p., [frontis].
    Mainly connections with Gainsborough and Holbeach, but some reminiscences of Bishop King.

4641. ELTON, Lord
Edward King and our times
London: Geoffrey Bles, 1958. 143p., 4 leaves of plates.

4642. COOK, A.M.
Bishop Edward King: his memory is still green in Lincoln
p.10: ill. in *Church times*, 4 March, 1960.

4643. CHADWICK, Owen
Edward King: Bishop of Lincoln, 1885–1910
Lincoln: Friends of Lincoln Cathedral, 1968. 31p., [frontis].
(Lincoln Minster pamphlets. Second series, 4)

4644. LEE, Walter
'I think I would like my photograph taken', said Bishop King, 'in the pouring rain'
p.31: ill. in *Lincolnshire life*, vol.8, no.5, July, 1968.
    Author's experience of photographing the Bishop whilst still an apprentice.

4645. NORMAN, E.R.
Anti-Catholicism in Victorian England
London: George Allen and Unwin, 1968. 240p.
(Historical problems: studies and documents, 1)
    pp.110–121: prosecution of Edward King.

4646.   CHADWICK, Owen
The Victorian church.   Part II
2nd ed.
London: A. & C. Black, 1972.   vii, 510p.
Originally published: 1970.   Includes index.
    Includes much on Edward King.

4647.   NEWTON, John A.
Search for a saint: Edward King
London: Epworth, 1977.   128p., [frontis].
ISBN 0716202816

4648.   BENTLEY, James
Ritualism and politics in Victorian Britain: the attempt to legislate for belief
Oxford: Oxford University Press, 1978.   xii, 162p.: ill.
    pp.117–120: Edward King.

4649.   NEWTON, John
Edward King
London: Church Literature Association, 1983.   16p., [frontis].
(Oxford prophets, 6)
ISBN 0851911714

4650.   CROFT, Bernard
Lincolnshire worthies.   No.48: Bishop Edward King
pp.34–35: ill. in *Lincolnshire life*, vol.24, no.12, March, 1985.

4651.   WILGRESS, G.F.
Edward King: Bishop of Lincoln, 1885–1910
[Lincoln]: Bishop of Lincoln's Appeal Fund, [1911?].   30p., [frontis].
    Written to be translated into French for La Vie Intellectuelle.

4652.   OVERTON, J.H.
Bishops of Lincoln: Dr. Benjamin Laney, 1663–1674
by Canon Overton.
pp.214–216 in *Lincoln diocesan magazine*, vol.IV, no.26, June, 1888.

4653.   PERRY, George G.
Mediaeval Bishops of Lincoln: Henry de Lexington, 1254–1258
by Canon Perry.
pp.21–24 in *Lincoln diocesan magazine*, no.3, July, 1886.

4654.   ——————
Mediaeval Bishops of Lincoln: Marmaduke Lumley, 1451
pp.114–117 in *Lincoln diocesan magazine*, vol.VII, no.64, August, 1891.

4655.   ARUNDALE, R.L.
Richard Niele: Bishop of Lincoln, 1614–1617
Lincoln: Honywood Press, 1987.   27p., [frontis].

4656.   PHIPPS, Simon
Our new Bishop: [*Lincolnshire chronicle* supplement, 24th January, 1975]
Lincoln: Lincolnshire Chronicle, 1975.   XXp.: ill.
    Includes notes on former Bishops.

4657.   TIPPING, Ruth
The Induction of the Rt. Rev. Simon Wilton Phipps as 69th Bishop of Lincoln
pp.46–49: ill. in *Lincolnshire life*, vol.14, no.13, March, 1975.

4658.   **GIRALDUS CAMBRENSIS**
Giraldi Cambrensis opera
edited by James F. Dimock.
London: Longman, 1877.
(Rerum Britannicarum Medii Aevi scriptores)
Includes index.   Text in Latin, with English preface.
> Vol.VII: 'Vita S.Remigii et vita S.Hugonis'.   Giraldus was resident in Lincoln, 1196–99.

4659.   **PERRY, George G.**
Mediaeval Bishops of Lincoln: Philip Repyngdon, 1405–1419
pp.67–69 in *Lincoln diocesan magazine*, vol.VI, no.49, May, 1890.

4660.   **ARCHER, Margaret**
Philip Repingdon, Bishop of Lincoln, and his Cathedral Chapter
pp.81–97 in *University of Birmingham historical journal*, vol.IV, no.2, 1954.

4661.
Memorials and character, together with the lives of divers eminent and worthy persons
[by John Wilford?].
London: [The Author?], 1741.   788, 42p.
> pp.197–206: Bishop Sanderson.

4662.   **SANDERSON, Robert**
The Life of Bishop Sanderson
London: John and Charles Mozley, 1850.   36p.: ill., [frontis].

4663.   **OVERTON, J.H.**
Bishop Sanderson
by Canon Overton.
pp.117–119 in *Lincoln diocesan magazine*, vol.III, no.20, December, 1887.
Continued: pp.133–135 in vol.III, no.21, January, 1888.

4664.   **PERRY, George G.**
Mediaeval Bishops of Lincoln: Oliver Sutton, 1280–1299
pp.2–6 in *Lincoln diocesan magazine*, vol.III, no.13, May, 1887.
Continued: pp.21–24 in vol.III, no.14, June, 1887.

4665.   **VENABLES, Edmund**
The Opening of the tomb of Bishop Oliver Sutton, and the discovery of a chalice, paten
and episcopal ring
pp.354–358 in *AAS reports and papers*, vol.19, 1887–88.

4666.   **HILL, Rosalind M.T.**
Oliver Sutton, Dean of Lincoln, later Bishop of Lincoln, 1280–99
Lincoln: Friends of Lincoln Cathedral, 1950.   36p.: ill.
(Lincoln Minster pamphlets, 4)

4667.   **SWAYNE, W.S.**
Parson's pleasure: [autobiography]
Edinburgh: Wm. Blackwood, 1934.   ix, 319p., [frontis].
> pp.257–298: Lincoln.

4668.   **OVERTON, J.H.**
Bishops of Lincoln: Thomas Tewison
pp.83–85 in *Lincoln diocesan magazine*, vol.V, no.50, June, 1890.

4669. ——————
Bishops of Lincoln: William Wake
by Canon Overton.
pp.35–38 in *Lincoln diocesan magazine*, vol.VII, no.59, March, 1891.

4670. SYKES, Norman
Bishop William Wake's primary visitation of the diocese of Lincoln, 1706
pp.189–206 in *The Journal of ecclesiastical history*, vol.II, 1951.
> Most of the article consists of a transcription of Wake's own record of his installation and visitation, including that of Lincoln itself.

4671. ——————
William Wake, Archbishop of Canterbury, 1657–1737
Cambridge: Cambridge University Press, 1957. 2 vols.
Includes index.

4672. HACKETT, John
Scrinia reserata: a memorial offer'd to the great deservings of John Williams, D.D., who some time held the places of Ld. Keeper of the Great Seal of England, Ld. Bishop of Lincoln, and Ld. Archbishop of York
London: printed by Edw. Jones for Samuel Lowndes, 1693. 230p., [frontis].

4673. ROBERTS, B. Dew
Mitre & musket: John Williams, Lord Keeper, Archbishop of York, 1582–1650
London: Oxford University Press, 1938. xii, 300p., [frontis].

4674. OVERTON, J.H.
Post Reformation Bishops of Lincoln: Thomas Winnitt
by Canon Overton.
pp.163–164 in *Lincoln diocesan magazine*, vol.VI, no.55, November, 1890.

4675.
The Pastoral staff presented to the Lord Bishop of Lincoln, October, 1872
Lincoln: James Williamson, printer, 1872. 17p.: ill., 1p. of plates.
> Contains detailed description of the staff and its presentation and a list of the subscribers. Bishop in question was Christopher Wordsworth.

4676. WORDSWORTH, John
Love and discipline: a memorial sermon preached in the nave of Lincoln Cathedral, on Palm Sunday afternoon, March 29th, 1885, being the Sunday after the funeral of Christopher Wordsworth
Lincoln: printed James Williamson, 1885. 16p.

4677. OVERTON, John Henry
Christopher Wordsworth, Bishop of Lincoln, 1807–1885
by John Henry Overton and Elizabeth Wordsworth.
London: Rivingtons, 1888. xvi, 542p., [2] leaves of plates.

4678. BENSON, Arthur Christopher
The Leaves of the tree: studies in biography
London: Smith, Elder, 1911. vii, 332p.
> pp.260–283: Christopher Wordsworth, Bishop of Lincoln.

4679.   MARSH, P.T.
The Victorian church in decline: Archbishop Tait and the Church of England, 1868–1882
London: Routledge & Kegan Paul, 1969.   x, 344p.
Includes index.
ISBN 0710062427
References to Christopher Wordsworth, Bishop of Lincoln passim.

4680.   STRUDWICK, Victor
Christopher Wordsworth: Bishop of Lincoln, 1869–1885
Lincoln: Honywood Press, 1987.   32p., [frontis].
(Lincoln Cathedral publications)
ISBN 095050839X

FAMILIES

4681.
The Visitation of the county of Lincoln made by Sir Edward Bysshe, Knight, Clarenceux King of Arms in the year of our Lord, 1666
edited by Everard Green.
Lincoln: Lincoln Record Society, 1917.   xiv, 99p.
Includes about a dozen Lincoln families.

4682.   BENSON, E.F.
Our family affairs, 1867–1896
London: Cassell, 1920.
pp.27–58: Lincoln.

4683.   BENSON, Arthur Christopher
The Trefoil: Wellington College, Lincoln and Truro
London: John Murray, 1923.   297p., [8] leaves of plates.
Includes index.
pp.67–170: detailed descriptions of Cathedral and town.

4684.   NEWSOME, David
Godliness & good learning: four studies on a Victorian idea
London: John Murray, 1961.   291p., [12]p. of plates.
Includes index.
pp.148–194: 'The Exemplar: Martin White Benson'.

4685.   BENSON, E.F.
As we were: a Victorian peepshow
London: Longman, 1971.   355p.
Originally published: 1930.   Includes index.
pp.67–84: 'Lincoln and Truro'.

4686.   WILLIAMS, David
Genesis and exodus: a portrait of the Benson family
London: Hamish Hamilton, 1979.   x, 236p.
ISBN 0241101905
pp.49–64: time in Lincoln.

4687.
Blundell of Liverpool, Lincoln and Kingston-upon-Hull: [pedigree]
London: Mitchell Hughes and Clarke, 1906.   25p.

4688.   BINNALL, Peter B.G.
The Family of Blyton
pp.26–34 in *The Lincolnshire historian*, no.1, summer, 1947.

4689.   LAYTON, G.
Some notes on the Boole family
[1968].   27 leaves.
Ms.

4690.   HEMINGWAY, G.
The Caparns of Lincolnshire
[1977].   19 leaves.
Typescript.
    pp.7–8: Lincoln connections of Daniel Caparn, 1751–91; p.12: John Caparn, 1763–1806.

4691.   CARLINE, Richard
Corbet and the Carlines: Shrewsbury painters, sculptors and architects of the early 19th
century
ill. in *The Shropshire magazine*, March, 1958.
    Family originally from Carline Place, now Carline Rd., Lincoln.   Thomas Carline, Senior,
    moved to Shrewsbury in 1770.

4692.
*The Carline family: George, 1855–1920; Anne, 1862–1945; Sydney, 1888–1929; Hilda,
1889–1950; Richard; Nancy*: [catalogue]
Leicester: Leicester Galleries, 1971.   [26]p.: ill.
    Artistic family with Lincoln roots; George's father was mayor of Lincoln, but died when the
    boy was seven years old.   Hilda married Stanley Spencer.

4693.   HOLLES, Gervase
Memorials of the Holles family, 1493–1656
edited by A.C. Ward.
London: Camden Society, 1937.
(Camden third series, vol.LV)
    pp.216–217: account of fights in Lincoln between Sir Robert Swift and John Kingston.

4694.
[Notes on the Kettleborough family]
[19??].   [2] leaves.
Typescript.

4695.   GARTON, Charles
Lamb's paternal forebears
pp.420–421 in *Notes and queries*, vol.CCXIV, 1969.

4696.   NICHOLS, John Gough
The Descent of the earldom of Lincoln, with notices of the seals of the Earls
pp.253–279 in *Memoirs illustrative of the history and antiquities of the county and city of
Lincoln*, 1850.

4697.   RACE, Steve
We Races...
[1982].   32 leaves.
Typescript.

4698.
Graves of the Sibthorp family, discovered in April, 1830
[Lincoln]: [s.n.], [1830].   1 sheet: ill.
　　In St Mark's Church, Lincoln.

4699.　　**MADDISON, Arthur R.**
An Account of the Sibthorp family
Lincoln: printed James Williamson, 1896.　115p.
　　pp.47–93: Sibthorps of Canwick, including Charles De Laet Waldo Sibthorp.

4700.　　**SYKES, Christopher**
Two studies in virtue
London: Collins, 1953.　256p., map, [6] leaves of plates.
　　pp.19–106: Richard Sibthorp and Charles De Laet Waldo Sibthorp.

4701.　　**SWAN, John**
Pedigree of the Swan family
London: Waterlow, 1901.　13p.

4702.
Two Lincoln brothers
pp.40–41 in *Lincolnshire poacher*, vol.1, no.2, spring, 1953.
　　Refers to Henry Wake who was a stone-mason and Kyd Wake who was a printer.

4703.　　**GREEN, Everard**
Pedigree of the family of Willson of Hainton, Co. Lincoln, and of the city of Lincoln
[S.l.]: [s.n.], [1906].　[3]p.
　　Genealogical table.

DIRECTORIES

4704.
Universal British directory, 1791. Vol.III, no.42
[S.l.]: [s.n.], [1791]. pp.549–566.
Cover title: *Lincoln directory, 1791.*

4705. WHITE, William
History, gazetteer and directory of Lincolnshire, and the city & diocese of Lincoln...
Sheffield: The Author, 1842. 780p.

4706. ─────────────
*History, gazetteer and directory of Lincolnshire, and city and diocese of
Lincoln...boroughs, towns and ports...and a variety of other agricultural, biographical
and statistical information in one volume with a large map of the county*
2nd ed.
Sheffield: printed for the author by R. Leader, 1856. 900p.
Originally published: 1842. Includes index.
   pp.61–118: history of Lincoln; pp.118–130: list of streets; pp.120–143: directory.

4707. ─────────────
*History, gazetteer and directory of Lincolnshire, and the city and diocese of Lincoln,
comprising a general survey of the county...White's professional and commercial
advertising directory*
3rd ed.
Sheffield: William White, 1872. xvi, 884, 80p.
   pp.58–98: history of Lincoln; pp.99–100: Lincoln streets, lanes; pp.101–138: Lincoln street
   directory; pp.139–153: Lincoln professions and trades.

4708.
The Lincoln commercial directory and private residence guide
Lincoln: Victor and Baker, 1843. 51, [10]p., [2] leaves of maps.

4709.
Post Office directory of Lincolnshire, with Derbyshire, Nottinghamshire and Rutlandshire
London: W. Kelly, [1849]. pp.xii, 2371–3309, [10] leaves of maps.
   pp.3084–3094: Lincoln.

4710.
*The City of Lincoln directory, 1857: containing an alphabetical list of the principal
householders, a classified trade and professional list, a complete street directory, and a
list of carriers, etc.*
Lincoln: Charles Akrill, 1857. 102, [16]p.

4711.
The City of Lincoln directory, 1867: containing an alphabetical list...carriers, etc.
Lincoln: Charles Akrill, 1867. [10], viii, 129p.

4712.
The City of Lincoln directory, 1877: containing a new map of the city...a complete street directory...carriers, etc.
Lincoln: Charles Akrill, 1877.   [16], 175p., 1 folded map.
  Map is James Sandby Padley's map of 1842, new ed., corrected to 1868.

4713.
The City of Lincoln directory, 1881: containing a new and improved map of the city...street directory...carriers, etc.
Lincoln: Charles Akrill, 1881.   [12], x, 215p., map.

4714.
The City of Lincoln directory, 1885...
Lincoln: printed Akrill, Ruddock & Keyworth, 1885.   230p., folded map.

4715.
Directory of the city of Lincoln, with the surrounding district, containing street, court guide, alphabetical & classified trades lists, with map of county
compiled by Wells & Manton.
Lincoln: Akrill, Ruddock & Keyworth, 1888.   278p.

4716.
Directory of the city of Lincoln, with the surrounding district, containing street and alphabetical and classified trades lists, with map of the city showing the streets
Lincoln: Akrill, Ruddock & Keyworth, 1894.   xxxiv, 220p., folded map.

4717.
City of Lincoln and district...a complete street directory in alphabetical order...
Boston: W.J. Cook; Lincoln: Clifford Thomas, bookseller, 1895.   xxxii, 256, [18]p., map.

4718.
Directory of the city of Lincoln, with the surrounding district, containing street and alphabetical and classified trades lists, with map of the city showing the streets
Lincoln: J.W. Ruddock, 1897.   xxxii, 242p., 1 folded map.

4719.
Directory of the city of Lincoln...
Lincoln: J.W. Ruddock, 1899.   xxxii, 278p., map.

4720.
Directory of the city of Lincoln, with the villages within a radius of ten miles, containing street and alphabetical and classified trades' lists, with map of the city showing the streets
11th ed.
Lincoln: J.W. Ruddock, 1901.   xxxiv, 278p., 1 folded map.

4721.
Directory of the city of Lincoln...
12th ed.
Lincoln: J.W. Ruddock, 1903.   lxiv, 270p., 1 folded map.

4722.
Directory of the city of Lincoln...
13th ed.
Lincoln: J.W. Ruddock, 1905.   lxxii, 286p., 1 folded map.

4723.
Directory of the city of Lincoln...
Lincoln: J.W. Ruddock, 1907.   lxxx, 306p., 1 folded map.

4724.
Directory of the city of Lincoln...
Lincoln: J.W. Ruddock, 1909.   lxxxiv, 314p.

4725.
Directory of the city of Lincoln...
Lincoln: J.W. Ruddock, 1911.   lxxviii, 312p., map.

4726.
City of Lincoln directory...
17th ed.
Lincoln: J.W. Ruddock, 1913.   xcii, 334p., 1 folded map.

4727.
Directory of the city of Lincoln...
18th ed.
Lincoln: J.W. Ruddock, 1919.   lxxxviii, 352p., map.

4728.
Directory of the city of Lincoln
19th ed.
Lincoln: J.W. Ruddock, 1922.   xcvi, 378p.

4729.
Lincoln city year book and business directory, 1922
Lincoln: Lincolnshire Chronicle, 1922.   427p., [frontis].

4730.
Directory of the city of Lincoln...
20th ed.
Lincoln: J.W. Ruddock, 1928.   xcvi, 406p.

4731.
Directory of the city of Lincoln...
21st ed.
Lincoln: J.W. Ruddock, 1932.   xcvi, 398p.

4732.
Kelly's directory of Lincoln and neighbourhood
London: Kelly's Directories, 1937.   [58], 540p.
     'Incorporating Ruddock's *Directory*'.

4733.
Kelly's directory of Lincoln and neighbourhood
London: Kelly's Directories, 1939.   [54], 548p.

4734.
Kelly's directory of Lincoln and neighbourhood
London: Kelly's Directories, 1941.   [52], 554p.

4735.
Kelly's directory of Lincoln and neighbourhood
London: Kelly's Directories, 1946.   [52], 576p.

4736.
Kelly's directory of Lincoln and neighbourhood
London: Kelly's Directories, 1949.   [40], 640p.

4737.
Kelly's directory of Lincoln and neighbourhood
London: Kelly's Directories, 1952.   [38], 676p.

4738.
Kelly's directory of Lincoln
7th ed.
London: Kelly's Directories, 1955.   xiv, 714p.

4739.
Kelly's directory of Lincoln
8th ed.
London: Kelly's Directories, 1957.   38, 760p.

4740.
Kelly's directory of Lincoln and neighbourhood
9th ed.
London: Kelly's Directories, 1959.   xiv, 703p.

4741.
Kelly's directory of Lincoln and neighbourhood
10th ed.
London: Kelly's Directories, 1961.   xiv, 751p.

4742.
Kelly's directory of Lincoln and neighbourhood
13th ed.
London: Kelly's Directories, 1967.   xiv, 8, 769p.

4743.
Kelly's directory of Lincoln and neighbourhood
14th ed.
London: Kelly's Directories, 1968.   vi, 8, 739p.

4744.
Kelly's directory of Lincoln and neighbourhood
15th ed.
London: Kelly's Directories, 1969.   8, 744p.

4745.
Kelly's trade finder of Lincoln, 1970
Kingston-upon-Thames: Kelly's Directories, 1970.   pp.618–743.
Originally published: in *Kelly's directory of Lincoln*, 1970.

4746.
Kelly's directory of Lincoln and neighbourhood
17th ed.
London: Kelly's Directories, 1971.   iv, 742p.

4747.
Kelly's directory of Lincoln and neighbourhood
18th ed.
London: Kelly's Directories, 1972.   iv, 739p.

4748.
Kelly's trade finder of Lincoln, 1972
Kingston-upon-Thames: Kelly's Directories, 1972.   pp.614–740.
Originally published: in *Kelly's directory of Lincoln*, 1972.

4749.
Kelly's directory of Lincoln and neighbourhood
19th ed.
London: Kelly's Directories, 1973.   iv, 718p.

4750.
Kelly's directory of Lincoln and neighbourhood
20th ed.
London: Kelly's Directories, 1974.   732p.

4751.
Kelly's directory of Lincoln and neighbourhood
21st ed.
London: Kelly's Directory, 1975.   728p.

4752.
Kelly's trade finder of Lincoln, 1975
Kingston-upon-Thames: Kelly's Directories, 1975.   pp.626–728.
Originally published: in *Kelly's directory of Lincoln*, 1975.

ALMANACS

4753.
Cousans and Gale's Lincolnshire compendium
[Lincoln]: [Cousans and Gale], [18??].   [11]p., [c.36] leaves.
Bound with: *Old Moore's almanack.*
>Includes: 'Blanche Le Beck: a local tale of the thirteenth century', which is set in the city.

4754.
The Lincolnshire annual rememberancer, from the shop of John W. Drury, bookseller, printer and bookbinder
Lincoln: J.W. Drury, [1841].   12p.

4755.
Stainton's literary and commercial advertising sheet, or Companion to the almanack
Lincoln: J. Stainton, 1845.   Various pagings.
Bound with: *Old Moore's almanack* and *Noble's almanack compendium.*

4756.
Stainton's almanack advertiser for 1846
[Lincoln]: [J. Stainton], 1846.
Bound with: *Old Moore's almanack* and *Noble's almanack compendium.*

4757.
Stainton's almanack advertiser for 1848
[Lincoln]: [J. Stainton], [1848].   [c.28] leaves.
Bound with: *Old Moore's almanack* and *Noble's almanack compendium.*

4758.
W. and B. Brooke's Lincoln companion to the almanack: [for the years 1858, 1860, 1861, 1862, 1863, 1864]
Lincoln: W. and B. Brooke, 1858–64.   Various pagings.

4759.
Loder's Lincoln budget: [for the years 1860, 1861, 1875]
Lincoln: R. Loder, 1860–75.   Various pagings.
>1860 said to be 23rd year of publication.   Lists: town council and magistrates; market carriers; fairs; country feasts.

4760.
Lincoln budget and almanack for the year 1868
Lincoln: F.J. Clarke, [1868].   [c.56] leaves.

4761.
Woodcock's Lincoln family almanack and annual advertiser, 1868
Lincoln: Page D. Woodcock, 1868.

4762.
Lincolnshire compendium: [1873]
[Lincoln]: [s.n.], [1873].   [c.85] leaves.

4763.
George Gale's Lincolnshire companion to the almanacks, 1876
Lincoln: George Gale, [1876].   c.85 leaves.
Accompanies: *Old Moore's almanack.*
>   Includes short story: 'The Cook of St Catherine's: a legend'.

4764.
Lincolnshire companion to the almanacs, 1901
[Lincoln]: [George Gale], [1901].   [c.60] leaves: ill.

4765.
Akrill's Lincoln budget
Lincoln: Akrill, Ruddock, 1903.

4766.
The Lincoln budget: [Ruddock's Lincoln budget for 1907, 1910, 1927, 1928, 1932, 1936]
Lincoln: J.W. Ruddock, 1907–36.   Various pagings.
>   1910 issue said to be 57th year of publication.

4767.
The Lincoln temperance almanack for 1911
Lincoln: issued by Theo. P. Starke, 1911.
>   Inside is general temperance almanack.

4768.
Lincoln and Lincolnshire almanac, 1920
Lincoln: Lincolnshire Chronicle, [1920].   95p.: ill.

4769.
*The **Lincolnshire chronicle** almanack for Lincoln and Lincolnshire, together with a compendium of local information and a photographic record of the year 1924*
Lincoln: Lincolnshire Chronicle, [1924].   104p.: ill.
>   Foreword states that there was a lapse of 3 years and in 1922 the almanack was experimentally replaced by a yearbook and directory of wider scope.

4770.
Ruddock's Lincoln budget, 1930
Lincoln: J.W. Ruddock, 1930.   160p.
Bound with: *Raphael's prophetic almanac* and *The Humorous companion.*

4771.
Critch's annual
Lincoln: Critch, 1933–34–   .
Originally published: 1901–19; restarted: 1934.

NEWSPAPERS

4772.
The Lincoln gazette or weekly intelligencer
Vol.1, no.14, 6–13 March, 1728; no.44, 6–16 October, 1729; no.45, 16–23 October, 1729.
Contains: London weekly bill of mortality; list of books published in London; news from abroad.

4773.
Two Lincoln newspapers
Louth: printed J. Jackson, 1808. 8p.
Anonymous advertiser writing against a new newspaper which is set to rival the 'old county paper of the Messrs Newcombs'.

4774.
The Lincoln and Lincolnshire cabinet and annual intelligencer of public business, &c., for 1827: with a monthly retrospect of the principal events and occurences of the county, for 1826
Lincoln: J.W. Drury, 1827. iv, 189p., [4] leaves of plates.

4775.
The Lincoln and Lincolnshire cabinet and annual intelligencer of public business, &c., for 1828: with a monthly retrospect of the principal events and occurences of the county, for 1827
Lincoln: J.W. Drury, 1828. viii, 250p., [5] leaves of plates.

4776.
The Lincoln and Lincolnshire cabinet and calendar of public business, for 1829, with lists of the public officers and public institutions in all parts of the county
Lincoln: J.W. Drury, 1829. 146p.
Cover title: *The Lincolnshire red book.*

4777.
[Letter announcing that new paper, the *Lincolnshire chronicle and county advertiser*, is to be established, with questionnaire about best place for publication: Boston, Stamford or Lincoln]
[Lincoln]: [s.n.], [1832]. 2 sheets.

4778.
The Lincoln cabinet
Vol.1, no.1, February 1, 1832-no.12, April, 1832.
Lincoln: Robert Ely Leary, 1832.
A weekly 'literary journal' which was also intended to be published in monthly parts.

4779.
The Lincoln mirror of useful and entertaining knowledge
Vol.1, no.1, Wednesday, September 26, 1832–no.7, Wednesday, November 7, 1832.
Bound with: *The Lincoln cabinet.*
   'The proprietors of the *Mirror* announce their intention of publishing an annual list of their
   subscribers and they indulge a hope that the names of the necessitous and truly sordid will
   alone be found wanting.'

4780.
The Penny blue citizen
Vol.1, no.1, Saturday, November 16th, 1844.
[Lincoln]: [s.n.], [1844].   8p.
   Agitation over city politics.

4781.
J.B. Smith's Lincolnshire estate register: insurance, emigration and trade reporter
Vol.1, no.4, Monday, January 6, 1851.
Lincoln: printed Charles Keyworth, 1851.   22p.

4782.
Lincoln journal
Tuesday, 22 December, 1874.
[Lincoln]: [s.n.], [1874].

4783.
Old Lincolnshire: an antiquarian magazine: [a pictorial quarterly magazine]
Vol.1, March, 1883-June, 1885.
edited by George H. Burton.
Stamford: Old Lincolnshire Press, [1885].   256p.: ill., [10]p. of plates.
Includes index.

4784.
Lincoln recorder
Vol.1, no.1, July/August, 1952–vol.6, no.3, May/June, 1957.
Lincoln: Lincoln National Unionist Association, 1952–57.   Various pagings.
   Incomplete run held in Lincoln Central Library.

4785.
The Westminster Press provincial newspapers
edited by A.P. Duncan.
London: Westminster Press, 1952.   84p., 27p. of plates.
Includes index.
   pp.39–40: *Lincolnshire chronicle* and Lincolnshire Newspapers Ltd.

4786.
Lincoln city new announcer
Vol.1, no.1, Wednesday, 6th February, 1963–
[Lincoln]: [s.n.], [1963–   ].
Issued weekly.

4787.
Lincoln pride
No.1, April, 1972–no.2, May, 1972.
[Lincoln]: [s.n.], 1972.

4788.

Catalogue of the Newspaper Library, Colindale. Volume 2: England and Wales, Scotland, Ireland

London: British Museum Publications, 1975.
> Includes Lincoln entries.

4789.   **NEWTON, David**

Men of mark: makers of East Midland Allied Press

Peterborough: East Midland Allied Press, 1977.   xv, 239p., [48]p. of plates.

Includes index.

ISBN 0950595403
> pp.16–17: brief references to *Lincoln leader & county advertiser* which merged with *Lincolnshire chronicle* in January, 1930.

4790.

West end news

Vol.1, no.1, November 15, 1978–

[S.l.]: [s.n.], [1978–   ].

Issued fortnightly.

4791.

Anniversary souvenir: [LSG supplement]

Lincoln: LSG, 1983.   20p.: ill.
> Includes facsimile of 1st issue of the *Lincolnshire chronicle*.

4792.

The Newspaper centre: [LSG supplement, February 25, 1983]

Lincoln: LSG, 1983.   8p.: ill.
> About new premises of the Lincoln Standard Group.

MISCELLANEOUS

NOTICES OF SALE

4793.
Freehold estate, Bail of Lincoln: to be sold by private contract
Lincoln: printed J.W. Drury, 1805. 1 sheet.

4794.
Land in Lincoln field: to be let in small lots
Lincoln: printed J.W. Drury, 1805. 1 sheet.

4795.
To be sold by auction...at the house of Mr Robert Capp, the Rein-deer Inn, in the city of Lincoln, on Friday, the 8th day of February next: January 14th, 1805
Lincoln: printed J.W. Drury, 1805. 1 sheet.

4796.
To be sold by auction by Mr Preston, on Wednesday, the 23rd of January, 1805, on the premises of the late Mrs Heneage near St Peter's Church, city of Lincoln: all the household furniture
Lincoln: printed J.W. Drury, 1805. 1 sheet.

4797.
To be sold by auction...on Friday, the 15th day of February next...
Lincoln: printed J.W. Drury, 1805. 1 sheet.

4798.
Cheap blankets, &c., to be sold by auction, February 19, 1805, by Mr Chalk at the house of Mr John Bailey, the Sign of the Crown, in the Butchery Lane
Lincoln: printed J.W. Drury, 1805. 1 sheet.

4799.
To be sold by auction by Mr Preston, on Friday, 5th day of April, 1805, at the house of Mr Ranshaw, the White-Hart Inn, Above-hill, Lincoln...an excellent piece of land
Lincoln: printed J.W. Drury, 1805. 1 sheet.

4800.
To dealers, brewers, publicans and all other consumers of hops: to be sold by auction by Mr T. Chalk, on Friday, the 26th of April, 1805...at his warehouse on the Corn Market hill...
Lincoln: printed J.W. Drury, 1805. 1 sheet.

4801.
To builders and others: to be sold by auction by Mr Preston, on the premises, on Friday, tenth of May, 1805, the whole of the materials of four tenements in St Paul's Lane...and...of four tenements, on the site of the new city gaol
Lincoln: printed J.W. Drury, 1805. 1 sheet.

4802.
To be let and entered upon immediately, a very good garden...near the Falcon Inn, and late in the occupation of J.T. Bell, Esq., May 15, 1805
Lincoln: printed J.W. Drury, 1805.   1 sheet.

4803.
City of Lincoln: to be sold by auction by Mr Preston on Thursday, the 16th of May, 1805, on the premises of Mr John Smith, in Newport, Above-hill, Lincoln: all the farming stock, manure, hay, eat of land, &c.
Lincoln: printed J.W. Drury, 1805.   1 sheet.

4804.
City of Lincoln: to be sold by auction by Mr Preston, on Saturday, the 18th and Monday, the 20th of May, 1805, at the dwelling-house of Mr Firth, Above-hill, in the field near the Cold Bath, all the neat and valuable household furniture...
Lincoln: printed J.W. Drury, 1805.   1 sheet.

4805.
To be sold by auction by Mr Preston, on Tuesday, the 3rd of September, and the following day, at the dwelling-house of the late Mr Walker, in the parish of St Peter-at-Gowts, city of Lincoln: all the household furniture...
Lincoln: printed J.W. Drury, 1805.   1 sheet.

4806.
To be sold by auction, on Monday, November 11, 1805, on the premises of Mr Thomas Chalk, liquor merchant, Cornhill, Lincoln: a general assortment of household furniture
Lincoln: printed J.W. Drury, 1805.   1 sheet.

4807.
To be sold by auction by Mr Chalk, on Friday, the 15th day of November, 1805, and the following days, on the premises of Mr Francis Martin, linen draper, near St Peter's Church, Lincoln, all the stock in trade, household furniture, shop fixtures, &c.
Lincoln: printed J.W. Drury, 1805.   1 sheet.

4808.
[Sale by auction of billiard table]
Lincoln: printed W. Brooke, 1833.   1 sheet.

4809.   **CITY ARMS HOTEL**
[Notice of postponement of letting, November 3rd, 1837]
Lincoln: printed J.W. Drury, 1837.   1 sheet.

4810.
Lincoln: to be sold by auction by Mr W. Widdowson...freehold and leasehold estates:
[March, 1838]
Lincoln: printed T.J.N. Brogden, 1838.   1 sheet.

4811.
Deanery, Lincoln: valuable library of books, curious and rare gold, silver and copper coins, choice cellar of wines...a quantity of household furniture, and brewing plant, to be sold by auction by Mr Hitchins, on...December 2 & 3, 1845...
Lincoln: printed W. and B. Brooke, 1845.   28p.

4812.
Excellent and valuable household furniture...books, pictures, &c...a gig horse, an excellent milch cow...to be sold by auction by Mr Hitchins, on Tuesday, the 20th of May, 1845, on the premises of W.H. Ward, Esq., 141, St Peter-at-Gowts...
Lincoln: printed J. Stainton, 1845.   16p.

4813.
Extensive sale: Grecian Place, Lincoln: the household furniture, glass, china...library of books...to be sold by auction by Mr Hitchins, on...the 11th & 12th of June, 1845, on the premises late in the occupation of Mrs Hutton...
Lincoln: printed J. Stainton, 1845.   36p.

4814.
St Peter-in-Eastgate, Lincoln: household furniture and effects...to be sold by auction...on Tuesday, the 24th day of June, 1845 by Mr Hitchins, on the premises of Mrs Noel Bromhead
Lincoln: printed J. Stainton, 1845.   1 sheet.

4815.
New Road, Lincoln: sale of valuable household furniture...choice paintings by old masters, curious and rare engravings, library of books...to be sold by auction by Mr Hitchins, on...September 30th, and October 1st, 1846, on the premises of the late Mrs Nelson
Lincoln: printed W. and B. Brooke, 1846.   15p.

4816.   **CITY ARMS HOTEL**
[Auction of building material, October 29th, 1847]
[Lincoln]: [s.n.], [1847].   1 sheet.

4817.
Important and extensive sales...of most valuable and desirable freehold property: [June 7th, 1847]
Lincoln: printed W. Peck, 1847.   1 sheet.

4818.   **LINCOLN CORPORATION**
Important sales...of freehold property: [poster, March 10th, 1847]
Lincoln: printed T.J.N. Brogden, 1847.   1 sheet.

4819.
Particulars of valuable and important freehold and other property in the city of Lincoln, to be sold by auction by Mr Hitchins, at the Guildhall, on Thursday, June the 17th, 1847...
Lincoln: W. Peck, [1847].   [4]p.

4820.
Saint Mary-le-Wigford, city of Lincoln: valuable & modern household furniture...to be sold by auction by Mr Hitchins, on...April 7th and 8th, 1847, on the premises of the Rev. S.B. Bergne, 331, High Street, Lincoln
Lincoln: printed J. Stainton, 1847.   18p.

4821.
Sales of property in April
Lincoln: printed T.J.N. Brogden, 1847.   1 sheet.

4822.
Subdeanery, Lincoln: new & elegant household furniture...works and engravings connected with the topography of Lincolnshire...to be sold by auction by Mr T.J.N. Brogden, on...March 20, 21 and 22...
Lincoln: printed T.J.N. Brogden, [1848].   26p.

4823.
James' Street, Lincoln: superior household furniture...library of books with valuable Mss...to be sold by auction by Mr T.J.N. Brogden, by order of the executors of the late Mrs Bromehead...on the 16th, 17th, 18th and 19th, Sept., 1850
Lincoln: printed T.J.N. Brogden, 1850.   32p.

4824.
Particulars and conditions of sale of a freehold messuage, shop & premises, in Silver Street, in Lincoln, which will be sold by auction...by Messrs Brogden & Son, at the Saracen's Head Hotel, Lincoln, on Thursday, the 29th day of August, 1861
[Lincoln]: [T.J.N. Brogden], [1861].   [4]p.
    Refers to no.39, Silver Street.

4825.
Subdeanery, Lincoln: splendid household furniture, plate, wines, pictures...to be sold by auction by Mr Hitchins, at the Subdeanery, the residence of the late Thomas Manners Sutton...on Dec. 17th, 18th. 19th and 21st
Lincoln: printed W. and B. Brooke, [19??].   25p.

4826.
By order of Lincoln Hotels, Ltd., Lincoln, Henry Spencer and Sons are instructed to hold an important four days sale by auction of the contents of the Saracen's Head Hotel, at the Hotel, on...8th, 9th, 10th and 11th December, 1959...
Retford: Henry Spencer, [1959].   [70]p., [3] leaves of plates.

4827.
Henry Spencer & Sons are instructed to include and to sell by auction in the Saracen's Head Hotel, Lincoln, sale, on the first day, Tuesday, 8th December, 1959, additional items of choice furniture
Retford: Henry Spencer, [1959].   [3]p.

4828.
By order of Trust House Hotels, Ltd., London: the Great Northern Hotel, Lincoln: Henry Spencer & Sons are instructed to hold a two days sale by auction on the premises...3rd and 4th October, 1963: [catalogue]
Worksop: Henry Spencer, 1963.   [34]p., 4p. of plates.

4829.
By order of the executors of Miss B.M. Kennedy, deceased: to be sold by auction, at the Central Market, Lincoln, on Tuesday, 14th February, 1967: the whole of the valuable contents of 8, James Street, Lincoln...
Lincoln: A. Jackson, 1967.   15p., [2] leaves of plates.

4830.
Lincoln: to be sold by auction, in Eastgate Parish Hall, on Friday, 8th December, 1967, antique furniture, silver, plate, china, glass, books and pictures removed from 8, Minster Yard, Lincoln, for convenience of sale
Lincoln: Geo. L. Tinsley & Laverack, 1967.   12p.

4831.
Henry Spencer & Sons are instructed to sell by auction at their saleroom ...Wednesday, 16 July, 1969, the Wells collection of fine Nailsea coloured glass removed...from the house in Minster Yard, close to Lincoln Cathedral
Retford: Henry Spencer, 1969. [11]p.

4832.
Instructed by the executor of the late Lieutenant-Colonel L.B. Shepherd Folker, O.B.E.: the furnishing contents of his home at the Eastgate Parish Hall, Eastgate, Lincoln, Thursday, 2nd September, 1971
Lincoln: T.J.N. Brogden, 1971. [22]p.

4833.
By order of the Right Reverend, the Lord Bishop of Lincoln, Doctor Kenneth Riches, D.D. and Mrs Riches: the Bishop's House, Lincoln...Henry Spencer & Sons are instructed to sell by auction...on Wednesday, 9th October, 1974, the major portion of the contents...
Retford: Henry Spencer, [1974]. [20]p.

SALE CATALOGUES

4834.
Catalogue of the household furniture, &c., on the premises of Mr Thomas Chalk, Cornhill, Lincoln: to be sold by auction, on Monday, the 11th day of November, 1805
Lincoln: printed J.W. Drury, 1805. 1 sheet.

4835.
A Catalogue of the elegant and modern household furniture and other effects of the late Mr John Spyve, in the High-Street, near the Stone-bow, Lincoln, to be sold by auction by F. Hopkinson
Lincoln: printed W. Brooke, 1811. 1 sheet.

4836.
Important sale: catalogue of the valuable household furniture, plate, linen, glass, china and other effects, which will be sold by auction, on Monday, the 4th day of August, 1845, on the premises of Mr Thomas Bousfield, a bankrupt, High Street, Lincoln
Lincoln: printed T.J.N. Brogden, [1845]. 8p.

4837.
Catalogue of part of the library of the Rev John Nelson, late of the Vicars' Court, in the Close of Lincoln, deceased, which will be offered for sale by auction...Tuesday, the 12th day of August, 1845, in the Great Room at the White Hart Inn,...
Lincoln: printed W. and B. Brooke, [1845]. 12p.

4838.
264, High Street, St Martin's, Lincoln: catalogue of the superior modern and nearly new household furniture...to be sold by auction by Mr Hitchins, on...Feb. 25th & 26th, 1851, on the premises of Anderson Mason, Esquire
Lincoln: printed at the Times, 1851. 20p.

4839.

Catalogue of the choice collection of works of art and vertu, and a portion of the service of plate, of the late Colonel Sibthorp, M.P., which...will be sold by auction by Messrs Christie & Manson...April 9, 1856...
London: Christie & Manson, 1856. 80p.

4840.

Catalogue of the highly important collection of ancient and modern pictures and water-colour drawings of Joseph Ruston...auction by Messrs Christie, Manson & Woods
London: Christie, Manson & Woods, 1898. 42p.

4841.

A Catalogue of part of the contents of the Old Palace, Lincoln, which, by the direction of the executors of the Right Reverend King, D.D., late Lord Bishop of Lincoln, will be sold by auction on the premises by Mr Robert N. Whaley, on...25th May, 1910
Lincoln: printed Critch, [1910]. 32p.

4842.

A Catalogue of the contents of 4, Vicars' Court, Lincoln, which, by the direction of the executors of the late Rev Canon A.R. Maddison...will be sold by auction at the City Sale Room...3rd July, 1912
Lincoln: printed Echo and Gazette, 1912. 16p.

4843.

Catalogue of the collection of modern pictures and water colour drawings, the property of Alfred Shuttleworth, Esq., J.P, deceased, late of Eastgate House, Lincoln, which will be sold by auction by Messrs Christie, Manson & Woods...Friday, February 5, 1926
[London]: [Christie, Manson & Woods], [1926]. 22p.

4844.

By the order of the administrators of George Doughty, deceased...catalogue of antique and modern furniture...to be sold by auction on 10th–12th Feb., 1959, by A. Jackson & Son
Lincoln: A. Jackson, 1959. 48p., 3 leaves of plates.

4845.

The Eastgate Hotel, Lincoln: catalogue of the sale by auction: the entire contents of the Hotel.... 29th and 30th October, 1963
Retford: Henry Spencer, 1963. [24]p., [4] leaves of plates.

4846.

By instructions of the executors of the late Miss S.M. Shipley, 'The Mount', Wragby Road, Lincoln: J. Hunter & Sons...will sell by auction on the premises, on Tuesday, 28th September, 1965, the major portion of the contents...: [catalogue]
[Lincoln]: [R. Hunter], [1965]. 20p.

4847.

By direction of the trustees of the late Mrs M.B. Wells-Cole, Lincoln: catalogue of the main contents of the residence...to be sold by auction by Woodroffe Walter & Son... 24th May, 1966...
Horncastle: Woodroffe Walter, 1966. [13]p.
　　Residence was Dunstall House, Greetwell Road.

FICTION

4848.   COOKE, William
The Cheating age, or Leonard of Lincolne's journey to London to buy wit
London: published by E.A. for John Wright, [pre-1626].

4849.   TRUSWELL, Mr.
The Fortune of France, from the prophetical predictions of Mr Truswell, the recorder of Lincoln, and Michael Nostradamus
London: printed for Jonathan Edwin, 1678.   25p.
> Concerns ancient prophecy 'said to have been found in the ruins of a religious house at or near Lincoln, and given to Mr Truswel, the recorder of that city, from whom it now borrows the name...'.

4850.   SCRIBLERUS, Martin
The Prospect: a lyric essay
London: printed for the author and published by Lewis Tomlinson, 1769.   28p.
> Poem inspired by dream of being 'convey'd in an instant to the top of the northern tower of Lincoln Cathedral'.

4851.
The Lincoln newscarrier's Christmas address to his customers
[Lincoln]: [s.n.], [1790].   1 sheet.

4852.   SCRUTATOR
An Address to the city of Lincoln: [poem]
[Lincoln]: [s.n.], [18??].   1 sheet.

4853.   SMART, W.
Lincoln: [poem]
Lincoln: printed W. Fox, [18??].   1 sheet.

4854.   JOHNSON, Richard
The History of Tom a Lincoln, the Red Rose Knight
London: William Pickering, 1828.   xv, viii, 133p.
(Ancient English fictions)
Facsimile of 7th impression, originally published: 1635.

4855.   BULWER-LYTTON, Edward George
A Strange story; and The haunted and the haunters
New ed.
London: Routledge, Warne & Routledge, 1864.   viii, 343p., [frontis].
> Set in provincial city of L_____ which has low town and the hill.

4856.
A Legend of old Lincoln
[edited by Edward Walter].
Lincoln: printed James Williamson, 1876.   iv, 69p.
> Legend of the origin of the Lady Chapel, which turns into a polemic against Rome and an exhortation to rally round the Church of England.

4857.   WINN, Henry
Winceby fight, and sketches of the Civil War in Lincolnshire: [verse]
Horncastle: printed Watson Joll, 1885.   24p.
> Starts with Cromwell's men desecrating the Cathedral.

4858. —————
Lindum: an historical sketch: [verse]
Horncastle: printed Hugh Willson, 1890.   17p.

4859.   **FROST, Arnold**
The Ballad of the wind, the Devil and Lincoln Minster: a Lincolnshire legend
3rd ed.
Lincoln: Boots, 1898.   16p.: ill.
Originally published: 1897.

4860.   **DYE, Cecil**
Love and the Lincoln Imp: a tale of old Lincoln
Lincoln: printed W.K. Morton, [19??].   16p.: ill.

4861.   **HOWDEN, William Spittlehouse**
[Scrapbook]
[19??].   222, [25]p.
  Has contents page and chronological listing of titles of poems.   Mainly newspaper cuttings,
  including items on Lincoln city and cuttings of Howden's own poems.

4862.   **WILLS, S.**
*Bracebridge boys: lines recited by the author at the Bracebridge and Boultham Pig Club
supper, held in the Gatehouse Hotel, Bracebridge, September 14th, 1900*
[Lincoln]: [The Author], [1900].   [4]p.

4863.
The Proclamation at Lincoln: [verse]
p.250 in *Lincolnshire poacher*, vol.1, no.11, April, 1901.
Originally published: in *Ironmonger*, March 9th, 1901.

4864.   **KESSON, H.J.**
The Legend of the Lincoln Imp: [verse]
Lincoln: J.W. Ruddock, 1904.   [12]p.: ill.

4865.   **GUTCH, Mrs.**
*Country folklore.   Vol.V: Printed extracts, no.VII: examples of printed folk-lore
concerning Lincolnshire*
collected by Mrs Gutch and Mabel Peacock.
London: published for the Folk-Lore Society by David Nutt, 1908.   xxiii, 437p.
(Publications of the Folk-Lore Society, vol.LXIII)
  pp.59–63: Devil looking over Lincoln and other references.

4866.   **TOMBLESON, John**
Bothasberg and other verses
London: Walter Scott Publishing, 1910.   124p.
  Includes poems, entitled: 'Ermine Street'; 'The Lincoln Imp'; 'Lincoln Castle'; 'Lincoln
  Cathedral'.

4867.
The Lay of Havelock the Dane
re-edited from Ms. Laud Misc. 108 in the Bodleian Library, Oxford by Walter W.
Skeat.   2nd ed.
Oxford: Clarendon Press, 1915.   xl, 171p.
Includes index.

4868.   **WOOD, Charles Lindley**
Lord Halifax's ghost book: a collection of stories of haunted houses, apparitions and supernatural occurences
made by Charles Lindley, Viscount Halifax.
London: Geoffrey Bles, 1946.   2 vols.
Originally published: 1937; collected ed.: 1939.
>   Vol.2 contains: 'Bishop King's escape' and 'The Rustling lady of Lincoln'.   Both stories were
>   sent to Viscount Halifax by Miss A.E. Nash.

4869.   **THOMPSON, Stanbury**
Ghost stories
Stapleford: Thompson, 1958.   136p., 1 port.
(3rd series)
>   pp.68–74: 'Gold Dust' refers to Lincoln and concerns Ye Olde Cross Keys, a tavern.

4870.   **ALLISON, M.H.G.**
Lincolnshire's link with the Lawrences
pp.29–31: ill. in *Lincolnshire life*, vol.8, no.7, September, 1968.
>   D.H. Lawrence and T.E. Lawrence, both of whom visited the city.

4871.   **EASTOE, Ethel**
The Lincoln Imp legend
p.26: ill. in *Lincolnshire life*, vol.8, no.11, January, 1969.

4872.   **TRAVIS, Edmund**
Swans at Lincoln: [poem]
p.43: ill. in *Lincolnshire life*, vol.13, no.5, July, 1973.

4873.   **COX, Dallas Denton**
Lincolne mine own contrey: the story of a manuscript written by John [i.e. Thomas]
Heywood of Ashby-cum-Fenby
pp.40–41: ill. in *Lincolnshire life*, vol.14, no.2, April, 1974.
>   Ms. is a play by Thomas Heywood, which features the character Tom a Lincoln, an illegitimate
>   son of King Arthur.   Adapted from Richard Johnson's novel of 1599, *The most pleasant
>   history of Tom a Lincolne, the renowned soldier of the Red Rose Knight*, but the latter only
>   mentions Lincoln as the birthplace.

4874.   **RAINES, K.**
Souvenir of Lincoln: [poem]
p.40: ill. in *Lincolnshire life*, vol.15, no.3, May, 1975.

4875.   **FISK, Roy**
Abe and the Imp: [short story]
pp.38–39 in *Lincolnshire life*, vol.19, no.6, September, 1979.

4876.   ———————
Abe and Roman Lincoln: [short story]
pp.40–41: ill. in *Lincolnshire life*, vol.20, no.8, November, 1980.

4877.   ———————
Abe on the hustings: [short story]
pp.32–33: ill. in *Lincolnshire life*, vol.20, no.10, January, 1981.

4878.   **HAWORTH, Gilbert**
My Lincoln Imp
pp.26–27: ill. in *Lincolnshire life*, vol.20, no.10, January, 1981.
>   War time reminiscence, featuring Lincoln Imp trinket.

4879.   RUTHERFORD, Maurice
Lincoln red bull: [poem]
p.22 in *Lincolnshire life*, vol.21, no.12, March, 1982.

4880.   ENGLISH, Jim
The Lincoln Imp
p.8: ill. in *Picture postcard monthly*, no.62, June, 1984.
    Legend and representation on postcards.

4881.
Ghosts, mysteries and legends: a light hearted look at some of Lincoln's folklore
Lincoln: Lincoln, Recreation and Leisure Department, [1987].   1 sheet: ill.

CORONATION FESTIVITIES, ROYAL VISITS

4882.
[Notice that address to His Majesty is awaiting signature, December 26th, 1820]
Lincoln: printed W. Brooke, 1820.   1 sheet.

4883.
To George Steel, Esq., the mayor of Lincoln: [letter requesting meeting to discuss presentation of address to His Majesty, 11th December, 1820]
Lincoln: printed Drury, 1820.   1 sheet.

4884.
The Queen: the city of Lincoln address and Her Majesty's answer
Lincoln: printed W. Brooke, [1820].   1 sheet.

4885.
The Queen!: [notice of celebration in Cornhill in 'honor of the abandonment of the odious proceedings against the Queen by her prosecutors']
Lincoln: printed W. Brooke, [1820].   1 sheet.

4886.
[Account of meeting held to celebrate the 'triumph of the Queen', November 15, 1820]
Lincoln: printed W. Brooke, 1820.   1 sheet.

4887.
[Letter to mayor to request meeting to discuss best means of enabling humbler classes to participate in the festivities of the day of His Majesty's coronation, August 31st, 1831]
Lincoln: printed J.W. Drury, 1831.   1 sheet.

4888.
[Resolutions of meeting to arrange festivities on day of coronation of Their Majesties, September 6th, 1831]
Lincoln: printed W. Brooke, 1831.   1 sheet.

4889.
[Resolutions of meeting for arranging celebration of Queen's coronation]
Lincoln: printed W. and B. Brooke, [1837?].   1 sheet.

4890.
Celebration of the coronation in Lincoln, June 28th, 1838: programme of the procession on the day of Her Majesty's coronation
[Lincoln]: [s.n.], [1838].   1 sheet.

4891.
[Poster about telegraphing of Queen's speech to Lincoln so that it will be available in the second edition of the *Lincolnshire times*]
Lincoln: printed W. Bellatti, [1847].   1 sheet.

4892.
Programme of proceedings on the intended visit of His Royal Highness the Prince Albert: [April, 1849]
Lincoln: printed W. Bellatti, 1849.   1 sheet.

4893.
To His Royal Highness, field marshal, the Prince Albert, K.G., &c, &c.: [letter from the mayor, aldermen and citizens of the city of Lincoln]
[Lincoln]: [s.n.], [1849].   1 sheet.

4894.
Celebration of the marriage of the Prince of Wales with the Princess Alexandra of Denmark, March the 10th, 1863: [programme]
Lincoln: printed Edward R. Cousans, 1863.   1 sheet.

4895.
Celebration of Her Majesty's jubilee: programme
Lincoln: printed C. Keyworth, 1887.   [3]p.

4896.
Marriage of Princess Victoria Mary of Teck with H.R.H. the Duke of York, July 6th, 1893: official programme of celebration in Lincoln
Lincoln: printed Cooper, [1893].   [4]p.

4897.
Celebration of the coronation of King Edward VII and Queen Alexandra, June 26th and 27th, 1902: official time table of festivities and programme of the sports
Lincoln: printed Keyworth, 1902.   [24]p.: ill.
   Includes short history of city.

4898.
City of Lincoln...programme and souvenir of the local festivities, on the occasion of the coronation of Their Most Gracious Majesties, King George V and Queen Mary in the Abbey Church of St.Peter at Westminster, Thursday, 22nd June, 1911
Lincoln: printed Ruddock, 1911.   54p.: ill.

4899.
City of Lincoln and county of the same city: programme and souvenir of the local festivities, on the occasion of the coronation of...King George V and Queen Mary...22nd June, 1911
Lincoln: Lincoln Corporation, [1911].   56p.: ill.
   Includes watercolours by Arthur C. Payne.

4900.
Coronation celebrations souvenir programme, 1937
Lincoln: Lincoln Corporation, 1937.   25p., [7]p. of plates.

4901.
*Coronation souvenir: supplement to the **Lincolnshire chronicle and leader***
Lincoln: Lincolnshire Newspapers, 1937.   32p.: ill.
   p.32: 'Royal visit to Lincoln'.

4902.
Coronation celebrations: souvenir programme, 1953
Lincoln: Lincoln Corporation, 1953.   30p.: ill., [frontis].

4903.
One thousand boys and girls from Lincoln School dance for Her Majesty Queen
Elizabeth II at the City Football Ground, Lincoln, on 27 June, 1958: [programme]
Lincoln: Lincoln, Education Committee, 1958.   [9]p.: ill., [frontis].

4904.
Visit of Her Majesty Queen Elizabeth II and His Royal Highness the Duke of Edinburgh,
27th June, 1958: programme of events: [working programme for rehearsal to be held on
Sunday, 1st June]
[1958].   Various pagings.
Typescript.

4905.
Visit of Her Majesty the Queen and His Royal Highness the Prince Philip, Duke of
Edinburgh, 27th June, 1958, the Castle, Lincoln: [programme]
[Lincoln]: [Lincoln County Council], [1958].   [5]p.

4906.
*The Royal visit to Lincoln: a **Chronicle** supplement*
Lincoln: Lincolnshire Chronicle, [1976?].   20p.: ill.

4907.
[Top twenty entries from Age Concern, 1977 essay competition on the subject of royal
occasions]
[1977].
Typescript.
        Many mention royal visits to the city.

4908.
The Queen in Lincoln: [an LSG supplement, October, 1980]
Lincoln: LSG, 1980.   xxp.: ill.

EXHIBITIONS

4909.
Supplement to the first edition of the catalogue of the Lincoln exhibition
Lincoln: printed Chas. Akrill, 1861.   8, [16]p.

4910.   **LINCOLN EXHIBITION OF ARTS, SCIENCE & MANUFACTURES**
The Catalogue of the Lincoln Exhibition of Arts, Science & Manufactures, held in the
Temple Gardens, opened July 30th, 1861
Lincoln: printed Charles Akrill, [1861].   25, [21]p.

4911.
Catalogue of pictures and works of art, exhibited at the School of Art, Lincoln,
November, 1867
Lincoln: printed W. Doncaster, [1867].   25p.

4912.
Report of the Lincolnshire Exhibition, June 16th to August 30th, 1887
Lincoln: Akrill, Ruddock & Keyworth, [1887].   103, [57]p., [2] leaves of plans.

4913.   **LINCOLNSHIRE EXHIBITION**
Lincolnshire Exhibition, 1887: catalogue
Lincoln: printed Akrill, Ruddock & Keyworth, [1887].   103, [57]p., [2] leaves of plans.
pp.8–9: short memoir of Peter De Wint, by G.T. Harvey; pp.10–15: brief history of Lincoln, by Edmund Venables.

4914.
The Lincolnshire Exhibition of fine arts
pp.52–53 in *Lincoln diocesan magazine*, vol.III, no.16, August, 1887.

4915.
Twelfth annual art & industrial exhibition, August 22nd, 23rd, 24th & 25th, 1905, Municipal Technical School, Monks' Road: catalogue
Lincoln: printed Keyworth, 1905.   63p.
_____   eleventh...1904.
_____   thirteenth...at the Grey Friars...1906.
_____   fourteenth...Municipal Technical School...1907.

4916.
Lincoln fifteenth annual art and industrial exhibition held under the auspices of the Lincoln City Education Authority, at the Municipal Technical School, Monday to Saturday, November 23rd to 28th, 1908
Lincoln: printed Critch, [1908].   68p.

4917.
Lincoln Engineering Society jubilee exhibition
[1973].   [2]p.
Typescript.
Exhibition at Museum of Lincolnshire Life, organized jointly by the Lincoln Engineering Society and the Lincolnshire Association.

EVENTS

4918.   **TRANSFIELD'S AMERICAN CIRCUS**
Special commemorative programme, Friday, December 29th, 1899
[S.l.]: [The Circus], [1899].   1 sheet.
Issued on silk.
Circus on Monks Road.

4919.
A Festival of folk dance at the Castle, Lincoln, June 4th, 1953 at 7.30pm.
Lincoln: Lincoln, Education Committee, 1953.   8p.: ill.
Includes programme and pictures.

4920.   **LINCOLN SHAKESPEARE FESTIVAL**
Lincoln Shakespeare Festival, 5th to 25th April, 1964: [programme]
[Lincoln]: [Lincoln Shakespeare Festival Office], [1964].   1 sheet: ill.
Includes information on Lincoln connections with Richard II.

4921.   **ELVIN, Laurence**
The Cake Ball
pp.7–10: ill. in *The Fireside magazine*, vol.3, no.5, February, 1966.

4922.   **PALMER, Cyril**
Lincoln at Christmas
pp.10–12: ill. in *Britain*, vol.27, no.12, December, 1972.
> Events centred round the Cathedral.

4923.   **POACHER '77**
Camp news, 31st July, 1977
[S.l.]: [s.n.], [1977].
> Guide and Scout camp held in Lincoln.

4924.
Lincoln annual antiques fair celebrates 10th anniversary
p.23: ill. in *Lincolnshire life*, vol.18, no.4, July, 1978.

4925.   **KAYE, David**
The Lincolnshire year: Lincoln water festival
pp.20–22: ill. in *Lincolnshire life*, vol.22, no.12, March, 1983.

VARIOUS

4926.   **MILNER, T.**
The Substance of an address on British colonial slavery, delivered October 17, 1830
Lincoln: printed W. Brooke, 1830.   21p.

4927.   **BROGDEN, J. Ellett**
Provincial words and expressions current in Lincolnshire
London: Robert Hardwicke, 1866.   241p.

4928.   **LINCOLN, Bishop of**
Speech delivered by the Lord Bishop of Lincoln at a meeting held in the Corn Exchange, Lincoln, on Monday, February 28, 1870
Manchester: Central Association for Stopping the Sale of Intoxicating Liquors on Sundays, 1870.   15p.
> Uses the 'working men of Lincoln' as one of his examples.

4929.
Register of furnished houses and apartments to be let: [Royal Show, Lincoln, 25th to 29th June, 1907]
issued by Robert N. Whaley.
Lincoln: printed J.W. Ruddock, [1907].   89p.: ill., folded map.

4930.   **MOREY, Geoffrey**
The Lincoln kangaroos
London: Hodder & Stoughton, 1962.   78p.: ill.
> Lincoln mentioned in tables but not in text.

4931.   **FAIERS, Roy**
The Lincoln kangaroos
p.38 in *Lincolnshire life*, vol.2, no.2, summer, 1962.
> About the article which Geoffrey Morey wrote about his pet kangaroos.

INDEX

Note: The numbers used here and in the Table of Contents refer to records rather than pages. Entries in upper case derive from the headword of one or more records, those in lower case from the title or notes. Bold entries derive from section headings.

Grey, Bishop William   4574
Greyladies   4548
GRIDGEMAN, N.T.   4336
GRIFFIN, D.   1367, 1368
Griffith   4182
GRIFFITH, P.   3454, 3457, 3462
Grilles   2622
Grimm, S.H. of Burgdorf   4434
Grimsby to London by rail   1152
GRIMSHAW, P.   1516
GRINLING, C.H.   1121
Griscom, A.   390
Grocer   1344, 1345
GROSE, F.   884
Grose, Sir N.   3082
GROSSE, G.H.   3825
Grosseteste, Bishop Robert   114, 116,
     426, 521, 590, 778, 1064, 1234,
     1312, 1413, 2872, 3022–3028, 3224,
     3676, 3884, 4162, 4575–4591
  defender of liberties   4583
  letters   4578
  life and times   4579
  philosophical remains   4577
  re canonization   4590
  table manners   4587
  tomb   4591
  visitation   4588
GRUNDY, J.   977, 979, 980, 1040
Grundy, Rev.J.   4277
GUARDIANS OF THE POOR
     2757–2761, 2764
GUDSBY, F.L.   1364
Guest house   2619
Guide   115, 527, 563, 566, 600, 615, 618,
     619, 624, 627, 628–634, 636, 637,
     638–643, 645, 647, 649–653, 655,
     656, 658, 659, 662, 664, 665, 668,
     671, 676, 678, 679–682, 684, 685,
     686–689, 691, 692, 693–699, 701,
     702, 703, 706, 709, 716, 723, 726,
     800, 802, 803, 805, 807, 809, 810,
     815, 819, 820, 1115, 1116, 1151,
     1152, 1275, 1329, 1467, 1624, 2556,
     2582, 2585, 2591, 2592, 2596, 2719,
     2723, 2870, 3350, 3394, 3416, 3544,
     4011, 4065, 4081, 4155, 4708, 4715,
     4923
  illustrated guide   566, 636, 641, 642,
     647, 658, 659, 716, 726, 1115, 1116,
     3394
  pocket guide   649–652, 676
Guide and Scout camp   4923

GUIDES FOR SPECIAL OCCASIONS
     718–730
GUIDES, OFFICIAL   678–701
GUIDES, POST-1820   619–677
GUIDES, PRE-1820   603–618
Guild   71, 367, 374, 727, 770, 849–851,
     866, 946, 1259, 1277, 1333, 2689,
     3171, 3637, 3886, 4100, 4211
Guildhall   14, 71, 104, 105, 132, 492,
     501, 852–855, 903, 905, 1017, 1019,
     1069, 1655–1658, 2363, 2447, 2463,
     2520, 2685–2688, 2690, 2691, 2694,
     2696, 2698, 2741, 2892, 3547, 4099,
     4125, 4819
Gunn, A.   806
Gunsmith   4452
GUNSTONE, A.   314, 321, 326, 327,
     329
GUTCH, Mrs   4865
Gutters   2512
Gwyllym, St J.   4599
Gwynnes Pumps   1524, 1526
Gynwell, Bishop John   4558
Gyula, R.   1427
H.& P.P. lines   4249
H.M.Inspectors of Education
  Lincoln City School   2947
  report on Educn.Dept., H.M.Prison
     Lincoln   3196
  S.Faith's First School   3002
  S.Peter & S.Paul High School   3001
Haberdashery   1343
HACKETT, F.E.   4329
HACKETT, J.   4672
HADDERSLEY, C.R.   2304
HADFIELD, C.   1065
HADLEY, J.   4162
HAIGH, M.   3813
Hainton   4539, 4703
Hair-cutter   1351
Halfpenny
  Lincoln's own   328
  of Henry Wanless of the Two
     Dolphins   328
Halifax, Viscount   4868
HALL, B.C.   4406
Hall, C.   1639
HALL, G.J.   1871
HALL, J.   2211
Hall, L.G.   2414
HALL, R.   2455, 4407, 4408
Hall, T.   2875
Hall, Thomas   3086
Hall, William   3110

Lighting and Paving Act 2517, 2520
Lighting Order 2721
Lighting, Building and Improvements
Committee 3231
LILBURN, R. 2182, 2398, 2487
LILLICRAP, C.A. 3574
Limestone 38, 39
Lincoln; government 514
Lincoln 'green'; colour of 755
LINCOLN & DISTRICT MENCAP
SOCIETY 2841
LINCOLN & DISTRICT SPASTICICS
SOCIETY 2838, 2839
LINCOLN & LINDSEY BANK 1296,
1297, 1299, 1301
LINCOLN & NOTTINGHAM
ARCHITECTURAL SOCIETY 3645
Lincoln Ancaster High School 2995
LINCOLN AND DISTRICT ANGLING
ASSOCIATION 3810
LINCOLN AND DISTRICT CITIZENS
ADVICE BUREAU 2814
LINCOLN AND DISTRICT MARRIAGE
GUIDANCE COUNCIL 2813
LINCOLN AND DISTRICT TABLE
TENNIS LEAGUE 3865, 3866
Lincoln and Lincolnshire almanac for
1920 4768
Lincoln and Lincolnshire Freehold Land
Society 1394
Lincoln and Lincolnshire Insurance
Office 1395
Lincoln and Nottingham Railway 1114
Lincoln and nuclear weapons 2725
Lincoln and Pyewipe junction 1127
Lincoln and Wakefield Railway 1112
Lincoln arboretum 2497
Lincoln Archaeological Research
Committee 92, 155, 160, 225, 269,
274
Lincoln Archaeological Trust 74, 75, 96,
105–108, 111, 112, 236, 267, 279,
295, 315, 412
Lincoln Area Volunteer Bureau 2795
LINCOLN ASSOCIATED
PHYSICALLY HANDICAPPED
SOCIETY 2837
Lincoln Association for the Abridgement
of the Hours of Business 1389
LINCOLN BENEFIT BUILDING
SOCIETY 3774
Lincoln Blue-Coat School 2949
Lincoln Brick Co 1529

Lincoln budget and almanack for the year
1868 4760
LINCOLN Burials Board 2495, 2664
Lincoln bypass 289
Lincoln cabinet 4778, 4779
Lincoln Canoe Club 1054, 3812, 3813
Lincoln Castle 63, 105, 106, 266, 280,
293, 366, 480, 713, 730, 791, 792,
793, 794, 796, 797, 799, 800,
801–803, 805, 806, 807, 809, 810,
811–816, 818, 819, 820–822, 882,
947, 2305, 3117, 3128, 3172–3176,
3178, 3181, 3182, 3189, 3190, 3193,
3386, 4252, 4424, 4866
fortification, 1642 480
siege of 366
Lincoln Cathedral – see Cathedral
LINCOLN CENTRAL CIRCUIT 4241
Lincoln Central Library xvi, xvii, xviii,
530, 557, 605, 615, 1270, 1315,
2469, 3556, 3560, 3589, 4000, 4784
LINCOLN CENTRAL SCIENCE
CLASSES 3044
Lincoln Chamber of Commerce 680,
681, 1219, 1242
LINCOLN CHORAL SOCIETY 3594,
3598
Lincoln Christ's Hospital 2931, 2933,
2940, 2952, 2981, 2984, 2992, 3207,
4472, 4493, 4494
Lincoln Christ's Hospital Girls' High
School 2952, 2984, 4472
LINCOLN CHRIST'S HOSPITAL
SCHOOL 2981, 2992, 3207
Lincoln City and County Museum 173,
210, 211–214, 216, 310, 780, 3391,
3395
LINCOLN CITY COUNCIL, Housing &
Estates Dept 1246
Lincoln City Engineer 4502
LINCOLN CITY FOOTBALL CLUB
3824, 3827, 3830, 3831, 3838
LINCOLN CITY GAOL 3183, 3193
Lincoln city new announcer 4786
LINCOLN CIVIC AWARD TRUSTEES
3528
Lincoln Civic Trust xiii, xv, 72, 403,
711, 781, 782, 836, 837, 854, 855,
1053, 2571, 3516, 3517–3529, 3531,
3532, 3533, 3535, 3539, 3545, 3547
Lincoln Civic Week 2666
LINCOLN CIVIL DEFENCE CORPS
2723
LINCOLN Civil Defence Division 2729